A REFERENCE GUIDE TO
MODERN FANTASY
FOR CHILDREN

A REFERENCE GUIDE TO MODERN FANTASY FOR CHILDREN

PAT PFLIEGER

HELEN M. HILL, *Advisory Editor*

GREENWOOD PRESS

Westport, Connecticut • London, England

Library of Congress Cataloging in Publication Data

Main entry under title:

A Reference Guide to modern fantasy for children.

Bibliography: p.
Includes index.
1. Fantastic fiction, English—Dictionaries.
2. Fantastic fiction, American—Dictionaries.
3. Children's stories, English—Dictionaries.
4. Children's stories, American—Dictionaries.
I. Pflieger, Pat. II. Hill, Helen, 1915-
PR830.F3G84   1984   823′.0876′099282   83-10692
ISBN 0-313-22886-8 (lib. bdg.)

Library of Congress Catalog Card Number: 83-10692
ISBN: 0-313-22886-8

First published in 1984

Greenwood Press
A division of Congressional Information Service, Inc.
88 Post Road West, Westport, Connecticut 06881

Printed in the United States of America

10   9   8   7   6   5   4   3   2   1

For my family, whose fantasies have sustained me

CONTENTS

FOREWORD

Few reference works can be read just for pleasure, but this guide to modern fantasy for children is a book that can give pleasure to the general reader as well as to the specialist. Those most likely to consult it, of course, will be teachers, students, and librarians, but anyone interested in children's fantasy will find the book not only useful but enjoyable.

Part of the pleasure of browsing through this volume comes from finding such full coverage of a story, not only in the plot entries, but also in the entries on each of the characters. If, after reading a plot summary here, the reader follows through and reads about each of the characters, he will come to a fuller understanding of the whole book than he could possibly get from just a summary of the story. When information overlaps, as it sometimes must, there is no stale repetition. To present views of the same material more than once, even when those views are to be looked at from a new perspective each time, to write about each character with sympathy and enthusiasm, as Ms. Pflieger does, is an admirable achievement. It is an additional pleasure that the author's enthusiasm for fantasy in general and for these books in particular never flags, and that her writing remains fresh and lively throughout.

One of the hazards of making an anthology or reference work is that inevitably some readers will ask, "Why wasn't my favorite book (or poem or story) included?" The answer lies in the limits of space and the dictates of personal choice. This book is not comprehensive, but selective; yet most readers will surely agree that the authors Ms. Pflieger has chosen to write about are significant writers of modern fantasy for children. The two most noticeable absentees are Lewis Carroll and A. A. Milne. Although modern fantasy did not begin with Carroll in 1865, the Alice books are the most spectacular early examples, and for most English-speaking readers they remain the high point in fantasy. But Ms. Pflieger believes with Tolkien that "if a waking writer tells you that his tale is only a thing imagined in his sleep, he cheats deliberately the primal desire at the heart of Faërie: the realization, independent of the conceiving mind, of imagined wonder."[1] It is Alice's dream, of course, not Carroll's, and the viv-

1. J.R.R. Tolkien, *Tree and Leaf* (London: George Allen and Unwin, 1964), p. 19.

idness of the fantasy is not dispelled when the reader learns that Alice has dreamed it all. Still, Carroll tells us that the fantasy was a dream; and dream fantasies have been excluded here. Other readers may miss the stories abut Christopher Robin and Winnie-the-Pooh, which have been excluded on the ground that they are more clearly short stories than a continuous narrative with a visible plot; and the Oz books, which, as Ms. Pflieger points out in her preface, have been much written about by others. The omission of such well-known favorites is rare, however, and with Alice and the Oz books, at least, one can read about them in much greater detail elsewhere.

These omissions granted, one can find here a remarkably full picture of more than a century of fantasy for children, both English and American, from Charles Kinglsey's *The Water-babies* in 1863 to Mary Norton's *The Borrowers Avenged* in 1982. Though there are and always will be some books that are didactic, this has been a century in which the writing of good books for children has become a serious concern of the literary artist whose primary aim is not to be didactic, but to write books that entertain, yet at the same time have the qualities of human understanding and literary skill that we ask for in the best books for adults. It will be a pleasure for anyone interested in fantasy for children to read about the books included here, to refresh his memory about old favorites, and to discover new writers for future reading.

Helen M. Hill

PREFACE

A Reference Guide to Modern Fantasy for Children is intended to form an introduction to the work of thirty-six nineteenth- and twentieth-century British and American authors, who have among them written over one hundred works of fantasy for children. As such it fills a gap between general works such as Margery Fisher's *Who's Who in Children's Books* and such specific works as Paul F. Ford's *Companion to Narnia* and Robert Foster's *The Complete Guide to Middle-earth*. This work should be useful to the student approaching the subject of fantasy for children for the first time or to the scholar needing a ready reference to the books and authors included. It will also be of use to those needing a survey of the fantasies for children by a particular author; the title of a work in which a particular character, place, or magical object appears; or a synopsis of a difficult-to-find work. The dictionary format of the book, with its entries on authors, books, characters, places, and magical objects, makes it relatively easy to find that elusive person, place, or thing.

Because a complete guide to the works of all the authors of fantasy would run to many volumes, I have been forced to be selective. I have chosen not to include science fiction in this work, though science fiction and fantasy overlap in such books as Madeleine L'Engle's *A Wrinkle in Time* and Robert O'Brien's *Mrs. Frisby and the Rats of NIMH*. Because L'Engle's book has elements of high fantasy and O'Brien's work is essentially an animal story, they have been included here. As there is no complete agreement on whether works in which fantastic events are the result of a dream or vision should be considered fantasy, I have chosen not to include them, agreeing with J.R.R. Tolkien that since fantasy "deals with 'marvels', it cannot tolerate any frame or machinery suggesting that the whole story in which they occur is a figment or illusion."[1] Thus, Charles Dodgson's *Alice's Adventures in Wonderland* and *Through the Looking-Glass* are not included here, for they are clearly dream stories. Both works have been discussed at length in several works, among them *Lewis Carroll*, by Richard Kelly, and *The Annotated Alice*, edited by Martin Gardner. Because of limited space, I have also chosen to discuss only "full-length" fantasies, "full-length" in this case meaning any work one hundred pages or longer; no collections of short stories or works that are not essentially continuous narratives are included.

This has made it necessary to leave out A. A. Milne's *Winnie-the-Pooh* and *The House at Pooh Corner* which (especially the former) are clearly short stories about Christopher Robin's animals, being told to the boy by an anonymous narrator. The Mowgli stories in the Jungle books by Rudyard Kipling, on the other hand, have been included because they form a continuous narrative and have been published separately as such. Beyond these concerns, the authors selected for this guide are outstanding practitioners of their craft; their works have the three-dimensional characters, plausible plots and settings, rich themes, and vivid styles we usually associate with good literature. For this reason, the works of L. Frank Baum have been omitted. Though the first of Baum's fantasies has remained popular since its publication, the Oz books lack the literary crafts-manship of the other works included here. Moreover, his life and books are discussed fully in such works as *The Oz Scrapbook*, by David L. Greene and Dick Martin, and *The Wizard of Oz and Who He Was*, by Martin Gardner and Russell B. Nye; and the characters in Baum's fourteen Oz books are fully described in Jack Show's *Who's Who in Oz*, which the present guide comple-ments. Many of the authors included in the guide have been honored with a Newbery Award, a Carnegie Medal, or a National Book Award for the quality of one of their works. In most cases the award was for a work of fantasy, and almost all the award winners have been included here.

Select as they are, the works included represent well several kinds of fantasy for children. Fantasies can be purely entertaining, or they can deal seriously and thoughtfully with important issues, ideas, and themes. Mary Norton's Borrower series presents us with the joys and tribulations of someone six inches high living in an over-sized world. *Miss Hickory*, by Carolyn Sherwin Bailey, chronicles the adventures of a sharp-natured doll created from a hickory nut and an apple twig. *Peter and Wendy* and *Peter Pan in Kensington Gardens*, by James M. Barrie, celebrate youthful exuberance. E. Nesbit Bland's works are humorous and delightful, for in them magic is as apt to backfire as it is to go right. Other works of fantasy deal seriously with important issues and themes. The nature of good and evil is explored in such works as the Chronicles of Narnia, by C. S. Lewis, Susan Cooper's Dark Is Rising series, and the Time trilogy, by Madeleine L'Engle. In *Charlotte's Web*, E. B. White deals with the realities of friendship and death through an animal story, making it easier for children to accept death as part of life; Natalie Babbitt's *Tuck Everlasting* exposes and explores our romantic dreams about immortality. Ursula LeGuin discusses death, love, and growing up in her Earthsea trilogy. Child abuse is at issue in *A Chance Child*, by Jill Paton Walsh. The frailties of human nature are also recognized in these fantasies; T. H. White exposes the human propensity to possess in *Mistress Masham's Repose* and the inclination toward violence and a belief that might is right in *The Sword in the Stone*. In *The Hobbit*, J.R.R. Tolkien depicts the workings of greed.

Works of fantasy may be classified in several ways according to content.

These categories sometimes overlap; the works themselves may fall into more than one category. Each category is well represented in this work.

One division is place fantasy, in which the action of the work occurs in a world or place other than our own. In such fantasies, the author creates through realistic details an imaginary world where what is impossible in our own world can be real. Narnia, in C. S. Lewis's Chronicles of Narnia, is a completely realized landscape through which the reader could travel if he had the chance; in Ursula LeGuin's Earthsea trilogy, it is the homely details of daily life—the rushwashtea and the wheatcakes toasted beside an open fire—that bring that realm into our experience and make it real to us. The locales in which such fantasies occur are as rich and varied as the imaginations of their creators. The Neverland of James M. Barrie's *Peter and Wendy* is an island created from the dreams of children; here fairies and mermaids live among the Indians and pirates, and children can fly. Jean Ingelow's Fairyland in *Mopsa the Fairy* is a place strangely sweet and savage, where glittering air fairies flutter in the night sky and stony-hearted people literally turn to rock until their time of penance is done. Astarlind, in *The Wolves of Aam*, by Jane Louise Curry, which has a landscape much like ours, is populated by giants and humans, talking wolves, and the small, nomadic Tiddi.

Among those fantasies that take place in our own world are time fantasies, in which characters move accidentally or at will between various centuries. Time, in these books, is not a straight track to be followed; rather, it encircles us: we live in our own present moment and can step from one time to another because all other moments are around us. Thus we find Creep, in Jill Paton Walsh's *A Chance Child*, following a canal from the twentieth century into the early nineteenth century, and Tom Long, in Philippa Pearce's *Tom's Midnight Garden*, stepping out each night that the grandfather clock strikes thirteen into a garden of the turn of the century. Twentieth-century Penelope Cameron, in Alison Uttley's *A Traveller in Time*, often finds herself in Elizabethan times, as does Tommy Bassumtyte, in *The Bassumtyte Treasure*, by Jane Louise Curry. Seventeenth-century Johanna Vavasour "kneads" time to bring John Webster from the twentieth century to help her out of her trouble, in Robert Westall's *The Devil on the Road*.

In high fantasies the basic conflict is between good and evil—not only the good and evil of individual characters or personalities, but a more absolute evil and a more absolute good. Lloyd Alexander, in his Chronicles of Prydain, narrates the struggles of the inhabitants of Prydain to break the power of Arawn, the Lord of Death; Susan Cooper, in her Dark is Rising series, records the never-ceasing battle between the Dark and the Light. Many of these struggles take place in a world other than our own, as in Alexander's works, C. S. Lewis's Narnia books, and Ursula LeGuin's Earthsea trilogy. This does not mean that high fantasy cannot occur in our own world. Susan Cooper's works are set in the British Isles, and Penelope Lively's *The Whispering Knights* is set in the

British countryside. Jane Louise Curry's Abáloc novels have their setting on the North American continent, and Madeleine L'Engle's works begin in North America, if they do not always stay there. Just as some high fantasies overlap with place fantasy, so do a few overlap with time fantasy. In L'Engle's *A Swiftly Tilting Planet*, Charles Wallace Murry journeys into the past to save the present; in several of Curry's Abáloc novels, children of the twentieth century find themselves taking part in adventures that have occurred centuries before they were born.

Sometimes overlapping with the first three types of fantasy are those works using traditional characters or themes. Some authors look to Celtic and Scandinavian mythology for themes and characters. J.R.R. Tolkien borrows the names of his wizard and dwarves from Scandinavian mythology for *The Hobbit*. T. H. White retells the Arthurian tales in *The Sword in the Stone*; we also find Arthur in Jane Louise Curry's *The Sleepers*, William Mayne's *Earthfasts*, and Susan Cooper's *The Grey King* and *Silver on the Tree*. The Wild Hunt haunts Cooper's *The Dark Is Rising* and *Silver on the Tree*, Alan Garner's *The Moon of Gomrath*, and Penelope Lively's *The Wild Hunt of Hagworthy*. The Horned King in Lloyd Alexander's *The Book of Three* seems to be based on the traditional appearance of the Hunt's leader. Figures from the Welsh *Mabinogion* serve to name many of the inhabitants of Lloyd Alexander's Prydain and appear in Alan Garner's *The Owl Service*, which takes as its basic plot a reworking of the tragic tale of Blodeuwedd. In *Elidor*, Garner has also used the traditions explicated in Jesse Weston's *From Ritual to Romance*: Malebron is his Fisher King; the blasted landscape of Elidor, made to blossom at Findhorn's death, is his Wasteland. Other works take Christian mythology as their theme. George MacDonald's sometimes-elusive *At the Back of the North Wind, The Princess and the Goblin*, and *The Princess and Curdie* discuss faith and obedience to a higher good. In the Narnia books, C. S. Lewis explores redemption and resurrection in works reflecting Christian theology. Charles Kingsley's *The Water-babies* examines allegorically the basic tenets of Christianity.

In some fantasies, incredible beings live or find their way into our own world. They can be workers of magic born in our world or visitors from beyond it; they can also be inanimate objects, usually toys, brought to life. Miss Eglantine Price is an everyday woman who has always had a talent for witchcraft, though it is many years before she develops it, in Mary Norton's *The Magic Bed-Knob*. P. L. Travers's Mary Poppins comes from no place in our vocabulary. The Psammead in E. Nesbit Bland's *Five Children and It* is in our world but not of our everyday reality, as are the borrowers in Mary Norton's Borrower series. The Twelve Young Men in Pauline Clarke's *The Twelve and the Genii* once were toy soldiers; Miss Hickory, in Carolyn Sherwin Bailey's book by the same name, was a doll. Sometimes the visitors into our world were once part of it but are now part of another reality or level of existence: Samuel Stokes, in *The Revenge of Samuel Stokes*, and Thomas Kempe, in *The Ghost of Thomas Kempe*, both by Penelope Lively, are the spirits of men who have died.

Animal fantasies have as their characters animals who speak among themselves and have their own culture, though they may not communicate with humans. Although most act and think as animals, their problems and emotions are ones the human reader has sympathy for. Toad, the Mole, the Water Rat, and the Badger, in Kenneth Grahame's *The Wind in the Willows*, are almost more human than animal, taking pride in their neatly furnished homes and living like country gentlemen; Toad converses with humans and is accepted as one of them until he proves differently. Amos, the mouse in Robert Lawson's *Ben and Me*, chatters with Ben Franklin and writes his own memoirs, seated at a mouse-sized Chippendale desk. He retains, however, the tastes and prejudices of a mouse. In many books, animals and humans do not converse, and the animals themselves live less like people than animals. The creatures in Lawson's *Rabbit Hill* and *The Tough Winter* retain most of their animal characteristics, though Little Georgie and his family live in a rabbit burrow neatly fitted with shelves and bunks. Richard Adams, in *Watership Down*, writes of rabbits who behave as do those we are familiar with but who have a culture all their own, with their own rules and rituals, and a hero, El-ahrairah, about whom they spin legends. The experimental rats of *Mrs. Frisby and the Rats of NIMH*, by Robert O'Brien, are still seeking to develop their own culture, but they are more socially advanced than are the creatures around them. The creatures in E. B. White's *Charlotte's Web* and Penelope Lively's *The Voyage of QV 66* have little or no social order. Such fantasies allow us to see ourselves and our institutions through new eyes. *Watership Down* gives us a look at leadership and how it affects society; the Jungle books by Rudyard Kipling present us with an ideal society, where common sense and fair play are the rule. Lively shows us our artifacts, seen anew through the eyes of animals, and ridicules human prejudices and foibles: most of the animals are as biased against those unlike them as humans are.

The works included in this guide also represent a century crucial in the development of fantasy as an art form. Before the 1860s, fantastic literature for children was usually restricted to literary fairy tales patterned after traditional folk tales, and to the ''autobiographies'' of animals and inanimate objects. Most were numbingly edifying: animal stories such as *The Life and Perambulations of a Mouse* (1783-1790), by Dorothy Kilner, and *Fabulous Histories* (1786), by Sarah Trimmer, extoll obedience to parents and kindness to animals; literary fairy tales were often meant to be allegorical, as William Gardiner reminds his readers in *The Magic Spell* (1819?), which is ''meant to symbolize the virtuous and evil propensities of the mind, and that the happiness or misery of the human condition depends on their different agencies.'' With Charles Kingsley's *The Water-babies* (1863), entertainment became an important goal for authors of fantasy for children. This did not mean that fantasies could not present moral or mystical teaching. In *The Water-babies*, Tom the chimney sweep learns better behavior and Christian virtue in his adventures in the sea and in various strange lands. The works of George MacDonald are tales of adventure imbued with mysticism. But liveliness and a good story are the key. Jean Ingelow's *Mopsa the Fairy* (1869) has lessons on morality for those who will listen, but the emphasis is on entertainment. Though Mary Molesworth's *The Cuckoo Clock* sometimes concerns itself with the lessons in manners that its young heroine must learn, these moments are passed over lightly; *The Tapestry Room* is sheer dream-like fantasy meant to delight. Rudyard Kipling, in *The Jungle Book* and *The Second Jungle Book*, presents his reader with the tenets of an ideal world, where law and common sense prevail in an animal civilization; but Mowgli's adventures in this society often overshadow the lessons Kipling wants to teach.

The twentieth-century works in this guide represent several trends in fantasy for children. One is an even greater emphasis on entertainment. E. Nesbit Bland's chronicles of the hilarious adventures of children in the realm of magic hold no lessons, though some, such as *The Story of the Amulet* and *Harding's Luck*, dip into social commentary. What lessons later fantasy works teach are well couched in wonder or adventure, and they are likely to be lessons about life and the position of the individual, or about the nature of evil. Ursula LeGuin's Earthsea trilogy and Lloyd Alexander's Chronicles of Prydain are as much about becoming a mature person as they are about defeating a great evil. The Chronicles of Narnia, by C. S. Lewis, and Madeleine L'Engle's Time trilogy explore the workings and responsibilities of the moral individual as he deals with a corrupt universe. But many fantasies are sheer entertainment, such as Carolyn Sherwin Bailey's *Miss Hickory*, or any of the works of Robert Lawson. *The Revenge of Samuel Stokes*, by Penelope Lively, is light humor; Mary Norton's *Are All the Giants Dead?* sometimes satirizes the fairy tales from which its characters spring. High fantasy is a fairly recent development; C. S. Lewis's Narnia books, of the 1950s, are the earliest included in this guide. The number of high fantasies has increased markedly since the early 1960s, probably because of the success of J.R.R. Tolkien's adult trilogy, *The Lord of the Rings*. Another recent development is the use of figures from mythology and Celtic tradition as characters. Fairies and brownies appear in such nineteenth-century works as Jean Ingelow's *Mopsa the Fairy*, but they come from no readily identifiable tradition. Today, as we have seen, writers are more likely to use figures from traditional material as part of their basic plots. The same troubles and trials found in realistic fiction are becoming more and more a part of fantasy fiction as well. Jill Paton Walsh's Creep, in *A Chance Child*, is a badly abused young boy. Anne Melton, in *The Watch House*, by Robert Westall, is so disturbed at the breakup of her parents' marriage that she unwittingly unleashes a ghost; in another book by the same author, *The Wind Eye*, a family is on the verge of breaking up until it feels the touch of a seventh-century saint. Eleanor Cameron's *The Court of the Stone Children* is as much about Nina Harmsworth's finding a place to live and friends to feel close to in alien San Francisco as it is about her aiding a troubled spirit.[2]

This guide includes all the full-length fantasies of each author discussed. The works themselves are synopsized as briefly as possible. Characters, places, and magical objects that have entries elsewhere are indicated by an asterisk: * . In several cases, where two or more characters having the same last name are listed together, the same number of asterisks follows, indicating that each character has a separate entry: for example, "Edmund, Lucy, Peter, and Susan Pevensie****." References to each entry are included in the index; the user looking up "Wilbur," for example, will find references to the entries for other characters in which his name appears. Characters are cross-referenced in the work according to first name, followed by the title of the works in which they appear, for the convenience of the user who cannot remember a character's last name: thus, "Betty Arden (*The House of Arden*). *See* Arden, Betty." Entries dealing with the books themselves include bibliographical information about the first edition of the work and, where pertinent, information on revisions or earlier printed versions, as well as the brief synopsis. The synopses themselves have been made from first editions of the works in all cases. Entries dealing with authors include a short biography of the writer; a brief discussion of major themes in the full-length fantasy works he or she has produced; a primary bibliography; and a secondary bibliography of selected studies primarily on the author or his or her works of fantasy for children. The primary bibliographies are of books only and are listed in chronological order according to the date of the first editon.

In additon to the text, there are three appendices: a list of works dealing with fantasies for children; a chronological list of the fantasies themselves, with birth and death dates of the authors; and a list of illustrators of the first editions of the fantasies.

NOTES

1. J.R.R. Tolkien, "On Fairy-Stories," in *The Tolkien Reader* (New York: Random House, Ballantine Books, 1966), p. 42.

2. Fantasy and realistic fiction converge in a recent type of fiction, not included in this guide, which Lois Kuznets has termed *psychofantasy* (Lois R. Kuznets, "Games of Dark: Psychofantasy in Children's Literature," *The Lion and the Unicorn*, 1 [1977], pp. 17-24). In psychofantasy, the main character takes refuge from the real world and its problems by stepping into a fantasy world of his own creation, where magic can solve his problems or at least keep them at bay; Eleanor Cameron's *Beyond Silence*, William Mayne's *A Game of Dark*, Robert Westall's *The Scarecrows*, and Eloise McGraw's *A Really Weird Summer* are all works of this type.

ACKNOWLEDGMENTS

More people have a hand in a finished work than anyone can possibly imagine, for no writer likes to suffer alone but feels he must be generous with the pain and spread it around some. So I would like to thank and acknowledge the help of the following people: Jackie Donath and Randy Cox, for providing copies of books; Dr. Norine Odland, for advice; the staff of Inter-Library Loan at the University of Minnesota—Twin Cities; the staff of the Southeast Branch of the Minneapolis Library and of the George Sverdrup Library, Augsburg College; Dr. Karen Hoyle, Margaret Nevinski, Susan Gorman, and the rest of the staff of the Kerlan Collection, University of Minnesota—Twin Cities, especially Brad Trusty, Laureen Baker, Gerald Barnaby, and Roberta Maas, who paged above and beyond the call of duty; Didi Johnson, who listened loyally and long and sometimes got a wise word in edgewise; Helen Hill, who patiently squinted through reams of bad photocopies and often saw the forest where I found only trees; and especially Jo Ann Pflieger, who provided love, encouragement, and index cards when things looked impossible. Any errors in this work should not be blamed on them but are all my own creation.

THE GUIDE

ABADAN, a place in *The First Two Lives of Lukas-Kasha**, by Lloyd Alexander*. The capital of this monarchy is Shirazan, which holds the splendid royal palace. Rich in water and agricultural lands, for years Abadan had traded food for gold and jewels from metal-rich Bishangar*. King Afrasyab, growing greedy, had begun to demand more and more gold. When the Queen of Bishangar refused, Afrasyab had captured Bishangar's capital city and proclaimed Bishangar a province of Abadan. The conflict between the two states ends during the reign of Lukas-Kasha*, who, after he is nearly deposed by his Grand Vizier, makes peace with Bishangar.

ABÁLOC, the ancient setting of the Abáloc novels*, by Jane Louise Curry*. It had been a great kingdom called Ebhélic* in eastern North America. In this kingdom lay the City of the Moon Under the Mountain* and Inas Ebhélic*. Its people are descended from the mysterious Aldar*, who had intermarried with the native Americans in the Ohio Valley. In the fourth century, the kingdom had fought the Northern Wars against Aztalán. After this the kingdom's strength had faded because the Abalockians followed the false oracle of Katóa*, an ancient evil force. Ordered by the oracle to destroy their books, the people had thus been forced to rely on their wise men, who had gotten their wisdom from the oracle. By the twelfth century, Abáloc has dwindled to a small village beside the Ohio River, in West Virginia; its gentle people pay tribute to Cibotlán*, the great empire to the south. Madauc*, a Welsh explorer, and his men help the Abalockians to defeat Cibotlán and then remain in the land, intermarrying with the Abalockians. Perhaps from Madauc's stories come the European legends of Avalon, a wonderful land of apple trees beyond the sea. By the twentieth century, Abáloc has been forgotten, though its name lingers: Apple Lock* is built on the site of the village.

ABÁLOC NOVELS, seven loosely connected novels by Jane Louise Curry* which have the North American continent as their locale. In order of internal chronology they are: *The Wolves of Aam**; *The Watchers**; *The Birdstones**; *The Daybreakers**; *Over the Sea's Edge**; *The Change-Child**; *Beneath the Hill**.

ACHREN, a character in Lloyd Alexander's* *The Book of Three*, *The Castle of Llyr**, and *The High King**. Her consort had been Arawn*. Achren had once ruled Prydain* from Annuvin*, a reign characterized by the torment of those who had not worshipped her, and by blood sacrifices. Having learned from Achren all the magic she knew, Arawn had taken the throne. Eventually Achren had come to live at Spiral Castle, there raising Eilonwy*, a young enchantress, and biding her time. When Achren takes prisoner Gwydion*, war leader of the High King of Prydain, and Taran*, his young companion, she suffers a defeat, for Eilonwy helps Taran escape, and Spiral Castle falls into ruin after they take a mighty sword from its resting place. Achren flees to Caer Colur, off the coast of the Isle of Mona*. Here again she makes a bid for power, kidnapping Eilonwy and seeking to control the girl's powers of enchantment. Thwarted by Eilonwy herself, Achren becomes a broken woman, living at Caer Dallben* and trying no more enchantments. During Arawn's final bid for control of Prydain, Achren starts out to kill him. Finally she leads Taran and a small band to Annuvin, where she is killed trying to slay Arawn.

ADA MAY, MRS. (the Borrower series). *See* May, Ada (Mrs.)

ADAMS, RICHARD (1920-   ), British writer. He was born in Newbury, Berkshire, on 9 May 1920 to Evelyn George Beadon and Lilian Rosa (Button) Adams. He was educated at Bradfield, and he served in the British Army for five years. Adams later earned a B.A. from Worcester College, Oxford, in 1948, and an M.A. in 1953. On 26 September 1949 he married Barbara Elizabeth Acland; they have two daughters. Adams has worked in the Ministry of Housing and Local Government and was assistant Secretary in the Department of the Environment; now he is a free-lance writer.

Of Adams's three works which children enjoy, two are in verse; *Watership Down** is a fantasy. This story of the adventures in survival of a handful of rabbits is a quest story for an ideal place—a place where they can live in dignity as rabbits. In the world of Adams's rabbits, survival can be difficult, but survival with dignity can be even more so.

Whether or not a warren survives depends on its leader; whether or not the rabbits of the warren live as rabbits or not also depends on the leader. How he reacts to threats to the warren can make a difference between its life and death, and how it lives or dies.

A leaderless state can be filled with despair and a sense of hopelessness in a time of emergency. Cowslip's* warren, which Hazel* and his friends visit during their search for a place to live, is in a constant state of siege. It is a dystopia, a place where all seems fair but is not. The rabbits of the warren never need to worry about food, for it is always available, brought to them by the farmer who owns the land. The price they pay for this security is dreadful, for the farmer traps them for food. The culture they have developed is more man-like than rabbit-like: they sing and press stones into the burrow walls to make pictures, they laugh, and they carry things from one place to another. Their despair at their fate is expressed through poetry—something Hazel and the others have little experience of. The warren has no leader to help them. Though they stay where they are because of the food, a leader might be able to organize them to get them away. Having no leader, they despair and try to develop a will to accept their fate. They do not tell the stories of El-ahrairah, the rabbit culture hero, perhaps because they do not wish to be reminded of his courage, which helps him and his people to survive. The comparison between him and them is too painful.

A warren with a leader may be little better, depending on the leader. The warren Hazel and his friends set out from is fairly healthy and the rabbits seem happy. They tell their tales of El-ahrairah and live as best they can. The Threarah appears to be a good leader, but he has his faults and they are fatal for the warren. He is cool, detached, and clever, but he is impersonal; when Hazel and Fiver* come to warn him of the danger the warren is in, he forgets their names and relationship throughout the conversation. He seems to do little but stay in his burrow, sending his Owsla, or guards, for lettuce, and depending on them for reports of what is happening in the warren and around it. He is uninterested in things he has not thought of himself or in things that might disturb the warren's status quo. As a result, the warren is unprepared when men come to clear the way for a new housing project, and it is destroyed.

Under a strong, ambitious leader, a warren can thrive, but its individuals can live in a state that would make death preferable. Efrafa* is such a warren. Built as a model of efficiency, it is so well hidden that no human seems to know it is there, so safe that it becomes overcrowded. The rabbits there have little or no say in their daily lives—in when they will eat or whom they will mate with or where they will live. Any action they take to free themselves is ruthlessly quelled. As a result they have become deadened, unthinking objects that somehow survive. General Woundwort* is the Efrafan leader, and he reacts to the threat humans pose to the warren in the way that to him seems most likely to succeed. His control of Efrafa is one key to its survival. Woundwort's control also satisfies a need in himself. Ambitious, he longs to rule a kingdom and he sets out to do just that: because the warren cannot be extended, Woundwort sends out patrols to control its neighborhood and kill the rabbits' traditional enemies. To help them to survive and to satisfy his own ambitions, Woundwort makes the rabbits other than they are: the strong become stronger, but the majority exist in a kind of numb despair.

Perhaps the best leader is strong and clever, gentle and ingenious, able to take advice and to inspire his followers to greater feats of body and imagination, and able to adapt. Hazel shows himself to be all these during the rabbits' journey from the Threarah's warren to their place on Watership Down, and afterward, as the warren establishes itself. Leader by accident, he knows when and how to take the advice of those around him and how to use their special talents: Fiver's visions, Bigwig's* strength and experience, Blackberry's ingenuity. Under pressure he stays cool, though his emotions are never very far from the surface. He is considerate and fair, taking the needs and feelings of others into consideration. Hazel is adaptive—using a boat, having his bucks dig though it is traditionally the does' job, seeing the possible uses of mice and a gull in the new warren's struggle to survive—but never does he force his followers to do anything against rabbit nature. Unlike the Threarah, Hazel rules by love and respect; unlike Woundwort, he does not rule by force. The warren on Watership Down thrives, and it is free enough for all its inhabitants to be happy.

Adams's book is rich in incident and suspense and in a sense of the countryside where the action takes place. Of the characters, Hazel is very convincing; Woundwort, though the very image of the dictator, is convincing also. But some of the characters are more types than anything else, and a few are merely names. Kehaar* is among the types, as the conventional foreigner; Bigwig is the rabbit of action but few thoughts; the does seem to exist only to become mothers. Where the work shines is in its evocation of a culture entirely different from our own but reflecting aspects of our own, seen from a viewpoint none of us could know. Details of the lapin language and way of life are fresh and original, as are the stories of El-ahrairah.

Works

Juvenile full-length fantasy: *Watership Down* (1972).
Juvenile non-fantasy: *The Tyger Voyage* (1976); *The Adventures and Brave Deeds of the Ship's Cat on the Spanish Maine* (1977).
Adult works: *Shardik* (1974), novel; *Nature Through the Seasons* (1975); *The Plague Dogs* (1977), novel; *Nature Day and Night* (1978); *The Girl on the Swing* (1980), novel.

Secondary Works

Adams, Richard. "Some Ingredients of *Watership Down*," in *The Thorny Paradise: Writers on Writing for Children*, ed. Edward Blishen (Harmondsworth, England: Kestrel Books, Penguin Books, 1975), pp. 163-73.
Fritz, Jean. "An Evening with Richard Adams," *Children's Literature in Education*, 29 (Summer, 1978), pp. 67-72.
Hammond, Graham. "Trouble with Rabbits," *Children's Literature in Education*, 12 (Sept., 1973), pp. 48-63.
Thomas, Jane Resh. "Old Worlds and New: Anti-Feminism in 'Watership Down,' " *The Horn Book Magazine*, 50 (Aug., 1974), pp. 405-8.

ADAON, a character in Lloyd Alexander's* *The Black Cauldron**. He is the son of Taliesin, chief bard in Prydain*, and is bethrothed to Arianllyn. Adaon is a warrior, calm and wise, who has prophetic dreams and sees more than others see. This is due, probably, to the magical iron brooch* he wears, which gives its wearer the ability to see beyond what lies around him or her. Adaon has done everything from sailing beyond the known lands to weaving to working at a forge. He knows well the ways of the forest animals and can play a harp with great skill. Though he dreams of his own death, Adaon sets out on a mission to find and destroy the Black Crochan*, from which Arawn*, the Lord of Death, is creating an invincible army. Adaon leads Taran*, a young warrior, and Ellidyr*, a young prince, as part of his company, and his intercession keeps them from coming to blows at times. Adaon is mortally wounded saving Taran from one of the Huntsmen*, Arawn's warriors, and he gives the brooch to Taran before he dies.

AEDDAN, a character in *Taran Wanderer** and *The High King**, by Lloyd Alexander*. He is the son of Aedd and the husband of Alarca; he is the father of Amren, who had died in battle. Though Aeddan is a farmer in the Valley Cantrevs of southern Prydain*, which long ago had been fertile and rich, he is poor, for he has little knowledge of farming and his crops have failed for two years. Aeddan puts his hope in one last crop, only to have it destroyed by the warriors of Lord Goryon* and Lord Gast*, battling over possession of a herd of cows. Taran*, a young man whom Aeddan has helped, persuades their king, Smoit*, to sentence the two lords to helping the farmer farm his land and giving him Cornillo, the best in the herd of disputed cows. Aeddan prospers.

AGA, NAHDIR, a character in *The First Two Lives of Lukas-Kasha**, by Lloyd Alexander*. He is the Commander of the Guards for the king of Abadan*. This brutal man nearly kills Lukas-Kasha* (Lukas) when the young man washes ashore; he may be responsible for the deaths of two other prospective rulers of Abadan as well. When Lukas, having fled the palace and started to Bishangar*, stumbles on Abadani troops, Nahdir imprisons him and almost kills him. In Lukas's escape, Nahdir is set aflame and perishes.

AGES, MR., a character in *Mrs. Frisby and the Rats of NIMH**, by Robert O'Brien*. This white mouse had been one of the experimental animals at Nimh*, where his lifespan and intelligence were made greater. When the rats in the experiment escape, he goes with them; he and Jonathan Frisby* are the only two mice to escape. Mr. Ages settles near the colony the rats form, using his considerable skills at healing to help the creatures of the neighborhood. He introduces Mrs. Frisby* to the rats when she needs their help.

ALAN COLLET (*Poor Tom's Ghost*). *See* Collet, Alan

ALBANAC, a character in *The Moon of Gomrath**, by Alan Garner*. He is one of the Children of Danu, the best of men, who had come to the world long ago. Like all the Children of Danu, Albanac spends his days in the cause of good, but he never sees his work fulfilled; it is the doom of the Children of Danu that they never see the end of what they have begun, for then their bright natures might be tarnished and their power used for selfishness. Albanac seems a strange man, dressed in black, wearing a gold earring, and riding a black horse named Melynlas, and people who do not know him think he is mad. He is a brave fighter, helping to battle the Morrigan*, an evil witch. Wounded by Pelis the False* in a final stand against the Morrigan, he leaves before the battle is over, to heal his wound. Because the Children of Danu are never gone for long, he will be back.

ALBERT WIGG (the Mary Poppins books). *See* Wigg, Albert

ALDAR, a race of people in *The Watchers** and *The Birdstones**, by Jane Louise Curry*. They came to North America before the native Americans, settling in what is now Ohio and West Virginia. Tall, dark, and silver-eyed, the Aldar had lived longer lives than most people and knew of great powers: it was they who had bound Katóa*, a ravening power that held the land before them, beneath the mountains of Ebhélic* and then in Tûl Isgrun*. When men came to Abáloc*, the Aldar had moved on to the City of the Moon Under the Mountain*, to live there before departing forever to lands beyond the northern seas. Not all went: Elzivir* had been among those who stayed at Berinir Gair* to guard Tûl Isgrun, and Alida, Dalea's* mother, had delayed her journey until she grew too lonely to wait. The descendants of the Aldar are dark and pale-eyed and live exceptionally long lives. The families at Twilly's Green Hollow* are perhaps the last of these.

ALEXANDER, LLOYD (1924-   ), American writer. He was born 30 January 1924 to Alan Audley and Edna (Chudley) Alexander and was educated at West Chester State College and Lafayette College, Pennsylvania, and at the Sorbonne, Paris. On 8 January 1946, Alexander married Janine Denni; they have one daughter. He has been author-in-residence at Temple University, Philadelphia, a translator of French works into English, and the director of the Carpenter Lane Chamber Music Society; Alexander is also a member of the editorial advisory board of *Cricket* magazine.

   Most of Alexander's works for children are fantasy, or connected in some way with his ten full-length fantasy works. *Coll and His White Pig, The Truthful Harp*, and *The Foundling* all tell the adventures of characters in the Chronicles of Prydain*. His other works include short stories and novels. Of his full-length fantasies, five—the Prydain Chronicles—are high fantasy; the other five are not, though they hinge on a struggle between good and evil people. Though most of Alexander's ten full-length fantasies take place in different places and times, all turn on the theme of youth entering adulthood: in the books, adventure becomes a rite of passage.

   If one type prevails as the hero of Alexander's tales, it is the endearing bumbler, stumbling his way through a world not of his own making, possessed of few special talents or none, but prevailing by dint of goodness, earnestness, and a sense that justice must win out. Few of the heroes operate in a world in which they have grown up. Sebastian*, in *The Marvelous Misadventures of Sebastian*, has been sheltered in a manor all his life and begins his marvelous adventures when he is fired. Lionel*, in *The Cat Who Wished to Be a Man*, has grown up as a cat and enters the world of men after he begs his master to transform him into a youth. Lukas-Kasha*, in *The First Two Lives of Lukas-Kasha*, is transported from his own village to an exotic land. Jason*, in *Time Cat*, finds himself in past times and civilizations. Taran*, in the Prydain Chronicles, has been raised on a small farm where, though he is not completely shut off from the rest of the world, he is still not prepared for some of its vagaries or realities. If there is, therefore, a single shortcoming that besets most of these heroes, it is innocence. In some cases innocence is coupled with idealism, for Taran romanticizes war and noble causes, and Mallory*, in *The Wizard in the Tree*, dreams that magic will set her free.

The world, the Alexander hero discovers, has good people, but corruption can gain ascendancy. Often in these books an absolute ruler of some sort makes himself felt, and by accidentally joining the outlaw opposition, the young hero brings him down. Lionel knows nothing of Mayor Pursewig's* domination of Brightford* when he meets and joins Gillian*, whom the mayor is persecuting. Sebastian hears of Count Grinssorg's* iniquities and of "Captain Freeling's" fight against him but does not realize that the Captain is the man he has been traveling with, nor does he know until later Isabel's real identity. Mallory knows Squire Scrupnor* is reprehensible, but she never dreams that by allying herself with a wizard she could defeat the squire. Lukas sides with those who defy the treacherous Grand Vizier, Shugdad Mirza*, by choice, finding them amusing companions and never thinking he will be instrumental in ending Shugdad's reign. Of Alexander's heroes, Taran alone chooses his side at the beginning and with the most idealistic motives.

When the hero is male, he often finds himself siding with a young woman in trouble. Sometimes she is mysterious and her real identity is not known; always she is an individual who makes her own demands and fights many of her own battles and is a source of both irritation and delight. Lukas is often spurned by Nur-Jehan* but remains fascinated, not learning until later that she is the queen of Bishangar*. Taran's first meeting with Eilonwy* leaves him utterly bewildered, at once angry and disarmed. Sebastian finds Isabel's hauteur frustrating, but he agrees to help her, after he learns who she really is. Lionel finds Gillian oddly attractive, for a human, though he does not always understand her, even after he takes her side. Brief though their acquaintance is, Jason grows very fond of blunt, opinionated Diahan*.

Innocent, sometimes idealistic, always friendly, Alexander's heroes are also unlikely. Mallory is a serving-girl, Sebastian is a fiddler, and Lukas is a reprobate. Only Lionel, because of his cat's skills, has any special talents one might expect of a hero. Sebastian has little idea of how to fight. Lukas would rather run or talk his way out of trouble; in this he is like the trickster/rogue of traditional tales. Taran learns to fight and becomes king, but his rise is not inevitable, for he could have been a hero or a knave. Like King Arthur*, Taran does not know his parentage and proves his worth by drawing a sword hidden under a stone, but he does not know whether he is of royal blood or not. Alexander's unlikely heroes achieve their goals seemingly by accident. Detailed as his plans are, something is bound to go wrong, and the hero finds himself trapped, thereby destroying the villain. Sebastian finds himself in Grinssorg's hall and is ordered to play the music that kills the count. Lionel happens to find Mayor Pursewig trapped in the burning inn and makes him promise to resign. Mallory accidentally finds the gold ring that gives back Arbican's* powers. Taran finds himself trapped by Arawn's* deathless soldiers and, in desperation, strikes the only blow that will turn the battle.

As is traditional in folk tales, by helping another the hero always helps himself. Mallory frees Arbican and is in turn freed from her slavery. Lukas helps a merchant, and he in turn helps rescue Lukas at a critical moment. The kitten Sebastian saves rescues him in turn by bringing him a key to open his cell. Taran nurses a wounded gwythaint* back to health and is rewarded when it saves him from falling into a chasm. But the hero helps himself in another way, too, by learning from his experiences. As each goes through a series of adventures, he or she learns about life both from the events themselves and from the people he or she meets. Jason's adventures are a result of his growing up; Gareth* takes him through time to teach the boy what he will need to know as an adult. The Prydain Chronicles record Taran's growth from a callow youth infatuated with glory and excitement to a mature young man cognizant of his own weaknesses and strengths. Both Sebastian and Lionel, in their adventures, are completely innocent of the ways of the world—Sebastian because he has been sheltered all his life, and Lionel because he has just been changed from a cat to a man. Each, by the end of his adventure, has learned how to survive in a sometimes-hostile world. Mallory and Lukas are more experienced to begin with, but each has a lesson to learn, too. Mallory learns to depend on herself, and Lukas discovers for the first time what it is to be responsible. As a result of these adventures, each of Alexander's protagonists is ready to take his or her place in the world.

Alexander's tales are lively and fast-moving, full of action and excitement. Though certain types of characters appear over and over in the works—the earnest, if clumsy, young hero; the irritating but fascinating heroine; the ridiculous adult who turns out to be not as much a fool as others think—each has his or her own personality. Characters and dialogue are colorful and full of life.

Works

Juvenile full-length fantasy: *Time Cat* (1963) as *Nine Lives* (England); *The Book of Three* (1964); *The Black Cauldron* (1965); *The Castle of Llyr* (1966); *Taran Wanderer* (1967); *The High King* (1968); *The Marvelous Misadventures of Sebastian* (1970);

The Cat Who Wished to Be a Man (1973); *The Wizard in the Tree* (1975); *The First Two Lives of Lukas-Kasha* (1978).

Juvenile non-fantasy: *Border Hawk: August Bondi* (1958); *The Flagship Hope: Aaron Lopez* (1960); *Coll and His White Pig* (1965), picture book; *The Truthful Harp* (1967), picture book; *The King's Fountain* (1971), picture book; *The Four Donkeys* (1972), picture book; *The Foundling, and Other Tales of Prydain* (1973); *The Town Cats and Other Tales* (1977); *Westmark* (1981); *The Kestrel* (1982).

Adult: *And Let the Credit Go* (1955), novel; *My Five Tigers* (1956); *Janine is French* (1959); *My Love Affair with Music* (1960); *Park Avenue Vet* (1962), with Louis J. Camuti; *Fifty Years in the Doghouse* (1964) as *Send for Ryan!* (1965).

Secondary Works

Alexander, Lloyd. "The Flat-Heeled Muse," *The Horn Book Magazine*, 41 (April, 1965), pp. 141-46.

———. "The Grammar of Story," in *Celebrating Children's Books*, ed. Betsy Hearne and Marilyn Kaye (New York: Lothrop, Lee and Shepard Books, 1981), pp. 3-13.

———. "High Fantasy and Heroic Romance," *The Horn Book Magazine*, 47 (Dec., 1971), pp. 577-84.

———. "Newbery Award Acceptance Speech," *The Horn Book Magazine*, 45 (Aug., 1969), pp. 378-81.

———. "No Laughter in Heaven," *The Horn Book Magazine*, 46 (Feb., 1970), pp. 11-19.

———. "Seeing with the Third Eye," *Elementary English*, 51 (Sept., 1974), pp. 759-65.

Carr, Marion. "Classic Hero in a New Mythology," *The Horn Book Magazine*, 47 (Oct., 1971), pp. 508-13.

Colbath, Mary Lou. "Worlds as They Should Be: Middle-earth, Narnia, and Prydain," *Elementary English*, 48 (Dec., 1971), pp. 937-45.

Durell, Ann. "Who's Lloyd Alexander?" *The Horn Book Magazine*, 45 (Aug., 1969), pp. 382-84.

Glass, Rona. "*A Wrinkle in Time* and *The High King*: Two Couples, Two Perspectives," *Children's Literature Associaton Quarterly*, 6 (Fall, 1981), pp. 15-18.

Lane, Elizabeth. "Lloyd Alexander's Chronicles of Prydain & the Welsh Tradition," *Orcrist*, 7 (1973), pp. 25-28.

Rossman, Douglas A., and Charles E. Rossman. *Pages from "The Book of Three": A Prydain Glossary*. Baltimore, Md.: T-K Graphics, 1975.

West, Richard C. "The Tolkienians: Some Introductory Reflections on Alan Garner, Carol Kendall, and Lloyd Alexander," *Orcrist*, 2 (1967-1968), pp. 4-15.

ALEXANDER OLDKNOW (the Green Knowe books). *See* Oldknow, Alexander

ALISON BRADLEY (*The Owl Service*). *See* Bradley, Alison

AMES, HARRIET, a character in E[lwyn] B[rooks] White's* *Stuart Little**. This tiny girl—just two inches tall—is of a prominent family in the town of Ames' Crossing. The family fortune seems to have been made by an ancestor in Revolutionary times who had ferried anyone who could pay across the stream at Ames' Crossing. So pretty is Harriet that she catches the attention of Stuart Little*, a mouse-like person only two inches tall himself. He invites her to come canoeing with him, but their plans are spoiled when Stuart's canoe is ruined.

AMMARN, a type of tree in Jane Curry's* *The Birdstones**. These trees were planted by the Aldar*; there were many on Inas Ebhélic*. They seem to have been symbols of fruitfulness; a stone copy of an ammarn tree surrounded by a ring of carved stone water stands in the Tree-Chamber of Inas Ebhélic even into the twentieth century, reflecting a symbol found several places in Curry's Abáloc novels*. The destruction of the last ammarn tree on the island clears the way for Tekla* to dedicate there a shrine to Katóa* in the fourth century. The stump sends out a shoot, finally, in the twelfth century, and it grows into a magnificent tree by the twentieth century. By placing three birdstones* in this tree, Dalea* and Thiuclas* are able to make the magic to send them from the twentieth century back to their home in fourth-century Abáloc*.

AMOS, the "me" in Robert Lawson's* *Ben and Me**. This mouse is the oldest of twenty-six children, some of whom are named Bathsheba, Claude, Daniel, Ephraim, Xenophon, Ysobel, and Zenas. He and his family live in the vestry of Old Christ Church in Philadelphia, in the eighteenth century. During the winter of 1745, the family is so poor that Amos decides that as the oldest he must leave and make his own way in the world. He meets Benjamin Franklin* (Ben) and becomes that learned man's close friend and adviser, and the sometimes unwitting participant in some of Ben's experiments. Amos does the actual observing when Ben flies a kite during a thunderstorm, and Amos is responsible for Ben's diplomatic coups as ambassador to France. While he is in France, Amos aids an aristocratic mouse named Sophia*. As the years pass, Amos desires less and less to travel everywhere with Ben, hidden in his fur cap, as he has done; on the eve of Ben's eighty-first birthday, Amos presents him with a tricorner hat. After Ben's death, Amos writes his own version of events. The manuscript is found in the twentieth century beneath the bedroom hearthstone in an old Philadelphia house.

AMULET, THE, an object in E[dith] Nesbit Bland's* *The Story of the Amulet**. This charm is in three parts: two halves and a pin that holds them together. The amulet was shaped thousands of years ago from a red stone thrown out to sea when the volcano of Atlantis* erupted. For centuries it was worshipped in a succession of shrines by several peoples, for the complete amulet guarantees the fertility of the land and people; drives away the things that make people unhappy; gives strength, courage, and virtue; and grants individuals their heart's desire.

Finally the amulet was captured, along with its priest, by invaders. The priest made it invisible, keeping it safe until it was returned to the broken shrine. There its power was enslaved by someone who knew a greater word of power. When the shrine was being rebuilt, a stone was dropped on half the amulet, and it and the pin were ground into dust. The other half lay in the desert for thousands of years, to be found in Egypt after Napoleon took his army there. It was brought to England and eventually sold to the owner of a curio shop. Here Robert*, Anthea*, Cyril*, and Jane* buy it in the twentieth century in order to get their heart's desire—the return of their parents and baby brother. Because half the amulet is missing, they use their half to travel through time by using the words of power: "Ur Hekau Setcheh." Their search for the missing half is complicated when they meet unscrupulous Rekh-marā*, an Egyptian priest who is also search- ing for it. Finally the children and the priest find a time when the amulet was whole and unguarded, and they take it. Under the arch of the joined amulet, the souls of Rekh-marā and Jimmy*, a twentieth-century scholar, are joined. At their parents' return, the children give the amulet to Jimmy. It eventually goes on display in the British Museum.

AMULET, THE. *See Story of the Amulet, The*

ANALDAS, UNCLE, a character in Robert Lawson's* *Rabbit Hill** and *The Tough Winter**. He is the uncle of Molly and the great-uncle of Little Georgie*; he is perhaps the father of Mildred. Crotchety old Analdas lives in bachelor squalor after Mildred's marriage, until Molly invites him to come live on the Hill with her family. Here Analdas is sometimes more trouble than he is worth, grumbling about unnecessary things like tidiness. When Georgie is hit by a car and taken in by the Folks in the house on the Hill, who care for him, Analdas spreads the word that he is being mistreated. In a subsequent autumn, he takes great pleasure in announcing that the following winter will be a hard one and is darkly pleased when it turns out so. During that winter, Analdas decides to go south to the bluegrass country to fetch back the Folks, who have gone there, and he sets out to do just that, ending up in Tim McGrath's* barn. Here he stays for a time before going home. During his journey, his left ear is frost-bitten, making his appearance even more disreputable than before. After this sojourn, he thinks of the bluegrass country as a veritable paradise, where he will spend all his winters from now on.

ANDREW, a dog in the Mary Poppins books*, by P[amela] L[yndon] Travers*. This silky little lapdog belongs to Miss Lark, the rich woman living next to the Banks family on Cherry Tree Lane. Miss Lark pampers Andrew excessively. He has four little overcoats and two pairs of tiny boots; he has cream every day for every meal; he sleeps on a silk pillow and goes to the hairdresser twice a week in a chauffeur-driven car. All the neighborhood people think Andrew is a ninny. This embarrasses him, for he longs to be a common dog; though he is fond of Miss Lark, he is bored by his rich life. Andrew makes friends with all the common dogs he can, especially with Willoughby, half Airedale, half retriever, and the worse half of both. One day Andrew brings Willoughby to live with him and Miss Lark. With Mary Poppins* translating, he makes Miss Lark agree to his demands that he neither wear overcoats nor go to the hairdresser again. Miss Lark does not give up her fussing, but between them Andrew and Willoughby manage her quite well.

ANDREW, EUPHEMIA (MISS), a character in P[amela] L[yndon] Travers'* *Mary Poppins Comes Back**. She was the governess of George Banks, and he remembers her as a holy terror. She is one, too: strict, always right, loving to put everyone in the wrong about everything. This large woman with a deafening voice is very careful of her health; she brings lots of medicines with her when she visits people. Miss Andrew not only deafens the ear: she deafens the personality, too, and people find themselves giving in to her with great alacrity. She keeps a lark in a cage and wonders why it will not sing. Descending on the Banks family, Miss Andrew more than meets her match in Mary Poppins*, their nanny. When Miss Andrew insults her, Mary Poppins frees the lark and uses it and its cage for a bit of revenge. Totally terrorized, Miss Andrew leaves and the Banks family never sees her again.

ANDREW KETTERLEY *(The Magician's Nephew). See* Ketterley, Andrew

ANDY BATTLE *(The Three Mulla-mulgars). See* Battle, Andy

ANGELA PAFF *(The Daybreakers; The Birdstones). See* Paff, Angela

ANGHALAC, the name of a horn in Alan Garner's* *The Moon of Gomrath**. This ivory-colored horn with rim and mouthpiece of gold is the third best thing of price ever won. It had been given by Moriath to Finn, who gave it to Camha, who gave it to Angharad Goldenhand*, who gives it to Susan*. Anghalac is to be blown only in time of great need, for the sound of it is too sweet for mortal heart to hear and have rest again. Susan blows it when she is pursued by the Brollachan*, an evil force; the horn calls Garanhir* and his Herlathing (the Wild Hunt*), who destroy the Brollachan. *See also* hunting horn.

ANGHARAD, a character in *The Foundling, and Other Tales of Prydain* who is mentioned in *The Castle of Llyr** and *Taran Wanderer**, by Lloyd Alexander*. She had been of the House of Llyr* and was the daughter of Regat; she was the wife of Geraint and the mother of Eilonwy*. Against Regat's wishes Angharad had followed her heart and had run away to marry the only one of her suitors she could love, carrying with her a book of spells and the Golden Pelydryn*, a magical golden ball. After Eilonwy was born and Geraint died, the child had been kidnapped, and Angharad had searched long and hard for her. One winter night, ill and exhausted, Angharad had taken refuge with Morda*, a sorcerer, but she died before the night was done. From her Morda had taken the book and her only jewel, a magical emblem of the House of Llyr; Angharad had given the Pelydryn to her daughter. Morda uses the emblem for evil until he is killed.

ANGHARAD GOLDENHAND, a character in *The Weirdstone of Brisingamen** and *The Moon of Gomrath**, by Alan Garner*. She is the wife of a great captain who sleeps in Fundindelve* until he is to wake and help defeat a great evil. Fair and gentle Angharad is the Lady of the Lake of Redesmere, near Alderley, England, and here she helps those in need of her, on her invisible island floating in the lake. Angharad bears a silver bracelet of power, and her powers are linked to the moon, for when it is full her magical powers wax. She helps Susan* and Colin*, two human children, and their companions, several times. When they are in danger of being captured by evil forces during a difficult but necessary journey in midwinter, Angharad takes them on her island to save them, giving them food and warm cloaks; and to Susan she gives the Mark of Fohla*, a powerful bracelet. During a subsequent adventure, Angharad explains the bracelet's powers to Susan and gives the girl Anghalac*, a magic horn, to blow when she is in mortal danger.

ANGUS TUCK *(Tuck Everlasting). See* Tuck, Angus

ANIMAL FAMILY, THE. Randall Jarrell. Decorations by Maurice Sendak. New York: Pantheon, 1965. 180 pp. American.

In a little log house between the forest and the sea, a hunter* lives by himself. Because his parents have died, he has become lonely, for there is no one with whom to share the beautiful things he sees. One night he hears singing from the ocean, but when he calls out it stops. The next night he again hears the singer in the sea; it is a mermaid* and night after night when she sings he goes to her. Gradually she comes to trust the hunter, and they teach each other their languages. Because she learns his so easily, they soon confine themselves to that, though the mermaid sometimes has trouble because the land and the sea are so different, both physically and in the attitudes the inhabitants hold toward many things. As they spend time together, the mermaid accustoms herself to living on the land, and finally she goes to live in the cabin.

The hunter and the mermaid live together and are happy as they come to know one another better. They are different—the mermaid cannot understand the hunter's regret at his parents' deaths, for she had not regretted that of her sister—but so different are they that they seem alike, and they live together quite contentedly. Then the hunter begins to dream that he is his father's shadow and the mermaid is his mother's, but there is no child. This, the mermaid explains, must mean he wants a boy, to complete the family. One night, coming in late, he laughs that he has done just that. He has brought a bear cub. When the hunter had accidentally come between a mother bear and her cub, he was forced to kill the mother to save his own life. The cub soon becomes part of the family, growing in a clumsy, haphazard way into a fine, big bear* who eats, sleeps, and once brings home some furious bees.

On a winter day when the bear is hibernating and the mermaid has been visiting her family in the sea, she returns to find that the hunter has caught a lynx* kitten. Much more gracefully than the bear, the lynx grows up, loving all of them and not hesitating to show it. The cabin's rafters become the lynx's special place, where it can climb as in a forest of trees.

After a terrible storm, the lynx finds a small boat on the beach, and in it are a dead woman and a small, live boy*. Because the hunter and the mermaid are out, the lynx brings the bear to the boat, and the boy is fascinated. Clutching the bear's fur, the boy follows the lynx to the cabin, where he is found later by the mermaid and the hunter, curled up asleep beside the bear. When the hunter buries the woman, he is reminded of his mother.

The boy grows up in a home he does not see as strange, learning the ways of the mermaid and the hunter, believing that he is their son, not simply a child found by the lynx. He is perfectly happy without knowing he is happy. One morning, leaving the boy in the cabin, the hunter and the mermaid go for a swim and a walk. Each is awkward out of his or her element. But, to the mermaid, the land is better. She speaks to the hunter of how the land has grown familiar to her and of how the sea is always the same, as is life there. The day after her sister had died, she had forgotten, but now she is different, for her heart would break if the boy or the hunter died. The land has made her different; the land is always different, and to her it is better. When they return to the cabin, she tells the boy a story about a little mermaid and how the boy has been part of their family always, even longer than the lynx or the bear.

ANNABEL BANKS (the Mary Poppins books). *See* Banks, Annabel

ANNE BOLEYN (*The House of Arden*). *See* Boleyn, Anne

ANNE MELTON (*The Watch House*). *See* Melton, Anne

ANNUVIN, a place in the Chronicles of Prydain* and *Coll and His White Pig*, by Lloyd Alexander*. This castle lies in the western part of Prydain*, near Mount Dragon*. Achren* had ruled Prydain from here; Arawn*, the Lord of Death, rules now from its skull-shaped throne. Annuvin is a place of darkness and winding halls lit only by torches. It holds a great treasure-trove gathered by Arawn; the treasure includes not only jewels and gold but secrets of crafts and magical implements besides. Hen Wen*, an oracular pig, is taken here and rescued by her master, Coll*; the Black Crochan* also resides here for a time. During Arawn's final bid for control of Prydain the battle comes to the very gates. Glew*, a greedy former giant, inadvertently starts a fire in the treasure room; when he grabs some of the jewels there, the walls burst into flame. At Arawn's death, the castle shatters and burns.

ANTHEA, a character in E[dith] Nesbit Bland's* *Five Children and It*, *The Phoenix and the Carpet*, and *The Story of the Amulet*. She is the sister of Robert*, Jane*, Cyril*, and the Lamb*. Anthea's nickname is "Panther." She and the others have several adventures with magic, discovering a Psammead* who grants wishes, a wishing carpet* in which is rolled the egg of the Phoenix*, and half of an amulet* that takes them back through time to find its other half. Like her brothers and sister, Anthea is not especially clever, attractive, or good, and she has a great talent for getting into mischief without meaning to. Anthea is almost always polite and becomes the particular favorite of the Psammead and of Jimmy*, a scholar. She is responsible for several of the children's transformations, asking the Psammead to make them beautiful and, later, wishing they had wings. She also visits the cook* on her tropical island to see how the woman is making out. Anthea's kindness makes it easy for Imogen* to talk to her and reveal her problem.

ANTHONY BABINGTON (*A Traveller in Time*). See Babington, Anthony.

ANVARD, a place in the Chronicles of Narnia*, by C[live] S[taples] Lewis*. It is the castle from which the kings of Archenland* have ruled for generations. This many-towered stronghold has gates that face east; it has no moat. During the reign of King Lune*, Anvard is the scene of a great battle between the forces of Archenland and the army of Calormen*; after the Calormenes are defeated, their leader, Rabadash*, is here changed into an ass by Aslan*, the great lion-protector of Narnia*.

APPLE, SILVER, an object in *The Magician's Nephew*, by C[live] S[taples] Lewis*. It is also called the Apple of Life and the Apple of Youth. The apples grow on a tree in a walled garden on a green hill far west of Narnia*, a magical land. They shine with a light of their own, and the tree is very beautiful. Though the sweet-smelling apples confer immortality on all who eat them, those who pick them at the wrong time or without permission soon wish they had not, for the immortality the apples confer is filled with misery; the fruit is good, but the eater loathes it forever after. Digory Kirke*, a young boy from Earth, is sent by Aslan*, Narnia's great lion-creator, to pluck an apple from the tree so that it may be planted to keep Jadis*, an evil queen, from entering Narnia. Though he is tempted, he does not eat an apple himself. Jadis does and becomes immortal; this immortality is more a burden than a gift. From the tree planted in Narnia, Digory is allowed to pluck an apple to give to his mother, to make her well. The core of this apple is planted in London, and when that tree finally falls, its wood is made into a magic wardrobe* that takes those who enter it into Narnia.

APPLE ISLAND, a place in Jane Louise Curry's* Abáloc novels*. This island is in the middle of the river just across from Apple Lock*, Ohio. Once known as Inas Ebhélic*, twentieth-century Apple Island still bears traces of its history. Here grows the last ammarn* tree, and here lies the ancient Tree-Chamber, which is sealed up in the twentieth century.

APPLE LOCK, a place in Jane Louise Curry's* *The Birdstones*, The Day-breakers*, and *The Watchers*. This small town is on the Ohio bank of the Ohio River. It was settled in the early nineteeth century on the site of ancient Abáloc*. Apple Lock is an industrial town with the plagues such towns are heir to, for industry has eroded the ancient beauty of the landscape. The town has two public elementary schools and a private school; Poole College is nearby.

APPLE WOMAN, THE, a character in *Mopsa the Fairy**, by Jean Ingelow*. Though homesick for the world, she lives in Fairyland* because the world is filled with pain and suffering. In Fairyland she is valued greatly, for she alone can make the fairies cry. The old apple woman becomes quite fond of Mopsa* and helps her and Jack*, a human boy, to run away when the fairy girl is in danger.

APPLETON, ARTHUR AMORY, a character in *Mr. Twigg's Mistake**, by Robert Lawson*. He is the son of Arthur and Helen Appleton and the nephew of a scientist named Amory. Arthur is sometimes called Squirt. He is an active, imaginative, and ingenious boy whom his father seems to regard as every plague and calamity ever visited upon humankind, all in one child. Arthur enjoys archery, sometimes ambushing the garbage truck when it comes by, and he has several other games based on adventure. When Arthur finds a mole, he decides to make a pet of it, naming it General de Gaulle* and feeding it Bita-Vita Breakfast Food*. To Arthur's surprise the mole soon grows as tall as he is; they become close friends and play together. When General de Gaulle finds an oil well and then disappears, Arthur knows he will be the richest boy at his boarding school, but he would rather have de Gaulle back.

ARABELLA BABINGTON (*A Traveller in Time*). *See* Babington, Arabella

ARABLE, FERN, a character in E[lwyn] B[rooks] White's* *Charlotte's Web**. Her parents operate a small farm; she is the sister of Avery and the niece of Homer L. Zuckerman*. Eight-year-old Fern becomes so upset when her father is about to kill the runt of a litter of pigs that he gives the piglet to her to raise. Fern names him Wilbur*, the most beautiful name she can think of, and she loves him so much that when Wilbur is sold to Mr. Zuckerman, she visits him often. Sensitive Fern understands the speech of the farm animals, and she listens and watches for hours as they go about the business of living. Her mother becomes worried when Fern reports the doings of the farm animals, and she visits a doctor who reassures her, telling Mrs. Arable that Fern will eventually become interested in boys. At the county fair, she does, riding the ferris wheel with Henry Fussy and carrying the memory of those rides with her for a long time.

ARAVIS, a character in *The Horse and His Boy** and *The Last Battle**, by C[live] S[taples] Lewis*. She is the daughter of Kidrash; she becomes the wife of Cor* and the mother of Ram the Great. Aravis is a girl of noble birth in Calormen*; her father is lord of Calavar and has the right to remain on his feet in the presence of the Tisroc*, the king. Like most noble ladies of her culture, she is proud and willful, unable to think of her slaves as people with feelings and unwilling to look beneath her station. When her stepmother arranges a marriage between Aravis and Ahoshta, an old Calormene lord, the girl runs away, drugging the slave set to watch her. She and Hwin*, her talking mare, go toward Narnia*, where both will be free. They soon fall in with Shasta and Breehy-hinny-brinny-hoohy-hah*, the horse who accompanies him. Together the four journey north and there warn the king of Archenland*, the land between Narnia and Calormen, of an impending invasion by the Calormenes. On this journey Aravis learns humility and consideration for others, receiving from Aslan*, Narnia's great lion-protector, scratches equal to the stripes received by the slave she had drugged. Shasta discovers that he is really Cor, a prince of Archenland, and Aravis lives with his family at Anvard*, the palace. She and Cor get on so well together, fighting and making up, that they get married after several years so as to do it more conveniently. Aravis is among those in Aslan's country when Narnia comes to an end.

ARAWN, a figure in Celtic lore who appears as a character in Lloyd Alexander's* Chronicles of Prydain*, *Coll and His White Pig,* and *The Foundling, and Other Tales of Prydain.* He is also known as the Lord of Death. Arawn was the consort of Achren*, queen of Annuvin*. Once she had taught him magic, he took the throne and became king of Annuvin. Early in Prydain's* history, Arawn took from it certain secrets of metal-forging, clay-working, and cultivation, as well as magical implements for doing these things. From his castle near Mount Dragon*, Arawn seeks control of Prydain, playing on the greed of some of its chieftains and winning their allegiance. One is the Horned King*, who becomes Arawn's champion for a time. Arawn gets use of the Black Crochan*, a huge cauldron in which dead warriors are made into the ruthless, deathless Cauldron-Born*; for the Crochan, he pays a high price to its owners. After the Horned King's death, Arawn uses the Crochan to strengthen his army until its owners take it back from him because he has refused to give it up when he was supposed to. Finally Arawn makes a final, desperate bid for control of Prydain, leaving his stronghold and changing his shape to get Dyrnwyn*, a great sword that is the only weapon that can kill him. This shape-changing is a power Arawn uses only when no other will serve, and it makes him as vulnerable as the shape he becomes; when Taran*, a young warrior, bears Dyrnwyn into Arawn's castle, he slays the king when he takes the shape of a great serpent. Where Arawn's body falls and fades, the ground becomes seared and wasted.

ARBICAN, a character in *The Wizard in the Tree**, by Lloyd Alexander*. He is an ancient enchanter. When the other wizards sailed to Vale Innis*, Arbican was left behind, for he had been imprisoned inside a tree when he tried to pull off one of its branches to use as a walking stick. Centuries later the tree is felled and Arbican is rescued by Mallory*, an orphaned serving girl. By this time, Arbican's powers have become erratic with disuse, and getting to Vale Innis becomes a problem. Arbican cannot stay in this world, for he will die, as he has already lived out a lifetime. In trying to help Mallory, Arbican adds to his problems when Squire Scrupnor* decides to frame the wizard for a murder he himself has committed. After humiliating adventures during which he is transformed into a goose, a stag, and a pig, Arbican regains his powers as a wizard by an old method: Mallory gives him a gold ring. He realizes that Scrupnor is the murderer and accidentally annihilates him when the squire touches Arbican as his powers reach their peak. Arbican builds his boat and sails, at last, to Vale Innis.

ARBIE MOAR *(The Watchers). See* Moar, Russell Boyd

ARCHENLAND, a place in C[live] S[taples] Lewis's* Chronicles of Narnia*. This mountainous kingdom between Narnia* and Calormen* had been settled early in Narnia's history; the second son of King Frank* had been its first king. For the most part Archenland has been at peace with Calormen, though during King Lune's* reign this peace is broken when Rabadash* leads his army to take over Archenland; they are halted at Anvard*, the palace of the king. Lune is succeeded by his son, Cor*, who is succeeded by Ram the Great, the land's greatest king; many years later King Nain reigns in Archenland. In Archenland is Mount Pire, a twin-peaked mountain formed of the remains of Pire, a two-headed giant; Stormness, a great mountain on which a wild bear has lived, is also here. Near Anvard the Hermit of the Southern March* has his dwelling.

ARCHIMEDES, a character in *The Sword in the Stone**, by T[erence] H[anbury] White*. He is a tawny owl and the pet of Merlyn*, a wizard. Because they get little company, Archimedes is shy with strangers; it takes a little time before he is willing to talk to the Wart (Arthur*), who visits Merlyn. Archimedes hates to be called "Archie." When Merlyn becomes the tutor of the Wart and his foster brother, Kay*, Archimedes goes along, helping once in the Wart's education by taking the boy—who has been changed into an owl—to meet Athene*. Archimedes later marries and raises several families. When the Wart is crowned king of Britain, the owl sends his great-great-grandson to perch on the back of the throne and make messes.

ARDASHIR, a character mentioned in *The First Two Lives of Lukas-Kasha**, by Lloyd Alexander*. He was the son of Tamina and the father of Nur-Jehan*. Ardashir was one of the greatest kings of Bishangar* until he was killed in battle. For many years his death is kept a secret because the kings of Abadan*, who fear him, would overrun Bishangar once they knew they would not have to face him. Because of the great battles and raids attributed to Ardashir, the Abadani begin to fear him even more.

ARDEN, BETTY, a character in *The House of Arden**, by E[dith] Nesbit Bland*. She lives in Arden Castle* in 1707. Vain, flighty, and not terriby quick-witted, Betty almost collapses when her coach is robbed by Edward Talbot* as she travels from Arden House* to Arden Castle. When Edward, posing as James III, the "rightful" heir to the throne, seeks shelter in Arden Castle, Betty hides him in a secret room and manages a convincing faint when men dressed as soldiers come looking for him.

ARDEN, EDRED, a character in *The House of Arden** and *Harding's Luck**, by E[dith] Nesbit Bland*. He is the son of Edred Arden and the brother of Elfrida Arden*. The day before Edred's tenth birthday, he and Elfrida visit Arden Castle*, and here Edred learns that because his father is missing he will inherit the title of Lord Arden and live at the dilapidated castle. Hidden in the castle, legend has it, is a long-lost treasure, and if Edred speaks a certain spell at sunset between his ninth and tenth years, he will get the help he needs to find the treasure. Edred speaks the spell and thus makes the acquaintance of the Mouldiwarp*, the white mole on the Arden badge, who tells Edred and Elfrida how to travel into the past to find the treasure. During their adventures, Edred sometimes has his ego bruised because he is not as brave and bold as Elfrida, though he begins to be braver and wiser after he talks with Sir Walter Raleigh in the Tower of London. Edred makes a difficult decision when he learns that his father is alive and that if the children use their magic to rescue him, they will never again be able to travel into the past. When Edred and Elfrida choose to rescue their father, they do not regret their decision, though Edred regrets the hesitation he had experienced while making it. He later makes another difficult decision when, on the advice of the Mouldiestwarp*, Edred braves the dark night to rescue kidnapped Dickie Harding*, the true Lord Arden, knowing that in doing so he will help reveal Dickie's true position and his father will lose his title. Edred has one more adventure in the past when he and Elfrida travel back in time with Dickie, via some magical moonflower* seeds, and finally see the treasure being hidden.

ARDEN, ELFRIDA, a character in E[dith] Nesbit Bland's* *The House of Arden** and *Harding's Luck**. Her father is Edred Arden; her brother is also named Edred Arden*. Twelve-year-old Elfrida proves her bravery many times when she and Edred travel into the past to find the long-lost treasure of the

Ardens. Her boldness and ready sympathy get her into several difficulties. In the sixteenth century, taken with Anne Boleyn's* beauty and happiness, she warns the queen of her tragic fate and provokes the wrath of Henry VIII*; in 1605, Elfrida and her brother are locked in the Tower of London when she unwittingly reveals the details of the Gunpowder Plot before it is discovered, and she must be rescued after Edred is freed; in 1708, Elfrida unknowingly helps Edward Talbot* win a bet by hiding him in Arden Castle*, thinking he is James III, the "rightful" heir to the throne. After she and Edred rescue their missing father, their time travel is over, except for an adventure with Dickie Harding*, who uses his magical moonflower* seeds to take them back to the time when the treasure had been hidden.

ARDEN, RICHARD, a character in *Harding's Luck** and *The House of Arden**, by E[dith] Nesbit Bland*. This boy of seventeenth-century England is the son of gentry. After a long illness, he is "replaced" by Dickie Harding*, a boy from the twentieth century who travels back in time and lives as Richard. Richard's life is a rich one; he learns not only from his tutor, Mr. Parados*, but from a shipbuilder who was at the battle against the Spanish Armada, and once he meets the king and queen at court. When Edred and Elfrida Arden**, two time travelers from the twentieth century, visit Richard, appearing as his cousins, Richard narrowly escapes being imprisoned in the Tower of London as Elfrida demonstrates a too-intimate knowledge of the Gunpowder Plot on the very day it is discovered. He later helps her to escape from the Tower. Richard grows to be a man loyal to England and to his name, his memories mixed with those of Dickie Harding.

ARDEN CASTLE, a place in E[dith] Nesbit Bland's* *The House of Arden** and *Harding's Luck**. This beautiful castle was built before 1508. In the sixteenth century the castle is visited by Henry VIII* and Anne Boleyn*. During the English civil war, the castle had been overrun by Cromwell's Roundheads, and the treasure of the Ardens had been hidden, not to be found until 1908. In 1707 Edward Talbot* wins a bet by staying overnight in one of the castle's secret rooms while pretending to be James III, the "rightful" heir to the throne. The threat of a French invasion in 1807 keeps all who live in the castle in a state of readiness, though the only Frenchmen who land here are shipwrecked. By the early twentieth century, the family fortunes have fallen and Arden Castle is in a state of disrepair. After Edred and Elfrida Arden** and their cousin, Dickie Harding*, find the long-lost Arden treasure, the new lord of the castle restores it to its former splendor, aided by photographs taken by Edred and Elfrida on one of their journeys back in time.

ARDEN HOUSE, a place in E[dith] Nesbit Bland's* *The House of Arden** and *Harding's Luck**. This townhouse in London was built before 1605. Here Edred and Elfrida Arden** and Dickie Harding*, time travelers from the twentieth century, meet; and here Edred and Elfrida and the Arden family are arrested for high treason when Elfrida unwittingly reveals the details of the Gunpowder Plot before it is discovered.

ARDIS, a character in Natalie Babbitt's* *The Search for Delicious**. When the world is still very young, this little mermaid comes to live in a lake created by a spring discovered by a dwarf*. Ardis promises the dwarfs she will watch over the spring, in exchange for a doll they make for her of linked stones with a fern for hair. Every day she blows a whistle* that opens the door of the now-flooded rockhouse built over the spring and plays in the rockhouse with her doll; at night she leaves the rockhouse, blows the whistle to close the door, and sleeps. Because all the streams of the kingdom flow from the lake, the waters of the land belong to Ardis. One day a man comes by and, finding the whistle, blows it, thus closing the door with Ardis's doll inside the house. Because he takes the whistle away, she cannot get into the house. For centuries Ardis mourns her lost doll, and someone writes a song about her sadness, but no one can help. At last Vaun-gaylen*, a young boy, receives the whistle and brings it to her; in return for the whistle, Ardis may be responsible for the destruction of a dam which an evil man named Hemlock* has had built across the streams flowing from the lake. Though she is centuries old, Ardis looks like a beautiful child, smelling of lilies and gleaming with water.

ARE ALL THE GIANTS DEAD? Mary Norton. Illus. Brian Froud. London: Dent, 1975. 119 pp. British.

James* wakes one night to find Mildred*, his guide to adventure, in his room. She leads him through the streets of his village to the Land of Cockayne*, where the characters of fairy tales live happily ever after. While visiting at the castle, James meets Dulcibel*, a princess, playing cup and ball beside a well. Such play is dangerous for her, for if the ball falls into the well, she will have to marry the toad that lives there and brings it to her.

Mildred and James go through the forest to Much-Belungen-under-Bluff*, where they visit a nameless inn and where James is introduced to Jack-the-Giant-Killer* and Jack-of-the-Beanstalk*, now old men who run the inn. The bane of Jack-the-Giant-Killer's existence is a pair of red dancing shoes* that dance into the inn whenever the door is open; Jack-of-the-Beanstalk thinks they are trying to say something. Mildred goes to report on a royal wedding, and James stays overnight at the inn. The next day he follows the red shoes into the forest; they lead him to Dulcibel, who has run away from the castle. Her ball has finally fallen into the well and she must marry the toad in a week or the castle and all who live there will vanish into thin air. Though Mildred has explained again and again that the toad will become a prince, Dulcibel is unequal to the situation.

To help Dulcibel, James decides to find a special toad with a jewel in its head, which the toad in the well had been in love with; perhaps the toad will prefer to marry its own kind. He and Dulcibel visit Hecubenna*, an old witch who is supposed to have the toad—which is really a frog—but she has lost it to a giant* living on top of the Bluff above the village. The only way to the top of the Bluff is through a crevice filled with hobgoblins*. Dismayed but not dissuaded, James takes Dulcibel to the inn, where she explains her situation to the two Jacks. That night, after he and Dulcibel go to bed, James hears the two old men go out.

The next day the children explore the crevice in the Bluff. The hobgoblins, though ugly, prove to be gentle creatures, and James and Dulcibel make their way to the top of the Bluff. Here they see the giant's castle. Evening comes and a thunderstorm is whipped up by an evil fairy. James and Dulcibel spend the night in the crevice. In the morning they find that a boulder loosened by rivulets has blocked the lower part of the crevice, and they cannot get back to the inn. Thirsty, they climb out onto the Bluff and find a pool—and the giant, intently fishing for something. The giant flips out the jeweled frog, which falls into Dulcibel's lap. James grabs it, and the two children run. The giant chases Dulcibel but falls, felled by Jack-the-Giant-Killer, who has reached the top of the Bluff by climbing a beanstalk grown from one of Jack-of-the-Beanstalk's beans.

When they return to the inn, James makes Dulcibel promise to marry the toad, for while she has the frog nothing will harm her; and after she promises to marry the toad, if she loses the frog, it will not matter as much. After Dulcibel starts for the castle, James, in shock, sees that the frog has somehow escaped from her, but he cannot catch it. That night Mildred comes back to the inn. After the wedding she had gone to the castle and there witnessed Dulcibel's return. The girl had promised to marry the toad, and all but Mildred were surprised to see a handsome prince spring from the well. Exhausted by the day's events, Mildred, James, and the two Jacks go to bed; James, lying awake thinking, suddenly realizes that he is home.

ARHA. *See* Tenar

ARKENSTONE, THE, a fabulous stone in *The Hobbit**, by J[ohn] R[onald] R[euel] Tolkien*. Found by dwarves* delving into the heart of the Lonely Mountain, the Arkenstone has become their greatest treasure. Huge and clear, it shines with a light of its own, and its facets glitter in the light with a brilliance of a thousand rainbows. The Arkenstone becomes part of the hoard of Smaug*, a dragon, when he takes the treasure of the king under the Lonely Mountain. Bilbo Baggins*, accompanying Thorin Oakenshield* and a party of dwarves to recover the ancient treasure, finds the stone and keeps it for himself; he later gives it to the men of Lake-town*, to bargain with when Thorin refuses to acknowledge their claims on the treasure. This plan fails. After Thorin's death the Arkenstone is placed on his breast as he lies in his tomb.

ARMAMENTARIUM, an object in *The Cat Who Wished to Be a Man**, by Lloyd Alexander*. This chest is the property of the illustrious Dr. Tudbelly*, who carries it with him from town to town. In its many drawers and cubbyholes are the ingredients he uses in his sometimes inconsistent concoctions.

ARMINTA HALLAM (*Mindy's Mysterious Miniature*). *See* Hallam, Arminta

ARREN, a character in *The Farthest Shore**, by Ursula K. LeGuin*. His real name is Lebannen. Arren's father is the Prince of Enlad and the Enlades on Earthsea*; his mother is called Rose. Arren's lineage is old and respected, for he is descended from Morred and Serriadh, two great kings. He has inherited the sword of Serriadh, an ancient enchanted weapon never drawn except in the service of life; from this sword he has received the name "Arren," which means "sword." When spells and sorcerers seem to be failing in the Enlades, Arren's father sends the boy to the island of Roke*, to consult the mages there. Arren travels with Ged*, the Archmage, on a long and dangerous journey across Earthsea, searching for the cause of the leaching out of magic from the land. On this journey Arren visits islands he has only heard of and meets and speaks with dragons and with the mysterious Children of the Open Sea*. Along the way he grows from a boy infatuated with Ged and his magic to a young man aware of his own failings and strengths. At last he follows Ged out of Earthsea into the land of the dead and there helps the mage to seal the opening between the worlds of the living and the dead. Then Arren manages to drag the exhausted Ged across the Mountains of Pain back to the world of the living. In doing so, he fulfills a prophecy spoken by Maharion, the last king to rule all Earthsea from Havnor*—that the next king to rule would be the one who "has crossed the dark land living and come to the far shores of the day" (p. 20). Arren becomes the King of All the Isles.

ARRIETTY CLOCK (the Borrower series). *See* Clock, Arrietty

ARTAIR, a legendary British king who appears as a character in *The Sleepers**, by Jane Louise Curry*. He is the brother of Margan* and the uncle of Medraut*; he is the husband of Gwynhyfar and the father of Anir. After their last battle against the Saxons, Artair and his men tethered their horses in an underground chamber and slept there until the time when Britain would need them. In the twentieth century they are wakened because Margan and her son have discovered the chamber and are planning to kill them and take the *Brenhin Dlyseu**, the Thirteen Treasures of Prydein, which lie in the chamber. Because Medraut has the valuable Ring of Luned*, which he captured in the battle, Artair leads his men against Margan and her minions. The Ring secured, Artair and his men sail with the Treasures to a place of safety beyond the seas. *See also* Arthur

ARTHUR, a legendary British king who appears as a character in several works. In T[erence] H[anbury] White's* *The Sword in the Stone**, he is the son of Uther Pendragon and is taken by Merlyn* to Sir Ector, who raises him as his own son. From Kay*, Ector's real son, Arthur gets the nickname "the Wart," because it almost rhymes with Art. He does not like having no mother or father, for it makes him different, and Kay has taught him that being different is wrong.

Loving, honest Wart admires Kay and loves Sir Ector. He is a hero-worshipper and a born follower. Though no braver than any other boy, Wart tries to do what he believes is right, and this fervor makes him do many things that are brave. When one of Sir Ector's hawks is lost in the Forest Sauvage*, the Wart goes after it because he knows how bad the falconer will feel. Here he meets King Pellinore* and the Questing Beast* and finds Merlyn, a wizard who comes to the castle to be the boys' tutor. After this, life and the Wart's lessons are rarely quiet; Merlyn changes the boy into a perch so he can learn about despotism; into a merlin to learn about courage; into a snake so that he can learn about responsibility and the power to kill; into an owl, to learn of the violence men are capable of; and into a badger so that he can learn about men and, incidentally, about the powerful and the helpless. Interspersed are adventures with witches, Robin Wood*, and everyday life. When the time comes, Kay is made knight and the Wart chokes down his own feelings and becomes Kay's squire. Though Merlyn has tried to erase the Wart's romanticism about chivalry, the Wart, were he made a knight, would like to battle all evil by himself. When he accompanies Kay to a tournament in London, the Wart draws from the stone the sword that makes him king over all Britain—a shattering experience, for he cannot stand to see Ector bow before him. But he becomes king, with Merlyn to advise him.

In William Mayne's* *Earthfasts*, Latin-speaking Arthur and his men sleep among their treasures in a chamber beneath the castle at Garebridge. In the middle of the Round Table is a stone socket in which sits a candle* that holds time still for Arthur and his men. While it is in its place, they sleep, appearing to the rest of the world as stalactites and stalagmites. When Nellie Jack John Cherry* (John), an eighteenth-century soldier, enters the chamber in search of the treasure, he takes the candle, for his own has burned out. With the candle out of its place, time begins again for Arthur and his men, and they wake. They are out of joint with the twentieth century, however, and appear as ghosts. Arthur or one of his men snatches David Francis Wix*, a boy who has looked deeply into the candle and seen the vision it holds, into the chamber where they have slept. When Arthur appears to Keith Heseltine*, who takes the candle after David vanishes, he makes the boy understand that the candle must be put back. As Keith goes to the passage leading to the chamber, the king and his army become more and more a part of the boy's world, until they no longer move as ghosts. Arthur decides he will arise now, and he tries to keep Keith from putting the candle back in place, cutting the boy with Excalibur in the process. Keith succeeds, and Arthur and his men sleep once more.

In *The Grey King** and *Silver on the Tree**, by Susan Cooper*, Arthur is the husband of Guinevere and the father of Bran Davies*. Because she had known he would not believe Bran is his own son, Guinevere had taken the child to twentieth-century Wales, with the help of Merriman Lyon*, Arthur's friend and adviser. Arthur wins the Battle of Badon with the aid of the six powerful Signs of the Light*, but his peace does not last, and the Dark, which he has defeated for a time, rises in power again. Arthur is one of the three Lords of High Magic who keep a golden harp* until Bran comes and wins it by right; this is the first time Arthur and his son meet. Arthur may have something to do with Herne*, the leader of the Wild Hunt*, for Herne's eyes are very like Bran's, and where Herne disappears Arthur appears, after the final battle between the Dark and the Light. Once this battle is done, the king sails with the forces of the Light in the *Pridwen* to the peaceful land in back of the north wind, there to rest and be happy among the apple trees. Though Bran chooses to stay in the world of men, Arthur feels he has made the right choice. *See also* Artair

ARTHUR, ARTHUR (DUB), a character in Jane Louise Curry's* *Beneath the Hill** who is also mentioned in *The Daybreakers** and *The Birdstones**. "Dub" is short for "Double," an apt nickname because of his double name. When practical Dub discovers Nūtayē (the City of the Moon Under the Mountain*) and its inhabitants during a visit with his cousin, Margaret Arthur*, he has trouble believing they are real and that a true evil is sealed beneath the mountain. At last he does believe, and he helps *y Tylwyth Teg**, the Fair Folk*, to escape to Tir na'nOg*, riding in their boats to his own home. The Folk give him a gift: a book written in an unknown language and bound with covers of rose quartz—*The Book of the Kings of Abáloc**—which they had found in Nūtayē. Dub vows to translate the book someday, though this may prove to be the work of a lifetime.

ARTHUR, MARGARET (MIGGLE), a character in *Beneath the Hill**, by Jane Louise Curry*. She is the cousin of Arthur Arthur* and of Stevie Griffith*. Though Miggle is impulsive and often illogical in her thinking, she likes to control things; when she finds a strange key* in the family spring, she concocts a treasure hunt with it as a prize. Because Miggle has a special feeling for old tales, she readily accepts Nūtayē (the City of the Moon Under the Mountain*) and its inhabitants, realizing before the other children do how valuable is the key she has found. Miggle helps *y Tylwyth Teg**, the Fair Folk*, to escape to Tir na'nOg*, rediverting the underground river they have used so that it covers the Bane*, where an ancient evil force is trying to break out. Realizing that she is not always as wise as she should be and that she might lose the powerful key, Miggle melts it in her mother's kiln.

ARTHUR AMORY APPLETON (*Mr. Twigg's Mistake*). *See* Appleton, Arthur Amory

ARTHUR TURVEY (*Mary Poppins Comes Back*). *See* Turvey, Arthur

ASLAN, a character in the Chronicles of Narnia*, by C[live] S[taples] Lewis*. He is the son of the Emperor-Beyond-the-Sea. Aslan has nine names, among which seem to be "Bridge Builder" and "King of the Wood." Though he can appear as any creature imaginable, he usually appears as a lion with a rich, golden mane and a rich, golden voice. He sings Narnia* into being and becomes its protector-ruler, though he does not always stay there. Whenever he is needed, Aslan comes. He breaks the grip of the evil White Witch's* winter by bringing the spring, he makes sure Archenland* is warned when an army from Calormen* seeks to invade it, and he reawakens the old Narnia which has been oppressed into sleep by the conquerors from Telmar*. When Narnia's Prince Rilian* is lost, Aslan brings Jill Pole* and Eustace Clarence Scrubb* to find him. Aslan is the power of life and of growing things, and his country is a place where all are happy forever. When Edmund Pevensie* must be slain by the White Witch because he is a traitor, Aslan takes his place on the Stone Table* and is slain by her instead; because he is blameless, the Table breaks, death reverses itself, and he is resurrected, to become more powerful than before. Though Aslan is good, he is not safe, for he is ferocious with his enemies and daunting to his followers. He can be playful, though he is royal; it is like romping with a thunderstorm. At the time of the last battle of Narnia, Aslan calls an end to all things and leads his chosen ones into his country.

AT THE BACK OF THE NORTH WIND. George MacDonald. Illus. Arthur Hughes. London: Strahan and Co., 1871. 378 pp. British.

Diamond*, the son of a coachman, sleeps in the stable loft above his father's favorite horse. One night the North Wind* speaks to him and tells him to meet her outside, but when he goes, she is not there. The next week, the Wind, a lovely lady, comes again and takes him out. That night he watches as she frightens a bad nurse, and the Wind grows large and carries Diamond with her as she flies over London. Seeing a ragged little girl, Nanny*, Diamond wants to help her, so the Wind leaves him, but when he walks Nanny home, the door is locked against her. The children take shelter in a barrel and then wander for a time; Diamond comes to his home and Nanny goes off to work. A week later Diamond gets a chance to give her a penny when they meet in the daytime. One evening Diamond sees the Wind, tiny now, helping a bee out of a flower, and that night he is wakened by the Wind, huge now, who takes him out. She is going to sink a ship, and the boy does not want to see, so she puts him into a cathedral. Here Diamond sleeps and in his sleep hears the stained-glass apostles maligning the Wind. He wakes in bed.

When Diamond is sent to stay with his aunt, he again meets the Wind, and he asks to be taken to the country at the back of the north wind*. That night he falls ill. The Wind comes for him and, since of course the North Wind cannot blow north, puts him onto various ships and, finally, onto an iceberg going in the right direction. When the iceberg comes to land, he finds the Wind sitting on the doorstep of her country. Passing through her, Diamond comes to the country, where nothing goes wrong but nothing is quite right, though all will be right some day. After a time Diamond longs to go home; he meets the Wind, and she takes him to his aunt's. He has been quite ill.

His father's employer has gone bankrupt because of the ship the Wind had sunk, and Diamond's father becomes a cabman. Meanwhile Diamond's little brother is born, and the family goes back to London. Here Diamond becomes a favorite with the other cabmen, learning to drive and to take care of the horse. One day he meets Mr. Raymond*, who gives him a book after he learns to read. Not seeing Nanny for several days, Diamond learns she has been sick, so he gets Mr. Raymond to take her to the hospital. When his father falls ill, Diamond takes the cab out himself. He has trouble at a strange cabstand until a cabman he had once helped intervenes. During the two weeks he drives, Diamond brings home enough to help his family and even reunites a pair of lovers. When he visits Nanny in the hospital, he hears Mr. Raymond tell the children there a story about a cursed princess.

Mr. Raymond makes a bargain with Diamond's father that if the family takes in Nanny the father will get use of Mr. Raymond's horse. Nanny tells Diamond of a dream he has had: how the North Wind had blown her into a garden, where she had gone inside the moon and kept clean the windows there until she had peeked where she should not have. She does not believe the dream. Nanny comes to live with Diamond and his family, and so does the horse, who proves to be more trouble than he is worth, for he lames himself. When the Wind calls Diamond to the stable one night, he hears Mr. Raymond's horse telling his father's horse that he is an angel-horse who has hurt his ankle to grow fat. The next day Mr. Raymond comes for his horse and decides to hire Diamond's father as his coachman, for the man has been obedient and the two horses will make a fine pair, after a little work.

All go to live at Mr. Raymond's house. One night Diamond again meets the North Wind, who tells him of her many names, including Bad Fortune, and reveals that he has seen only a shadow of her country. The Wind pays several more visits. The next night she comes again and takes him to his old home, now dreary and dark, then she takes him back to Mr. Raymond's house. Another night Diamond wakes and finds the Wind in his room, looking at him. Finally she comes again and at last he goes to the country at the back of the north wind, though people think he is dead.

Note: This work was originally serialized in *Good Words for the Young* in 1870.

ATHENE, a goddess in Greek and Roman mythology who appears as a character in *The Sword in the Stone**, by T[erence] H[anbury] White*. She is the goddess of wisdom and the mother of owls. Athene lives by herself, though she is beyond solitude, and she is very unhappy, though she is beyond sorrow. In her unhappiness she is never anything but merciful and protecting toward those around her. She has a beauty that is neither of youth nor of age, and one can be aware of this beauty even though she is invisible. Archimedes*, an owl belonging to Merlyn*, a wizard, takes a young boy called the Wart (Arthur*) to Athene, and she shows him the graceful, slow Dream of Trees and the gritty Dream of Stones.

ATLANTIS, a legendary island that appears as a place in E[dith] Nesbit Bland's*
The Story of the Amulet*. The people on this lovely, garden-filled island feel
blessed by the gods, particularly by Poseidon, to whom they make sacrifices.
They are ruled by ten kings. All the buildings in Atlantis are made of marble;
many are covered with gold and oricalchum. Woolly mammoths are used by the
people as steeds. During a visit to Atlantis by Anthea*, Robert*, Jane*, Cyril*,
and Jimmy*, who are searching for the missing half of a powerful amulet*, the
mountain on which Atlantis is built erupts and a tidal wave destroys the island.
A piece of rock thrown out by the volcano falls onto a ship that manages to
escape to Egypt, and it is later carved into the amulet.

ATUAN, a place in Ursula K. LeGuin's* Earthsea trilogy*. This island in the
eastern part of Earthsea* is part of the Kargish Empire. On the island is the
Place of the Tombs of Atuan, where stand the tombstones of the nine Nameless
Ones* who ruled Earthsea before the creation of men. Long before the empire
was created, kings would come to Atuan to seek the counsel of the Nameless
Ones, who spoke through their nameless Priestess. With the rise of Priest-Kings
and the coming of Godkings*, Atuan came under their rule. Because the Godking
is himself a god, he has less need to consult the Nameless Ones, and by the
time Tenar* becomes Priestess here, the temple is almost in ruins. The better-
kept temples of the Twin Gods and of the Godking stand not far away. Below
the tombstones lies the vast Undertomb*; from it branches and coils the great
Labyrinth* designed to confuse those who would seek the Treasure of the Tombs.
In this Treasure lies half of the Ring of Erreth-Akbe*. For this reason, several
sorcerers have crossed the desert surrounding the Place of the Tombs to find the
Treasure. The last of these is Ged*, who succeeds in his quest with the help of
Tenar. At his success, so angry are the Nameless Ones that they destroy the
Tombs, trying to destroy him.

AWIN, a character in Lloyd Alexander's* *Time Cat**. Her father is Maughold.
This sixteenth-century woman of the Isle of Man is convinced she is ugly because
she has one brown eye and one blue. Believing Baetan* wants to marry her out
of pity, Awin discourages his visits, though this makes her miserable because
she loves him. Jason*, a boy from the twentieth century, proves to Awin that
the different can also be considered beautiful, pointing out that Dulcinea*, the
tailless cat Awin takes in, is odd-looking but still beautiful. Finally accepting
her looks, Awin also accepts Baetan's love.

AY, ROBERTSON, a character in the Mary Poppins books*, by P[amela]
L[yndon] Travers*. He is also known as the Dirty Rascal, a wise fool who knows
that dry facts are not what is most important. As the Rascal, he comes to the
court of King Ethelbert and teaches the king his own brand of wisdom. The
Rascal then crosses the rainbow, leaving Ethelbert on top of it. The Rascal
wanders the world, thinking only as far ahead as the immediate moment, taking

service with kings or living among ordinary folk, and bringing good fortune to all he stays with. As Robertson Ay, he works for the Banks family at Number Seventeen Cherry Tree Lane. Robertson's doctor has told him he has a weak heart, so he takes life easy, doing his work his own way and sleeping more than he works. He has a perfect genius for sleeping anywhere at any time. Because they love him, Jane Caroline and Michael George Banks** protect him by covering for him. Mr. Banks, however, has no reason to love Robertson, for the young man has been known to black Mr. Banks's bowler hat, polish one shoe with black and the other with brown, and clean only one shoe in a pair. But Mr. Banks never fires him, and Robertson never gives notice.

BABBITT, NATALIE (1932-   ), American writer. She was born in Dayton, Ohio, on 28 July 1932, to Ralph Zane and Genevieve (Converse) Moore and was educated at Smith College, in Northampton, Massachusetts. On 26 June 1954 she married Samuel Fisher Babbitt; they have two sons and a daughter. Babbitt has been an instructor in writing and illustrating for children at Kirkland College, in New York; she has also illustrated several works not her own.

Babbitt's nine works for children include two in verse, one picture book, and a collection of short stories. Her full-length novels all verge on the fantastic to some extent, but *The Search for Delicious** and *Tuck Everlasting** are full-fledged fantasies. Different as they are in setting and scope, each features a young person learning about the world, both its pain and its rewards.

Both Winifred Foster* (Winnie), in *Tuck Everlasting*, and Vaungaylen* (Gaylen), in *The Search for Delicious*, have grown up sheltered in some way. Winnie's parents—especially her mother and grandmother—fuss over her, keeping her home and worrying about her clothes, warning her that she could not manage without them, making her feel as if she is in prison; Gaylen has grown up in a castle, the beloved and pampered child, and has never been outside, among people who do not care for him. As a result, Winnie is afraid of the world outside her neighborhood, convinced that she could not take care of herself and fearful of kidnappers. Gaylen, on the other hand, trusts too much, convinced that he knows the world and can take care of himself. Each leaves home for a time, having adventures in an unknown world. Winnie spends the night with the free-and-easy Tucks, who are the antithesis of the Fosters and who trust her good sense enough to tell her their secret. Gaylen proudly rides beyond the castle walls through a kingdom that teaches him hostility, distrust, and indifference.

Their respective journeys teach them much about the world and their place in it. Gaylen, to his dismay, finds that not all people are good and that not all are trustworthy. He does meet people who are true and good-hearted, but he also comes up against people who are suspicious, indifferent, and downright hostile. But Gaylen discovers that he can transcend this and overcome it in himself, and thus he finds out something about his own place in the world. Winnie, on the

other hand, learns that she can trust herself and manage very well. The kidnapping
Tucks prove trustworthy and lovable, and for the first time Winnie has ties to
people outside her family, experiences they have not shared. Winnie learns that
she can take care of herself, and also of the Tucks, as she helps manage Mae
Tuck's* escape from jail.

Having learned about themselves, Winnie and Gaylen have also learned about
life. Living is painful, for it means getting involved with others, and it means
dying and accepting death, as well. But the alternative can be worse. Gaylen,
anguished and tired in a world where people can start a war over a word in the
dictionary, seeks to be away from it, living apart in the mountains. He will be
like the woldweller* living alone in the forest, or like the winds blowing free
over the kingdom. But if these have freedom and quiet, they also have indifference—to the people in the war, and to the people Gaylen loves. Ardis*, the
small mermaid Gaylen bargains with to defeat the enemy, and the dwarfs* who
live alone in the mountains are also indifferent. They had been here long before
men had come, and they are not of men, so they live apart and they do not care.
Caring hurts Gaylen, but he cannot be indifferent, especially to those he loves.
By caring he can help them, but by remaining indifferent he cannot. The pain
of caring has a part in life. Winnie, who cannot see a fish killed for her breakfast,
decides to drink the water that will keep her young and safe forever. Life can
be frightening, but a sip from the spring* the Tucks have found erases that fear,
for those who drink it cannot be hurt. Death is also frightening, but the spring
destroys that, too. The alternative, though, is eternal life in a world that is always
changing around you, an eternal saying-goodbye to those transient people you
have loved. It means loneliness of a peculiar kind. As Angus Tuck* makes clear,
all things change, grow, develop; all life is dynamic; and death is an important
part of it. Eternal life, though, is static, with little or no room for change. Eternal
life can be a death of the soul. Before she turns seventeen, Winnie has realized
this. Dying can be painful, but, like caring, it is worth it, for it is a part of life.

Babbitt's works move swiftly and surely; her prose is vivid and descriptive.
Characters are well realized. The dialogue is very convincing, especially in *Tuck
Everlasting*, where Babbitt captures well the cadence of country speech.

Works

Juvenile full-length fantasy: *The Search for Delicious* (1969); *Tuck Everlasting* (1975).
Juvenile non-fantasy, short stories, and verse: *Dick Foote and the Shark* (1967); *Phoebe's
    Revolt* (1968); *Kneeknock Rise* (1970); *The Something* (1970); *Goody Hall* (1971);
    The Devil's Storybook (1974); *The Eyes of the Amaryllis* (1977); *Herbert Rowbarge*
    (1982).

Secondary Works

De Lucca, Geraldine. "Extensions of Nature: The Fantasies of Natalie Babbitt," *The
    Lion and the Unicorn*, 1 (Fall, 1977), pp. 47-70.

Hirsch, Corinne. "Toward Maturity: Natalie Babbitt's Initiatory Journeys," *Proceedings of the Seventh Annual Conference of the Children's Literature Association* (1980), pp. 107-13.

Mercier, Jean F. "Natalie Babbitt," *Publisher's Weekly*, 208 (28 July 1975), pp. 66-67.

BABINGTON, ANTHONY, a character in Alison Uttley's* *A Traveller in Time**. He is the son of Mistress Foljambe and the older brother of Francis Babington*; he is the husband of Mary Babington and the cousin of Arabella Babington*. Anthony is the master of sixteenth-century Thackers* and the doomed courtly lover of Mary Stuart*. Despite his wife's pleadings, he struggles to free Mary Stuart and plots to bring her from nearby Wingfield Manor* through ancient tunnels to Thackers. His plans are thwarted when the tunnel entrance at Wingfield is discovered, but no evidence is found that will implicate him. Through his relationship with Penelope Taberner Cameron*, a twentieth-century girl who slips into Elizabethan Thackers, Anthony realizes he is doomed, but still he works to free the queen, until he is executed for treason against Elizabeth I. After Anthony's death, part of the manor house is pulled down.

BABINGTON, ARABELLA, a character in Alison Uttley's* *A Traveller in Time**. She is the cousin of Anthony and Francis Babington**. Her father prophesied a short life for Anthony. Arabella takes an immediate dislike to Penelope Taberner Cameron*, a twentieth-century girl who travels back in time, and she traps Penelope in a tunnel, leaving her to starve. Penelope is rescued by Jude*, the Babingtons' deaf-mute servant.

BABINGTON, FRANCIS, a character in *A Traveller in Time**, by Alison Uttley*. He is the son of Mistress Foljambe and the younger brother of Anthony Babington*; he is the cousin of Arabella Babington*. Francis lives at Thackers*, the Babingtons' manor house, which he loves very much. Francis longs to be master here and resents Anthony's neglect of the place. He also worries about Anthony and his dangerous efforts to free Mary Stuart*, Queen of Scots, though he helps Anthony because Francis loves the queen in his own way. Francis is popular among the common folk of Thackers and the surrounding area. He shares a warm relationship with Penelope Taberner Cameron*, a twentieth-century girl who visits Elizabethan Thackers.

BACCHUS, a Roman god who appears as a character in the Chronicles of Narnia*, by C[live] S[taples] Lewis*. He is a wild boy who occasionally makes merry in the moonlit forests of Narnia* with Silenus and his female followers. Though subordinate to Aslan*, Narnia's great lion-protector, he has powers of his own: he can make streams run wine instead of water and make grapevines grow thick. During the War of Deliverance when the tyrannical conquerors from Telmar* are driven from the land, Bacchus helps Aslan liberate Beruna* by causing grapevines to grow there in profusion and bring down its bridge and some of the houses as well. He and his maenads later dance the creation of a rich feast when the Narnians celebrate their victory. Bacchus's wildness can be alarming, but Aslan keeps him completely under control.

BADGER, THE, a character in *The Wind in the Willows**, by Kenneth Grahame*. He is an unsociable animal who lives by himself in the Wild Wood. The Badger's comfortable home is a maze of ancient tunnels dug by his ancestors in the ruins of an ancient city, and he is very proud of his heritage and of the fact that while men may come and go, animals are patient and endure. The shy Badger is fond of his friends and is always willing to help them. He takes Toad* in hand when the latter's mania for motorcars is making him more foolish than usual, though the Badger fails to cure Toad of his passion. Toad, the Mole*, and the Water Rat* look up to the Badger and rely on his wisdom, coming to him for help; he plans and leads the successful rout of the weasels and stoats from Toad Hall. Though mothers use the Badger's fierce reputation to make their children behave, he is really quite fond of children.

BAETAN, a character in *Time Cat**, by Lloyd Alexander*. This black-haired, blue-eyed young fisherman on the sixteenth-century Isle of Man is in love with Awin*, who refuses his courting because she thinks he pities her. Convinced that she is ugly because she has one blue eye and one brown, Awin cannot believe that anyone could love her. When Jason*, a boy from the twentieth century, helps her to accept her looks, Awin is able to accept and return Baetan's love.

BAGGINS, BILBO, the main character in J[ohn] R[onald] R[euel] Tolkien's* *The Hobbit** and *The Lord of the Rings*. He is the son of Bungo and Belladonna Took Baggins; he is the cousin of Otho and Lobelia Sackville-Baggins; he is the uncle of Frodo Baggins; he is the great-great-great-grandnephew of Bullroarer Took, inventor of golf. Bilbo is a quiet hobbit*, fond of good food and comfort, and living in a lovely hobbit hole called Bag-end, in Hobbiton. He is fond of maps and runes and quiet, and of pipefuls of good tobacco. Bilbo's quiet life is shattered when Gandalf*, an old wizard, suggests him as a suitable treasure hunter and burglar for a party of dwarves* going to the Lonely Mountain to steal back their treasure from Smaug*, a dragon. Much to his own surprise, Bilbo finds himself setting off on an adventure through unknown lands, dealing with goblins*, trolls*, elves*, and men, as well as with Smaug himself. On his journey, Bilbo wins a magic ring* in a riddling contest with Gollum*; this ring stands him in good stead, for it makes its wearer invisible. During his adventure, Bilbo learns how well he can manage on his own and finds himself actually a little sad to see the journey end. He quickly resumes his quiet life in Hobbiton; but his reputation is destroyed, and he does not regain it, for he takes to writing poetry and visiting elves. On his eleventy-first birthday, Bilbo leaves the Shire; on his one-hundred-and-thirty-first, he travels with the elves and Gandalf to a shining land beyond the ken of men.

BAGHEERA, a character in the Jungle books*, by Rudyard Kipling*. He is a black panther who was born among men; his mother had been owned by the king at Oodeypore, India. When he had one night felt his own strength and power, Bagheera broke the lock on his cage and freed himself. He still bears the mark of a collar: a bald spot on his jaw. Bagheera is cunning, bold, and reckless, and few creatures in the jungle care to cross him. When Mowgli*, a human baby, is to be ritually adopted by the Seeonee wolf pack, Bagheera buys his life with that of a bull, thus allowing the child to be adopted. The panther also takes a hand in Mowgli's education, teaching him to climb trees, among other things. Bagheera loves Mowgli deeply and will do anything for him. When the boy is seventeen and it is time for him to leave the jungle, Bagheera kills another bull, thus freeing him.

BAILEY, CAROLINE SHERWIN (1875-1961), American writer. She was born 25 October 1875 in Hoosick Falls, New York, to Charles Henry and Emma Frances (Blanchard) Bailey. Bailey was educated at home until she was twelve, when she was sent to Lansingburgh Academy. She attended the Teacher's College, Columbia University, graduating in 1896; the Montessori School, Rome; and the New York School of Social Work. She taught in schools in Springfield, Massachusetts, and in New York, New York, and was a social worker at the Warren Goddard House in New York City. Bailey also was editor of the children's department of the *Delineator* and edited *American Childhood* for a time. She married Eben Clayton Hill in 1936. Bailey died 23 December 1961.

Of the approximately ninety-seven books Carolyn Sherwin Bailey was responsible for, all but seven are for children, and her seven books for adults deal with aspects of childhood and of children's education. Bailey wrote primers, plays, and stories for children, books of games, and some historical fiction, but it is for the Newbery Award-winning *Miss Hickory** that she is best remembered.

This is a memorable little book, both for its evocation of the New England countryside and for its lively, hard-headed little heroine. Miss Hickory's* body may be made of a flexible apple twig, but it is her hard, pointed hickory-nut head that gives her her sharp-tongued inflexibility. Miss Hickory's words, even to her friends, are often as pointed as her hickory-nut nose, and the hardness of the nut that forms her head makes it difficult for her to accept what she cannot see with her own eyes. Both of these traits give her cause for remorse: Miss Hickory's obstinacy keeps her from believing that the Brown family has left her until she is shown, and it causes her to miss not only the fun of seeing Cow being dosed for a stomach ache, but the wondrous miracle in the manger on Christmas Eve; because Miss Hickory cannot conceive of living life any differently than she has, she falls into despair when Chipmunk takes over her little corncob house and is rescued only by Crow's* intervention when he finds a place for her to live. Her sharp words give Miss Hickory a special reason for regret: nettled at last by her scolding, starving Squirrel* pulls off her nut head and eats it. As he does so, the head berates both itself for being so stubborn and Miss Hickory for not putting it to good use. Her apple-twig body, freed of the obstinate, shrewish head, happily climbs an apple tree and there finds a permanent home.

Such a home is what Miss Hickory lacks through most of the book. Her winter home is vacated by the people who usually take her in; the little corncob cabin she lives in the rest of the year is taken over by Chipmunk; the robin's nest Crow finds for her is reclaimed by its rightful owners when they return in the spring. Miss Hickory's progress from home to home is a progress toward independence. When first she learns that she has lost not only the large, warm house where she usually winters but also the small cabin that has been built for her, she sinks into despair so deep that it is almost the end of her, and only Crow's intervention saves her; when Miss Hickory is chased from her winter home by the robins, she realizes that she cannot depend on someone else to help her and so takes on the responsibility of finding a new home herself. The little cabin Miss Hickory lives in at the beginning is provided for her by a child, and it is made comfortable by dollhouse furnishings provided by another child; on her own in the robin's nest that winter, Miss Hickory must fend for herself, and she learns to do so with wonderful self-reliance.

Miss Hickory's progress is not only toward independence: it is also a progress back to where she truly belongs—back to the world of nature. She gives up her cabin for a robin's nest and her gingham dress for clothes made of natural materials; she learns to do without a stove and stores her food raw, without canning it. Miss Hickory learns independence from civilization and comes close to nature, her true heritage. In the end she literally becomes a part of it, her hickory-nut head eaten by a squirrel, her apple-twig body grafting itself onto an old apple tree. Miss Hickory's head has accused her of being selfish; in her final acts she is subsumed and helps others at the same time, for her head feeds starving Squirrel and her grafted body revitalizes the old tree. The little country woman's final, permanent home is the only one possible for her; the apple twig that is her body comes to rest in a place very like that from whence it came.

Bailey skillfully evokes the country life of New England. Through her rich descriptions, she recreates the beauty of the countryside. Though *Miss Hickory* is basically a happy book, concerning itself with the brightness of its world, it also presents the darker side, as Fawn's mother is killed by a hunter. The characters are strongly drawn, especially the book's hard-headed but oddly touching heroine.

Works

Juvenile fantasy: *Miss Hickory* (1946).
Juvenile non-fantasy: *The Peter Newell Mother Goose* (1905); *For the Children's Hour*

(1906), with Clara M. Lewis; *The Jingle Primer* (1906), with Clara L. Brown;
Firelight Stories (1907); *Stories and Rhymes for a Child* (1909); *Boys' Make-at-Home Things* (1912), with Marian Elizabeth Bailey; *Girls' Make-at-Home Things* (1912); *The Children's Book of Games and Parties* (1913); *Every Child's Folk Songs and Games* (1914); *Songs of Happiness* (1914), with Mary B. Ehrmann; *Stories for Sunday Telling* (1916); *Boys and Girls of Colonial Days* (1917); *Hero Stories* (1917); *Stories for Any Day* (1917); *Once Upon a Time Animal Stories* (1918); *The Outdoor Story Book* (1918); *Stories for Every Holiday* (1918); *What to Do for Uncle Sam* (1918); *Broad Stripes and Bright Stars* (1919), stories, as *Boy Heroes in the Making of America* (1931); *Everyday Stories* (1919); *Folk Stories and Fables* (1919); *Legends from Many Lands* (1919); *Stories of Great Adventures* (1919); *The Enchanted Bugle and Other Stories* (1920); *Wonder Stories* (1920); *Merry Tales for Children* (1921); *The Touch of Courage and Other Stories* (1921); *Flint* (1922); *Bailey's In and Out-door Play-games* (1923) in *Sixty Games and Pastimes for All Occasions* (1928); *Friendly Tales* (1923); *Reading Time Stories* (1923); *Surprise Stories* (1923-1930; 1936), series; *When Grandfather Was a Boy* (1923), stories; *All the Year Play Games* (1924) in *Sixty Games and Pastimes for All Occasions* (1928); *Boys and Girls of Pioneer Days* (1924); *Lincoln Time Stories* (1924); *Little Men and Women Stories* (1924); *Stories from an Indian Cave* (1924), legends; *The Wonderful Days* (1925); *The Wonderful Tree and Golden Day Stories* (1925); *Boys and Girls of Discovery Days* (1926); *The Wonderful Window and Other Stories* (1926); *Untold History Stories* (1927); *Boys and Girls of Today* (1928); *Forest, Field, and Stream Stories* (1928), reader; *Boys and Girls of Modern Days* (1929); *Garden, Orchard, and Meadow Stories* (1929); *Read Aloud Stories* (1929); *The Little Rabbit Who Wanted Red Wings* (1931); *Plays for the Children's Hour* (1931); *Tell Me a Birthday Story* (1931); *Pets* (1934), reader; *Our Friends at the Zoo* (1934), reader, with Alice Hanthorn; *Picture Work Book* (1934), reader; *My First Little Book* (1934), reader; *My First Story Book* (1934), reader; *Little Folk Tales* (1934), reader; *My First Work Book* (1934), reader; *Adventure Stories* (1934), reader; *Everyday Stories* (1934), reader; *My Book of Games* (1934), reader; *My Second Work Book* (1934), reader; *The Story-telling Hour* (1934); *Toys* (1934), reader; *Children of the Handicrafts* (1935); *Marionettes* (1936), with Ditzy Baker; *Tops and Whistles* (1937); *From Moccasins to Wings* (1938); *Li'l' Hannibal* (1938); *Homespun Playdays* (1941); *Country-Stop* (1942) as *Wishing-Well House* (1950); *Pioneer Art in America* (1944); *Old Man Rabbit's Dinner Party* (1949; rev. 1961); *Enchanted Village* (1950); *A Candle for Your Cake* (1952), stories; *Finnegan II, His Nine Lives* (1953); *The Little Gray Lamb* (1954); *The Little Red Schoolhouse* (1957); *Flickertail* (1962).

Adult: *Daily Program of Gift and Occupation Work* (1904), with Clara M. Lewis; *For the Story Teller* (1913); *Montessori Children* (1915); *Everyday Play for Children* (1916); *Letting in the Gang* (1916); *The Way of the Gate* (1917), with others; *Tell Me Another Story* (1918).

Secondary Works

Bailey, Carolyn Sherwin. "Miss Hickory: Her Genealogy," *The Horn Book Magazine*, 23 (July, 1947), pp. 239-42.

The Carolyn Sherwin Bailey Historical Collection of Children's Books: A Catalogue, ed. Dorothy R. Davies. N.p.: Southern Connecticut State College, 1967.

Davies, Dorothy R. *Carolyn Sherwin Bailey*. Privately printed, 1967.

Lindquist, Jennie D. "Books and an Apple Orchard," *The Horn Book Magazine*, 23 (July, 1947), pp. 243-49.

BALOO, a character in Rudyard Kipling's* Jungle books*. This old brown bear eats only nuts and honey and so is welcome among the wolves of the Seeonee wolf pack. He teaches the laws and ways of the jungle to the young wolves. When Mowgli*, a human child, is ritually shown to the pack, Baloo speaks up for him, saving him from the tiger, Shere Khan*. Baloo later teaches Mowgli all he needs to know to live in the jungle, from how to steal from wild bees to the words he must know in all the jungle languages to keep himself safe. Baloo is sometimes a tough teacher, for he realizes that Mowgli, having neither claws nor sharp fangs, must know these things to survive. As the years pass, Baloo becomes stiff and blind with age, but his widsom endures. He helps Mowgli realize that his place is no longer in the jungle, but with men.

BANE, THE, a place in Jane Louise Curry's* *Beneath the Hill**. It is a ravaged piece of land which is being strip-mined for coal. The Bane runs so deep that it threatens to set free an ancient evil force that lies bound beneath the mountains of Pennsylvania. In the Bane lies a deep lake which seems to suck into it all that comes too close; when Stevie Griffith* is pulled in, his uncle forces the mine owner to fill in the lake, threatening the man with a lawsuit. Thus the evil force is resealed beneath the mountain. By using a key* she found in the family spring, Margaret Arthur* turns the waters back to the Bane, flushing it and restoring the springs and streams that once flowed here, allowing the Bane to grow green again.

BANKS, ANNABEL. a character in P[amela] L[yndon] Travers* *Mary Poppins Comes Back** and *Mary Poppins Opens the Door**. She is the youngest child of George and Caroline Banks; her older brothers and sisters are Barbara, Jane Caroline, John, and Michael George Banks****. When she is born at Number Seventeen Cherry Tree Lane, Annabel is certain she will remember the long journey of her birth, but she forgets it in a week, though she does remember how to talk to birds. Annabel is too young to take part in the adventures which happen whenever her nanny, Mary Poppins*, is around, but sometimes she is present as an interested spectator.

BANKS, BARBARA, a character in the Mary Poppins books*, by P[amela] L[yndon] Travers*. She is the second daughter of George and Caroline Banks; she is the twin of John and the sister of Annabel, Jane Caroline, and Michael George Banks****. She was born on a Tuesday. Like her brother, until she is a year old Barbara can speak to and understand birds, sunlight, and the wind;

after her first birthday she loses this ability. Young as she is, Barbara takes part in several of the adventures that happen when Mary Poppins*, her nanny, is present.

BANKS, JANE CAROLINE, a character in P[amela] L[yndon] Travers's* Mary Poppins books*. She is the oldest child of George and Caroline Banks; she is the sister of Annabel, Barbara, John, and Michael George Banks****. Jane was born on a Wednesday. Usually she enjoys being the oldest, but sometimes she feels this position carries with it unpleasant duties and responsibilities. When she is taken into a Royal Doulton bowl* and given the chance to be the youngest of a family, though, she opts for home, deciding that being the oldest is not so bad when you are among people you love. This is only one of many adventures Jane has when Mary Poppins*, her tart, magical nanny, is around. With her brothers and sisters, Jane gets a glimpse of Mary Poppins's wonderful world and comes to realize how marvelous the world itself is. She learns other things, too, from her adventures with animals, stars, and Mary Poppins's amazing relatives. Though her nanny goes away, Jane remembers her lessons for a long time.

BANKS, JOHN, a character in the Mary Poppins books*, by P[amela] L[yndon] Travers*. He is the youngest son of George and Caroline Banks; he is the twin brother of Barbara and the brother of Annabel, Jane Caroline, and Michael George Banks****. He was born on a Tuesday. John is usually quite polite, though he has his tantrums. Until he is a year old, John can speak and understand the language of birds, sunlight, and wind. Young as he is, John participates during the first few years of his life in several of the adventures that happen when his nurse, Mary Poppins*, is around.

BANKS, MICHAEL GEORGE, a character in P[amela] L[yndon] Travers's* Mary Poppins books*. He is the older son of George and Caroline Banks; he is the brother of Annabel, Barbara, Jane Caroline, and John Banks****. Michael was born on a Monday and is considered quite handsome, though plump. As does any young boy, he sometimes gets into trouble with adults, especially with expressive nannies. Mary Poppins* is different, and Michael is soon caught up in the adventures that occur whenever she is around. From his adventures with the odd and fascinating animals and people Mary Poppins knows, Michael learns many things, among them that the world is a wonderful, magical place. Michael remembers her and her lessons often after she goes away.

BARBARA BANKS (the Mary Poppins books). *See* Banks, Barbara

BARBER, a character in *The Marvelous Misadventures of Sebastian*, by Lloyd Alexander*. His real name is unknown. Sent by Count Grinssorg* to find Princess Isabel Charlotte Theodora Fredericka* (Isabel), this man, disguised as a barber, follows her in her journey across Hamelin-Loring*. He murders an over-inquisitive innkeeper and almost kills Sebastian*, the young fiddler who tries to help Isabel. The barber once captures Isabel and Sebastian and almost gets them back to the count's castle before they are rescued. Finally, during a brief and ugly fight with Sebastian on a pier, the barber is accidentally set on fire and falls into the water. Nothing more is heard of him.

BARNABAS DREW (*Over Sea, Under Stone; Greenwitch; Silver on the Tree*). *See* Drew, Barnabas

BARNABAS, TABERNER (*A Traveller in Time*). *See* Taberner, Barnabas

BARRIE, SIR JAMES M[ATTHEW], BART. (1860-1937), British writer. He was born 9 May 1860 in Kirriemuir, Scotland, to David and Margaret Ogilvy Barrie. He was educated at Glasgow Academy (1868-1870), Forfar Academy (1870-1871), Dumfries Academy (1873-1878), and Edinburgh University (1878-1882), from which he received an M.A. Barrie was the leader-writer for the *Nottingham Journal* (1882-1884) and wrote articles for many publications. On 9 July 1894 he married Mary Ansell; they were divorced in 1909. They had no children, but in 1910 Barrie adopted the five orphaned sons of a friend. He received honorary degrees from St. Andrews University (1898) and Edinburgh University (1909). Barrie received a baronetcy in 1913 and was Rector of St. Andrews University from 1919 to 1922. In 1922 he received the Order of Merit. Barrie was Chancellor of Edinburgh University from 1930 to 1937. He died 19 June 1937.

Both Barrie's fantasies for children started out as something else: *Peter and Wendy** is a novelization of the play *Peter Pan; Peter Pan in Kensington Gardens** comprises six chapters of an adult novel, *The Little White Bird*. Both works have in common their main character, Peter Pan*, that erratic but endlessly charming child who will never become an adult. In *Peter Pan in Kensington Gardens*, he is the confused little "betwixt and between"—no longer a bird but not really a human—who steals the hearts of all the female fairies and thus gains free rein of the Gardens at night. In *Peter and Wendy*, Peter is the essence of youth, a force to be reckoned with, lord in his own right of the wonderful island of Neverland*; he seems the synthesis of what young boys long to be, in a world where daydreams are real.

Central to both works is a veneration of mothers and motherhood. When he decides to leave Kensington Gardens and return to the everyday world, it is—understandably—to his mother that Peter wants to go, just as it is to her mother that Maimie Mannering* wants to return after her adventures. It is as mothers that fairy folk of the Gardens first react to Peter: because he is a baby, the female fairies respond to him, and the males, who follow the females in everything, agree to accept him. The veneration of mother is more pronounced in *Peter and Wendy*. Mrs. Darling* is the very picture of the devoted mother as she tidies her children's minds every night, laughs with and delights in them, and leaves the nursery window open for weeks, waiting for their return. The Never bird*, Captain Jas. Hook* tells us, is a good example of a mother, for though her nest falls into the water, she does not desert her eggs but floats in her nest around the lagoon. Nothing but motherless Peter's desperate plight will induce her to leave her eggs. Young as she is, Wendy Darling* herself becomes a mother-figure. The lost boys*, who have been longing for their mothers, accept her immediately as their mother, and a cozy little family is formed, with Wendy and Peter as the parents and the lost boys as the children. Wendy takes to mothering with ease and seems never to tire of it, dispensing "medicine," telling stories, sewing and darning for the boys after they have gone to bed. Even the pirates think of Wendy as a mother. Hook plots to carry her off and make her the mother of the pirates, and when he has captured the lot and is preparing to have the boys walk the plank, he brings up Wendy for "a mother's last words to her children." Though Peter desires only to marry Maimie Mannering, he can react to Wendy only as does a son to his mother; he comes to the Darlings' house not to look at her but to listen to the stories, and he only takes Wendy to Neverland because she knows many stories he does not. Peter becomes nervous at Wendy's game that he and she are the parents of the boys, and he is vastly relieved to be assured that it is not true. Though consciously Peter does not seem to need mothering, he really does need it; unconscious of Wendy's cuddling, he accepts it when he is asleep in the throes of a nightmare. In fact, Maimie Mannering aside, Peter reacts to all the women in his life as possible mothers, bewildered by Tinker Bell's* jealousy of Wendy and wondering what Tinker Bell and Tiger Lily* want to be to him that is not his mother.

Fathers do not come off nearly so well. The lost boys do not talk about them, preferring, instead, to try to remember their mothers. In fact, the only father to appear in either book—Mr. Darling*—appears to be as much a child as his daughter and sons, and Mrs. Darling treats him accordingly.

In *Peter Pan in Kensington Gardens*, the emphasis is on the faery. The Gardens, Barrie assures us, are a place of magic and mystery, where fairies frolic and the birds who become children are hatched. Peter is a part of this world. Half human, half not, he becomes accepted by the fairies, playing his pipes at their balls and riding his goat around the Gardens at night, searching for lost children and taking them to the small house the fairies build for their protection. Like the fairies, he is an unseen force in the Gardens—elusive, but not shy.

In *Peter and Wendy*, Peter is a force in a realm of daydream. Neverland is a world of the imagination; each child has a Neverland where he can spin out his fantasies but which at night becomes frighteningly real. The Neverland to which Peter takes Wendy and the boys seems to be a synthesis of every child's fantasy. There are plenty of possibilities for adventure: the citizens of the island include Indians, pirates, wild beasts, mermaids, and fairies—all eager for battle or for fun. And there are no interfering parents to haul one out of danger just as things get exciting. Adventure there is, and killing, too, but it is as gloriously bloody yet bloodless as in a daydream.

And Peter himself is the stuff of daydreams. A good flier, a good swordsman, enough of a boy to make mistakes yet braver and bolder than many can ever hope to be, Peter is perhaps what a boy dreams of being. Though he is lamentably conceited, he has something to be conceited about; he is respected by the fairies, the mermaids, and all his enemies. Though they try to kill him, still he can master them all. In Kensington Gardens, Peter was a "betwixt and between"; in Neverland, he is all boy, with something added: he is not just "ordinary boy," he is "wonderful boy." And in being that wonderful boy, he becomes all that is joyful and young and heartless—a symbol of the eternal child.

Barrie's prose is probably best suited to a more sentimental time. His women are ministering angels; his children are never graceless, sullen, or deliberately provoking. In themselves, the works have good stories and make good reading, but they are marred by situations and remarks by the author that border on the cute, and all the sweetness of the books seems saccharine. Under the author's touch, the works become too charming, and perhaps this is their major failing. Barrie's characters are stock ones, but he breathes into them a kind of life that makes them memorable. The action scenes are full of gusto and both works move fairly swiftly, though they are sometimes slowed by Barrie's whimsy.

Works

Juvenile fantasy: *Peter Pan in Kensington Gardens* (1906), from *The Little White Bird* (1902); *Peter and Wendy* (1911).
Juvenile non-fantasy: *Peter Pan* (1904), play.
Adult: *Caught Napping* (1883), play; *Auld Licht Idylls* (1888); *Better Dead* (1888); *When a Man's Single* (1888); *An Edinburgh Eleven* (1889); *A Window in Thrums* (1889); *My Lady Nicotine* (1890); *Ibsen's Ghost* (1891), play; *The Little Minister* (1891), novel; *Richard Savage* (1891), play, with H. B. Marriott Watson; *A Holiday in Bed, and Other Sketches* (1892); *The Houseboat* (1892) as *Walker, London* (1921); *Allahakbarries C. C.* (1893); *An Auld Licht Manse* (1893), novel; *Becky Sharp* (1893), play; *Jane Annie* (1893), play, with A. Conan Doyle; *A Lady's Shoe* (1893); *A Tillyloss Scandal* (1893); *The Professor's Love Story* (1894), play; *Scotland's Lament* (1895); *Margaret Ogilvy* (1896); *Sentimental Tommy* (1896), novel; *The Little Minister* (1897), play; *The Allahakbarrie Book of Broadway Cricket for 1899* (1899); *Tommy and Grizel* (1900), novel; *The Wedding Guest* (1900), play; *The Little White Bird* (1902), novel; *Little Mary* (1903), play; *Alice Sit-by-the-Fire* (1905), play; *Pantaloon* (1905); *Josephine* (1906); *Punch* (1906); *What Every Woman Knows* (1908); *George Meredith* (1909); *Old Friends* (1910), play; *A Slice of Life* (1910), play; *The Twelve-pound Look* (1910), play; *The Dramatists Get What They Want* (1912), also as *The Censor and the Dramatists; Rosaline* (1912), play; *The Adored One* (1913) as *The Legend of Leonora* (1914), shortened into *Seven Women* (1917); *Half an Hour* (1913); *Quality Street* (1913); *The Will* (1913), play; *The Admirable Crichton* (1914), play; *Der Tag* (1914), play; *Charles Frohman: A Tribute* (1915); *The Fatal Typist* (1915), play; *The*

New Word (1915), play; *Rosy Rapture* (1915), play; *A Kiss for Cinderella* (1916), play; *The Real Thing at Last* (1916), play; *Shakespeare's Legacy* (1916), play; *Dear Brutus* (1917); *The Old Lady Shows Her Medals* (1917), play; *Reconstructing the Crime* (1917), play; *Who Was Sarah Findley? by Mark Twain, with a Suggested Solution of the Mystery* (1917); *Echoes of the War* (1918); *La Politesse* (1918), play; *A Well-remembered Voice* (1918), play; *Mary Rose* (1920), play; *The Truth About the Russian Dancers* (1920); *Shall We Join the Ladies? (1921); Courage* (1922), address; *The Ladies' Shakespeare* (1925), address; *Neil and Tintinnabulum* (1925); *Cricket* (1926), address; *Barbara's Wedding* (1927); *The Entrancing Life* (1930), address; *The Greenwood Hat* (1930), repr. articles written as James Anon; *Farewell Miss Julie Logan* (1931), novel; *The Boy David* (1936), play.

Secondary Works

Asquith, Cynthia. *Portrait of Barrie*. London: N.p., 1954.

Birkin, Andrew. *J. M. Barrie & the Lost Boys: The Love Story That Gave Birth to Peter Pan*. New York: Clarkson N. Potter, 1979.

Blake, Kathleen. "The Sea Dream: *Peter Pan* and Treasure Island," *Children's Literature*, 6 (1977), pp. 165-81.

Chalmers, Patrick R. *The Barrie Inspiration*. London: P. Davies, [1938].

Cutler, B. D. *Sir James M. Barrie: A Bibliography*. New York: Greenberg, Publisher, 1931.

Darlington, W. A. *J. M. Barrie*. London and Glasgow: Blackie and Son, 1938.

Darton, F. J. Harvey. *J. M. Barrie*. London: Nisbet and Co., n.d.

Dunbar, Janet. *J. M. Barrie: The Man Behind the Image*. Boston: Houghton Mifflin Company, 1970.

Egan, Michael. "The Neverland of Id: Barrie, *Peter Pan*, and Freud," *Children's Literature*, 10 (1982), pp. 37-55.

Fraser, Morris. "Narcissus and the Lost Boys," *New Society*, 46 (19 Oct. 1978), pp. 144-46.

Garland, Herbert. *A Bibliography of the Writings of Sir James Matthew Barrie, Bart., O. M.* London: Bookman's Journal, 1928.

Geduld, Harry M. *Sir James Barrie*. New York: Twayne Publishers, 1971.

Green, Roger Lancelyn. "Barrie and Peter Pan," *Junior Bookshelf*, 24 (Oct., 1960), pp. 197-204.

———. *Fifty Years of "Peter Pan."* London: Peter Davies, 1954.

———. *J. M. Barrie*. London: Bodley Head, 1960.

———. "James Matthew Barrie," in *Tellers of Tales* (Leicester, England: Edmund Ward, 1946), pp. 206-19.

Griffith, John. "Making Wishes Innocent: *Peter Pan*," *The Lion and the Unicorn*, 3 (Spring, 1979), pp. 28-37.

Hammerton, J. A. *Barrie: The Story of a Genius*. New York: Dodd, Mead and Company, 1929.

Karpe, M. "The Origins of Peter Pan," *Psychoanalytic Review*, 43 (1956), pp. 104-10.

Letters of J. M. Barrie, ed. Viola Meynell. New York: Charles Scribner's Sons, 1947.

Mackail, Denis. *Barrie, the Story of J.M.B.* London: P. Davies, 1941.

Marsh, Corinna. "Eleven Little Girls and Peter Pan," *The Horn Book Magazine*, 31 (June, 1955), pp. 199-205.

Master, Helen. "Peter's Kensington,"*The Horn Book Magazine*, 10 (Sept., 1934), pp. 316-21.

Moult, Thomas. *Barrie*. New York: Charles Scribner's Sons, 1928.

Roy, James A. *James Matthew Barrie: An Appreciation*. New York: Charles Scribner's Sons, 1938.

Skinner, John. "James M. Barrie, or, The Boy Who Wouldn't Grow Up," *American Imago*, 14 (Summer, 1957), pp. 111-41.

Starkey, Penelope Scott. "The Many Mothers of Peter Pan," *Research Studies*, 42 (1974), pp. 1-10.

Williams, David Park. "Hook and Ahab: Barrie's Strange Satire on Melville," *Publications of the Modern Language Association*, 80 (Dec., 1965), pp. 483-88.

BARTHOLOMEW, HARRIET MELBOURNE (HATTY), a character in *Tom's Midnight Garden**, by Philippa Pearce*. She is the cousin of Hubert, James, and Edgar Melbourne; she becomes the wife of Barty Bartholomew and the mother of two sons killed in World War I. Orphaned at an early age, Hatty is sent to live with her aunt. The woman has no love for her and lets Hatty know it at every occasion; Hatty grows up shy, lonely, and desperately afraid of her aunt. She does have one companion, however: Tom Long*, a boy from the twentieth century staying in a flat which in that century is part of the house Hatty inhabits in the nineteenth century. Though he appears only at odd, spaced intervals, Tom gives Hatty the friendship and approval she needs. After she falls as they are making a treehouse together, James decides that she must go out into society. She does, making friends and going to new places. Tom continues to visit Hatty, but he seems to her more and more transparent, as if she can see through him. During the great frost in 1895 he and she skate down the river to the next town; on the way back they meet Barty, and for the first time she really enjoys talking with him. A year or so later they are married on Midsummer Day. Things go well for them, though they lose both sons in World War I. Barty buys the house Hatty had grown up in from James and converts it into flats; after he dies, she goes to live in one. Here she dreams of her childhood; and because of this and of his own loneliness, Tom, who has come to stay in one of the flats, is able to enter the garden and be her companion.

BASSUMTYTE, MARGARET, an Elizabethan character in *The Bassumtyte Treasure**, by Jane Louise Curry*. She is the wife of Sir Thomas Bassumtyte and the mother of Thomas Bassumtyte. A supporter of Mary Stuart*, Queen of Scots, she helps to hide the queen's son by adopting him into the family, calling the child Thomas Bassumtyte* (Small Thomas). Because she cannot bear to lose Small Thomas and because Mary may never come into power, Lady Margaret and her husband hide the boy's identity not only from the rest of the world but from him as well. Perhaps in an effort to remind the boy of his heritage, she panels his room with needlepoint tapestries depicting King Arthur* and the rescue of ladies in distress. One of these panels is by Mary, his mother; Lady Margaret overstitches the monogram. In what she thinks of as "dreams," she journeys forward into the twentieth century, helping Tommy Bassumtyte* to find the Bassumtyte treasure and thus keep Boxleton House* from being sold. Because she is an insatiable scribbler, her household books, journals, and letters fill a shelf in Boxleton's library.

BASSUMTYTE, THOMAS, the name of several characters in *The Bassumtyte Treasure**, by Jane Louise Curry*. Small Thomas Bassumtyte lived in Boxleton House* in Elizabethan England; though his last name was Bassumtyte, he was actually the son of Mary Stuart*, Queen of Scots, brought to Boxleton House for safety and adopted into the family. He is the ''Bassumtyte treasure'': the clues to his identity were hidden away, their whereabouts hinted at in a rhyme passed down through generations of Bassumtytes. Twentieth-century Tommy Bassumtyte* looks almost exactly like his ancestor.

In the twentieth century, a Thomas Bassumtyte again lives at Boxleton; he has inherited the house from his father, but high taxes and maintenance costs, coupled with a loss of income after his mountain-climbing accident, make him fear he will have to sell the place. When Tommy Bassumtyte, Thomas's second cousin, comes to live with him, his troubles are solved, for in the boy's search for the Bassumtyte treasure, objects are uncovered that bring enough money to save Boxleton. Thomas marries Gemma Harvey*, the vicar's niece.

BASSUMTYTE, TOMMY, a character in Jane Louise Curry's* *The Bassumtyte Treasure**. Tommy lives with his grandmother and cousin until he is ten, when they are judged too old to care for him. Before the law can step in, the two send him to live with his second cousin, Thomas Bassumtyte*, in Boxleton House*, in England. Here Tommy feels immediately at home, and he diligently searches for the treasure of the Bassumtytes so that Boxleton House will not have to be sold. Tommy finds more than he bargained for, however, when he discovers that his Elizabethan look-alike ancestor, Thomas Bassumtyte*, was really the son of Mary Stuart*, Queen of Scots, and that he is therefore descended from her.

BASSUMTYTE TREASURE, THE. Jane Louise Curry. New York: Atheneum, 1978. 130 pp. American.

When ten-year-old Tommy Bassumtyte's* grandmother and cousin are deemed too old to care for him, he is sent to England to live with his second cousin, Thomas Bassumtyte*. Thomas lives in Boxleton House*, the Tudor house where generations of Bassumtytes have lived, but taxes and maintenance costs are so high that he might be forced to sell to either Britain's National Trust or to a foreign prince who will pay any price. Tommy loves the house from his first sight of it and is fascinated by its antique furnishings—from the room panelled in needlepoint tapestries worked by Lady Margaret Bassumtyte* in Elizabethan times to the portrait of her grandson, Thomas Bassumtyte* (Small Thomas), who looks exactly like Tommy.

That first night, as Tommy lies homesick in bed, he is comforted by an elderly woman who reminds him of the rhyme Tommy's grandfather used to say to him: that the key to "Bassumtyte's treasure" is shut in a box. The next morning Tommy diligently searches for boxes with keys, with no luck. That afternoon, as he watches Thomas bargain with the representative of the prince who wants to buy Boxleton House, Tommy becomes aware of the woman who had comforted him the night before; she now appears to be upset by the prince's representative and urgently tells Tommy to "get to his box," before she disappears.

The woman, Thomas tells him, was Lady Margaret, Small Thomas's grandmother. The history of the Bassumtytes is full of tragedy; Lady Margaret's son returned one night to Boxleton from a stay in London, with a wagon bearing Small Thomas, his newborn son, and the body of his young wife, who was laid at rest in the family chapel. When the boy was ten years old, his father had been executed for treason, for plotting to put Mary Stuart*, Queen of Scots, on the English throne. Queen Elizabeth forced Small Thomas's grandfather to pay a heavy fine in order to keep Boxleton House, and the family withdrew from the rest of the world, living quietly in the country. For generations there have been rumors that Mary Stuart's treasure is at Boxleton, with the medallion Tommy had received from his grandfather and the rhyme the old man had taught him as clues to its whereabouts. Realizing that the "box" Lady Margaret spoke of to Tommy must refer to the box bed in his room, the boy investigates and finds a passageway leading not only to the secret room Thomas knows is beneath the stairs but to a windowseat in the library.

When Gemma Harvey*, the vicar's niece, who works in a museum, comes to see Boxleton, she is interested not only in the portrait of Small Thomas's mother but in the needlepoint panels. One panel, she discovers, was worked by Mary Stuart; the queen's monogram has been neatly overstitched in one corner. This would make the house important enough to be sold to the National Trust. Despite Thomas's polite refusal to sell, the foreign prince has not given up; the next day he sends a team of appraisers, posing as tourists, through the house, and Thomas discovers that not only can the bank—which has suddenly acquired new owners—not extend his debts, but that the prince has started proceedings to buy the family chapel, which has belonged to the Church since Elizabethan days. Because Small Thomas's mother is buried there, the prince cannot take "vacant possession" of it.

But Gemma has a theory and proves that no body was ever in the coffin; "Grace Bassumtyte" never existed. Her portrait in Boxleton House is proved to be that of Mary Stuart, doctored to look different; perhaps she was to escape to some other country via Boxleton House and sent the painting as a gesture of thanks. The secret passage would have hidden her, and the rumors of her treasure might have been true.

The next morning Tommy is found at the foot of the tree in the middle of the overgrown Tudor maze-garden. Lady Margaret had gotten him up the night before to look at something, he says, but he cannot remember what it was.

Whem Tommy wakes again later that morning, in his own bed, all looks strange, and when he looks out his window at the maze—now neatly trimmed—he realizes that it appears to be a nest of boxes, with the tall tree in the middle like a key in a lock. Thomas and Gemma are startled when they come into his room, for he seems to be half there and half not, but Thomas "draws him back" into his own world. The tree in the center of the maze *is* the key, for in an iron box grown into a crotch of the tree, where it was placed in Elizabethan times, are, among other things, portraits of Small Thomas and Mary Stuart, a gold toy cannon, and a letter from Mary to "her own true Tomas." Small Thomas, Gemma has already realized, was the child Mary is rumored to have borne— the "treasure" kept safe at Boxleton. Twentieth-century Boxleton will have a new mistress, for Gemma has agreed to marry Thomas. The portrait of Mary Stuart is worth so much that Boxleton House will be safe; she was not saved by any of the Bassumtytes, but she has surely saved them.

BATTISTO, a character in Lloyd Alexander's* *The First Two Lives of Lukas-Kasha**. This mountebank performs magical tricks in the villages he travels through. When he comes to Zara-Petra*, Battisto sends Lukas-Kasha* (Lukas) to Abadan* by pushing the young man's head into a pot of water, and then brings him back. Because it appears to the crowd that Lukas has not really gone anywhere, the people chase Battisto out of town.

BATTLE, ANDY, a character in Walter de la Mare's* *The Three Mulla-mulgars**. He is an Oomgar, or man. This Englishman, who now lives in a hut in a tropical forest, longs for his home and looks forward to the day when he will return there. When he captures Ummanodda* (Nod) in a snare, lonely Andy makes a friend of him, teaching Nod English and living with him as a comrade. Nod rewards his kindness by destroying the Immânala*, the terrible beast who seeks to kill Andy. Realizing how lonely Nod is for his brothers, Andy reluctantly allows the little Mulgar* to go free, giving him many presents.

BAUBLE, THE. *See* Golden Pelydryn

BEALE, JAMES, a character in *Harding's Luck**, by E[dith] Nesbit Bland*. He becomes the husband of Amelia; Beale's father lives near Arden Castle*. Beale is a tramp, living as best he can by begging and stealing. When he and his partner plan to burgle Talbot Court, Beale is sent to find a small boy to help them; he comes upon orphaned, unhappy Dickie Harding* and invites the boy to come with him. The two become fond of one another. When the burglary goes wrong, Beale escapes and is later joined by Dickie. Uncomfortable at the dishonesty of their life, Dickie tries to change it, carving boxes to earn their living and encouraging Beale to keep dogs. Soon the two have settled down together and live quite comfortably. When his business outgrows the premises and the wandering urge hits him, Beale talks Dickie into looking for a bigger place. They come to Arden Castle, and Beale settles down with his father, marrying and raising dogs.

BEAR, THE, a character in Randall Jarrell's* *The Animal Family*. When the hunter* accidentally gets between a mother bear and her cub, he is forced to kill the mother to save himself. He takes the cub home to the mermaid* who shares his cabin and they raise the bear as their child. His upbringing is awkward; the bear is clumsy and tends to make messes, but he has a knack for making the best of anything from his clumsy way of climbing trees to the upset bees whose hive he robs. Clumsy and messy as he is, the bear is dearly loved by the hunter and the mermaid and by the boy* who also joins their family.

BEASTS, a race of beings in *A Wrinkle in Time*, by Madeleine L'Engle*. They live on Ixchel, a dark planet in the same system as Camazotz*. Because there is little light, the beasts have no need of it; they have no eyes, though they do have faces. The tall beasts have four arms with many tentacles instead of fingers; through these tentacles they speak and seem to sense. Instead of hair and ears, they have more tentacles. The beasts are covered with downy gray fur that smells fresh and springlike. They seem able to sense the reality of things rather than just see the outside surface, and they can hear the music of the stars. The beasts seem to be filled with infinite love. Mr. Murry*, in a desperate attempt to get away from IT*, a monstrous power on Camazotz, lands himself, his daughter, Meg Murry*, and their friend, Calvin O'Keefe*, on Ixchel; the beasts welcome and care for them until Meg goes back to Camazotz to rescue her younger brother.

BEAVER, MR., a character in C[live] S[taples] Lewis's* *The Lion, the Witch, and the Wardrobe* and *The Last Battle*. He and Mrs. Beaver are a cheerful old couple living in a snug beaverhouse at Beaversdam, on the Great River in Narnia*. Mr. Beaver is one of the talking beasts of that magical land, and when Edmund, Lucy, Peter, and Susan Pevensie**** come to the land, he welcomes them into his home and hides them from the evil White Witch*, who would like to kill them. He explains to the children much about Narnia and its mighty ruler, Aslan*. Mr. Beaver and his wife lead the children to the Stone Table* to meet Aslan; he probably takes part in the later battle against the White Witch. The Beavers are among those in Aslan's country after Narnia comes to an end.

BEAVER, SAM, a character in E[lwyn] B[rooks] White's* *The Trumpet of the Swan*. He lives with his parents on a ranch in Montana. This eleven-year-old is very fond of animals and is happy watching them. He also likes to be alone in the woods. When he and his father go camping in Canada, Sam discovers a pair of nesting trumpeter swans and meets Louis*, one of their cygnets, who cannot talk. Sam has already driven off a fox menacing the female swan; as

Louis grows up, he looks to Sam for help several more times. Sam talks a teacher into teaching Louis to read and write; he also gets Louis the first job he needs to pay for the trumpet Louis's father has stolen. Sam helps Louis make an agreement with a head keeper at the Philadelphia zoo so he and his mate will be set free. As soon as he is old enough to work, Sam gets a job at the Philadelphia zoo.

BED-KNOB, MAGIC, an object in Mary Norton's* *The Magic Bed-Knob** and *Bonfires and Broomsticks**. This globe-shaped bed-knob is part of a brass bed bought in 1903 by the aunt of Carey, Charles, and Paul Wilson***. It is ordinary until the children come to stay with their aunt during a summer holiday; Paul, discovering that the knob will unscrew, takes it off and it is enchanted by Eglantine Price*, who is trying to bribe the children to keep quiet about her study of witchcraft. Back on the bedpost, the knob will transport the bed and its contents anywhere Paul wishes, in the present or the past, depending on which way it is turned. After a hair-raising experience on a South Sea island, the children and the bed return in such disarray that the children's aunt sends them home in disgrace. Paul, however, takes the bed-knob with him. Two years later the bed-knob again works magic when the children stay with Miss Price, who now owns the bed. This time, they are transported into the past, where they meet Emelius Jones*, a necromancer. The bed and bed-knob finally become seventeenth-century furnishings when they transport Emelius and Miss Price to that century to live permanently.

BED-KNOB AND BROOMSTICK. *See Bonfires and Broomsticks; The Magic Bed-Knob*

BEDONEBYASYOUDID, MRS., a character in *The Water-babies**, by Charles Kingsley*. She is the ugly "sister" of Mrs. Doasyouwouldbedoneby*. As old as Eternity, she will remain ugly until people do as they should. This fairy rewards the good and punishes the bad, punishing those who do wrong without knowing better less severely than those who knowingly do wrong. She teaches Tom*, a water-baby*, to be good and also helps Mr. Grimes* to repent of his bad deeds. Mrs. Bedonebyasyoudid is merely one facet of a being whose real name is too dazzling for mortals to know. Mrs. Doasyouwouldbedoneby is another facet, as is Mother Carey*.

BEEZIE O'KEEFE (*A Swiftly Tilting Planet*). *See* O'Keefe, Branwen Zillah Maddox

BELL OF RHÛN, an object in Jane Louise Curry's* *The Sleepers**. This bronze bell is chased with the figures of animals; its handle is a snake with its tail in its mouth; its sound is too sweet for mortal heart to bear. It was made long ago and was buried above the chamber where Artair*—King Arthur*—

and his knights sleep until they are needed. The ringing of the Bell is meant to wake them. When Henry Peter Huntington* and his companions dig beneath the Eildon Tree*, they find the Bell; Henry later rings it to wake Artair and his men to save them from Margan*, Artair's sister and enemy. The Bell of Rhûn goes with the other *Brenhin Dlyseu**, the Thirteen Treasures of Prydein, to safety beyond the seas.

***BEN AND ME*.** Robert Lawson. Ill. Robert Lawson. Boston: Little, Brown and Company, 1939. 113 pp. American.

In a tiny concealed chamber in a Philadelphia house are discovered the memoirs of Amos*, a mouse, who tells the story of his relationship with Benjamin Franklin* (Ben):

Amos is the eldest of the twenty-six children of a church mouse. During an especially hard winter, he leaves home to make his fortune and comes to Ben's house. Here Amos sleeps in Ben's fur hat and the next day gives him the idea for the Franklin stove. So taken is Ben with Amos and his ideas that he makes an agreement with the mouse to provide for Amos's family and allow Amos to live in the fur cap, which is modified to accommodate him.

Amos's life with Ben is filled with small adventures, such as the time Ben goes swimming. Amos, left on the streambank with the hat, scampers up a tree when a dog trots up and takes the cap. Ben, partially dressed, chases the dog, thinking Amos is in peril. Meanwhile some men happen by and, seeing the clothes, decide Ben has drowned. They take the clothes back to town and return with a crowd to the stream, only to find Ben there—scratched and as dignified as a nearly-naked man can be. To Ben's joy, Amos is well and returns to his hat. Another adventure ensues when Amos edits *Poor Richard's Almanack*, changing the tide tables and giving himself credit for the proverbs. The mob that forms when the tide tables are discovered to be wrong is quelled when Ben points out that this obviously is not the true *Poor Richard's*; Amos hides from Ben for two days.

By this time Ben is experimenting with electricity—experiments Amos enjoys not at all, though he does manage some enthusiasm when Ben arranges an exhibit for the governor; Amos "helps" Ben by fixing the wiring, thereby giving the governor an exhilirating jolt. Ben is interested in lightning, too, attaching rods to the house to collect it but terrified when the rods do their work. Undaunted, though, Ben makes more observations—sending Amos up on a kite to do the observing. After this awful experience, Amos stomps home to his family, to return only when Ben promises to stop experimenting. When Ben makes his trip to Britain, however, Amos stays home because Ben has equipped the ship with lightning rods. After his return, Ben presents to a committee the Declaration of Independence, which he has altered from the declaration written by a rebellious mouse friend of Amos's.

Amos goes with Ben to France, where he spies for popular Ben and thwarts diplomatic plots against him. Here he meets Sophia*, an aristocratic mouse seeking to rescue her children held at Versailles, so that she and they can rejoin her husband in America. When he and Ben are invited to a ball at Versailles, Amos sees his chance; he gathers an army of peasant mice and others, and they secret themselves in Ben's clothes and the wig of Sophia's mistress. At the ball, the mice go into action, provoking hysteria in the humans, and after a great battle, Amos and his army are victorious. Ben, the man who had dripped mice, is shunned by one and all. At home, he is a great hero and is more than content.

As the years pass, Amos no longer wants to go everywhere with Ben; he presents him with a tri-corner hat to replace the ragged fur cap Amos has spent so much time in. After all, Amos figures, at eighty-one Ben is old enough to go out by himself.

BENEATH THE HILL. Jane Louise Curry. Illus. Imero Gobbato. New York: Harcourt, Brace and World, 1967. 255 pp. American.

Determined to impress her cousin, Arthur Arthur* (Dub), who has come to visit, Margaret Arthur* (Miggle), concocts a treasure hunt in which the treasure is a strange key* she has found in a nearby spring. At first the hunt goes well, though the clues are subtly different from what Miggle had made them and though the children are being followed by a strange, silvery-eyed boy. Finally they find that the place where Miggle had hidden the treasure has disappeared— destroyed by strip-mining—and Miggle admits what she did. While the others go home, Dub goes looking for Terwilliger* (Willy), the dog, who has wandered off. Willy leads Dub to an ancient patch of woods, where he meets Káolin*, the boy who has been following the children. Káolin wants to trade something for Willy, who appears to be the dog in an old prophetic rhyme, but Dub will not trade.

The next day the children explore the Bane*, the strip pits left by the mining. When Stevie Griffith*, the cousin of Miggle and Arthur, is sucked into a deep lake, Káolin rescues him and takes the children to his house for lunch. There they meet mysterious and beautiful people—y Tylwyth Teg*, the Fair Folk*— from Wales. Long ago these people were separated from others of their kind on a long journey to Tir na'nOg*, the Fortunate Isles. Landing in America, they were intrigued by Indian tales of others like them and traveled to Nūtayē (the City of the Moon Under the Mountain*), beautiful caverns where they live still. Now the Folk are not sure they will ever reach the Isles, for they are trapped by the civilization that has grown up around them. Miggle and the others are taken through the lovely caves, past an underground river, to a place where an evil force is sealed beneath the mountain; the Folk fear that the coal mining will accidentally free it.

When they get home, the children learn that Miggle's father has found the box with the "key" in it; it was on top of the chicken coop, apparently thrown there by blasting. When Miggle goes to get it, she is almost attacked by weasels, which seem to be after the box instead of the chickens. Though driven away, they come back that night and try to get through Miggle's bedroom window.

Having thwarted them, the frightened children go to the boys' room, where they watch a thick fog drifting from the Bane. When one of the Fair Folk, appearing out of the fog and beckoning Miggle to follow her, turns out to be an illusion of the mist, the children realize that something wants the "key" desperately; it must be more important than they had thought.

The next day, on the way to Nūtayē, the children find themselves in a thick patch of fog. Each time they try to find their way out of it, they discover themselves to be at the Bane. Finally Willy finds them and leads them home, out of a tiny patch of fog they have been lost in. The children try again the following day, riding their horses so they will not have to carry a two-year-old who is under their care. To the Folk, the children appear as figures out of legend, and they bear the same key those legendary folk had had—Miggle's "key" controls the waters in the land. By fitting the key into its "lock" in the cavern wall near the underground river, the water can be diverted into an old channel and the Bane will be flooded; the evil force will be resealed and the land will grow green again. But if the key is turned further, the river will be diverted into another channel and the Folk will be able thereby to float to an aboveground river and thence to the sea and to Tir na'nOg.

Because the mining company is filling in the Bane to stave off a lawsuit by Miggle's father, thus sealing the evil force again, the children decide to help the Folk go free by diverting the underground river away from the Bane, though this will mean that nearby springs will dry up and the land will stay barren. But the Folk decide to divert the waters only long enough to get them on their way; once they are at the river, the children can redivert the waters onto the Bane. To protect it from intruders, the Folk seal all but one of the entrances of Nūtayē: this last entrance will close at the hour by which the children will be out of the caves. Dub, who has to go back home early, will pretend to catch the bus at the station but will really slip back to Nūtayē and travel with the Folk, who will float down the river past his house.

All goes as planned. Miggle and Stevie watch as Dub and the Folk sail away, then they redirect the waters and hurry out of the caverns before the gate closes and the entrance vanishes. Later that night, Miggle, aware that the key can be misused, destroys it by melting it in a pot in her mother's kiln. Arthur reaches home and is given a gift by the Folk: a lovely book in an unknown language with covers of rose quartz, which they had found in Nūtayē. Someday, he promises himself, he will read it. The Bane eventually grows green again, and the Folk finally reach Tir na'nOg.

BENJAMIN FRANKLIN (*Ben and Me*). *See* Franklin, Benjamin

BEORN, a character in *The Hobbit**, by J[ohn] R[onald] R[euel] Tolkien*. He is a skin-changer who appears as either a great black bear or as a huge, black-haired man. Some think he is a bear, but probably he is a man. Beorn is a solitary man with few friends, living apart from men in a great house he shares with the animals who serve and talk to him. He lives primarily on honey and cream, fruit, and nuts, never eating meat. Beorn makes a very bad enemy. When Thorin Oakenshield* and his companions lose their ponies and supplies to goblins*, whom Beorn hates fiercely, he loans them ponies as far as the great forest of Mirkwood, and he keeps close watch on them to be sure the ponies are treated well. Beorn gets his chance to battle with goblins at the Battle of Five Armies, when goblins and wild wolves sweep down on the four armies gathered at the Lonely Mountain to claim part of the great treasure Thorin has regained. Beorn battles in the shape of a bear and his wrath is terrible, especially after Thorin falls. Beorn becomes a great chief in the lands between Mirkwood and the Misty Mountains, and for many generations his descendants have the power to change into bears. Though some of them are bad, most are as kindly as Beorn, though perhaps not as gruff or strong.

BERINIR GAIR, a place in Jane Louise Curry's* *The Watchers*. Though this ancient castle or fortress looks European, it was built in ancient America by the mysterious people who lived in the valley above Tûl Isgrun*, on the lush mountaintop which in the twentieth century is called Up Top*. The people who lived here spoke a language akin to Welsh. By the twentieth century, the building is in ruins; only one tower still stands. Here are kept ancient books and documents. The people who live in Twilly's Green Hollow* call this place "the Gare."

BERNARD, a character in *Wet Magic*, by E[dith] Nesbit Bland*. He is the brother of Francis*, Mavis*, and Kathleen*. Bernard is one of those unlucky people who always get caught whenever they are doing something beyond the pale. He is an excellent planner, however; he plans the rescue of Freia*, a captured mermaid, and it comes off without a hitch. When the children visit Freia's home, Merland*, Bernard and the others are captured defending it from the Under Folk*; he helps the others to rescue Freia's father and bring about peace between the sea peoples after centuries of war.

BERT (the Mary Poppins books). *See* Herbert Alfred

BERT ELLISON (*The Ghost of Thomas Kempe*). *See* Ellison, Bert

BERTRAM, a character mentioned in Alan Garner's* *The Owl Service*. He was related to Alison Bradley*. Handsome, dashing Bertram was caught up, in his time, in an ancient triangle of love and jealousy first acted out by Blodeuwedd*—a mythical woman made of flowers—her husband, and her lover. Having won the love of Nancy*, a Welsh servant in Bertram's house, Bertram planned to marry her; Huw Hannerhob*, jealous and tired of Bertram making him look foolish, took the brake blocks from the refurbished motorcycle Bertram rode up and down the driveway, hoping to send him skidding into the bushes. Instead Bertram rode over a dangerous pass and was killed coming around a bend. Nancy never forgave Huw for this, nor he, himself; Bertram is the "dark raven" of Huw's "unreason." From Bertram, Alison's father inherited the house that he gave her before he died. Bertram's presence seems to be felt still in the valley where he lived. When Blodeuwedd's story begins to play itself out again in the next generation, Roger Bradley* takes a picture which may show him on his motorcyle, and a motorcycle engine is sometimes heard in the valley.

BERTRAND STUDDARD (*The Wind Eye*). *See* Studdard, Bertrand

BERUNA, a place in C[live] S[taples] Lewis's* Chronicles of Narnia*. Here there are fords in the Great River, where the river becomes very shallow and wide. The Fords of Beruna is the site of the battle in which the evil White Witch* is defeated by Aslan*, the great lion-protector of Narnia*. Later a small town called Beruna springs up here. A bridge is built across the fords by conquerors from Telmar*, who do not like open water. The town is later "liberated" by Aslan during the war that puts Caspian X* on the throne: the bridge is destroyed and the bad people are forced from Beruna. The bridge is rebuilt by Caspian, but the town stays liberated.

BETH STUDDARD (*The Wind Eye*). *See* Studdard, Beth

BETTY ARDEN (*The House of Arden*). *See* Arden, Betty

BETTY LOVELL (*The House of Arden; Harding's Luck*). *See* Lovell, Betty

BIDDLE, MRS. a character in E[dith] Nesbit Bland's* *The Phoenix and the Carpet*. Miserly and sour-tempered, Mrs. Biddle takes out her temper on those who cannot fight back. At the church bazaar she unknowingly buys a wishing carpet* for her parlor floor—saying it is for the servants' quarters—and refuses to sell it back to Robert*, Anthea*, Cyril*, and Jane*, who had not intended to sell it. When the children use the carpet to wish on her a better temper, Mrs. Biddle's humor sweetens and she gives the carpet to them.

BIGGIN, MAUD (DR.), a character in *The River at Green Knowe*, by Lucy Boston*. She is the great-aunt of Ida*. Maud is an archaeologist who believes that giant men once roamed the earth. Such a professional is she that she constantly searches the ground for artifacts; she detests vacuum cleaners because they leave nothing for her to discover. Near-sighted, she never straightens up; all the books and notes she consults are left at a convenient level and she moves among them. When she needs more books, Maud goes to the library on her little motorcycle. Looking for a peaceful place to write her book on ancient man, Maud rents Green Knowe* with her friend, Sybilla Bun. Because there is so much room, she sends for Ida and two displaced children to spend the summer. Certain that the children can take care of themselves, she leaves them to their own devices. Because Maud hopes to prove the existence of giant prehistoric men, the children leave the tooth of Terak*, a giant boy they have met, where she will find it; when she does, it sets off a great controversy among her colleagues. Despite her hopes, when the children take Maud to see Terak, now a clown in the circus, she decides that he is a fake; she cannot believe giants can exist now and not just in the past.

BIGWIG, a character in Richard Adams's* *Watership Down**. This rabbit's name is Thlayli, which means "furhead," because he has a heavy growth of fur on the crown of his head. Bigwig is one of the Owsla, the team of strong rabbits that wield authority, at the Sandleford warren. His duties become distasteful, for Bigwig gets tired of doing sentry duty and stealing lettuce for the Chief Rabbit. When Fiver* has a vision of the warren being destroyed and Bigwig allows him to see the Chief Rabbit at an inconvenient time, the Chief's anger is the last straw and Bigwig decides to leave the warren. He goes with Fiver, Hazel*, and eight others, eventually ending up at Watership Down. Bigwig's strength comes in handy, especially when the rabbits realize that their warren has no does, and Bigwig is finally sent to the nearby warren of Efrafa* as part of a plan to get some from there. In the process he makes a fool of General Woundwort*, the Efrafan leader. When Woundwort and his forces attack Bigwig's warren, Bigwig and Woundwort have a terrible fight, and, though Bigwig is dreadfully injured, Woundwort loses. Bigwig becomes the captain of the Owsla in the warren at Watership Down.

BILBO BAGGINS (*The Hobbit*). *See* Baggins, Bilbo

BILL WINGARD (*Parsley Sage, Rosemary & Time; The Magical Cupboard*). *See* Wingard, William

BINKY, a dog in Jane Louise Curry's* *The Sleepers**. This small but valiant terrier belongs to the archaeologist grandfather of Gillian and Ellen Peresby**. When Jennifer Huntington* uncovers the passage to the chamber where Artair*— King Arthur*—and his warriors lie sleeping, Binky falls into it. In rescuing him, the children find Artair.

BIRD WOMAN, a character in P[amela] L[yndon] Travers's* *Mary Poppins** and *Mary Poppins Opens the Door**. She is the mother of the park keeper, Fred. The Bird Woman sells bags of crumbs for tuppence outside St. Paul's Cathedral. So long has she done this that all she can say to customers is "Feed the Birds, Tuppence a Bag!" even for greetings. Though Mary Poppins* contradicts them, Jane Caroline and Michael George Banks** know that when all is still each night, the doves and pigeons fly down and nestle under the woman's skirts, where they sleep snug and warm as under a broody hen.

BIRDSTONES, THE, three magical stones in Jane Louise Curry's* *The Bird-stones*. Each of these bright stones is in the shape of a bird, and each has a name: Annit, Pannit, and Dree. The stones are handed down through her mother to Dalea*, a girl of fourth-century Abáloc*. When set in the ammarn* tree on Inas Ebhélic* or its stone double in the Tree-Chamber under the island, the stones become real birds and control time, if the proper dance and chant are performed. Thiuclas* and Dalea use the power of the stones to come to twentieth-century Apple Lock*, Ohio, and then to get back to their own place in time.

BIRDSTONES, THE. Jane Louise Curry. New York: Atheneum, 1977. 204 pp. American.

It is fall, and school is just opening in Apple Lock*, Ohio. This schoolyear seems unpromising, for one of the town's two elementary schools has burned down, so students will have to crowd into the other. Callista Lee Rivers* (Callie) and her friends decide that the best thing they could do to buoy their spirits would be to hoax everyone. When Anna Maria D'Agostino* (Teeny) tells the other girls about the "invisible" student her sister and her friends had made up and registered at the local college, the girls know they have their hoax, and so "Dayla Jones" is born. Meanwhile, Michaelangelo Pucci* (Pooch) discovers on Apple Island*, where his family has a garden, an oval of sycamores which surrounds a wild garden with a huge tree in the center. Pushing through a thorn-hedge, the boy finds himself at the tip of the island, where he hears a lovely birdsong and sees moss-covered steps leading down into a cave. Here Pooch finds a beautifully carved bird of stone—a birdstone*.

Because the classes are so crowded, Callie and her friends have little trouble hoaxing the teachers. Dayla's homework is divided between the girls. One day they find that somebody is disturbing "Dayla's" locker; some cookies and a lunch and some schoolbooks are missing, and a strange sweater has taken their place. The girls are not sure who to blame, but Angela Paff* thinks it is part of a local crime wave in which only food has been stolen.

Suddenly the crimes take a more serious turn; when the Pucci's grocery store is broken into, the little museum the children formed above it last year is ransacked. Only objects having to do with Abáloc*, the twelfth-century place the children had visited the year before, have been damaged. The local high school has also been vandalized. The next week, the mystery of Dayla's locker deepens as the girls find that the food that was taken has been replaced. Angela and Teeny see someone wearing the sweater found in Dayla's locker, but they do not see where she goes. Intrigued by the turn the crime wave has taken, the girls and boys in the class who had shared their adventure compile a list of those who have suffered burglaries and match them up with people who had bought Abalockian objects at auction. The local cop is very interested.

While the boys concentrate on finding the burglar, the girls concentrate on "Dayla," who apparently is doing her own homework: lovely pictures of birds found only in Abáloc—part of a class assignment—appear in the locker, and

Callie finds that "Dayla" has written an essay about Abáloc for class. Then one day the lock is changed; Teeny learns in the principal's office that "Dayla" has complained that someone was rummaging in her locker, and when Teeny sees her folder with its photograph, she recognizes a small, shy girl who is new in the class.

Thoroughly confused, the girls tell the boys. The new girl has been seen with Pooch, who has been acting mysteriously, so all decide to confront him with the matter. When they reach the grocery store, they find there three dark men dressed in what are obviously mismatched rummage sale clothes; the mysterious men are obviously up to no good, but they leave quietly when the policeman comes. Pooch tells the children that he has been followed all week and reveals how he found the birdstone and then descended the steps into a cave with a central pillar carved to look like a tree, its branches carved into the ceiling and a stream carved into the floor around the circumference of the cave. For a moment he had glimpsed a woman with singing birds in either hand; then she was gone, but a girl named Dalea* was there instead.

In the fourth century, a strange drama unfolds. Tekla*, the queen of Kanhuan*, seeks the power she needs to take over New Aztalán*. She hopes to gain the power of Katóa*, an evil force, by making it a shrine at Inas Ebhélic*, the Island of Abáloc, where Katóa was before the Aldar* came and imprisoned him. Having destroyed, she thinks, the last of the Aldar, Tekla will also destroy the last ammarn* tree, which they had planted on the island, and thereby prepare it for the shrine. Dalea, living with her grandfather, Thiuclas*, on the island, dreams that enemies come in boats to Abáloc. Waking to find her grandfather gone, Dalea searches for him, sees the boats coming, and warns the village, but it is destroyed. Dalea spends the night in the great ammarn tree at the center of the island and goes home to find the note Thiuclas has left for her: preparing to go to the City of the Moon Under the Mountain*, a place of refuge, he has first taken the five *Books of the Kings of Abáloc** to a safe place. She is to wait in the Tree-Chamber under the island for him. Here, her mother had shown her, three birdstones come to life when they are put into niches in the stone tree and a certain dance and chant are performed. Dalea is seen and chased by Tekla's men, who are felling the ammarn. Fleeing to the Tree-Chamber, she sees that the birdstones are in their places; she sings the song and dances the dance. The birds sing, and Dalea finds herself in the twentieth century, discovered by Pooch when one of the birds flies out of the cave and becomes stone again.

Dalea has been staying with Mr. Douglass, the eccentric old man who runs a plant nursery in Apple Lock, helped by Pooch to slip into the gap left by "Dayla Jones." The children realize that the warriors of Kanhuan who chased Dalea into the cave are trapped in this time as well, for they need the birdstones to get back. Dalea has the three stones, but she cannot go to the island, for the men will find her. The children decide to hold a Halloween costume party on the island and smuggle her there that way.

The town librarian has been acting oddly for some time, for Tekla has possessed her. Overhearing the Halloween plans, she takes the place of one of the chaperones. Angela Paff, who knows the librarian better than the others do, realizes that something is wrong with her and follows her to the ammarn tree. She is astonished when the woman curses the tree in a strange language and calls up some sort of dreadful power. Angela follows the woman to the end of the island and is grabbed there by Tekla's men.

Pooch, Teeny, Dalea, and Mr. Douglass, who is carrying a mysterious knapsack, also witness the curse and decide that they cannot waste time. Because, as Mr. Douglass tells them, the tree in the cave is a copy of this one, which sprouted from the one cut down by Tekla and the men sixteen hundred years ago, they are able to use the power of the birdstones. As they touch the tree, the stones come alive; they sing away the evil, and sing a sleep onto the others on the island. As Pooch and Teeny watch, Dalea vanishes—with Mr. Douglass.

The next day they piece together what had happened. Mr. Douglass was really Thiuclas, who had come to the twentieth century to hide the books and was trapped here when Dalea brought away the birdstones. Tekla's men have been captured by the police, thanks to Angela, and the librarian has no memory of Tekla's possession. The children discover that Dalea and Thiuclas did indeed reach their own time, for wrapped around an Abalockian book found in the Pennsylvania mountains is a bookbag on which is printed "Sam's News"— which Dalea had used as Dayla Jones.

BISHANGAR, a place in Lloyd Alexander's* *The First Two Lives of Lukas-Kasha**. This mountainous province is rich in gold and jewels but poor in water. Its people are proud, and its women are equal in importance to its men. Under the reign of King Neriman, the place was rich and peaceful, trading with the country of Abadan* for food and grain. During this time Jannat al-Khuld, a great city, was built. When Neriman's daughter, Queen Tamina, succeeded him, the king of Abadan began to demand more and more for Abadani goods, and when she finally refused to pay, the Abadanis declared war and captured Jannat, claiming Bishangar as a province. Tamina died in battle. Her son, Ardashir*, and his people hid in the mountains and harassed the Abadani army, planning to retake Jannat when their forces were great enough. Nur-Jehan*, Ardashir's daughter and heir, brings peace to Bishangar by bargaining with the Abadani king, Lukas-Kasha*, after he regains control of his country. Namash*, a resourceful Abadani waterseller-turned-merchant, discovers a large stream under Jannat which will help make the countryside productive.

BISM, a place in C[live] S[taples] Lewis's* *The Silver Chair**. It lies deeper under the land of Narnia* than the deepest mines ever go. It is very hot and very bright: rubies, diamonds, silver, and gold are living here, and edible; the rivers run fire. In these rivers live salamanders, who speak very eloquently from them. Bism is the land of the Earthmen*, and all other lands seem cold to them by comparison. They leave Bism only at the commanding spells of the Queen of Underland* and are very glad to get back to their native land once she is killed.

BITA-VITA BREAKFAST FOOD, a concoction in Robert Lawson's* *Mr. Twigg's Mistake*. This cereal is often called Bities, for short. It is made of toasted peanut shells, corn silk, and coffee grounds, mixed with Vitamin X, a miraculous vitamin that promotes growth and is fantastically good for you. Bities are very popular, for over 870 million boxes are sold each year; they are eaten by stage, screen, and radio stars, athletes, and the most aristocratic people. Mr. Twigg is responsible for the proper mixing of Bities with Vitamin X, and he takes his job very seriously. One day, though, he has a headache and forgets to mix the vitamins with the Bities in one batch. As a result, two and three-fourths pounds of undiluted Vitamin X are emptied into one package of Bities. This package is eventually delivered to the house of Arthur Amory Appleton*; when he feeds it to General de Gaulle*, his pet mole, the animal grows to the size of a man.

BITIES. *See* Bita-Vita Breakfast Food

BLACK CAULDRON, THE. Lloyd Alexander. New York: Holt, Rinehart, and Winston, 1965. 222 pp. American.
It is autumn, and an important council meets at Caer Dallben*, the farmstead of Dallben*, an old and powerful sorcerer. The council is called by Gwydion*, the war leader of the High King of Prydain*, and present are kings and warriors from all over the land: Fflewddur Fflam*, a king and would-be bard; Doli*, one of the Fair Folk*; Smoit*, king of a southern cantrev; Adaon*, son of Prydain's chief bard; Morgant*, king of a northern realm; and Ellidyr*, a young prince full of bitter pride. Gwydion has gathered them for a dangerous quest—the destruction of Arawn's* magical cauldron, through which the evil king of Annuvin* is creating an ever-increasing army of deathless warriors called the Cauldron-Born*. Despite Morgant's protests that the cauldron be taken to his realm, it is decided that the warriors will go to Annuvin, seize the cauldron, and bring it to Caer Dallben to be destroyed. With them will go Taran*, the orphaned young man living at Caer Dallben. Smoit will ready his warriors to cover the retreat.
The journey to Annuvin is punctuated by flare-ups between Ellidyr and Taran, whom the prince scorns. When the group reaches its objective, the two are left with Adaon to guard the horses, and they are soon joined by Eilonwy*, a fierce-tempered young princess, and Gurgi*, a hairy creature of uncertain antecedents—both upset at being left behind at Caer Dallben. Suddenly Fflewddur and Doli return without the others; the cauldron is gone, stolen by someone else. The little band is attacked by Huntsmen*, vicious Annuvinian warriors, and the group flees. It finds refuge in one of the Fair Folk's way posts, manned by Gwystyl*,

who, prompted by Kaw*, his crow, tells them that the cauldron is in the hands of Orddu*, Orwen*, and Orgoch*, in the marshes. Taran decides to go after it.

During their journey, Ellidyr, who longs for glory, leaves the band to find the cauldron on his own. As they follow him, the others are attacked by a band of Huntsmen, whom Fflewddur and Doli lead away after Adaon is wounded. The young man dies, giving Taran a magical brooch*. As he, Gurgi, and Eilonwy travel toward the marshes, the brooch makes Taran become especially sensitive to the world arounnd him and gives him prophetic dreams; they find Fflewddur where he had dreamed they would. When they come to the marshes and are attacked by Huntsmen, Taran is able to lead them safely through the bog.

In the middle of the marshes, they find the three sisters—Orddu, Orwen, and Orgoch—three old and eccentric witches who had loaned the Black Crochan*— the cauldron—to Arawn and then had to steal it back from him. Now it sits in the shed where the travelers spend the night—a night during which Taran sees the hags appear as maidens, one carding, one spinning, and one weaving. The next morning, having failed to steal the Crochan, the travelers trade for it the most precious thing they have: Adaon's brooch. Hammers do not break the Crochan; it can only be destroyed if a living being, knowing what he is doing, climbs inside; but the Crochan's destruction will also destroy the person who climbs into it.

Disheartened, the companions start for Caer Dallben, lugging the Crochan with them. It is a hard journey. At a river crossing, the Crochan slips from its harness and falls on Fflewddur, breaking his arm. The Crochan sinks into the mud and cannot be budged. When Ellidyr happens on them, he is maddened because they have found the Crochan and robbed him of glory; after he helps them move it to land, he tries to kill Taran, who falls and hits his head on a rock. When the boy wakes, Ellidyr has taken the Crochan, having tried to kill the others too.

As the companions travel home, they come across Morgant's warriors; Morgant and the others who had gone into Annuvin have escaped Arawn's warriors and have learned from Gwystyl of Taran's journey to the marshes. Ellidyr and the Crochan are with Morgant. When the companions reach camp, however, they find Ellidyr battered and bound and are themselves taken prisoner. Morgant plans to use the Crochan to make a powerful army, and he wants Taran to join him, or all the companions will be made into Cauldron-Born. Taran has the night to consider Morgant's offer. The next morning, however, Doli—who has the power to become invisible—comes and frees them. Ellidyr battles the guards around the Crochan and throws himself into it, dying with its destruction. Suddenly Smoit, Gwydion, and the other warriors arrive, and Morgant is killed in the ensuing battle. Having raised barrows over Morgant and Ellidyr, the others ride back to Caer Dallben, Taran with Kaw on his shoulder—a present from Gwystyl.

BLACK CROCHAN, the title object in Lloyd Alexander's* *The Black Cauldron*. This great, battered black cauldron is large enough to hold a man. It belongs to Orddu*, Orgoch*, and Orwen*, three mysterious witches living in the Marshes of Morva. For a time they lend it to Arawn*, the evil lord of Annuvin*, and he uses it to create an army of invincible Cauldron-Born*, for any corpse put into it becomes a deathless, heartless warrior. After this, all the Crochan is good for is making the Cauldron-Born. When the time comes for him to give it up, he does not, and the three witches take it from him. Seeking to destroy the Crochan, young Taran* and his companions come to the Marshes and bargain with the women, trading the Crochan for a magical brooch*. They cannot destroy the cauldron, for only a living man, in full knowledge of what he is doing, can destroy the Crochan by climbing into it. In doing so he will die. The cauldron is finally destroyed when Ellidyr*, a proud prince repenting of his pride, climbs into it.

BLACK RIDER, THE, a character in Susan Cooper's* *Over Sea, Under Stone*, *The Dark Is Rising*, and *Silver on the Tree*. He is one of the greatest of the evil Lords of the Dark and has been on the earth since its beginning. Handsome, with auburn hair and blue eyes, he is usually dressed in black and rides a black horse. Sometimes he takes on another form; once he appears as Mr. Hastings, a vicar. In every age, the Black Rider has sought to defeat the Light—the powers of good—a struggle in which he is not always successful. As Mr. Hastings, he seeks to get from Barnabas, Jane, and Simon Drew*** a grail* and a manuscript* they have found that prophesy the coming of King Arthur* to defeat the Dark, but he fails. He also tries to keep Will Stanton*, one of his enemies, from getting the six Signs of the Light* and fails again, this time to be harried and chased by Herne* and his Wild Hunt*. The Black Rider, scarred by this encounter, and aided by the White Rider*, bitterly tries again to defeat the Light. Because those of the Light reach the midsummer tree* and, cutting its flower, are able to defeat their enemies, the Black Rider and the White Rider are sent out of time forever.

BLACKIE. *See* Lucy

BLAJENY, a character in *A Wind in the Door*, by Madeleine L'Engle*. He is a Teacher from the Veganuel galaxy. Blajeny's school is the entire universe, and his pupils are everyone from a cherubim to a farandola* to some humans. Tall and dark as night, with amber eyes, he radiates quiet, confidence, and strength. Blajeny teaches Meg and Charles Wallace Murry**, their friend Calvin O'Keefe*, and a cherubim named Proginoskes*, leading them to discover for themselves how best to help themselves.

BLAND, E[DITH] NESBIT (1858-1924), British writer. She was born on 15 August 1858 and was educated in France, Germany, and Brighton. In 1880 she married Hubert Bland; they had two sons and a daughter and adopted a daughter and a son. Hubert died in 1914, and she married Thomas Terry Tucker on 20

February 1917. Bland was a writer, a journalist, and a painter of greeting cards. She was poetry critic for the *Athenaeum* magazine in the 1890s, co-editor from 1907 to 1908 of the *Neolith*, and general editor of the Children's Bookcase series for Oxford University Press from 1908 to 1911. Bland was also a founding member of the Fabian Society. She died 4 May 1924.

Most of Bland's works are episodic fantasies dealing with good and bad in the individual. *Five Children and It**, *The Phoenix and the Carpet**, and *The Story of the Amulet** concern the adventures of five children. *The House of Arden** and *Harding's Luck** dovetail with one another; the other three stand by themselves. What sets Bland's novels apart from all others is their warm blend of the real world and the fantastic one—a blend spiced with humor.

In Bland's novels, the world of magic is never very far away; by finding the proper key—a carpet, a ring, an amulet, a magical creature—the children in the works discover the undercurrent of fantasy in their own world. Statues which look ordinary by day come to life at night, revealing themselves only to the wearer of a magic ring*. An old Persian carpet bought for a pittance from a London used furniture dealer is actually a wishing carpet* harboring the egg of the Phoenix*. In a sandpit in the English countryside is discovered a wish-granting Psammead*. The seeds of a flower grown from birdseed, used with an old silver rattle* and a signet, magically transport one through time. A few lines from Milton call up a mermaid.

If magic reveals itself as an undercurrent in the world we know, it also reveals itself as something chancy and temperamental. The magical creatures in the novels are usually garrulous and vain. The Psammead does not like to be bothered and grants wishes with a singular ill-will, though Anthea* can get into its good graces through flattery and special attention. The Mouldiwarp* is fiercely proud of the Ardens and of its own position on their crest, and brooks no criticism of either. When Edred and Elfrida Arden** call it by chanting poetry, it usually arrives with a sour review of their verse. The Phoenix is more equanimous, but this is mostly due to its extreme vanity: because it is vastly superior to all other creatures, it feels that it can afford to be tolerant. All three creatures can be depended upon when the children are in trouble, however. The Psammead exhausts itself getting Robert*, Anthea, Jane*, and Cyril* out of a mess they get into with Lady Chittendem's* jewels; the Mouldiwarp exerts its power over white things to rescue Eldrida from a secret passage; and the Phoenix can be counted upon to get just the wish from the Psammead which will save the children from whatever jam they are in.

For jams are frequent occurrences when one is dealing with magic, in Bland's works. Granted wishes are apt to be pleasant at first, but their drawbacks are soon apparent. If you wish to become "as beautiful as the day," no one recognizes you; wish for wings and you find that the people you meet are apt to be afraid of you. Invisibility proves inconvenient for those around you, and a crowd of dummies wished to life can be horrifying. Magic must be precise in order to have the proper effect; when Robert wishes he were bigger than the butcher's boy, he becomes ten feet tall; when Jimmy (James*) uses a magic ring to wish himself rich, he becomes a wealthy old gentleman with no time for the other children. The magic of the ring, a statue of Apollo tells Kathleen*, must be precisely demarcated or confusion will result.

Time travel also can prove hazardous to the unwary, as Elfrida Arden discovers. Touched by the happiness of Anne Boleyn*, she warns the doomed queen and upsets her, igniting the wrath of Henry VIII*. On 5 November 1605, she reveals an intimate knowledge of the Gunpowder Plot, which was yet to be discovered that day, and is put into the Tower of London. Even if one resists the impulse to prophesy, there are other dangers; for example, if the key to the time transport is lost, one can get stuck in that other time, as Robert, Anthea, and Cyril discover when they are imprisoned in a cell in ancient Babylonia, far from Jane and the magic amulet*.

Despite its quirks, magic can help restore lost fortunes or make people happy. Aided by magic, Edred and Elfrida Arden find their lost father and the treasure needed to restore Arden Castle*. Lame Dickie Harding's* forays into the past allow him to live as a strong, healthy boy and, finally, to take up a life of happiness. Robert, Anthea, Cyril, and Jane use magic to restore a family's fortune and bring their own family, scattered through necessity, back together; they also help a student of ancient history and a priest of dynastic Egypt gain their hearts' desires, and find a mother in prehistoric Britain for an orphaned child. Gerald*, Jimmy, Mabel*, and Kathleen use a magic ring to reunite a pair of lovers.

The beneficial effects are also felt on a wider scale, for the adult heroes in many of Bland's works use their fortunes to help the poor, once their own needs are taken care of. In most of the novels, the plight of the working-class poor is a strong element. The hardships of Dickie Harding and his ilk are keenly described, and adult heroes are strongly aware of them. Lord Arden makes plans to create a "model village." In the utopian future the children visit in *The Story of the Amulet*, as well as in paradisiacal Atlantis*, the needs of the poor are seen to and all are clean and bright.

The blend of humor and seriousness in the novels is skillfully handled, as in the balance of realism and fantasy. Bland's novels soar without losing sight of the earth. The style is fresh and humorous. The most outstanding characters in Bland's novels are her magical creatures, with their quirky personalities; the children, while realistic, are for the most part undifferentiated from one another. The plots have the inescapable logic that is the hallmark of good fantasy: incidents arise from situations, and their credibility and humor are not strained.

Works

Juvenile fantasy: *Five Children and It* (1902); *The Phoenix and the Carpet* (1904); *The Story of the Amulet* (1906); *The Enchanted Castle* (1907); *The House of Arden* (1908); *Harding's Luck* (1909); *The Magic City* (1910); *Wet Magic* (1913).
Juvenile non-fantasy, stories, etc.: *Songs of Two Seasons* (1890); *Voyage of Columbus*,

1492 (1892), verse; *Listen Long and Listen Well* (1893), with others; *Our Friends and All About Them* (1893), verse, with others; *Sunny Tales for Snowy Days* (1893), with others; *Told by Sunbeams and Me* (1893), with others; *Fur and Feathers* (1894), with others; *The Girl's Own Birthday Book* (1894); *Hours in Many Lands* (1894), with others; *Lads and Lassies* (1894), with others; *Tales That Are True, for Brown Eyes and Blue* (1894), with others; *Tales to Delight from Morning till Night* (1894), with others; *Doggy Tales* (1895); *Dulcie's Lantern* (1895), stories, with others; *Pussy Tales* (1895); *Treasures from Storyland* (1895), with others; *As Happy as a King* (1896), verse; *The Children's Shakespeare* (1897); *Dinna Forget* (1897), poems, with G. C. Bingham; *Royal Children of English History* (1897), with Doris Ashley; *Tales Told in the Twilight* (1897), with others; *A Book of Dogs* (1898); *Pussy and Doggy Tales* (1899) as *Pussy Tales* and *Doggy Tales*, with additional material; *The Story of the Treasure Seekers* (1899); *The Book of Dragons* (1900), with additional material as *The Complete Book of Dragons* (1972); *Nine Unlikely Tales* (1901); *To Wish You Every Joy* (1901), verse; *The Would Be Goods* (1901); *The Revolt of the Toys* (1902), stories; *The Rainbow Queen, and Other Stories* (1903); *Cat Tales* (1904), with Rosamund Bland; *The New Treasure Seekers* (1904); *Oswald Bastable and Others* (1905); *Pug Peter* (1905); *The Railway Children* (1906); *The Old Nursery Stories* (1908); *My Sea-Side Story Book* (1911), with G. C. Bingham; *The Wonderful Garden* (1911); *The Magic World* (1912), stories; *Our New Story-Book* (1913), with others; *Children's Stories from English History* (1914); *Five of Us—and Madeline* (1925).

Adult: *The Prophet's Mantle* (1885), as Fabian Bland, with Hubert Bland; *Autumn Sketches* (1886), with others; *Lays and Legends* (1886); *Spring Sketches* (1886), with others; *Summer Sketches* (1886), with others; *Winter Sketches* (1886), with others; *The Lily and the Cross* (1887), poem; *The Star of Bethlehem* (1887), poem; *The Better Part and Other Poems* (1888); *By Land and Sea* (1888), poems; *Easter-Tide* (1888), poems, with Caris Brooke; *Landscape and Song* (1888); *Leaves of Life* (1888), poems; *The Message of the Dove* (1888), poems; *The Time of Roses* (1888), poems, with others; *Corals and Sea Songs* (1889); *Lilies Round the Cross* (1889), verse, with Helen J. Wood; *Life's Sunny Side* (1890), poems, with others; *Twice Four* (1891), stories, with others; *Lays and Legends* (1892), second series; *Sweet Lavender* (1892), poems; *Flowers I Bring and Songs I Sing* (1893), poems, with others; *Grim Tales* (1893); *Something Wrong* (1893); *The Butler in Bohemia* (1894), stories; *Holly and Mistletoe* (1895), poems, with others; *A Pomander of Verse* (1895); *Rose Leaves* (1895), poems; *In Homespun* (1896), stories; *Songs of Love and Empire* (1898); *The Secret of Kyriels* (1899), novel; *Thirteen Ways Home* (1901), stories; *The Literary Sense* (1903), stories; *The Rainbow and the Rose* (1905); *The Incomplete Amorist* (1906), novel; *Man and Maid* (1906), stories; *Ballads and Lyrics of Socialism, 1883-1908* (1908); *Jesus in London* (1908), poem; *Daphne in Fitzroy Street* (1909); *Salome and the Head* (1909) as *The House with No Address* (1914); *Fear* (1910), stories; *Ballads and Verses of the Spiritual Life* (1911); *Dormant* (1911), novel; *Wings and the Child* (1913); *The Incredible Honeymoon* (1921); *The Lark* (1922), novel; *Many Voices* (1922), poems; *To the Adventurous* (1923), stories.

Secondary Works

Ayers, Lesley. "The Treatment of Time in Four Children's Books," *Children's Literature in Education*, 2 (July, 1970), pp. 69-81.

Bell, Anthea. *E. Nesbit*. London: Bodley Head, 1960.

Bland, Edith Nesbit. *Long Ago When I Was Young*. London: Whiting and Wheaton, 1966.

Crouch, Marcus S. "E. Nesbit in Kent," *Junior Bookshelf*, 19 (Jan., 1955), pp. 11-21.

———. "The Nesbit Tradition," *Junior Bookshelf*, 22 (Oct., 1958), pp. 195-98.

Croxson, Mary. "The Emancipated Child in the Novels of E. Nesbit," *Signal: Approaches to Children's Books*, 14 (May, 1974), pp. 51-64.

de Alonso, Joan Evans. "E. Nesbit's Well Hall, 1915-1921: A memoir," *Children's Literature*, 3 (1973), pp. 147-52.

Eager, Edward. "Daily Magic," *The Horn Book Magazine*, 34 (Oct., 1958), pp. 349-58.

Ellis, Alec. "E. Nesbit and the Poor," *Junior Bookshelf*, 38 (April, 1974), pp. 73-78.

Green, Roger Lancelyn. "E. Nesbit: Treasure-Seeker," *Junior Bookshelf*, 22 (Oct., 1958), pp. 175-85.

———. "Edith Nesbit," in *Tellers of Tales* (Leicester, England: Edmund Ward, 1946), pp. 196-205.

Lynch, Patricia. "Remembering E. Nesbit," *The Horn Book Magazine*, 29 (Oct., 1953), pp. 342-43.

Manlove, Colin N. "Fantasy as Witty Conceit: E. Nesbit," *Mosaic*, 10 (Winter, 1977), pp. 109-30.

Moore, Doris Langley. *E. Nesbit: A Biography*. London: E. Benn, 1933. [Rev. ed., London: Ernest Benn, 1967.]

Prickett, Stephen. "Worlds Within Worlds: Kipling and Nesbit," in *Victorian Fantasy* (Bloomington and London: Indiana University Press, 1979), pp. 198-239.

Strange, Mavis. "E. Nesbit, As I Knew Her," *The Horn Book Magazine*, 34 (Oct., 1958), pp. 359-63.

Streatfield, Noel. *Magic and the Magician*. London: Ernest Benn, 1958.

———. "The Nesbit Influence," *Junior Bookshelf*, 22 (Oct., 1958), pp. 187-93.

Walbridge, Earle F. "E. Nesbit," *The Horn Book Magazine*, 29 (Oct., 1953), pp. 334-41.

BLENKINSOP, REVEREND SEPTIMUS, a character in E[dith] Nesbit Bland's* *The Phoenix and the Carpet*. This reserved young man lives in London with his two maiden aunts. He believes he has gone mad when a wishing carpet* appears in his study and he has what he thinks is a dream during which he marries a man and a woman on a tropical island. Reverend Blenkinsop is unnerved when Robert* and Jane*, whom he recognizes from his "dream," appear at his home. He is even more unnerved when they suddenly vanish before his eyes.

BLODEUWEDD, a character in the Welsh *Mabinogion* who appears as a character in *The Owl Service*, by Alan Garner*. She was the wife of Lleu Llaw Gyffes and the lover of Gronw Pebyr, Lord of Penllyn. Lovely Blodeuwedd was created from the powers and the flowers of oak, broom, and meadowsweet by Gwydion*, a wizard, for Lleu, but she did not love him, falling in love instead with Gronw. Gronw threw a spear at Lleu to kill him; instead, Lleu changed into an eagle, to be changed back into a man by Gwydion. Seeking his revenge, Lleu threw a spear at Gronw, killing him though he crouched behind a stone. In retribution for her betrayal of Lleu, Gwydion changed Blodeuwedd into an owl. Though the story is an ancient one, the triangle of love and jealousy is recreated in subsequent generations, as the powers from which Blodeuwedd had been created build themselves up in the valley where she lived, to be unleashed through three people. Though Blodeuwedd "wants to be flowers," each time jealousy and hatred prevail and she "is made owls," and the unleashing of the powers has tragic results. Though Huw Hannerhob* and at least two other men have tried to thwart the powers, they have failed. Somehow some of Blodeu-wedd's power seems to become part of a set of oddly patterned plates* made by Huw's grandfather; when the plates are found by Gwyn* and Alison and Roger Bradley**, the old story of love and hate begins again. Though Alison, through whom Blodeuwedd's power manifests itself, sees only Blodeuwedd's owl-like, destructive side, when the power finally flows full-force through her, Roger manages to persuade Alison of Blodeuwedd's gentler, flower nature, and it seems that things will turn out well.

BOAT, an object in *The Wind Eye**, by Robert Westall*. It is the *Resurrectio Vitaque Sum*—"I am the resurrection and the life"—a single-sailed oak boat used since the seventh century to fetch the dead from the Farne Islands, off the coast of England. The monks of the nearby monastery use it to bring the body of St. Cuthbert* (Cuddy) to his first resting place. It seems to have been kept at Monk's Heugh for centuries, guarded by generations of Studdards descended, perhaps, from Stitheard, one of those who had attended Cuddy's body. In the twentieth century, Henry Studdard sails in the boat and disappears; the boat itself is found, empty, on the sea. When they vacation at Monk's Heugh, Beth, Michael, and Sally Studdard*** discover that the *Resurre*—as her prow now reads—can take those who sail in her back through time, to see whatever seventh-century event has taken place in the sea near the islands. They and their father, Bertrand Studdard*, use the boat to visit Cuddy, who helps each in a different way.

BOBBIN BOY, an object in Alison Uttley's* *A Traveller in Time**. It is a small wooden figure carved in the shape of an Elizabethan gentleman by Jude*, a servant in Elizabethan Thackers*, to show his acceptance of Penelope Taberner Cameron*, a twentieth-century girl who travels back through time. Through the bobbin boy, Penelope contacts Jude when Arabella Babington* imprisons her under an old barn. Penelope receives the figure again in the twentieth century, when she finds it in Cicely Ann Taberner's* sewing box. It has been used to hold silk thread.

BOGGART, a creature in *Earthfasts**, by William Mayne*. This mischievous house spirit is about the size of a cat. It has lived at Swang farm for centuries, alternately plaguing the Watson family or sleeping. Once it sleeps for many years, waking when a candle* that holds time still for King Arthur* and his knights is taken away in the twentieth century. Though once it had been of some use around the house, sweeping up or doing other chores, now it is lazy and mischievous, playing pranks on everyone, especially the family cat and Frank Watson, the farmer. The boggart takes particular delight in making as much of a mess as possible. The only person it seems to respect and obey is David Francis Wix*, who has looked into the candle and who feels an understanding of the creatures it controls. When Frank Watson becomes angry one day and calls down the wrath of God on the boggart, it settles down, helping as well and as meekly as it can, though it does spoil all the eggs it washes. The Watsons, however, learn to live with it and humor it. When the candle is put back in its place, the boggart becomes lazier and lazier, finally going to sleep under the bedroom floor, though it will knock back if someone knocks on the board above it.

BOLEYN, ANNE, a consort of Henry VIII*, who appears as a character in E[dith] Nesbit Bland's *The House of Arden**. When she and the king visit Arden Castle*, Anne is warned of her tragic future by Elfrida Arden*, a young time traveler from the twentieth century. She becomes upset at the warning, causing the king to seek vengeance against Elfrida, but the girl escapes.

BOLT, a character in *The Wizard in the Tree**, by Lloyd Alexander*. He is Squire Scrupnor's* unscrupulous gamekeeper. When Bolt captures Arbican*, an enchanter Scrupnor is framing for a murder he himself has done, the gamekeeper tries to claim the substantial reward Scrupnor has offered for the killer. Scrupnor kills Bolt with a poker.

BOND-RUNE, THE, a symbol in *The Tombs of Atuan** and *The Farthest Shore**, by Ursula K. LeGuin*. It is also called the Sign of Peace, the Lost Rune, and the King's Rune. This symbol of dominion and peace is one of nine Runes of Power inscribed inside the Ring of Erreth-Akbe*. When the Ring was broken during a battle between Erreth-Akbe* and a Kargish priest, the rune was broken, too; as a result, the power of the kings at Havnor* declined and the Priest-Kings of the Kargad Lands became powerful. Dissension was rife in Earthsea*. Though the rune is restored when the Ring is made whole by Ged*, a sorcerer, almost twenty years pass before Arren* comes to rule over all of Earthsea.

BONFIRES AND BROOMSTICKS. Mary Norton. Illus. Mary Adshead. London: J. M. Dent and Sons, 1947. 119 pp. British.

One morning, Carey, Charles, and Paul Wilson*** see an exciting advertisement in the London *Times*: Eglantine Price*, a would-be witch they had met two years before, is taking in children to board during the summer holidays. The three children talk their parents into sending them to her for the summer.

When they arrive, they learn that she has given up magic, but they find in her room a certain bed she must have bought at the sale of their aunt's estate—the bed they had used two years before the travel to distant places, magically transported by an enchanted bed-knob*. They have kept the bed-knob and hope to use it again, but Miss Price takes it.

Carey, up early one morning, finds the bed, Miss Price, and Peter gone; on their return, she and Charles learn from Peter that Miss Price had wanted to see if the bed-knob still worked. Indignant that she should keep it from them, the children talk Miss Price into allowing them to take the bed into the past—something they had not had a chance to do before. Reluctantly she agrees.

They find themselves in London in 1666, where they meet Emelius Jones*, a necromancer afraid of being persecuted for his witchcraft and made doubly nervous by the thought that he has conjured up the children and that his magic might actually work. They talk until the children have to leave, and they become fond of one another. Miss Price, having spent a sleepless night worrying about the children, is provoked to find that they have brought Emelius back with them, but she is intrigued by the fact that he is a professional. Emelius, in turn, is fascinated because Miss Price's spells actually work.

Emelius stays for a week, and though he finds modern times sometimes frightening, he enjoys talking magic with Miss Price. Miss Price, too, enjoys it, and when the time comes for Emelius to leave, she is sad, but she takes him back to his own time and leaves him there, rather abruptly. Soon she begins to worry, though, because the Fire of London may have left him homeless, so Miss Price and the children go back in time to make sure he is all right.

They find him in a hopeless state of affairs, for, one of the scapegoats after the fire, he has been tried for witchcraft and is sentenced to be burned at the stake. Miss Price and the children cannot get the bed into his cell to rescue him, but they promise to save him. Miss Price leaves the children with the bed as she goes to see what she can do. Uneasy because she has not returned and because a storm is brewing, the children go to find her. They find, instead, a crowd gathered around Emelius, who is tied to a stake. Helpless, they watch as a fire is set at his feet. Suddenly Miss Price appears, flying on her broom, swooping over the crowd and dispersing it. Soldiers fire at the figure on the broom, and it falls. Rain pours down as Charles releases Emelius and the four go in shock and sorrow back to the bed. Here they find Miss Price, anxious, but in perfect health; she had sent her clothes on the broomstick to frighten the crowd, but she was not in them. They take Emelius to the twentieth century.

Emelius asks Miss Price to marry him, and she accepts. They will go back to Emelius's time and live there on the small farm he has inherited from his aunt. They travel back, via the bed, carrying some luxuries of the twentieth century. The saddened children go to the ruins of the farm on the hill, where Carey envisions Emelius and Miss Price standing in the garden—and jumps back in alarm to hear Miss Price's calm voice across the centuries, ordering her out of the lettucebed.

BONNIE YANTO (*The Watchers*). *See* Yanto, Bonethy

BOOK OF THE KINGS OF ABÁLOC, the title of five books in which is written some of the history of Abáloc* in many of Jane Louise Curry's* Abáloc novels*. The ancient title is *E plagro tane menet e kintisamos or penque plévroues or Rigóues o Abáloc*. In the fourth century, these books are in the keeping of Thiuclas*, who takes them to safety in the twentieth century when Abáloc is attacked by Tekla* and her warriors. When Thiuclas returns to his own century, he takes the books to the City of the Moon Under the Mountain*. Sometime before the twelfth century, the oracle at Inas Ebhélic* tells the people to destroy all books and writings, so that by the twelfth century only one volume of the five survives, handed down from mother to daughter until it reaches Erilla*, who takes the book back to the City of the Moon in the twelfth century. There it remains until the twentieth century, when *y Tylwyth Teg**, the Welsh Fair Folk* who have taken refuge there, give it to Arthur Arthur*. Fascinated by the beauty of its rose quartz covers and its strange, multicolored writing, the boy vows to learn to read it.

BOOK OF THREE, THE, a book of magic in the Chronicles of Prydain*, *Coll and His White Pig*, and *The Foundling, and Other Tales of Prydain*, by Lloyd Alexander*. It has this title because it tells the future, the present, and the past, but its prophecies are not certain, for they do not chart the future but only reveal its possibilities. The book is ancient; when it comes into the hands of Dallben*, an enchanter, it is already very old. He is the only one who can touch it, for it will not let itself be handled or opened by anyone else. Taran*, Dallben's young ward, touches the book and gets blistered fingers from the heat of its cover; Pryderi*, an ambitious king, seizes the book and is destroyed by lightning from it. When Taran becomes High King of Prydain*, the book's prophecies are finished and it becomes a book of history and heritage. Dallben leaves it with Taran when the wizard goes to the Summer Country* to live forever.

BOOK OF THREE, THE. Lloyd Alexander. New York: Holt, Rinehart and Winston, 1964. 217 pp. American.

Orphaned Taran*, impatient, impetuous, and eager for glory, lives with Coll* and Dallben*, a magician, at Caer Dallben* in the land of Prydain*. Evil threatens this magical land: the Horned King*, an evil war leader, is gaining power, though the Sons of Don*, under their war leader, Gwydion*, still protect Prydain. One day, at Caer Dallben, the farm animals become unreasonably terrified. When Dallben tries to consult Hen Wen*, his oracular pig, she runs in terror into the forest. Taran follows her and comes upon the Horned King and his men, who wound the young man. He is tended by a gentle yet commanding man: Gwydion, come to consult Hen Wen. Arawn*, the evil king of Annuvin*, is threatening Prydain, using the Horned King as his champion.

The next morning, as Taran and Gwydion trail the pig, Taran is attacked by Gurgi*, a hairy, groveling creature who directs them to the place he last saw Hen Wen. Taran and Gwydion do not find the pig, but they do find the Horned King's camp and witness a dreadful ritual. Gwydion realizes that the King has allied himself with the rulers of Prydain's southern kingdoms, who are rising against the High King of Prydain. Gwydion and Taran avoid the Horned King's men, but they are captured, after a fearful fight, by the warriors of Achren*, an evil queen, and taken to her castle. There, when she fails to lure Gwydion onto her side, Achren imprisons them separately.

In the dreadful dungeon, Taran makes an unlikely friend: Eilonwy*, Achren's niece, a flighty, courageous girl who is learning sorcery from her hated aunt. She agrees to free Taran and the other prisoner in the dungeon, leading them separately through the maze of secret passages under the castle. As she guides him to freedom, Taran stumbles into a passage leading to the barrow of the king who had built the castle; to protect himself, he takes a sword from one of the dead warriors, and Eilonwy takes the king's sword. Above them the castle begins to break apart, and the two barely escape.

To Taran's dismay, the other prisoner Eilonwy has rescued is not Gwydion; it is Fflewddur Fflam*, a hapless bard. Realizing that Gwydion must have been trapped inside the castle, Taran searches the ruins but finds nothing. The next morning the three set off to Caer Dathyl* to warn the Sons of Don of the uprising. They are accompanied by Gurgi, and they bear with them Fflewddur's harp, which keeps him honest by snapping its strings when he stretches the truth, and Dyrnwyn*, the sword Eilonwy had borne from the barrow, which can be drawn only by one of royal blood.

Their journey is hard, for the Cauldron-Born*, deathless warriors controlled by Arawn, follow them until the warriors reach the limits of that lord's control and must turn back. Wolves take up the pursuit, and Gurgi is badly injured in an accident. Finally Taran allows Gwydion's horse to lead the travelers to safety through Prydain's mountains, and the horse takes them to Medwyn*, an old man beloved by animals, who heals Gurgi's hurt and sets the travelers on their way. As they pick their way through the shallows of a great, black lake, the travelers are sucked into it and emerge underground. There they are taken prisoner by the Fair Folk*, and Taran manages to bargain for their freedom, for provisions, and for a guide. In the realm of the Fair Folk, Gurgi finds Hen Wen, and the pig joins the group, now guided by Doli*, a dwarfish character who ought to be able to turn invisible, but cannot.

As they travel, they find a young, wounded gwythaint*, one of the huge birds Arawn uses as spies. Taran insists on helping it instead of killing it, and he feels real loss when it eventually escapes. One day's journey from Caer Dathyl, the travelers come upon the Horned King's army and manage to repulse an attack by a handful of his warriors. Another, larger troop comes upon them, and Hen Wen flees as Fflewddur sends Taran and Eilonwy ahead on the horse. They are pursued by the Horned King and are knocked from the saddle; in the ensuing fight, Taran's sword is shattered and, despite Eilonwy's protests, he draws Dyrnwyn. The sword blazes fiercely and knocks Taran down, burning his arm. Suddenly a voice speaks a single word and the Horned King bursts into flame.

Taran recovers in Caer Dathyl, where he is overjoyed to learn that not only are his companions all right, but so is Gwydion. When the castle had fallen on the removal of Dyrnwyn, Gwydion was in another stronghold. Because he had endured the torments there, to him were revealed secrets of life and death, and the walls of his prison had melted away. Traveling to Caer Dathyl, Gwydion had met a young gwythaint which told him of Hen Wen and the others and sent him to their aid. Finding the pig, Gwydion learned from her the Horned King's true name, and he used it to destroy the man, for once one knows evil's name, it is powerless. Eilonwy has given Dyrnwyn to Gwydion.

He in turn gives them gifts: to Fflewddur he gives an unbreakable harp string; to Doli goes the power of invisibility; to Gurgi he gives a never-empty wallet of food; to Eilonwy he gives a gold ring*. Taran is granted his dearest wish, which is to go home to Caer Dallben. He has another wish granted, too, when Eilonwy goes with him to live there.

BOOK PEOPLE, a race of beings in *Wet Magic**, by E[dith] Nesbit Bland*. They are characters of books who live in the rocks of the Cave of Learning*, just outside the golden door to Merland*, beneath the sea. Just as there are heroes and villains in books, there are good and bad Book People. Among the bad ones are Mrs. Fairchild, of *The History of the Fairchild Family*; Eric, of *Eric, or Little by Little*; Mr. and Miss Murdstone, from *David Copperfield*; and Mrs. Barbauld, author of didactic literature in the eighteenth century. The only defense against them is ignorance of them; it strikes like a spear and wounds their vanity. These people cannot kill; they can only stupefy. Porpoises guard the door into Merland, for porpoises are so ignorant that the Book People cannot get past them. When land children man the gates during a visit to Merland, the Book People accidentally get in. The heroes of their books are called up against them and manage to save Merland by pushing the bad Book People back into their books.

BORROWER SERIES, five books by Mary Norton* that deal with the adventures of miniature people called borrowers*. *See The Borrowers; The Borrowers Afield; The Borrowers Afloat; The Borrowers Aloft; The Borrowers Avenged.* A related shorter work is *Poor Stainless*.

BORROWERS, a race of beings in Mary Norton's* Borrower series*. They seem to be an ancient race which got smaller and smaller with every generation, becoming tinier and more hidden because they were so frightened of human beings. At last they had reached a size that would be comfortable living in a dollhouse. Not only are their bodies small: they are perfectly formed for their lifestyle; borrowers' hands and feet are longer in proportion to their bodies than are humans', making it easy for them to climb. Despite their fear of humans, borrowers believe that these giants were put on Earth for their use, and they live off humans as best they can, "borrowing" what they need. There are several kinds of borrowers. Some live wild, free lives outdoors, and some live staid, comfortable lives in human houses, choosing only those houses which have a regular routine borrowers can depend on. Firbanks, a country manor, once supported several families of borrowers, who took their names from the places where they lived; thus, the Overmantels lived above the mantelpiece in the morning room, the Harpsichords lived in the wall behind where the harpsichord used to stand, and the entrance to the Clocks' home was beneath the grandfather clock. When borrowings became slim at Firbanks, most of the families moved away. Out of necessity, all borrowers are very ingenious, making do with what they can borrow and turning what humans would call junk into furniture and clothes. Necessity is also the basis of the rules of borrowers: that no borrower steal from another, for borrower life is too precarious; and that no borrower ask a strange borrower where he or she lives, for their homes must be secret and hidden from humans. Borrowers are most afraid of two things: owls and cats.

BORROWERS, THE. Mary Norton. Illus. Diana Stanley. London: J. M. Dent and Sons, 1952. 159 pp. British. Carnegie Award winner.

From Mrs. Ada May*, who is living with Kate* and her parents, the girl hears a curious story about borrowers*, miniature people whom Mrs. May's brother* knew and helped when he was a boy:

Pod, Homily, and their daughter, Arrietty Clock***, are the last of many borrowers living in a country manor, existing on what they can "borrow" from humans. One night Pod comes home shaken; he has been seen by Mrs. May's brother. This could prove disastrous for the tiny people, who stay away from humans. Sheltered Arrietty, finally told of the realities of borrower life, wants to emigrate, as other borrowers have done, for she feels closed in in her home beneath the kitchen floor. Reluctantly Pod agrees instead to take her borrowing with him.

Three weeks later Arrietty gets her first glimpse of the world of humans and finds it gloriously adventurous. The outdoors is particularly exciting, especially when Arrietty meets and talks to the human boy who had seen her father. Hearing from Arrietty of Lupy* and Hendreary*, the parents of a family of borrowers now living in a badger's den in a nearby field, the boy agrees to take them a letter Arrietty will write. The next time Pod takes her borrowing, Arrietty leaves the letter to be found by the boy. A few nights later she overhears Mrs. Driver*, the cook, complaining about the boy, who has been seen crawling down badger holes. Arrietty manages to get up to the boy's bedroom and there learns from him that he has delivered the letter and gotten an answer: a note from Hendreary asking the Clocks to tell Lupy to come home. Pod catches Arrietty with the boy and is furious, for she has endangered the family by telling the boy where they live. Later that night the boy lifts the ceiling of their home; he has brought furniture from the dollhouse for them.

After that a regular routine is set up; the boy brings the borrowers furniture, and Arrietty repays him by reading to him. All is well until the boy takes valuable little pieces from the drawing room. Mrs. Driver, missing them, gets up one night to keep watch and hears the boy make his visit. She discovers the Clocks in their home and, deciding they are nasty little creatures, calls the rat catcher. The night before he is due to come, the boy warns the three borrowers. The Clocks decide to emigrate to the badger's den, and the boy agrees to bring the dollhouse furniture before he leaves the next day for India. Mrs. Driver comes upon him and whisks him off to bed, and he never sees the borrowers again. The rat catcher comes and prepares to smoke out the borrowers. Just in time the boy breaks a grate so the trapped family can escape, but he is hurried to the station before they come out.

To calm Kate, upset over the ending of the story, Mrs. May expresses her belief that the family had escaped. Having heard the story from her brother, when she visited the house as a child she had taken furnishings from the dollhouse to the field and left them; when she went back, they had been gone and she had found the diary Arriety had kept. Mrs. May is not completely convinced, however, for her brother had a talent for making up stories, and the writing in Arrietty's diary was very like his own.

BORROWERS AFIELD, THE. Mary Norton. Illus. Diana Stanley. London: J. M. Dent and Sons, 1955. 194 pp. British.

Eleven-year-old Kate* has almost forgotten the stories Mrs. Ada May* has told her of the borrowers*, tiny people who "borrow" what they need from humans. Then one day Mrs. May takes Kate to see a cottage she has inherited, and Kate meets Tom Goodenough*, who knows about borrowers and had even talked to one of them, Arrietty Clock*, when he was a boy. He tells Kate their story:

Having been smoked out of their home under the floor of a mansion, Arrietty and her parents, Pod and Homily Clock**, escape to a nearby field where relatives are said to be living in an abandoned badger's den. They do not find them that day; when evening comes and rain begins to fall, the three take refuge in an old boot. This boot becomes their temporary home, which they drag behind them as they search the field for the others. The three camp near a stream and the boot is wedged between the roots of a stump where it will be safe.

The day after they move the boot, the three walk around the field but find nothing. When they return to the boot, they discover that someone has been inside and taken some of their belongings. The next day Pod looks for the den. Arrietty is delighted with this new outdoor world, revelling in its freedom and beauty. Climbing a hedge, she meets Dreadful Spiller* (Spiller), an orphaned borrower grown up wild. Despite his good intentions, Spiller makes a bad impression on Homily, who flies into hysterics at his appearance. When Pod returns, Spiller is gone. Pod's news is bad: the den is full of foxes and the borrowers are gone.

Spiller redeems himself the next day. Pod and Homily, hearing humans, hide the boot by pulling down a sapling to cover it. Arrietty is out drawing water, and they are worried. Spiller slips in when the sapling is pulled down, explaining that Arrietty will come later; he had seen a dog stalking her and put her into his small boat, sending her whirling safely downstream. The boat will come up against an obstacle and she should be home soon. Arrietty does return soon, to find that Homily is impressed with Spiller's courage.

The boy provides the family with meat over the following weeks as summer turns to chilly fall. Spiller goes to get the winter suit someone has made for him, and before he returns it snows and the family runs out of food. They drink elderflower wine Spiller has borrowed for them and sleep soundly. Then Arrietty wakes to find that they and the boot are under a bed in a gypsy caravan. Mild Eye*, the gypsy to whom the boot once belonged, has reclaimed it. He gets a surprise, however, when he finds small people in it—small people who run and hide and whom he cannot catch. The three borrowers spend a dreadful day dodging Mild Eye, his cat, and a gypsy woman, who almost get them before young Tom Goodenough arrives. He seems to be helping Mild Eye capture the three, but when Tom gets close to them, he tells them to get into his pocket, where Spiller is already. The gypsies see them run, but Tom gets away.

He takes the four borrowers to his grandfather's cottage, where Tom has "collected" other borrowers: Lupy*, Hendreary*, and their four children, who had once lived in the badger's den. In the wall of the cottage they have a well-furnished place, and Homily recognizes furnishings from the home she once had. The Clocks will live above them. Suddenly feeling hemmed in by the furnishings and crowd of people, Arrietty goes back the way she came and shyly introduces herself to Tom.

BORROWERS AFLOAT, THE. Mary Norton. Illus. Diana Stanley. London: J. M. Dent and Sons, 1959. 176 pp. British.

As Mrs. Ada May* looks at the cottage she has inherited, Tom Goodenough* tells Kate* about the tiny people, borrowers*, who had stayed in the cottage when he was a boy:

Because other borrowers live here, Dreadful Spiller* (Spiller), a wild orphan, has brought Pod, Homily, and Arrietty Clock*** to the cottage. Lupy* and Hendreary*, their relatives, are friendly, but Pod, Homily, and Arrietty are not happy because they feel unwelcome. One night Homily finds that Arrietty has been talking to young Tom Goodenough and has learned that the boy and his grandfather will leave and shut up the cottage. This will be disastrous, for borrowers live on what humans leave behind, and they may starve. Pod, Homily, and Arrietty decide to leave.

The night they are to leave, they find their only exit blocked by a ferret Tom had lost. The three do not know what to do until Spiller suddenly arrives; he has come for his summer clothes. Spiller will help them by taking the three out of the cottage via the drain; then he will take them downstream in his knifebox boat to Little Fordham*, a legendary model town where the borrowers can live in ease. The ride in an aluminum lid down the drain takes all night, becoming monotonous, but then suddenly getting exciting when bath water unexpectedly pours out from one of the side drains. The four borrowers are forced to abandon the lid and hang onto branches Spiller had wedged inside the drain, as the water pours around them and washes away their luggage and boat. It is a short walk to the end of the drain, where they recover their things and dry out.

Spiller is going upstream to load up his boat with supplies, so Pod, Homily, and Arrietty wait for him in the rusted kettle in which he lives. The first two days are warm and sweet but on the third day it begins to rain. The rain comes for three days, and the stream rises; when the borrowers wake the fourth morning, the kettle is afloat and they are swirling downstream. They get out on top and watch the world sail past them. At last the kettle comes against a little island of sticks in the middle of the stream and stays there; the three borrowers make the best of things as they wait for Spiller to come looking for them.

With the evening comes danger, for a poacher is fishing from the bank above them. Once the hook catches Homily's skirt and, after a struggle, Pod and Arrietty manage to get her free—though the fisherman gets the skirt. The fisherman is Mild Eye*, a gypsy who has caught them once before, and he has seen the struggle. Mild Eye casts for them, and his hook catches bits of the island and manages to sink the kettle before they can cut his line. The gypsy tries to wade in and get them, but the stream is too deep and cold, so he stretches a rope across the stream and holds onto it as he gropes through the water. As Mild Eye catches hold of the island, the rope breaks and he lets go, falling into the water. A passing policeman spots Mild Eye, finds the fish, and runs him in for poaching.

Spiller comes in the boat. He, too, had seen the struggle for Homily and had cut Mild Eye's rope. The four borrowers start downstream for Little Fordham, the boat loaded with supplies for a new life there.

BORROWERS ALOFT, THE. Mary Norton. Illus. Diana Stanley. London: J. M. Dent and Sons, 1961. 154 pp. British.

Having abruptly retired because of a disability, Mr. Pott*, a former railway man, builds himself a model village for enjoyment. Little Fordham* is wonderfully detailed, and, to Mr. Pott's dismay, it soon becomes an attraction for tourists. Sidney Platter*, a former undertaker, builds a tiny village to attract tourists and finds himself hard put to keep up with and surpass Mr. Pott. Then one day he discovers tiny people living in Little Fordham and fears ruin.

The tiny people are a family of borrowers*: Pod, Homily, and Arrietty Clock***. After much wandering and hard times, they have come to Little Fordham to live, guided here by Dreadful Spiller* (Spiller), a wild orphan borrower. For a time their lives are peaceful, as they go about their lives undisturbed. But they are not unseen, for Miss Menzies*, who believes in fairies, has watched them and spoken with Arrietty. Miss Menzies finally convinces Mr. Pott of the borrowers' existence. Mr. Platter, meanwhile, steals the little people for his own village and takes them to his house to imprison them in the attic. Mr. Pott and Miss Menzies, dismayed to find them gone, decide to refurbish the house for their return.

Pod, Homily, and Arrietty are having a miserable time of it in the attic, for exploration of it has revealed no escape route. By pretending to be unintelligent, they allay the Platters' fears and learn that they are to be put on exhibit in the model village. The winter passes, and the borrowers are no closer to getting out, though they have learned to open the attic window. Then Arrietty, who has been reading old issues of the *Illustrated London News*, realizes that they might escape by making a balloon. Immediately the three go to work, improvising an escape balloon from a toy balloon, a net, and a strawberry basket, and using gas from the light fixtures to inflate the balloon.

One balmy day they leave and drift to Little Fordham, where they manage to moor on a fence Mr. Pott has built around his village. Pod goes ahead to check their house and finds Spiller there. When Homily comes to the house, Arrietty reveals that she has talked to Miss Menzies and that the house was furnished specifically for them. Pod becomes upset. He does not like the idea that humans know they are here, for humans are untrustworthy and always prying; the house is more like a cage. The borrowers need a place to be private and look after themselves; they will move to a quiet mill Spiller has told him about. Pod makes Arrietty promise not to talk to humans again, but after she does so she becomes upset, for her friend, Miss Menzies, will never know what has happened to them. Spiller, though shy and wary of humans, will tell the woman, for Arrietty's sake.

BORROWERS AVENGED, THE. Mary Norton. Illus. Pauline Baynes. London: Harcourt Brace Jovanovich, 1982. 298. 298 pp. British.

When Homily, Pod, and their daughter, Arrietty Clock***, suddenly vanish from Little Fordham*, a miniature village, their friend, Miss Menzies*, has trouble convincing the local constable that the tiny borrowers* ever existed, and she soon gives up hope of ever hearing of the family again. When spring comes, the Clocks, having spent the winter imprisoned by greedy Sidney Platter* and his wife, escape and make their way back to Little Fordham. They cannot stay here, however, for the Platters, greedy for the money they could earn by showing the tiny people, will be searching for them. An old mill the family had thought to live in is in ruins, but Pod and Dreadful Spiller* (Spiller), a wild young borrower, have found the large rectory near the local church, inhabited only by a caretaker couple.

The journey to this place is difficult but worthwhile, for her first morning there Arrietty meets another young borrower, Peregrine Overmantel* (Peagreen), a lame young man living by himself in the rectory. Having moved to new quarters in the house's abandoned aviary, Peagreen offers the Clocks his old home, an enchanting, light-filled place inside a windowseat in the library. With Peagreen's and Spiller's help, the Clocks move into their new home. Meanwhile, the Platters are almost caught while searching Little Fordham for borrowers.

During the days that follow, the Clocks improve their new home. Arrietty is happy here, even getting used to the rectory ghosts. At last the family visits relatives—Hendreary*, his wife, and their son, Timmis*—living in the nearby church. The days pass and Arrietty is happy in her new home, helping Pod and Spiller borrow for the two families and playing with young Timmis.

One day, at his wife's insistence, Mr. Platter takes Homily's left-behind apron to a "finder," a woman able to tell where people are by touching something they have owned. They meet in the church, where they are observed by Timmis and Arrietty. Though the woman can tell nothing from the apron because it has been washed and ironed, Miss Menzies, who is with her, recognizes the little garment and realizes that the borrowers had been taken by the Platters but have escaped. Staying behind after the others leave, the Platters almost catch Timmis, who finally takes refuge in the collection box. But the caretaker's wife locks the box in the vestry and shooes the Platters out of the church.

That night the Platters break into the church and into the cupboard where the collection box and church valuables are kept. Hidden, Arrietty listens as the Platters discover that Timmis has escaped from the collection box, then she watches the mayhem as Timmis runs into the church and is chased by the Platters into the bell chamber. Suddenly the bell begins to sound. Called by the caretaker, the constable finds the Platters in the bell chamber and the valuables out of their cupboard; the Platters have a lot of explaining to do. Timmis, however, is safe: he had run up the bell rope, and the Platters had accidentally rung the bell while trying to get him. What finally happens to the Platters the borrowers never know, but they may have gone to Australia. Meanwhile, the borrowers are as safe as they ever really are.

BOSTON, LUCY [MARIA] (1892-   ), British writer. She was born in 1892 to James and Mary (Garrett) Wood and was educated at Downs School, Sussex, and Somerville College, Oxford. She served as a nurse in France during World War I. In 1917 she married Harold Boston; the marriage was dissolved in 1935.

Most of Boston's novels for children are fantasies. Her shorter fantasies, like her longer ones, carry Boston's distinctive blend of the familiar and the fabulous, of everyday life and rich, strange transformations. In *The Sea Egg*, two boys find an egg that hatches into a triton who takes them on a journey through the wondrous sea. *The Castle of Yew* details the adventures of two boys who suddenly shrink to only a few inches high. A young boy has strange adventures when he enters a strange house in *The Guardians of the House*; and *The Fossil Snake* comes wonderfully alive when it is warmed by a radiator. The Green Knowe books*, Boston's longer fantasies, are perhaps her most famous; rich in incident, they are also filled with a sense of mystery and the unknown, and with a sense of continuity.

They have as their focus Green Knowe* itself, a manor house dating back to the twelfth century. It is the sum of all its history. The alterations its owners have made on it can be seen; the orginal stone manor has been added to over the centuries, and one brick wall with high windows remains from the additions made in the eighteenth century. Inside is the accumulation of centuries of living, the furniture and odds and ends of everyday life. The toys in the nursery may just as well have belonged to a seventeenth-century child as to a twentieth-century one. Scraps of eighteenth-century materials that make up part of a patchwork curtain are finally replaced two hundred years later. Many have lived and died here, and their presences are still felt. Linnet Oldknow* and her brothers play their pranks on Green Knowe's twentieth-century inhabitants, though they had died in the seventeenth-century; the voices of children who have lived here are heard one stormy winter night when Green Noah*, a cursed tree, comes to rampaging life.

The house is more than just a physical presence, and its history is manifested by more than just the objects it contains. Green Knowe is a center of power: a temple of the moon once stood here and on some full-moon nights it returns; the river that flows past it has wonders of its own; and two ancient stones nearby can transport people into the future or the past. The house has an aura no ordinary house has. Mrs. Linnet Oldknow* furnishes it not with objects that please her own taste, but with things that belong here: with "uncomfortable" pictures and objects that smack of the uncanny. To draw the curtains at Green Knowe does not keep out the unfathomable night but keeps it in, for the house seems to be in touch with and accepts the secrets of the universe, so it can transmute the laws of the universe. A small wooden mouse can squeak or a topiary deer become real, if only for an instant. When Oskar Stanislawsky* decides to make a mouse nest from the inside in Green Knowe's garden, he is able to do so, becoming smaller and smaller in the process, until he is as tiny as a mouse himself. Time shifts and doubles back on itself at Green Knowe. Tolly (Toseland*) climbs a tree and is heard singing in the eighteenth century, two hundred years away. As he and Mrs. Oldknow talk in one room, they hear a baby being sung to sleep in the next, and they themselves join the singing as, in another century, the baby goes to sleep. The Norman hall in the house has a "habit of slipping back into its own century" when left empty for several hours, and many of the children who have lived here gather to play in the garden, wondering aloud, "Who's real this time?", as other children might wonder whose yard they should play in. At Green Knowe, all times are present, and all things are possible.

But not for everyone. Belief is a factor in the house's mysteries. Most of the children who live here believe in and can witness its secrets. Jacob*, a black child, can hear but not see the other children who manifest themselves at Green Knowe, perhaps because he can believe in them but is not related to them. When Ping (Hsu*), a Chinese refugee, is in the house, the children from other centuries do not appear, but a three-hundred-year-old mirror* does reflect prophecies. Like most grownups, Dr. Maud Biggin* cannot believe that wonders can exist in her own life, so she does not believe in the giant who is presented to her. Piers Madely*, however, an artless vicar, sees Green Knowe transform itself in the moonlight, and Mrs. Oldknow, who has grown up at the place, is still able to accept its mysteries. To the child and the child in heart, Green Knowe's secrets are revealed.

Boston's style is richly descriptive, and Green Knowe and its inhabitants are deftly brought to life. Boston's characters do not always seem full of the nuances and contradictions of life, but they have nooks and crannies in their personalities that are not completely explored. The children in the works are very child-like and their actions are deftly observed: Susan Oldknow* playing with her new fan as she talks to her father, Tolly leaving sugar for Feste* and taking a wooden mouse to bed with him, Linnet Oldknow teasing him as he reads a book she once owned—all have the ring of life and truth. The mood of these works—so important if they are to succeed for the reader—is exactly right.

Works

Juvenile full-length fantasy: *The Children of Green Knowe* (1954); *The Chimneys of Green Knowe* (1958) as *The Treasure of Green Knowe* (America); *The River at Green Knowe* (1959); *An Enemy at Green Knowe* (1964); *The Stones of Green Knowe* (1976).
Juvenile short fantasy and novels: *A Stranger at Green Knowe* (1961); *The Castle of Yew* (1965); *The Sea Egg* (1967); *Nothing Said* (1971); *The Guardians of the House* (1974); *The Fossil Snake* (1975).
Adult: *Yew Hall* (1954); *Persephone* (1969) as *Strongholds* (America); *The Horned Man* (1970), play; *Memory in a House* (1973); *Perverse and Foolish* (1979), memoir.

Secondary Works

Boston, L. M. "Christmas at 'Green Knowe,' " *The Horn Book Magazine*, 31 (Dec., 1955), pp. 471-73.
———. "A Message from Green Knowe," *The Horn Book Magazine*, 39 (June, 1963), pp. 259-64.
———. *Perverse and Foolish: A Memoir of Childhood and Youth*. London: Bodley Head, 1979.
———. "The Place That Is Green Knowe," *Junior Bookshelf*, 26 (Dec., 1962), pp. 295-301.
Chambers, Aidan. "The Reader in the Book,"*Signal*, 23 (May, 1977), pp. 64-87.
Crouch, Marcus. "Lucy Boston at 80," *Junior Bookshelf*, 36 (Dec., 1972), pp. 355-57.
———. "A Visit to Green Knowe," *Junior Bookshelf*, 26 (Dec., 1962), pp. 303-5.
Robbins, Sidney. "A Nip of Otherness, Like Life: The Novels of Lucy Boston," *Children's Literature in Education*, 6 (Nov., 1971), pp. 5-16.
Rose, Jasper. *Lucy Boston*. London: Bodley Head, 1965.

Rosenthal, Lynn. "The Development of Consciousness in Lucy Boston's *The Children of Green Knowe*," *Children's Literature*, 8 (1979), pp. 53-67.
Townsend, John Rowe. "L. M. Boston," in *A Sense of Story* (Boston: The Horn Book, 1971), pp. 28-38.

BOSTWEILER, SAMANTHA, a character in *Mindy's Mysterious Miniature** and *The Lost Farm**, by Jane Louise Curry*. Five-year-old Samantha is one of the eight citizens of Dopple*, Pennsylvania, who happen to be home when Professor Willie Kurtz* gets revenge on the village by miniaturizing it with his reducing machine in 1915. Though Samantha grows up in a stifling atmosphere of secrecy and fear, with only adults around her, she never loses her liveliness or sense of adventure. Nimble Samantha clambers up and down from the table on which the village is now exhibited, as she forages for things the secret villagers need. She and the others endure fifty-five years of being small; finally, under the influence of Arminta Hallam* and Mrs. Mary Buckle Bright*, the eight hoax the professor's nephew, who has inherited eveything, into making them normal-sized again. Two years later Samantha finds Pete MacCubbin*, also a victim of the reducing machine, and she restores him to normal size. They marry and live on the farm, selling the preserves and syrups they make from his grandmother's recipes.

BOXLETON HOUSE, a place in Jane Louise Curry's* *The Bassumtyte Treasure**. Built by Sir Thomas Bassumtyte in 1561 on the site of an earlier house, Boxleton has since sheltered many generations of Bassumtytes. When his son is executed for plotting to put Mary Stuart*, Queen of Scots, on the throne of England, Sir Thomas is forced to pay a heavy fine to Queen Elizabeth in order to keep the house, and to give up the family chapel. In the twentieth century, his descendant, Thomas Bassumtyte*, has similar problems: high taxes and maintenance costs may force him to sell the house to either the National Trust or an unscrupulous foreign prince. His second cousin, Tommy Bassumtyte*, who loves the house and is fascinated by its beautiful antiques, secret room and passageway, and room panelled in needlepoint tapestries, solves the riddle of the Bassumtyte treasure, which provides enough money to keep the house in the family.

BOY, THE, a character in Randall Jarrell's* *The Animal Family**. His mother dies after she and he are shipwrecked; the lifeboat, with them inside, is washed up on the beach and found by the lynx*, who uses the bear* to get the boy back to the cabin both share with the hunter* and the mermaid*. The boy calls the mermaid "Mama," but he does not yet know a word to call the hunter. The boy grows up, accustomed to his special family and seeing nothing strange about it. He learns to run and hunt from the hunter; he learns to swim and speak the language of the mermaid; and he is almost as good at both as each of them. The boy does not remember his real mother; though they tell him that the lynx found him, the boy knows that the hunter is his father and the mermaid his mother, and that he has been part of their family for a long time.

BRADLEY, ALISON, a character in Alan Garner's* *The Owl Service*. She is the daughter of Margaret and the stepdaughter of Clive Bradley; she is the stepsister of Roger Bradley*. Alison's life seems fairly secure; ambitionless, she is content to live the quiet life that has been planned for her. Before Alison's father had died, he turned over to her a house he inherited from Bertram*. When her mother remarries, the family comes to the house for a holiday, and here odd things happen. When he investigates scratching coming from the ceiling of Alison's room, Gwyn*, the son of the cook, finds some oddly patterned plates*. Alison sees and begins to trace the figures of owls in the flowery patterns. Soon this becomes a compulsion, for Alison begins to feel a strange tension build, which is released only when she traces the owls or when her rage expresses itself in a kind of telekinesis. Certain powers in the valley have built themselves up and must be unleashed through her, Roger, and Gwyn. The powers are ancient ones, originally unleashed in the violent struggle of Blodeuwedd*, a mythical woman made of flowers, her husband, and her lover; and for generations the struggle has been repeated. This time, through Alison, Blodeuwedd's powers are manifested. Because Alison has seen the pattern as owls instead of flowers, the results will be tragic; tragedy is narrowly averted when Roger is able to persuade Alison that the pattern is flowers.

BRADLEY, ROGER, a character in *The Owl Service*, by Alan Garner*. He is the son of Clive and the stepson of Margaret Bradley; his stepsister is Alison Bradley*. Roger loves his mother very much and is very sensitive because she has walked out on the family. Still, he gets on fairly well with his stepsister and stepmother when Clive remarries. Roger is happiest when things and people act predictably and rationally. Though he enjoys taking and developing photographs, he does not plan to do it for a living, preferring instead the security of working with his father; though he does not look forward to his father's kind of life, Roger will not press the issue. When the Bradleys go on holiday to a cottage that Alison owns, Roger is caught up in a series of strange events as certain powers in the valley where the cottage stands build themselves up and must be unleashed through him, Alison, and Gwyn*, the cook's son. The powers are ancient, originally unleashed in the violent struggles of Blodeuwedd*, a mythical woman made of flowers, her husband, and her lover; and for generations the struggle has been repeated. Tension rises between Roger and Gwyn, and Roger begins to bait the other boy. Because Alison sees only Blodeuwedd's destructive nature, the results will be tragic; finally Roger overcomes his own hatred of Gwyn and persuades Alison of the woman's gentle side, and it seems that things will be well.

BRAN DAVIES (*The Grey King; Silver on the Tree*). *See* Davies, Bran

BRAN MADDOX (*A Swiftly Tilting Planet*). *See* Maddox, Bran

BRANDON LLAWCAE (*A Swiftly Tilting Planet*). *See* Llawcae, Brandon

BRANWEN ZILLAH MADDOX O'KEEFE (*A Swiftly Tilting Planet*). *See* O'Keefe, Branwen Zillah Maddox

BRANZILLO, MADOG, a character mentioned in *A Swiftly Tilting Planet**, by Madeleine L'Engle*. He is descended from Madoc*, a twelfth-century Welsh prince who had fled his kingdom and come to the New World with his brother, Gwydyr*. Branzillo is the leader of Vespugia*, a small South American country. In the book he is two entities, one ravaging and one peaceful, because he has two ancestries. Originally descended from Bran Maddox*, a descendant of Madoc, and Zillie*, a descendant of Gwydyr, Branzillo is a bloodthirsty tyrant whose nickname is El Rabioso and who threatens nuclear war with the United States in retribution for its overuse of the world's resources. When Charles Wallace Murry* travels through time to alter history, Branzillo's ancestry changes as well; he is descended from Bran Maddox and Zillah Llawcae*, another descendent of Madoc. Branzillo himself is a man of peace, whose nickname is El Zarco, "the Blue-eyed." He sets up a Congress for the fair distribution and use of the earth's resources.

BREEHY-HINNY-BRINNY-HOOHY-HAH (BREE), a character in C[live] S[taples] Lewis's* *The Horse and His Boy** and *The Last Battle**. This talking horse was born in Narnia*, a land of talking beasts; wandering into Archenland* and beyond, he was captured and taken to Calormen*, where he was sold to Anradin, a Calormene lord. In Calormen Bree was a warhorse and took part in several battles, in which he was very brave. Bree has longed to return to Narnia, so when he meets Shasta (Cor*), a young boy Anradin wants to buy, he warns the boy about the man's cruelty and they run away together, north to Narnia, traveling with Aravis* and her horse, Hwin*, and coming to Archenland just in time to warn its people of impending invasion by Calormen. Though he is brave in battle, Bree is intensely afraid of lions; he is also very conceited and displays this at every opportunity. A horse of great logic, he proves to himself that Aslan*, the great lion-protector of Narnia, is not a lion at all, being too powerful to be a mere beast. Aslan disproves this theory by appearing suddenly and frightening him, and this also teaches the horse humility. Bree later leaves Shasta and goes to live in Narnia, later marrying. Bree is one of those in Aslan's country when Narnia comes to an end.

BRENHIN DLYSEU, thirteen traditional objects that appear in *The Sleepers**, by Jane Louise Curry*. They are the Thirteen Treasures of Prydein. Whoever holds these objects controls Britain. They are the Cauldron of Tyrnoc, a bronze cauldron rich with blue enamel and pearls; the lance, *Rhongomyniad*; the beautiful gold-trimmed *cib*, the drinking horn that holds the Best of All Drink; the sword, Caledvwlch, or Excaliburn; the Horn of Brân, made in the shape of a dragon; the lovely gold *graal*, or platter, of hospitality; the shield, *Wynebgwrthucher*, emblazoned with a shining face; the Golden Game, a chessboard which represents life in miniature; the Great Seal; the whetstone of great power; a horse harness of leather and beaten silver; the Ring of Luned* which Artair*—King Arthur*— is to wear; and the Bell of Rhûn*, which will wake Artair and his men when Britain needs them. All but the Ring and the Bell were to be loaded onto the *Pridwen* and sent to a place of safety beyond the circle of the moon; but because the Ring was taken by Medraut*, the Treasures stayed for centuries in the chamber where Artair and his men slept. In the twentieth century, Margan*, Artair's sister, and her son seek to destroy Artair and gain possession of the Treasures; they are thwarted, and the Treasures are loaded onto an old and venerable boat, which Myrddin*—Merlin—Artair, and his men sail to safety.

BRIGHT, MRS. MARY BUCKLE, a character in Jane Louise Curry's* *Mindy's Mysterious Miniature** and *The Lost Farm**. She is the widow of William Bright. Mrs. Bright grew up in an old house in Brittlesdale, Pennsylvania; this house disappears during the summer of 1915, after she rejects Willie Kurtz*, a peddlar of spurious patent medicines and an inventor of medical machines that do nothing. Kurtz uses his reducing machine to miniaturize the house, and Mrs. Bright does not see it for fifty-five years. Then she and Araminta Hallam* (Mindy) are accidentally made miniature and help to free the eight citizens of Dopple*, Pennsylvania, who were miniaturized when Kurtz decided to make the town into an exhibit. Because her house, were it installed in its original setting, would be too close to a highway, Mrs. Bright decides to live in Dopple.

BRIGHTFORD, a town in Lloyd Alexander's* *The Cat Who Wished to Be a Man**. This bustling little place lies close to a river where there is a tollbridge; on the other side of the river lies Dunstan Forest. To this town comes Lionel*, a young cat turned into a man by his master, Magister Stephanus*. After several adventures Lionel succeeds in ending the greedy rule of Brightford's mayor, Pursewig*. Fuller, the head of the town council, succeeds Pursewig.

BROLLACHAN, THE, an evil force in Alan Garner's* *The Moon of Gomrath**. This black form, with eyes and a mouth, but no shape, is always blacker than the night. It is one of the Old Evils, long imprisoned in a pit at the foot of Alderley Edge; it had escaped and had been recaptured and re-imprisoned long before being accidentally set free by some workers digging a trench. Because it has no shape, it takes that of others, changing and warping them before they become husks and it abandons them for another. It does not willingly abandon a shape until the shape is beyond repair; and the Brollachan's mind is slow to

change, so that sometimes it retains the memory of another shape and super-
imposes that one on a subsequent shape. The Morrigan*, an evil witch once
thwarted by two children, Colin* and Susan*, uses the Brollachan to revenge
herself on Susan, but the creature is driven from the girl by a powerful bracelet.
The witch sends the Brollachan after her enemies at the end of a great battle,
but Susan thwarts her revenge by blowing Anghalac*, a magical hunting horn*:
the Wild Magic of the Herlathing (the Wild Hunt*) fills the Brollachan and
consumes it.

BROOCH, an object in *The Black Cauldron**, by Lloyd Alexander*. On this
iron clasp is engraved the bardic symbol with its lines for knowledge, truth, and
love. Ordinary as it looks, it is full of power, for Menwy Son of Teirgwaedd,
who fashioned it, filled it with dreams, visions, and wisdom; its wearer can see
the future and feel the wonder of the world. The brooch eventually belongs to
Adaon*, a wise young warrior who, at his death, gives it to another young man,
Taran*. Though wearing it is a delight, Taran trades the brooch for the Black
Crochan*, which he has sworn to find and destroy. Because he gives it willingly
to Orddu*, Orgoch*, and Orwen*, three hags who own the Crochan, the brooch's
powers remain intact.

BROWN, MISS, a character in T[erence] H[anbury] White's* *Mistress Masham's Repose**. She becomes the wife of Mr. Hater*; she is a very distant
relative of Maria*. Miss Brown met Mr. Hater at a public school, where she
was matron and he was housemaster. Later Miss Brown became Maria's governess. This hateful woman with pebble-colored eyes is a subtly cruel tyrant,
devising torments for Maria that play on the girl's shyness and natural energy.
Miss Brown owns thirty pairs of black, sharp-toed shoes. For pleasure she reads
J. Taylor's *Holy Living*, George Fox's *Journal*, Bunyan's *Pilgrim's Progress*,
and a Victorian book called *The Daily Light*. Like a toad, she spreads when she
sits down. She and Mr. Hater had begun a search for a parchment regarding the
inheritance of Malplaquet*, Maria's ancestral home, hoping that if it were altered
Maria's inheritance would come to Miss Brown. Their plans are thwarted, though,
by Maria and her friend, the Professor*. Because she has treated Maria cruelly
and has helped Mr. Hater embezzle money Maria should have had, Miss Brown
gets a heavy sentence. When that is served and she marries Mr. Hater, the two
live near Whitby, being refused drinks in pubs and beeing booed at by small
boys.

BROWNIE, a character in *Peter Pan in Kensington Gardens**, by James M.
Barrie*. Brownie is a fairy, a plain street singer who seeks to fire the cold heart
of the Duke of Christmas Daisies*. When Maimie Mannering* helps her out of
a difficulty and gives the fairy encouragement, Brownie gains the confidence
she needs to win the Duke's love. Brownie pleads for Maimie's life when angry
fairies try to kill the girl.

BULL FROG, a character in *Miss Hickory**, by Carolyn Sherwin Bailey*. Tough Bull Frog grows tired of people throwing stones at him, so one fall he leaves his pond and makes his way to a nearby stream. Here Miss Hickory*, a little countrywoman formed of an apple twig and a hickory nut, finds him next spring, frozen in the ice, and rescues him, pulling off his old skin in the process. Resplendent in his new skin, Bull Frog goes back to his pond, which seems safer than the stream.

BURDICK TENCH (*The Wizard in the Tree*). *See* Tench, Burdick

BURGLAR, a character in *The Phoenix and the Carpet**, by E[dith] Nesbit Bland*. This good-humored man is the son of a farmer. In London he lives with his brother and quick-tempered sister-in-law. He sells oranges until one night someone steals the money he has earned; then, recalling a conversation he has overheard, he goes to what he thinks is an empty house, to try his luck at burglary. What he finds are a cow, 197 hungry Persian cats, and Robert*, Anthea*, Cyril*, and Jane*; and this is so much for him to bear that the burglar swears off burgling once and for all. He helps the children by milking the cow to feed the cats, then he and a friend take away the cats to sell and thus get rid of them for the children. The police, however, arrest the burglar on suspicion of stealing the cats. The children rescue him by using their wishing carpet*, and they take him to a tropical island, where he meets and marries a cook* and settles down to be a farmer.

BUTTER CRASHEY (*The Twelve and the Genii*). *See* Crashey, Butter

BUTTERFLY-LAND, a place in *The Cuckoo Clock**, by Mrs. Mary Molesworth*. It is inhabited by butterflies. Here grows a garden filled with flowers in every possible tint and shade; the butterflies use color from these flowers to paint all the flowers in the world before the fairies pack up the flowers and send them where they are to go. The butterflies work hard here, getting only three months off in summer. They live on the scent distilled from the many flowers in butterflyland. Griselda* is brought to this land by the magical cuckoo* living in her great-aunts' clock, after she expresses a desire to see the place, for she believes the butterflies have nothing to do all day but fly. Her visit soon changes her mind.

C

CADELLIN SILVERBROW, a character in Alan Garner's* *The Weirdstone of Brisingamen** and *The Moon of Gomrath**. He is the brother of Grimnir*. Cadellin is an ancient wizard of white magic who has had many names in the world. Centuries ago 140 pure warriors were put into an enchanted sleep in Fundindelve*, to stay there until the time when they would be needed to defeat Nastrond, the ancient Spirit of Darkness. Cadellin watches over the sleepers and the cave, waiting until it is time to rouse them and send them forth. Because at the time their sleep was put on them only 139 white mares were found for the warriors to ride, Cadellin long waited for another, finally bargaining for one with a greedy farmer. The farmer had turned out to be more greedy than Cadellin knew, for he had taken Firefrost*, the powerful stone in which the enchantment of the warriors' sleep is held. Centuries later Cadellin regains the stone after a dreadful battle in which he is forced to kill evil Grimnir. Cadellin is reluctant to allow Colin* and Susan*, the two children who have borne Firefrost, to take part in a subsequent struggle to defeat the Morrigan*, an evil witch, for humans have lost what defenses they had had against the forces of evil. But events force the children into the battle. Cadellin himself stays at Fundindelve, for only he can wake the sleepers, and they must be kept safe at all costs.

CAER DALLBEN, a place in the Chronicles of Prydain*, by Lloyd Alexander*. This little cottage just south of the Great Avren River in Prydain* is one of only two places which stand against the evil Lord Arawn*, who cannot himself enter here. It is owned and protected by Dallben*, an old and powerful enchanter; here, too, live Hen Wen*, an oracular pig, and Taran*, an orphan raised by Dallben. Caer Dallben's fields are tilled by Coll*, a warrior-turned-farmer. This little cottage is the scene of meetings of great import in the fight against Arawn; here Pryderi*, who was won over to Arawn's side, meets his death. Here, too, Taran weds Eilonwy* and is proclaimed High King of Prydain.

CAER DATHYL, a place in Lloyd Alexander's* Chronicles of Prydain* and *The Truthful Harp*. It is the place from which the High King of Prydain* rules

his land. It was built early in that land's history by the Sons of Don*. This
beautiful stronghold in the Eagle Mountains holds the greatest treasures of Prydain. Here also are preserved the memories of great men: their memorials and
weapons, and, in the Hall of Lore, the songs the bards have written of them.
Caer Dathyl is destroyed in war when Arawn*, an evil lord, makes his final bid
to rule Prydain.

CAESAR, JULIUS, Roman emperor (100–44 *B.C.*) who appears in E[dith]
Nesbit Bland's* *The Story of the Amulet*, *Wet Magic*, and *The Magic City*.
In *The Story of the Amulet*, when Robert*, Anthea*, Cyril*, Jane*, and Jimmy*
travel back in time to the Britain of 55 *B.C.* to take Imogen* to someone who
will want her, they visit Caesar after Jimmy wishes to see him. When they arrive,
he has just decided not to bother with Britain because it is full of barbarians.
After conversation with Jimmy and Jane, he is impressed with what Britain may
have to offer and decides to invade anyway. In *Wet Magic*, Caesar is one of the
good Book People* who come out of their volumes to save Merland* from the
evil Book People. In *The Magic City*, he is again a person from a book. When
the wicked Pretenderette* takes over the city of Polistopolis*, Philip Haldane*
opens *De Bello Gallico*, which he had used to construct the city, and calls from
it Caesar and his legions. After the Romans disperse the Pretenderette's soldiers,
Caesar sentences the woman to go to Somnolentia*, to teach the Great Sloth*
there to love its work and to make the people of that city love her. For a moment
Philip sees in Caesar a resemblance to his new brother-in-law, whom he has
resented.

CAFALL, a character in *The Grey King*, by Susan Cooper*. He is a dog
belonging to Bran Davies* and is greatly loved by the boy. Silver-eyed Cafall
can see the wind; once he saves Bran and his friend, Will Stanton*, from the
malicious wind of the Grey King*, a force of evil. In a burst of rage and hatred
Caradog Prichard*, who hates Bran and is possessed by the evil Grey King,
shoots Cafall, accusing the dog of stealing sheep.

CAIR PARAVEL, a place in C[live] S[taples] Lewis's* Chronicles of Narnia*.
It is a shining castle on the east coast of Narnia*, near the mouth of the Great
River. From it rule most of Narnia's kings and queens. This beautiful castle is
used until conquerors from Telmar* take over Narnia. The peninsula on which
it has stood has been cut through so that the castle stands on an island, and the
Telmarines will have little to do with open water. After ten generations Caspian
X* comes to the throne, and he rebuilds the now-ruined castle. All who come
after him seem to rule from it. Cair Paravel is taken, just before the end of
Narnia, by warriors from Calormen*, Narnia's enemy.

CAKEBREAD, GOODY, a character in *Parsley Sage, Rosemary & Time*,
by Jane Louise Curry*. Her husband was the miller for Bennickport, Maine, in

the seventeenth and eighteenth centuries; her son is Thomas Cakebread*. When she was married, Goody Cakebread's grandmother-in-law gave her a magical cupboard* that gives its owner whatever he or she needs, and it served the Cakebreads well when they imigrated to America to settle in a colony. In 1710 Goody Cakebread's son, Thomas, ran away to sea; seven years later she became a widow and came to live quietly in a little cottage not far from Bennickport. In 1722 her quiet, poverty-filled life is shattered when Rosemary Walpole*, Hepsibah Sagacity Walpole*, and William Wingard* travel in time from the twentieth century and find themselves at her house. Amazed at the strange children and astonished when William is accidentally changed into a pig and back again by the cupboard, Carolanna*, an Indian slave, spreads the story that Goody Cakebread is a witch, and the woman is jailed. Among her accusers is Thanatopsis Grout*, who had begun preaching against her after she refused to sell him some valuable land. When Carolanna helps her to escape, Goody Cakebread goes to her friends among the Indians, to stay with them until things settle down. Thomas comes back, however, possessor of a fortune and angry at those who have imprisoned his mother. Rich young Thomas clears his mother of all charges and builds a house, where Goody Cakebread lives out the rest of her life in comfort with her son and daughter-in-law.

CAKEBREAD, JUDITHA, a character in Jane Louise Curry's* *Parsley Sage, Rosemary & Time**. She is the wife of Thomas Cakebread*. Because her father owns five sugar plantations in Barbados, Juditha is wealthy in her own right; when she marries Thomas, she increases their fortune through shrewd investments. Juditha is a witch. When she comes to America with Thomas, she recognizes the Dreaming Trees* as magical and orders a double wall built to enclose them. Nearby she has a house built for herself, Thomas, and his mother, Goody Cakebread*. Near the trees Juditha plants a little herb garden, adding to it a small patch of time*. Only by using this herb can one walk through time between the trees.

CAKEBREAD, THOMAS, a character in *Parsley Sage, Rosemary & Time** and *The Magical Cupboard**, by Jane Louise Curry*. His mother is Goody Cakebread*; his wife is Juditha Cakebread*. In 1710, when Thomas was fifteen, he ran away to sea. Having made a fortune in the rum and molasses trade, he married Juditha and added her fortune to his own. In 1722 he returns to Bennickport, Maine, and discovers that his father has died and that his mother has been accused of witchcraft. Enraged, Thomas influences the authorities to drop the charges; impressed by his fortune, they prove very amenable. Thomas settles down in Bennickport, building a large house that comes to be known as "Wychwood," where he and Juditha live with his mother.

CALICO, MISS, a character in P[amela] L[yndon] Travers's* *Mary Poppins Opens the Door**. She is a good friend of Mary Poppins*. Miss Calico has not walked for centuries, nor have any of her family, for they all prefer riding. For this purpose she sells peppermint walking sticks made of the finest sugar, to be used as hobby horses. For each stick her customers pay her a pin, which they stick into tiny, tough little Miss Calico's dress; her dress glitters and sparkles with thousands of pins. The hobby horse peppermint sticks fly through the air and are steeds as steady as any could wish. Miss Calico collects her sticks at night, riding through the sky and calling them to her from those who have bought them.

CALLISTA RIVERS (*The Daybreakers; The Birdstones*).   *See* Rivers, Callista Lee

CALORMEN, a place in the Chronicles of Narnia*, by C[live] S[taples] Lewis*. This land south of Archenland* is bounded on two sides by mountains; on the east lies the Eastern Ocean. Calormen was settled early in the history of Narnia* by outlaws from Archenland. Their descendants are dark people with a formal culture, ruled by the Tisroc* from his palace at Tashbaan. Calormene society is highly structured, with slaves at the bottom, free men above them, and Tarkaans and Tarkeenas just below the Tisroc. The Calormenes seem to worship several gods and goddesses, the most powerful and terrible being Tash*, a bird-headed god whose rites require human sacrifices. There are no talking beasts in Calormen, and its people are very practical. Calormen is often either at war with Narnia, or in a kind of insecure peace, for the Narnians do not believe in slavery or human sacrifice, and the Calormenes long for empire. During the reign of the father of Rabadash*, Calormen tries to invade Archenland and, from there, Narnia, but these efforts fail. Rabadash, when he takes the throne, does not pursue the attempt, for he is under an enchantment of Aslan*, Narnia's omniscient lion-protector, and will change into a donkey if he goes ten miles from Tashbaan. His reign is the most peaceful Calormen knows. Later Calormenes invade Narnia economically at the request of Shift*, a Narnian ape, before invading physically and taking Narnia's capital; after this last battle, Narnia and Calormen come to an end.

CALVIN O'KEEFE (the Time trilogy). *See* O'Keefe, Calvin

CAMAZOTZ, a planet in *A Wrinkle in Time*, by Madeleine L'Engle*. Physically it is very like Earth; psychically it is a dystopia. Having given in to the powers of evil that are trying to take over the universe, Camazotz's inhabitants have given up their individuality; all submit to the will of IT*, a monstrous brain which does all thinking for the planet. Camazotz's inhabitants are all alike; those who are different are given a horrible lesson in conformity. As a result there is no war on Camazotz. There is no illness, either, for the sick are "put to sleep." If there is no unhappiness on Camazotz, neither is there happiness; but Camazotz's people do not seem to miss it. To this planet Mr. Murry* accidentally comes while he is trying to transport himself to Mars, and he resists IT as well as he can. He does not know how long he is here before he is rescued by his children, Meg and Charles Wallace Murry**, and their friend, Calvin O'Keefe*, for time on Camazotz is turned in on itself, inverted in some way.

CAMERON, ELEANOR (1912–   ), American writer. She was born in Winnipeg, Manitoba, Canada, on 23 March 1912, to Henry and Florence (Vaughan) Butler. She attended the University of California at Los Angeles and the Art Center School at Los Angeles. In 1934 she married Ian Stuart Cameron; they have one son. She has been a library clerk at the Los Angeles Public Library and the Los Angeles Schools Library, and a special librarian and research librarian at an advertising agency. Cameron has also been a member of the editorial board of *Cricket* magazine.

Cameron's works for children include four science fiction novels, several realistic novels, a psychofantasy, and a fantasy, *The Court of the Stone Children*. A ghost story, it also explores the mysteries of time and the unknown.

In this work, time is not a stream flowing swiftly in a strictly bounded channel from here to there; it is, as the title of a Chagall painting indicates, "a river without banks," flowing in ways not always easy for the mind to comprehend but which the heart can sometimes understand. Nina Harmsworth*, a young girl who admires the painting, knows the truth of what it says. She has a special affinity for the past and a special love of museums, and sometimes when she touches an object from the past she gets her "museum feeling," a sense that there are no years between herself and those who have touched it in the past. Wandering through the recreated rooms in the French Museum, Nina feels a sense of timelessness, as if she is free of her own present moment and, perhaps, of time itself. Others she meets also sense that time does not flow swiftly from the past to the present but sometimes seems to swirl and eddy on itself. Gil Patrick, though as young as Nina, already has explored the nature of time and has realized that it is not the straight path we usually think it is. Mrs. Henry, searching for a place to house her huge art collection, had stood looking at a piece of property her husband owned and had seen, in a vision, the French Museum she would later build there. Mrs. Kendrick searches mirrors for the girl she once was, whose image, she feels, is buried somewhere in the layers of time and reality that are reflected there. Dominique de Lombre* (Domi), the French girl who died early in the nineteenth century, exists in a layer of time different from that of Nina and her friends, a layer of awareness they cannot always see. Though her body has died, she is still learning, still discovering, as unable to see ahead as she was when she was alive. We are in the bankless river, surrounded by the future and the past, but we cannot always see it or feel it, except in certain moments.

In dreams we can transcend our own level of awareness and see a distant time as well as we see our own. After her father, Clovis Antoine de Lombre* (Kot), dies, Domi dreams of being in the French Museum and seeing there Nina, who,

Kot tells her, will help them; years later this dream comes true. Nina dreams of going up a staircase and finding a picture important to Odile Chrysostome*, and weeks later she walks up a stairway to discover the painting that will clear Odile's fiance, Kot, of the murder he is said to have committed. In dreams we change our level of awareness about the world and thus can see times hidden from us in everyday life.

It is more difficult, but sometimes possible, to transcend our own awareness while we are awake. Mrs. Henry does it as she looks at a plot of land and sees there her museum—a vision of the future. Kot and Nina each have a different waking experience, for each, only for a moment, shares a oneness with the world and all its creation that transcends time and space to fill them with the "serene grandeur" of the universe.

As the world in the book works on several layers, so does the book itself. Its complex theme is woven through a suspense-filled story that is as engrossing as any mystery story could be. For at heart it is a mystery story which transcends itself as it explores deep themes. The characters seem real and three-dimensional, if, in some places, a touch idealized: many adults in the book are more understanding than many children could hope for. Nina is a believable young girl trying to make her own place in a city where she feels she does not belong. Cameron is adept at catching the mood of the moment and conveying it to the reader in rich, descriptive prose.

Works

Juvenile fantasy: *The Court of the Stone Children* (1973).
Juvenile science fiction, novels, etc.: *The Wonderful Flight to the Mushroom Planet* (1954); *Stowaway to the Mushroom Planet* (1956); *Mr. Bass's Planetoid* (1958); *The Terrible Churnadryn* (1959); *A Mystery for Mr.Bass* (1960); *The Mysterious Christmas Shell* (1961); *The Beast with the Magical Horn* (1963); *A Spell Is Cast* (1964); *Time and Mr. Bass* (1967); *A Room Made of Windows* (1971); *To the Green Mountains* (1975); *Julia and the Hand of God* (1977); *Beyond Silence* (1981), psychofantasy; *That Julia Redfern* (1982).
Adult: *The Unheard Music* (1950); *The Green and Burning Tree* (1969); *The House on the Beach* (1972); *A Place of Mischief* (1972); *The Young Widow* (1973).

Secondary Works

Cameron, Eleanor. "Into Something Rich and Strange: Of Dreams, Art, and the Unconscious," *Quarterly Journal of the Library of Congress*, 35 (April, 1978), pp. 92–107.
———. "Of Style and the Subject," *The Horn Book Magazine*, 40 (Feb., 1964), pp. 25–32.
———. "Why *Not* for Children?" *The Horn Book Magazine*, 42 (Feb., 1966), pp. 21–33.

Nodelman, Perry. "The Depths of All She Is: Eleanor Cameron," *Children's Literature Quarterly*, 4 (Winter, 1980), pp. 6–8.

CAMERON, PENELOPE TABERNER, the main character in Alison Uttley's *A Traveller in Time**. Young Penelope loves to tell stories. Like her grandmother, she has "second sight" and can sometimes see people who lived long ago; while at Thackers*, the farm belonging to her great-uncle and aunt, Penelope slips back and forth through time to become involved in the lives of her Elizabethan forebears. She becomes the confidante of Anthony Babington*, who is struggling to free Mary Stuart* and who will eventually be accused of plotting against Queen Elizabeth and hanged. Penelope finds herself drawn to Anthony's younger brother, Francis Babington*, who shares her great love of Thackers. Though she knows what will happen to Anthony and to Mary, Penelope is unable to change the past and avert their doom.

CANDLE, an object in William Mayne's* *Earthfasts**. This yellow wax candle has stood for centuries in its stone socket in the center of the Round Table in the chamber where King Arthur* and his knights sleep. It burns hot, as a candle should, for it is in its own present time, but it burns slowly. As long as it burns in its place, Arthur and his men, and giants, and other forces sleep, appearing as stones to the outside world. In 1742 Nellie Jack John Cherry* (John) enters the chamber, searching for Arthur's treasure, and he takes the candle, for his own has burnt out. The tunnel collapses behind him, and he presses on, emerging from underground in the twentieth century. Here the candle is out of its time, a fossil, and its white flame burns cold, needing no air and igniting nothing. It is studied by David Francis Wix*, who falls under its fascination, for when he gazes into the flame he seems to look into infinity, seeing everything at once. The giants wake, as does at least one boggart*. David understands these things and has some affinity for the newly liberated forces because he has looked into the candle. When David is snatched away by Arthur or one of his men, Keith Heseltine* takes the candle, and its light reveals to him Arthur and his army. The flame of the candle begins to resist the air in some way, to have weight, and it gets heavier and heavier. Keith realizes that he must put the candle back where it belongs, and that Arthur and his men must not touch it, for their time has not yet come. He takes the candle back to the chamber and sets it again in its socket, and Arthur, his men, and all the things that had slept and wakened sleep again.

CARADOG PRICHARD (*The Grey King*). *See* Prichard, Caradog

CAREY, MOTHER, a character in *The Water-babies**, by Charles Kingsley*. She sits on a throne in the middle of Peacepool, behind Shiny Wall* in the Arctic, and gazes into the water, making the water creatures make themselves.

Tom* comes to her to learn the way to the Other-end-of-Nowhere*. Mother Carey is an old woman with white hair and blue eyes; she is one facet of a being whose real identity is too dazzling for mortals to know. Mrs. Bedonebyasyoudid* and Mrs. Doasyouwouldbedoneby* are two other facets.

CAREY, PAUL (DR.), a character in E[lwyn] B[rooks] White's* *Stuart Little*. He is, appropriately enough, a surgeon-dentist. Dr. Carey's hobbies include building model boats and cars. He loves to sail his boats on the sailboat pond in Central Park, and here the bane of his life is a fat, sloppy boy who allows his boat to bump into Dr. Carey's. One day Dr. Carey meets Stuart Little*, a mouse-like person two inches high, who offers to sail Dr. Carey's schooner, the *Wasp*, against the one owned by the fat boy. To the doctor's delight Stuart wins the race. When Stuart runs away from home to find Margalo*, a bird he loves, Dr. Carey provides him with a lovely little yellow car with a gas engine and a button that makes it invisible.

CAREY WILSON (*The Magic Bed-Knob; Bonfires and Broomsticks*). *See* Wilson, Carey

CAROLANNA, a character in Jane Louise Curry's* *Parsley Sage, Rosemary & Time*. She becomes the wife of Gunty. This eighteenth-century native American girl is from Carolina, and her name reflects that. She is the slave of Thanatopsis Grout*. Young and sometimes foolish, Carolanna gets Goody Cakebread* into trouble by accusing her of being a witch after the girl witnesses the transformation of William Wingard* from a piglet, via the old woman's magical cupboard*. Immediately contrite when Gunty will have nothing to do with her because of what she has done, Carolanna helps Goody Cakebread escape to safety. Gunty and Carolanna are married after the girl runs away from her master.

CARPET, WISHING, an object in E[dith] Nesbit Bland's* *The Phoenix and the Carpet*. This Persian carpet was the treasured property of caliphs and kings and sultans and was kept in rich chests, wrapped in luxurious cloth. In about 100 B.C., an enchanter gave the carpet to a pair of lovers, who used it to take them to the wilderness. Here they met the Phoenix* and gave to it the magic carpet. Weary of burning itself and being born again every five hundred years, the Phoenix had laid its egg on the carpet and wished that it would take the egg to a place where it would not be found for two thousand years. In the twentieth century the carpet is bought by the mother of Robert*, Anthea*, Cyril*, and Jane* at a used furniture shop. The Phoenix, who hatches from the egg rolled inside the carpet, explains the workings of its magic: the carpet will grant three wishes each day. It can also be sent on errands if a note explaining the errand is pinned to the carpet, word-side down, so that the carpet can read it. Because it is magic, the carpet communicates with the Phoenix and expresses its wishes and needs. The children use the carpet to have adventures and help people in need: they take their baby brother to a tropical island to get over his cough and incidentally take along the cook*; they travel to France and restore a fortune to a poor family; and they help a burglar* out of jail and take him to the cook's tropical island. The carpet also saves the children from a burning theater. All its adventures have a detrimental effect on the carpet, and finally the children are forced to relinquish it. The Phoenix lays its egg on the carpet and sends it to a place where the egg will not be found for another two thousand years.

CASPIAN X, a character in *Prince Caspian*, *The Voyage of the "Dawn Treader"**, *The Silver Chair**, and *The Last Battle**, by C[live] S[taples] Lewis*. He is the son of Caspian IX and the nephew of Miraz* and Prunaprismia; he is the husband of the daughter of Ramandu* and the father of Rilian*. He is also called "Caspian the Navigator" and "Caspian the Seafarer." Though a descendant of the conqueror from Telmar* who took the throne in Narnia* and killed or drove into hiding its magical beasts, Caspian longs for the old days when talking beasts and the spirits of trees and fountains roamed the land, for he has heard of these things from his old nurse. Caspian is raised by Miraz in ignorance of his true heritage, for the king had killed Caspian's father and taken the throne. Doctor Cornelius*, Caspian's tutor, tells the boy of his true heritage and helps him regain the throne. During his reign Caspian revives the old Narnia and sails the Eastern Ocean in the *Dawn Treader**, searching for seven lords Miraz had sent to explore the sea beyond the known lands. On this voyage he meets his future wife. The rest of Caspian's reign is fairly peaceful, save that his son mysteriously vanishes after the queen's death. Caspian, now an old man, sets sail to Terebinthia to ask the advice of Aslan*, Narnia's great lion-protector; Aslan sends him back home, where Caspian lives just long enough to greet Rilian, who has been found. On his death, Caspian is taken to the mountain of Aslan and there revived and rejuvenated by a drop of the lion's blood; he helps the two children from Earth who had found Rilian wreak vengeance on their tormentors. Caspian is one of those in Aslan's country after Narnia comes to an end.

CASTLE COX, a place in Jane Louise Curry's* *Poor Tom's Ghost**. Built in 1603 for Tom Garland*, this house is haunted by him in the twentieth century. By that time, the house has been enlarged and "improved" until it is unrecognizable. Originally called "New House," the house is jokingly dubbed "Castle Cox" by the aunt of Tony Nicholas*, who inherits it from the Cox family.

CASTLE OF LLYR, THE. Lloyd Alexander. New York: Holt, Rinehart and Winston, 1966. 201 pp. American.

Having lived at Caer Dallben*; with Dallben*, an enchanter, and Taran*, his orphaned ward, for a time, Eilonwy*, a princess of the House of Llyr*, leaves to live on the Isle of Mona* and learn to be a princess. With her on her journey go Taran and Gurgi*, a strange, hairy escort, Rhun*, the cheerfully clumsy prince of Mona, and when they reach the island, Taran's irritation does not decrease. Here he finds old friends: Fflewddur Fflam*, a king who lives the wandering life of a bard, and Gwydion*, the war leader of Prydain's* High King, now disguised as a shoemaker. Gwydion warns Taran that Achren*, an evil sorceress, may seek Eilonwy's life, but he is not to tell the girl. That night Taran follows Magg*, the Chief Steward, as the man leaves the castle, and watches as the steward signals a ship. Gwydion is there, too; Achren is on the ship but Gwydion does not know what is happening, and he sends Taran back to the castle to keep an eye on Eilonwy.

The next morning, however, the girl vanishes. She had been seen riding out of the castle with Magg. As search parties are formed, Rhun's father, aware of his unfitness to be a leader, makes Taran swear to help Rhun learn to be a man and a king, for it is the king's wish that eventually Rhun and Eilonwy will marry. During the search, Rhun, certain he is leading the group, gallops into some woods. In trying to find him, Taran, Fflewddur, and Gurgi get lost; the next day, they find the prince in a deserted cottage where they find a blank book and a book of potions and spells to make things grow. Glew*, the sorcerer who had lived here, evidently tried them out on Llyan*, his cat, and seems to have vanished soon after the cat grew too big for the cottage. The group is attacked by a huge cat and soon realizes that it is Llyan. When Fflewddur plays his harp, she is fascinated and the others are able to escape; the bard joins them later, having played Llyan to sleep. Because the horses have gone, the companions walk toward the castle.

Suddenly Kaw*, Taran's talking crow, comes upon them. He has seen Eilonwy at a nearby river. By the time they get there, however, she is gone; they find the magical golden sphere she carries with her, half-hidden in the sand. Evidence shows that she was taken by boat, so Taran and the others build a raft and start downstream. The raft hits a rock and breaks up. Collecting wood to repair it, Rhun opens up and falls into a large pit; his companions, realizing they cannot pull him out, slip in and try to help him. A sudden slide seals the pit, and the travelers find themselves in a lovely cave, made visible by the light from Eilonwy's sphere. As they search for a way out, they meet Glew, the sorcerer, who had drunk a potion while in the cave and is now a giant, too big to fit through the entrances. The blank book they found in his cottage, he explains, is from Eilonwy's ancestral home, now a ruin at the mouth of the river, and is supposed to be full of spells. Promising to help them get out of the cave, Glew instead imprisons the four in a dead-end passage, explaining that one of them must die to provide an ingredient for a new potion and begging them to decide who it will be. Instead, the companions find a small passage high in the wall and manage to get Rhun into it to go for help. When Glew opens their prison, the other three attack him. Just as he is about to capture Taran, a bright light dazzles the giant's eyes; it is the light of Eilonwy's sphere, wielded by Rhun. Rocks, dislodged by Glew's surprised shout, fall and knock him out and open an entrance to the outside world.

Having repaired the raft, the companions float to the mouth of the river and the island that lies there. Here they meet Gwydion, who has discovered that Eilonwy is being kept at the ruined palace as Achren's prisoner. The golden sphere is the Golden Pelydryn*, the light of which reveals the spells in the blank book, and Achren wants both. Because the spells will work only for a daughter of the House of Llyr, she has kidnapped Eilonwy. At nightfall, Gwydion, Taran, and the others go to the island and hide the book and the Pelydryn to keep them safe. Kaw has found Eilonwy in a tower, but when Taran climbs up to rescue her, she does not remember him, for she is under a spell. Eilonwy alerts the guards and a melee ensues, during which the companions come face to face with Achren.

The sorceress has bound Eilonwy's life with her own and intends to use the girl to rule Prydain. After Rhun blurts out that they have hidden the magical objects Achren needs, Gwydion tells her, finally, where they are, and the book and sphere are brought. When the Pelydryn is put into her hands, Eilonwy goes through a terrible internal struggle and, as she drops the book, it bursts into flame, setting the room on fire. Eilonwy faints, and Taran, carrying her, flees the castle, for Magg has opened the gates to the sea and the fortress is crumbling. All are swept into the sea. When Taran wakes, he is on shore; Llyan, following Fflewddur, has fished them all out and is now quite tame. To Achren, who has been losing her powers of enchantment, Gwydion offers the peaceful refuge of Caer Dallben. After many anxious hours, Eilonwy wakes and knows them all. While she had held the Pelydryn, she had known that they wanted her to destroy the book of spells, but she had to struggle against her desire to keep the book for herself. Kaw finds them; in his claws is the Pelydryn, rescued from the sea. Because she must, Eilonwy will learn to be a lady, though she hates the prospect, and she gives to Taran a hunting horn* cast up by the sea as a pledge that she will not forget him. To Taran's relief, Eilonwy has no intention of being betrothed to Rhun.

CAT. *See* Cathound

CAT, a character in *Mary Poppins Opens the Door**, by P[amela] L[yndon] Travers*. This white cat appears one day at the court of King Cole*, who is neglecting his wife and people in search of knowledge. In a contest of wit and knowledge, the cat proves to King Cole that it is wiser than he and wins from him his kingdom. By looking into the cat's eyes, King Cole also learns who he really is. The cat gives him back the kingdom in exchange for the queen's flower necklace, which she winds around its body, and for permission to come and see her whenever he wants to. Now he wanders the world, seeking those who will return his gaze and staying with them long enough to show them who they really are. The cat stays for a time with Michael George Banks*, in the guise of a china cat painted with a chain of flowers.

CAT WHO WISHED TO BE A MAN, THE. Lloyd Alexander. New York: E. P. Dutton and Co., 1973. 107 pp. American.

Lionel* is the young cat belonging to Magister Stephanus*, a wizard who has no use for humans because they pervert everything he gives them. When Lionel pesters him about turning him into a man, however, the wizard obliges. Stephanus makes him promise to come home without delay after his visit to Brightford*, the nearby town, and gives Lionel a magic wishbone* so he can help himself if he needs to; if broken it will take Lionel wherever he wishes to be. Full of excitement, the young man hurries to Brightford but has no money for the tollbridge. As the people behind him on the bridge grumble at both the delay and the heavy tolls, the panicky guards call Swaggart*, their boss, who tells Lionel that since he insists he is a cat, he can surely leap over the high, barbed tollgate; if he does, all can come across the bridge free. To Swaggart's dismay, Lionel leaps the gate with no difficulty.

Lionel finds Brightford exciting. When he accidentally catches a pickpocket, the man pays him to let him go, and Lionel soon increases this amount by winning at a game of chance. The young man loses his money when Swaggart swindles him out of it. If he wants dinner, the man tells him, Lionel should go to a nearby inn and ask for it, paying Gillian*, its keeper, with a kiss. This the young man does, and he is amazed at her violent reaction to what he finds is a surprisingly pleasant experience.

Dr. Tudbelly*, a traveling quack who carries his remedies in a wooden chest, or Armamentarium*, also comes to Gillian's inn for dinner, but there is nothing to eat. Mayor Pursewig*, who owns most of the town, is trying to ruin Gillian so she will sell him her inn. Because she cannot afford to repair damage Pursewig had sent his men to do, Gillian has been forced to close the inn, and she has nothing to feed them with. Undaunted, Dr. Tudbelly and Lionel go out and collect food for dinner by collecting people to bring it and eat it. As word spreads that the inn is reopening, others come and a party starts, only to be broken up by Pursewig and Swaggart. Slightly hurt by Swaggart before Gillian can get the man out of her inn, Lionel is given a soothing syrup by Dr. Tudbelly, and when he wakes it is morning—hours later than he had promised Stephanus to return.

Before he goes, Lionel chases out the rats Pursewig has put into Gillian's cellar and is elated when the rodents scurry into the mayor's house. Sad because he does not want to leave Gillian, Lionel tries the magic wishbone, which he has lost and then found. To his surprise, it does not work. When Pursewig's men come to arrest him, Lionel flees with Dr. Tudbelly, who insists on bringing the Armamentarium. Because the tollgate is closed, they escape by swimming the river—which is distasteful to Lionel. In the Armamentarium Lionel finds the real wishbone, but he does not use it; he will go back and help Gillian. Some friendly tradesmen hide him and Dr. Tudbelly in their wagon and take them to the inn, where Gillian is being held prisoner. The two are caught and are tried and sentenced by Pursewig in an illegal trial.

When a member of the city council intervenes, Lionel and Dr. Tudbelly are put into jail for jumping off the bridge and not paying the toll, and Pursewig's ownership of the bridge is investigated, for Lionel reveals that Stephanus, his master, had built the bridge for the entire town. In the cell, Dr. Tudbelly mixes up a solvent to dissolve the bars, but in typical fashion the solvent belies its purpose and becomes a glue which grows hot and, when Lionel throws it down, explodes and blows a hole in the outer wall. Tudbelly gets away, but Swaggart captures Lionel, puts him into a sack, and tosses him into the river. Lionel uses his wishbone to go to Gillian and immediately finds himself in the burning inn, locked in with Gillian and the potboy. With difficulty he saves them and then goes after Pursewig, who is trapped in the cellar. Desperate, the man promises anything if he is rescued and is forced to keep his word, taking down the tollgate, resigning his position, and helping Gillian in the inn. Swaggart gets away.

Though he would like to stay with Gillian, Lionel must go back to Stephanus. Gillian and Dr. Tudbelly accompany him into the forest, where they meet Swaggart, who tries to kill Lionel. Chasing the man, Lionel finds Swaggart's crossbow and almost uses it, but he cannot. Stephanus comes upon him and, despite the protests of Gillian and Dr. Tudbelly, is determined to change Lionel back into a cat. He has already changed Swaggart into a skunk. When Stephanus tries to transform Lionel, though, the spell does not work; Lionel has felt so much human emotion that he has become human inside as well as out. Excited by the prospect of his new life, Lionel leaves with Gillian and Dr. Tudbelly to live in Brightford.

CATHOUND (CAT), a character in *The Wolves of Aam**, by Jane Louise Curry*. She is an orphan found in a boat by the Tiddi* and raised as one of them. Cathound was named after the cathound found guarding her in the boat. Cat grows up to become a hunter. Though she is small she is not like the other Tiddi; Cat is taller than they and quiet and solitary, with long feet and straight hair; her senses are not as sharp as those of the Tiddi. When Runner-to-the-Sky's-Edge* is kidnapped, Cat goes after his captors, helping him and the Wolves of Aam* rescue Lek*, the conjuror captured by the evil Lord Naghar's* men and taken to the fortress of Gzel*.

CAULDRON-BORN, THE, a type of warrior in Lloyd Alexander's* Chronicles of Prydain*. These deathless, heartless men are not born so; once, each was an ordinary warrior who had died; after his death he was put into the Black Crochan*, a magical kettle, by Arawn*, the Lord of Death, and had come out of the kettle alive, though speechless, emotionless, and deathless. Arawn creates a great army of these creatures by raiding barrows and by murdering men, to put the bodies in his cauldron. The longer and farther they are from Arawn, the more their powers wane, but they are terrible to come up against in battle because they cannot be hurt or killed. One thing only finally causes the death of the

Cauldron-Born; Taran*, a young man, strikes one with Dyrnwyn*, a powerful sword, and the warrior falls dead; as he does so, all the Cauldron-Born fall as well.

CAVATICA, CHARLOTTE A., the title character in *Charlotte's Web*, by E[lwyn] B[rooks] White*. She is a gray barn spider about the size of a gumdrop who builds her web in the doorway of Homer L. Zuckerman's* barn. From there she watches Wilbur*, his pig, and makes herself known to him when he is feeling lonely and friendless. Though Wilbur is at first horrified because Charlotte drinks the blood of insects, the two become fast friends. Charlotte is level-headed, ingenious, and a good weaver, and all these qualities come into play when she works to save Wilbur's life. By writing into her web words and phrases flattering the pig, she makes Mr. Zuckerman feel that Wilbur is so special that he spares his life. Charlotte does not live to enjoy this, having lived out her natural lifespan. She dies alone on the fairgrounds of the county fair the day after the fair is over. Her egg sac, with its 514 eggs, is taken by Wilbur back to Mr. Zuckerman's farm, and here her children hatch. Three of Charlotte's daughters, Joy, Aranea, and Nellie, become Wilbur's friends, and so do some of her grandchildren and their children. But none replace Charlotte in Wilbur's heart.

CAVE OF LEARNING, a place in E[dith] Nesbit Bland's* *Wet Magic*. It lies just outside the golden gate of Merland*, beneath the sea. The walls of the cave are rocks made of books, and its atmosphere is full of learning, which leaks out of the rocks. The cave is dark at its beginning and gets lighter close to the golden door.

CAW, SOLOMON, a character in James M. Barrie's* *Peter Pan in Kensington Gardens*. Solomon is a bird who lives in Kensington Gardens and is responsible for sending babies to people. Old Solomon reveals to Peter Pan* that the boy is no longer a bird and helps him to talk the thrushes into building a nest that Peter can use as a boat. Solomon looks forward to retiring from the baby business and keeps his treasures in an old sock.

CAXTON, a character in Lucy Boston's* *The Chimneys of Green Knowe*. He is the butler of Captain Oldknow* in eighteenth-century Green Knowe*, but he has great ambitions. Caxton sells young village men to the press gangs and also employs young boys as poachers, all for his own profit. At Caxton's urging, Sefton Oldknow*, the Captain's son, has gone into debt betting on horses, and Caxton hopes eventually to have such a hold on Sefton that when the Captain dies the family fortune will be Caxton's. Then he will marry Susan Oldknow*, Sefton's blind younger sister, and take over the house as well. When one of Caxton's young poachers tells Captain Oldknow of the butler's dealings, Caxton is dismissed. The night before he is to leave, Caxton steals the family jewels. He does not profit from the theft, though, for that night a fire breaks out in Green Knowe and Caxton dies in it, trying to save his hoard.

CELEMON, a traditional figure in Celtic lore who appears as a character in *The Moon of Gomrath**, by Alan Garner*. She is the daughter of Cei, of the moon. Celemon and the eight other Shining Ones are from Caer Rigor. They ride across the sky on horses, with their hawks and hounds. For a time they seem to have been kept by the lords of High Magic at the back of the north wind, but Susan*, a human girl, inadvertently brings them back into the world; she rides with them and they come back with her when her spirit is recalled to her body. Celemon and her riders later join Garanhir* and his Wild Hunt*, and they ride across the sea to Caer Rigor.

CERDIC LONGTOOTH (*Time Cat*). *See* Longtooth, Cerdic

CHANCE CHILD, A. Jill Paton Walsh. London: Macmillan, 1978. 158 pp. British.

On a gloomy, rainy day, an abused child called Creep* seeks shelter. He finds it in a little metal hut beside a canal; after the rain stops, he learns from a man that the hut is really a little boat that can be pulled down the canal. Creep follows the canal, pulling his boat past grimy buildings. He comes to a lock, where a little girl comes out of a cottage to help him. The second lock he comes to— which is located under a building—he manages by himself, and he comes out in a place with houses and horses and a blacksmith and a church. Around the bend in the canal lies a world with trees and meadows and cows, far lovelier than Creep has ever imagined.

Meanwhile Chris* and Pauline*, Creep's half-brother and -sister, are looking for him. The man who had spoken to Creep shows them which way the boy went. They go past the first lock with its now roofless, deserted cottage; they go under the building and past the church, which is now surrounded by factories.

Creep wakes and finds coal barges being towed down the canal. He catches a tow from a passing boat, then finds that the current in the canal is enough to move the boat alone. It goes past a factory town, where the clear water is tainted by pollution, and finally the boat glides off the canal and down an underground passage, past a wharf where coal is being loaded, and into a cave where Creep hears the sound of crying mingled with the sound of picks. Creep searches for the crying child and finds her just as adult searchers come upon her. The searchers, who do not seem to see Creep, take the child, and Creep follows the search party. When it comes upon a miner mistreating his apprentice, the man is bundled off; Creep takes the boy, Tom Moorhouse*, to his boat and steers it out of the mines and back onto the canal.

Chris, in the meantime, is puzzled and discouraged. He feels that he has passed Creep somewhere, but he knows there is no reason for Creep to want to come back: the child was mistreated by their mother, probably because she came to hate Creep's father, who had fathered the child while she was married to the father of Chris and Pauline. Chris comes upon a couple who are traveling the canals in a boat, and he learns from them about the canals. The next day he persuades Pauline to help him follow an overgrown offshoot of the canal.

Creep's little boat, meanwhile, has stopped near a foundry. He and Tom find a little cottage and beg food from a woman, though Creep is not hungry. The woman does not seem to see him. There is no work for Tom at the foundry, so the boys go to the next town for work. Here Tom gets a job as an apprentice to a nailer, a man who forges chains, who does not see Creep, either. Also helping the man is Lucy*, who is called Blackie because of a great black burn scar that disfigures her face, from when she had fallen asleep on the job and fell into a fire. After working all night on a special order, Tom decides this job is as bad as the one in the mines, and he runs away again, taking Blackie. On their journey down the canal, the three cut Creep's name into a stone bridge, to serve as a mark for Chris. They decide to find work at a pottery plant, for Blackie once met a girl who worked at one and who praised the place.

Chris, tramping a little ahead of Pauline, comes to the bridge where Creep's name is cut. The name has been overgrown by moss, and weeds have grown up around it. Frantic, Chris runs down the canal, which finally is silted in, and at last he comes to a rotting metal boat. Chris realizes where Creep has gone, but he does not know how to find him.

Creep, Blackie, and Tom come to a pottery plant, where Blackie and Tom are hired until the regular boy recovers from his illness. They help in the making of plates, and the work is exhausting, though Creep tries to help as much as he can. He is not like the others: he is never hungry, never tired, never hot, and he never laughs; nor does he seem to feel any emotion. Fall comes. Blackie longs to work in the warm, friendly room where the china is painted, and she has many plans for Tom and herself, including marriage. Tom dismisses this immediately, saying she is too ugly for him. At last Blackie gets her chance to work in the painting room, but the first day is a disaster, for Tom, feeling unwell, drops a basket of china and is dismissed. Blackie goes with him. They again travel down the canal in the little boat.

Meanwhile, Chris has his own problems; Pauline and his mother are pretending Creep never existed, and because no one else has seen him, it is as though the boy never did exist. But Chris is determined not to deny Creep, and he learns from a history teacher where to find information about ordinary people in the nineteenth century. Eagerly he hunts for information about Creep.

Creep's little boat stops near a bridge, and there Tom finds work in a mine safer than the one he was first employed in. He also finds a place to live. But there is no room for Blackie, so Tom leaves her and Creep. After Tom leaves the boat floats down the canal and they come to a cotton mill, where Blackie gets a job in the spinning room, mending the broken threads. Creep helps her in this tiring work. In the mill, as elsewhere, the children see him, but the adults cannot. One day a boy gets his sleeve caught in the machine and is brutally beaten when he is freed. The next day his angry mother berates the boy's master. After she leaves, the boy is beaten again, for telling, and someone slips out and calls back his mother. All the workers are secretly pleased when the mother takes a roller and belabors the master with it, but Creep laughs out loud—and suddenly all can see him. He is sent out of the factory and waits with a pinched belly for Blackie. The next day he walks her to the mill and then trudges down the canal, pulling his boat, looking for work. At the end of the canal, he finds work with the crew that is cutting a channel for the canal.

In his own century, Chris finds a little pamphlet written by Nathaniel Creep and realizes that he has at last found his half-brother. The pamphlet tells how Creep had escaped from the closet when a hole was made in the wall as the house next door was being torn down, and he escaped from his house; how he had worked cutting the canal until he was crippled by an accident; how he learned to read and became a printer; how he went back to find Blackie and married her. He had had a hard life but a happy one and one day went back to leave a farewell message on a bridge, for he felt even as a boy that someone was looking for him.

Chris and Pauline go to look for the message. On the way they meet a social worker who has found Creep's birth certificate, but Chris tells her that Creep died before any of them were born. When Chris and Pauline get to the bridge where Creep had carved his name, they also find four lines of a poem—Creep's farewell message to his brother.

CHANGE-CHILD, THE. Jane Louise Curry. Illus. Gareth Floyd. New York: Harcourt, Brace and World, 1969. 174 pp. American.

Because twelve-year-old Eilian Roberts* is lame and golden-haired and *different*, the superstitious farmers and villagers who live in that part of Wales call her a changeling, believing that she has the powers of witchery because she is actually a fairy child changed for a mortal one. Taunted and hated by the others, Eilian leads a miserable life, hiring out her services as a maid-of-all-work far from her home so that she can contribute to the household. After a puzzling encounter with Simon Rastall*, a nobleman's son, Eilian travels home to discover that she is no longer simple Eilian Roberts; she is an heiress and will inherit a nearby manor at her father's death. Because Simon, who has his eye on the manor himself, will not stop short of kidnapping Eilian and forcing her to marry him in order to get it, she is sent with her grandmother, Mamgu*, the "Queen" of the "Red Fairies"*, to be kept safe in the wood where the old woman lives.

The Red Fairies are lovely, golden-haired people who live on the edge of the wood and are all related to Eilian. They live by their wits, on what they can steal, and they dwell near the mysterious wood in order to take advantage of the old tales of the Fair Folk* believed to dwell there. Harried by justices, they are trapped in their way of life, for if they leave the safety of the wood, they will be caught and punished. For Eilian, finally receiving the love she has sought, time flits by. Every day Mamgu works on her lame foot, making it stronger.

One morning Eilian has Emrys*, her uncle, take her into the mysterious, frightening wood. When he leaves her for a short time, Eilian meets Goronwy*, a boy who had helped her earlier on her journey home. But Emrys, seeing Goronwy when he comes back to Eilian, is wary; the boy is one of the Children of the Great Dark Wood, of whom the Red Fairies are as frightened as they are of the justices. The next day Eilian is to go home. Emrys is sent off early, to carry a letter to a nearby town, but he is stopped by Goronwy and is sent after Mamgu and Eilian, catching up with them just in time to keep the drugged and docile girl from being handed over to Simon Rastall. Mamgu had thought to buy the safety of the Red Fairies by giving up Eilian. In the ensuing fight, Emrys is badly wounded, and he, Eilian, and Pilipala*, another of the Red Fairies, are taken by Goronwy to a secret valley in the center of the wood.

In this lovely valley Eilian meets *y Tylwyth Teg**, the true Fair Folk, the Children of the Great Dark Wood, who are lovely and remote and ageless. Unable to live alongside mortals, they have sought sanctuary here. But they are upset by the arrival of Eilian, for it means they must leave; once, a singer stole away the wife of one of the lords of the Folk, and when the lord found them he killed the singer and cursed the offspring of the illicit union, dooming them to eternal wandering; the grief-stricken wife responded with another curse, declaring that one of these offspring would drive the Folk from Middle Earth. The Red Fairies are the wandering descendants of the lady and the singer, and Eilian is the force that drives the Folk from their sanctuary, for when Simon, having been cursed by Mamgu, is killed in a fall from his horse, his father orders the wood destroyed so that it will no longer harbor the Red Fairies. The forest is set on fire, and the Folk must leave it.

They leave our world as well. One night as Eilian gets ready to go to bed in the great manor house, she feels a strange sort of call and leaves the house, finding Emrys and Pilipala, now husband and wife, abroad, too; they also have been called. At the river they discover that the Folk are gathering to sail in great coracles to mystical Tir na'nOg*, where they can live in peace forever. Only Goronwy stays behind, and the four watch as the Folk sail away. In later years they and their children after them gather on this spot every Midsummer Eve to sing the spring on its way with lovely songs of time passing, though they are content with the present.

CHARLES WALLACE MURRY (the Time trilogy). *See* Murry, Charles Wallace

CHARLES WILSON (*The Magic Bed-Knob; Bonfires and Broomsticks*). *See* Wilson, Charles

CHARLOTTE A. CAVATICA (*Charlotte's Web*). *See* Cavatica, Charlotte A.

CHARLOTTE'S WEB. E[lwyn] B[rook] White. Illus. Garth Williams. New York: Harper and Brothers, Publishers, 1952. 184 pp. American.

Because Fern Arable* becomes so upset when she learns that her father is going to kill the runt of a litter of pigs his sow has given birth to, he gives the piglet to her. Fern names it Wilbur* and tenderly raises him until he is five weeks old, when Wilbur is sold to her uncle, Homer L. Zuckerman*. Fern takes every opportunity to visit Wilbur in his new home, where she sits in the barn and watches and listens to the animals. Though he appreciates Fern's visits, Wilbur one day becomes bored and is shown by a goose how to escape from his pen; despite the excitement of the chase, Wilbur is glad to be lured back into the pen. The next day is rainy and Wilbur feels lonely and friendless. That night he hears a voice promising that its owner will be his friend, and the next morning Wilbur meets Charlotte A. Cavatica*, a gray spider who, to Wilbur's horror, drinks blood.

Spring turns to summer and a nestful of goslings hatches. One egg is a dud and it is given to Templeton*, a rat who collects such things. Wilbur becomes close friends with Charlotte, whom he comes to admire. Then one day Wilbur learns that he is being fattened for slaughter at Christmas, and such is his hysteria that Charlotte promises to help him. Fern, whose mother is worried because she spends so much time in the barn, watches as one day Wilbur tries—and fails—to spin a web. Charlotte, still working on her plan, advises him to work on building himself up as a pig.

At last Charlotte hits upon her plan, and that day Fern's brother tries to catch the spider. In doing so he accidentally breaks Templeton's egg and the smell of the rotten egg drives him away. That night Charlotte reworks her web, and the next morning the words SOME PIG appear there. Mr. Zuckerman accepts this as a supernatural sign that Wilbur is indeed special, and people come from miles around to see the pig. A few nights later Charlotte holds a meeting of the farm animals to come up with a new word, and Templeton is recruited to bring words from the dump. After Charlotte writes TERRIFIC in her web, Mr. Zuckerman decides to take Wilbur to the county fair. Fern's mother is so worried about her daughter that she goes to a doctor, who reassures her about Fern.

Summer is ending, and people still come to see Wilbur, who, thanks to a soapbox Templeton has found, is now RADIANT. Charlotte is getting ready to lay her eggs, but she goes with Wilbur to the fair, talking Templeton into coming, too. They travel with Wilbur in his crate. At the fair, Wilbur is put into a pen next to a tremendously large pig who is sure to win a prize. When night comes, Fern's mother is gratified to see her daughter with a boy, and Charlotte weaves her last word—HUMBLE—into her web. She also makes her egg sac. The huge pig in the next pen wins a ribbon the next day, but Wilbur gets a special prize; during the ceremony he faints and Templeton rouses him by biting his tail. The last day of the fair comes, and Charlotte is dying. Wilbur bribes Templeton to bring down her egg sac, which he carries back to the farm in his mouth. The next day Charlotte dies alone.

Wilbur watches over the egg sac all that winter, and he is pleased when spring comes and the eggs hatch. A few days later, Charlotte's children float away on streamers of web; three of her daughters stay behind. As the years pass, Wilbur is well cared for and always has friends as new spiders replace the old. None, however, can replace Charlotte in his heart.

CHERRY, NELLIE JACK JOHN (JOHN), a character in *Earthfasts**, by William Mayne*. He is the son of Jack, the son of Nellie; he had a brother named Thomas. John was born in Low Eskeleth, Arkengathdale, England, in the eighteenth century. In order to be near his sweetheart, Kath, he enlisted as a drummer boy in the army stationed at Garebridge. Under the castle at Gare-bridge, King Arthur* and his knights supposedly sleep among their treasures, so when a fallen wall uncovered a passage, John entered it one May night in 1742. He beat his drum as he marched, for two friends to follow the sound so they would know where to dig for the treasure. Because his candle burned out, when he got to the chamber John took a short candle* burning there; because the tunnel collapsed behind him, he pressed on, beating his drum. John feels he has only been gone an hour or so, but he comes out from under the earth in a field in the twentieth century, in front of two astonished boys, Keith Heseltine* and David Francis Wix*. At first John does not believe he is in the twentieth century, but when he is convinced, he re-enters the earth where he had come out, hoping to walk through the passage back to his own time. Because John is afraid of the dark, he takes David's bicycle lamp. Walking against the flow of time is difficult and he makes very little progress; when they later encounter him in the passage, Keith and David turn John around and take him back with them. Though he does not want to stay in this century at first, John decides to stay when Frank Watson and his wife take him into their home.

CHILDREN OF GREEN KNOWE, THE. Lucy Boston. Illus. Peter Boston. London: Faber and Faber, 1954. 157 pp. British.

Toseland* (Tolly) goes to stay with his great-grandmother, Mrs. Linnet Old-know*, at the ancient family manor, Green Knowe*. He arrives by rowboat because the nearby river has flooded. The next day he spends learning about the place and about two brothers and a sister who lived there in the sixteenth century: Toseland Oldknow* (Toby), who kept a horse named Feste*, Alexander Old-know*, who loved music, and Linnet Oldknow*, who loved animals. That night, as Tolly lies in bed, he hears them; and the next day, as he explores the house grounds, he hears them again. That night Mrs. Oldknow tells Tolly a story about Toby and Feste: how Toby rode for the doctor one night because Linnet was sick, and how Feste refused to cross a certain bridge. As they swam the river, the flood-weakened bridge collapsed. Feste got Toby safely to the doctor's.

The day after the story, the three children tease Tolly, letting him hear them but not letting him get close; once, he catches a glimpse of Alexander and Linnet in a mirror, but they vanish. That evening it snows, and as Tolly and Mrs. Oldknow sit by the fire, they hear children singing carols; but when Tolly opens the door, no one is there. The three children will allow him to be with them when they are sure of him, Mrs. Oldknow tells him. The next day Tolly makes stronger contact; a chaffinch he has befriended finds the lost key to a toybox, and in it are things that belonged to Toby, Alexander, and Linnet. As Tolly watches in fascination, the children's dominoes set themselves up in a line and then topple over; when he reads Linnet's book, she puts her hands over his eyes and then vanishes.

As they sit by the fire that night Mrs. Oldknow tells Tolly a story of how a gypsy once sneaked into the stable to steal her father's fine horse. Seeing Feste in his old stall, which had always been left empty since his death, the gypsy tried to steal him, unaware that Feste was not an ordinary horse. Feste picked him up and dropped him, injuring the man's leg, and the gypsy was captured.

Tolly makes contact with the children from the past the next morning, when he goes outside and finds them feeding the animals in the snow. When the loud, arrogant peacock comes, they vanish and the animals leave. That evening Mrs. Oldknow tells Tolly a story about Linnet, how the girl saw the statue of St. Christopher* that stands near the house moving across the fields one Christmas Eve, taking the Christ Child on its shoulder to Mass.

When Tolly again goes to find the children, they warn him about Green Noah*, a yew tree shaped like Noah to go with the topiary animals near the house; but before Tolly can ask about it, they vanish. Mrs. Oldknow's story that night is about Alexander and how he sang for the king, who gave him a flute. When Tolly goes to bed, he opens the window of his room and calls in songbirds to stay there so they will be sheltered from the cold. He wakes in the night to hear Linnet shoo away an owl that is trying to get in. The truth about Green Noah comes out the next afternoon when Tolly reads in an article that the tree had been cursed by the mother of the gypsy who tried to steal Feste.

Christmas is near and they get ready for it, hearing as they decorate the tree the sound of a woman singing to a baby centuries ago in the next room. It is stormy that evening as Tolly goes out to put sugar in Feste's old stall. In the dark he gets lost and sees Green Noah coming blindly after him; Tolly calls Linnet, who calls on St. Christopher, and lightning strikes Green Noah. On Christmas Eve, when they go to Midnight Mass, Tolly falls asleep and opens his eyes to see himself and Mrs. Oldknow at a church service with Toby, Linnet, and Alexander. St. Christopher stands in the shadows. Mrs. Oldknow wakes Tolly, and neither knows whether or not they have been dreaming.

When he wakes Christmas morning, Tolly finds Toby's old coat thrown over his clothes. He puts it on and goes out to the stable, feeling that Feste, being Toby's horse, will appear to him. Tolly keeps his eyes closed, and, for a few thrilling moments, he touches wonderful Feste. As Tolly goes back to the house, he meets Toby, Linnet, and Alexander, and he realizes when they vanish that they will be back; they will always be there. One of Tolly's presents that day is a puppy like the one Linnet owned. Tolly names it Orlando*, like hers. He gets other presents that day, too; he is not to go back to the boarding school but will go to a school nearby and be able to come to Green Knowe for all his holidays; and Tolly's father wants him to learn to ride.

CHILDREN OF THE OPEN SEA, THE, a race of people in Ursula K. LeGuin's* Earthsea trilogy*. Large-eyed and thin, they are truly children of the sea, for they live on large rafts beyond the southernmost islands of Earthsea*. Once a year they come to land at the Long Dune, where the people refit their rafts before they follow the whales north each autumn. After spending the winter apart from each other, the rafts come together again in the spring and drift southward together until it is time to journey northward. Time for these people is a great circle of days. The people marry young, and their children learn to swim as soon as they learn to walk. Nilgu, a type of seaweed, is gathered by both the men and the women and is used for food and to make cloth and rope. Fresh water is a precious commodity. These people have little contact with landsmen, and their first instinct when they come on Ged*, an injured mage, and Arren*, his companion, adrift on the open sea, is to leave them to drift; but the Children of the Open Sea care for them and restore not only their physical but their mental health. In turn Ged and Arren help them when, on the night of the Long Dance*, their chanters forget the songs of the sea that they must chant.

CHIMNEYS OF GREEN KNOWE, THE. Lucy Boston. Illus. Peter Boston. London: Faber and Faber, 1958. 186 pp. British.

When Toseland* (Tolly) comes to Green Knowe* to stay with Mrs. Linnet Oldknow* for the Easter holidays, he finds a change: Toby, Alexander, and Linnet Oldknow***, the three children whose spirits he played with on his last visit to the house, are gone, because Mrs. Oldknow has lent their portrait. She may sell the painting to pay for some of the upkeep of Green Knowe, for the jewels the family once owned and which she would sell before she sold the painting vanished long ago. As Mrs. Oldknow repairs an old family quilt with scraps of material, she tells Tolly about Susan and Sefton Oldknow**, the children of Captain Oldknow*, who lived in the house in the eighteenth century.

The next day Tolly searches for treasure and finds Susan's things in a window seat. He goes to tell Mrs. Oldknow and returns to find a young girl in the room, but she vanishes when he goes down again to Mrs. Oldknow, for, Mrs. Oldknow tells him, it was Susan. That night she tells him more. Susan, being blind, was not allowed to do things for herself for fear she would hurt herself. She was also thought to be an idiot, but she realized more about people than they thought. Captain Oldknow had got her a tutor.

Because his dog, Orlando*, barks under a certain tree much of the time, Tolly decides to climb it; here he finds the initials "S" and "J" carved high in the tree, along with a little hoard of pretty things. The things, Mrs. Oldknow tells him, belonged to Jacob*, the black child Susan's father bought to keep him from slavers and brought to Green Knowe to be Susan's companion. Tolly realizes that the "J" stands for Jacob and that Orlando knows that is Jacob's special tree. He picks some flowers for Susan and takes them upstairs in her mug; she is there when he gets upstairs, but she vanishes.

Mrs. Oldknow tells Tolly more about Jacob and Susan: how Jacob learned lessons with her and how Sefton, Susan's sarcastic older brother, as a joke, ordered for Jacob clothes like those of an organ-grinder's monkey. To get back at him, Jacob stole one of Sefton's buttons and hid it in the tree; he and Susan stole things from Sefton every day to irritate him. Tolly begins to see Jacob, too; he watches as Jacob catches a moorchick for Susan and disappears. The next days are busy, but each ends with a story: one day, sent by Sefton up the chimney to retrieve a wounded duck, Jacob discovered the space just under the roof in the brick wing which Maria Oldknow*, Susan's mother, had added to Green Knowe. Jacob explored the series of chimneys and trapdoors and found one leading into his tiny room; cleaning himself up and going out, he found a dead hen and dropped it down the chimney for Sefton.

One day Tolly's dog brings him an arrow that is not his; when he shoots it, he cannot find it again. Mrs. Oldknow tells him another story about Jacob: finding the hedgehog Tolly had left under a pot for Susan, and hearing him sing but not seeing him, Jacob concluded that Tolly was a ghost, and he and Susan made "juju" to placate him, until they were caught. One afternoon when Mrs. Oldknow is gone, Tolly finds nearby a "hideout" with a tunnel below it, which he follows to a pool of water before returning. By the time he gets out, it is evening, and he goes into the house to find Susan and Jacob there. They are in a quandary; the gardener's son is hiding in the tunnel because he has almost been caught poaching for Caxton*, the malicious butler, and they have no way to take food to him. Tolly takes him a basket of food and then falls asleep in the hideout. He is wakened by Mrs. Oldknow, who tells him what had happened that night so long ago: Captain Oldknow and Maria had come home and heard from Susan what happened; to protect the gardener's son, the Captain made him one of his sailors.

The next tales Tolly hears from Mrs. Oldknow are just as exciting: Jacob made a rope ladder and helped Susan to climb trees. The Captain dismissed Caxton just before leaving on his next sea voyage; Caxton was to leave the next day. That night Maria came home from a party to discover that her jewels were missing. That night, too, the new wing of the house caught fire and burned completely down. Susan, caught there, was rescued by Jacob, who brought her down a chimney. Caxton, however, was lost in the fire. Distraught at the loss of her jewels, Maria asked a gypsy woman how to find them. The woman told her to sew a picture of the house, using hair from the heads of all who were there the day the jewels were lost and saying a charm with each stitch. The picture took two years to stitch, but the jewels were never found.

The last day before he is to leave, Tolly explores under the tiles of the house, where Jacob went, and in a flue leading to an unused room, he finds a sack containing the jewels. The picture of Toby, Alexander, and Linnet is returned. The day Tolly leaves, he again sees Susan and Jacob, and he also sees Toby. Because Susan wants to touch a real deer, Tolly asks him to call his pet deer, and for an instant, though Jacob does not see this, a topiary deer in the garden turns real for Susan to touch. Mrs. Oldknow tells Tolly the end of the tale: Susan grew up to marry her kind tutor; Jacob grew up to have a wife from the Barbados; and both his family and hers were devoted to one another.

CHITTENDEM, LADY, a character in E[dith] Nesbit Bland's* *Five Children and It*. This immensely rich woman tries to kidnap the Lamb* after the Psammead* grants Robert's* wish that everyone would want the child. Later Lady Chittendem's jewels are stolen, and this sparks another unfortunate incident after Jane* wishes her mother would find them. After some hasty and judicious wishes by the children that smooth matters over again, Lady Chittendem "discovers" that the jewels were not stolen, after all.

CHRIS, a character in *A Chance Child*, by Jill Paton Walsh*. Chris is the brother of Pauline* and the half-brother of Creep*. Though their mother abuses Creep, Chris loves him and tries to ameliorate what she does. When Creep escapes from the house, Chris searches for him in the twentieth century; finally, realizing what has happened, he looks through the Parliamentary Papers for records of his brother and finds both the records he seeks and the messages Creep has left behind. Though his mother and Pauline deny that Creep ever existed, Chris cannot deny his brother, and he is glad when he finds that Creep led a rich and happy life in the nineteenth century.

CHRISTINE, a character mentioned in *The Driftway*, by Penelope Lively*. She is the stepmother of Paul* and Sandra*. Christine is a real homebody, doing all she can to make a home for herself, her new husband, and her new step-children. Her husband becomes more visibly happy than he had been before their marriage, but Christine is regarded as an intruder by Paul, who tries to shut her out of his life. Finally he comes to realize how miserable he has been making them all, and he resolves to change his actions toward her.

CHRISTOPHER, ST., the patron saint of travelers in the Catholic calendar. A statue of him carrying the Christ Child on his shoulder stands at the entrance of Green Knowe* in Lucy Boston's* Green Knowe books*. The statue is made around 1120 in order to invoke the saint's protection for Bernard d'Aulneaux, the oldest son of the house, who is far away. The small, quiet sculptor who makes it is a man given to sudden flashes of humor; so talented is he that it seems as if he endows the statue with more than just shape; at least twice in the next eight hundred years the statute moves. Once, in the seventeenth century,

Linnet Oldknow* sees it carry the Child to Christmas Eve Mass; in the twentieth century Toseland* calls on St. Christopher to protect him from evil Green Noah*, and the statue is seen moving after Green Noah is destroyed. Because Bernard had come home safely, a chapel was built and dedicated to St. Christopher at Green Knowe; though by the twentieth century this chapel is ruined, the statue, weathered, still stands. Behind it Mrs. Linnet Oldknow* hides a disgusting object Dr. Melanie Delia Powers* tries to use to curse the house.

CHRONICLES OF NARNIA, seven books by C[live] S[taples] Lewis* which have the magical land of Narnia* as their locale. *See The Magician's Nephew; The Lion, the Witch, and the Wardrobe; Prince Caspian; The Voyage of the "Dawntreader"; The Silver Chair; The Horse and His Boy; The Last Battle*

CHRONICLES OF PRYDAIN, a five-book cycle of stories by Lloyd Alexander*, concerning the imaginary land of Prydain*. *See The Book of Three; The Black Cauldron; The Castle of Llyr; Taran Wanderer; The High King.* Related works include *Coll and His White Pig, The Truthful Harp,* and *The Foundling, and Other Tales of Prydain.*

CHRYSOSTOME, ODILE, a character mentioned in Eleanor Cameron's* *The Court of the Stone Children*. She was the daughter of Jean Louise Baptiste Chrysostome, a painter, and his wife; she was the sister of Gabrielle, Cyprian, and Simone; and she was the wife of a farmer named Hyppolyte Calome Carondel. Odile was born in France around 1787. When she was fifteen she began to keep a journal. Odile had always been fond of her father's friend, Clovis Antoine de Lombre* (Kot), but when she was about seventeen, she realized that she loved him as a woman loves a man. Odile did not reveal her love to Kot until December of 1804, when they realized their love for each other and made plans to marry. Odile's father painted a picture of them coming in to tell the family the news. Kot was a critic of Napoleon, and on 10 December 1804, a week after their betrothal, he was executed for a murder he did not commit. Four days later Odile heard the news. Heartbroken, she did not protest the marriage with Carondel which her father arranged for her. Because the Chrysostome family was pledged to secrecy about Kot's visit to them, they could not reveal that he had been with them the night the murder took place. Odile's journal is later published, but because she had used the initial "K" for Kot's nickname, instead of his real name, no reader has realized that the journal proves Kot's innocence. Only in the twentieth century, when the painting is discovered, does Mrs. Helena Hampton Staynes* realize that the "K" of the journals is not Julien Korin but Antoine de Lombre.

CHUCK MADDOX (*A Swiftly Tilting Planet*). *See* Maddox, Chuck

CIBOTLÁN, a powerful empire in twelfth-century America, the scourge of Abáloc* in Jane Louise Curry's* *The Daybreakers** and *Over the Sea's Edge**. Cibotlán's influence extends over most of the Ohio River Valley and further south. In this empire are seven cities: Natilchizcó, Tushcloshán*, Etowán, Cutivachcó, Ranoacán, Quanatilcó*, and Tucrikán. The people of Cibotlán worship the Sun Serpent (Katóa*), to which they offer up human sacrifice. For this purpose the rulers of Cibotlán demand and get a tithe of children from the tribes absorbed into the empire. Cibotlán is ruled by seven priest-kings. The people of Cibotlán tattoo their bodies according to their rank, with simple patterns or complex designs. The Cibotlán influence is responsible for the mounds in Moundsville, West Virginia. The empire falls in the twelfth century when a terrible plague sweeps its cities.

CICELY ANN TABERNER (*A Traveller in Time*). *See* Taberner, Cicely Ann

CICELY TABERNER (*A Traveller in Time*). *See* Taberner, Cicely

CITY OF THE MOON UNDER THE MOUNTAIN (Nūtayē; Avel Timrel), a place in Jane Louise Curry's* Abáloc novels*. It is an ancient haven in what is now the Pennsylvania mountains. In the beginning of time it was called *Te Aveli te Mirel Issur Garath*, or Avel Timrel; in fourth-century Abáloc* it is called *A Tunom ir Tlegro ten'a Manat*; in the twelfth century it is known as *Dunom o'r Plagro Tan'e Menet*, or Nūtayē. In all ages its name is translated as "City of the Moon Under the Mountain." In this great, beautiful cave, at the beginning of time, rested Mirelidar*, the moon, one of twelve powerful sky-stones*. Avel Timrel was built in the caves of Rothin under Uval Garath, the Opal Mountain, by Basadil and his followers, who were of a magical race called the Silvrin. After the War of the Silvrin against Aam, the Wolves of Aam* lived here and, later, when ice had covered the land, Basadil and his people left, sealing the cave. In the second age of Abáloc, the Aldar*, another magical race, had gone to the City of the Moon, gathering here before journeying to lands beyond the world. In the fourth century, Abalockians again had taken refuge in the City, but they had left at the urging of an oracle at the shrine of Katóa*, a great evil. In the twelfth century Erilla*, an Abalockian queen, and her people go to the City, accompanied by Dewi ap Ithil* and other Welsh explorers who have come to North America, but they do not stay long in the City's empty halls. They leave behind in the City the *Book of the Kings of Abáloc**. It is found in the sixteenth century by a band of *y Tylwyth Teg**, Welsh Fair Folk*, who get lost in their journey to Tir na'nOg*, the Fortunate Isles, and take refuge in the City. They live here until the twentieth century, ever wary of an evil force that is imprisoned in the mountain. In the twentieth century Margaret Arthur* and her cousins help the Folk to resume their journey. To protect the City, the Folk seal all entrances to it.

CLARA CORRY (*Mary Poppins; Mary Poppins Opens the Door*). *See* Corry, Clara

CLARKE, PAULINE (1921–   ), British writer. Pauline Clarke was born 19 May 1921, at Kirkby-in-Ashfield, to Charles Leopold and Dorothy Kathleen (Milum) Clarke. She graduated from Somerville College, Oxford, with a B.A. with honors. Clarke married Peter Hunter Blaire in February, 1969. A free-lance writer since 1948, Clarke has written children's books, short stories, and plays for adults, and has been a book reviewer for the *Times Literary Supplement*.

Though she has written several books for children under her own name and that of "Helen Clare," it is for *The Twelve and the Genii**, winner of the Carnegie Medal for 1962, that Clarke is most often cited. Her works include volumes of poetry, works of historical fiction, and several doll stories. *The Twelve and the Genii* is of this last genre but transcends it, treating of creativity and the nature of genius.

The Twelve (Twelves*) of the title are twelve wooden soldiers once owned by Branwell Brontë. Invested with personalities by their owner and his sisters, Anne, Emily, and Charlotte, the soldiers were led through adventures the four made up for them. So great were the children's imaginations and the powers of their genius that the soldiers not only came to life but became individuals in their own right. The Twelves seem to be less toys able to move and speak as real people, than real people able to freeze into toys at the first hint of danger. Such are the dignity of Butter Crashey*, the bravery of Stumps*, the confidence of Cheeky, and the moroseness of Gravey—for whom nothing goes right—that they become, for the reader, more than toy soldiers; they become small individuals with all the rights thereof. The creative powers of the Brontë children invested them with movement and life; the genius of the children invested them with souls. Thus the title by which the Twelves know the children—as Genii—is apt in both its senses; the Brontës are the magical beings who guard and govern the little soldiers' lives, and they are also the inspiring powers who give life to them.

Because the Twelves are soldiers, they are brave, willing to take any chance for the sake of adventure—except, of course, for poor Gravey. But perhaps because they were brought to life by children, they have the flexibility of childhood, and are able to accommodate changes in their lives. For the soldiers, dying and being brought back to life are not incredible, though they are unusual. When Frederic I dies and is brought to life again as Frederic II, the unlikeliness of the action is not commented upon by the soldiers; rather, his change is another adventure in a world of adventures. For if the soldiers have the flexible minds of children, they also have a child's sense that life is a series of adventures. Because they are so small, all things *are* adventures: descending a flight of stairs has all the danger of an Alpine exploration. But these little men have a sort of "heroic" attitude about life—that it is one big adventure to be savored. Like the knights of old or the heroes of epic tales, the Twelves do not let a chance for excitement go by unexplored, and when they feast or play they do it with intensity and verve. These devil-may-care young men are noble, but delightful. Their courage is the courage of soldiers, but their playfulness and supple imaginations are those of children playing a game of let's pretend.

Though the Twelves are small, because they are such realistic little individuals they command respect. Max Morley* is like an adult with them, worrying over them, helping them, seeing to their happiness. He treats them almost as a child would wish adults to treat him; Max guides, protects, and advises the Twelves, but he does not interfere or take over their actions. To do so might make them freeze forever into wooden soldiers, but to do so would also betray the trust they have in him and negate their dignity as individuals.

This is a well realized fantasy convincing in all its details. The soldiers seem to be soldiers of the early nineteenth century, no other time; events reported as they see them seem absolutely right. Characters in the tale are three-dimensional, and the story moves swiftly and smoothly to a satisfying conclusion.

Works

Juvenile fantasy: *The Twelve and the Genii* (1962) as *The Return of the Twelves* (America). Juvenile non-fantasy, short stories, etc.: *The Pekinese Princess* (1948); *The Great Car* (1952); *The White Elephant* (1952); *Five Dolls in a House* (1953), as Helen Clare; *Merlin's Magic* (1953), as Helen Clare; *Smith's Hoard* (1955) as *The Golden Collar* (1967); *Bel the Giant, and Other Stories* (1956), as Helen Clare; *The Boy with the Erpingham Hood* (1956); *Five Dolls and the Monkey* (1956), as Helen Clare; *Sandy the Sailor* (1956); *Five Dolls in the Snow* (1957), as Helen Clare; *Hidden Gold* (1957); *James, the Policeman* (1957); *Five Dolls and Their Friends* (1959), as Helen Clare; *James and the Robbers* (1959); *Poems from Sherwood Forest* (1959); *Torolv the Fatherless* (1959); *The Lord of the Castle* (1960); *The Robin Hooders* (1960); *Seven White Pebbles* (1960), as Helen Clare; *James and the Smugglers* (1961); *Keep the Pot Boiling* (1961); *Silver Bells and Cockle Shells* (1962), poetry; *Five Dolls and the Duke* (1963), as Helen Clare; *James and the Black Van* (1963); *Crowds of Creatures* (1964); *The Bonfire Party* (1966); *The Two Faces of Silenus* (1972).

Secondary Works

Clarke, Pauline. "The Chief Genii Branwell," *Junior Bookshelf*, 27 (July, 1963), pp. 119–23.

CLEWAREK, DURHAM (DREAM), a character in Jane Louise Curry's* *The Watchers**. He is married to Star; he is the father of Rainelle, June Ann, Mary-Mary, and Jody. Dream is Ray Siler's* uncle. It is he who takes the boy in when he is sent to live away from home. Dream gets his name through a slurring of his real name and because he always seems to be in a dream.

CLIFFE, HARRY, a character in *Poor Tom's Ghost**, by Jane Louise Curry*. This Elizabethan actor is determined to steal Katherine Purfet Garland* from her husband, Tom Garland*. Harry's deception with Jack Garland*, Tom's brother, starts the events that culminate in Tom's unhappy ghost haunting Castle Cox*.

CLOCK, ARRIETTY, a character in Mary Norton's* Borrower series*. She is the daughter of Pod and Homily Clock**. Arrietty is a borrower*, one of a race of miniature people who "borrow" what they need from humans. She and her family live beneath the kitchen of a country manor that once housed many borrowers. Because humans are dangerous to the tiny people, Arrietty is never allowed outside her home, and she grows up longing for the freedom of the outdoors, which she can glimpse through a grating. When she is fourteen, Arrietty gets what she longs for after she and her family are discovered and barely escape with their lives. They take to the surrounding fields and, helped by Dreadful Spiller* (Spiller), finally find relatives who take them in. Forced to leave this place as well, Arrietty and her parents make their way to Little Fordham*, a borrower-sized village, where they live in comfort until they are captured by Sidney Platter*. After the family escapes from Mr. Platter, the borrowers decided to move to a mill to live. By this time Arrietty is almost seventeen and, to Homily's horror, she vows to marry Spiller, preferring his adventurous life outdoors to a staid, tame one in a house. Arrietty's longing for adventure leads her to speak to humans, something no borrower should ever do because of the danger involved; Pod finally makes her promise not to do it again. And she does not. When the Clocks go to live in a quiet rectory, Arrietty is very happy, learning to borrow and living in freedom. Here she also loses her fear of ghosts, for the rectory has three. Having learned caution from her family and friends, Arrietty does not try to talk to humans again.

CLOCK, GRANDFATHER, an object in Philippa Pearce's* *Tom's Midnight Garden**. It stands in the hall of the house which had once belonged to the Melbourne family in Victorian times and which has been divided into flats owned by Harriet Melbourne Bartholomew* (Hatty). On the clock's dial is pictured an angel with one foot on water and one on land, holding a book open before his glowing face. Below him is written the citation for the Bible chapter and verse in which he appears: Revelations X:1-6. On the pendulum of the clock is written "Time no longer." The clock seems sometimes to take this literally, for though it keeps good time, it strikes whatever hour it chooses. When the house is sold after Hatty's aunt dies, the clock goes with it, for the screws that hold it to the wall have rusted so badly that it cannot be moved. In the twentieth century, Tom Long*, a boy staying at one of the flats, learns that when the clock strikes thirteen he can go downstairs and into the Victorian age, where he and Hatty provide companionship for each other.

CLOCK, HOMILY, a character in the Borrower series*, by Mary Norton*. She is the wife of Pod Clock* and the mother of Arrietty Clock*. Homily is a borrower*, one of a race of miniature people who "borrow" what they need from humans. Her maiden name was Bell-Pull. When Homily married Pod, she had a pleasant time being rich; this lasted until their home flooded and Pod got sick, and Homily was forced to give away their things in return for help from other borrowers. Homily says she is not house-proud, but she does like a well-ordered room with elegant furnishings, though she is happy enough in her snug, plain home under the kitchen. Cursed with a nervous temperament, Homily does not mind being shut away from the freedom of the outdoors, which she equates with insects, snakes, and danger. When the family is discovered at Firbanks, however, Homily is forced to take to the fields with the others. Complaining sometimes even when she explains she is not complaining, Homily nevertheless rises to the occasion and makes the best of things. She is ecstatic, however, when the family comes to Little Fordham*, a miniature village, and she has a proper house again. When Pod insists that the family move on to a quiet mill where it will be safer, though, Homily agrees. When the family moves into a quiet rectory instead, however, Homily is happy to have a roof over her head and is particularly proud of the kitchen that Pod rigs up for her. Now Homily quietly lords it over her more opulent sister-in-law.

CLOCK, POD, a character in Mary Norton's* Borrower series*. He is the husband of Homily Clock* and the father of Arrietty Clock*. Pod is a borrower*, one of a race of miniature people who live by "borrowing" what they need. His family has always lived beneath the kitchen of Firbanks, a country manor. Pod is better educated than his father, being able to count almost to a thousand. He makes shoes and is an excellent borrower; when he was young, Pod could walk the length of the humans' dining room table after the gong was rung and take something from every dish before the diners arrived. Later he borrows many things from the bedridden old woman who owns Firbanks. He walks on her bed and talks to her; she thinks Pod comes out of the decanter of Fine Old Pale Madeira she drinks every evening. Because of his skill, Pod and his family are the last to leave Firbanks after the borrowings become lean, and then it is only because the family is in danger. When the borrowers take to a nearby field, Pod's ingenuity is taxed again and again as he strives to keep his family safe and fed. Borrowing is Pod's life; when his family takes refuge with relatives and he is not allowed to borrow, he becomes unhappy. Nor is he happy when the family moves to a toy village and he learns that humans know where they live. At Pod's insistence, they move on to a quiet rectory where he happily resumes borrowing and uses his ingenuity to create a special home for his family.

CLOUGH, LUCY, a character in Penelope Lively's* *The Wild Hunt of Hagworthy**. She is the niece of Mabel Clough; her parents are divorced and Lucy lives with her father. When Aunt Mabel invites her to spend the summer with her at Hagworthy, Lucy is nervous at the thought of reacquainting herself with the people she had known there five years before, particularly Kester Lang*. Things soon prove more difficult than she might have imagined, for Kester has grown into a rude, sarcastic youth and the girls Lucy had known are interested only in horses. There is an uneasy tension, too, between Kester and the other boys in the village; and Lucy is caught in the middle as tension rises and strange things happen in the weeks before the Horn Dance*, long associated with the Wild Hunt*, takes place. Though she does not understand what is going on, Lucy tries to protect Kester. She succeeds on the day of the Dance by stopping the dancers before he can be hurt, and by keeping him from the Hunt when it comes upon him.

CLOVIS ANTOINE DE LOMBRE (*The Court of the Stone Children*). See de Lombre, Clovis Antoine

CLUMP, SARAH (MRS.), a character in P[amela] L[yndon] Travers's* *Mary Poppins Opens the Door**. She is a landlady in London; Mr. Fred Twigley* is her tenant. Unpleasant, greedy Mrs. Clump wants to marry Mr. Twigley because on certain days he has seven wishes come true; she wants him to wish for them a golden palace and peacock pie. Finally one day he does, but he wishes for it his way; she becomes a tiny mechanical person in a tiny golden palace, eating a tiny tin pie each time a penny is dropped into the slot Mr. Twigley fixes on the side of the palace—part of the entertainment on Brighton Pier.

COALA, a character in *Over the Sea's Edge**, by Jane Louise Curry*. She is the sister of Tochtlú; she becomes the wife of Madauc* and the mother of Rien. Coala is a princess in twelfth-century Cibotlán* and a priestess of the serpent cult. When Tochtlú is to be sacrificed to the Sun Serpent (Katóa*), she flees with him, coming upon the band of Welshmen seeking gold with Madauc, a dispossessed prince in Wales. Convinced that blond Madauc is the god Matec, she guides him to Abáloc*, where there is a powerful oracle. Puzzled at Madauc's search for gold and disappointed to find that he is not a god, Coala is attracted to Madauc and marries him when he returns from a journey to Wales. Unhappy in Cibotlán, Coala finds true happiness in Abáloc.

COB, a character in *The Farthest Shore**, by Ursula K. LeGuin*. Though the people of Earthsea* thought he was only a sorcerer, Cob was a great mage, able to summon the spirits of the dead. Once he was seen doing this by Ged*, a sorcerer, who in anger dragged Cob into the land of the dead, terrifying him so that he promised never to do it again. After his experience, Cob went to the island of Paln. He was not humbled, as Ged thought, but, having seen death, he had made up his mind to refuse it and cast a spell that would allow him to journey between the worlds of life and death. In this casting he dies, but a doorway is opened between the lands of the living and the dead, and through this door Cob journeys back to life. Here he terrifies the living and promises them eternal life; using their fear, he is able to draw from them magic and life. For, though Cob exists, he has lost his selfhood and seeks to regain it by drawing the world after him into the land of death. Disturbed by the leaching out of magic and vitality from the people of Earthsea and the madness and listlessness this has caused, Ged, now an Archmage, journeys to Selidor* and follows Cob far into the land of death. He closes the door at the cost of his own powers.

COB, THE, a character in *The Trumpet of the Swan**, by E[lwyn] B[rooks] White*. He is the father of Louis* and of several other cygnets. The cob is a trumpeter swan and proud of the fact, taking every opportunity to express his satisfaction with his place in the world. More than a little vain, he is also quite verbose and fond of stringing together well-turned phrases. Though the cob has a very fine voice, his son, Louis, cannot speak. Desperate to help him, the cob flies through the window of a music shop in Billings, Montana, and steals a trumpet so Louis will be able to communicate with the other swans. Louis's conscience bothers him, however, and he works to earn enough money to repay the storekeeper. When the cob comes to give the money to the man, the store-keeper, thinking his store is again being attacked, shoots the cob, who is rushed to a hospital. His wound is only superficial, and he flies home.

COBHAM, MATTHEW, a character in *The Driftway**, by Penelope Lively*. He is the son of William Cobham; his brother is also named William. Seven-teenth-century Matthew is of Colchester, England. Believing he can no longer simply stand aside in the civil war, Matthew becomes a musketeer in Denzil Holles's force, on the Parliamentary side. His first battle is fought at Edgehill, near the town of Kineton. It is an experience so shocking that Matthew will never forget it; finally he throws down his gun and runs away. Though he hears that his side has won the battle, Matthew feels that he has really lost. So shocked has he been that his story becomes a shadow on the driftway* he wanders, to be re-experienced in the twentieth century by Paul*, a runaway traveling the road.

COLE, KING, a nursery rhyme figure who appears as a character in *Mary Poppins Opens the Door**, by P[amela] L[yndon] Travers*. A handsome, robust, loving man who lives in a crystal palace, he wooed and won his queen. Then, in the midst of comparing her eyes to stars, her cheeks to roses, and her teeth to pearls, he had begun to wonder about stars, roses, and pearls and to seek to find out about them and a great many other things, too. He neglects his queen and his people, studying his books so hard that he becomes short-sighted, thin, and prematurely old. Mice infest the palace and its crystal walls become dim because the servants and courtiers are kept busy thinking; the queen grows lonely. The king learns so much that he becomes absent-minded. One day a white cat* comes to the palace, and after a contest of wisdom with it, King Cole realizes that he is not the wisest man in the world after all, and that with all his knowledge he does not know himself. By looking into the cat's eyes, he learns that he is not a thinking man but a merry old soul; he grows cheerful and handsome and young, calls for his pipe and his bowl, and sets his fiddlers three to fiddling. Forever after his subjects make merry, sing, and love one another dearly, because it is law.

COLIN, a character in *The Weirdstone of Brisingamen** and *The Moon of Gomrath**, by Alan Garner*. He is the brother of Susan*. When their parents go abroad for six months Colin and Susan go to Alderley Edge to stay with Bess and Gowther Mossock*. Here they have adventures with wizards and witchcraft as they return a powerful stone to its rightful owner and seek to re-imprison an ancient evil. Colin finds his adventure exhilirating and finds great beauty in the world of magic. He accidentally calls up the Wild Hunt*; he also follows one of the ancient roads to pluck the Mothan*, a magic flower, to help Susan.

COLL, a character in the Chronicles of Prydain* and *Coll and His White Pig*, by Lloyd Alexander*. He is the son of Collfreur. Once a mighty warrior, Coll was sickened by the violence and bloodshed and settled down on a small farm, Caer Dallben*. Here he concerned himself with raising turnips instead of war and was quite happy. Once, when Hen Wen*, his oracular pig, is kidnapped and taken to Annuvin*, realm of the evil lord of death, Coll rescues her. When Dallben*, a wizard, comes to live at the farm, Coll cheerfully works for him, helping him raise Taran*, an orphan. Coll loves the land and his work and tries to teach Taran the arts of farming and crafts useful to a farmer, though the boy is sometimes a difficult pupil. Much as he dislikes it, Coll joins the battle against Arawn* when that evil king tries to gain control over Prydain*. On the final campaign he is killed and is buried at Red Fallows, a once-rich land made barren by war.

COLLET, ALAN, a character in *Poor Tom's Ghost**, by Jane Louise Curry*. He is the husband of Jemima. Alan's research helps to uncover the ultimate destinies of Jack, Tom, and Katherine Purfet Garland***, three Elizabethans whose destinies become entwined with Tony Nicholas*, a twentieth-century actor friend of Alan's.

CONWAY, JEFFERSON D., a character in E[dith] Nesbit Bland's* *The Enchanted Castle**. This American millionaire hears that Yalding Castle* is for rent and decides to try it—provided it has a ghost. When Mabel Prowse* uses a magic ring* to provide one, though, Mr. Conway, though impressed by the ghost, finds it too lively and "ill-mannered" for his liking. He decides not to rent the castle after all.

COOK, THE, a character in *The Phoenix and the Carpet**, by E[dith] Nesbit Bland*. This woman with a tart disposition has her patience worn thin by the antics of Robert*, Anthea*, Cyril*, and Jane*. When the children use a wishing carpet* to take their brother to a tropical island to get over his whooping cough, the cook is accidentally taken along. She thinks the journey is a marvelous dream, especially when the natives proclaim her their queen and beg her to stay with them. In this relaxed and relaxing land, the cook is happy, gently ruling her subjects and teaching them the rudiments of cooking. When the children bring a burglar* to the island to escape unjust punishment, the cook marries him.

COOKSON, HENRY (THE OLD FELLER), a ghost in Robert Westall's* *The Watch House**. He was born in 1844 in Garmouth, England. When he was ten years old, Henry witnessed the murder of Major Scobie Hague* for a boxful of gold. Henry never told anyone, and later went to where the box was buried and dug it up, perhaps taking one or two coins left inside. The murder and his feeling of being somehow as guilty as the thieves preyed on him, and he did all he could to repay Hague, gradually replacing the money in the box, founding the Garmouth Volunteer Life Brigade in 1870, and working to make safer the rocks on which the ships wreck. In doing so Henry became a man driven by an obsession. Having inherited a fine business, married, and had three children, Henry seemed set for life. But the Brigade took all his time and he lost his business and family. Though Henry lost all trying to placate Hague, Hague became ever more powerful for the frail little man; Henry's guilt built Hague into a monster that haunted him. After Henry caught rheumatic fever, his heart went bad. Finally, one stormy night in 1903, from inside the Watch House* on the cliff, Henry was so terrorized by Hague that he died of heart failure. He haunts the Watch House after that, making sounds and moving things and being ignored by the men on the Life Brigade, who affectionately call him "the Old Feller." Still he is haunted by Hague. When Anne Melton*, a lonely girl needing someone to help and protect, comes to the Watch House, Henry gets her attention. The attention Anne and her friends, Pat Pierson* and Timothy Jones*, pay to Henry gives him more power than before, and his manifestations become more violent. Finally Hague's ghost is laid and Henry departs, not to be seen or heard from again.

COOPER, SUSAN [MARY] (1935–   ), American writer. She was born on 23 May 1935, in Burnham, Buckinghamshire, to John Richard and Ethel May (Field) Cooper. She was educated at Somerville College, Oxford. On 3 August 1963 she married Nicholas J. Grant; they have a son and a daughter. Cooper has been a reporter for the *Sunday Times*, London, as well as being a free-lance writer in New York.

Although she is also the author of a historical novel and a picture book for children, Cooper is probably most famous for her five high fantasies, The Dark

Is Rising series*, set in the British Islands but touching on worlds beyond the ken of humans. Much of the action takes place in the physical landscape of our own world, but it is a landscape transformed, remembering its mythic past, and beneath the level of day-to-day living lie magic and mystery. At the beginning of the world, magic was in everything, and the memory seems to dwell here still. In a lake where King Arthur* once defeated a monster, the beast still lives; in the Chiltern Hills of England grows a tree that can be seen only once every seven hundred years; a cleft in a mountain opens into a realm of magic.

Through this landscape move figures of myth and magic: Herne* the Hunter leads the Wild Hunt* each Twelfth Night; Tethys, the Lady of the Sea, dwells in its dark reaches; and six warriors sleep in the Welsh mountains. Other powers dwell there, too, and fight a long, hard battle with each other: the good Old Ones of the Light, and the evil Lords of the Dark. They are opposites, ancient and eternal, and have been fighting each other since the beginning of the world. Neither force can hurt or destroy individuals of the other; they seek instead to gain control of forces already in the world, of the magic in the land and of men's souls. Only thus can the balance of power between the two be altered and one defeat the other on Earth.

Throughout the history of the world they have struggled to control men's minds. The Old Ones are born of humans but are more than human, for they are also born into their destinies as forces of the Light. As such they are in the world but not of it; they serve an absolute good that is above the charity and good-heartedness we admire in our world and that is, rather, like the all-consuming white fire of the sun or the sharp blade of justice; it destroys evil but can also destroy what is not evil. It is keen and nothing can withstand it. An Old One cannot let his own feelings stand in the way of the triumph of the Light; Will Stanton*, one of the Old Ones, is made ill by the Light so that he may be in the proper place at the proper time. This is hard for humans to accept, because immediate deeds are all they can see, and the future good is hidden. The Light has influenced history in subtle ways and has kept alive the force of good in men in the times when the Dark has held the land. Those who have invaded Britain wreak the havoc the Dark desires, but the Light eventually gentles them and wins them to the land. The Lords of the Dark create themselves. They are not evil from birth but make themselves so; only the Black Rider* has been in the world from its beginning. The Dark cannot hurt those related to the Old Ones, but it can cause them to hurt themselves, as Will discovers when his mother is made to fall down some steps. Using magic, the Lords of the Dark can insinuate their will into someone else's, as the Black Rider does to Will's mother and sister. But the Dark has other, subtler means as well. Its minions can play on men's souls by offering things the Light will not. The Light is a harsh force to follow, and so is the Dark, but the Light makes no promises and does not seek to hide its harshness; the Dark has no such scruples. Hawkin*, though of the Light, is tempted into the service of the Dark by the blandishments of a young witch. The extremes of emotion can also be used by the Dark. Blind hate creates a channel through which the Dark can take over a man's mind, and so does blind idealism. Caradog Prichard's* hate-twisted soul can thus be used by the Grey King*. Whether the Dark or the Light controls a person depends on the choices that person makes, consciously or not.

Just as the human mind can be in the service of the Light or the Dark, so can the Wild Magic, High Magic, or Old Magic of the land. All are neutral, existing only for themselves and making no conscious choice between the Light and the Dark. They exist beyond the struggle between the two. Herne rides the winter sky because he must, and the Greenwitch's* wild power is only an extension of itself; the golden harp* of High Magic releases its power for whoever holds it, and the midsummer tree* flowers for itself. These are the forces of the land itself and are neutral because nature is neither bad nor good. The powers of Herne and the Greenwitch, the harp and the midsummer tree are not consciously turned to the Dark or the Light by themselves but can be used by whoever gets to them. Herne's cruelty is turned toward the Dark because the Light wakes him, and the harp must be won in a contest judged by three lords before the Light gets its use. The power of the midsummer tree will be turned toward whomever cuts its flower. The Greenwitch's Wild Magic overcomes the man of the Dark who tries to control it, but the memory of the pity of a young girl turns it to the service of the Light.

By controlling powers of magic and people, the Light turns the balance and defeats the Dark, but the battle is not over. The Lords of the Dark fall out of time and the Old Ones leave the world, to rest and to do battle in other places, but the battle between good and evil still goes on and will go on as long as humans remain. Man is left to take care of himself in a world imperfect because he is imperfect. Magic is gone and will not help him, and he must do his best. The Dark will not work its wiles on the human mind, but human frailty might accomplish what the Dark had desired. Yet as long as the good in human beings remains, the world will survive.

Cooper's five books are rich and uneven. The use of tradition and of altered tradition gives them the resonance of myth. Prose is richly descriptive. Characterization is a problem; the depiction of the Drew children and of the Stantons is very true to life, but that of the forces of the Light and the Dark is less well realized and believable. In places the works are vague and confusing; conversation and, sometimes, the prose itself seem stilted.

Works

Juvenile full-length fantasy: *Over Sea, Under Stone* (1965); *The Dark Is Rising* (1973); *Greenwitch* (1974); *The Grey King* (1975); *Silver on the Tree* (1977); *Seaward* (1983) [not included].

Juvenile novel and picture book: *Dawn of Fear* (1970), novel; *Jethro and the Jumbie* (1979), picture book; *The Silver Cow* (1983).

Adult: *Mandrake* (1964), novel; *Behind the Gold Curtain* (1965); *J. B. Priestley: Portrait of an Author* (1970).

Secondary Works

Cooper, Susan. "Escaping into Ourselves," in *Celebrating Children's Books*, ed. Betsy Hearne and Marilyn Kaye (New York: Lothrop, Lee and Shepard Books, 1981), pp. 14–23.
———. "Newbery Award Acceptance," *The Horn Book Magazine*, 52 (Aug., 1976), pp. 361–66.
Gilderdale, Betty. "Susan Cooper, *The Dark Is Rising*, and the Legends," *Children's Literature Association Yearbook*, 1978, pp. 11–23.
McElderry, Margaret K. "Susan Cooper," *The Horn Book Magazine*, 52 (Aug., 1976), pp. 367–72.
Philip, Neil. "Fantasy: Double Cream or Instant Whip?" *Signal*, 35 (May, 1981), pp. 82–90.

COR (SHASTA), a character in *The Horse and His Boy** and *The Last Battle**, by C[live] S[taples] Lewis*. He is the son of King Lune*; he is the twin brother of Corin*. Cor becomes the husband of Aravis* and the father of Ram the Great. He was born in Archenland*. When he was a week old, Cor and his brother were taken to a centaur to be blessed; the centaur prophesied that Cor would save Archenland from its greatest danger. Lord Bar, an unscrupulous courtier in the pay of the king of Calormen*, decided that the child must be put out of the way because of the prophecy, so he kidnapped Cor and put out to sea. After a hard chase, Lune captured Bar's ship in battle. But the child and one of Bar's knights had already been set adrift in a tiny boat; the dead knight and the living child were found by Arsheesh, a Calormene fisherman who named the child Shasta and raised him as his own. There is no love lost between the two, and when Anradin, a Calormene noble, offers to buy the boy, Arsheesh agrees. Warned by Breehy-hinny-brinny-hoohy-hah*, Anradin's talking horse, of the man's cruelty, Shasta flees with the horse to Narnia*, the magical land to the north. On the way they meet Aravis and her horse, Hwin*, and, aided by Aslan*, Narnia's great lion-protector, Shasta comes to Archenland just in time to warn Lune of an impending Calormene invasion, thus saving the land from a great danger. To his dismay Cor is educated and eventually becomes king.

CORIAKIN, a character in C[live] S[taples] Lewis's* *The Voyage of the "Dawn Treader"**. Once a star, he committed a crime and was put onto the island of the Dufflepuds* as punishment. Here he is a great magician living in a large house on the island. He rules and tries to teach the lazy, stubborn Dufflepuds, though they do not appreciate his lessons. When they become fractious and refuse to do his bidding—though it is for their own good—Coriakin makes the conceited little dwarfs* into creatures with one leg and an enormous foot, and they admire him even less than before. Strict as he is with the Dufflepuds, he is quite fond of them and is a kindly man at heart. He welcomes Caspian X* and his companions into his home and makes a magical feast for them, sending them on their way with a map magically drawn from their descriptions of the lands they have seen and explored.

CORIN, a character in *The Horse and His Boy** and *The Last Battle**, by C[live] S[taples] Lewis*. He is the son of King Lune*; he is the twin brother of Cor*. Rambunctious, impulsive, adventurous Corin is as good at getting out of scrapes as he is at getting into them. He grows up expecting to inherit the throne of Archenland*, though he is younger than Cor by a few minutes, for Cor has been missing since soon after their birth. Corin accompanies Susan and Edmund Pevensie** when they travel to Tashbaan, in Calormen*, at the request of the prince there; here he defends Susan's honor when a Calormene boy slights it, by knocking down the boy (twice) and his older brother (once) and then getting away from the Watch. He meets Shasta, a young boy who is really Cor, and thinks of the great fun they would have being mistaken for one another, but Corin helps Shasta get on his way. Corin is present at the subsequent battle in Archenland when the Calormene army tries to invade it, though he is told not to be. When Shasta is revealed as Cor, Corin is very pleased, for now he can have fun and will not have to take the throne. Corin is very good at boxing; when he grows up he is called "Corin Thunder-fist," for he boxes the Lapsed Bear of Stormness into submission during a match of thirty-three rounds. A song is made of this adventure. Corin is among those in the country of Aslan*, Narnia's* great lion-protector, when Narnia comes to an end.

CORNELIUS, DOCTOR, a character in C[live] S[taples] Lewis's* *Prince Caspian*. He is part dwarf* and part human, but he passes successfully as human. Cornelius has much wisdom and a little magic; he uses both to find the hunting horn* of Susan Pevensie*, left behind in Narnia* when she went back to her home on Earth long before. Cornelius becomes the tutor of Caspian X*, a young prince whose throne has been usurped by his uncle, Miraz*. From Cornelius the boy learns of his true heritage and of the old Narnians, the talking beasts and magical creatures that had been killed or gone into hiding when the conquerors from Telmar* took over Narnia. When Miraz decides that Caspian must die, Cornelius helps the boy escape and, later, he helps him gain the throne. Because of his ancestry Cornelius is not immediately trusted by the true dwarfs, but they soon find he can be trusted. Cornelius becomes one of Caspian's best advisers.

CORRY, CLARA (MRS.), a character in *Mary Poppins** and *Mary Poppins Opens the Door**, by P[amela] L[yndon] Travers*. She is the mother of Fannie and Annie Corry. Though she is a spring chicken compared with her grandmother, Mrs. Corry was barely out of her teens when the world was created. She remembers this and everything that has happened since. Mrs. Corry has advised King Solomon, listened to William the Conqueror, danced with Henry VIII*, and learned what Guy Fawkes had for dinner every second Sunday. She is also a good friend of Albert Wigg* and Mary Poppins*. When Jane Caroline and Michael George Banks** meet Mrs. Corry, she sells gingerbread made from a recipe she got from Alfred the Great, a good cook though once he burned the cakes. Now a peppery little old woman, Mrs. Corry still moves quickly and gaily and completely terrorizes her two gigantic daughters. Mrs. Corry's fingers are sweets, and when she breaks one off, another immediately grows in its place. Her customers pay her by sticking coins onto her black coat. After selling gingerbread stars to the children, she comes in the night and, with Mary Poppins, glues the gilt paper stars from the cookies onto the sky.

COUNTRY AT THE BACK OF THE NORTH WIND, THE, the title place in George MacDonald's* *At the Back of the North Wind**. This country lies behind the North Wind*, and entrance into it through her is bone-piercingly cold. Several people have been here: Herodotus, Durante, Kilmeny, and Diamond*, a young London boy. It is different for each. In the country, it is always spring. Though there is no sun or moon, the country is filled with light. Here flowers bloom and a river flows over grass, singing a song into the hearts of the people who live here. The people whom others think they have lost live in this country; though they are not sad, they are not happy, but they know they will be some day. They communicate without words, and all they wish is good, for none can want anything bad. If anyone wishes to see how those he has left behind are, all he must do is climb a certain tree, from which his loved ones can be seen. Lovely as this country seems to Diamond, it is really lovelier still; on his journey he had not seen the real country, only a picture of it. Finally the North Wind takes Diamond to her country to stay forever; his parents and friends think he has died.

COUNTRY OF THE NODDING MANDARINS, a place in Mrs. Mary Molesworth's* *The Cuckoo Clock**. This country behind the Chinese cabinet in the great saloon of the house belonging to Griselda's* great-aunts is inhabited by mandarins who nod to communicate. Griselda visits this rich and lovely land one night, when she is brought here by the magical cuckoo* living inside her great-aunts' cuckoo clock.

COURT OF THE STONE CHILDREN, THE. Eleanor Cameron. New York: Dutton, 1973. 191 pp. American. National Book Award, 1974.

Nina Harmsworth* has lived in her new home for four months but still longs for the old one and has trouble making friends. The day she realizes that she wants to become a museum curator, she learns about a museum devoted to things French. Here she finds recreated rooms from a French villa and meets a young girl but must leave because the museum is closing. The next morning Nina returns to the museum and again meets the girl. Because a group of schoolchildren is touring the museum, the two separate, to meet in the museum courtyard. Puzzled, Nina realizes that a ring she has seen on the girl's finger also appears in a painting. The girl's name is Dominique de Lombre* (Domi) and the court-yard's statues of children had once been at her home in France, as had the recreated rooms. The painting in which Nina has seen Domi's ring is of Domi herself. Domi had once dreamed of the museum and seen Nina; she had also seen her dead father, Clovis Antoine de Lombre* (Kot), who told Domi that Nina would help them, though now she cannot figure out how. Before she leaves, Domi tells Nina that she must tell Helena Hampton Staynes*, the museum registrar, who is writing a biography of Kot, what she can. Nina, though, is even more puzzled, for she finds that Mrs. Staynes has Domi's ring, and she does not understand why.

Days later, Nina returns to the museum but does not meet Domi. She does find a copy of the journal of Odile Chrysostome*, the daughter of a nineteenth-century French painter, and takes it when the museum closes. Realizing that the book belongs to the curator, Nina brings it back and meets Domi. Mrs. Staynes has lost the ring, and Domi shows Nina where it is, explaining that it can belong to both of them because Domi had died long ago. The shock of realizing that Domi is a ghost overwhelms Nina, and she faints, to be found by the museum curator, who takes Nina home and loans her Odile's journal. That night Nina dreams Odile is trying to show her something at the top of a staircase.

The next time she goes to the museum and meets Domi, Nina is afraid, but her fear soon vanishes. Mrs. Staynes has finished her book but is convinced that Kot was a murderer. Domi tells Nina his story. Possessed of a deep social conscience, Kot had criticized Napoleon. One night after he had been gone for two weeks, Domi had heard him come in. The next morning Kot's valet was found, murdered, and a week later Kot had been accused of murder and of conspiracy against Napoleon; he was court-martialed and shot. The night he died, Domi had had her strange dream. She had never been able to prove Kot's innocence. When Nina leaves, she wishes she could help Domi.

To her joy, Nina gets a summer job at the museum and finds an apartment that suits her family better than the one they already have. The next time she sees Domi, Nina tells her about Odile's journal and together they explore the second volume, in French. Here they learn that Kot had been with the Chry-sostome family before he was shot. He and Odile had realized their love for each other, and Odile's father had painted a picture of them in their happiness. Then Kot went to see Napoleon, swearing them all not to tell about his visit, to keep the family safe. After his death, Odile had been married to a farmer. Because Odile had used the initial "K" instead of Kot's real name, Mrs. Staynes had not realized the relationship. Domi and Nina realize that the painting of Kot and Odile would prove that "K" had been Kot and that the journal would vindicate him, but the painting is probably gone.

Over the next days, Domi tells Nina much about her life and home. Then one day Nina goes with Mrs. Staynes to the home of an old woman who is giving items to the museum. At the top of the staircase she had seen in her dream, she finds a painting of Odile and the farmer and realizes that this is the painting in the journal. X-rays reveal that beneath the farmer's face appears Kot's and that the painting had had a title mentioning "Kot." Mrs. Staynes realizes that she must reread Odile's journal and rewrite her book. At a small celebration Nina is given a copy of the second volume of Odile's journal, to teach herself French, and to everyone's surprise she reads from it with Domi's accent. For a moment that night she feels her life enmeshed with all things; though she realizes Domi will not come back to her, she is not sad.

COWSLIP, a character in *Watership Down**, by Richard Adams*. Like all the rabbits in his warren, Cowslip is fat and well-fed and evasive, because the warren is fed by a farmer who traps the rabbits. Unable to face their inability to leave the rich life of the warren or to know when or where they themselves will be killed, the rabbits in the warren choose not to think about their destinies. Like the others, Cowslip is urbane and feels that he is more sophisticated than normal rabbits, for in their despair the rabbits have developed music and art, like men. Cowslip brings to his warren Hazel*, Five*, Bigwig*, and eight other rabbits whom he finds traveling near the warren.

CRADDOC, a character in *Taran Wanderer**, by Lloyd Alexander*. He is a widower. A shepherd in the mountains of southern Prydain*, beside the Small Avren River, Craddoc helped defend his rich valley from invaders, being lamed during the fighting. Despite the fact that the land is no longer rich and that others had left it to try elsewhere, Craddoc stayed on, desiring the freedom here. His wife died giving birth to their son, who died with her. For many years Craddoc has struggled to survive. Then Taran*, a young man searching for his heritage, comes to the valley, and, to keep him here, Craddoc tells Taran that he is his father. Miserable as Taran is sharing Craddoc's life in the valley, he stays and helps the man, ready to take up his life. When Craddoc slips and is mortally injured falling onto a ledge, Taran tries to help him and is hurt also. In despair Craddoc tells him the truth. Though Taran uses a magical hunting horn* to call for help, it arrives too late, for Craddoc dies.

CRASHEY, BUTTER, a character in Pauline Clarke's* *The Twelve and the Genii**. He is one of the Twelves*, a dozen wooden soldiers once owned by Branwell Brontë who came to life through the creative genius of the boy and his sisters, Charlotte, Anne, and Emily. Butter got his name because once he fell into some butter. He is the oldest of the Twelves, being 140 years old, and they honor him for his dignity and his wisdom and because Branwell made him privy to secrets the other Twelves would never know. Butter introduces Max Morley*, the twentieth-century boy who finds the soldiers hidden in his attic, to the other Twelves and acts as go between for the boy and the other soldiers.

When the Twelves journey back to their old home, Haworth, Butter almost does not make it; he is found by a farmer while out foraging but is taken back to Max, who helps him to rejoin the others.

CREEP, the main character in *A Chance Child**, by Jill Paton Walsh*. He is the brother of Chris* and Pauline*; he becomes the husband of Lucy*. As an adult, he calls himself Nathaniel Creep. Creep is the child of an illicit affair of a married woman; perhaps because of her hatred of his father and the subsequent desertion by her husband, the woman keeps Creep in a small closet under the stairs until he is freed when a hole is made in the side of the house by a crew tearing down the house next door. He has no real name; "creep" is what she calls him. After Creep's escape, he makes his way to an old canal. He finds himself in a totally new world and does not notice when, in his journey down the canal, he leaves the twentieth century and enters the early nineteenth. Even though he becomes involved with Tom Moorhouse* and Lucy, two abused child workers, Creep is strangely detached, not eating or showing much emotion. Adults cannot see him. Finally, when the mother of a boy abused in a factory goes after the boy's master with a roller, Creep laughs at the sight, and abruptly becomes part of the nineteenth century. Soon after this he leaves Lucy and gets a job cutting the canal. Crippled by an accident, he learns to read and becomes a printer. Finally he goes back to find Lucy and marries her. They have ten children, four of whom reach adulthood.

CROCODILE, THE, a creature in James M. Barrie's* *Peter and Wendy**. This crocodile once swallowed a clock, so it ticks until the clock finally runs down; Peter Pan* and the other boys in Neverland* find out the time by following the beast until the clock strikes. Because Peter has fed the crocodile the hand of Captain Jas. Hook*, the beast seeks the pirate high and low, for it liked the taste so much it wants more. When the clock runs down and Peter and Hook wage their last battle, the crocodile gets what it has been waiting for.

CROW, a character in Carolyn Sherwin Bailey's* *Miss Hickory**. Though, like most of his crow friends, he can be rowdy (he is the organizer of the annual, boisterous Old Crow Week each spring), Crow has a gentler side. He helps Miss Hickory* find a home when she loses her little house to a chipmunk, and he takes her on her first air trip, flying her over the countryside to see that spring is arriving.

CUCKOO, THE, a character in *The Cuckoo Clock**, by Mrs. Mary Molesworth*. It lives in a cuckoo clock created by the grandfather of Sybilla. The cuckoo itself may be "fairyfied"; wherever the clock hangs, that house has good luck. This sometimes curt, always mysterious little bird becomes the object of fascination for Sybilla's granddaughter, Griselda*, and she finds in him a magical companion who entertains her and takes her to strange lands. The cuckoo thinks

Griselda has much to learn, and he teaches her patience, duty, and obedience. Finally he helps her to meet a companion, Phil*, and because Griselda now has friends who will understand her and help her to work and play, the cuckoo leaves.

CUCKOO CLOCK, THE. Mary Louisa Molesworth. Illus. Walter Crane. London: Macmillan, 1877. 242 pp. British.

Griselda*, a little girl, comes to live with her great-aunts in their huge old house. It is quiet and lonely for a child, though Griselda becomes fascinated by the cuckoo* in her aunts' cuckoo clock. One day, though, she throws a book at it because it seems to mock her, and the cuckoo stops cuckooing. The next night Griselda apologizes to the bird, who accepts her apology and seems sympathetic when Griselda explains that she is not quite happy because she has no one to play with. The next night Griselda wakes suddenly and is guided to the clock. Here the cuckoo invites her in, and she is small enough to enter his cozy little home. He loans her a feather mantle and agrees to take her to different places; all she must do is use the mantle and make a wish. Griselda wishes to go the Country of the Nodding Mandarins*, behind the cupboard where her aunts keep some nodding Chinese dolls. Here she is dressed for a wonderful ball and has a lovely time before the cuckoo throws the mantle over her and she wakes in bed, finding in the bed one of the tiny shoes she had worn.

Days later Griselda is nursing a cold in a room near the clock. To relieve her boredom the cuckoo shows her images of the maker of the cuckoo clock and his granddaughter, Griselda's grandmother, of her grandmother as a young woman, and of her grandmother's funeral. Griselda is ill for the next few days and becomes spoiled and cross, wishing to go to butterfly-land*, where it is never winter and no one must do lessons or work. That night she wakes in time to rescue a half-frozen bird, the cuckoo, from the garden. He invites her into the frosty garden but she declines; when he leaves, though, she follows through a strange door into the bright, lovely garden that is butterfly-land. Here Griselda learns that the butterflies work hard using the colors of the flowers in the garden to paint all the flowers of the world. After a banquet and a dance, Griselda becomes frightened when the butterflies all want to kiss her. Acting on the cuckoo's advice, she claps and wakes in bed.

At last spring comes. Griselda is still lonely, for the cuckoo does not comes to her. One day a little boy comes upon Griselda in the woods; it is Phil*, led to her by the sound of a cuckoo. His mother is sick, so he is staying at a nearby farm and is lonely. The two decide to meet every day to play. Because Griselda does not ask her great-aunts politely, they withhold their permission, though a maid persuades them to reconsider. Griselda will not be able to meet Phil the next day and is so upset by this that the cuckoo takes her that night to Phil, and she tells him as he sleeps not to come the next day. The cuckoo then takes her to the silent sea on the other side of the moon, where Phil is rowing in a little boat. He vanishes, and Griselda falls asleep and wakes in her bed.

Though it is difficult, Griselda is good all that day, and the next day she is allowed to meet and play with Phil in the woods. When they get lost coming out, the cuckoo guides them with his voice. Phil's mother, now well, has come to the farm and will stay there. That night Griselda dreams that the cuckoo comes to her and says goodbye, for now she has friends who will help her as it has.

CUDDY. *See* Cuthbert, St.

CUPBOARD, MAGICAL, an object in *Parsley Sage, Rosemary and Time** and *The Magical Cupboard**, by Jane Louise Curry*. It was made long ago in England by Mat Cakebrede. The richly carved cupboard is handed down in the Cakebread family through generations, finally coming to Goody Cakebread* and going with her family to colonial America. This cupboard has certain magical properties; it gives its owner whatever he or she needs and takes what is not needed. When it turns William Wingard* (Bill) into a piglet and back again, Goody Cakebread is accused of being a witch and is jailed. Though charges against her are dropped, the cupboard, seized as evidence, is stolen by Thanatopsis and Sufferana Grout**, who hope to make a fortune by using it to get gold. The sometimes-tempermental cupboard thwarts them. It also thwarts David Hollybush* when he tries to increase the Grouts' small store of gold. The cupboard later belongs to Goliath Hollybush* and Felicity Parmenter* and chooses the site of their house during a journey when it comes to a certain place and refuses to go any further. The Hollybushes build their house to accommodate the cupboard and there it stays for over two hundred years, waiting to be claimed by Bill and Hepsibah Sagacity Walpole*, whom Felicity had seen looking for the cupboard one cold night in 1722. Crawling into the cupboard to get warm, Felicity discovered inside it a cosy little room with a window into the twentieth century and overheard the two in their search. In 1976 Bill and Hepsibah and their niece, Rosemary Walpole*, find the cupboard and claim it.

CURDIE PETERSON (*The Princess and the Goblin; The Princess and Curdie*). *See* Peterson, Curdie

CURRY, JANE LOUISE (1932–   ), American writer. She was born in East Liverpool, Ohio, in September, 1932. She studied for a year at the University of London, reading medieval English literature, and received her Ph.D. from Stanford University in 1969. She has been an art instructor in the Los Angeles public school system, an assistant in a bookstore, and an acting instructor at Stanford University.

Curry is one of the most prolific American writers for children at work today, having produced eighteen books in eighteen years. Among her works are two mystery-suspense novels, a retelling of California Indian tales, and fourteen fantasies, most of them involving time travel or time shifts. Several of Curry's works are high fantasies taking place in North America in times ranging from the Ice Age to the twentieth century. In *The Wolves of Aam**, the setting is Astarlind, a great land in eastern North America populated by men, by a race of small folk called the Tiddi*, and by the gigantic Icelings*, all of whom have distinctive cultures shaped by the ice that covers much of the land. In *The Birdstones** and *The Watchers**, Ebhélic* has replaced Astarlind in fourth-century North America; in the twelfth century the same land is called Abáloc*, as in *The Daybreakers** and *Over the Sea's Edge**. By the twentieth century, these ancient names are forgotten, though the Fair Folk* in *Beneath the Hill** live in and near the City of the Moon Under the Mountain*, a legendary haven mentioned in each of the other works. *The Change-Child** takes place in England but is a companion piece to *Beneath the Hill*. The rest of Curry's works are also companion pieces. Of these, *The Lost Farm** is a companion piece to *Mindy's Mysterious Miniature**, and *The Magical Cupboard** is a companion to *Parsley Sage, Rosemary & Time**. In these companion works, as in the Abáloc novels, neither book depends on the other, but the two together make a much greater whole.

In many of Curry's high fantasies, the individual is compelled to fight for his rights against a force of greed and oppression. The good characters in Curry's works have individual needs, quirks, and failings; they are creative, and love each other and the land around them. The people of Abáloc, beset by enemies bent on enslaving them, are gentle people who still take delight in the world around them; though Lincoas* and his small band are pursued by Cibotlán* warriors, they find joy in the song of a bird and amusement in a small raccoon kit. When Callista Lee and Harry Rivers** and Melissa Mitchell*, three twentieth-century children, meet the Abalockians, their first instinct is to protect the people as worried parents would their children. The large family in Twilly's Green Hollow* warily avoids contact with strangers but welcomes Ray Siler* with such warmth that he soon responds in kind. The villains of the works, though individuals in their own right, are often subsumed by greed or by a greater force, such as Katóa*, a ravening power that has lain in the land since its beginning. Cibotlán, a nation that worships Katóa, is also an empire bent on enslaving its neighbors; its people cover themselves with tattoos that mask their individuality. Tekla*, in the fourth century, uses Katóa to help her gain an empire and does not care how many lives she must take before she gains it. The coal-mining company in *Beneath the Hill* is a faceless conglomerate; Russell Boyd Moar* (Arbie) and his friends give their consciences and wills to Katóa. In many works, villainy goes hand in hand with desecration of the land, especially in the twentieth century. The coal company, though not conscious of its role in freeing the evil force beneath the Bane*, is a sinister presence destroying the landscape; Arbie Moar, in his attempt to free Katóa, tries to bring his coal-mining company into the beautiful Hollow. The forces of good in Curry's high fantasies respect and appreciate the land and each other too much to do either any harm, but the forces of evil have no such scruples.

In Curry's time fantasies—*The Daybreakers, Over the Sea's Edge, The Watch-*

ers, Parsley Sage, Rosemary & Time, The Magical Cupboard, The Birdstones, Poor Tom's Ghost*, and *The Bassumtyte Treasure**—the past and the present are inextricably intertwined, for "the past is never dead. It's not even past" (*The Daybreakers*, pp. 157–58). Events of one age often seem to play themselves out over again in a successive generation. As learning is lost in Abáloc, it seems to be in danger of being lost in its modern equivalent, Apple Lock*. A twentieth-century Shakespearian actor must break the cycle begun by his troubled Elizabethan counterpart. People of the past and present are also linked; often a character in the twentieth-century drama is the mirror-image of someone in the past and therefore is able to act in that other time. In *Over the Sea's Edge*, David Reese* (Dave) must exist in order that Dewi ap Ithil* may come forward in time; Dewi must exist for Dave to go back. In *The Watchers*, through Ruan* Ray Siler is able to witness events in the fourth century; by becoming Jack Garland*, Roger John Nicholas* travels into the Elizabethan age to alter history in *Poor Tom's Ghost*. Where there is no such "door," the time travelers often remain invisible to the period into which they journey, until someone in that period realizes they are there.

Curry's books make entertaining and satisfying reading. Her prose style has grace and power; her descriptions are particularly vivid. She is adept at handling the realistic background in her works, giving the reader a sense of life and realism beyond the bounds of fantasy. The Elizabethan world of *The Change-Child, Poor Tom's Ghost*, and *The Bassumtyte Treasure* is particularly well drawn. Characterization, however, is often a weak point; and where there is more than one protagonist, characters may tend to blur into one another. On the whole, the child characters are very true, bickering in the face of danger, keeping up their spirits through humor, wonderfully unsentimental and non-sentimentalizing.

Works

Juvenile fantasy: *Beneath the Hill* (1967); *The Sleepers* (1968); *The Change-Child* (1969); *The Daybreakers* (1970); *Mindy's Mysterious Miniature* (1970); *Over the Sea's Edge* (1971); *The Lost Farm* (1974); *The Watchers* (1975); *Parsley Sage, Rosemary & Time* (1975); *The Magical Cupboard* (1976); *The Birdstones* (1977); *Poor Tom's Ghost* (1977); *The Bassumtyte Treasure* (1978); *The Wolves of Aam* (1981); *Shadow Dancers* (1983) [not included].

Juvenile non-fantasy: *Down from the Lonely Mountains* (1965); *The Ice Ghosts Mystery* (1972); *Ghost Lane* (1979).

Secondary Works

Curry, Jane. "On the Elvish Craft," *Signal: Approaches to Children's Books*, 2 (May, 1970), pp. 42–49.

CUTHBERT, ST. (CUDDY), a saint in the Catholic calendar who appears as a character in Robert Westall's* *The Wind Eye**. In the seventh century he lives on Inner Farne, an island off the coast of England. Here he lives a life of prayer and praise, holding off the little devils who ride goats and pester him. Because, like all saints, Cuddy is someone God cannot say no to, he is able to call up storms and his curses have great effect; he can change the living but not the dead, and that, to him, is the difference between himself and a sorcerer. When a nearby monastery is attacked by Vikings, Cuddy destroys them in a storm; he spends the next ten years, until his death, repenting. Living on bread and onions and whatever else he finds, Cuddy seeks to live far from those who would seek his power. Against his wishes, after his death, the monks take Cuddy's body, on the *Resurrectio Vitaque Sum*, to their church to be buried by the altar. His remains are later moved to Durham, where, it is said, he makes the inscription over his resting place appear. Later, when a prostitute touches his grave, Cuddy causes a stone to fall from the roof, just missing her. Cuddy does not belong only to his own time; he can come at will into any century, Michael, Beth, and Sally Studdard*** learn, just as the *Resurre* can be used to go back to Cuddy's time. Cuddy, in different ways, helps the children and their parents, Bertrand and Madeleine Studdard**, though he prefers not to use his powers, regarding them as a snare to tempt him from his hermit's life. To Madeleine, Cuddy gives peace after years of suffering; to Beth, he gives comfort and advice; Cuddy heals Sally's horribly burned hand; and he gives Bertram something besides the dry and competitive twentieth century. Michael wants nothing from him.

CYNRIC, a character in *The Driftway**, by Penelope Lively*. He is the son of Cynwulf and the brother of Edric. This Saxon boy was born and grew up in a small settlement on rich land; his father was a ceorl, a free man. Sent one day to the nearby settlement of Culworth, Cyrnic arrives as the ravaging Norsemen are burning the place. Terrified, he gallops down the driftway* to warn the other settlements. When the Danes reach his settlement, Cynric fights them with the rest of the men, seeing his kinsmen die and suffering a wound before he runs into the forest to escape the Danes. There, in shock and despair, he joins the women, boys, and old men who are all that are left of the people in the settlement. Cynric's story remains as a shadow on the driftway, re-experienced by Paul* in the twentieth century, when he runs away from home and travels the road.

CYRIL, a character in *Five Children and It**, *The Phoenix and the Carpet**, and *The Story of the Amulet**. He is the brother of Robert*, Anthea*, Jane*, and the Lamb*. Cyril is nicknamed "Squirrel." He often takes charge in the adventures the children have with magic, when they discover a Psammead* who grants wishes, a wishing carpet* with a Phoenix's* egg rolled inside it, and half of an amulet* that takes them through time to find its other half. Like his brothers and sisters, Cyril has a talent for getting into mischief without meaning to. Cyril tries hard to do the good and noble thing, though sometimes it is difficult. After reading *The Last of the Mohicans*, Cyril wishes there were Indians in England and is frightened when the Psammead grants his wish. When Robert becomes a giant, Cyril exhibits him at a local fair in order to earn pocket money for the children. His possession of a cap pistol proves lucky during the children's search for the amulet; when he fires it, the sound so impresses the ancient Egyptians that they allow the children access to the precious charm.

D

D'AGOSTINO, ANNA MARIA (TEENY), a character in *The Daybreakers** and *The Birdstones**, by Jane Louise Curry*. Shy and small for her age, she is called "Teeny Weeny Scallopini" or just "Teeny." She is one of the girls who travel into twelfth-century Abáloc* and rescue Lincoas* and his companions; Teeny is also present at the rescue of Conway Tapp*. Having heard her sister tell about the fictional student she helped shape at the local college, Teeny is instrumental in the creation of "Dayla Jones." She later helps Dalea*, the fourth-century Abalockian girl who fills "Dayla's" persona temporarily, to get back to her own place in time. Though she will never be as bold as some of the others, Teeny's exploits give her more confidence.

DALEA, a character in *The Birdstones**, by Jane Louise Curry*. She is the daughter of Alida and the granddaughter of Thiuclas*. Dalea lives with her grandfather on Inas Ebhélic* in fourth-century Abáloc*. When Tekla*. the queen of Kanhuan*, attacks the island and the village, Dalea uses the birdstones* her mother left her to escape to twentieth-century Apple Lock*, Ohio. There she is found by Michaelangelo Pucci* (Pooch), who helps her to fit into twentieth-century life and to slip into the personality of "Dayla Jones," a fictional student created by some of the girls in Apple Lock to liven up an otherwise dull school year. Dalea finds Thiuclas, who has been living as Mr. Douglass, the eccentric owner of a plant nursery, and together they elude their pursuers and escape back to their own time. There they reach the safety of the City of the Moon Under the Mountain*.

DALLBEN, a character in the Chronicles of Prydain* and *The Foundling, and Other Stories of Prydain*, by Lloyd Alexander*. His parents are unknown; as a baby he was found in a wicker basket in the Marshes of Morva by Orddu*, Orwen*, and Orgoch*, three witches, who raised him. When one day they were making a special potion for wisdom, Dallben accidentally got a taste of it and immediately knew as much as the three witches. They sent him out into the world with *The Book of Three**. He became a great wiseman and enchanter, settling down, finally, to live quietly at Caer Dallben*. From there he made a long journey of many years, searching for the High King mentioned in *The Book of Three* and finding, finally, a baby who, like the future king, had no station in life. This child Dallben took to Caer Dallben and raised, calling him Taran*. By the time Taran becomes a youth, Dallben is 380 years old, content to live quietly on his little farm with Coll*, a warrior-turned-farmer, and Hen Wen*, an oracular pig. When the evil lord Arawn* threatens Prydain*, Dallben is ready with advice for the land's defenders, and he himself narrowly escapes death at the hands of Pryderi*, who comes to Caer Dallben to slay the enchanter and take *The Book of Three*. After Arawn's death, the Sons of Don* leave Prydain and Dallben goes with them to the Summer Country*, having proclaimed Taran High King of Prydain.

DANCING SHOES, RED, two objects in Mary Norton's *Are All the Giants Dead?*\. These shoes do not need someone in them to dance; they dance by themselves in the Land of Cockayne*, where fairytale people live happily ever after. The shoes plague Jack-the-Giant-Killer* because they take every chance they can to dance into the inn he owns with Jack-of-the-Beanstalk*. Because Jack-of-the-Beanstalk thinks the shoes want to tell them something, James*, a visitor to Cockayne, follows them through the forest; they lead him to Dulcibel*, a princess who needs his help. After they lead the two children to Hecubenna*, a witch, where they have some of their questions answered, the dancing shoes are not seen again.

DARK IS RISING, THE. Susan Cooper. Illus. Alan E. Cober. New York: Atheneum, 1973. 216 pp.
   The day before his eleventh birthday, Will Stanton* is given an oddly shaped buckle to "keep safe." For some reason, animals suddenly seem afraid of him, and he feels oddly menaced for no reason that night. The next morning Will hears music as he wakes, and when he looks out his window, the winter landscape changes to that of a wintry forest. He goes out into it, following the sound of hammering to a forge where he meets a rider dressed in dark clothes, with a black horse: the Black Rider*. The man tries to get Will into his power but fails. Will feels he must find someone called the Walker, and he does, recognizing him as an old tramp some rooks had chased the day before. The Rider finds them, but a white mare Will had seen at the smithy saves Will and takes him to a hill where wooden doors stand.
   Through the doors Will finds a great hall, where Merriman Lyon* (Merry) and a frail old woman, the Lady*, await him. Will has inherited the power of the Old Ones and has certain powers he must use. He is to find the six Signs of the Light*, a circle enclosing a cross, and defeat the Dark, an awesome force. He had received one, the Sign of Iron, the day before. Though Will is in the hall, the Dark tries to get at him, but with the Lady's help, he and Merry break

free. Before he leaves, Merry tells him that the next sign will come from the Walker.

The next two days are peaceful. Coming back from Christmas shopping, Will meets the Walker, who does not trust him but who finally gives Will the Sign of Bronze. A farmgirl, one of the Dark's minions, tries to get the Signs, but Merry suddenly appears and drives her away, using her true name. When Christmas Eve comes, Will and his brothers and sisters go carolling. At the manor of Miss Mary Greythorne*, an old woman, Will is surprised to find Merry acting as her butler. As they sing, things seem to stop, and Merry takes Will into the Christmas of 1875, where Miss Greythorne renews the Sign of Wood, which is hidden for Will to find in his own century. Here Will reads an ancient book and learns all he must know to be an Old One. He and Merry watch as Hawkin*, Merry's liege man, is tempted by a woman of the Dark; he will betray Merry and the rest. Merry and Will go back to the twentieth century, and here Will gets the third Sign.

On Christmas Day Will receives an odd present from his brother, who is stationed overseas: an antlered mask an old man had given him to send to Will. It is a thing of the Old Ones and bears the imprint of the Signs. A friend of Will's father, the Black Rider in disguise, brings a bracelet for his mother. During the church service that day, Will feels the Dark outside. He, the other Old Ones, his brother, and the rector are the last to leave, and Will uses the Signs to drive back the Dark; when they glow the Sign of Stone, hidden in the church, is revealed. As they all leave, Will's brother and the rector having been made to forget what has happened, a rook leads Will to the Walker, lying in the snow; he is taken to Will's house.

A terrible snowstorm starts. That night Will wakes to find Merry outside, and they go to see the ancient hunting of the wren, where the bird is the Lady and Will is warned to beware of the snow. Over the next days the snow continues falling and the villagers go to Miss Greythorne's manor, where Will and his father take the Walker. At the manor Will, through a spell, sees a puzzling vision of the Lady, who tells him he must get the Sign of Fire; the candles will show him. When the Rider comes to the manor, he is driven away by a brand the Sign of Iron had given Will. The Walker, though, summons the Dark, and in a different time Will sees nine flames, the candles of winter, burn cold. Merry tries to get the Walker—Hawkin—to come back to the Light, but the man refuses. In the twentieth century the electricity is off and the manor is growing cold; the candles of winter seem to become clearer as the cold increases. They are independent powers used by the Dark, and when the Walker is given a sedative so that the Dark loses access to the house, the Old Ones grab the candles. Suddenly the Lady's hall is all around them, and the candles are put into their places on a candelabrum; the Sign of Fire is revealed.

When Will takes it, he is suddenly in the twentieth century, where it is raining and warmer. At home, Will's mother has fallen and been injured, and one of his sisters is missing. Will looks for her. One of the Old Ones takes him to a certain place; Will is to take the white mare to the Hunter. Puzzled, when he finds the mare Will allows her to take him where she will, and she takes him to an island in the flood-swollen river. Hawkin is there; the Rider rides up with Will's sister on his horse. He offers her in exchange for the Signs, and when Will refuses he tries to kill her, but Merry snatches her away. Before Will's wondering eyes, the island begins to break apart and a ship bearing the body of a king is revealed. From his hands Will takes the Sign of Water, and the ship floats downstream, set aflame by the wrath of the Rider.

Merry, having taken Will's sister to safety, takes Will to the oak where the Wild Hunt* rides each year. The Dark follows. The mare is sent to Herne*, who leads the Hunt, and Will gives him his mask, washed out of the Stanton house by the flood. On Herne's shoulders the mask becomes real. Herne gathers his hounds and rides into the sky, after the Dark. Fleeing, the Rider casts Hawkin down and the man dies. In a bubble of time between the thirteenth and the twentieth centuries, the Old Ones gather and the Signs are joined in a chain and given to the Lady. Back in the twentieth century, Will finds that everything is well.

DARK IS RISING SERIES, five books by Susan Cooper* that chronicle the battle between the forces of the Dark and the Light. In chronological order they are: *Over Sea, Under Stone*; *The Dark Is Rising*; *Greenwitch*; *The Grey King*; *Silver on the Tree**.

DARLING, JOHN, a character in James M. Barrie's* *Peter and Wendy**. John is the middle child of Mr. and Mrs. Darling**; he is the brother of Wendy and Michael Darling**. John flies to Neverland* with his brother and sister and Peter Pan* and has many adventures, returning from Neverland to grow up and have children of his own.

DARLING, MICHAEL, a character in *Peter and Wendy**, by James M. Barrie*. He is the youngest child of Mr. and Mrs. Darling**; he is the brother of Wendy and John Darling**. Michael flies off with his brother and sister and Peter Pan* to Neverland*, where, since he is the youngest, he must play the baby of the household. After he returns from Neverland, Michael grows up to become an engine-driver.

DARLING, MR., a character in James M. Barrie's* *Peter and Wendy**. Petulant, overbearing, and childish, Mr. Darling is sometimes quite a handful for Mrs. Darling*. He ties Nana*, the children's dog/nurse outside, thus unwittingly clearing the way for Peter Pan* to lure Wendy, John, and Michael Darling*** to Neverland*. Mr. Darling, contrite, moves into the dog house and swears he will not come out until the children return. When they do return, bringing the lost boys*, he adopts the boys and raises them as his own.

DARLING, MRS., a character in *Peter and Wendy** by James M. Barrie*. Mrs. Darling is a motherly and understanding woman; any woman would have to be whose husband is Mr. Darling* and whose children are Wendy, Michael, and John Darling***. Though her children go to Neverland* for many weeks, Mrs. Darling keeps the nursery ready for their return. She adopts the lost boys* and wants to adopt Peter Pan*, but he refuses, not wanting to grow up.

DARLING, WENDY MOIRA ANGELA, the title character in James M. Barrie's* *Peter and Wendy**. She is the daughter of Mr. and Mrs. Darling** and the older sister of John and Michael Darling**. From the age of two, Wendy has known she must grow up. She is a motherly little person who takes advantage of her flight to Neverland* to play mother to the lost boys*. She wants to be something more to their leader, Peter Pan*, and this earns her the jealousy of Tinker Bell*, the fairy who loves Peter. Even the pirates want Wendy to be their mother, but she refuses. While John and Michael are on the island, Wendy tries to make them remember Mr. and Mrs. Darling; finally she insists that they leave before their mother decides that they will never come back. Back from Neverland, Wendy grows up to have a child of her own, Jane*, whom she tells about Neverland and sends to do Peter's spring cleaning.

DA SOUZA, FATHER, a character in Robert Westall's* *The Watch House**. This stocky Catholic priest is American; he is visiting Garmouth, England. His curacy here is boring, as he is fond of complaining to his Anglican friend, Father Fletcher*. Both take delight in playing tennis with each other, cheating whenever possible; Father da Souza plays a merciless game. When he meets Anne Melton*, things take a different turn. Realizing that she is trying to communicate with the ghost that haunts the Watch House*, Father da Souza tries to warn her of the danger. When things get out of hand, Anne goes to the priest, and after a terrible struggle, helped by Father Fletcher, he successfully exorcises the ghost of Major Scobie Hague*.

D'AULNEAUX, ROGER, a character in Lucy Boston's* *The Stones of Green Knowe**. He is the son of Osmund and Eleanor (de Grey) d'Aulneaux; he has two sisters and two brothers: Bernard and Edgar. Roger was born around 1109 in England; his mother is Norman and his father is half Saxon. Because Roger will be a fighting knight when he grows up, he learns fencing and jousting and serves his father at table. When Roger is eleven, the large and beautiful stone manor his father has built is completed. Roger loves the new house with all his heart and is glad that he will inherit the estate. When one day he discovers the Stones*, two ancient stone thrones on a nearby hill, he begins a series of journeys into the future and the past, meeting the inhabitants of the manor, which comes to be called Green Knowe*. Roger is alarmed by the future, in which the house sometimes seems to be in danger of being destroyed, though it survives into the twentieth century. Finally he meets the young girl who will become Mrs. Linnet

Oldknow*, and extracts from her a promise that she and her grandson, Toseland* (Tolly), will work as hard as they can to keep Green Knowe safe. In exchange, she gives Roger a ring to give to his future wife; it will be handed down by his descendants until it becomes hers again. Lonely at home, Roger becomes very fond of the descendants he meets on his journeys, particularly of Tolly, who resembles him.

DA VINCI, LEONARDO, a character in *Time Cat**, by Lloyd Alexander*. His father is Piero da Vinci; his uncle is Francesco da Vinci. Lively, coppery-haired Leonardo is fascinated by everything he sees in Renaissance Italy and investigates it all with great enthusiasm. Though the boy wants to be a painter, his father wants to apprentice him to a notary. After Leonardo meets Jason*, a boy from the twentieth century, and Gareth*, his cat, he paints a picture of Gareth that so impresses his father that he apprentices the boy to a painter, Andrea Verrocchio.

DAVID FRANCIS WIX *(Earthfasts). See* Wix, David Francis

DAVID HOLLYBUSH *(The Magical Cupboard). See* Hollybush, David

DAVID REESE *(Over the Sea's Edge). See* Reese, David

DAVID WATSON *(Elidor). See* Watson, David

DAVIES, BRAN, a character in Susan Cooper's* *The Grey King** and *Silver on the Tree**. He is the son of Guinevere and King Arthur*. Knowing that Arthur would not believe Bran is his child, Guinevere asked Merriman Lyon* to help her take the child somewhere safe, and he had chosen twentieth-century Wales. Here Bran is raised as the son of Owen Davies, who fell in love with Guinevere and now loves Bran as his own son, though he feels some guilt because Guinevere had lived in his tiny cottage with him for a few days, and they were not married. For this reason he does not tell the boy the truth about himself and raises him in an atmosphere of guilt. The only thing the boy has to love is Cafall*, his dog, who is killed by Caradog Prichard*. Bran is different in looks from others, for he has pale hair and skin, and tawny eyes that cannot take bright light. Because he is the Pendragon, inheritor of his father's responsibilities, Bran has certain powers against the forces of evil, but until he bears Eirias*, a crystal sword, he does not have his true power. At the last battle between the Dark and the Light, Bran uses Eirias to cut the blossom of the midsummer tree*, which allows the Light to destroy the Dark. Though Arthur expects Bran to go with him beyond the world of men, Bran refuses, staying in the world of men, where he feels he belongs, though here he will endure sorrow and death.

DAVVY HOLLYBUSH *(The Magical Cupboard). See* Hollybush, David

DAWN TREADER, THE, the title ship in *The Voyage of the "Dawn Treader"**, by C[live] S[taples] Lewis*. Though not as large as the ships that once sailed the ocean off Narnia*, it represents the best technology available in the early years of the reign of Caspian X*, after there was a lapse of several generations in ship travel. The *Dawn Treader* is shaped like a great, green dragon, with a bow in the shape of a dragon's head and the tail tapering off behind the poop deck. Though it has a square purple sail to drive it, there is also space for rowers. Caspian sails in the *Dawn Treader* when he goes beyond the known lands in the Eastern Ocean to find seven lords his uncle had sent there.

DAYBREAKERS, THE. Jane Louise Curry. Illus. Charles Robinson. New York: Harcourt, Brace and World, 1970. 191 pp. American.

Callista Lee (Callie) and Harry Rivers** and their family have moved from Texas to Apple Lock*, Ohio. Callie is unhappy in her new town; it is ugly and cold, and she does not fit in, for the Riverses are one of only a few black families in Apple Lock. One morning Callie wakes to her first real snowfall and goes out early to enjoy it. She makes her way to the woods growing on the hill that dominates the town, where her rage at the town seems to intensify. Compulsively she makes seven snowmen that somehow seem threatening when they are done. While in the woods Callie discovers Conway Tapp* (Sonny) torturing a small rabbit. Chasing the seven-year-old, she meets his cousin, Melissa Mitchell* (Liss), who is in Callie's class at school and who has nothing good to say about Sonny. That night Callie hears insistent voices calling her, and when she looks out the seven snowmen she has built are in the yard.

Next morning Callie goes to the woods to verify that the snowmen actually moved, and she is dismayed to find them gone. She meets Liss, who is following Sonny's tracks to find out where he had been the day before. When Callie falls through the surface of the mound on which Sonny had killed the rabbit, miraculously clear of snow, the two investigate further. In the mound the girls discover Indian artifacts, including a blue-green stone*. Suddenly they find themselves in ancient Abáloc*, at the burial of Tepollomis*, whose grave is at the other end of the mound the girls invade in the twentieth century.

Callie and Liss listen as Neolin*, a priest, exhorts the reluctant crowd to provide a sacrifice to be buried with the dead king. The two girls are apprehensive when Neolin points them out as maidens of the moon and the sun sent by the Sun Serpent (Katóa*) to be the sacrifice. They are caught, as is Harry, Callie's brother, brought through time by the force of her need for him.

The three children are taken to the village of Abáloc, where they will stay before being taken to Cibotlán*, there to be sacrificed. Talking with Erilla*, who opposes their sacrifice, they reveal that they come from the future. Erilla confesses that she has yearned for someone to come help her people and tells them of the troubles Abáloc faces; Cibotlán wants to rule Abáloc, one of the last free places in the Ohio River Valley. Tepollomis was killed when the small band of young people he was leading was attacked by Cibotlán warriors; the youths, among them Lincoas*, their son, were carried off. Neolin seems to be leading the people away from their traditional customs and into the ways of Cibotlán, but no one dares challenge him, for he is the only man who knows the old ways. The art of writing has been lost, and superstition precludes it being learned again. Erilla, though, possesses the ancient *Book of the Kings of Abáloc**, secretly handed down over the centuries. She shows the book to the children, who copy the hieroglyphics from the title page along with their ancient pronunciation. Erilla longs to take her people to Nūtayē (the City of the Moon Under the Mountain*), a traditional sanctuary from whence came her ancestors.

That night the children are carried to Quanatilcó*, where they meet seven priests in whom Callie recognizes the seven snowmen. Callie and Harry are hailed as the dark children spoken of in an ancient hymn to the sun, but the priests want Sonny, to be sacrificed with Liss. Suddenly Lincoas, one of the captive Abalockians, recognizes Harry. Startled, Callie drops the stone, and Lincoas picks it up as the children vanish.

They reappear in Apple Lock ten minutes after they left. Lush, unspoiled Abáloc seems a paradise compared with snowy, polluted Apple Lock. The children are not sure all their experiences were real, but they are anxious about the simple people of Abáloc. The children get a long, unexpected vacation after Thanksgiving because there is not enough money to keep school in session. Harry and his friends break the code of the characters secured from Erilla's book and rediscover the Abalockian alphabet. When Harry tells the boys what happened, they scoff at him, but all the children are intrigued by the artifacts and set up a small museum in an unused storeroom above the town grocery.

Callie becomes increasingly anxious about the fate of Abáloc, and after Liss tells a group of unbelieving girls about their experience, Callie decides to go back, if she can, to help. The girls follow her to the mound, where she again finds the blue-green stone that carries them all back, one girl clutching choir robes her mother has entrusted to her care.

The boys, too, go to the mound, but they dig at the other end. The girls seem to have used a stone from Erilla's grave; Harry hopes that a stone Callie and Liss had seen buried with Tepollomis will take them to an earlier time. Harry's strategy works, for the boys find themselves near the camp of Tepollomis and the band of young people, who are hunting and gathering food in the forest. Harry warns them of the imminent attack and Tepollomis is understandably suspicious, but Lincoas and the others are fascinated by the alphabet Harry offers to teach them. Each person learns a separate letter of the alphabet before the band is suddenly attacked by Cibotlán warriors; in the battle Tepollomis is killed and some of Harry's friends are hurt. When Harry drops the stone beside Tepollomis, the boys find themselves in their own century, unharmed.

The girls, too, have an adventure, finding themselves in a deep forest and following the smell of food to a Cibotlán outpost on a trail. Along the path come bearers carrying Lincoas and the other youths, whom the girls rescue by dressing in choir robes and pretending to be ghosts. When Lincoas sees the stone Callie carries, he brings out the stone he had picked up in Quanatilcó; they are the same. The two stones come together, and the girls vanish into Apple Lock. Lincoas and his group start back to their village.

The little museum the children have started becomes the outlet for their enthusiasm about Abáloc. When an archaeologist from a local college visits, he is overwhelmed by the artifacts they have found in the mound and organizes a dig that turns up priceless artifacts, and the fact that the center of the mound had once been a sacrificial altar. The children realize, with sinking hearts, that this must mean that Lincoas and his new knowledge never got back to Abáloc, that Neolin must have won out. There is some good news, for Liss has discovered that the mound, thought to be on her grandfather's land, actually belongs to the school district, and any profit from the sale of artifacts would belong to the schools.

That night Sonny vanishes. He has told Liss of strange dreams of people calling him and of seven doctors operating on him. Now, searching for the boy, Liss finds a badly spelled note indicating that "they" had said they would help him to be stronger than the rest if he would go to them at dark. Liss goes to the mound, where she feels Sonny's fear; she cannot help him, for the stones will not work any more. The other children gather at the mound, too. As they stand near the sacrificial stone they suddenly find themselves in Abáloc, where Sonny is crouched on the altar and Neolin is triumphantly haranguing the crowd in the early dawn. As Liss reaches for Sonny and the others turn on their flashlights, the awed crowd sees two children of the moon on the altar and what appear to be stars come down from the sky. Harry points out the strange boats on the Ohio River that are carrying Lincoas and the youths back to Abáloc with the light of knowledge. As the sun rises, the children vanish.

Back in Apple Lock, they are disgruntled to realize that they may never know exactly what happened to their friends in Abáloc, but they understand that there are no endings; an ending is the beginning or middle of something else. They are excited, though, when their teacher shows them the book they first saw in Erilla's hands in Abáloc, which had been found at Nūtayē.

DAYLA JONES (*The Birdstones*). *See* Dalea

DEADMAN'S BROOK, a place in *Rabbit Hill**, by Robert Lawson*. This brook has proved a trap for many unwary rabbits, for none has been able to jump it. One spring morning, Little Georgie*, pursued by the Old Hound, makes a leap of eighteen feet to become the first rabbit to jump it.

DE GAULLE, GENERAL, a character in Robert Lawson's* *Mr. Twigg's Mistake**. This mole is named after the French general, who had been the head of the French underground, for moles are underground creatures. When de Gaulle is first found by young Arthur Amory Appleton*, he is an ordinary mole with a penchant for biting fingers. For want of any other food, Arthur feeds him Bita-

Vita Breakfast Food*, not knowing that, instead of cereal, the box is full of Vitamin X, a miraculous vitamin. De Gaulle begins to grow, becoming at last as tall as Arthur. Very intelligent, he quickly understands and enters into the imaginative games Arthur makes up for them to play. His worst enemy is Mr. Snarple, the next door neighbor, and he takes several opportunities to get even with that annoying man. As he grows larger, de Gaulle begins to go farther and farther afield; once he is mistaken for a bear. One day after he has been gone for some time, the ground rumbles and oil shoots into the air from a field near the house; de Gaulle seems to be swimming in it, up into the air, until he disappears behind the clouds, still rising. What eventually becomes of him is not known.

DE LA MARE, WALTER (1873–1956), British writer. He was born on 25 April 1873 in Charlton, Kent, to James Edward and Lucy Sophia de la Mare. He was educated at St. Paul's Cathedral Chorister's School. De la Mare worked in the Anglo-American Oil Company. In 1899 he married Constance Elfrida Ingpen; they had two daughters and two sons. He died on 22 June 1956.

De la Mare is best known for his many volumes of poetry for children and adults. His one full-length fantasy for children reflects a poet's feeling for language; *The Three Mulla-mulgars** is a lyrical quest story, a prose poem about a search for what lies beyond the boundaries of the known world.

The known world in this case is one of mountains and jungles—one of the Mulgars*, or monkeys. In the mountains lie the legendary Valleys of Tishnar*, the unknown. From these valleys comes a Mulla-mulgar, a royal monkey, named Seelem*; he is different from the Mulgars who live in the forest, and he teaches his sons to be different, too: unlike other monkeys they do not climb trees, nor do they have tails. They wear jackets in the cold and understand the making of fire; they walk upright and never eat meat. More like men than monkeys and more like monkeys than men, they are more like themselves than either. When Seelem returns to the Valleys, he leaves his sons their heritage and special injunctions against eating meat, walking on all fours, and climbing trees or growing tails, except in danger and despair—in short, against a tendency to fall into the ways of their neighbors and deny their special heritage.

And, through their trials and their tribulations, the three obey him. The fire they use gets out of hand one day, burning down their hut and forcing them to live in the trees, but they do not descend to the level of the monkeys who also live there. Instead they seek Seelem, in the Valleys of Tishnar. The journey is hard, long, and painful, full of despair and sometimes with temptation to give up their quest, but the three persevere, longing to find not just their father but something more, something other than what they find in the forest or with its denizens. Ummanodda* (Nod), because he is a Nizza-neela and therefore somehow special, and because he carries the Wonderstone*, one of Tishnar's fabulous jewels, can sometimes see beyond the world in which they travel, as when in the harsh mountains he sees that the ghouls that glower down on them are but tree trunks, and that the space behind the trees is not a snowy glade, but a small meadow of flowers and fruit-laden trees. With the stone he makes his companions see these things as well. Through their adventures with the creatures of the forest and of the mountains, the three small Mulgars prove their worth, and they triumph over the sleep that comes to them in the caves beneath the mountains, to come awake in the Valleys of Tishnar.

Their quest is a physical one for their father but also a spiritual one for what lies beyond death. Tishnar is something more than can be thought about or expressed; she is the unknown, and all that is beautiful comes from her; the last sleep of the world also comes from her. Her valleys are rich and sunfilled and those who are there live peaceful lives. Though some are born there and come out, none can enter except by going through the long, dark caves in which runs a river that makes those who drink of it sleep as in death. It is as much the lure of Tishnar and of the valley that draws the Mulgars on their quest as the hope of finding their father.

This work is written in a style as rich in meaning and as rhythmic as lyric poetry. The world of the Mulgars is well imagined. Of the characters themselves, Nod stands out in the memory as being the best realized, but those he meets, such as Andy Battle*, the Quatta hare, and the little moon-eyed, mouse-faced Minimuls*, are truly memorable.

Works

Juvenile full-length fantasy: *The Three Mulla-mulgars* (1910) as *The Three Royal Monkeys* (1935).

Juvenile poems, short stories, etc.: *Songs of Childhood* (1902); *A Child's Day: A Book of Rhymes* (1912); *Peacock Pie* (1913), poems; *Crossings* (produced 1919; pub. 1921), play; *Down-Adown-Derry* (1922); *Broomsticks and Other Tales* (1925); *Miss Jemima* (1925); *Lucy* (1927); *Old Joe* (1927); *Told Again: Traditional Tales* (1927) as *Tales Told Again* (1959); *Stories from the Bible* (1929); *Poems for Children* (1930); *The Dutch Cheese and the Lovely Myfanwy* (1931); *The Lord Fish and Other Tales* (1933); *Letters from Mr. Walter de la Mare to Form Three* (1936); *This Year, Next Year* (1937), poems; *Bells and Grass* (1941), poems; *The Magic Jacket and Other Stories* (1943); *The Scarecrow and Other Stories* (1945); *The Dutch Cheese and Other Stories* (1946).

Adult: *Henry Brocken* (1904), novel; *Poems* (1906); *M. E. Coleridge: An Appreciation* (1907); *The Return* (1910), novel; *The Listener and Other Poems* (1911); *The Old Men* (1913), poems; *The Sunken Garden and Other Poems* (1918); *Motley and Other Poems* (1918); *Flora* (1919), verse; *Rupert Brooke and the Intellectual Imagination* (1919), lecture; *Poems 1901 to 1918* (1920); *Memoirs of a Midget* (1921), novel; *The Veil and Other Poems* (1921); *Lispet, Lispett, and Vaine* (1923), short stories; *The Riddle and Other Stories* (1923); *Some Thoughts on Reading* (1923), lecture; *Thus Her Tale* (1923), poem; *A Ballad of Christmas* (1924); *Ding Dong Bell* (1924); *The Hostage* (1925), poetry; *Two Tales* (1925); *The Connoisseur and Other Stories* (1926); *Poems* (1926); *Alone* (1927), verse; *Stuff and Nonsense and So On* (1927), verse; *The Printing of Poetry* (1927); *At First Sight* (1928), novel; *The Captive and Other Poems* (1928); *Self to Self* (1928), poems; *A Snow-drop* (1929), poems; *On the Edge* (1930), short stories; *News* (1930), poems; *Desert Island and Robinson Crusoe* (1930); *Seven Short Stories* (1931); *To Lucy* (1931), verse; *Two Poems* (1931); *Lewis Carroll* (1932); *The Fleeting and Other Poems* (1933); *A Froward Child* (1934), short stories; *Poetry in Prose* (1935), lecture; *Poems 1919 to 1934* (1935); *Early One Morning in Spring* (1935); *The Wind Blows Over* (1936), short stories; *Poems* (1937); *Memory and Other Poems* (1938); *Two Poems* (1938); *Arthur Thompson* (1938); *An Introduction to Everyman* (1938); *Haunted* (1939), poem; *Behold, This Dreamer!* (1939); *Pleasures and Speculations* (1940); *Collected Poems* (1941); *The Burning-Glass and Other Poems* (1945); *Inward Companion* (1950), poems; *Winged Chariot* (1951), poems; *Private View* (1953), essays; *O Lovely England and Other Poems* (1953); *The Winnowing Dream* (1954), poems; *A Beginning and Other Stories* (1955); *The Morrow* (1955), poems.

Secondary Works

Bianco, Pamela. "Walter de la Mare," *The Horn Book Magazine*, 33 (June, 1957), pp. 242–47.

Clark, Leonard. *Walter de la Mare*. London: Bodley Head, 1960.

Farjeon, Eleanor. "Walter de la Mare," *The Horn Book Magazine*, 33 (June, 1957), pp. 197–205.

Gulliver, Lucile. "Walter de la Mare," *The Horn Book Magazine*, 2 (Nov., 1925), pp. 36–42.

Hopkins, Kenneth. *Walter de la Mare*. New York: Longmans, Green and Co., 1953.

McCrosson, Doris Ross. *Walter de la Mare*. New York: Twayne Publishers, 1966.

Mégroz, Rodolphe L. *Walter de la Mare: A Biographical and Critical Study*. London: Hodder and Stoughton, 1924.

Reid, Forrest. *Walter de la Mare: A Critical Study*. London: Faber and Faber, 1929.

Walter de la Mare: A Checklist. New York: Cambridge University Press, 1956.

DEL GATO HERRERA Y ROBLES, DON DIEGO FRANCISCO HERNÁNDEZ (DON DIEGO), a character in Lloyd Alexander's* *Time Cat**. Though he came to Peru with Pizarro and the conquistadores, Don Diego is not interested in either gold or the army; his parents bought him a commission as a captain. He makes a bad captain, unable to instill respect even in his orderly. Fascinated by the Incas he is supposed to be fighting, Don Diego is writing a history of them and a dictionary of their language. When Jason*, a boy from the twentieth century, and Gareth*, his cat, visit sixteenth-century Peru, Don Diego takes them in, thinking Gareth is the cat he sent for. The two are captured and held for ransom by the Incas, and the Spaniard bargains for their release, promising the Incas that he will try to help them. He keeps his promise when he becomes adviser to the Spanish Viceroy sent to Peru.

DELLY MATTICK (*The Watchers*). *See* Mattick, Delano

DE LOMBRE, CLOVIS ANTOINE (KOT), a character mentioned in Eleanor Cameron's* *The Court of the Stone Children**. He was the husband of Marie-Laure and the father of Dominique de Lombre* (Domi). Kot was born around 1769. Quiet and intense, Kot became embroiled in politics and came to be called the conscience of Napoleon, for he did not hesitate to speak out against injustice. Kot was gentle and loving, deeply in touch with the pattern of the seasons at his chateau near Saint-Sauveur, in Burgundy, France, and filled with love for his wife and daughter. When Napoleon began to look toward Italy for its treasures, Kot protested, though it did no good. Around 1803, Kot's wife died in childbirth and Kot was heartbroken. He began to confide in Domi, though he did not tell her everything for fear she would be in danger. Kot was more and more distrustful of Napoleon and was always fighting against his injustices. On 3 December 1804, Kot stayed with his good friend, Jean Louis Baptiste Chrysostome, a painter, because, having criticized Napoleon, he was in danger. That evening he declared his love for Odile Chrysostome*, Jean's daughter, and they became engaged. Though he realized the danger, Kot went to see Napoleon on 10 December 1804, only to find himself accused of conspiracy to kill the emperor and of the murder of Maurice, Kot's valet, the week before. Refusing to reveal where he had been, Kot was court-martialed and shot that day. The next night Domi dreamed of him; he told her that a young girl would help them. Though Domi had tried during her lifetime to prove Kot's innocence, she had not succeeded, for the Chrysostomes had been sworn to silence; not until the twentieth century does new information come to light, revealing the truth.

DE LOMBRE, DOMINIQUE (DOMI), a character in *The Court of the Stone Children**, by Eleanor Cameron*. She is the daughter of Marie-Laure and Clovis Antoine de Lombre* (Kot). Domi is Comtesse de Bernonville. She was born around 1791 and her childhood near Saint-Sauveur in Burgundy, France, was very happy and full of love. When Domi is twelve, her mother dies in childbirth; after this, Domi's life is more solemn, especially since Kot makes her his confidante, and his chilly, repressive mother takes charge of the house. When Domi is thirteen Kot is shot on a false charge of murder and conspiracy against Napoleon, and she dreams of him and of a strange young girl he says will help Domi clear his name. Though she tries during her lifetime to prove her father's innocence, Domi is unsuccessful before she dies giving birth to her third child. After her death Domi wanders the corridors and rooms of her beloved home with her cat, Lisabetta. When the furnishings and wall panels are sold to the French Museum in San Francisco, California, Domi goes with them, unable to bear watching the "modernizing" of her old home. She finds the twentieth century harsh and noisy and bewails the sterility of the recreated rooms. When Domi meets Nina Harmsworth*, the girl in her dream, she does not understand how Nina can help her father, but Domi helps Nina as well as she is able to, until Kot's name is cleared. Then Domi leaves and Nina does not see her again.

DEREK POOLEY (*The Devil on the Road*). *See* Pooley, Derek

DEVIL ON THE ROAD, THE. Robert Westall. London: Macmillan London, 1978. 248 pp. British.

Having finished his first year at college, John Webster* takes off on his motorcycle, looking for adventure. He finds it for a moment in a re-enactment of a battle, then he goes on, outrunning a storm and finally finding an old barn to shelter in. Here he finds a man dressed for battle, trying to kill a kitten, and John deals with him, turning to find his cycle gone. Another man appears and fires a gun at John, blowing away John's helmet, and, after being blinded for a time, John realizes that the cycle is still in the barn, but the men are not. There are no signs of a fight. John's head hurts and he is helped by Derek Pooley*, who asks him the next day to caretake at the barn. When Derek brings him a new helmet, John decides to stay. After a week spent making friends with the kitten, which he names News*, John is ready to leave, but he realizes that he cannot find a home for News, so he stays.

Behind what he had thought was a harness board, John discovers a settle with kitchen equipment on it, shoved into a great fireplace, and he realizes that the barn was once a house. In the fireplace is scratched a man's name and a hundred-year-old date. John cleans the place. Strange things begin to happen. The next time John goes into town he finds the local people oddly glad to help him, and that night someone leaves a rabbit for him. The next day Derek tries to explain the rabbit and the kitchen furniture but does it badly. On his advice John takes News to a nearby ring of oaks, where he sees the marks of carts and horses in the track and where what had been a man hangs in a gibbet. A young girl comes by. The next minute the girl and the gibbet are gone, and the oaks are twice as tall; John realizes he has just seen them centuries younger.

When he gets back to the barn, he finds presents of food there, and that evening a girl comes with eggs and asks for something to help her win back her boyfriend. The next day a man comes, asking for help for his boy, and he mistakes Derek's wife, who is visiting John, for the "herb mother." When John finds a book that may tell him what is going on, he finds that the name the locals have for him, "Cunning," is the word for a white warlock, and that a strange carving he has found on the barn door means "witch." Frightened, John decides to leave, but his motorcycle works only when he is headed for the barn, so he goes back, to find local men bringing him furniture. One night, News leads John out of the twentieth century into the seventeenth, where he meets the girl he had seen at the gibbet. She is Johanna Vavasour*, and she is afraid he will be taken for a witch because of his strange clothes; she knows he is out of his time. When News touches John, he comes back to his own century.

The next time he time travels, John tries to dress the part. This time he pretends to be Johanna's servant, and they visit an old woman who sings him a song to cast off a spell of love. Their visit over, Johanna begs him to find out about a man called Hobekinus, and John finds himself in his own time. At a bookshop he finds a book on Hobekinus—Matthew Hopkins*, a witch hunter who had plied his trade for profit. In a list of those Hopkins had accused of being witches, John finds the old woman he and Johanna had visited and Johanna herself, though her fate is uncertain. That night the sound of knocking leads John to a trapdoor into an empty room, where he finds Johanna. Outside they hear Hopkins, who is sent to the village. John tells Johanna all he has learned about the man and then finds himself in his own time.

In the twentieth century the room beneath the trapdoor is remarkably well preserved, and here John finds Johanna's herbal, with her notes. When he re-enters the room, he finds Johanna there. Hopkins is trying witches, and she is going to the trial. John goes as her dumb servant. At the trial she turns the crowd against Hopkins's assistant and stands up to Hopkins himself, taking her place with the accused witches because she knows he will not prosecute a gentlewoman such as herself. The court spectators poke fun at Hopkins until two men he has sent to search Johanna's house return with a tale of a fight there with the Devil; John recognizes them as the two he had saved News from, and the remains of the helmet they hold up is his. He tries to attack Hopkins and is struck; when he wakes, John learns that Johanna is to be hanged. News leads him to Johanna's house, and as he changes clothes there his century changes also.

Getting a shotgun, John goes back to Johanna, who is being led, with the other accused women, past the house to be hanged. There are so many soldiers there that John does not know what to do, and he slips back into his own century. Going again to Johanna, he realizes that he can do anything in the twentieth century and still come back to a certain point in Johanna's time. Gathering explosives, fireworks, and his motorcycle, he goes to Johanna's century and prepares a trap for Hopkins. When it is set off, the soldiers think the Royalists are coming and go to fight them; Johanna introduces John to the terrified Hopkins as the Devil and makes him do homage, assuring the man that John will come back for him. When the soldiers return one shoots at John but gets News instead, before the women are hustled into the barn. Suddenly it is a few years later, and the village is deserted because of a plague. Johanna sends the women out into the world; she herself goes with John to the twentieth century.

In his own century John is uneasy with Johanna because of her strange powers, though Derek is oddly pleased with her presence. Though Johanna wants him, John cannot love her because it would be permanent. When one day they go to the sea, John's motorcycle quits near the grave of Hopkins, who had gone mad and who was himself persecuted as a witch. Johanna's face, as she kneels by his grave, frightens John. That night he learns from her that she had sent News to him and had made him come to the barn. The next morning News comes back to him, though she does not know him, brought by Johanna out of another past to please him. John realizes that News has been used—as he has been used to get Hopkins, and as the man who had carved his name in the fireplace had been used—and he wonders if the mounds behind the barn are the graves of Johanna's other men. After finding a poppet Johanna has made of him, John tries to leave. The weather tries to stop him, until he sings the old woman's song to break Johanna's spell of love. Going back to the barn, he finds men taking away the furnishings; Johanna is gone. Like John, many others have failed her before him; she has kneaded time before to get help, but all have failed her somehow. John realizes that she would not have hurt him, but it is too late for him. He scratches his name in the fireplace and leaves.

DEWI AP ITHIL, a name shared in the twelfth century by two personalities in *Over the Sea's Edge**, by Jane Louise Curry*. The original Dewi is born in twelfth-century Wales to Ithil, a friend of Madauc* (an unrecognized son of the king) and of Llywarch ap Llewellyn*, a pig-boy who became a poet. From his father Dewi inherits a silver pendant*. Dewi is timid and unsuited for the rough life of the twelfth century; he longs for the quiet life of a scholar and, by means of the pendant, he trades places with David Reese*, a twentieth-century American boy who resembles him and who feels stifled in his own time. This new Dewi inherits the old one's reputation as a dreamer, but he is much bolder; he joins Madauc when the young man seeks fabled lands to the west, and finds adventure there. Content in lovely Abáloc*, Dewi decides to stay there, and he and some of Madauc's men settle, taking native wives and raising children. Dewi marries Siona*, and they have a daughter, Elen. He leaves his story written on parchment and sealed in a jar.

DIAHAN, a character in *Time Cat**, by Lloyd Alexander*. Her father is King Miliucc*. She lives in Ireland in 411 A.D. This lively red-headed girl is curious and opinionated about everything. She brings Jason*, a boy from the twentieth century, and his cat, Gareth*, to her village and is saved by Gareth from a snake, thus prompting Miliucc to name Jason his sorcerer and inducing jealousy in Lugad*, his magician. Jason comes to like Diahan very much before he leaves.

DIAMOND, a character in George MacDonald's* *At the Back of the North Wind**. He is the oldest child of Joseph and Martha; he has a brother and a sister. Joseph is a coachman, and when Diamond is born, he names the child after his favorite horse, a great creature named Diamond. The boy sleeps in a bed in the hayloft above the horses in the stable. Here he is visited by the North Wind*, a beautiful, sometimes terrifying, lady who carries Diamond with her on strange journeys. Always gentle, Diamond becomes more so after he falls ill and travels to the country at the back of the north wind*. Because he has been there, he is never miserable, not even after his father loses his job because his employer has gone bankrupt. Though the family moves to a rough section of London, Diamond is unaffected by the squalor that surrounds him; though he hears bad language, it does not stick, and he does what he can to help the family of a drunken cabdriver. At first they mistake his innocence for idiocy, but the cabdrivers make a favorite of Diamond, and he is soon looked upon as a kind of angel. The boy proves as good a cabman as his father, taking over the cab when his father falls ill. Diamond is frightened of nothing, probably because he has been at the back of the north wind. Sometimes he dreams about this place, and these dreams make him feel very good. When his father is hired by Mr. Raymond*, Diamond becomes the page in Mr. Raymond's house, reading the stories he writes to see if they are good or not. The boy has quiet wisdom and comes to be called "God's baby" by Nanny* and Jim, two children he has helped. Finally Diamond seems to die, but actually he goes to country at the back of the north wind.

DICKIE HARDING (*The House of Arden; Harding's Luck*). *See* Harding, Dickie

DIEGO (*Time Cat*). *See* del Gato Herrera y Robles, Don Diego Francisco Hernández

DIGORY KIRKE (*The Magician's Nephew; The Last Battle*). *See* Kirke, Digory

DOASYOULIKES, a race of people in Charles Kingsley's* *The Water-babies**. The Doasyoulikes lived in a rich country and did nothing all day but sleep and eat. When a volcano erupted, destroying the food-bearing trees, the people were too lazy to go elsewhere and work to live. Gradually they evolved into apes.

DOASYOUWOULDBEDONEBY, MRS., a character in *The Water-babies**, by Charles Kingsley*. This fairy is the kind and beautiful "sister" of Mrs. Bedonebyasyoudid*. She snuggles and loves the water-babies* and tells them stories. Mrs. Doasyouwouldbedoneby is but one facet of a being whose true name is too dazzling to know, as are Mrs. Bedonebyasyoudid and Mother Carey*.

DOCTOR PROFESSOR POLOPODSKY (*The Fabulous Flight*). *See* Polopodsky, Doctor Professor

DOLI, a character in the Chronicles of Prydain* and *The Foundling, and Other Tales of Prydain*, by Lloyd Alexander*. He is one of the Fair Folk*. All Doli's family can turn invisible at will, but Doli cannot, which makes him disgusted at himself and the world. He is usually chosen for, he thinks, the worst jobs; everybody always depends on "good old Doli" to take the worst tasks. Guiding Taran*, a young warrior, and his companions to Caer Dathyl* is a profitable task, for as a reward for Doli's help in the battle against the evil Horned King*, Doli is given the power of invisibility by Gwydion*, the war leader of the High King of Prydain*. Invisibility has its drawbacks, for the effort of doing it makes Doli's ears ring, people who cannot see him constantly run into him, and he is called upon more than ever to help. "Good old Doli"acts disgusted by all this, but he is secretly pleased. Doli helps Taran in the mission to find and destroy the Black Crochan*, from which Arawn*, the Lord of Death, makes an invincible army. He also finds Morda*, an enchanter who poses a danger to the Fair Folk, and is changed by him into a toad for a miserable time, to be rescued by Taran. Doli fights in the last battle against Arawn. After Arawn's defeat, when magic leaves Prydain, Doli returns to the realm of the Fair Folk, which is being closed to men forever.

DOMI DE LOMBRE *(The Court of the Stone Children)*. *See* de Lombre, Dominique

DONALBAIN MACCUBBIN *(The Lost Farm)*. *See* MacCubbin, Donalbain

DOPPLE, a place in *Mindy's Mysterious Miniature**, by Jane Louise Curry*. When the bankers in this little Pennsylvania town refuse to back his research, Professor Willie Kurtz* makes the village into a traveling exhibit by miniaturizing it with his reducing machine in 1915. Eight of the original inhabitants are also miniaturized; they bide their time for fifty-five years until they are able to hoax Kurtz's nephew into making them normal size. The buildings of Dopple are restored to their old sites and the little town is spruced up and modernized.

DORATH, a character in *Taran Wanderer** and *The High King**, by Lloyd Alexander*. He is the leader of a band of outlaws in the Hill Cantrevs of Prydain*. These men are soldiers for hire, but they take pleasure in killing even when they are not working for pay. Vicious and cruel, Dorath takes whatever he wants and has great pleasure in taking it violently. Taran*, a young man searching for his place in life, comes upon Dorath and his band and loses a cherished sword to Dorath in an unfair fight. Later Taran helps some of the people of the Free Commots* repulse an attack by the outlaw band on their farms. Taran and Dorath meet again at the Mirror of Llunet*, but their fight there is inconclusive, for Dorath's stolen blade splinters against one Taran has forged for himself. Much later, when Eilonwy*, Taran's sweetheart, falls into the hands of the outlaws, Dorath sees his chance for revenge, but he and his men are killed by wolves charged with the protection of Eilonwy.

DOUGLASS, MR. *See* Thiuclas

DRAGON, a character in Robert O'Brien's* *Mrs. Frisby and the Rats of NIMH**. He is a large orange and white cat belonging to Mr. Fitzgibbon*. Dragon is the terror of the neighborhood, adeptly stalking just about any animal he can find. To get him out of the way when they need to be abroad, the rats of a nearby colony—experimental animals who escaped from Nimh*—put sleeping powder into his food; Jonathan Frisby* lost his life doing this.

DRAGON'S RUN, a place in the Earthsea trilogy*, by Ursula K. LeGuin*. This group of islands near Selidor* in the westernmost part of Earthsea* is the home of many dragons, including ancient Kalessin*. It is filled with shoals and weirdly shaped rocks. Few men come here; Ged*, a great sorcerer, comes here twice, the second time at the behest of Orm Embar*, the mightiest of dragons. Here he learns that the dragons are being made mad and robbed of their speech by Cob*, a deathless man who terrifies them.

DRAUT, M. E. (*The Sleepers*). *See* Medraut

DREAM CLEWAREK (*The Watchers*). *See* Clewarek, Durham

DREAMING TREES, two elms in Jane Louise Curry's* *Parsley Sage, Rosemary & Time*. They are ancient; they were planted in America centuries before the Abenaki came to live here. Between these trees is a doorway through time, and many who walk between the trees find themselves in another time and do not return. For this reason it is forbidden for any but wisemen to go between them. Three children from the future use them in 1722 to return to the twentieth century; later in 1722 the path between them is closed when Juditha Cakebread* has a wall built around the trees. Nearby she plants a special garden. These ancient trees are still standing in 1976.

DREEGO, PENN, a character in *The Watchers*, by Jane Louise Curry*. He is married to Mavee. Penn is very active, despite his 111 years. He tells Ray Siler* about some of the family traditions and takes the boy Up Top* to show him the remains of Berinir Gair*. Penn lives close to Up Top and feels it was a mistake for the families to have moved to Twilly's Green Hollow*.

DREW, BARNABAS (BARNEY), a character in Susan Cooper's* *Over Sea, Under Stone*, *Greenwitch*, and *Silver on the Tree*. He is the youngest child of Dick and Ellen Drew; he is the brother of Jane and Simon Drew**. Barney seems to have inherited his mother's talents as an artist. Since he learned to read, Barney's heroes have been King Arthur* and his knights, and he knows a lot about them. Thus he is excited when he and his family visit Merriman Lyon* (Merry), a friend, in Cornwall, a place associated with Arthur. The trip turns out to be even more thrilling than he had hoped, for the children are soon on a treasure hunt for a grail* and an ancient manuscript*, which only Barney is small enough to get to in the tiny cave where they are hidden. This is not the last of Barney's adventures with Merry and the other servants of the Light, the power of good in the universe; Barney and his brother and sister revisit Cornwall, where they regain the manuscript, which had been lost; the three also help Will Stanton*, another servant of the Light, to gain the last things needed to finally defeat the Dark. Like his brother and sister, Barney is made to forget his adventures with magic.

DREW, JANE, a character in *Over Sea, Under Stone**, *Greenwitch**, and *Silver on the Tree**, by Susan Cooper*. She is the daughter of Ellen and Dick Drew; she is the sister of Barnabas and Simon Drew**. Warm-hearted, sympathetic Jane is not a good sailor, for she is easily made seasick. On a visit with her family to Cornwall, Jane is caught up in the eternal battle between evil and good, when she and her brothers follow a map to a grail* and an ancient manuscript*. On a subsequent trip to Cornwall, Jane witnesses the making of the Greenwitch*, a figure made each year of rowan and hawthorn and then sacrificed to the sea; instinctively feeling the figure's loneliness, when it is time to wish on it Jane wishes for the Greenwitch's own happiness and is later rewarded when the figure brings to her the manuscript, which had been lost. Because of her name and because she is female, Jane has special ties with the Lady*, one of the forces of good. The Lady chooses her to bear a message instructing Will Stanton*, another of the forces of good, in what he must do to gain the last things needed to defeat the Dark, the forces of evil. Like her brothers, Jane is made to forget her strange adventures.

DREW, SIMON, a character in Susan Cooper's* *Over Sea, Under Stone**, *Greenwitch**, and *Silver on the Tree**. He is the son of Dick and Ellen Drew and the brother of Barnabas and Jane Drew**. Simon loves boats. He also enjoys teasing his sister, just like any other boy. While on a trip to Cornwall with his family, Simon gets involved in the struggle between the Light and the Dark, good and evil, as he and his brother and sister search for a mysterious grail* and a manuscript*. On a subsequent visit, after the grail has been stolen, Simon helps Will Stanton* and Merriman Lyon*, two of the forces of the Light, to recover it. Later he is called upon to help Will find the last things needed to finally defeat the Dark. The battle over, Simon is made to forget his part in it.

DRIFTWAY, THE, a type of road that appears as the subject of Penelope Lively's* *The Driftway**. Parts of this ancient road are thousands of years old: it was made by people who needed to get from one place to another, and had gradually become a road wide enough to drive cattle and sheep along. It is not used much now except by the local people, for it is not paved. This quiet lane has seen many travelers, some of whom have left the shadow of their experiences behind for certain people to relive later. A nameless prehistoric boy has realized the common humanity of a stranger here; Cynric* has ridden the road in terror to warn his settlement of raiding Norsemen; Matthew Cobham*, a soldier on the Parliamentary side of the civil war, has stumbled along this road in horror of war; Jennet Haynes and her child have been shuttled from parish to parish along this road, with nowhere to go; James Tobias Hooker* has been a highwayman here, as has Jack Trip*, for a night; and a young woman has walked the driftway in inexpressible joy, to meet her sweetheart, who has returned from a war. When Paul*, a young boy running away from home, rides the driftway with his sister and Old Bill*, he experiences these long-ago hopes and terrors and comes to a better understanding of himself.

DRIFTWAY, THE. Penelope Lively. London: Heinemann, 1972. 140 pp. British.

Paul* is miserable because his father has remarried a woman named Christine*. He is buying things to keep her out of the room he shares with his sister, seven-year-old Sandra*, when they are accused of shoplifting. The two escape and Paul decides they will go to their grandmother, who will hide them. The first road they travel is so busy it makes Paul nervous, so when they get a chance they leave the man who had picked them up. They find a quiet road and are walking down it when a terrified boy gallops past on a horse. Paul and Sandra get a ride with Old Bill*, who is driving a horse-drawn cart, and to his surprise Paul finds himself telling the man about Christine and about the terrified boy. The driftway*, Bill tells him, is an ancient road, and those who have used it have left messages of a sort for certain people to hear later.

When they stop for some tea, Paul sees the boy again and understands his story: he is Cynric*, who had been sent to fetch some oxen from a hearby settlement. Arriving, he sees Norsemen there, so he rides back to his home to warn them. Despite the warning, the Norsemen loot the settlement, and its survivors are on their own. When Paul tells Bill Cynric's story, Bill makes Paul realize that for the first time he is thinking of someone besides himself—a sign of maturity. They go on and stop at an inn, and here Paul senses another story, that of Jack Trip*, an eighteenth-century stableboy who steals to augment his salary. Hearing two cattlemen plotting to kill a third and blame it on "Driftway Jim," a highwayman, Jack masquerades as Jim and robs them, only to be robbed by the real highwayman.

Old Bill starts off again, and they eventually stop to eat at an old woman's house, where Paul senses the story of a starving family, reduced to poaching. As they travel on, Paul begins to regret his decision to leave. When night comes he feels another story, of a prehistoric boy who finds a sick stranger and almost kills him; recognizing the man's humanness, the boy does not, an alien reaction to an alien emotion. When they stop to have the cart fixed, Paul hears of another person who had also heard the stories of the driftway. As they go on, Old Bill tells Paul about the civil war battles once fought here; Paul stops the cart because he sees a young man sprawled in the hedge. It is Matthew Cobham*, a soldier on the Parliamentary side. A battle with the king's men has been fought here, and though his side has won, Matthew does not feel victorious, only horrified.

As he grows more tired, Paul begins to regret more and more what he has done and how he has acted toward Christine. Suddenly Driftway Jim, James Tobias Hooker*, is keeping pace beside them on a horse, and he tells Paul his story. The drover whom the other two had decided to murder came to James and made a bargain; he would leave the two and have James rob them; then they would share the money. When James goes to rob the drovers, he sees Jack Trip and robs him. The spoils have been divided, and James is confident he can elude the men hunting him. Paul hears the pursuit of James, on the spot where he had been caught, betrayed by a boy who had been his confederate.

Paul has a crisis of his own when, stopping for Sandra to go to the bathroom, the two come upon two fugitives and give them their money. As he and Sandra walk back to the cart, Paul has a sudden glimpse of a happy woman walking down the road in the sunshine. He, Sandra, and Old Bill travel on, and as they do, Paul senses the story of a pregnant widow with a child, being shuttled from parish to parish and belonging nowhere. He is moved and realizes that things do not happen to just one person; they can affect everyone, including Christine. James Hooker's story has already made Paul realize that each story has more than one side.

When they come to Paul and Sandra's grandmother's house, she is not surprised. Their parents know where they are, having been told by the police Bill had talked to earlier. Paul realizes that the happy woman he had seen walking had been his grandmother, going to meet his grandfather, home from the war. Paul and Sandra will go home the next day, and Paul knows that, however hard it will be, he will greet Christine.

DRIFTWAY JIM. *See* Hooker, James Tobias

DRIP, THE. *See* Tapp, Conway

DRIVER, MRS., a character in *The Borrowers**, by Mary Norton*. She becomes the housekeeper at Firbanks, a country manor, after the last maid is dismissed for pilfering. Mrs. Driver is not above a little pilfering herself but thinks it well within her rights. She is a harsh woman when she wants to be; when Mrs. May's brother* comes to Firbanks, Mrs. Driver threatens many times to "take a slipper to him." Discovering that he has been taking things from the drawing room cabinets, she watches one night and thus discovers the existence of the borrowers*, tiny people who live by "borrowing" what they need. Fiercely afraid of these "nasty" creatures, Mrs. Driver calls in a rat catcher to kill them. He does not succeed; the borrowers escape.

DUB. *See* Arthur, Arthur

DUDU, a character in Mrs. Mary Molesworth's* *The Tapestry Room**. This raven is at least three or four hundred years old and has seen many things. Dudu has always lived at the house of Jeanne's* family, in France. He is more than just an ordinary raven; when Hugh*, Jeanne's cousin, comes to stay, Dudu is responsible for the adventures they have some nights. He also tells the two about their great-grandmother and her English friend. At first Jeanne does not trust

Dudu, believing him to be a bad fairy, but later the girl comes to accept him, though she is never polite to the raven. Saddened by a world that can change so much over the years, Dudu leaves.

DUFFLEPUDS, a race of beings in *The Voyage of the "Dawn Treader"**, by C[live] S[taples] Lewis*. These dwarfs* on an island in the Eastern Ocean are stubborn, lazy, and not very bright. They plant boiled potatoes to save themselves the trouble of cooking them once they grow; they wash the dishes before the meal to save washing up afterward. Originally they had called themselves Duffers, and their leader is the Chief Duffer. From him they have learned to be conceited. When Coriakin*, a magician who had been a star, is set to rule over them, the Duffers resent him, though what he does is for their own good, and they defy him every way possible. Finally he makes them into one-legged dwarfs with a huge foot, as a punishment. The Duffers feel so ugly after this that they sneak into his house and read a spell to make themselves invisible; when this palls, they force Lucy Pevensie*, a voyager on the *Dawn Treader** and a visitor to the island, to go into the house and read a spell to make them visible again. The dwarfs are pleased to find that no one on the ship thinks they are ugly and are equally pleased to be called "Monopods"; they get the new name mixed up with their old one and call themselves Dufflepuds forever after.

DUKE OF CHRISTMAS DAISIES, a character in James M. Barrie's* *Peter Pan in Kensington Gardens**. This oriental fairy is unable to fall in love until he comes to Kensington Gardens and meets Brownie*. His Grace has, for practicality, a trapdoor through which the temperature of his heart can be taken. Brownie's homeliness is such a refreshing sight to him that his heart becomes too hot to touch.

DULCIBEL, a character in Mary Norton's* *Are All the Giants Dead?**. She is the daughter of Beauty and the Beast; she becomes the wife of Florizel. When she was christened, a bad fairy, Pinprickel, put a spell on Dulcibel that meant that she would have to marry a toad in the palace well if her ball ever fell into the water. Kept at home, Dulcibel grows up lonely, playing cup and ball near the well for lack of anything else to do. Finally the unthinkable happens and Dulcibel must marry the toad within a week or the castle and all who live there will vanish. Though Mildred*, a level-headed reporter, has explained several times that the toad will turn into a prince, Dulcibel is frightened and she runs away. She is helped by James*, a visitor to the Land of Cockayne*, who helps her find the charmed frog with a jewel in its head and sends her back to the palace with it. Because James has made Dulcibel promise to say she will marry the toad, she speaks to it and is surprised when it becomes a prince named Florizel. Having the frog—or, rather, thinking she does—gives Dulcibel the courage to do what she knows she must.

DULCINEA, a character in *Time Cat**, by Lloyd Alexander*. She is a tailless cat who is shipwrecked with her kittens on the Isle of Man when the ship she is on in the Spanish Armada sinks. Because of her bad experience, Dulcinea avoids the sea for some time afterward. She and her kittens find a home with Awin* and her father, Maughold. Though she has given up the sea, Dulcinea changes her mind when she realizes that she could give luck by going with the fishermen, who have been having trouble finding fish.

DUNY. *See* Ged

DURATHROR, a character in *The Weirdstone of Brisingamen**, by Alan Garner*. He is the son of Gondemar. Though he is a dwarf*, Durathror is a great friend of the elves*. When the elves left for the northern lands, Durathror sought to go with them, renouncing his heritage, but they did not allow him to. The elves gave him Valham, a cloak of feathers that allows its wearer to fly, and he gave them Tanhelm, a helmet that makes its wearer invisible. Angered that his son gave away this great treasure, Gondemar had cast him out, and Durathror wandered for many years, coming at last to Cadellin Silverbrow*, a great wizard, and helping him in a quest against evil. Durathror has a lust for battle, and he is never afraid in a fight. He wields his sword, Dyrnwyn*, with great skill. Durathror is killed in battle at the pillar of Clulow Cross by the minions of Nastrond, a great evil lord, but he manages to slaughter many before he dies. When Fenrir, a great wolf, is sent by Nastrond to swallow up those who have defied him, Durathror's body is swallowed up as well.

DURHAM CLEWAREK (*The Watchers*). *See* Clewarek, Durham

DUTHBERT MORTMAIN (*A Swiftly Tilting Planet*). *See* Mortmain, Duthbert

DWARF, a being traditional in Celtic and Nordic lore who appears in several works. In Natalie Babbitt's* *The Search for Delicious**, these small men mine the mountains and create lovely things of metal and stone. They seem to be ageless, living for centuries, and they are always busy, for they have much to do. They have names like Bevel, Pitshaft, and Thwart. Making no distinction between good and evil, the dwarfs will help whomever asks them, for the affairs of men mean nothing to them. It is a dwarf who discovers the spring that floods its valley to become a lake; the dwarfs also make a little rockhouse over the spring. Bevel fashions the whistle* that opens and closes its door. When men come to the area made fertile by the streams running from the lake, the dwarfs retreat to the mountains, where they hammer and forge and ignore the world of men.

In *The Hobbit** and *The Lord of the Rings*, by J[ohn] R[onald] R[euel] Tolkien*, they are small people, a little larger than hobbits*, who love gold and fine things and excel in the crafting of metal. Dwarves (sic) are very strong for their height and can carry large burdens. They dig and delve in the earth, living in homes cut from the rock and working underground. Though dwarves are fine metal-workers, they are clever in other ways as well: they invent moon-letters, runes which when written with a silver pen under a certain moon, can be read only in the light of that moon. The solemn dwarves have little to do with elves*, for they consider elves foolish. They are not heroic, but they do have a good idea of the value of money, and when greed touches their hearts they are bold and fierce. A dwarf will do anything for revenge or to recover what is rightfully his, even if it means tackling a dragon; Thorin Oakenshield* leads a band of twelve dwarves and a hobbit to the Lonely Mountain to recover the treasure and ancestral hall of his people, which had been taken by Smaug*.

In *The Weirdstone of Brisingamen** and *The Moon of Gomrath**, by Alan Garner*, dwarfs are miners and good fighters, a hardy people who are terrible in battle. Masters of bird lore, they also use birds to spy for them.

In C[live] S[taples] Lewis's* Chronicles of Narnia*, dwarfs are small, hardy miners very clever with their hands; they make the crowns for the first king and queen of Narnia* from gold and silver trees that had grown from coins dropped by Andrew Ketterley*. The tough little dwarfs can walk a day and a night without tiring. There are two kinds of dwarfs: red and black, according to the color of their hair and beards. Though many in Narnia do not look favorably on the dwarfs, several dwarfs have given aid in her battles against evil. During the last battle in Narnia, most of the dwarfs take neither the side of the Narnians nor that of the men from Calormen*, believing that neither has anything to offer them. Always a stubborn race, they decide to live for themselves only, but this gets them nothing; they are too blind to see Aslan*, Narnia's mystical lion-protector, when he comes to them, and they cannot see his country, which lies all around them.

DWELLERS BY THE SEA, a race of beings in *The Magic City**, by E[dith] Nesbit Bland*. They live by the sea in Polistarchia*, about three days' ride from the city of Polistopolis*. Polistarchia is a land built of various objects by Philip Haldane*; the Dwellers were created when a book he used fell open and an image of happy people "leaked out." They are children, living in a sand castle Philip once built, and their lives are a round of play and more play, hunting for themselves and taking care of themselves, for the most part; heavy work is done by M.A.'s, men who work so hard at college that they take a holiday here. The one fear of the Dwellers is that the sea will wash away their castle. When Philip magically shrinks and enters Polistarchia, he ends the Dwellers' fear as one of seven tasks he must accomplish. Calling on Noah*, Philip has an ark made for the Dwellers to get into if the sea rises. Soon after the ark is finished, the sea does rise, but the Dwellers are safe. Eventually they float to the Island-where-you-mayn't-go*, which Philip gives them as a permanent home.

DYRNWYN, a sword in Celtic lore that appears in several works. In Alan Garner's* *The Weirdstone of Brisingamen**, it belongs to Durathror*, a dwarf*.

When his body disappears down the throat of Fenrir, a great, sky-filling wolf, it presumably vanishes as well.

In the Chronicles of Prydain* and *The Foundling, and Other Tales of Prydain*, by Lloyd Alexander*, it is a magical sword. Dyrnwyn was made by Govannion the Lame, for King Rhydderch Hael, to protect the land of Prydain*. On the black scabbard is inscribed, "DRAW DYRNWYN, ONLY THOU OF NOBLE WORTH, TO RULE WITH JUSTICE, TO STRIKE DOWN EVIL. WHO WIELDS IT IN GOOD CAUSE SHALL SLAY EVEN THE LORD OF DEATH." An enchantment had been laid on the powerful sword so that no one but those who would use it wisely and well could draw it; any other would be destroyed. Finally Dyrnwyn came to King Rhitta, Rhydderch's grandson. Rhitta, who had committed evil, did not draw the sword, though he marred the inscription on the scabbard. One night as he lay in his chamber beneath Spiral Castle, Rhitta drew the sword and was instantly killed. For centuries Dyrnwyn lay in Rhitta's grasp beneath Spiral Castle, becoming a legend in the memories of men. It is found and taken by Eilonwy* when she and Taran* make their way out of Spiral Castle; at its removal, the castle falls into ruins. When Taran tries to draw it to defend himself from the Horned King*, Dyrnwyn burns his arm. Eilonwy gives the sword to Gwydion*, the war leader of the High King of Prydain; he bears it until it is taken by Arawn*, the Lord of Death, who hides it on Mount Dragon*. Here Dyrnwyn lies until Taran accidentally finds it. This time he draws it without injury, and he uses it to kill Arawn's deathless warriors, the Cauldron-Born*, and, later, Arawn himself. After this the normally glowing blade becomes dull, its enchantment gone. Taran keeps the sword as he rules as High King.

EARTHFASTS. William Mayne. London: Hamish Hamilton, 1966. 154 pp. British.

On a warm summer evening Keith Heseltine* and David Francis Wix* investigate a mysterious mound which has cropped up in a field. From the mound comes a sound like drumming, which gets louder and louder. As the boys watch, the ground stirs and out comes a strangely dressed boy holding a candle* and beating a drum. He is Nellie Jack John Cherry* (John), a soldier, who speaks to them in a dialect as strange to them as theirs is to him. He had gone into a tunnel at what is now a ruined castle, and when his candle burned out he had picked up the one he now holds; the tunnel had collapsed behind him so he had marched on. John is intent on getting back to his comrades, so he goes to the village, to the castle where they had been camped, tossing away the candle at the edge of town. But no one is at the castle, and David tells John what has happened to him: long ago John had gone into the passage to find King Arthur* and his knights, supposedly sleeping in a chamber full of treasure; as he had walked, he had played his drum so his friends could follow him above ground, but the drumming had stopped and he never came out. John has been gone two hundred years. Not wanting to believe him, John runs away into the dark and the boys cannot find him. The next morning, when they find him, John still does not believe, and he sets off for home. Keith and David, following, see John rebuffed at the cottage where his sweetheart had lived; this convinces him that he is in a different century. Believing he will come out in his own time, John re-enters the mound, playing his drum. Keith and David feel strangely bereft. Realizing that the candle is evidence of their experience, they find it, still burning with a cold flame. David takes the candle to study it.

Autumn comes. One day the boys read an article about the Jingle Stones*, a circle of stones which appears to have moved; when they investigate, they find that the stones have not only moved but cracked, taking the appearance of giants. Over a hill two miles away they see a giant striding away. As the boys go home, they come across a pack of hounds out alone and follow them to a rock which has just come out of the ground. Something the dogs can see but the boys cannot flattens the grass and chases away the hounds; nervous, the boys hurry to David's house. Here they learn that a boggart* which had plagued a certain farmhouse for years has recently started making mischief again; the family in the house soon becomes resigned to its pranks.

More excitement is to come. Two days later all the pigs in the area are silently stolen during the night, and the next market day police searching for the pigs chase into the village a huge wild boar that goes on a rampage before it is shot. The next day, remembering an old story of a giant who had once stolen pigs in the area, David and Keith follow a set of huge footprints to the remains of a fire where a pig had been cooked. A policeman follows and grabs them, but he sets them free.

David continues to be fascinated by the candle, in the flame of which he sees things moving. After looking into it long and deeply, he can see and understand things Keith cannot; when the boys, reinvestigating the Jingle Stones, see seven giants but no stones, David realizes that, for the stones, time is a wind that has stopped, so that now they can move. When they visit the boggart-haunted farm, the boggart likes and obeys David, and the boys see a creature invisible to the rest, disturbing the sheep. On the way home, David sees a vision, and before Keith's horrified eyes a crack appears in the air and swallows David up. Unconscious in a fit, Keith is taken to the farmer's house; when he wakes, he is told that he and David had been struck by lightning, which had vaporized David.

Keith goes to David's house and gets his notes and the candle, walking into something invisible as he goes home. Though he has many sudden urges to look into the candle flame, Keith does not for a day; when he does, he sees strange shapes all day. A month after David's death, the inquest is held, and that evening, walking home, Keith walks into a horse. Suddenly he realizes that he had walked into a horse the night he brought home the candle, and he recalls that one of the witnesses at the inquest had told of seeing a horse and rider just before lightning struck the boys. Early the next morning, Keith realizes that the man on the horse may have had something to do with King Arthur, and the candle in his room shines through the window onto an army in the yard. During the day Keith sees the shadows and creatures David had seen. The candlelight seems much brighter, and the candle itself is heavier; the flame seems to resist the air and actually hangs in midair.

That evening Arthur appears in Keith's room and vanishes, and again Keith sees the army in the garden; this time Arthur is there. Looking into the king's eyes, Keith learns that he is to take the candle back to where John had gotten it. He does that night, accompanied by Arthur's ghostly soldiers, who soon become as real as he is. Keith realizes that when John had taken the candle, he had disturbed all that had been sleeping through time. As Keith goes down the passage, the candle gets lighter and lighter and begins to burn warm instead of cold. Suddenly he is chased by Arthur and his men, who do not want to be bound in sleep again; reaching the chamber, Keith jams the candle into its socket just as Arthur strikes him with his sword—and all the men freeze into stones.

David is there, too, and no time has passed for him. As the boys leave, they find John, who is pushing against time, and they turn him around and take him with them. The three come out into a snowstorm. When they get Keith to David's house to be cared for by David's father, a doctor, they learn that it is February and that Keith has been missing several months. The day after he had disappeared, many standing stones had been found in roads and in new circles, and the next day most of the pigs had suddenly returned, some of the sows with piglets resembling the wild boar. John goes to live with the boggart-haunted farmer, the boggart itself eventually sleeps again, and things are mostly quiet.

EARTHMEN, a race of beings in *The Silver Chair**, by C[live] S[taples] Lewis*. These grotesque-looking men scarcely seem to be of the same race: some have horns, some have tails, some are small, and some are very tall. They come from Bism*, a bright world beneath the world of Narnia*. The Queen of Underland*, needing expert diggers, brings them to just below the surface, where they are very uncomfortable, to be her slaves. Though they obey her, the Earthmen are terrified at the thought of breaking through into the open air of Narnia and being made to help take that land over. When Jill Pole*, Eustace Clarence Scrubb*, and Puddleglum* come to Underland* and defeat the Queen, the Earthmen are only too happy to go back to their glowing world, where rubies and diamonds are their food.

EARTHSEA, the world of Ursula K. LeGuin's* Earthsea trilogy*. Earthsea is mostly water; the only land is its hundreds of islands, which are divided into the Archipelago, Kargad, and the North, South, East, and West Reaches. On many of the islands specialized crafts are practiced; Lorbanery* is famous for its silks, and on Roke* is the school where wizards learn their trade. Not all the inhabitants live on land, for the Children of the Open Sea* drift on the seas beyond the Western Reach on great rafts, landing once a year to refit the rafts. Several racial types live on Earthsea, and at least three languages are spoken; one of them, the Old Speech, is spoken now only by dragons and wizards, and in this language are words of power used to make magic. Everything and every place in Earthsea has a special name, and if a sorcerer knows that name, he can control it. Essential to Earthsea's perpetuation is the Equilibrium, the Balance, which must be taken into account by any wizard doing true magic that is not an illusion. His magic must be for a good cause, for the effects of his changing what already exists may be terrible. At least once in Earthsea's history, this Balance is threatened: Cob*, a sorcerer who is afraid to die, opens a door between the world of the living and the land of the dead, and much evil occurs before the door is closed by Ged*, the Archmage at Roke. Though there are many islands, through much of its history Earthsea has been ruled by one king at Havnor*. For an eight-hundred-year period, after the Bond-Rune* was destroyed with the breaking of the Ring of Erreth-Akbe*, no man was strong enough to rule all of Earthsea. Seventeen years after the restoration of the Ring and the Rune, Arren*, descended from the ancient kings, takes the throne as King of All the Isles.

EARTHSEA TRILOGY, three novels by Ursula K. LeGuin* which chronicle the adventures of Ged* in Earthsea*. See *A Wizard of Earthsea; The Tombs of Atuan; The Farthest Shore*

EBHÉLIC, a place in Jane Louise Curry's* *The Watchers**. This seems to be the ancient place name of what in the twelfth century is known as Abáloc*. Katóa*, a ravening force of destruction, was bound under the mountains here until it got away, to be bound again before the fourth century at Tûl Isgrun*.

ECHTHROS, a type of being in *A Wind in the Door** and *A Swiftly Tilting Planet**, by Madeleine L'Engle*. The Echthroi are what Earth mythology would call fallen angels; they are the un-Namers, uncreators intent on destroying the universe. The Echthroi are a void that can negate, or "X", all they touch. The first Echthros had wanted all the glory of creation for itself and so had become bad; others have followed. The business of the Echthroi is war and hate, and they fuel this by making people not know who they are, for he who really knows does not need to hate. When someone is not loved, the Echthroi can move in and use him. The only way they can be totally vanquished is if all the universe is Named. Knowing that by destroying the balance they can destroy the universe, the Echthroi concentrate on individual entities; while he is still a child, they seek to kill Charles Wallace Murry* by killing his mitochondria; to do this, they affect a farandola*, which the mitochondrion needs to survive. Here they are thwarted by Meg Murry*, Charles's sister; Proginoskes*, a cherubim; and Mr. Jenkins*, a bewildered adult who has already been host to an Echthros. Later the Echthroi try and fail to stop Charles in his quest to alter events and keep Madog Branzillo* from destroying the world.

EDMUND PEVENSIE (the Chronicles of Narnia). *See* Pevensie, Edmund

EDRED ARDEN (*The House of Arden; Harding's Luck*). *See* Arden, Edred

EDWARD TALBOT (*The House of Arden*). *See* Talbot, Edward

EFRAFA, a place in *Watership Down**, by Richard Adams*. This rabbit warren is a model of efficiency and safety, having been created so by its leader, General Woundwort*, and his adviser, Snowdrop. Woundwort's lust for power has led him to start a warren of his own, a large one which he can rule. Efrafa is so set up that humans have no idea that it exists. The burrow entrances are cleverly hidden; one is in an abandoned drain tile and, if this pipe were moved, the entrance would collapse, keeping it secret. The rabbits of the warren are divided into several Marks, according to permanent scars on chin, flank, or paw that they bear from kittenhood; each Mark has a separate burrow and feeds at different times of the day or night, to keep the number of rabbits from being known by any observor. All droppings are buried for the same reason. Though the warren is overcrowded, with many more does than bucks, no rabbits are allowed to leave to start new colonies of their own, because they might attract the attention of men; any who run away are horribly punished. As a result, most rabbits are docile and apathetic. To compensate for keeping his warren to a size smaller than he would wish, Woundwort institutes Wide Patrols, using his stronger rabbits to police the area aboveground, killing predators and bringing in any strange rabbits who happen to wander into the area. To Efrafa come rabbits from Watership Down, and after they succeed in helping several does escape, Woundwort leads an army after them. After Woundwort's probable death, Campion takes over, and things are not as coldly efficient. Some Efrafans and some rabbits from Watership Down form another warren.

EGLANTINE PRICE (*The Magic Bed-Knob; Bonfires and Broomsticks*). *See* Price, Eglantine

EILDON TREE, a hawthorn tree in *The Sleepers**, by Jane Louise Curry*. Beneath this tree Thomas the Rhymer met the Queen of Elfland; in this tree Myrddin*—Merlin—was imprisoned by Nimiane*. All that remains of it in the twentieth century are the stump and roots, which cover the Bell of Rhûn* and an inscribed stone which reveals that further below the ground lies the chamber where Artair*—Arthur*—and his men sleep beside the *Brenhin Dlyseu**, the Thirteen Treasures of Prydein. Though little of the tree remains, Myrddin is trapped inside it until he tricks Ellen Peresby* into disenchanting him.

EILIAN ROBERTS (*The Change-Child*). *See* Roberts, Eilian

EILONWY, a character in Lloyd Alexander's* Chronicles of Prydain*. She is the daughter of Angharad* and Geraint; she becomes the wife of Taran*. Because Eilonwy is of the House of Llyr*, she inherits magical powers, along with the Golden Pelydryn* and a book of powerful spells. Achren*, seeking power in order to revenge herself on evil Arawn*, kidnaps Eilonwy when she is a child, hoping to get the girl under her power and thereby control her powers of enchantment. Eilonwy hates Achren and, when Taran is brought to Spiral Castle, she helps the young man and Fflewddur Fflam* to escape, accidentally bringing down the castle by taking with her Dyrnwyn*, a magical sword. Taran finds himself both irritated and enchanted by strong-willed, flighty, fire-haired Eilonwy, who talks her way into many adventures, including a quest for the Black Crochan*, a great cauldron in which are made the Cauldron-Born*. Eilonwy is handier with the sword than the needle, and she is more comfortable sleeping on the ground than in a bed, but because she is a princess, she must learn to be a lady. She is sent to the Isle of Mona* to be taught by the queen there, and Achren again tries to get the girl under her power but fails. After a year spent learning to be a lady, Eilonwy is ready for adventures, and she gets them during Arawn's final bid to control Prydain*, when she sets into motion the fulfillment of a prophecy. After Arawn's defeat Eilonwy gives up her magical powers by use of a gold ring* to marry Taran, now High King, and advise him.

EIRIAS, a crystal sword in Susan Cooper's* *Silver on the Tree**. Its name means "a blaze," and is appropriate, for the gold-hilted sword blazes almost with a light of its own, burning blue in the presence of evil. It was made by Gwyddno, the king of the Lost Land, at the command of the Light, the forces of good. But the Dark, the forces of evil, made Gwyddno doubt himself, and he has taken Eirias into his crystal tower, shutting out all who would speak to him. Finally Bran Davies*, for whom the sword had been made, comes to claim it, breaking the four barriers between him and the sword by saying the six lines carved in the wall above where Eirias lies. When Bran takes Eirias, the Lost Land is flooded at the Dark's behest. Bran bears Eirias because he is the Pendragon, inheritor of King Arthur's* might and responsibility, and he uses it during the final battle between the Dark and the Light to cut the flowering branch of the midsummer tree* and defeat the Dark. When Arthur sails to the peaceful land behind the north wind, he takes the sword with him.

ELF, a type of being in traditional Celtic lore. They appear as characters in several works. In J[ohn] R[onald] R[euel] Tolkien's* *The Hobbit** and *The Lord of the Rings*, there is more than one kind of elf. The High elves are the Light-elves, the Deep-elves, and the Sea-elves, who had gone to the land of Faerie in the west; here they had grown wiser and more fair, inventing their magic before returning to the world. Their singing is lovely, and to some they may seem foolish, though they are not. The Wood-elves had not gone to Faerie, preferring to stay in their forests. They love to ride and hunt at the edges of their woods, and, as humans have taken over the world, they have taken to doing their business in the dusk. The elves of Mirkwood hold Thorin Oakenshield* and his dwarf* friends for a time, for they do not trust dwarves. The dwarves are rescued by Bilbo Baggins*, a hobbit*. The elves later make a claim on part of the treasure Thorin and his companions win back from Smaug*, a dragon who had taken the hoard long ago. After defeating Sauron in that evil king's attempt to regain his magic ring*, many elves journey to a shining land beyond the ken of men.

In *The Weirdstone of Brisingamen** and *The Moon of Gomrath**, by Alan Garner*, elves are also called the lios-alfar. About four feet high, they have eyes like goats. They are good fighters and are merciless without being kindly. They are silent and calm in battle. Some things about them are incomprehensible, the more so because they do not need to speak to communicate with one another.

Elves avoid humans almost entirely, for their own safety; the pollution of industry is fatal to them, and they have been driven to quieter places in the northern part of England.

ELFRIDA ARDEN *(The House of Arden; Harding's Luck). See* Arden, Elfrida

ELIDOR, the title place in *Elidor**, by Alan Garner*. This magical land was once a glorious place, rich and shining, created from fire. Part of that flame is in four Treasures* essential to Elidor's well-being. The Treasures were kept in four castles: Gorias, Findias, Falias, and Murias. Elidor is subtly linked with our world, and in certain places that are neither one thing nor another, access between the worlds is possible if the right musical note is played. In Elidor are the Hill of Usna, the Hazel of Fordruim, and the Forest of Mondrum, but here also is the Mound of Vandwy and its standing stones, where evil finds a place. Slowly the powers of darkness have infected the land, so that, finally, Mondrum is a swamp and Findias, Falias, and Murias are in ruin; the land is waste and only in Gorias still shines what once was. Realizing that *The Lay of the Starved Fool* is a chaotic prophecy, Malebron*, a king in Elidor, brings David, Helen, Nicholas, and Roland Watson**** to Elidor to rescue three of the four Treasures, now in the Mound of Vandwy. Only the dying song of Findhorn*, a unicorn, can bring life back to the land, where music has certain properties. At Findhorn's song, the rivers of Elidor begin again to flow and life springs anew in the wasted land.

ELIDOR. Alan Garner. Illus. Charles Keeping. London: Collins, 1965. 159 pp. British.

Playing with a street map, David, Nicholas, Roland, and Helen R. Watson**** become intrigued by the name of a street and set out to find it. The street is a disappointment, for its buildings are deserted and are being torn down. Near an abandoned church the children find a football left by the workmen; when kicked, it goes through the church window and, one by one, all but Roland go to get it. Finally, when no one comes out, he goes in, but no one is there. A lame fiddler they have seen on a nearby corner enters the church and when Roland touches his bow to lead him in, he sees visions. The fiddler plays a wild dance and asks Roland to open a locked door. When the boy does, the church vanishes and he is on a seashore.

On a nearby cliff is a ruined castle, where Roland finds the football. Hearing singing, he follows it up a tower, from which he sees the fiddler, outside on a road. Roland runs down and follows him through a bleak and blasted landscape, only to lose him. Roland sleeps and wakes and comes upon some standing stones, from which he sees a shining, golden castle. Starting toward it, he finds, on a mound, sticking out of the ground and embedded in quartz, Helen's glove. Suddenly a lame man with a glowing spear approaches. He is Malebron*, a king in Elidor*, who had been the fiddler. There is a darkness in the land, and only the shining castle shows what once was; Roland must help Malebron and save Elidor by bringing back the light. Each of four castles in Elidor once held one of four Treasures* which in turn held the light of Elidor. Now three are buried in the mound, and Malebron holds the fourth; Roland is to get the other three.

Roland forms in his mind the image of a door—the door to the Watsons' new house—and that door becomes the door into the mound. He will find the other three children, who have each gone in and failed, inside the mound. Malebron gives Roland the spear for comfort. Inside the mound, Roland finds the others staring, entranced, at a crystal apple blossom hanging from the ceiling, which they beg him to touch. He does, with the spear, and the blossom shatters, shattering the trance, too. The children find the Treasures—a sword, a stone, and a cauldron—and leave. Malebron shows them an ancient book of prophecy in which they are pictured and which foretells their coming; it also reveals that things in Elidor will get worse until the song of Findhorn* is heard. When Malebron and the children go back to the ruined castle, they are nearly caught by the enemy. Malebron sends the children back to their world with the Treasures, to keep them safe; when they emerge into their own world, the church through which they had reached Elidor crumbles.

The Treasures have changed to parodies of themselves: the spear is a length of rusty iron; the sword, two sticks nailed together; the stone, a brick; and the cauldron, a chipped cup. Because the family is moving to a new house and their mother would never allow these things to be packed up, the children hide them in the old house. When Roland goes back for them a few days later a puzzled repairman is there; something from the house is generating enough power to jam television sets, radios, and the like in the neighborhood. After the man leaves Roland gets the Treasures and suddenly sees shadows emerging into the air of the empty house. He runs. When the Treasures are hidden in the garage of the new house, neither the television nor the radio works right, and the car starts by itself as it sits in the garage. Realizing that the Treasures are acting as generators, the children bury them in the garden, and the happenings cease.

A year passes, and Elidor does not seem to matter to anyone but Roland. The front door buzzes strangely at times, and once Roland sees an eye peering through the letterbox, but no one is there. The garden is full of static electricity, and birds seem to avoid the place over the Treasures. One day Roland sees shadows in the garden, and that night someone rattles the door, but no one is there when it is opened. Over the next days the rattling goes on; once, trying to surprise whoever is doing it, the children's father jerks it open on what Roland recognizes as night on Elidor before the door slams shut. Early the next morning Roland gets up and peers out through the letterbox, seeing tents and men; he realizes that the enemy has found them, having found the door Roland had used to open the mound. Since he has made it, he can also unmake it, and this Roland does as the men batter at the door to get it open. Though in Elidor the door is destroyed, in Roland's world it bears gashes from the men's axes.

The children go to a party and here receive party favors resembling the treasures, though only Roland believes the connection. During a seance at the party, the planchette draws a unicorn and writes "Findhorn"; as they walk home, the others accuse Roland of doing it himself. Suddenly they are almost run down by a white creature they recognize as a unicorn, bleeding from gashes. The next day David realizes that there is static electricity in the garden because the enemy is trying to find the Treasures in Elidor. All the children are in the garden when two shadows appear; two men come through them and run away. Nicholas and David want to give the men the Treasures and thereby get them out of the way, but Roland, aghast at what had been done to Findhorn, wants to help Malebron.

Two days later their parents go out and the children dig up the Treasures. When someone tries to get into the house, they take the Treasures and leave, feeling that they will be safe with others. On a bus, they find one of the men on the demolition crew for the church; he has seen a horse with a horn and shows them where he saw it. The children get off the bus. Roland runs ahead and finds Findhorn, but when he begs him to sing, the unicorn attacks him, and Nicholas saves him. The men of Elidor come and attack Findhorn, who kills one; the other flees. Berserk, Findhorn nonetheless comes to Helen because she is a maiden, and puts his head on her lap. As Roland implores him to sing, the Elidorian returns and strikes Findhorn with his spear. Dying, the unicorn sings, and the children see Elidor springing to color and to life, but it is not enough. The children throw the Treasures into Elidor, the light fades, and they are left alone in a slum.

ELIZA, a character in *The Enchanted Castle**, by E[dith] Nesbit Bland*. She is the maid at the school where Kathleen*, Gerald*, and James* stay over the holidays. When Eliza finds in Gerald's room a magic wishing ring* he has lost, she slips it onto her finger and becomes invisible without realizing it. Eliza becomes understandably upset when her sweetheart is unable to see her. To keep her out of the way until the ring slips off her finger, the children take Eliza on a picnic at Yalding Castle*, where she is charmed to see the statues come to life at sunset—until she touches one and is terrified. Because of her experience, Eliza vows never to borrow someone else's ring again.

ELLEN PERESBY (*The Sleepers*). *See* Peresby, Ellen

ELLIDYR, a character in Lloyd Alexander's* *The Black Cauldron**. He is the youngest son of King Pen-Llarcau. Because his brothers have inherited the family wealth, Ellidyr has nothing but his horse, his sword, and his enormous strength. He is proud but unhappy and tormented, lashing out at everyone around him. Ellidyr is called to be one of a party of warriors seeking to destroy the Black Crochan*, a cauldron from which an evil lord is producing an invincible army. To his dismay he is put in league with companions he feels are beneath him. Ellidyr soon leaves them and seeks the Crochan by himself, and when his companions find it first, he takes it from them so as to win the glory for himself.

Instead, he is captured by King Morgant*, who wants the Crochan. Realizing how his pride has destroyed him, Ellidyr destroys the cauldron, killing himself in the process.

ELLIE, a character in Charles Kingsley's* *The Water-babies**. She is the daughter of Sir John and My Lady. Ellie lives in a splendid old manor in the country, sleeping in a lovely room where all is clean and white. When Tom*, a grimy chimney sweep, accidentally comes out in Ellie's room as he is cleaning the chimneys, he realizes for the first time how dirty he is and resolves to become clean. Some time later My Lady takes her children to the seaside, and here Ellie is taught by Professor Ptthmllnsprt*. As she tries to recapture Tom, who has become a water-baby*, Ellie falls and hurts her head; she dies a week later. After her death, Ellie again meets Tom, teaching him how to get rid of his ill-temper. By doing this, which she had not wanted to do, Ellie earns a place in a wonderful land. By the time Tom earns a place here, both are grown up, and they fall in love.

ELLISON, BERT, a character in Penelope Lively's* *The Ghost of Thomas Kempe**. Taciturn and heavily built, Bert's advertised trade is that of builder, and he works in everything from wood to masonry. Bert has an unadvertised sideline, however, as a wart charmer, water diviner, and sometime exorcist which he apparently had learned from his father. When the spirit of Thomas Kempe*, a seventeenth-century sorcerer, manifests himself in the twentieth century, Bert is asked by James Harrison* to exorcise him. Bert's attempts fail. Then Thomas, uneasy with twentieth-century life, asks James to "help him go" by laying the remains of his spectacles and pipe on his grave. Bert finds Thomas's coffin where it has been sealed in a vault beneath the floor of the church and lays the possessions there.

ELZIVIR, a character in Jane Louise Curry's* *The Watchers**. He is one of the Aldar*, living at Berinir Gair* in the fourth century. Elzivir is the Watcher there, keeping watch over Tûl Isgrun*, where a ravening force, Katóa*, lies sealed. He is killed by Tekla* and her men when they are brought by Ruan* to Tûl Isgrun.

EMELIUS JONES (*Bonfires and Broomsticks*). *See* Jones, Emelius

EMETH, a character in C[live] S[taples] Lewis's* *The Last Battle**. He is the seventh son of Harpha. Emeth is of Tehishbaan, in Calormen*, the traditional enemy land of Narnia*, a magical land. Since he has been a boy Emeth has served Tash*, the great Calormene god, and has desired to know more of him. He has hated Aslan*, Narnia's great lion-protector, as he has hated Narnia. When Rishda*, a Calormene lord, gathers a company to invade Narnia, Emeth is glad to be part of it, though he does not enjoy going as a merchant and invading with lies and deceit, rather than as a warrior, and invading with more honorable battle. When he gets to Narnia and finds that Rishda is mocking Tash, Emeth likes things even less. One night it seems that Tash has really appeared in the stable on Stable Hill*, and Emeth, with joy, goes to meet him. Instead he comes through the door into a land of sunshine and peace and here meets Aslan himself. Expecting the lion will kill him, Emeth is overjoyed to find that, to Aslan, all the good the young man had done for Tash is counted as service done for him, for nothing good can be done in the name of Tash and nothing evil can be done in the name of Aslan. To his joy, Emeth lives in Aslan's country forever.

EMRYS, a character in *The Change-Child*, by Jane Louise Curry*. He is the son of Mamgu* and the uncle of Eilian Roberts*. Emrys is one of the Red Fairies* who live near the Great Dark Wood. Though he is in love with Pilipala*, he does not admit it, for Mamgu would send the girl away. In thwarting his mother's plans to give Eilian to Simon Rastall*, the unscrupulous nobleman's son the girl is fleeing, Emrys is badly wounded; he is healed by *y Tylwyth Teg*, the Fair Folk*, who live in the middle of the wood. Emrys finally marries Pilipala.

ENCHANTED CASTLE, THE. E[dith] Nesbit Bland. Illus. H. R. Millar. London: T. Fisher Unwin, 1907. 352 pp. British.

Because their cousin has the measles and they cannot go home, Gerald*, James* (Jimmy), and Kathleen* spend the school holidays at Kathleen's empty school, watched over by the French teacher, Mademoiselle*. Exploring the surrounding countryside, the three children find a passage through a bank that brings them to a lovely garden place with statues, surrounding a castle. They follow a thread through a maze to the center, where they find a girl dressed as a princess. She is sleeping, and she wakes when Jimmy kisses her. The princess takes the children to the castle, where she shows them a room full of treasure hidden behind secret panels that only she knows about. One of the treasures is a ring* which, she explains, will make its wearer invisible. The princess is distraught, however, when she puts on the ring and really does become invisible; she confesses that she is really Mabel Prowse*, niece of the housekeeper at Yalding Castle*, playing at magic while everyone is away. Because Mabel cannot get the ring off and her aunt would not understand her present predicament, Gerald, Jimmy, and Kathleen take the girl to stay with them, leaving a note in which Mabel explains that she has been adopted and may not return.

The next day, the four visit Mabel's aunt and are surprised to learn that she believes the note. To earn money for Mabel's food, Gerald acts as a magician at the fair, with Mabel as his invisible assistant. At the end of the show, Mabel realizes that she can slide the ring off her finger, and Gerald uses it to get away from the pressing crowd. Gerald and Mabel go to the castle, where Mabel's aunt is overjoyed to see her and hasn't any idea why she was so calm about her disappearance. Night falls as Gerald walks through the castle gardens, and he watches as the marble statues come alive, frightened only after he touches one of them. He goes into the castle and finds burglars there, but his hasty note tied to a rock tossed through an open window fails to impress Mabel's aunt. Gerald follows the burglars and watches them hide the loot before he creeps into his own room and goes to bed.

The next morning the ring slips from Gerald's finger and is lost. He shows a friendly constable the burglars' hiding place; the man will catch the thieves when they come to divide the loot. Gerald cannot bear the thought of anyone in prison and he warns the men off, warning them also that if they steal any more, he will turn them in. The children discover that Eliza*, the school maid, has found the ring and put it on. To keep her out of the way while she is invisible, they take her to Yalding Castle for a picnic, and she is charmed to see the statues come to life. The children realize that only those who wear the ring can see the living statues, but if one touches the wearer, he becomes afraid. Terrified when she touches a statue, Eliza runs back to the school and slips off the ring. Later the children realize that the ring will no longer make people invisible.

When they put on a play for Eliza, Mademoiselle, and an audience of stuffed dummies, the children learn that the ring has become a wishing ring when Mabel, wearing it, wishes the dummies were alive. The Ugly-Wuglies* are horrible to be near but very, very respectable, and Gerald lures them to Yalding Castle by telling them that he is taking them to a really good hotel. Once there he shuts them in the secret passage behind the Temple of Flora* in the garden, aided by a cheerful young man who does not believe the story of the ring. When the children visit the temple the next morning, hoping the wish has worn off, they find the young man unconscious there and the Ugly-Wuglies gone. All but one Ugly-Wugly become dummies again; the most respectable had found his way down the passage and into a really good hotel and has become human as a result. The children are excited by the former dummy's wealth; after they help the young man, Jimmy, wearing the ring, wishes he were rich and immediately becomes an elderly rich man who does not know his brother and sister. Gerald follows Jimmy and the Ugly-Wugly to London. Using Mr. U. W. Ugli*, the Ugly-Wugly, Gerald gets the ring from Jimmy and wishes them both back to the castle.

The children realize that the ring is what they say it is, and to prove it Mabel says it will make the wearer twelve feet high—a height that proves inconvenient. Kathleen makes the ring a wishing ring again and wishes she were a statue because they do not seem to mind the hot day. Jimmy and Gerald leave the two waiting to become disenchanted. That night Mabel's enchantment wears off, and Kathleen joins the other statues in a night of play. After a statue explains the limitations that can be put on the magic of the ring, Kathleen wishes Mabel were a statue until dawn and wishes the same for the boys when they come. On the island in the middle of the castle lake, they have a delightful feast until dawn, when the others return to their pedestals, telling the children to meet them at the Temple of Strange Stones* in two weeks. The children become themselves on the island and realize that they are stranded there; none of them can swim, though they could as statues, and Psyche* has the ring. When they find a passage in the tunnel that leads them to the Hall of Granted Wishes* where Psyche's statue stands, they take the ring from the statue and wish themselves home.

On a picnic with the young man who helped with the Ugly-Wuglies, they meet Mademoiselle, who is as surprised and pleased to see the young man as he is to see her; he is young Lord Yalding*, and she is the woman he was forbidden by his father to marry. Leaving the two alone, the children go to the castle, where they meet Jefferson D. Conway*, an American millionaire who intends to rent the impoverished Lord Yalding's castle, if it has a ghost in it. When the children wish a ghost on him that night, he finds it to be more than he wants and does not take the castle. The children reveal to Lord Yalding how rich he is, showing him the hidden treasure and giving him the ring. When he sees the statues that night and his wishes come true, the lord decides that he is mad and breaks his engagement with Mademoiselle.

The next night is the night they are to go to the Temple of Strange Stones. All go and witness the moonrise over a standing stone and suddenly see it as a light of eternity and understanding. Statues of gods and demons from all over the world come to worship the light, and the humans fall into a magical sleep. The next morning they go to the Hall of Granted Wishes, where Mademoiselle wishes the magic done by the ring undone and that the ring will become the charm that binds her and Lord Yalding. Many changes are made; parts of the castle built by wishing vanish, and a certain Mr. U. W. Ugli disappears. The lord and Mademoiselle are married and live at the castle on the money from the sale of the treasures.

Note: This work first appeared in *The Strand Magazine*, nos. 192–203 (Dec., 1906–Nov., 1907).

ENEMY AT GREEN KNOWE, AN. Lucy Boston. Illus. Peter Boston. London: Faber and Faber, 1964. 150 pp. British.

Toseland* (Tolly) and his Chinese friend, Hsu* (Ping), are staying at Green Knowe* with Mrs. Linnet Oldknow*, Tolly's grandmother. Because he does not know where his father is, Ping has become almost one of the family. Their first night at Green Knowe, Mrs. Oldknow tells the boys about those who lived at Green Knowe long ago: Dr. Wolfgang Vogel*, a sorcerer and scholar, was brought in 1630 to tutor the son of the master of the house, a sickly child who became so ill under Dr. Vogel's tutelage that he was sent to his grandmother to recover. So fearful did Dr. Vogel finally become of his own black arts that he confessed to Piers Madely*, a local vicar, and burned his books of magic. That night a scream was heard and Dr. Vogel disappeared, never to be seen again.

The next day Ping and Tolly, looking at an ancient mirror*, realize that it reflects not the room they are in but that room at another time. Suddenly they see reflected a woman's sneering face. The boys take the mirror to their room to keep an eye on it. That afternoon Dr. Melanie Delia Powers*, a scholar looking for books belonging to Dr. Vogel, comes. She is very nosy and becomes almost hostile at the end of the visit when Mrs. Oldknow and the boys make it clear that they do not want her searching Green Knowe. Ping recognizes her as the woman in the mirror; Tolly sees her magically steal a small cake at tea. That night Ping sees reflected in the mirror a strange little shape running about the moonlit lawn.

The next day Miss Powers enters the house without being asked but leaves after being shown where Dr. Vogel worked. When the boys take Mrs. Oldknow out on the river that day, she acts strangely and does not feel herself, though this feeling passes when Ping puts on her the Stone of Power* he and Tolly had found while on holiday. When they return to Green Knowe, Miss Powers is there, and she tries to trick Mrs. Oldknow into selling the house and its contents, but fails. After she has left, Ping and Tolly explore Dr. Vogel's room and find a secret passage in which they discover a book made of a bat and a mouse-gnawed copy of an old magic book. These they show to Maitland Pope*, a medieval scholar renting a place to work at Green Knowe. He gathers the pieces of the book and reads part of it—a spell for diminishing a demon—to them.

That night Miss Powers goes out "to gather night flowers," and the next morning the gardens at Green Knowe are invaded by maggots, which the birds eat. Later that day black cats invade the gardens, catching the birds, which Miss Powers hangs on a line in her garden. That night Ping calls the ghost of Hanno*, a gorilla who had escaped from the zoo and been killed at Green Knowe, to frighten away the cats. It works. The next day the orchard is full of snakes guarding what turns out to be an egg in which is a charm to call snakes; the boys throw it into the river and the snakes follow it. That day Miss Powers asks them to come to her at dusk. They go to spy on her and discover in the shed near their house a tall, inscribed pole; Mrs. Oldknow helps them to decipher its inscription, which turns out to be Miss Powers's secret name. That night Tolly wakes to find Susan Oldknow*, a young girl who had lived at Green Knowe in the eighteenth century, taking the mirror from his room. Miss Powers has used old scraps of material she found in the trashbin to compel someone from the house to bring the mirror to her; the scraps were from Susan's nightgown. When Tolly uses Miss Powers's secret name to ask Susan to give him the mirror, she does so and vanishes.

A day passes without Miss Powers's magic, and the boys plan what to do against her. The next day there is to be an eclipse of the sun, and that morning Mrs. Oldknow finds tacked to the door the skin of a human palm with a curse written on it, which she shuts in a prayer book and hides behind the statue of St. Christopher* that stands at the front door. Ping and Tolly see reflected in their mirror Miss Powers making a tremendous effort of will. As the eclipse starts, the boys see "fingers" prying at the roof of the house, breaking stones and tiles. Mr. Pope, who has pierced together an invocation of power, reads it aloud and the fingers vanish. When Miss Powers comes by later, Tolly and Ping see reflected there Tolly's father with Ping's father, whom Ping had thought dead, coming through the garden gate.

ERILLA, a character in Jane Louise Curry's* *The Daybreakers* and *Over the Sea's Edge*. She is the wife of Tepollomis* and the mother of Lincoas*. Erilla is the queen of twelfth-century Abáloc*. A warm, gentle woman, she tells Callista Lee (Callie) and Harry Rivers** and Melissa (Liss) Mitchell* of the troubles Abáloc faces. Erilla is the guardian of the *Book of the Kings of Abáloc**, which she hopes the children will be able to decipher. It is Erilla's great need of someone to save Abáloc that draws the children to her ancient time. Her burial mound is the first to be discovered by Callie and Liss.

ERNIE GOBLE (*The Lost Farm*). *See* Goble, Ernie

ERRETH-AKBE, a character mentioned in Ursula K. LeGuin's* Earthsea trilogy*. He was the greatest wizard and dragonlord who ever lived in Earthsea*, and many songs are sung and stories told of his deeds. One of these was the defeat of the Firelord, who tried to stop the sun at noon. Somehow Erreth-Akbe came to possess the Ring of Erreth-Akbe*. In the Kargad Lands in eastern Earthsea, he joined with rebels in Awabath, from which the Kargish Empire came to be ruled; here he fought the High Priest of the Inmost Temple of the Twin Gods of Kargad and lost. In the battle, the Ring was broken. Half remained with the Priest; Erreth-Akbe gave the other half to Thoreg of Hupin, one of the rebels. Erreth-Akbe escaped from Kargad and went to the western island of Earthsea; here, on Selidor*, he battled with Orm, a great dragon. His power lost, Erreth-Akbe was killed by Orm, but so powerful was the mage that the dragons still remember him. The sword of Erreth-Akbe is set as a pinnacle on the highest tower in the city of Havnor*; pointing skyward, it shines before anything else in Havnor when the sun rises and after anything else at sunset.

ESGAROTH. *See* Lake-town

ESTARRIOL. *See* Vetch

EUPHEMIA ANDREW (*Mary Poppins Comes Back*). *See* Andrew, Euphemia (Miss)

EUSTACE CLARENCE SCRUBB (*Chronicles of Narnia*). *See* Scrubb, Eustace Clarence

FABULOUS FLIGHT, THE. Robert Lawson. Illus. Robert Lawson. Boston: Little, Brown and Company, 1949. 152 pp. American.

Peter Peabody Pepperell III* is a normal little boy until he reaches the age of seven, when he has a fall that affects one of his glands, causing him to grow smaller instead of larger. Another shock might cure Peter, but nothing else will. As the years pass, he gets tinier. Peter makes friends with the small wild animals in the area, who, because of his size, are not afraid of him, and he trains them in military exercises. When they show off at one of his parents' parties, though, the result is disaster. At thirteen, Peter is just four inches high, and he takes up sailing in his father's model boat, on the lake. Here he meets Gus*, a seagull fond of travel who would like to go abroad but who has no one to go with. Peter and Gus become good friends and Gus sometimes takes Peter flying, on his back.

Peter's father is worried, for a scientist has developed a terrible explosive, and his government wants to use it to subjugate the world. The scientist has threatened to explode the substance if anyone tries to steal it. Peter offers to go and steal it, the United States government finally agrees, and his father makes for Peter a little car that straps to Gus's back and that Peter can ride in. Gus and Peter wing their way to London, where Peter receives part of the information he needs; he learns that the scientist's name is Doctor Professor Polopodsky*. He and Gus are then sent to Copenhagen, where Peter learns the name of the country he is to go to; then they are sent to Paris, where he learns the location of the castle where the professor is.

Peter and Gus finally reach the castle, and here Peter makes a startling discovery; Dr. Polopodsky is dead, and his place has been taken by Fisheye Jones*, a smooth operator from Chicago. This man has made two capsules, one filled with sugar and one containing the explosive. He is using the explosive to blackmail the country and will cut in an old confederate who comes upon him. Peter cannot open the safe, so he waits two days for a chance to steal the explosive. When at last Fisheye's comrade opens the safe, intending to use the capsule to blackmail the world, Peter sticks him with a special hypodermic sword, grabs the capsules, and gets away on Gus's back.

On the way home, Peter and Gus detour through Italy. Gus, who has been disappointed in one way or another by every city they have already visited, is equally disappointed in those of Italy. Because the explosive is too terrible for anyone to have, Peter and Gus drop it into the Atlantic Ocean. Despite their maneuvers, they are hit by the resulting blast and Peter falls from Gus's back into the sea, where he floats until Gus finds him. After a hard journey Peter arrives home and all are glad to see him. He is given a medal for his mission and is assured that he had made the right decision in getting rid of the explosive. But, best of all, the shock of falling into the sea has cured his gland problem, and Peter will grow again.

FAIR FOLK, a race of beings in the Chronicles of Prydain*, by Lloyd Alexander*. They are also called y Tylwyth Teg*, the Happy Family, and a dozen other names they find insipid. Some are dwarfs*, some are lake spirits, and some are tall, undefinable creatures; some have wings, though others do not. Once the Fair Folk had all of Prydain* to themselves, but when the race of men came they had been driven underground. The Folk are ruled by King Eiddileg, a harried monarch who feels that his people are unappreciated by the humans in Prydain, who grab any Fair Folk treasure they can get. The Folk themselves are erratic, unreliable, and quarrelsome, but they always come through in a crisis; Doli*, a dwarf, and Gwystyl*, who is in charge of a way post, are among those who help Prydain when Arawn*, an evil king, seeks to control it. With the passing of magic from the land of Prydain, the realm of the Fair Folk is closed to humans.

FAIRYLAND, a place in *Mopsa the Fairy**, by Jean Ingelow*. Fairyland has two entrances; Jack*, a boy who takes four fairies to meet their queen, must take the back way, through the bay where ships associated with evil lie becalmed, up the river that flows inland.

FARANDOLA, a type of being in Madeleine L'Engle's* *A Wind in the Door**. The farandolae are tiny, tiny creatures; they are part of the mitochondria inside the human cell, too small to be seen with even a micro-electron microscope. They are aqueous, deciduous, spore-reproducing, fruit-bearing, and coniferous. When they are young, they have the power to move about their mitochondrion at will. During adolescence, though, the farandolae root themselves and Deepen, becoming mature; now they are called farae. Though they cannot move physically, the farae can move by kything*, or communicating with others in a language deeper than words. By kything the farae are one with each other and with the stars. The farae are essential to the health of the mitochondrion, for when their number drops, hydrogen transport is impaired and the mitochondrion, its cell, and its living host die through energy lack. The temptation of a farandola is to remain immature; an Echthros*, a force of uncreation in the universe, takes advantage of this to talk some farandolae into refusing to Deepen and even into killing some of the farae, thus endangering Charles Wallace Murry*, their host. The Echthros is thwarted by Meg Murry*, Charles's sister, and her companions, Calvin O'Keefe*, Mr. Jenkins*, and Proginoskes*.

FARTHEST SHORE, THE. Ursula K. LeGuin. Illus. Gail Garraty. New York: Atheneum, 1972. 223 pp. American. National Book Award, 1973.

On the island his father rules in the world of Earthsea*, wizards' spells are going sour, so Arren* travels to Roke* to seek advice from the master magicians there. The Archmage—Sparrowhawk, whose real name is Ged*—decides to seek the source of the problem, which, he feels, has to do with an upset of the natural Equilibrium of the world. Arren goes with him.

They go to Hort Town*, where there are no more wizards. One old man who gave up his power offers to take Sparrowhawk to the place where he had lost it; while the mage is in a trance, he and Arren are attacked by three robbers, and the boy is captured and taken onto a slave ship. From here Sparrowhawk rescues him and they travel on. The old man was no guide. They go to Lorbanery*, where things have gone wrong, and there meet an old witch woman who has lost the words of a craft and speaks of a great man of darkness who lives forever. Here, too, they meet Sopli*, the woman's mad son, who has seen the way into the place Sparrowhawk seeks and the enemy he must defeat. They will find them on Obehol*. The two take Sopli onto their boat and sail west.

As they sail, Arren comes to mistrust Sparrowhawk, who does not seem to care if he dies. Those who gave up their powers did so to gain eternal life and Arren, who does not want to die, feels that the mage is leading them into death to keep immortality from them. Finally the three come to Obehol and, trying to land, are attacked by the islanders; Sparrowhawk is wounded. Frantic to get to shore, Sopli leaps into the water and drowns. Arren exhausts himself trying to get away from the island and they drift for several days with little water. Finally they are rescued by the Children of the Open Sea*, who wander the ocean on rafts. Peaceful days follow while Sparrowhawk heals. Then, during the Long Dance* on the shortest night of the year, the chanters suddenly forget the words to the sacred songs and Arren sings the song of Creation to finish the Dance. At dawn that day Orm Embar*, a great dragon, comes upon them, seeking Sparrowhawk's help.

They leave the rafts and come to Dragon's Run*, where dragons are being driven mad and speechless by a man who has come among them. That man, Orm Embar explains, returns from death no matter how many times he is killed, and he is taking their speech—the Speech of Making in which are the words of power—from the terrified dragons, so that they revert to their true natures and attack each other. Sparrowhawk, now Ged, and Arren come to Selidor*, the westernmost island, and there they are met by a sending of the man with eternal life. Ged recognizes him as Cob*, a wizard whom he once knew on Havnor* who summoned the dead to this world but was terrified when Ged dragged him into the world of the dead. Orm Embar, the dragon, goes in search of the real man; after walking for a day, Ged and Arren sleep and wake to find the dead gathered around them, for the dead must obey Cob. Ged sets them free with words of unbinding.

Arren and the mage travel on. When Orm Embar comes upon them, he has been struck dumb, but he leads them to the remains of a dragon, where Ged summons his enemy. The man appears and tries to kill him with an enchanted blade, but Orm Embar intercedes and is killed instead, crushing his enemy as well. The man is not dead but leads Ged and Arren into the cold, dry, dull-colored land of death. Though they lose him at first, deep in this land the two find Cob, who had long ago rejected death and woven a great spell, dying in the attempt but coming and going through a door into the world of the living that had once been closed. Being neither alive nor dead, he seeks to fill his emptiness by drawing the world in after him.

Fleeing Arren and Ged, Cob runs to the open door. With all his strength, Ged closes the door between the worlds and releases Cob from his summons. The journey back to life is long and agonizing, but together the two crawl over mountains separating the dead land and the live world, Arren at last dragging Ged back to the beach on Selidor. Here the mage lies like one dead until a dragon, Kalessin*, wakes him with his name. The dragon flies them to Roke, where they leave Arren, who will become the King of All the Isles of Earthsea, then Kalessin takes Ged home to Gont*. Arren is eventually crowned at Havnor. Of what finally becomes of Ged, more than one story is told.

FATA MORGANA. *See* Margan; Morrigan, the; Fay, Morgan le; Fay, Morgan the

FAY, MORGAN LE, a character in Penelope Lively's* *The Whispering Knights*. She is the sister of Arthur*; for a time she is married to Mr. Steel, a rich industrialist in the twentieth century. Morgan is only one of several identities this witch has had; she is Circe, Duessa, the Ice Queen, and the Witch in Snow White, among others. She is the evil side of the world and is very, very old. Morgan dislikes the laws of nature and tries to work against them according to her own will; though she cannot control the weather, she can use it to suit her purposes. She also dislikes reason. Over the centuries, Morgan's powers change, so the tools to be used against her must change; though once the sign of the cross was effective against her, it is no longer. Morgan has had several places in which to work, for she thrives on the credulity of people, and as their belief in her weakens, she moves on to another place. For a time she lived in what is now a barn in a small village. Here she was rampant in the seventeenth century; in the eighteenth century she was called back and then driven away; in the twentieth she is again called, accidentally, by William*, Martha Timms*, and Susan Poulter*. The last two times it is through children that she has come, for they are vulnerable to her. In the twentieth century, Morgan marries a millionaire and causes a six-lane road to be planned to go through where the barn now stands, knowing that she can control that spot and work her evil on it. Though Morgan is unreceptive to new ideas, she exercises great powers over such things as televisions and cars. Working, as always, on their weaknesses, Morgan attempts to get the children who have called her, succeeding only with Martha. The others rescue the girl and eventually lead Morgan into the circle of the Hampden Stones*. Here a great battle takes place between Morgan and the Stones, and she is defeated, though she will return again, in another generation. *See also* Fay, Morgan the; Margan; Morrigan, the

FAY, MORGAN THE, a figure in traditional Celtic lore who appears as a character in T[erence] H[anbury] White's* *The Sword in the Stone**. She is the queen of the fairy folk, the Queen of Air and Darkness, and she lives in a castle, the Siege of Air and Darkness, to the north of the Forest Sauvage*. When Kay* and the Wart (Arthur*) enter the castle to rescue some friends who are imprisoned there, Morgan tries to tempt them into eating, which will put them under her power, but she fails. Much the two boys see in Morgan's castle has not yet been invented, and she herself appears as a glamor queen of the 1930s. Because she is one of the fairy folk, Morgan cannot stand the touch of iron; when the boys try to touch her with their daggers, she vanishes. *See also* Margan; Fay, Morgan le; Morrigan, the

FELICITY PARMENTER (*The Magical Cupboard*). *See* Parmenter, Felicity

FENODYREE, a character in Alan Garner's* *The Weirdstone of Brisingamen**. He is also called Wineskin or Squabnose, according to the humor of his friends. This dwarf* bears a sword called Widowmaker, though he is no born fighter, preferring merriment. His father was one of few who knew the ways of the ancient dwarf mines, and he had taught them to Fenodyree. This knowledge comes in handy when he and another dwarf, Durathror*, take Colin* and Susan*, two human children, through the caves to safety to keep a powerful stone, Firefrost*, out of the hands of evil creatures.

FERN ARABLE (*Charlotte's Web*). *See* Arable, Fern

FESTE, a horse in *The Children of Green Knowe** and *The Stones of Green Knowe**, by Lucy Boston*. This magnificent chestnut animal is owned by Toseland Oldknow* (Toby) in the eighteenth century. When one stormy night Toby goes for the doctor, Feste carries him safely, refusing to cross a bridge that moments later collapses. Toby also rides him when he rides with Roger d'Aulneaux*, the Norman boy whose father builds Green Knowe* and who visits the seventeenth century through the magic of the Stones*. Even after he dies Feste does not really leave Green Knowe. His old stall is always kept empty for him, and sometimes he uses it; once, in the nineteenth century, a gypsy horsethief sees Feste in his stall and tries to steal him, and the horse throws him so that the man is injured and easily captured. The thief's mother puts a curse on the Oldknows that lasts into the twentieth century. Toseland*, who lives at Green Knowe in the twentieth century, leaves sugar for Feste, and the horse eats it. By putting on Toby's old coat and entering the stable with closed eyes, the boy touches Feste for a thrilling moment.

FFLAM, FFLEWDDUR, a character in the Chronicles of Prydain* and *The Truthful Harp*, by Lloyd Alexander*. He is the son of Godo. Fflewddur is the ruler of a small kingdom in the northern part of Prydain*; weary of the life of a king, he studied to be a bard. Because he did poorly in the examinations, he was not admitted as a true bard, but the Chief Bard of Prydain gave him a beautiful harp; Fflewddur loves the harp, for it has a good tone and sometimes seems almost to play by itself; but he is forever repairing its strings, for when he "embellishes" the truth, the harp strings break, reminding him that he is lying. Fflewddur's playing is not to everyone's taste; when he plays for Achren* at Spiral Castle, she casts him into her dungeon. From here he is rescued by Eilonwy*, Achren's charge, who mistakes him for Gwydion*, the war leader of the High King of Prydain. Saddened because he thinks his own life has been bought at the expense of Gwydion's, Fflewddur goes with Taran* to warn the High King of the uprising of Prydain's southern kings and gets more adventure than he bargained for. He and Taran become close friends and share many adventures, among them a quest for the Black Crochan*, a cauldron in which are created the deathless Cauldron-Born*, and a search for the kidnapped Eilonwy. During this adventure Fflewddur proves the soothing powers of music when he gains the affections of Llyan*, a gigantic cat, by playing his harp. Llyan's attentions are not always welcome, but she becomes Fflewddur's loyal steed, bearing him when he travels with Taran in search of that young man's parents and when he rides with Taran's warriors in a desperate mission to delay the advance of Arawn's* unstoppable troops. In that final great struggle to halt Arawn's takeover of Prydain, Fflewddur makes his greatest sacrifice, burning his beloved harp to keep his companions warm during an unexpected blizzard. After Arawn's defeat, because he is distantly related to the Sons of Don*, Fflewddur goes with them to the Summer Country*, there to be forever happy.

FFLEWDDUR FFLAM. *See* Fflam, Fflewddur

FIELDMOUSE, WILLIE, a character in *Rabbit Hill** and *The Tough Winter**, by Robert Lawson*. This cheerful little mouse is one of a large family that lives on Rabbit Hill. He helps Mole by warning him of traps and poisons and by describing things to him; in return, Mole tunnels through flower beds, where Willie finds the crisp, delicious flower bulbs he so loves. When New Folks come to the Hill, Willie eavesdrops on them from an open window, to learn what they plan to plant. One night he falls into the rain barrel and is fished out in the nick of time by the Folks, who care for him until he is able to leave. Thinking the Folks have killed Willie, Mole rampages through the Folks' yard, crisscrossing it with tunnels, but after Willie's return he repents. Willie's bravery and good humor come in handy during a subsequent tough winter, when he stays with Little Georgie* and his family and keeps up their spirits. Having fought through that winter, Willie is determined to stay on the Hill no matter what and fight through the others as well.

FINDHORN, a unicorn in *Elidor**, by Alan Garner*. He lives in the high places in Elidor*, a magical land. Findhorn is mentioned in *The Lay of the Starved Fool*, an ancient work of prophecy; his song will bring the life back to Elidor. Findhorn is found and attacked by men in Elidor, and in desperation he breaks through into the London of David, Helen, Nicholas, and Roland Watson****. Here this great shining beast with a mane of light and a glorious horn enchants Roland, though, wild with fear, he attacks whomever comes near. In true unicorn fashion, though, he comes to Helen, a virgin, and puts his head in her lap. Roland tries desperately to get Findhorn to sing, but only when he is fatally wounded by a man from Elidor does the unicorn sing, a great, shimmering song that brings life back to Elidor.

FINDRAL, a character in Jane Louise Curry's* *The Wolves of Aam**. He is the pup of Rovanng and Renga* and is one of the few remaining Wolves of Aam* to have the powers of speech. After helping to rescue Lek* from the fortress of Gzel*, Findral guides the conjuror to the City of the Moon Under the Mountain*.

FIREFROST, the title object of *The Weirdstone of Brisingamen**, by Alan Garner*. It is a tear-shaped crystal holding what appears to be a thin, never-ending blue flame. This ancient spellstone turns cloudy when in the presence of evil, and Nastrond, the Great Spirit of Darkness, is powerless against it. It has been imbued with even more power by many wizards; realizing that only purity of heart will withstand the final might of Nastrond, the wizards bound in enchanted sleep 140 pure-hearted warriors and put into Firefrost the power that holds the warriors in their sleep. For centuries the stone lay in its place in Fundindelve*, where the warriors sleep. But a greedy farmer with whom Cadellin Silverbrow*, who watches the sleepers, had bargained for a mare, took Firefrost when Cadellin was not looking. For years the stone was handed down through the farmer's family, from daughter to daughter, until it had come to Bess Mossock, a nurse who had given it to one of her charges, the mother of a girl named Susan*. Susan calls it the Tear and wears it on a bracelet. When she and her brother come to stay with Bess, near Fundindelve, after a terrible struggle the stone is returned to its place.

FIRST TWO LIVES OF LUKAS-KASHA, THE. Lloyd Alexander. New York: E. P. Dutton, 1978. 213 pp. American.

Lukas-Kasha* (Lukas) is Zara-Petra's* village idler. When one day a mountebank named Battisto* comes to the village and, during his show, plunges Lukas's head into a pot of water, the boy finds himself suddenly swimming in the sea, far from Zara-Petra. Coming to land, Lukas, realizing that this is no dream, finds he has real problems; sword-bearing horsemen chasing a girl on horseback suddenly pursue *him*. Trying to defend himself, Lukas slips and hits his head on a rock. He wakes in a lavish tent, tenderly cared for and proclaimed the king of Abadan*. When the last king died without an heir, Locman*, an astrologer, had predicted where the next king would be found. His first predictions were bad, for the prospective kings were dead when Nahdir Aga*, commander of the guards, found them; it was with difficulty that Locman made Nahdir realize that Lukas was indeed the king and not a runaway Bishangari slave like the girl they were pursuing.

Lukas has a pleasant life as king, though Shugdad Mirza*, his Grand Vizier, makes him uncomfortable and Nahdir's brutality appalls him. The slave girl is caught and Lukas tries to help her, but Nur-Jehan* is rude to him. It has always been thus, Shugdad explains, between the inhabitants of Abadan and Bishangar*; the ignorant Bishangari live in mountains filled with gold and jewels and resent the Abadani trying to exploit them, so there is fighting between the countries. Lukas discovers just how ineffectual his kingship is when he tries to stop the fighting, but he succeeds in slowing preparations for war. Lukas does get a chance to halt the execution of a satirical poet, Kayim*, by freeing him and making him his personal servant; Kayim makes him realize that Shugdad may have had the other two prospective monarchs killed. Lukas discovers that he, too, is in danger when he is attacked after dressing in rags and spending an eventful afternoon in the city's bazaar. Realizing that his attacker was Shugdad, Lukas decides to leave the palace, sending Kayim to fetch Nur-Jehan while he makes ready. The two are just in time to save Lukas from Osman*, his personal guard, who, under orders from Shugdad, tries to garrot the king.

Once they are safely out of the palace, the three set off toward the mountains, where they hope to join a caravan and get safely out of the country. Hard travel brings them to the caravan, which, they find, has been robbed by Shir Khan*, a mountain bandit. Here they also find a friend—Namash*—whom Lukas has helped and who now helps him. When the caravan reaches a city, Lukas tricks an unscrupulous horse trader into giving him Nur-Jehan's purloined horse, but she rewards him by galloping off, leaving Lukas and Kayim to wander on their own. They travel from town to town for several weeks, hearing that Shugdad has declared Lukas dead and himself king, and has commanded all able-bodied men to join the army. In a tiny village they find Locman, who fled the palace when Shugdad threatened him for refusing to cast a false prediction and who is now mayor of the tiny town he lives in. After Locman reminds Lukas that he is still king, Lukas decides to find Ardashir*, the elusive king of Bishangar, and try to settle the conflict with him.

As he and Kayim travel, they are captured by Shir Khan, and Lukas manages to so stir the bandit's men that they kill their leader. Lukas and Kayim escape, taking with them Haki*, a Bishangari boy captured by Shir Khan. Haki leads them to his home, where the elders agree that the boy should lead Lukas and Kayim to those who will help, for Shugdad's invasion is almost ready. During the journey, Lukas is caught by a troop of Abadani soldiers and taken to a nearby city, where Nahdir has him locked up in the house he has made his headquarters. Before Lukas is killed, Shugdad wants him to sign a document declaring himself a traitor. The young man is rescued, however, by Kayim and Namash, who owns the house; Namash sets his own house on fire, and in the resulting melee, Lukas escapes after a terrible fight with Nahdir, who is consumed in flames. Lukas does not get far, for he and Kayim are captured as deserters by Abadani soldiers and put into a punishment troop commanded by Osman, his guard at the palace. Heartsick because he had betrayed his king, Osman agrees to obey Lukas's orders.

When the Abadani troop meets a troop commanded by Nur-Jehan, they make an uneasy truce, and Lukas discovers that Ardashir has been dead for many years and that Nur-Jehan, his daughter, is really queen of Bishangar. Things look bad for the Bishangari because of the superior numbers of Abadani forces, but Lukas realizes that if Shugdad is got out of the way, the soldiers will probably obey his orders. Lukas takes his few forces to meet Shugdad's army and himself lures Shugdad away from his men; he goes in the wrong direction, however, and narrowly escapes death at Shugdad's hands before Osman kills the man. Lukas is proclaimed the true king, and the Abadani forces are glad to have him in command.

Weary of settling affairs of state in Bishangar, Lukas goes back to his palace, meeting on the way Namash, who has found water under his burned house— valuable in this dry land. At home Lukas makes new and fairer laws. One day he slips away and goes to the beach where he had washed up and is excited to see Nur-Jehan riding toward him along the beach. A loosened boulder slips, however, and Lukas falls into the sea, raising his head to find himself back in Zara-Petra, exactly where and when he began. The townspeople, thinking Battisto is a fake, chase him out of town. Bereft and longing for his other life, Lukas begins a third life, journeying in search of Abadan, telling tales of it along the way to earn his living.

FISHEYE JONES (*The Fabulous Flight*). *See* Jones, Fisheye

FISSY PARMENTER (*The Magical Cupboard*). *See* Parmenter, Felicity

FITH, a character in Jane Louise Curry's* *The Wolves of Aam*. His father is Nee and his mother is Issa, queen of the small folk known as the Tiddi*. Shy and awkward, Fith feels he must prove his worth, and he does so when his friend, Runner-to-the-Sky's-Edge* (Runner), is kidnapped by Lord Naghar's* men. With Cathound*, the strange girl adopted by the Tiddi, Fith goes after Runner and eventually helps to rescue Lek*, a conjuror, from the fortress of Gzel*. Fith keeps a special pet, Tootoo, a little owl.

FITZGIBBON, MR., a character in *Mrs. Frisby and the Rats of NIMH**, by Robert C. O'Brien*. He is the father of Billy and Paul Fitzgibbon. Mr. Fitzgibbon is a farmer. In his garden live Mrs. Frisby*, a field mouse, and her family, and near his home is the burrow of a group of experimental rats who escaped from Nimh*; they have tapped into his electrical cable. When he hears about the rats who had chewed through a power cable in a hardware store, Mr. Fitzgibbon mentions his own colony and men from the government come to exterminate it.

FIVE CHILDREN AND IT. E[dith] Nesbit Bland. Illus. H. R. Millar. London: T. Fisher Unwin, 1902. 301 pp. British.

Robert*, Anthea*, Jane*, Cyril*, and their baby brother, the Lamb*, have accompanied their mother on vacation in the country. Soon after they arrive, their mother is called to care for their grandmother, and the children are left in the care of the servants. One day, digging in a nearby gravel pit, they find a Psammead*, an odd-looking creature thousands of years old who agrees to give one wish a day to all. At sunset the enchantment will fade. Anthea wishes they were as beautiful as the day, and the children are disconcerted to find that they do not recognize each other and neither do the servants. Shooed away from their own home, the children spend a long and hungry afternoon until they are restored at sundown.

The next day the children are careful to make the Psammead promise that the servants will not notice the gifts it gives them, and they wish to be rich. But the gold they get proves to be almost impossible to spend, for tradesmen think they have stolen it and either refuse it or refuse to give change. Finally a horse trader takes the children to the police. On the way they meet Martha*, one of the servants, who of course does not see the gold pieces and is triumphant when, at sunset, they reach the police station and the gold has vanished. The children are taken home in disgrace. They are unable to find the Psammead the next morning until Robert makes an unfortunate remark. Tired of the Lamb's mischievous behavior, he wishes that everybody would want him so the children could get some peace. And everybody who sees the Lamb *does* want him, from Lady Chittendem* to the gypsies in a nearby camp, who claim him as their own. At sunset, however, they change their minds.

Three days later the children decide that each will take turns wishing, if the others agree to the wish. Anthea wishes first and asks for wings to fly with. The children find flying delightful but soon discover, when they get hungry, that winged humans are too frightening for people to help. Finding a clergyman's house near a church with a tall tower, the children take food from the house, leaving money to pay for it, and eat it on the high, private tower. Exhausted, they sleep until after sunset and find that they cannot get down. Rousing the vicarage with their cries, they are rescued and taken home.

The next day they are punished by not being allowed outside. Only Robert is allowed out to "get something"—a wish from the Psammead. Unable to think of one, he wishes that the others would get whatever they wish and is surprised to return to the house and discover it has become a besieged castle. Robert is taken prisoner by the enemy, and his story is not believed. A soldier accompanies him back to the Psammead, and is astonished when Robert wishes he were with the others and vanishes. Though being in a besieged castle is exciting, the children grow frightened as they watch the enemy's war preparations and realize that there will be an attack. They are able to hold their "castle" until sundown, when all is set right.

While playing bandits the next morning, the children make the baker's boy angry and Robert fights him, only to lose and be kicked all the way to the sandpit. Furious, Robert wishes he were bigger than the other boy and immediately becomes ten feet tall and able to satisfactorily terrify the baker's boy. To get pocket money, the children show Robert at a nearby fair and have to do some fancy maneuvering at sundown to get him away without anyone finding out.

Two days later Cyril wakes early and visits the Psammead to ask it to grant them wishes wished even while they are not at the sandpit. Later that day, pestered by the Lamb, Cyril wishes that the baby would grow up then, and the children are horrified when he does—into a young man who wants to have nothing to do with them. Keeping him in sight that day is difficult, but they manage it and are rewarded just before sunset by the sight of Martha—who sees him as a tired baby—carrying the tiresome young man into the house and cooing babytalk to him.

Cyril again makes a wish the next morning when he absent-mindedly wishes there were Indians in England. Realizing what he has done, the girls arrange to get the Lamb and Martha to a safe place. When Indians appear at the house, the children dress as Indians and go out to pow-wow with Yellow Eagle* and his band. The Indians see through their disguises and chase them to the sandpit, where they prepare to scalp the children and burn them at the stake. Longing for his native land, Yellow Eagle wishes he and his warriors were there and immediately vanish. Martha, coming back from town, reveals shyly that she and her sweetheart are getting married.

The children's grandmother having recovered, their mother returns. That day, Lady Chittendem's jewels are stolen. Because her mother has little jewelry herself, Jane wishes that she will find the Lady's jewels in her room when she returns, and she does. When their mother hears that Lady Chittendem has lost her jewelry and that Martha's sweetheart has been at the house, she decides that he must have taken the jewels and hidden them there. Off she goes to tell the police. Horrified by the awful mess they have made of things, Anthea and Jane go to the Psammead and promise never to ask any more wishes if it will only grant them several that day. They wish that Lady Chittendem would find she has not lost her jewels, and that their mother would forget about the jewels and that Martha's sweetheart has been at the house. In turn, the Psammead asks them to make a wish for it: that they would not be able to tell anyone about it. Returning home, they find that all is well.

Note: This work first appeared as "The Psammead" in *The Strand Magazine*, nos. 136–144 (April–Dec., 1902).

FIVER, a character in Richard Adams's* *Watership Down**. He is the brother of Hazel*; he becomes the mate of Vilthuril. This rabbit's real name is Hrairoo, which means "little thousand," for he is the smallest of a large litter; to rabbits anything over four is a lot or "a thousand." Small and always tense, Fiver is psychic, having visions that he cannot always understand. He also gets inexplicable feelings about certain places, sensing their true natures. Fiver senses the danger his warren is in when land developers decide to build houses where the warren is, and so persuasive are his visions that Hazel and nine others join him on a journey that takes them to Watership Down. Fiver's visions help them along the way and also when they get there: he senses the dangers in Cowslip's* warren and finds Hazel when the latter has been shot; during the terrible battle between Hazel's rabbits and those of General Woundwort*, Fiver goes into a trance and unwittingly helps Hazel come up with a plan to save the warren. After this battle, Fiver is ruled more and more by that shadowy country from which his visions come, though he is devoted to Vilthuril. Threar, one of the four kittens in their first litter, inherits Fiver's psychic abilities.

FLEDGE, a character in C[live] S[taples] Lewis's* *The Magician's Nephew** and *The Last Battle**. His father was an officer's charger. He was born on earth and became a cabhorse; here his name is Strawberry. Being a London cabhorse is a miserable job, and Strawberry does not like it, nor does his owner, Frank*, like being a cabdriver. One day the two are magically taken into Narnia*, a magical world just being created. Its creator, Aslan*, chooses Strawberry to be one of the intelligent talking beasts in this land; he later gives the horse great copper- and chestnut-colored wings and makes him the father of all flying horses, giving him the name Fledge. Fledge takes Digory Kirke*, a boy from London, and his companion, Polly Plummer*, to the great walled garden west of Narnia, to pluck a silver apple* from one of its trees. He later appears in Aslan's country when Narnia comes to an end.

FLETCHER, FATHER, a character in *The Watch House**, by Robert Westall*. This Anglican priest has a church at Garmouth, England. Tall and handsome, he is well thought of. Father Fletcher is bored with his curacy, though he complains only to Father da Souza*, a Catholic priest. Father Fletcher is an old hand at organizing activities for his parishioners, especially for the teenagers. He sees only what he wants to see and is cheerfully dim about what goes on around him. When Father da Souza must exorcise the malevolent spirit of Major Scobie Hague*, he feels that he cannot call upon Father Fletcher, but the Father is called by da Souza's superior just in time to finish the exorcism when Father da Souza is temporarily blinded.

FOREST SAUVAGE, a place in *The Sword in the Stone**, by T[erence] H[anbury] White*. This huge forest is almost impenetrable in most places, and it is the home of strange, indescribable creatures, of wizards such as Merlyn* and Madame Mim*, of wild boars and wolves, of small dragons, and of outlaws, like Robin Wood* and his band. In a clearing in the forest is the castle of Sir Ector. When his ward, the Wart (Arthur*), goes after a hawk which has flown into the forest, the boy gets lost and meets King Pellinore* and the Questing Beast* and finds Merlyn. When Kay*, Sir Ector's son, wants an adventure of his own, he and the Wart are sent into the forest to have it.

FOSTER, WINIFRED (WINNIE), a character in Natalie Babbitt's* *Tuck Everlasting**. She is the only child of Mr. and Mrs. Foster; she marries a man whose last name is Jackson. Winnie was born in 1870 into a proud, respectable family. So overbearing are her mother and grandmother that when she is about eleven, Winnie feels smothered. She longs to be by herself for a change and decides to run away, though she later changes her mind. Seeking the source of what her grandmother calls "elf music," she comes to a tiny spring* in the family's woods and there meets Jesse Tuck*, a glorious young man whom she is immediately infatuated with. She also meets the rest of his family—Angus, Mae, and Miles Tuck***—and comes to love them for their warmth and their casual lifestyle. Winnie shocks her family by helping Mae, in jail for killing the stranger* menacing Winnie, to escape. Jesse begs Winnie to drink water from the spring when she is seventeen, so they can be together forever and have fun, though the rest of the family discourages this. Though she uses the water to protect her favorite toad, Winnie does not drink it herself; she marries, has children, and dies in 1948.

FRANCIS, a character in *Wet Magic**, by E[dith] Nesbit Bland*. He is the brother of Mavis*, Kathleen*, and Bernard*. His nickname is "France." Francis has been fond of water in any form since birth, exploring it in all its shapes, from puddle to horse trough to bath supply. When he buys an aquarium and his brother and sisters fix it up to look like a real seascape, Francis is surprised when what seems to be a mermaid appears and vanishes in it after he starts to recite a poem*. This poem vaults him into several adventures when he and the others go to the seaside, for when he says it a mermaid appears who asks him and Mavis to rescue Freia*, a mermaid captured by circus people. After the rescue, Freia takes all the children to her home, Merland*, which they defend from the dreadful Under Folk*. Francis and the others are captured by the Under Folk and help end the centuries-long war between the sea peoples by rescuing Freia's father, who pleads the cause of peace.

FRANCIS BABINGTON (*A Traveller in Time*). *See* Babington, Francis

FRANK, a character in C[live] S[taples] Lewis's* *The Magician's Nephew*. He is the husband of Helen; he becomes the father of several children. Frank was born in England, in the country, but because he could make no living there he went to London, to become a cabdriver. It is a bad job and he hates it, for he loves the country and hates the treeless, gray city. One day when Frank is out with his horse, Strawberry (Fledge*), Jadis*, an evil queen from a distant world, steals his cab. Pursuing her, Frank is accidentally pulled, with Strawberry, into Narnia*, a magical land just being created. It is a sumptuous place, just where Frank would love to live for the rest of his life. He does, for Aslan*, Narnia's great creator, brings Helen into Narnia and makes them its first king and queen. In Narnia Frank loses the cunning and quarrelsomeness he had picked up in London, and his natural kindness and courage come to the fore. His reign is a happy one. Frank's second son becomes king of Archenland*, the land to the south.

FRANKLIN, BENJAMIN (BEN), an eighteenth-century inventor and states-man (1706–1790) who appears as a character in Robert Lawson's* *Ben and Me*. In the winter of 1745, Ben meets Amos*, an intelligent, ingenious mouse who from that time on gives him the benefit of his advice. Ben is sorely in need of this advice, for, while brilliant, he does not always have his wits about him; Amos, ensconced in the fur cap Ben wears, is often called upon to get the great man safely across the street. Relations between Ben and Amos are sometimes strained by Ben's experiments, especially those which involve Amos as unwitting co-experimenter. Ben also tends to hog the glory that should be that of others; though Amos gives him the idea for the Franklin stove, Ben presents that idea as his own, and he also takes the credit for the Declaration of Independence, which he alters from a declaration written by Red Jefferson, a mouse friend of Thomas Jefferson's. Ben's success as ambassador to France is due to Amos, for the mouse discovers diplomatic plots against Ben and is able to warn him in time. Ben is as enthusiastic about new clothes and finery as he is about his experiments and statecraft and is as pleased as a small boy with the adulation he receives after his successes. On the eve of Ben's eighty-first birthday, Amos presents him with a tri-corner hat; it has no place for Amos to hide in it, but at eighty-one Ben is old enough to go out on his own. After Ben's death Amos writes the true story of the man's achievements.

FRED TWIGLEY (*Mary Poppins Opens the Door*). *See* Twigley, Fred

FREDA, a character in *The Voyage of QV 66**, by Penelope Lively*. She is a cow. Freda is one of the creatures left on Earth after the humans go to Mars to avoid a world-wide flood. Usually docile and unassertive, Freda can be dangerous when angered; when dogs try to attack Stanley*, a monkey which she and a friend, Pal*, have just discovered, Freda reacts violently. She becomes part of the small group that accompanies Stanley to London to find others like himself. Freda is not fond of things that are different or out of the ordinary, taking them as a personal affront. Though she is not vain, she loves hats and takes every chance to wear them. Sentimental, she tries to adopt all manner of young creatures.

FREDERICK C. LITTLE, MRS. (*Stuart Little*). *See* Little, Mrs. Frederick C.

FREE COMMOTS, a place in the Chronicles of Prydain*, by Lloyd Alexander*. This cantrev to the east of the Small Avren River is a rich and peaceful place. It is a land of small villages surrounded by rich farmland. Here live some of the greatest craftspeople in Prydain*: Annlaw Clay-Shaper, the finest potter; Hevydd, a master smith; Dwyvach, an excellent weaver; and Llonio, who excels at the art of making do and creating his own luck. Taran*, a young man seeking his true place in the world, comes to the Free Commots to find the Mirror of Llunet*, which reflects the truth about those who look into it. He later comes to raise the people of the Commots to battle Arawn*, the evil king seeking to rule Prydain. In that war Llonio and Annlaw are killed.

FREELING, CAPTAIN. *See* Nicholas

FREIA, a character in E[dith] Nesbit Bland's* *Wet Magic**. She is the sister of Maia and the daughter of the king and queen of Merland*. Because she is a princess, Freia has many responsibilities: keeping the rivers of the earth flowing, seeing to the rain and snow, setting free the winds, watching over the tides and whirlpools, and keeping the sea out of the kingdom of Merland. She also commands the Crustacean Brigade. Freia is captured by circus people with a rope made of llama hair, making it impossible for her to free herself; Mavis* and Francis*, two land children, rescue her. In gratitude, Freia brings them, their brother and sister, Bernard* and Kathleen*, and their friend, Reuben*, to Merland. After Francis, Mavis, Bernard, and Kathleen are captured by the Under Folk*, enemies of Merland, Freia becomes a prisoner too when Francis recites a poem* that calls her to him. In the kingdom of the Under Folk, Freia finds her lost father and rescues him, thus bringing about peace between the warring sea peoples. Though at first repulsed by what she thinks is his ugliness, Freia becomes engaged to Ulfin*, one of the Under Folk, after he removes the ugly armor he has always worn and reveals himself to be as fair as one of the Merpeople.

FRISBY, JONATHAN, a character in Robert O'Brien's* *Mrs. Frisby and the Rats of NIMH**. He was the husband of Mrs. Frisby* and the father of Martin, Teresa, Cynthia, and Timothy Frisby. Jonathan was an ordinary mouse until he became part of an experiment at Nimh*. There he learned to read and his intelligence and lifespan were increased. When Justin*, Nicodemus*, and the other experimental rats decided to escape, Jonathan went with them; of eight mice, only he and Mr. Ages* escaped. Jonathan stayed with the rats until he settled down to raise a family. Jonathan was killed one night when he was trying to put sleeping powder into the food of Dragon*, a cat, in order to get the animal out of the way for a while.

FRISBY, MRS., the title character in *Mrs. Frisby and the Rats of NIMH**, by Robert O'Brien*. She is the widow of Jonathan Frisby* and the mother of Teresa, Martin, Cynthia, and Timothy Frisby. Mrs. Frisby is a field mouse; after her husband's death she struggles along as best she can, living in the winter in Mr. Fitzgibbon's* garden. When Timothy catches pneumonia and is too delicate to travel during Moving Day, Mrs. Frisby takes desperate measures, for their house will be destroyed when the garden is plowed and she does not know what to do. Finally she is sent to the rats who live near the Fitzgibbon house and, enlisting their aid, learns things that answer many questions about her husband. Mrs. Frisby proves her bravery time and again as she goes to an owl for help, rides on the back of Jeremy*, a crow, and risks her life to put sleeping powder into the food of Dragon*, a cat. Her capture by Billy Fitzgibbon is a lucky accident, for she learns that the rat colony will soon be exterminated, and she is able to warn them in time.

FUJIWARA, a character in Lloyd Alexander's* *Time Cat**. His nephew is Ichigo*, boy-emperor of Japan in 998. As Regent and adviser to Ichigo, Fujiwara bullies the boy into submission to him. When Jason*, a boy from the twentieth century, and Gareth*, his cat, accompany a present of kittens to the Celestial Palace, Fujiwara does not approve of the gift. Unreasonably enraged when he discovers that the kittens have secretly been helping the local peasants by keeping down the rat population, Fujiwara demands their deaths, provoking Ichigo into humbling him and proving once and for all that he is Emperor.

FUNDINDELVE, a place in Alan Garner's* *The Weirdstone of Brisingamen** and *The Moon of Gomrath**. Once a great dwarf mine near what is now Alderley, England, Fundindelve has become the last stronghold of High Magic in our world. Long ago 140 pure-hearted warriors were put into an enchanted sleep, to sleep here until the time comes when they ride to defeat Nastrond, a great evil lord. Beside each warrior sleeps a white mare. In nearby caves lies a great treasure to help the king put right the evils of the world. Fundindelve is guarded by a great magic that keeps the warriors ever young; this magic was put into

Firefrost*, a crystal stone of power. When this stone is stolen by a greedy farmer, Cadellin Silverbrow*, who watches over the warriors in this enchanted place, searches for years to recover it. To Fundindelve come the elves* of the north when they need Cadellin's help.

GALAPAS, a figure in Arthurian lore who appears as a character in T[erence] H[anbury] White's* *The Sword in the Stone*. He has several daughters. Galapas is ten feet tall, extremely big for a giant, and he lives in a castle in the Forest of the Burbly Water. He has dug many pits in the forest and hidden them, so as to catch anyone who tumbles into them; anyone unfortunate enough to do so is either eaten, kept as a slave, or held for ransom. Galapas is a tyrant with a castle full of dreadful things, such as human corpses hanging in the game closets to age. He has many slaves. One of his captives, for a time, is King Pellinore*, who is rescued when the Questing Beast* comes looking for him, and Merlyn*, a wizard, and the Wart (Arthur*), his young companion, take this chance to open the dungeons. All Galapas's slaves go free while the Beast has him cornered in the castle tower.

GANDALF, a character in J[ohn] R[onald] R[euel] Tolkien's* *The Hobbit* and *The Lord of the Rings*. This old wizard converses with animals and performs certain kinds of magic with his wand. Having made a special study of enchantment with fire and lights, he is well known for his fireworks. Gandalf has been everywhere, from the mountains, where he once healed the eagle-lord, to the dungeons of the Necromancer, where he found the father of Thorin Oakenshield* and got from him a map showing the secret entrance to the halls Smaug*, a dragon, had overrun. Gandalf finds a burglar for Thorin when that dwarf* decides to recover the ancient treasure; he assures the dwarves that Bilbo Baggins's* meek exterior hides the heart of a warrior. Gandalf accompanies the group along part of the way, saving them from wild wolves and goblins*, and persuading Beorn* to lend them ponies. Then he joins a council of white wizards and helps them drive the Necromancer from his hold. He rejoins the questers in time for Thorin's final battle for possession of the treasure, though Gandalf does not fight for them. After many years in service to Middle-earth, Gandalf goes with the elves* to a country beyond the ken of men.

GARANHIR, a figure in traditional Celtic lore who appears as a character in Alan Garner's* *The Moon of Gomrath**. He is also called Gorlassar. Garanhir is at least seven feet tall and is powerfully built; on his head grows a set of the antlers of a stag. He is the leader of the Herlathing, the Wild Hunt*. Garanhir is of the Old Magic that cannot be controlled, and his power is of sun magic, moon magic, and blood magic. He is the power of all wild things: of lightning and of storm, of the seasons and the cycle of birth and death, of the need to make and to kill. He is the essential power of the earth. Like his twelve followers, Garanhir was made to sleep for centuries by the lords of High Magic, until Colin*, a young boy, rouses him by searching for the Mothan*, a magical plant growing on the mound where Garanhir sleeps. When his followers are roused, Garanhir leads them as before, coming to the aid of Colin's sister, Susan*, because she bears the Mark of Fohla*, a bracelet connected with the Old Magic, as he is. Finally he and the rest of the Hunt ride with Celemon* and her sisters to Caer Rigor, to be free forever. *See also* Herne

GARETH, a character in Lloyd Alexander's* *Time Cat**. He is a black cat with a white mark in the shape of an ankh on his chest. Cats do not have nine lives; they have the ability to visit nine different lifetimes—any place at any time period. Because Jason*, Gareth's owner, is growing up and must learn to be an adult, Gareth takes him on a journey to nine different countries and times, where the boy encounters many people and learns about himself and others.

GARLAND, JACK, a character in Jane Louise Curry's* *Poor Tom's Ghost**. Jack is the fourteen-year-old-brother of Tom Garland*; he is an Elizabethan boy-actor. His jealousy of Katherine Purfet Garland*, Tom's wife, grows into hatred. Hoping to break up the marriage, Jack deceives Tom into thinking his wife has deserted him, causing the man such misery that Tom's ghost haunts Castle Cox* into the twentieth century. Roger Nicholas*, a boy from the 1970s, finds himself a ghost in Elizabethan England and uses Jack to set things right, releasing Tom from his haunting. Jack dies of the plague in 1603.

GARLAND, KATHERINE PURFET, a character in *Poor Tom's Ghost**, by Jane Louise Curry*. She is the wife of Tom Garland*. Tom's devotion to her causes Jack Garland*, his brother, to hate her and concoct the plot that is Tom's downfall. She dies in 1642.

GARLAND, TOM, a character in Jane Louise Curry's* *Poor Tom's Ghost**. He is the husband of Katherine Garland* and the older brother of Jack Garland*. Tom is an Elizabethan actor whose devotion to his wife makes Jack so jealous that the boy plots to break up the marriage. Jack's plot leads to his brother's death of the plague in 1603, however, and Tom's ghost haunts twentieth-century Castle Cox* as it relives the man's grief at what he thinks is his wife's perfidy and seeks vengeance on the man whom he thinks stole her love. Tom pulls Tony

Nicholas*, a twentieth-century actor, into his story, thereby endangering Tony's life. After Roger Nicholas*, Tony's son, goes back to Elizabethan England and sets all right, Tom is able to avoid the plague and is reunited with Kate, dying six days after she does in 1642.

GARNER, ALAN (1935–   ), British writer. He was born in Congleton, Cheshire, on 17 October 1935, and was educated at Alderley Edge Primary School, in Wilmslow, Cheshire; at Manchester Grammar School; and at Magdalen College, Oxford. Garner married Anne Cook in 1956; they had one son and two daughters; the marriage was dissolved. In 1972 he married Griselda Greaves; they have one son.

Of Garner's eleven works primarily for children, four are full-length fantasies. *The Weirdstone of Brisingamen*, *The Moon of Gomrath*, and *Elidor* are high fantasy; *The Owl Service* is not. The realm of Garner's fantasies is one of beauty and terror, where the ordinary world and the fantastic one come together, sometimes in shattering collision.

In *The Weirdstone of Brisingamen* and *The Moon of Gomrath*, the fantasy world is an undercurrent of our own. The worlds of elves* and humans once were close, but humankind chose to master the world with what they could make with their hands; due to the resulting pollution, the elves have taken refuge in cleaner places, far from the smoking factories. Because humans have lost familiarity with the wild forces of magic and could be destroyed by them, the wizards and dwarfs* have withdrawn to protect them. Little contact is made between the worlds, and that contact is fraught with peril for each; in getting a milk-white mare for one of the knights who sleep in Fundindelve* until England has need of them, Cadellin Silverbrow*, a wizard, loses a powerful jewel to a greedy farmer; Colin* and Susan*, two human children drawn into Cadellin's world, make a mistake out of ignorance and unleash the uncontrollable Wild Hunt*. Another peril endangers the children, for the world of magic is a seductive one, and once they have acted in it they are not completely content in their ordinary lives. The bracelet Susan is given to protect her takes her farther and farther from human life; the brilliant call of a magical horn haunts Colin for the rest of his days. The world of magic is dangerous, for it is perilous fair.

The magical world of *Elidor* is just as fair and just as perilous. It is not part of our world, but the two touch at places that are neither one thing nor another, and the doors can be opened with music. Bleak and blasted, the land had a glory that now shines only in one of its castles, but even this echo is enough to inspire Roland Watson* to help Malebron*, an Elidorian king. Roland is the only one of the Watson children to do what Malebron requests, and, later, in his own world, he is the only one who can hold Elidor's* magic in his heart; his brothers and sister seem to dismiss their adventure there as a dream. To Roland, though, it is very real and very vital, and he cannot forget or dismiss Malebron and the charge he had laid on them. Elidor's magic lingers where it has touched his own life; in the door he has used as an entrance into a mound, in the common objects that shine as treasures in their own land. To Roland the shining castle of Gorias is as much a promise as it is a memory of what had been. The land will quicken again at a unicorn's song; evil will be defeated, and Elidor will be renewed. When the unicorn, Findhorn*, breaks through into the slum of Roland's world, it is a shining thing, reflecting the glory of its world, and Roland is awed. But to sing the unicorn must die, and the death of this bright creature is payment too much for the quickening of Elidor; in anger and in pain Roland hurls the treasure he has guarded for Malebron back into the glowing land. The magic world can touch lives with great beauty, but it can break them as well.

In *The Owl Service* the magical world is part of our own, but it intrudes into our reality not as a physical entity but as a power, a force for evil or for good. It is an ancient force—the power of the earth, of the fertile flowers that grow there—used long ago to create a woman, Blodeuwedd*. Her triangle of love, hate, and betrayal ended tragically; for succeeding generations the triangle has been played out again and again as the earth force has built up in the valley and must be released. Like the traditional Earth Mother, Blodeuwedd is able to nurture or to destroy, to love or to hate; she is the gentle, fertile flowers or the hunting owl; the power in the valley can be a power of life or of death. Each time the drama has been played out in successive generations, the hate has been emphasized, and tragedy has resulted. Finally it is the turn of Roger and Alison Bradley**, two English teenagers, and Gwyn*, the son of their Welsh cook. In their story, the triangle of love and betrayal is not just the clash of individuals; it is a conflict of cultures and classes. Though Blodeuwedd's flower aspect prevails and it seems that all will end happily, it is at Gwyn's expense, for he is so hurt by Alison's betrayal that he cannot even forgive her enough to help her when she needs him.

In their danger and their beauty Garner's fantasy worlds echo the traditional lore of the British Isles. *The Weirdstone of Brisingamen* and *The Moon of Gomrath* are based partially on Celtic lore; many of the names and figures are to be found in traditional lore, the places named are real, and the spells appear in old manuscripts. *The Owl Service* is based on the tale of Blodeuwedd in the *Mabinogion*. *Elidor* takes us to the Arthurian quest for the grail. In these tales we find prototypes of the lance, the sword, the stone, and the cauldron that hold the light of Elidor; Malebron is a type of lamed Fisher King; and the bleak and barren land quickens into life at the proper sacrifice. Roland is a type of perfect knight, faithful and true—but betrayed. For, as in traditional tales, the brush with the Other can be lovely and dangerous; beauty's exquisite edge can cut to the heart.

Garner's works are rich in incident and move surely to their conclusions. His lyrical style is well suited to his subject. Though some characters, such as Roland and Gwyn, are well realized and three-dimensional, others are fairly lifeless. This is especially true of the children in *The Weirdstone of Brisingame* and *The*

Moon of Gomrath, of Roland's brothers and sister, and of Roger and Alison in *The Owl Service*. Sometimes confusing, Garner's later works are more multi-layered and rich in theme than his earlier novels.

Works

Juvenile fantasy: *The Weirdstone of Brisingamen* (1960); *The Moon of Gomrath* (1963); *Elidor* (1966); *The Owl Service* (1967).
Juvenile short fantasy, novels, etc.: *The Old Man of Mow* (1966); *The Breadhorse* (1975), with Albin Trowski; *The Stone Book* (1976); *Granny Reardon* (1977); *Tom Fobble's Day* (1977); *Aimer Gate* (1978); *The Land of the Gad* (1981), retelling of folk tales.
Adult: *Red Shift* (1973).

Secondary Works

Berman, Ruth. "Who's Lleu?" *Mythlore*, 4 (June, 1977), pp. 20–21.
Cameron, Eleanor. "The Owl Service: A Study," *Wilson Library Bulletin*, 44 (December, 1969), pp. 425–33.
Garner, Alan. "Coming to Terms," *Children's Literature in Education*, 2 (July, 1970), pp. 15–29.
Gillies, Carolyn. "Possession and Structure in the Novels of Alan Garner," *Children's Literature in Education*, 18 (Fall, 1975), pp. 107–17.
McMahon, Patricia. "A Second Look: *Elidor*," *The Horn Book Magazine*, 56 (June, 1980), pp. 328–31.
Philip, Neil. *A Fine Anger: A Critical Introduction to the Work of Alan Garner*. New York: Philomel, 1981.
Rees, David. "Alan Garner: Some Doubts," *The Horn Book Magazine*, 55 (June, 1979), pp. 282–89.
Townsend, John Rowe. "Alan Garner," in *A Sense of Story* (Boston: The Horn Book, 1971), pp. 108–19. [Rev. in *A Sounding of Storytellers* (New York: J. B. Lippincott, 1979), pp. 81–96.]
Watkins, Tony. "Alan Garner's 'Elidor,' " *Children's Literature in Education*, 7 (March, 1972), pp. 56–63.
West, Richard C. "The Tolkienians: Some Introductory Reflections on Alan Garner, Carol Kendall, and Lloyd Alexander," *Orcrist*, 2 (1967–1968), pp. 4–15.
Whitaker, Muriel A. " 'The Hollow Hills': A Celtic Motif in Modern Fantasy," *Mosaic*, 13 (Spring/Summer, 1980), pp. 165–78.

GAST, a character in *Taran Wanderer** and *The High King**, by Lloyd Alexander*. He is a lord in Cantrev Cadiffor, in the southern part of Prydain*. Gast calls himself Gast the Generous, though he is generous only with himself; at his feasts he urges his guests to stuff themselves, though he gives them little food, while he eats heartily. Gast is proud of his possessions, though he does not always care for them and sometimes does not realize their true worth. During a dispute with Lord Goryon* over Cornillo, an extraordinary cow, and her herd, Gast's warriors and Goryon's men trample the only crop of Aeddan*, a poor farmer. Smoit*, their king, sentences the two lords to work alongside Aedden in his fields and to give to him Cornillo. Gast and his warriors later join in the battle against Arawn*, the Lord of Death, when he makes his final bid for rule of Prydain.

GAUDIOR, a character in *A Swiftly Tilting Planet**, by Madeleine L'Engle*. His name is Latin for "more joyful." This winged unicorn is from a planet with two moons. Like other time-traveling unicorns, Gaudior has hatched from an egg; he is a perfect creature with a light-filled horn, who lives on moonlight and starlight. When the world of Charles Wallace Murry* is in danger of being destroyed by a nuclear war started by Madog Branzillo*, he chants an ancient rune* and Gaudior is sent to help him. Together they travel ancient winds through time to alter the past and halt Branzillo's madness. The healing power of Gaudior's horn is used twice: once to keep Chuck Maddox* from dying of a fractured skull, and once to rouse Charles when the person he has "gone within" suddenly dies. Their mission accomplished, Gaudior makes those who have seen him forget him.

GAYLEN. *See* Vaungaylen (Gaylen)

GED, the main character in Ursula K. LeGuin's* Earthsea trilogy*. His father is the bronzesmith for Ten Alders, on the island of Gont*; his mother dies before he is a year old; he has six older brothers. Ged is also called "Sparrowhawk." When he is born he is named Duny, and he grows up impatient and wild, learning magic from the age of seven from his aunt, a sorceress. He takes pride in his knowledge and wants to learn as much as he can so he will have power no one else has. When he is twelve, the boy is apprenticed to Ogion*, who gives him his true name, Ged, when he is thirteen. Though he learns much from the man, Ged is impatient to learn more; once, Ogion must save the boy from a demon he calls up and cannot control. When Ogion gives Ged a choice—to stay with him or attend sorcerer's school at Roke*—Ged chooses the school. Here he learns much and is impatient to prove himself. Slighted by Jasper*, an older boy, Ged tries to prove his superior powers by calling up the dead, and he releases the shadow of his own pride and darker self, which attacks him and leaves him scarred in body and spirit. When Ged finishes his training, he takes a job on Low Torning, among a common people, before seeking out his shadow and finally accepting it and making it one with him. During his search for the shadow, Ged receives half of the Ring of Erreth-Akbe* as a gift; his search for the other half, to put together its Bond-Rune* and bring peace to Earthsea*, leads Ged to Atuan*, where he meets Tenar*, a young priestess, and frees her from her priestesshood. Ged becomes the greatest wizard of Earthsea and the only living Dragonlord; among his great deeds are the capping of the Black Well of

Fundaur and the building of the sea wall of Nepp. Because of these accomplishments, Ged is made Archmage at Roke. Five years later, because magic is seeping out of Earthsea, he seeks to mend things and finds that Cob*, a wizard Ged had once taken to the land of the dead to frighten him, has died making a spell to keep the door between death and life open. After much struggle, Ged mends the rift, expending his powers as he does so. He brings to Roke the young King of All the Isles, Arren*, and rides away on the back of a dragon. More than one story is told of what finally becomes of him; his life is told in *The Deed of Ged*.

GEDDER, a character in *A Swiftly Tilting Planet*, by Madeleine L'Engle*. He is descended from Gwydyr*, a twelfth-century Welsh prince who had come to the American continent and eventually made his way to what is now Vespugia*, a small South American country. Gedder is the brother of Zillie*. Their mother having died when they were young, the children were raised by an English sheep rancher. When a group of Welsh settlers comes to Vespugia in 1865, Gedder helps them plant and build houses. He has high ambitions and is soon lording it over the settlers. Strong, handsome, and flamboyant, Gedder attracts and is attracted to Gwen Maddox*, one of the settlers; he tries to get her brother, Bran Maddox*, interested in Zillie. One day, on a cliff, Gedder provokes a fight with Rich Llawcae*, who is also interested in Gwen. When Gedder pulls a knife, Rich takes it; lunging after it, Gedder falls over the cliff to his death.

GEMMA HARVEY (*The Bassumtyte Treasure*). *See* Harvey, Gemma

GEORGIE. *See* Little Georgie

GERALD, a character in *The Enchanted Castle*, by E[dith] Nesbit Bland*. He is the brother of James* (Jimmy) and Kathleen*. Because their cousin catches the measles, the children are forced to spend a school holiday at Kathleen's school. At nearby Yalding Castle* they meet Mable Prowse*, who has found a magic wishing ring*. Resourceful and quick-witted, Gerald is called on again and again to smooth over or undo the effects of the magic ring: he tricks the Ugly-Wuglies* the children have made and imprisons them in the Temple of Flora*; and he follows Jimmy, who has been changed into an adult, to London and brings him back again, transforming him back into young Jimmy as he does so. Gerald also witnesses Jefferson D. Conway's* struggle with the ghost of Yalding Castle.

GERALD RISHANGER (*The Sleepers*). *See* Rishanger, Gerald

GHAGRA, a character in Jane Louise Curry's* *The Wolves of Aam*. Though he is one of the huge Icelings*, he travels as one of Lord Naghar's* minions in order to keep a close watch on that evil lord's actions. Ghagra is one of the men who kidnap Runner-to-the-Sky's-Edge*; when he is ordered to kill the small Tiddi* hunter, Ghagra releases him instead. He also helps Cathound* escape from Gzel* by killing his commander, the Illigan*.

GHIBBA, a character in *The Three Mulla-mulgars**, by Walter de la Mare*. He is a Moona-mulgar* and leads the band that helps Thumma*, Thimbulla*, and Ummanodda* across the mountains, going with them, finally, to the Valleys of Tishnar*.

GHOST OF THOMAS KEMPE, THE. Penelope Lively. Illus. Anthony Maitland. London: Heinemann, 1973. 153 pp. Carnegie Award, 1973.

When James Harrison* and his family have lived in their new house for two weeks, odd things begin to happen. To a sign his mother has put up advertising apples for sale has been added an advertisement offering the services of a sorcerer, alchemist, physician, and finder of lost goods, for which James is blamed. Tim*, the dog who has adopted the family, has begun growling up at James's window. The next day, when James takes a prescription for cough syrup to be filled, he discovers that someone has altered it in the same handwriting that was on the sign. James is again blamed and sent to his room, where Tim behaves strangely. The boy finds an oddly spelled note detailing what his father should do to find his lost pipe.

That afternoon, digging to bury some trash, James finds among the fascinating junk long-buried in the garden some spectacles and part of a pipe. That night a message is written on his mirror: the writer, to whom the spectacles and pipe belonged, is going to practice his trade again; James had better make him a good apprentice. James realizes that he is dealing with a ghost. The next day, on a public bulletin board, a notice appears advertising the services of Thomas Kempe*, sorcerer, who lists James as his apprentice. That afternoon he gets a note from Thomas. When James explains that the twentieth century does not need Thomas's services, the sorcerer reacts so violently that James gives in.

Thomas makes his presence more noticeable than before; James intercepts a note to his mother explaining that Mrs. Verity*, who lives next door, is a witch responsible for her hayfever, and the doctor's office is vandalized by Thomas, who leaves a note. The next day Thomas leaves a note on the blackboard in James's classroom for his teacher, but fortunately for James the man merely compliments him on his seventeenth-century handwriting. James tries that evening to get help from his parents by telling them about Thomas, but they do not believe in ghosts. Thomas makes known his ire toward them by setting off their alarm clock at intervals all that night. When the vicar visits the next day, Thomas makes his presence felt again, for, he tells James, he "lykes not Priestes."

James, who is beginning to see himself being blamed for Thomas's doings for the rest of his life, gets unexpected help from Mrs. Verity, who tells him about Bert Ellison*, a sanguine carpenter who does exorcisms. His attempt to bottle Thomas fails, and Thomas tells James in a terse note that he will not be tricked like that twice. Realizing that Thomas has been exorcised before, James literally digs for clues in the garden, finding a diary that describes how, manifesting himself in 1856, Thomas was bottled and sealed in what is now James's room. Bert tries to use rowan to get rid of Thomas, but they are interrupted before the rowan works. Bert can do no more.

Thomas can, however. The next morning he writes on Mrs. Verity's fence, accusing her of being a witch; that evening James receives a note commanding him to have the local archaeology team give Thomas half the gold they find. There is trouble at the site when James makes a half-hearted visit, and inflammatory scrawls from Thomas appear at various places around town. The police come to see James because Thomas had left his name on a note tied to a brick heaved through the doctor's window, but James has an alibi. The next night he receives an appeal from Thomas, who does not understand the strange ways of the twentieth century. Before James can act, however, Thomas sets Mrs. Verity's house on fire; the firemen come in time to save everything.

Not knowing what to do, James asks Thomas and learns that he must find Thomas's resting place and put his pipe and glasses there, thus helping him to go. James takes the things to the churchyard but cannot find Thomas's grave. Bert Ellison remembers seeing it in the vault beneath the floor of the church, and when he digs, he finds Thomas's stone coffin. When Bert puts Thomas's things on the coffin, a small blue flame rests there for a moment and vanishes. Thomas Kempe is gone, and James goes home.

GIANT, a character in *Are All the Giants Dead?**, by Mary Norton*. The last of thirteen giants who once lived in the Land of Cockayne*, this disreputable creature escaped being killed by Jack-the-Giant-Killer* because it owned a frog with a jewel in its head—a lovely creature that confers protection on whoever owns it. The giant lives in a partially ruined castle on the Bluff above Much-Belungen-under-Bluff* and taunts Jack by throwing its garbage down the Bluff near the village, knowing that Jack cannot get through the crevice that is the only route to the top of the Bluff. James* and Dulcibel*, two children, can, and they climb to the top of the Bluff to get the frog for Dulcibel so that she will not have to marry a toad. Once the children have the frog, the giant is killed by Jack-the-Giant-Killer, who reaches the top of the Bluff by climbing a beanstalk grown by Jack-of-the-Beanstalk*.

GILLIAN, a character in *The Cat Who Wished to Be a Man**, by Lloyd Alexander*. This stubborn, fiery-tempered young woman runs an inn—The Crowned Swan—in the town of Brightford* and is noted for her excellent cooking. When greedy Mayor Pursewig* tries to take over the inn, Gillian resists as well as she can, not giving up even when she is forced to close the place because she has not enough money to run it. Practical Gillian is convinced that Lionel* is insane when the young man informs her that he has been changed from a cat, but she soon becomes deeply attached to him. When Lionel, having vanquished

Pursewig, goes back to Magister Stephanus*—the wizard who is his master—
Gillian discovers that he has been telling the truth. After Stephanus finds that
he cannot change Lionel back into a cat, Gillian gives the young man leave to
court her.

GILLIAN PERESBY (*The Sleepers*). *See* Peresby, Gillian

GINGER, a character in C[live] S[taples] Lewis's* *The Last Battle*. This
talking ginger tomcat does not believe in Aslan*, the great lion-protector of
Narnia*, a magical land. When he realizes that Shift*, an ape, and Rishda*, a
warrior from Calormen*—Narnia's traditional enemy—are reaping a great reward pretending to be Aslan's mouthpieces, Ginger joins them. Realizing that
Shift is less an asset than either wants, Ginger and Rishda plot to control him
and get things their way. They succeed until Ginger goes into the stable where
Tashlan, as they call Aslan, is supposed to be. Tash*, the Calormene god whose
name the two have slurred with Aslan's, is there, and Ginger is so frightened
that he ceases to be a talking beast and streaks from the stable as would any
terrified cat. When Narnia comes to an end, Ginger is not one of those who go
to Aslan's country; his ultimate, dark fate is unknown.

GLEW, a character in Lloyd Alexander's* *The Castle of Llyr** and *The High
King**. Mean-spirited Glew longs for greatness: he tries to be a great warrior
but cannot stand the blood or the battles; he tries to become a bard but cannot
bear the wandering life; he tries to be a hero, but the tiny dragon he tries to slay
bites him; he cannot become king because no princess will marry him. Longing
to become an enchanter, Glew buys from Morda* a book supposed to be full
of magical secrets, but the book is blank. Glew concocts his own potions to
make himself a giant, trying them out on Llyan*, his cat. After Llyan grows to
gigantic proportions, she chases Glew into a cave, where he takes his own potion,
intending to grow bigger than the cat. Bigger he becomes, but because he cannot
get through the small entrance, Glew is forced to live in the dark reaches of the
beautiful cave until Dallben*, an enchanter, sends him a shrinking potion, and
Glew becomes his original size. Glew's overwhelming interest in himself remains
as large as it was when he was a giant, and he longs for the days when he could
make people tremble. When the warriors of Prydain* gather to defeat Arawn*,
the evil lord of Annuvin*, Glew goes with Taran*, a young warrior, and his
companions. He causes trouble in a Fair Folk* mine by stealing gems from the
walls and bringing part of the mine down around the group's ears; but Glew's
greed yields rich results when he invades Arawn's treasureroom with Gurgi*,
who manages to rescue valuable secrets of craftsmanship before the castle crumbles. Because of his deeds, Glew accompanies the Sons of Don* to the Summer
Country*, there—one hopes—to finally find happiness.

GLIMFEATHER, a character in *The Silver Chair** and *The Last Battle**, by C[live] S[taples] Lewis*. This talking owl is present at the courts of King Caspian X* and his son, King Rilian*, in Narnia*. When Jill Pole* and Eustace Clarence Scrubb* are brought from our world to Narnia by Aslan*, Narnia's great lion-protector, to find Rilian, who has been lost for ten years, Glimfeather explains to them what has happened in the land and helps them make plans to search for the prince. Because he is a night creature and they will want to travel during the day, Glimfeather does not go with them. He is one of those in Aslan's country when Narnia comes to an end.

GOBLE, ERNIE, a character in *The Lost Farm**, by Jane Louise Curry*. Ernie is one of the children with Samantha Bostweiler* when she discovers that Pete MacCubbin* has been miniaturized by Professor Willie Kurtz's* reducing machine. Ernie finds the farm on his own and guards it that night, saving Pete from a weasel just in the nick of time. Concerned that hikers will find the farm, Ernie offers to move Pete and the livestock to his house, where they will live in his sister's abandoned dollhouse, but Pete refuses the offer.

GOBLIN, a type of being in traditional lore that also appears in several works. In J[ohn] R[onald] R[euel] Tolkien's* *The Hobbit** and *The Lord of the Rings*, the goblins are nasty, brutish creatures living in stuffy, filthy caves. Clumsy when it comes to making fine and lovely objects, they are very clever at making instruments of torture and death. They are good tunnellers and miners, though they prefer to use slaves for this. Goblins are always hungry and will eat anything, from a pony to a dwarf*. Often they come together with wild wolves to raid nearby settlements of men for slaves and prisoners. They hate and fear two swords, Orcrist and Glamdring, which they call Biter and Beater, for these swords have been used for many years to slay them. After the Great Goblin is slain by Gandalf*, a wizard who rescues some dwarves the goblins have captured, the goblins' natural hatred for the dwarves is fanned to a fury; and they sweep down on the dwarves, Thorin Oakenshield* and his companions, at the Lonely Mountain, to avenge the Great Goblin's death. Here they do battle with dwarves, men, and elves*, and are finally defeated when eagles join the fray. After that the goblins avoid men at all cost, though they do join Sauron's side when that evil lord seeks to regain his magic ring*.

In George MacDonald's* *The Princess and the Goblin**, the goblins are descendants of people who once lived above the ground. Because a king treated them with some severity, they took refuge in caves, coming out only at night to avoid people. Over the years they have become hideous and misshapen, cleverer and more mischievous. Now, though they look human, the goblins are far different: their heads are hard and their toeless feet are their weak points. Goblins are nine-tenths solid flesh and bone and do not need to eat every day. Still harboring resentment against those who live under the sun, the goblins wreak as much havoc as they can on those whom they catch in the mountains at night; but they can be driven away by verses or songs, for these they cannot abide, perhaps because they cannot make them up themselves. The goblins keep housepets which have become as grotesque as they, and they claim for their own the wild goats in the mountains—and any tame goats, too, which happen to fall into their traps. Seeking revenge on the descendants of the king who had driven their ancestors into the caves, the goblins plan the kidnapping of Irene (the princess)*, in order to marry her to their prince, but they are thwarted by Curdie Peterson*. A contingency plan to flood the silver mines and drown the miners there backfires on the goblins; Curdie and his father reinforce the wall the river is to batter through, and the water floods the goblins' caves instead. Many drown, and others escape; most of the survivors leave that part of the country. Most of those who remain become milder in character, with harder feet and softer heads and hearts, and they even become friendly with the people around them.

GODKING, THE, a character mentioned in *The Tombs of Atuan**, by Ursula K. LeGuin*. He rules the Kargish Empire in eastern Earthsea* from his place in Awabath. He is one of a line of Godkings who succeeded the Priest-Kings and have ruled for at least 150 years; under their rule the Kargish Empire was consolidated. Because they are divine, the Godkings have a richly appointed temple at the Place of the Tombs on the Island of Atuan*.

GOLDEN PELYDRYN, an object in Lloyd Alexander's* Chronicles of Prydain* and *The Foundling, and Other Tales of Prydain*. It is also called a bauble. It belongs to Eilonwy*, who had it from her mother, Angharad*. This golden sphere is more than the toy it seems, for it shines sometimes with a golden light that makes things clearer. Whether or not the Pelydryn lights up seems to depend on the attitude of the person holding it, for when he or she is thinking of another and not himself or herself, the light shines out from the bauble, growing brighter as the anxiety of the person holding it increases. When Prince Rhun* is anxious for his friend, Taran*, the bauble shines brightly; when Eilonwy later is anxious to save Taran's life, it blazes as brightly as the sun. In the Pelydryn's light some magical inscriptions are made clearer; the inscription on Dyrnwyn*, a powerful sword, is brought out, even the part that had been scratched out long ago; the bauble also reveals the spells of magic in a blank book. The power of Eilonwy and of the Pelydryn are closely bound, and when she gives up her powers to marry Taran, the light in the golden bauble winks out forever.

GOLIATH HOLLYBUSH *(The Magical Cupboard)*. *See* Hollybush, Goliath

GOLLUM, a character in *The Hobbit** and *The Lord of the Rings*, by J[ohn] R[onald] R[euel] Tolkien*. He gets his name from the "gollum" swallowing noise he makes. He also has been called Sméagol. Gollum calls himself "my precious," and he is the only creature to whom he is indeed precious. Once akin to hobbits*, living in the open air, Gollum killed for possession of a magic ring* and took refuge in a cave beneath a mountain. Here he lives on an island in the middle of an underground lake, paddling about in his boat and living off fish and young goblins*. Food is all he ever thinks of. Gollum is well adapted for his underground life; he has large pale eyes that shine and large feet for paddling his boat. Gollum is good at riddles, and when Bilbo Baggins* stumbles upon him, he and Gollum hold a riddling contest. Gollum loses and must show Bilbo the way out of the caves. Treacherous Gollum decides to eat Bilbo but cannot, for Bilbo has the ring, which makes its wearer invisible. Gollum inadvertently shows Bilbo the way out of the caves. In later years he seeks to regain the ring, only to meet a fiery death in Mount Doom.

GOLLY HOLLYBUSH (*The Magical Cupboard*). *See* Hollybush, Goliath

GONT, a place in the Earthsea trilogy*, by Ursula K. LeGuin*. On this island is born the young boy who comes to be known as Ged*; here also lives Ogion*, the wizard who apprentices him. Gont shelters both Tenar*, the former Priestess at the Tombs of Atuan*, when she leaves the Tombs, and Ged himself, when he finishes the work he has to do in Earthsea*.

GOODENOUGH, TOM, a character in *The Borrowers**, *The Borrowers Afield**, and *The Borrowers Afloat**. His grandfather was a gamekeeper. When he was young, Tom lived with him in a little cottage, which Tom later inherited. As a boy, Tom has a ferret and a "collection" of borrowers*, tiny people who "borrow" what they need from humans. He may have brought his ferret to Firbanks to catch Pod, Homily, and Arrietty Clock***, three borrowers, when the rat catcher comes to kill them. Tom later saves the Clock family from Mild Eye*, a gypsy. He has already made friends with Dreadful Spiller*, a borrower who has grown up in the wilds. Tom soon becomes friends with Arrietty, whom he warns when he and his grandfather must close up the cottage. When he is an old man, Tom tells his stories of the borrowers to Kate*, a young visitor.

GOODY CAKEBREAD (*Parsley Sage, Rosemary & Time*). *See* Cakebread, Goody

GORONWY, a character in Jane Louise Curry's* *The Change-Child**. He is one of *y Tylwyth Teg**, the Welsh Fair Folk*, though his maternal grandfather was a mortal. Goronwy aids Eilian Roberts* several times, helping her to get home, warning her uncle when the girl is about to be handed over to unscrupulous Simon Rastall* to be married to him, and taking Eilian, Emrys*, and Pilipala* to the safety of the center of the Great Dark Wood, where his people live. When the rest of the Fair Folk journey to Tir na'nOg*, Goronwy chooses a mortal's life and stays behind with Eilian.

GORYON, a character in Lloyd Alexander's* *Taran Wanderer** and *The High King**. He is a lord of Cantrev Cadiffor, in the southern part of Prydain*. He calls himself Goryon the Valorous, though his valor is mostly boastings; Goryon is not as bold as he claims to be. When Taran*, a young man in search of himself, happens on Goryon's border guards, they take from him his horse, Melynlas, and bring it to the lord. Melynlas proves unridable and, to Goryon's relief, Taran claims the beast as his own. For some time Goryon and Gast*, a nearby lord, have fought over the ownership of Cornillo, an extraordinary cow. During their final dispute, the warriors of the two lords trample the only crop of Aeddan*, a poor farmer. Though Smoit*, their king, wants to imprison the lords, Taran persuades him to sentence them to work alongside Aeddan in his fields. Later, when Arawn*, an evil lord, makes his final bid to rule Prydain, Goryon and his warriors join in the battle against him.

GOVANNON. *See* Grimnir

GOWTHER MOSSOCK (*The Moon of Gomrath*; *The Weirdstone of Brisingamen*). *See* Mossock, Gowther

GRAHAM, LUCY, a character in *The Magic City**, by E[dith] Nesbit Bland*. She is the daughter of Peter Graham; after her mother dies, she becomes the stepdaughter of Helen Haldane Graham and the stepsister of Philip Haldane*. When her father remarries, Lucy does her best to get along with Philip, but she is constantly rebuffed. Returning from a stay with an aunt, Lucy comes upon the model city Philip has built, and she rebuilds a part that has fallen. Thus she is able to shrink magically and enter the city when he does. Here Lucy and Philip have many adventures together, though at first Philip resents Lucy's company. Her problem-solving abilities soon sway him, for she helps him accomplish seven difficult tasks and become king. By the end of their adventures, Lucy and Philip are closer than they had thought they would be, and both are ready to start their new lives.

GRAHAME, KENNETH (1859–1932), British writer. He was born 8 March 1859, in Edinburgh, to James Cunningham and Elizabeth [Ingles] Grahame. Grahame was educated at St. Edward's School, Oxford. From 1879 to 1908 he worked at the Bank of England, becoming secretary of the Bank in 1898. During this time he also wrote for several publications, including *Yellow Book* (1894–1897). Grahame married Elspeth Thomson in 1899; they had one child. Grahame died 6 July 1932.

Grahame's output was not prodigious, and it consisted mostly of essays and articles directed toward adults; but it is for his single book for children, *The Wind in the Willows**, that he is best remembered. *Dream Days* and *The Golden Age* are often listed as children's books, but they were written for adults, and today adults usually enjoy them more than do children; *The Wind in the Willows* was written to please a child, and it pleases adults just as much. Since its publication in 1908 the book has not been out of print. *The Wind in the Willows* takes place in a world of motorcars, trains, and quiet country life, but it is a scaled-down world, a world that is the size of the animals that live in it. Grahame's world is more ordered, gentle, and tranquil than our own. Here everyone has a place; when one finds his place and is content there, all runs smoothly.

Thus, central to both the book itself and the animals who populate it is the importance of home. Home is more than a place to eat and sleep; it is a place where one is cosy and safe. The homes of the Rat* and the Mole* are not grand, but they contain everything those two animals need. The Badger's* house has a kitchen that is the epitome of all a cosy country kitchen should be. More than just a snug place to live, though, these homes are also a reflection of their owners—an extension of their owners' personalities. The River that is "brother and sister . . . aunts, and company, food and drink" to the Rat runs just outside the window of his best bedroom and sometimes invades the house itself; the music of its water lulls him to sleep. Toad Hall, with its Tudor windows, well-tended lawns, and huge banqueting hall, is as grand as rich Toad* could wish. The Badger's house is complex and ancient; it is comfortable and unostentatious, but solid, as he is himself. Dug and improved upon by generations before him in the ruins of an ancient city, the house reminds the Badger of his heritage and reinforces his view of man as a race that comes and goes while patient animals endure. The Mole's home, where he lives in genteel poverty, is humble but slightly elegant, like its owner. Each character takes pride in his home.

Most of the characters take as much pride in the community to which they belong as in the houses they dwell in there, for home, in the book, is not simply the place where one eats and sleeps; it is also the neighborhood in which one lives. For most of these animals, home is also the River that chatters and chuckles along its way, that provides food and recreation and almost everything else they need. The River is itself a "sleek, sinuous, full-bodied animal," and it is the center of both the community and the book.

For these animals, one's house and the neighborhood where it is found, are enough; they have no desire for anything else. To the Rat, the world beyond the River and the Wild Wood is a place no one in his right mind would want to explore, and indeed this attitude is important in the book. Foolish Toad seeks excitement beyond the borders of his home, and uncomfortable things happen to him, while those who stay behind live quietly and comfortably. The one time the Rat and the Mole venture beyond their River, their caravan is wrecked by a car; on his own in the wide world, Toad is thrown into jail and suffers humiliations and privations, though he also has the time of his life. It is almost as if one would have to be mad or possessed to leave home voluntarily, for it is Toad's enchantment with motorcars, during which time he acts as if possessed, that leads him to leave home; during the Rat's encounter with the mysterious, hypnotic Sea Rat*, the latter seems to possess him literally, even changing the color of his eyes, and Mole must act as a kind of exorcist.

Grahame's episodic novel gracefully intertwines two stories: quiet chapters dealing with the Mole's initiation into Riverbank society and his sometimes mystical adventures with the Rat alternate with chapters narrating Toad's rowdy adventures in the wide world. When the two stories come together, it is to show how the naive Mole has matured into a clever animal who can take care of himself and whom Toad can only envy. Grahame's style is fluid and graceful, and he is equally deft at evoking the sounds of the chattering, gliding River, the terror of a small animal at nightfall in the Wild Wood, the beauty of the countryside, and the awesomeness surrounding the appearance of the great god of all Nature. Though his animals are humanized, one does not forget that they are animals, and they remain in the memory not just as animals or as animals acting human but as spirited, three-dimensional personalities. Though Grahame uses a few recognizable types, he transcends stereotyping.

Works

Juvenile fantasy: *The Wind in the Willows* (1908).
Adult: *Pagan Papers* (1893), essays; *The Golden Age* (1895), essays; *Dream Days* (1898), essays; *The Headswoman* (1898).

Secondary Works

Baker, Margaret J. "Jo Meets the Secretary of the Bank of England," *Junior Bookshelf*, 10 (July, 1946), pp. 58–72.
Braybrooke, Neville. "Kenneth Grahame—1859–1932: A Centenary Study," *Elementary English*, 36 (January, 1959), pp. 11–15.
———. "A Note on Kenneth Grahame," *The Horn Book Magazine*, 46 (October, 1970), pp. 504–7.
Chalmers, Patrick R. *Kenneth Grahame*. London: Methuen and Co., 1933.
Clausen, Christopher. "Home and Away in Children's Fiction," *Children's Literature*, 10 (1982), pp. 141–52.
Forsyth, A. "*The Wind in the Willows*—50 Years Later," *Junior Bookshelf*, 22 (March, 1958), pp. 57–62.
Graham, Eleanor. *Kenneth Grahame*. London: Bodley Head, 1963.
Grahame, Kenneth. *First Whisper of "The Wind in the Willows,"* ed. by Elspeth Grahame. Philadelphia and New York: J. B. Lippincott Company, 1944.
Green, Peter. *Kenneth Grahame*. London: John Murray, 1959.
———. "The Rural Pan," *The Cornhill Magazine*, 170 (Winter, 1958–1959), pp. 293–304.
Green, Roger Lancelyn. "Kenneth Grahame and Beatrix Potter," in *Tellers of Tales* (Leicester, England, Edmund Ward, 1946), pp. 234–45.
———. "The Magic of Kenneth Grahame," *Junior Bookshelf*, 23 (March, 1959), pp. 47–58.
Kuznets, Lois R. "Toad Hall Revisited," *Children's Literature*, 7 (1978), pp. 115–28.
Meigs, Cornelia, et al. "A Landmark in Fantasy," in *A Critical History of Children's Literature*, rev. ed. (New York: Macmillan Publishing Co., 1969), pp. 328–37.

Milne, A. A. "Mr. Grahame, Mr. Roosevelt, and I," in *Booklets for Bookmen*, No. 1. New York: Limited Editions Club, Inc., 1940.

Moore, Anne Carroll. "Kenneth Grahame," *The Horn Book Magazine*, 10 (March, 1934), pp. 73–81.

Poss, Geraldine D. "An Epic in Arcadia: The Pastoral World of *Wind in the Willows*," *Children's Literature*, 4 (1975), pp. 80–90.

Sale, Roger. "Kenneth Grahame," in *Fairy Tales and After* (Cambridge, Mass.: Harvard University Press, 1978), pp. 165–93.

Smith, Kathryn A. "Kenneth Grahame and the Singing Willows," *Elementary English*, 45 (December, 1968), pp. 1024–35.

Sterck, Kenneth. "Rereading 'The Wind in the Willows,' " *Children's Literature in Education*, 12 (September, 1973), pp. 20–28.

Tucker, Nicholas, "The Children's Falstaff," in *Suitable for Children?: Controversies in Children's Literature*, ed. Nicholas Tucker (Berkeley and Los Angeles: University of California Press, 1976), pp. 160–64. [Reprinted from *Times Literary Supplement*, 26 June 1969.]

Williams, Jay. "Reflections on *Wind in the Willows*," *Signal*, 21 (September, 1976), pp. 103–7.

GRAIL, an object in Susan Cooper's* *Over Sea, Under Stone** and *Greenwitch**. This beautiful cup of beaten gold is richly engraved. In five panels, four stories of King Arthur* are told; the fifth bears an inscription presaging his final battle against evil. The grail was made near the time of Arthur's reign, to keep men from forgetting. While it exists, Arthur will come when the time is right. It was brought to Cornwall by Bedwin, one of Arthur's knights; he entrusted it to a good man who handed the grail down to his son, and he to his, until it came to a childless man. He hid the grail and the manuscript* that explains the inscription in a cave near what is now Trewissick, Cornwall; he made a map that leads to the grail. In the fourteenth century this crumbling map was found near a monastery and was copied by a monk. Six hundred years later it is found by Barnabas Drew*, who, with his brother and sister, Simon and Jane Drew**, finds the grail. It is put into the British Museum but is later stolen by servants of the Dark, forces of evil. One, a painter*, uses the grail as a cup for scrying. When the grail is again found by the Drews and their friends, who are of the forces of good, the inscription on the cup is translated, and its prophecy is revealed.

GRANDFATHER CLOCK. *See* clock, grandfather

GRANDMOTHER, THE. *See* Irene (the grandmother)

GRANDPA, a character in Penelope Lively's* *The Revenge of Samuel Stokes**. He is the maternal grandfather of Tim Thornton*. A widower for several years, Grandpa is able to indulge his proclivities for creative cooking and relaxed housekeeping. He also enjoys gardening, raising huge, gaudy flowers and thriving vegetables to show off his skill. He does not eat the vegetables because he considers them "rabbit food." Grandpa loves outings and is intensely interested in other people, about whom he speculates darkly. Because Grandpa's thinking process is so flexible, he realizes very soon what is happening when Samuel Stokes*, an eighteenth-century landscape designer, tries to drive off the people living in houses built on an old estate where he had created his finest achievement. With the help of Tim and of Jane Harvey*, Grandpa steers Stokes's attention away from the housing development and onto a nearby park.

GRANNY MACCUBBIN (*The Lost Farm*). *See* MacCubbin, Granny

GREAT SLOTH, a character in E[dith] Nesbit Bland's* *The Magic City*. It was once a picture in a book used by Philip Haldane* to build part of a city. When the book is accidentally opened in Polistarchia*, the land where all Philip's cities are real, the Sloth "leaks out" and makes its way to Briskford, a town in the northern part of the country. Here the Sloth so cows the citizens that they build it a temple of gold and sing it songs of praise, neglecting their fields and their work. The Sloth has such great influence that the citizens sleep when it does—which is almost all the time—and the town becomes known as Somno-lentia*. Philip and Lucy Graham* are sent to change this state of affairs by making the Sloth work all day. Lucy accomplishes this goal by tricking the Sloth into wishing for a machine to pump water eight hours a day, and because those who wish for machinery must use it, the Sloth must run the machine. Lucy makes sure the Sloth does not take revenge on its people by telling it that if it does, they will wish for machine guns which, of course, they will have to use.

GREEN KNOWE, the house that serves as the locale for Lucy Boston's* Green Knowe books*. On the site of Green Knowe once stood a prehistoric temple of the moon. The house itself is built about 1120 by Osmund d'Aulneaux to replace the cramped Saxon hall his family has always lived in. This stone house is very grand; it has two stories, with wide, double-arched windows in the second storey, where the family lives. Just as impressive is the fireplace, which is in the wall instead of in the center of the hall. Beneath its hearthstone are buried a piece of silver for wealth, a piece of iron to keep away the Little People, and a live toad for permanence. Most of Green Knowe is built of stone hauled from the midlands; one piece, though, is from a church destroyed by the Vikings and is included for luck. Roger d'Aulneaux*, Osmund's son, is very proud of the house and inherits it with the estate. Over the next eight centuries, Green Knowe changes as the family changes; the house is altered and added to suit the people who live there. In the seventeenth century, carvings of cherubs from an old monastery are added; in the eighteenth century, the old Norman house is hidden when additions in red brick are made to please Maria Oldknow*, but these additions burn in 1799. In the twentieth century, one brick wall with high windows remains. Green Knowe has two gardens: an informal one at the back of the house, and a formal, topiary garden on the side nearest the river. By the twentieth century, the house is showing its age: the masonry is crumbling a bit, and the adjoining chapel has fallen into ruins and has been repaired for secular purposes. The house holds onto its past; it is furnished with things that have been in the family for many generations; and past events replay themselves, for all time is one at Green Knowe. Green Knowe is more than just a house; it is on good terms with the mysteries of the universe and contains something bigger than itself. In the twentieth century, Mrs. Linnet Oldknow* struggles to preserve Green Knowe against those who would destroy it. Sometime in its history, the place becomes known as "Green Noah"* after a piece of topiary here; the names Green Knowe and Green Noah become interchangeable, though the former is most commonly used.

GREEN KNOWE BOOKS,   six books by Lucy Boston* that have as their locale Green Knowe*, an ancient English manor. In order of internal chronology they are: *The Children of Green Knowe**; *The Chimneys of Green Knowe**; *The River at Green Knowe**; *An Enemy at Green Knowe**; *The Stones of Green Knowe**. A non-fantasy in the series is *A Stranger at Green Knowe*.

GREEN NOAH,   a topiary tree in Lucy Boston's* *The Children of Green Knowe**. It stood in the garden at Green Knowe*. It was created in the late nineteenth century, when the topiary animals in the garden were created. When a gypsy horsethief was caught at Green Knowe and then deported, his mother, Petronella, cursed the tree and thereby got revenge on the men of the family living at Green Knowe; many had accidents when their horses bolted or shied from the tree, which sometimes moved at night. Though Green Noah is not trimmed after a time, it still proves a frightening figure. Eventually it gives its name to the house. In the twentieth century, the tree again comes alive, this time menacing Toseland*, the young boy living at Green Knowe, one stormy Christmas Eve. When the boy and other children who have lived at Green Knowe call on St. Christopher* to help him, lightning strikes the tree and destroys it.

GREENWITCH, THE,   a sacrificial figure in Susan Cooper's* *Greenwitch**. Sometimes it is called King Mark's Bride. Each spring it is made by the women of Trewissick, Cornwall, to insure a good harvest and good fishing. The vast figure of the witch is made of a framework of hazel, with rowan for the head, and a body of hawthorn. Stones in the body make it sink when it is sent into the sea as a gift for Tethys, the Lady of the Sea. Before it is sunk, those who want to can make a wish on it. The Greenwitch is a thing of Wild Magic, having nothing to do with the Light or the Dark, the forces of good or the forces of evil. It is ancient and awesome. When the Greenwitch is made one year, Jane Drew*, who senses its loneliness, wishes on it nothing for herself, as the others do; she wishes instead for its happiness. When it falls into the sea, the Greenwitch finds and keeps for itself a lead case containing a manuscript* essential in the battle between the Dark and the Light. Jealously protecting its "secret," the Greenwitch destroys a painter*, a minion of the Dark, who tries to get the manuscript away from it, by calling up the Wild Magic. Because Jane has pitied the witch, and because the manuscript is important to her, the witch gives her its "secret" in return for her wish, before it goes back to Tethys, in the depths of the sea.

GREENWITCH. Susan Cooper. Frontispiece by Michael Heslop. New York: Atheneum, 1974. 147 pp. American.

The grail* they had found the summer before has been stolen from the museum, and Barnabas (Barney), Simon, and Jane Drew*** visit the place, hoping to find a clue. Instead they find their great uncle, Merriman Lyon* (Merry), and they agree to help him find the grail. When they arrive in Cornwall, where the search is to begin, the three find, to their dismay, that eleven-year-old Will Stanton* has joined Merry. The Drews take an immediate dislike to Will, considering him a nuisance. One day when Barney is sketching, to his astonishment a painter* who comes by takes the sketch. He has also taken Rufus*, the dog belonging to Captain Toms*, and he leaves a note telling them all to stay away from the Greenwitch* if they want the dog alive.

Jane, because she is a girl, does go to the ceremony and watches the Greenwitch being formed of rowan and hawthorn. She feels its power and its loneliness, so when it is time to make her wish on it, Jane wishes for it to be happy. At dawn, the figure is sent into the sea. Will, Merry, and Captain Toms, all Old Ones—forces of good—have recognized the painter as one of the forces of the Dark and realize that he is after Barney. That day the painter returns Rufus, and the three Old Ones keep Barney from falling into his power. That night Jane dreams of the Greenwitch, that it has a secret in the sea, which it shows her; it is a small glowing stick, and she tells Merry about it.

The next morning Rufus leads Simon and Barney to the painter, who invites them into his caravan. They enter, in spite of Simon's unease, and have some soda, which only Barney drinks. Then the painter produces the grail, and he compels Barney to scry with it. Only Simon, not under the spell of whatever had been in the drinks, remembers what happens; that Barney sees in the grail that the Greenwitch has what the painter is looking for, and is gaining power, and that little time is left before the witch will slide into deep ocean and whatever it has will be lost. The painter makes Barney forget what has happened and sends the two boys away. When they have heard this, Will and Merry go into the sea to find the Greenwitch, to get from it its secret, which Merry has realized is a small manuscript* in a lead phial, accidentally thrown into the water. But the witch is gone.

That day the painter paints into dusk as Simon, Barney, Jane, and Captain Toms watch. The man is painting spells onto canvas, and when he finishes he uses it to summon the Greenwitch. It rises from the sea, a powerful figure. When the painter asks for the thing it holds, the witch refuses; when he tries to command it, the witch goes wild. That night Wild Magic is loose in the village, and Jane watches in terror the ghosts of times past being replayed. A strange ship sails over the village and across the moors. Will, Merry, and Captain Toms go down to the dock and call the Greenwitch. Having been reminded by Merry of Jane's wish for it, the witch causes the phantom ship to sail again across the sky and this time the painter is put aboard it, to sail out of time.

Jane speaks to the Greenwitch in her dreams. Because the witch's "secret" is important to her, the witch gives it to her; Jane will give it another "secret" in return. She wakes with the manuscript in her hand. At the painter's caravan that day, they find the grail. Together the manuscript and letters on the grail form the words of a prophecy concerning the downfall of the Dark. Merry destroys the manuscript, once it has been used, to keep the secret. That day Jane goes to the cliff above the sea to give the Greenwitch her bracelet, but Will gives her another gift to give instead—a line from a prophecy, engraved on bright, incorruptible gold.

GREY KING, THE, a force of evil in Susan Cooper's* *The Grey King*. He is also called the Brenin Llwyd. He is the most powerful of the Lords of the Dark, the forces of evil, but he rarely comes down from Cader Idris, the mountain in Wales where he has chosen to reside. He seeks to prevent those who would wake the six Sleepers*, warriors of the Light, who lie in enchanted sleep beside Lake Tal y Llyn. When Will Stanton*, one of the forces of the Light, comes to wake the Sleepers, the king sets out to stop him, sending his gray foxes and his coldest north wind, which "blows around the feet of the dead," and, finally, possessing Caradog Prichard*, a man full of hate. But the Sleepers are wakened, and at last the Grey King gives up his battle to stop them and to harm Bran Davies*, the son of King Arthur*. He sends his foxes into Tal y Llyn.

GREY KING, THE. Susan Cooper. Illus. Michael Heslop. New York: Atheneum, 1975. 208 pp. American. Newbery Award, 1976.

Will Stanton*, having been ill, is sent to his relatives in Wales, to recover. He has forgotten something important but can catch glimmers of it. Looking for a place that is somehow important, he finds a dog that catches him when he trips, and looking into its eyes Will remembers all, that what he has forgotten is a prophecy. The dog is Cafall*, and he belongs to Bran Davies*, a young boy who knows that Will is an Old One, one of the forces of good. Bran has learned from Merriman Lyon* (Merry) three lines of the prophecy, as a sign to Will, whom he is to help on his quest for a golden harp* that will aid the Old Ones in their final battle against the Dark.

One day Will is helping his uncle herd sheep. Something attacks one and they must leave it; when they return, the sheep is gone. Tension has been growing, and Will feels the malevolence of the Dark. More sheep are attacked over the next days, and Bran thinks it is the work of gray foxes, creatures of the malevolent Grey King* of the Welsh mountains. A fire starts on the mountain, and as they help fight it, Will follows Bran, who has seen a fox and thinks it is Cafall. The boys are trapped by the fire and must climb the mountain to escape. Foxes come, but so does Cafall, who holds them off so that the boys escape. The boys and Cafall enter a cleft in the rocks and come to a wall of rock which Will recognizes from the prophecy. In the wall is a door that Will opens and that takes them into a great hall; in the floor is a staircase which leads them through rock to a starlit landscape. Here they are scrutinized by the stars—a test of High Magic, for the harp belongs neither to the Light nor the Dark, but to the neutral High Magic. Suddenly they find themselves on the stairs again and descend them to a chamber where sit three lords of High Magic: one of the Light, one of the Dark, and one of neither—King Arthur*. They ask the boys three riddles, which they answer correctly, and Will claims the lovely harp for the Light. He must use it to wake the Sleepers*, who lie close to the Grey King's mountain.

Will, Bran, and Cafall leave with the harp, coming out in the cleft. A fierce wind rages, but it drops when Bran plays the harp. Rain comes; the fire is out. They start home. Suddenly a gray fox runs past, and Cafall chases it, followed by Bran. Will hides the harp. Cafall chases the fox down to the weary farmers, who cannot see it, and, thinking the dog is attacking the sheep, Caradog Prichard* shoots Cafall. The next day John Rowlands* tells Will about Bran's mother, who had come from nowhere with the baby and stayed only long enough to establish it with Bran's foster-father. Will goes to get the harp, and on the way back a mist forms that takes the shape of the Grey King, who threatens Will before leaving. Will hides the harp in his room. Prichard has been there, accusing John's dog of sheep-killing.

The next day Will and John take the dog to John's relatives for safety. The sheep that had vanished had been found here, dragged by a fox. Nearby is a lake which, Will learns, must be the one by which the Sleepers lie. Bran comes to warn them that Pritchard is coming to shoot the dog, and Will and Bran take it to a deserted cottage, where it becomes strangely paralyzed through the King's enchantment. Will goes to get the harp to break the spell. Bran, alone with the dog, is suddenly confronted by his father, and he learns the secret of his birth, having a vision of Merry and his own mother. Suddenly Bran realizes that he has powers of his own, and he speaks words to break the spell, running away with the dog.

Will, returning to the empty cottage, gets a vision, as Bran had, from the stone the Grey King uses for spying and learns that Bran is Arthur's son. Realizing that Bran has gone to the lake, Will follows. He is stopped by Prichard, through whom the King has channelled his forces. Prichard is keeping Will from the lake, so Will plays the harp where he stands; at its sound six horsemen, the Sleepers, ride from the mountain to rescue the world from the Dark, and they salute Bran before riding away. Prichard grabs the harp and throws it into the lake; he tries again to shoot the dog, but John is just in time to stop him. The Grey King gives up and leaves Prichard, who is now mad. A mist comes down from the King's mountain, and his foxes plunge into the lake.

GREYTHORNE, MARY (MISS), a character in Susan Cooper's* *The Dark is Rising** and *Silver on the Tree**. She is one of the Old Ones, the forces of the Light, and must have been born some time before the fifteenth century. In the nineteenth century she is very fashionable; she has gas lighting installed in her manor as soon as the system is developed. While she was still young, it is said, she was crippled when her horse fell with her, but Miss Greythorne refuses to be seen in a wheelchair. In the twentieth century she is the imperious, sometimes curt, but always dependable lady of her manor, taking in her neighbors when the power fails, and making sure all are provided for. In her house is hidden the Sign of Wood, one of the six Signs of the Light* Will Stanton*, youngest of the Old Ones, must find. After the final battle between the Dark and the Light, Miss Greythorne sails with the rest of the Old Ones beyond the world of men.

GRIFFITH, STEVIE, a character in Jane Louise Curry's* *Beneath the Hill**. He is the cousin of Arthur and Margaret Arthur**. Curious and open-minded, Stevie is able to take just about anything in stride, even mysterious Nūtayē (the City of the Moon Under the Mountain*) and its strange inhabitants, which the children discover while Stevie is visiting the Arthurs. When Stevie is sucked into the lake in the Bane*, where strip-mining has ravaged the land, his uncle threatens the mine owner with a lawsuit, forcing the man to have the lake filled in and incidentally sealing the entrance whereby an evil force bound beneath the mountain seeks to break free. Stevie, with the other, helps the Fair Folk* in Nūtayē escape to Tir na'nOg*.

GRIMES, MR., a character in *The Water-babies**, by Charles Kingsley*. Grimes is the brutal master sweep who apprentices Tom*. Full of wickedness and swagger, Grimes supplements his income by poaching and this leads to his death when he falls into a river and drowns after being surprised by officers of the law. Tom, having become a water-baby*, finds Grimes in the Other-end-of-Nowhere*, stuck in a chimney, having been given a dose of his own treatment of his sweep. Grimes's naturally surly temper is not sweetened by this treatment; his heart is so cold that is freezes everything that comes near him, even fire, and he therefore cannot keep his pipe lit; every evening a warm rain comes that turns to hail when it reaches him. Tom tries to free Grimes but fails. This is a place where each must help himself. Grimes achieves his freedom on learning that his aged mother, whose tears for him have provided the rain, has died; Grimes cries so that he is washed clean of soot and the bricks in the chimney crumble. After promising to be obedient, he is sent to Mount Etna to help keep it cleaned out.

GRIMNIR, a character in *The Weirdstone of Brisingamen**, by Alan Garner*. He is the brother of Cadellin Silverbrow*. Grimnir's real name is Govannon. Having studied under wise masters, he became a great loremaster. But Grimnir practiced black arts in his lust for knowledge, and this changed him into a monster before he went to live beneath Llyn-dhu, the Black Lake. Here he gained a master, Nastrond, lord of foul creatures in Ragnarok. Because he looks and sounds like Cadellin, his good brother, Grimnir never speaks, and he hides his form in a dark, hooded robe. Sent by Nastrond to find Firefrost*, a powerful stone once in Cadellin's keeping, Grimnir takes the stone for himself, planning to use it to gain power greater than Nastrond's. Though he does not like her witch magic, Grimnir gets the Morrigan* to help him. But he fails, losing the stone and, during a subsequent battle, his life, to Cadellin. Enraged at Grimnir's perfidy, Nastrond sends Fenrir, his great wolf, to swallow up Grimnir and those who have helped him.

GRINSSORG, COUNT, a character in Lloyd Alexander's* *The Marvelous Misadventures of Sebastian*. This handsome but inhuman man became Regent of Hamelin-Loring* after arranging the deaths of its rulers. While acting as Regent until their daughter, Isabel Charlotte Theodora Fredericka* (Isabel), comes of age, he announces their imminent marriage, causing the girl to run away. Grinssorg hates music; he dies as Sebastian*, a young fiddler, plays a magical violin*, perhaps because the power of music triumphs over his inhumanity.

GRISELDA, a character in Mrs. Mary Molesworth's* *The Cuckoo Clock*. She is the granddaughter of Sybilla and the great-niece of Tabitha and Grizzel; she is the only girl in the family of boisterous boys; her mother is dead. When Griselda is sent to stay with her great-aunts in England, she is lonely, for the old women are not the kind of company she is used to and Griselda misses her brothers. She finds an unexpected friend in the cuckoo* living in the cuckoo clock, and he teaches her lessons in patience and hard work by befriending her and taking her to a handful of fantastical lands. Finally Griselda finds a friend in Phil*, a little boy, and when Phil's mother comes to live nearby, the cuckoo leaves Griselda, for now she has friends who will help her and teach her what she still needs to learn.

GRITT. *See* Grout, Sufferana; Grout, Thanatopsis

GROMMET. *See* Grout, Sufferana; Grout, Thanatopsis

GROTTLE. *See* Grout, Sufferana; Grout, Thanatopsis

GROUND HOG, a character in Carolyn Sherwin Bailey's* *Miss Hickory*. He is greedy and surly and has no friends; consequently, he is afraid of everything, including his shadow. Miss Hickory*, a little countrywoman whose body is an apple twig and whose head is a hickory nut, reasons that Ground Hog is afraid because he steals from the farmers, and she sends the hen pheasant Ladies Aid Society with food for him. Devourkng the food, he does not run from his shadow because it is not there; this means that spring is on the way.

GROUT, SUFFERANA, a character in *The Magical Cupboard**, by Jane Louise Curry*. She is the wife of Thanatopsis Grout*. In her colorful career as the wife of a swindler, Mrs. Grout is also known as Mrs. Grottle, Mrs. Gritt, Mrs. Grommet, and Dorinda Plumtree. She particularly enjoys being Mrs. Plumtree because this alias allows her to be rich and fashionable; in her other aliases she is the dowdy wife of a poor clergyman. When Sufferana and her husband are forced to shut down the profitable orphanage they have been running, she goes to Boston to sell some valuables. Here she is recognized as Mrs. Grommet and is tried and sentenced to five years imprisonment. When her term is over, Sufferana journeys to the Connecticut River to rejoin Thanatopsis, only to find that he has lost his capacity for scheming and that the thriving fur trade which the Grouts thought one of their orphans had inherited is defunct. The Grouts go to Montreal, where they live in polite society.

GROUT, THANATOPSIS, a character in Jane Louise Curry's* *The Magical Cupboard** and *Parsley Sage, Rosemary & Time**. He is the husband of Sufferana Grout*. Thanatopsis's career is varied, but it is built around one theme: greed. In the 1690s, he was known as Parson Grommet and preached against witches, becoming rich from the witches' properties. Found out, he went to another place in New England, where, as Parson Gritt, he talked widows into leaving their money to him. In 1705 he was in Bennickport, Maine, as Parson Grout; because many of the orphans he was sending to their relatives had large inheritances, he decided to start an orphanage where he could keep the orphans and their wealth. Maintaining his identities as Grout and as Mr. Plumtree, the owner of the orphanage, Thanatopsis does well until 1722, when he preaches against Goody Cakebread* as a witch and finds himself fleeing her furious son. Thanatopsis manages to steal the widow's magical cupboard*, though it will not work for him. Forced to close the orphanage, Thanatopsis travels to the Connecticut River to take advantage of the inheritance of one of the orphans. Along the way, his group of travelers is attacked, and this, along with the discovery that Sufferana has been arrested, weakens his mind, so that he loses the capacity to scheme. At the Connecticut River, Thanatopsis reverts to his role as clergyman, preaching to the Indians and growing obese from too much of Mrs. Hollybush's* good cooking. When Sufferana is released from prison, she and Thanatopsis move to Montreal.

GRUMMORE GRUMMURSUM *(The Sword in the Stone)*. *See* Grummursum, Grummore

GRUMMURSUM, GRUMMORE (SIR), a character in *The Sword in the Stone**, by T[erence] H[anbury] White*. He is a good friend of Sir Ector. Sir Grummore is a public school man and proud of it. Gruff and hearty, he is as inveterate a quester as some are fox hunters, but he is sometimes disappointed when the villains he goes after give him a good run and then get away. On one quest he meets King Pellinore* in the Forest Sauvage* and invites him to joust; after the joust they become the best of friends and Grummore invites Pellinore to stay at his castle. Sir Grummore later takes a hand in the knighting of Kay*, Ector's son.

GUMERRY. *See* Lyon, Merriman

GUNGA-MULGAR, a type of being in *The Three Mulla-mulgars**, by Walter de la Mare*. Gungas are called "gorillas" in English. These great creatures speak a language all their own and often use the things of man. Thumma*, Thimbulla*, and Ummandodda* (Nod) meet a Gunga during their journey to the Valleys of Tishnar*; Nod tricks him into providing blankets and food for his brothers, and a boat for the three to cross a river, and he is hit by one of the enraged Gunga's arrows.

GURGI, a character in Lloyd Alexander's* Chronicles of Prydain*. He is neither animal nor human, but something in between, being covered with matted hair yet walking and talking like a man. His feet are as flexible as his hands. Gurgi longs to be clever and fierce, but he is neither. His admiration of those who are is vocal and persistent. Gurgi's major concern in life is eating. Though he at first tries to harm Taran*, Gurgi soon becomes the young man's loyal companion, helping him to find the Black Crochan*, the great cauldron in which are made the deathless Cauldron-Born*, and to rescue Princess Eilonwy* from her evil aunt. Gurgi also accompanies Taran on the young man's quest for his parents. As he experiences adventures and accumulates accomplishments, Gurgi becomes more and more human, learning generosity and love and coming to have moments of bravery and self-sacrifice. Gurgi's greatest accomplishment is accidental when, following greedy Glew* into the treasure room of the evil lord, Arawn*, Gurgi finds the secrets of craftsmanship, stolen by Arawn and hidden for centuries. For his part in Arawn's downfall, Gurgi accompanies the Sons of Don* to the Summer Country*, there to be happy and well fed forever.

GUS, a character in *The Fabulous Flight**, by Robert Lawson*. This seagull lives in Baltimore, Maryland, but Gus loves to travel; he has been almost everywhere on the east coast of the United States. His greatest ambition is to go abroad, though he does not want to go alone, so he has never made the trip. When Gus meets Peter Peabody Pepperell III*, a boy just four inches tall, he gets his chance, for the two are sent on a mission to Zargonia, to steal a powerful explosive developed by Doctor Professor Polopodsky*. Gus is disappointed by much of what he sees in Europe: London is too foggy, there are no sardines in Sardinia, Rome has too many ruined buildings, and there is no writing on the Rock of Gibralter. When he returns to the United States, he decides to stick to Baltimore.

GWEN MADDOX (*A Swiftly Tilting Planet*). *See* Maddox, Gwen

GWYDION, a figure in the *Mabinogion* who appears or is mentioned in several works. He is mentioned in Alan Garner's* *The Owl Service*. Here he is the creator of Blodeuwedd*, a maiden made of flowers for Lleu Llaw Gyffes. When Blodeuwedd's lover tries to kill Lleu and Lleu is changed into an eagle, Gwydion changes him back to a man. The wizard later punishes Blodeuwedd by changing her into an owl. Huw Hannerhob*, a twentieth-century laborer, may be descended from Gwydion; he certainly confuses himself with the wizard at times, claiming to have accomplished several of Gwydion's deeds.

In the Chronicles of Prydain*, by Lloyd Alexander*, Gwydion is one of the Sons of Don*. Prince Gwydion is the war leader of Math, the High King of Prydain*. Many of Gwydion's actions are dedicated to the destruction of Arawn*, the evil king who seeks to rule Prydain. When the Horned King* wreaks havoc in the land, Gwydion journeys to see Dallben*, a wizard, and consult Hen Wen*, his oracular pig; on the way he meets Taran*, Dallben's ward, and the two are captured and taken to Spiral Castle as prisoners of Achren*, an ancient sorceress. Enraged when he refuses to join her side, Achren takes him to the hideous fortress, Oeth-Anoeth, and Gwydion there endures unspeakable torment. Because he withstands his imprisonment, the secrets of death and life are revealed to him, and the walls of the prison melt away. Since he now understands the language of animals, Gwydion learns from Hen Wen the Horned King's secret name and is able to use it against him and destroy him. Gwydion later gathers warriors to find the Black Crochan*, from whence spring the death-less Cauldron-Born*. During Arawn's final bid for control over Prydain, he is stripped of Dyrnwyn*, the enchanted sword he carries, and is gravely wounded in the process; after his recovery, Gwydion rouses the Sons of Don against their foe, becoming High King when Math is killed. After Arawn's defeat, Gwydion accompanies the other Sons of Don to the Summer Country*, there to be eternally happy.

GWYDYR, a character in *A Swiftly Tilting Planet*, by Madeleine L'Engle* He is the sixth son of Owain, king of Gwynedd; he is the older brother of Madoc*. When Owain dies and his sons fight for the throne, Gwydyr would stay and take his chances, but he is persuaded to accompany Madoc on a journey away from the fighting and across the sea to the legendary North American continent. Here Gwydyr decides he will be king, and makes it appear to Madoc that he has died. Gwydyr becomes ruler over a tribe that lives beside a lake and seeks to extend his rule to the People of the Wind, who have lived in peace here for centuries. But he is defeated by Madoc and is sent in disgrace back to his tribe. They send him away and eventually Gwydyr finds his way to what is now Vespugia*, a small country in South America. Among his descendants are Gedder* and Zillie*. During his fight with Madoc, Gwydyr shows him an image of the future, of Madog Branzillo*, Vespugia's leader in the twentieth century, destroying the world in a nuclear war. This very nearly comes true, as Madoc's pure line is mingled with Gwydyr's tainted one, producing a Branzillo raging with hate and bloodlust. After Charles Wallace Murry* travels through time and changes history, Madoc's and Gwydyr's descendants do not intermarry, and Madog Branzillo is a man of peace.

GWYN, a character in *The Owl Service*, by Alan Garner*. He is the son of Huw Hannerhob* and Nancy*. Gwyn grows up in a city, raised by Nancy, who does not tell him about his father but tells him much about the village from which she had come. Thus it is that when Gwyn and Nancy come back to the house she once served in to do for the Bradley family, Gwyn feels he has come home. He is not completely happy, for he has ambitions beyond those Nancy has for him; he wants to be more than a clerk in a store, and she plans to take him out of school. Strange things begin to happen after Gwyn finds a set of oddly patterned plates* in the attic above Alison Bradley's* room. The story of Blodeuwedd*, a mythical woman made of flowers, and of her lover and her jealous husband, was played out in the valley long ago, and for generations after this triangle of love and jealousy has been replayed, each time with tragic results. Now Gwyn is caught up in it, loving Alison but considered unsuitable by her parents, and being baited by Roger Bradley*, Alison's stepbrother. Gwyn is proud of his Welsh heritage, but he also sees it as a stumbling block and is quick to take offense when the English Bradleys seem to mock him. Realizing what is happening to him, Alison, and Roger, Gwyn tries to leave leave the valley, to keep the ghastly drama from being played out again. When Huw reveals that he is Gwyn's father and that Gwyn must see the story to its end, the boy decides to stay and do what he can to keep events from turning out tragically. Finally, however, he cannot do even that; he has been hurt too much by Alison and her brother, and he cannot bring himself to help her when she needs it; Roger does it instead.

GWYSTYL, a character in Lloyd Alexander's* *The Black Cauldron* and *The High King*. He is one of the Fair Folk*, a tall creature who looks like a bundle of sticks with cobwebs for hair. Gwystyl is perpetually miserable, for he is always damp or sick, and events are always too much for him. Presented with a problem, he moans that it is too much to expect him to solve it. Yet Gwystyl has hidden qualities that soon come to the fore. King Eiddileg, king of the Fair Folk, has put him in charge of a way post near Annuvin*, the realm of the evil king Arawn*, and Gwystyl is to provide sanctuary for any Fair Folk who need it. He may bewail his lot, but he does his job, if pressed. Taran*, a young man, and his companions discover this when they take refuge with Gwystyl during a quest for the Black Crochan*, a cauldron from which Arawn makes his deathless warriors. From Gwystyl's crow, Kaw*, they get hints about the Crochan's whereabouts, and Gwystyl, hard-pressed, tells them where to find it. He later appears with some warriors just in time to save Taran and his friends. Because crows suddenly become too much for him, Gwystyl gives Kaw to Taran. Gwystyl later shows up just in time to help Taran's friends rescue the young man, and with him he has the necessary equipment, though it is some time before he gives it over. When the magic and the Fair Folk leave Prydain*, Gwystyl takes Kaw into the realm of the Fair Folk.

GWYTHAINT, a type of creature in Lloyd Alexander's* Chronicles of Prydain* and *Coll and His White Pig*. These great, black birds with curved beaks and terrible talons were once gentle, trusting creatures free as the air they flew in, but Arawn*, the evil lord of Annuvin*, lured them into his realm and imprisoned them, tormenting the birds until they began to serve him out of fear. Now he uses them as spies and as agents of terror in his battle to gain control of the land of Prydain*. Though savage, they can be gentle; Taran*, a young man, nurses a wounded gwythaint until it regains its strength and leaves him. Years later it saves him when he has slipped over the edge of a cliff on Mount Dragon* and carries him to safety, only to be killed trying to defend the young man.

GZEL, a place in *The Wolves of Aam*, by Jane Louise Curry*. This mountain was once part of Gazuldor, the land of the Icelings*, who built a small citadel here and mined the mountain for vindurn. When the glaciers came, Gzel was abandoned, to be inhabited again by the minions of evil Lord Naghar*. They enlarged the citadel and made it into a true fortress. It is to Gzel that Lek*, a conjuror, is brought to be questioned about the powerful stolen skystone*, Mirelidar*. When two Icelings, rescuing Lek, fire the fortress, the sleeping fires of the mountain wake, and Gzel becomes a volcano, destroying the fortress and Lord Naghar's men.

H. P. HUNTINGTON (*The Sleepers*). *See* Huntington, Henry Peter

HAGUE, SCOBIE (MAJOR), a ghost in *The Watch House**, by Robert Westall*. Huge, powerful Hague was originally from Garmouth, England; he became a member of the Fifty-fifth Regiment of Foot, serving in Australia. There he murdered Joseph Shears and his wife and fled Australia on the *Hoplite*. Somewhere he stole some gold sovereigns. When the *Hoplite* was wrecked off the coast of England, at Garmouth, in 1854, Hague volunteered to swim a rope from the ship to the shore, even then refusing to be parted from his gold. He made his way to shore, where he was set upon by five wreckers; after killing two of them, Hague himself was killed; his right hand was cut off to free the box it held, and the rest of his body was thrown into the sea. It was never found, and Hague was remembered as a hero. His murder was witnessed by ten-year-old Henry Cookson*, who may have taken what was left of Hague's gold after the wreckers divided it. Nourished by Cookson's feelings of guilt and terror, Hague haunted him, becoming the monster that finally killed him and even then would not let go. Because Hague's skull was found and put into the Watch House* on the cliff, most of his manifestations are there. When Anne Melton*, Pat Pierson*, and Timothy Jones* try to help Henry, Hague's manifestations become violent and he controls the actions of animals and inanimate objects; he sends a dog to disturb the graves of his murderers and causes a series of befuddling events in an attempt to keep his recovered skeleton from being buried. Finally Hague is exorcised by Father da Souza* and Father Fletcher*, who bury the cut-off hand, the last of Hague's remains.

HAKI, a character in Lloyd Alexander's* *The First Two Lives of Lukas-Kasha**. This orphan lives with his aunt and uncle in a tiny mountain village in Bishangar*. Captured by Shir Khan*, a mountain bandit, he escapes with Lukas-Kasha* (Lukas) and Kayim* after they trick the bandit's men into killing him. Haki guides the two through Bishangar, delighting and irritating them with his constant chattering about his relatives and his brother, Yussuf. When Lukas takes command of an Abadani troop, Haki leads Nur-Jehan* and her Bishangari soldiers to meet him.

HALDANE, PHILIP, a character in E[dith] Nesbit Bland's* *The Magic City**. His parents are dead; he was raised by his sister, Helen. Philip is happy until he is ten years old, when Helen marries a widower with a young daughter, Lucy Graham*. Resentful because he no longer has Helen to himself, Philip antagonizes those around him and he is left by himself with the servants during Helen's honeymoon. Miserable and bored, Philip builds a model city out of books, toy blocks, and anything else that comes to hand. One night he suddenly becomes small enough to enter it, and thus start many adventures in the city of Polistopolis* and the land of Polistarchia*. Philip rescues Lucy from a clockwork dragon as the first of seven deeds he must accomplish before he can become king and deliver the city from evil; Lucy, in turn, helps him to accomplish his tasks. As a result, they become closer than he had thought they would. In the course of one adventure, Philip decides to give up the Island-where-you-mayn't-go*, where he and Helen have lived happily together, though that means he will lose Helen in this magical world. Though Helen vanishes after Philip gives the island to the Dwellers by the Sea*, he feels he has done the right thing. After accomplishing his tasks and driving the usurping Pretenderette* from Polistopolis, Philip becomes king and is ready to go home to his new life.

HALFBACON, HUW. *See* Hannerhob, Huw

HALL OF GRANTED WISHES, a place in E[dith] Nesbit Bland's* *The Enchanted Castle**. This hall lies below the island in the lake in the gardens of Yalding Castle*. A passage leads to the hall from the Temple of Flora*, also on the grounds. The Hall of Granted Wishes appears differently to all who see it. All around it are arches through which can be seen pictures of the moment in which some soul has reached its destiny or its highest good, and at one end is a statue of Psyche*, from which radiates a soft light. To this hall comes one of the Ugly-Wuglies* made by Mabel Prowse*, Gerald*, James*, and Kathleen*, in search of a really good hotel, and it gets its wish, becoming almost human after spending a night there. In the hall Mademoiselle*, Lord Yalding's* sweetheart, makes the last wish that can be granted by a magic ring* and undoes all the magic it has done. When she does so, the hall fades into a rough cave, and the statue becomes the grave of the wife of Lord Yalding's ancestor, who built the place.

HALLAM, ARMINTA (MINDY), a character in *Mindy's Mysterious Miniature** and *The Lost Farm**, by Jane Louise Curry*. Mindy's father is a teacher, and her mother runs an antique store out of their home in Brittlesdale, Pennsylvania. Young Mindy buys a strangely perfect dollhouse at an auction and discovers that it is really a house made small by Professor Willie Kurtz*. With Mrs. Mary Buckle Bright*, Mindy is herself made tiny and helps to free the eight citizens of Dopple* who were miniaturized along with the town when the professor decided to make it into an exhibit. She becomes a good friend of Samantha Bostweiler*, one of the eight people.

HAMADRYAD, a character in *Mary Poppins**, by P[amela] L[yndon] Travers*. He is the cousin of Mary Poppins*. This great golden snake is the wisest and most terrible of all the animals in the zoo, and therefore is their lord. When Mary Poppins visits the zoo the night of her birthday, the Hamadryad casts its skin and gives it to her for a birthday gift.

HAMELIN-LORING, a place in *The Marvelous Misadventures of Sebastian**, by Lloyd Alexander*. This realm has Loringhold* as its largest city. Though a monarchy during much of its history, the country becomes more democratic during the rule of Isabel Charlotte Theodora Fredericka*.

HAMPDEN STONES, a circle of stones in *The Whispering Knights**, by Penelope Lively*. These prehistoric standing stones have several traditions attached to them. They are called the Whispering Knights because it is believed that they once were knights who drove away a bad queen and now protect the valley over which they look; it is believed that the Stones move in times of trouble. People also believe that anyone who moves them will have bad fortune forever, that the fairies dance around them and they themselves dance at midnight, and that no one counting the Stones comes up with the same total twice: though William*, Susan Poulter*, and Martha Timms* prove to themselves again and again that there are twenty-nine Stones. In the twentieth century the Stones must protect their valley when the three children accidentally call up Morgan le Fay*, who may have been the bad queen of the old story. The Stones move, and, finally, when Morgan follows the children into the circle, a great battle takes place, during which Morgan is defeated. After the battle, however, the Stones do not appear to have moved.

HANNERHOB, HUW, a character in Alan Garner's* *The Owl Service**. He is the father of Gwyn*. Huw is also called Huw Halfbacon or Huw the Flitch, but none of the three is his real name. Huw was an outdoor laborer on the staff of a house in Wales when Bertram*, an Englishman, owned it. The valley where the house stands had been the site of the tragic story of Blodeuwedd* (a mythical woman made of flowers), her husband, and her lover; in subsequent generations the tragedy of love and jealousy has replayed itself over and over. In Huw's time it was no different; jealous of Bertram's attentions to Nancy*, a pretty servant, Huw removed the brake blocks from Bertram's motorcycle, intending to send the man skidding into the bushes. Instead, Bertram was killed trying to negotiate a dangerous pass. Though Huw fathered Nancy's child, she left the valley, and this was his undoing; ever since he has been what some call mad, though the village people respect him because he is in some way the lord of the valley and responsible for it. The old tales and present realities all seem one to Huw. He sometimes confuses himself with Gwydion*, the wizard who created Blodeuwedd and who may have been Huw's ancestor; Huw's nickname comes from a story originally associated with Gwydion, who tricked a man into trading some pigs for enchanted toadstools—a barter Huw himself claims to have made. Huw stays at the house after Bertram's death, looking after the grounds. When Nancy and Gwyn return to serve the Bradleys, who have come to the house on vacation, Huw tries to help Gwyn and Alison and Roger Bradley**, through whom Blodeuwedd's story is again played out and the power in the valley unleashed.

HANNO, a character in Lucy Boston's* *A Stranger at Green Knowe* who is called upon in her *An Enemy at Green Knowe*. This gorilla was born in Africa; while still a baby he was captured and taken to a British zoo. Though he grew up in a cage, Hanno retained his dignity and some of his joy in life. When he is thirteen, he is seen by Hsu* (Ping), a Chinese refugee who immediately feels a kinship with the gorilla, for both are "displaced persons" and, to Ping's joy, he is allowed to feed Hanno a peach. When Hanno escapes, he makes his way to Green Knowe*, and here he and Ping meet again. Awed by the animal, Ping helps him to hide; remembering the peach, Hanno accepts the boy, saving his life when Ping is attacked by an angry cow. Because he thinks Hanno has injured Ping, the man who had captured him in Africa now shoots Hanno dead. Hanno's keeper gives Ping a few hairs from the gorilla's coat as a keepsake; when the evil Dr. Melanie Delia Powers*, who is menacing Green Knowe, sends cats into its gardens to kill the birds there, Ping uses the hairs to call Hanno, who comes and drives away the cats.

HARDING, DICKIE, a character in E[dith] Nesbit Bland's* *Harding's Luck* and *The House of Arden*. He is an orphan; when his father died, Dickie was left with one of his mother's relatives. Because she is unkind to him, Dickie leaves her to travel with James Beale*, a kindly tramp. Beale, however, has been sent to find a boy to help him and a partner burgle Talbot Court, and Dickie finds himself being pushed through a small window to unlock the door from the inside. When the burglary goes wrong, Dickie is captured and cared for by Lady Talbot*, but his only concern is to get back to Beale. Escaping, he makes his way back to the house he shared with the woman and gathers his treasures—an old silver rattle* and a broken sealing ring that both bear a curious crest, and the seeds of a moonflower*. When Dickie arranges them in a pattern to amuse himself, he is sent back in time to live the life of Richard Arden*, the son of a lord, whose life is as wonderful as Dickie's is bleak and who—unlike Dickie—is not lame. Dickie begins a double existence, living sometimes as Richard and then applying what he learns in that life to make his own and Beale's more comfortable. Dickie learns to love the Arden name and what it stands for and eventually comes to fight for it. Meeting Edred and Elfrida Arden**, two other time travelers, in Richard's world, Dickie helps them to find their father and then arranges to meet them in the twentieth century and help them find the long-lost Arden treasure. In the meantime, it is proved that Dickie is really Lord Arden, for he is descended from an Arden baby kidnapped three generations ago, which had become heir to the family name. Remorseful at taking the title from Edred and Elfrida's father and yearning to live as Richard Arden, Dickie uses his magic once the treasure is found to become Richard forever and make it appear that Dickie Harding is dead.

HARDING'S LUCK. E[dith] Nesbit Bland. Illus. H. R. Millar. London: Hodder and Stoughton, 1909. 281 pp. British.

Young Dickie Harding*, a lame orphan, lives with a woman he calls his aunt. Having spent time in the hospital, he comes home to find that she has pawned his treasure—an old-fashioned silver baby's rattle* given him by his father—so Dickie redeems it, trading a bunch of moonflowers* for it. The pawnbroker also gives him a broken sealing ring that bears the same crest as the rattle. That evening Dickie gets lost while buying wood and meets James Beale*, a kind-hearted tramp. Dickie accepts his invitation to travel with him, and the two make their way far from Dickie's aunt, begging to earn enough to live on.

Beale has been sent to get a small boy to burgle with, and Dickie finds himself being used by him and two other men to get inside a castle and open it. In the middle of the job, he repents of it. The men are surprised by the castle's inhabitants and escape, but Dickie is caught; because he is feverish, he is cared for by Lady Talbot*. The next morning, at breakfast, he notices that the emblem on his spoon is the same as that on his rattle, and the lady is very interested by this. Dickie wants to get back to Beale, so the maid helps him escape in a hamper which, as he sleeps in it, is delivered to a fruit shop, from which he also escapes. Making his way back to Beale, the boy passes his aunt's house and finds that she has gone. He spends the night there, taking his rattle from its hiding place and gathering the seeds of the moonflower. To amuse himself, he makes patterns on the floor with the seeds, forming a star around the rattle before he goes to sleep.

Dickie wakes to find himself in 1606. His name here is Richard Arden*, and he has been sick. As Dickie recovers, he learns from his nurse, Betty Lovell*, about Richard. Dickie loves his new life, especially as Richard is not lame. He feels guilty, however, because Beale is waiting for him, so he tells his nurse, who sends him to sleep and into that other life.

Dickie gets the pawnbroker to loan him the fare and returns to Beale. The man is very glad to see him but is puzzled because Dickie cannot bring himself to beg any more. Instead, Dickie uses skills he learned as Richard to make and sell wooden boxes. He and Beale make even more money when the man buys some puppies and sells all but one, which Dickie names True*. They go back to Dickie's aunt's house, where Dickie makes the symbol with the moonflower seeds, and again he wakes as Richard, realizing this time that it is not a dream, but magic; when he returns, no time will have passed. Richard's parents give him a horse and some gold pieces, and he wants to take the gold to Beale. Betty helps him by telling the boy where to bury it; if he lies over the spot, he will be able to find it in his own time. Sent to sleep by Betty's chants, he wakes as Dickie and helps Beale find the gold.

Now begins a new life. The two take Dickie's aunt's house and earn their keep. Dickie carves boxes and Beale keeps dogs. When again Dickie tries the magic, he finds himself in Richard's uncle's townhouse, with Edred and Elfrida Arden**, two other travelers in time. After Edred and Elfrida escape from prison, where they are confined for knowing too much about the Gunpowder Plot, they and Dickie trade stories. When soldiers come for Edred and Elfrida, Betty helps them escape by calling the Mouldiwarp*; and she tells Dickie about the Mould-iwarp and its powers, and how the two children have lost their father, Lord Arden. Dickie helps them to find him.

He then decides to help them find the treasure of the Ardens, lost centuries ago, and needed now to restore Arden Castle*. Using his magic, Dickie meets both the Mouldiwarp and the equally powerful Mouldierwarp* and asks to be sent back to live with Beale for a time and then find Edred and Elfrida, whom he will help to find the treasure. Dickie and Beale go tramping to Arden Castle, where they stay with Beale's father; Dickie meets Edred and Elfrida and is reacquainted with Lady Talbot, who realizes that the boy is really an Arden. He is brought to the castle to live. Beale, meanwhile, will marry and settle down in his father's house. Dickie uses his moonflower seeds to call up the Mouldierwarp, and he is puzzled to learn from it that the treasure will not be found until Lord Arden is lost and found again.

Then one night Dickie is kidnapped, and Edred and Elfrida call on the Mouldiestwarp*, the most powerful of all. It tells them that they must follow True to find Dickie, but that in rescuing him they will prove that he is the real Lord Arden. True leads the way to the cave where Dickie is a prisoner, and he is rescued. When his kidnappers are caught, on one is found a letter that proves that Dickie is Lord Arden. He is brought to live at the castle and travels, via the moonflower seeds, with Edred and Elfrida to the time when the long-lost Arden treasure was hidden from invading soldiers. Dickie marks the stone under which the treasure is put, but he is captured in the battle and put into the fuel shed before he and the others can travel to their own time. The Mouldiwarp rescues Dickie from the shed and sends the three back to their own time, where they find the hidden treasure, which includes title deeds to valuable estates, and Dickie is formally proclaimed Lord Arden. Because he has taken that title from Edred and Elfrida's father and because he is lame in his own time, however, Dickie decides to go to the seventeenth century and there live out his life. He leaves his clothes on the beach to make it look as if he has drowned, and uses the moonflower seeds to go back in time and take up life as Richard Arden.

Note: This work first appeared in *The Strand Magazine*, nos. 217–227 (Jan.–Nov., 1909).

HARFANG, a place in C[live] S[taples] Lewis's* *The Silver Chair**. It is a castle of giants in the mountains of the Wild Lands of the North, in Narnia*. It stands on a mound; below it lies the Ruined City. Harfang is the home of the giants who enjoy serving roast humans at their Autumn Feast. When Jill Pole* and Eustace Clarence Scrubb*, two human children, and their companion, Puddleglum*, stay at Harfang on the advice of the Queen of Underland*, they narrowly escape being the main course of that year's Autumn Feast.

HARMSWORTH, NINA, the main character in Eleanor Cameron's* *The Court of the Stone Children**. She is the only child of Nan and Christopher Harmsworth. Nina grew up in Silverspring, California, where she had friends and enjoyed working in the small museum there. Nina is a solitary person, never lonely, loving the hills around Silverspring, where she sometimes walked with her cat, Windy. When her accountant father fell ill and lost his clients, the family moved to San Francisco, where he had been offered a job. Nina hates the city, where there are few green places, and four months after the move, she is still miserable, hating their viewless apartment and unable to find friends who make her feel at home. One day Nina meets Gil Patrick, who tells her about the French Museum. Nina has always loved museums, and here she feels at home, meeting people who share her love of the objects people long dead have created or used. Here she meets Dominique de Lombre* (Domi), the girl who had lived in the museum's recreated rooms during the time of Napoleon, and helps Domi prove to Mrs. Helena Hampton Staynes*, who is writing a biography of Domi's father, that the man had not been a murderer. During her adventure, Nina finds a new home for her family and discovers new friends, settling at last in her new home.

HARP, GOLDEN, an object in *The Grey King**, by Susan Cooper*. It is one of the four things of power essential in the battle between the Light and the Dark, the forces of good and of evil. This small harp has been kept for a long time in a small cave, guarded by the three lords of High Magic; it has High Magic in it, and while it is played it defends those in its protection from enchantment or harm. Bran Davies* and Will Stanton*, who win the harp by passing the tests of High Magic, use it to wake the six Sleepers*, warriors of the Light. Caradog Prichard*, possessed by the Dark, throws the harp into the lake of Tal y Llyn.

HARRIET AMES (*Stuart Little*). *See* Ames, Harriet

HARRIET MELBOURNE BARTHOLOMEW (*Tom's Midnight Garden*).
See Bartholomew, Harriet Melbourne

HARRISON, JAMES, a character in Penelope Lively's* *The Ghost of Thomas Kempe**. He is the youngest child of Mr. and Mrs. Harrison; he is the brother of Helen. James is like most ten-year-old boys: curious, friendly, and slightly adventurous. He loves to eat, to dig, and to discover new things and sometimes pretends he is someone he is not. Things happen to James; once he fell through a bathroom floor, and another time he got his arm stuck in a grating. Thus it is that, two weeks after the family moves into their new house, James is blamed when Thomas Kempe*, a seventeenth-century sorcerer, begins to manifest himself as a poltergeist. Thomas wants to take up his profession again, with James as his assistant, and James endures the accusations of those around him when Thomas tries to order things to suit himself. With the help of Bert Ellison*, he finally puts Thomas's spirit to rest.

HARRY CLIFF (*Poor Tom's Ghost*). *See* Cliffe, Harry

HARRY RIVERS (*The Daybreakers; The Birdstones*). *See* Rivers, Harry

HARVEY, GEMMA, a character in Jane Louise Curry's* *The Bassumtyte Treasure**. She is the niece of the vicar near Boxleton House*. Because Gemma works in a museum, she has the background necessary to recognize the disguised portrait of Mary Stuart*, and the needlepoint panel the queen worked; gutsy Gemma's hunches and historical research lead her to realize that the ancestral "Bassumtyte treasure" was Mary's son, adopted into the Bassumtyte family. Gemma marries Thomas Bassumtyte*.

HARVEY, JANE, a character in *The Revenge of Samuel Stokes**, by Penelope Lively*. She is the oldest of the three children of Mr. and Mrs. Harvey. Ten-year-old Jane seems unimpressed when strange things happen, possibly because so much actually happens to her; she is a walking magnet for disaster, having a natural penchant for accidents and constantly being bumped, scratched, or scraped. Her glasses are often cracked. Jane, however, takes all this in stride. When Samuel Stokes*, the landscape designer of an eighteenth-century estate now converted to a residential area, tries to drive people away, Jane helps Tim Thornton* and his Grandpa* steer Stokes's attention away from the residential area and onto a nearby park.

HASTINGS, MR. *See* Black Rider, the

HATER, MR., a character in *Mistress Masham's Repose**, by T[erence] H[anbury] White*. He becomes the husband of Miss Brown*. Mr. Hater is a vicar. He was housemaster at a public school, where he delighted in caning the boys, but this pleasure could only be taken in moderation, because he has a weak heart. After this, Mr. Hater becomes the guardian of Maria*, and he makes a good living at it, for he not only draws a salary but embezzles money from Maria's estate. Mr. Hater gets Miss Brown a job as Maria's governess and spends much of his time searching the great house of Malplaquet* for a certain parchment, which he will alter to make Maria's inheritance go to Miss Brown, her distant relative. When they discover that Maria has found Lilliputians* living at Malplaquet, Mr. Hater and Miss Brown try to find them, to sell them to a circus; Mr. Hater decides, secretly, to sell the lot to three different circuses and leave the country, without telling Miss Brown. Thwarted by Maria, her friend, the Professor*, and the Lilliputians, Mr. Hater is sent to jail for embezzlement, along with Miss Brown. They marry when they get out, and their life together is miserable.

HATHI, a character in Rudyard Kipling's* Jungle books*. This elephant is very old and is the undisputed Master of the jungle who declares the water truce when drought shrinks the waterhole. No one wants to cross him. Hathi is called the Silent One because he thinks long before he speaks or takes action, doing a thing only in its proper time. He tells Baloo*, the bear who teaches the cubs of the Seeonee wolf pack, the master words in all the languages of the jungle, so Mowgli*, Baloo's human pupil, can learn them and so be safe in the jungle. Hathi once fell into a pit and almost was captured by hunters near Bhurtpore; in retaliation he and his three sons destroyed five villages there. For Mowgli's sake, they later destroy the village that had cast him out and harmed the woman who had been kind to him. Mowgli later saves Hathi from another pit; the elephant returns the favor the next day by rescuing him from a leopard trap.

HATTY (*Tom's Midnight Garden*). *See* Bartholomew, Harriet Melbourne

HAVNOR, a place in Ursula K. LeGuin's* Earthsea trilogy*. It is the heart of Earthsea*, from which the rulers of that world rule. Both a city and an island are called Havnor; the city lies at the center of the island, which lies at the center of Earthsea. The city is bright and colorful; its buildings have white marble towers and roofs of red tile and its bridges are covered with red, green, and blue mosaic work. The bright flags of princes flap from the towers. On the highest tower is set the sword of Erreth-Akbe*, pointing skyward, and it is the first thing to gleam in the morning and the last thing to shine at sunset. In that tower is the throne of the great kings of Earthsea. After the breaking of the Ring of Erreth-Akbe* and the destruction of the Bond-Rune* of dominion, no king rules from Havnor for eight hundred years; Maharion was the last. Finally the Ring is made whole again and brought to Havnor by Tenar* and Ged*, a sorcerer. Nearly twenty years later Arren* rules as King of All the Isles from Havnor.

HAWKIN, a character in *The Dark Is Rising**, by Susan Cooper*. He is also called the Walker. Hawkin was born in the thirteenth century; when his parents died, he was raised by Merriman Lyon* (Merry), one of the lords of the Light. To protect a powerful book of spells, Merry made Hawkin part of the ritual for retrieving it, and he trusted the man, knowing of Hawkin's love for him. When it is time for the last of the Old Ones to use the book, Hawkin is taken to the nineteenth century so that it may be retrieved. Here he realizes that Merry is willing to sacrifice his life to the demands of the Light, and Hawkin listens to the temptations of Maggie Barnes, one of the minions of the Dark. Merry takes Hawkin back to the century he had been born in and gives him the Sign of Bronze, one of the six Signs of the Light*, to keep safe across the centuries until it is taken from him by Will Stanton*. Hawkin becomes a hunted, haunted man, pursued until the twentieth century, where he appears as a fear-maddened old tramp terrified of Will. Once the Sign of Bronze has been taken from him, Hawkin rejoins the Dark; he dies when the Black Rider*, his master, casts him down from the sky to lighten his horse's burden as the Rider is pursued by the Wild Hunt*.

HAZEL, a character in Richard Adams's* *Watership Down**. He is the brother of Fiver*. Even as a yearling this rabbit knows how to take care of himself, and he has an air of quiet confidence. This confidence stands him in good stead when Fiver envisions their warren being destroyed and Hazel leads him, Pipkin, Hawk-bit, Bigwig*, Dandelion, Blackberry, Buckthorn, Speedwell, Acorn, and Silver out of the warren to a new one at Watership Down. Even Bigwig, though he has been a member of the Owsla—the strong rabbits who exercise authority—obeys Hazel. Hazel is a good leader, reasonable, quick to take good advice, and unwilling to put his followers into danger he will not himself experience. When Bigwig and some others go to the nearby warren of Efrafa* to get does, Hazel decides to lead a raid of his own and bring out the tame does at a nearby farm; though he is shot, he succeeds. Hazel cultivates the friendship of the field mice and of Kehaar*, a gull, and is rewarded when they help the warren. When General Woundwort*, the Efrafan leader, brings an army to destroy Hazel's warren, Hazel tries to reason with him but fails; under siege by superior forces, Hazel is inspired by a story of El-ahrairah, the rabbits' rogue/culture hero, and frees the dog at the farm, which probably kills Woundwort and decimates his army. Though most rabbits live only two or three years, Hazel lives longer, advising the rabbits in his warren and leading them admirably, until El-ahrairah comes for him and makes him an officer in his Owsla.

HECUBENNA, a character in *Are All the Giants Dead?**, by Mary Norton*. She is the last witch left in the Land of Cockayne*, where figures from fairy tales lives happily ever after. Because Hecubenna had owned the frog with a jewel in its head, she was protected and so remained in the forest in Cockayne. The frog was taken from her, however, by a giant.*. Once Hecubenna was a very successful witch, sending as many as twenty-seven bad fairies to do her wicked business; Rumpelstiltskin was one of these until he became too independent. After she lost the frog, Hecubenna's powers began to fade, though she was still able to stir up a powerful potion. By the time James*, a visitor to Cockayne, comes to her for help, Hecubenna is all but useless, having lost her powers. Old and deaf, she is cared for by Tabitha, who had come out of gratitude for the old witch's helping her husband. Hecubenna tells James of the crevice, the only way up the Bluff above Much-Belungen-under-Bluff*, where he will find the frog he seeks to help a princess.

HELEN R. WATSON (*Elidor*). *See* Watson, Helen R.

HELENA HAMPTON STAYNES (*The Court of the Stone Children*). *See* Staynes, Helena Hampton

HEMLOCK, a character in *The Search for Delicious**, by Natalie Babbitt*. He is the brother of a queen. Unpleasant Hemlock has no friends, only an obsession to rule. This desire leads him to a desperate plan: when the king's prime minister searches for a definition of "delicious," Vaungaylen* (Gaylen) is sent out to poll the kingdom; Hemlock rides ahead of the boy, on his gray horse, Ballywrack, and convinces the people that the poll is part of a plot by the king to ruin them. Soon the kingdom is split and all are suspicious of each other. Hemlock has the lake that feeds all the streams in the kingdom dammed, thus drying up the streams and causing more fear. He intends to hold the water hostage, agreeing to destroy the dam only if the people kill their king. Hemlock is thwarted, however; though he has sought to imprison Ardis*, the little mermaid who keeps watch over the waters of the spring that feeds the lake, he has failed, and she may be responsible for the dam breaking as he stands on it. Hemlock is only injured and will recover, but the king does not know whether to imprison or banish him.

HEN WEN, a character in Lloyd Alexander's* Chronicles of Prydain* and *Coll and His White Pig*. This white pig has oracular powers, though she is reluctant to use them. Hen Wen belongs to Coll*, a warrior-turned-farmer; when she was kidnapped by Huntsmen* and taken to Annuvin*, Coll followed and rescued her. At Caer Dallben*, she lives a contented life, cared for by Taran*, the young charge of Dallben*. Hen Wen has a mind of her own and is sometimes irritating to Taran; bathing her is a great chore, and once she is clean she often rolls in the dirt again. Gwydion*, the war leader of the High King of Prydain*, seeks her out to help him against the Horned King*; finally she gives him the evil king's real name, which Gwydion uses to destroy him. When Hen Wen is consulted during the final bid for power by Arawn*, the lord of death, the prophecy shatters the ash rods used to discover it, and after that her powers begin to fade. By the time a boar visits Caer Dallben and Hen Wen has a litter of seven piglets, her powers are gone, and the piglets are normal pigs. Hen could accompany Dallben to the Summer Country*, there to be happy forever, but her love for Taran keeps her in Prydain.

HENDREARY, a character in *The Borrowers**, *The Borrowers Afield**, *The Borrowers Aloft**, and *The Borrowers Avenged**, by Mary Norton*. He is the husband of Lupy* and the father of Eggletina, Timmis*, and two other sons; he is the brother of Pod Clock*. Hendreary is a borrower*, one of the race of tiny people who "borrow" what they need from humans. After his first wife died, leaving him with children, Hendreary married Lupy. A year after Eggletina disappeared, the family emigrated from the country manor where they lived to a badger's den in a nearby field. They later became part of Tom Goodenough's* "collection" of borrowers, living in the cottage the boy shares with his grandfather. Life here is hard, for the borrowings are slim, but the family is safe, so Hendreary is satisfied. Finally, however, the humans leave and so the borrowers are forced to find a new home. Hendreary, Lupy, and Timmis move to the vestry of the small church at Fordham; Eggletina and the older boys set up house in an old badger set. Getting older and becoming a victim of gout, Hendreary finds borrowing increasingly difficult and is pleased when his brother, Pod, and his family come to live in the nearby rectory, for Pod takes over much of the borrowing.

HENRY COOKSON (*The Watch House*). *See* Cookson, Henry

HENRY VIII, a king of England (1491–1547) who appears as a character in *The House of Arden**, by E[dith] Nesbit Bland*. When he and Anne Boleyn* visit Arden Castle*, Elfrida Arden*, a time traveler from the twentieth century, warns the queen of her tragic future. Upset by Anne's tears at the warning, the king searches for Elfrida, but she escapes.

   He also is mentioned in P[amela] L[yndon] Travers's* *Mary Poppins Opens the Door**. Sprightly little Mrs. Corry* remembers dancing with the king at one time during her long life.

HENRY PETER HUNTINGTON (*The Sleepers*). *See* Huntington, Henry Peter

HEPPLEWHITE, LETITIA (MISS), a character in *The Whispering Knights**, by Penelope Lively*. One of a large family, she now lives alone in her big house. She claims to be around eighty. Miss Hepplewhite was once thought to be quite daring; she was the first in the area to ride a bicycle. Though now her life is quieter, she still lives with a certain flair, wearing elegant, if old-fashioned clothes, and displaying a bright curiosity about modern things she has had no prior acquaintance with. She speaks beautifully and treats children as if they were adults. Miss Hepplewhite believes a hat should be allowed to mature; she has not bought one in twenty years and sometimes wears those her mother owned.

But Miss Hepplewhite is more than she seems; when Martha Timms*, William*, and Susan Poulter* recreate the witches' spell from *Macbeth* in Miss Hepplewhite's barn—which long ago had sheltered a witch—and thereby call up Morgan le Fay*, Miss Hepplewhite helps them keep out of Morgan's clutches. She reveals to them Morgan's secrets and guides them in their battle against her, maintaining good-humored optimism at all times. When the children, fleeing Morgan, take refuge at Hampden Stones*, they seem to see Miss Hepplewhite, young and very otherworldly, offering them sanctuary there, but when they press her about it later, she denies having visited the Stones for many years.

HEPSIBAH SAGACITY WALPOLE (*Parsley Sage, Rosemary & Time; The Magical Cupboard*). *See* Walpole, Hepsibah Sagacity

HERBERT ALFRED (BERT), a character in the Mary Poppins books*, by P[amela] L[yndon] Travers*. Herbert Alfred is the name he uses on Sundays. Bert has two professions: on wet days he sells matches, and on fine days he makes lovely chalk drawings on the sidewalk; when Mary Poppins* is around, these drawings come to life. Bert takes Mary to tea on her days out, for they are quite fond of one another.

HERMIT, THE, a character in *The River at Green Knowe**, by Lucy Boston*. He was a London bus driver until one holiday he sought a place where there were no people. The hermit came to a boggy place on the river near Green Knowe* and stayed there, weary of modern life. His first winter was hard until he learned to hibernate. When he woke, he saw visions of savage men and animals belonging to a long-ago past age; he still has these visions after he hibernates. The hermit lives without money or need of it, taking what he needs from the river and living in a treehouse to avoid paying rent. His life is peaceful and happy and he has no need of anyone else. When Ida*, Hsu*, and Oskar Stanislawsky* discover him, the hermit resents their intrusion; though he enjoys their company, he asks them not to return.

HERMIT OF THE SOUTHERN MARCH, THE, a character in *The Horse and His Boy**, by C[live] S[taples] Lewis*. Still hale at 109, this gentle man lives in Archenland*, not far from Anvard*, the castle of the king, in a little stone house beside a pool that reflects all that is happening in distant places. This peaceful man calls all animals "cousin" and lives in his little home in great contentment. He takes in Aravis* and her companions when they are driven here by Aslan*, the great lion-protector of Narnia*; the hermit heals her wounds and sends on Shasta (Cor*), her companion, to warn the king of Archenland about the imminent invasion of an army from Calormen*.

HERNE, a traditional figure in Celtic lore who appears as a character in Susan Cooper's* *The Dark Is Rising** and *Silver on the Tree**. He is the lord of the

Wild Hunt*, an awesome figure who is cruel because it is the nature of things that he be the Huntsman and harry the Dark. A tall, stag-horned man, Herne leads his pack of red-eyed, red-eared, white hounds each Twelfth Night, though for a thousand years they have nothing to pursue. In the twentieth century he rides after the Black Rider*, a lord of the Dark, and harries him; later Herne and his hounds join the six Sleepers*, six warriors of the Light, at the final battle between the Dark and the Light. Herne may have something to do with King Arthur*; Arthur's son, Bran Davies*, has golden eyes like Herne's. *See also* Garanhir

HESELTINE, KEITH, a character in William Mayne's* *Earthfasts**. His father is a lawyer. Keith is a good student and athlete, more clever than intelligent, but is not much noticed, unlike his best friend, David Francis Wix*. David and Keith get along well together, though David tends to dominate Keith, who feels this is only natural. Both enjoy playing chess, and here Keith keeps David on his toes because he sometimes makes moves that are not clever at all, which throws David's game. When Keith hears a strange rumbling sound from a mound which has just appeared, he and David investigate it and are present when Nellie Jack John Cherry* (John), an eighteenth-century drummer boy, emerges, bearing a strange candle* which affects time. Keith is fascinated by John and his reactions to his new time, forgetting that the other boy is in a strange time far from those he loves. John's removal of the candle from the chamber where King Arthur* and his men sleep precipitates a series of strange occurrences which only Keith and David even partially understand. When David is snatched away, Keith takes up the investigation of the phenomena alone, finally learning from Arthur what he must do to set things right. Though he does so in what he thinks is the space of an autumn night, he returns to find that months have passed.

HICKORY, MISS, the title character in *Miss Hickory**, by Carolyn Sherwin Bailey*. This little countrywoman has an apple twig for a body and a painted hickory nut for a head. Because her head is so hard, Miss Hickory is stubborn and slow to change, and she rarely believes what others are telling her. When a chipmunk moves into her corncob house while she is away, Miss Hickory spends the winter in an old robin's nest, enjoying her new independence from the trappings of civilization, helping some of her neighbors, and rebuffing the sometimes too personal attentions of Squirrel*. In spring, he gets his revenge when, chased from the nest by the newly arrived robins, Miss Hickory takes refuge in his house; starving Squirrel eats Miss Hickory's hickory-nut head. Now that it is free of her hard-headedness, Miss Hickory's body climbs the apple tree where she has lived and becomes attached to the tree, providing the graft that revitalizes it. Here Miss Hickory is happy, for she has found a permanent home.

HIGH KING, THE. Lloyd Alexander. New York: Holt, Rinehart and Winston, 1968. 285 pp. American. Newbery Award, 1969.

Taran*, the orphaned ward of Dallben*, and Gurgi*, his hairy companion, return to Caer Dallben* after a year-long quest and find there Eilonwy*, Taran's sweetheart; Rhun*, now King of Mona*; and Glew*, a small-hearted man recently changed back from a giant. Suddenly they are joined by Fflewddur Fflam*, a bard/king, who carries Gwydion*, the war leader of the High King of Prydain*; the two were set upon by Huntsmen* from the evil king Arawn*, and Gwydion, gravely wounded, was stripped of Dyrnwyn*, his sword. Because the sword is a weapon of power, they must get it back. Achren*, who taught Arawn her magical secrets before he usurped her, sees her chance for vengeance and rides off to Annuvin* while the others are consulting Hen Wen*, Dallben's oracular pig. Hen Wen prophesies that night will become noon and rivers burn before they get Dyrnwyn back.

Sending Kaw*, Taran's talking crow, ahead to find the sword, Gwydion starts to Annuvin to retrieve it. Taran, Eilonwy, Fflewddur, Rhun, Glew, Gurgi, and Coll*, Caer Dallben's warrior-turned-farmer, accompany him. When Glew, Fflewddur, Eilonwy, and Rhun do not catch up after going to Rhun's ship on errands, Coll, Taran, Gurgi, and Gwydion press on to the castle of King Smoit*. There they find the king imprisoned and Magg*, a servant of Arawn, on the throne. The four are imprisoned as well. Fflewddur, Eilonwy, Glew, and Rhun, coming to the castle, are uneasy and camp outside it. Sent into it as a bard to discover what he can, Fflewddur reports Magg's presence and the imprisonment of the others. Gwystyl*, one of the Fair Folk*, comes upon the little camp. From him the others get eggs full of smoke and mushrooms that make fire and use them to attack the castle and rescue their comrades. In the melee, however, Rhun is slain and Magg escapes.

Alarmed by Gwystyl's reports of trouble all through Prydain, Gwydion decides to rouse the Sons of Don* against Arawn's army, and he sends the others to rally the rest of Prydain. Kaw, meanwhile, wounded by gwythaints*—Arawn's spy birds—goes to Medwyn*, who has the trust of all animalkind and who sends his beasts to rally others against Arawn. Taran gets a taste of battle when, organizing the people of the Free Commots*, he fights a skirmish with Arawn's men that ends in a nearby village being burned and its inhabitants, including an old friend, being killed. Saddened, Taran meets the others at Caer Dathyl*, the castle of the High King of Prydain.

To the warriors gathered here comes Pryderi*, one of Prydain's greatest fighters. He demands their surrender; he has joined Arawn because the evil king will bring peace to Prydain. Refusing to surrender, the warriors fight Pryderi's men outside the castle and are routed when the Cauldron-Born*, Arawn's deathless soldiers, join the fray and destroy the castle, killing the king. Now High King, Gwydion regroups his army and leads them to attack Annuvin, certain that Arawn has sent so many warriors that Annuvin is unguarded. Taran leads a small band, including Fflewddur, Coll, Eilonwy, Gurgi, and Glew, to harry and delay the Cauldron-Born while Gwydion's army goes by ship to Annuvin.

Desperately Taran's band follows and skirmishes with the warriors who cannot be killed. Coll is slain, as are other men, and, after the Cauldron-Born attack the band, Eilonwy and Gurgi are reported missing. Grieving, Taran presses on. The band comes upon Doli*, an old friend, and other Fair Folk come to join them, leading Taran's men through an old Fair Folk mine that will bring them out ahead of the Cauldron-Born. But Glew, greedy for the mine's jewels, starts a slide that closes the exit, and they must go back through the mine and around. Meanwhile, Eilonwy and Gurgi, trying to follow Taran, are captured by Dorath* and his outlaws and are saved by wolves sent from Medwyn. The wolves guard them and lead them to a hill overlooking the valley at the entrance to the Fair Folk mine. Seeing that Taran's band, coming out, will encounter a passing band of Huntsmen, Eilonwy warns Taran by using her Golden Pelydryn*, a sphere that lights up the night as bright as day. Taran leads his band to safety as the frightened Huntsmen camp in a nearby gorge. Climbing above the camp, Taran's band uses fire and axes to free a frozen lake and send the flaming waters crashing down onto the camp, and Eilonwy, coming upon the band, realizes that Hen Wen's prophecies are coming true. Pryderi, meanwhile, has led his troops to Caer Dallben to slay Dallben, but he is himself slain trying to open the wizard's *Book of Three*.

Doli leads Taran's band to Annuvin, where, witnessing a battle between gwythaints and crows, Taran is overjoyed to find Kaw. Kaw leads them to Achren, who, though wounded, guides the band through secret ways to Mount Dragon*, from which they see Gwydion's army engaging Arawn's warriors at Annuvin. To Taran's dismay, the Cauldron-Born are almost upon Gwydion's men. Scrambling through the mountain pass, Taran slips, and his sword falls into the gorge. A gwythaint which he had saved long ago now saves him and carries him to the peak of Mount Dragon. A handful of Cauldron-Born start after him and, desperate for a weapon, Taran pushes a large boulder from its place and finds Dyrnwyn. Using it, he kills one of the deathless warriors, and the other Cauldron-Born fall as well. After that, Arawn's warriors are routed. Fighting his way into Annuvin, Taran searches for Arawn but finds Magg, who, crowning himself with Arawn's iron crown, is killed by it. Gwydion, Achren, and Taran find Arawn, who becomes a snake and kills Achren before Taran kills him. Glew and Gurgi, meanwhile, have found Arawn's treasure room. As Glew grabs Arawn's treasure, the room bursts into flames; Gurgi manages to get him out of the palace to join the others before Annuvin crumbles in on itself.

Back at Caer Dallben, Taran must make a decision. The Sons of Don must journey to the Summer County*, as must Fflewddur, Eilonwy, and Dallben. Because of their part in the battle, Taran, Gurgi, Hen Wen, and Glew can come as well. All enchantments must pass from the world and men be left to guide their own destinies. That night, Taran is visited by three lovely sisters: Orddu*, Orwen*, and Orgoch*, who give him the tapestry they have woven of his own life—with the end unfinished. By morning, though it grieves him, Taran has decided to stay and rebuild Prydain for the sake of those who have died. Joyful, Dallben reveals Taran's story: the wizard had found him beside a battlefield where many lay slain, and raised him, hoping he would become the High King *The Book of Three* spoke of, and by his actions he has proved to be that king. From his sad companions, Taran receives gifts, the most valuable being the box Gurgi found in Arawn's treasure room, which contains the secrets craftsmen have sought for long and hard. Eilonwy rebels against her destiny and is overjoyed to learn that a gold ring* Gwydion had given her will grant her deepest wish. Using it she wishes away her magic powers, and she and Taran plight their troth. Hen Wen, who now has a family, stays in Prydain when the others journey to the Summer Country, and Taran becomes the High King, accomplishing many tasks before his story becomes a tale that only the bards know the truth of.

HOBBIT, a race of beings in *The Hobbit** and *The Lord of the Rings*, by J[ohn] R[onald] R[euel] Tolkien*. Hobbits are smaller than dwarves* but bigger than Lilliputians*. They have no beards, but hair grows thick on their feet, which also have leathery soles, making it unnecessary for them to wear shoes. Hobbits wear bright colors and enjoy eating, especially dinner, which they have twice a day when they can. They are rarely seen by humans, for they live beneath the ground in bright, airy hobbit holes, and they can move quickly and quietly when necessary, to hide from humans. Above all things hobbits seem to prize a quiet, unadventurous life, though some, such as the Took family, disappear and have adventures that are quickly hushed up. When Bilbo Baggins* goes with dwarves to win back a treasure from Smaug*, a dragon, he comes home to find his reputation ruined, though he does not seem to mind.

HOBBIT, THE. J[ohn] R[onald] R[euel] Tolkien. Illus. J.R.R. Tolkien. London: George Allen and Unwin, 1937. 310 pp. Rev. ed., London: George Allen and Unwin, 1951. 315 pp. British.

In a hole in the ground lives a hobbit*, Bilbo Baggins*, a very quiet hobbit living a very quiet life until one morning Gandalf*, a wizard, comes by, announcing that he is going to send him on an adventure. To his surprise, Bilbo finds himself asking Gandalf to tea the next day, but he is even more surprised at his other guests: thirteen dwarves*, among them Thorin Oakenshield*. Flummoxed, Bilbo is nonetheless a good host, even after he learns that he is to go with the dwarves after a treasure stolen by Smaug*, an evil dragon, when he took over the ancient place where Thorin lived. The next morning Bilbo wakes late and suddenly finds himself running to go on an adventure, without even a handkerchief.

Bilbo and the dwarves travel long and hard. One miserable, rainy evening they see a light, and Bilbo is sent to investigate. It is the campfire of three trolls*, who catch Bilbo, and, later, the dwarves when they come up one by one to see what has happened. Bilbo manages to escape. Gandalf, who had gone ahead to scout, returns, and by trickery manages to keep the trolls wrangling until sunup, when they turn to stone. Traveling on, the group comes to the mountains and there lodges with elves* for two weeks. Here runes, revealed on the map they are using, tell how to find the back door into Smaug's lair.

They leave and travel through the mountains, sheltering from a storm in a shallow cave. Bilbo wakes from a dream to find that goblins* have opened a crack in the back wall of the cave and are pulling them into their caves. His shout warns Gandalf, who escapes, but the rest do not and are about to be killed when Gandalf suddenly appears and saves them. When they are pursued, Bilbo is separated from the rest. Crawling about in the dark, he finds a ring* which he puts in his pocket. Eventually he comes to a lake and here meets Gollum*, a slimy creature. They have a riddle contest: if Gollum wins, he will eat Bilbo; if Bilbo wins, Gollum will give him a present. Bilbo wins by asking an unfair riddle, but Gollum's present, a ring that makes its wearer invisible, has been lost. Bilbo realizes that *he* has it; to let Gollum off, he has the creature show him the way out.[1] Because goblins are watching the passage, Bilbo uses the ring and slips out, eventually finding the others.

They travel as far as they can without horses that day, and scramble into trees when the wargs—wild wolves—gather. The wargs are here to meet the goblins, for they are going to attack a village. When Gandalf lights pinecones and throws them at the wolves, far away eagles hear the ruckus. When the goblins come, they kindle fires to burn the trees Bilbo and the others are perched in, but in the nick of time the eagles rescue them. Gandalf is a friend of the eagles, so the birds take them a bit further on their way.

Gandalf is going to leave them, for it is not his adventure, but first he takes them to Beorn*, a huge friend of animals, who shelters the groups for a few days, giving them food and advice about the forest they will travel through, and lending them ponies. When they come to the great, dark forest, Gandalf leaves them, taking Beorn's ponies back and warning the travelers not to go off the track. Bilbo and the dwarves travel for days through the nasty, airless place, having a misadventure when one dwarf tumbles into an enchanted stream. They run out of food and water, and when one night they see fires gleaming through the trees, all stumble off the path after them. Around the fires are elves, feasting, but the fires are put out as they stumble into view. Again and again this happens, and finally Bilbo is separated from the others. He kills a great spider that is trying to catch him; in the morning Bilbo finds that the dwarves have not escaped capture, and he releases them, having drawn off the spiders. After a battle, all get away.

Thorin had not been captured by spiders; the elves have him and have put him into a dungeon. Later they capture the other dwarves and imprison them; invisible, Bilbo follows. He spends a lonely time in the elves' stronghold, finally finding the dwarves and helping them to escape inside empty barrels sent down-

---

1. Gandalf discovers later that, under the influence of the ring, Bilbo has lied about this adventure. Gollum promises not a present but to show Bilbo the way out. Having lost the game, Gollum decides to use the ring to surprise Bilbo and eat him, and when the hobbit slips on the ring, he learns of its power; Gollum accidentally shows Bilbo the way out. [Revised edition]

river to Lake-town*, a human town on the lake beneath the mountain where Smaug lives. Here they are warmly welcomed because of prophecies dealing with Thorin's return to his ancient home.

Two weeks later they leave and come to the mountain, finding the place where the secret door should be but not the door itself. As the last week of autumn begins, Bilbo understands the true meaning of the map runes, and the door is found. Bilbo enters, wearing his ring, and finds Smaug sleeping on his treasure. He steals a cup to show to the dwarves; when Smaug misses it and hunts for it, all take refuge in the tunnel. The next time Bilbo goes to reconnoiter, Smaug speaks to him, and before he leaves Bilbo learns of the dragon's only vulnerable spot. That night Smaug smashes the secret door, which the dwarves close just in time, and then he goes to Lake-town to deal with the humans there. He does not come back, and Bilbo makes another trip into the cave, finding and taking the fabulous Arkenstone* for his share. The dwarves brave the caves and explore, going through the ruined palace to the front gate, where they rest.

Three days have passed since Smaug has gone to Lake-town. Here he had been killed, though not before destroying the whole town. People have begun to speak against Thorin and the dwarves, and elves and men march to the mountain to claim the treasure. The dwarves hear of all this from a raven, and they fortify the gate, sending for help. The armies camp outside the gate and try to bargain for some recompense for what the people have suffered. Thorin refuses. Days pass, and a dwarf army approaches.

Restless one night, Bilbo slips out and visits the men, giving them the Arkenstone to bargain with. But Thorin refuses to bargain and sends Bilbo away. The next day the dwarf army arrives, and fighting starts. When goblins and wargs attack, the warring forces combine against them, but things go badly until the eagles come. Bilbo is knocked out, and when he wakes it is all over. The eagles and Beorn have helped turn the tide; the goblins have been driven away and many killed. Thorin, though, dies after forgiving Bilbo. After he is buried, the treasure is divided. Bilbo goes home, with Gandalf, to find that he has been declared dead and that all his belongings are being auctioned off; he manages to get back most of them (except some silver spoons), but he has lost his reputation. He is happy, though, writing poems and visiting elves, only a little figure in a very big world.

HOBGOBLINS, a race of creatures in Mary Norton's* *Are All the Giants Dead?**. These ugly little creatures look rather like gargoyles, having large snouts, wings, scaly bodies, and sad, glowing eyes. Dreadful as they look, they are very gentle and love to be stroked; they mate for life. The hobgoblins live in a crevice in the Bluff above Much-Belungen-under-Bluff*.

HOLLYBUSH, DAVID (DAVVY), a character in *The Magical Cupboard**, by Jane Louise Curry*. His mother is Mrs. Hollybush*; his brother is Goliath Hollybush* (Golly). Though he is Golly's twin, Davvy is almost his opposite:

small, dark, and concerned only with his own welfare, having learned from his mother how to cheat and trick people. Davvy discovers from Sufferana and Thanatopsis Grout** the many aliases they have used and turns this knowledge against them; when he hints that an officer of the law has been looking for them, the Grouts shut down the orphanage where Davvy's mother is housekeeper and flee, taking with them the Hollybushes and Felicity Parmenter*. On the way to the land Felicity has inherited, the little group is attacked by bandits whom, they suspect, Davvy has set on them in order to get a share of the wealth he thinks Mr. Grout is carrying. During the raid, Mrs. Hollybush and Mr. Grout become mentally incapacitated from their ordeal. When the house and fur trade Felicity has inherited prove to be long gone, Davvy, in a rage, flings all the money the group has into a magical cupboard* they have carried; finding that the cupboard has taken the money instead of increasing it, as he had hoped, Davvy leaves the others, perhaps going to join the bandits in Hutchinson's swamp.

HOLLYBUSH, FELICITY PARMENTER. *See* Parmenter, Felicity

HOLLYBUSH, GOLIATH (GOLLY), a character in Jane Louise Curry's* *The Magical Cupboard*. He is the son of Mrs. Hollybush*; he is the brother of David Hollybush* (Davvy). Golly becomes the husband of Felicity Parmenter* (Fissy). Golly was born early in the eighteenth century. Though he is Davvy's twin, they are almost complete opposites; Davvy is small, dark, and shrewd, and Golly is large, fair, and very kind to the orphans in the orphanage where his mother is housekeeper. He is especially nice to Fissy. Though Golly's mother and Sufferana and Thanatopsis Grout** think he is slow-witted, Golly knows more about their schemes than they give him credit for, and the only reason he goes with them when the Grouts close the orphanage is to watch over Fissy. Golly accompanies Mrs. Grout to Boston and returns just in time to save the others from bandits; when Mr. Grout and Mrs. Hollybush are mentally incapacitated by their ordeal, Golly leads the group to its destination. When they discover that the house Fissy has inherited is long gone, Golly rebuilds it and they settle down to farming and raising horses. Golly and Fissy marry on Fissy's seventeenth birthday. When the magical cupboard* they take as they later accompany the Grouts to Montreal refuses to leave a certain spot, Golly sells his farm and builds a house there in which generations of Hollybushes live.

HOLLYBUSH, MRS., a character in *The Magical Cupboard*, by Jane Louise Curry*. She is the mother of David and Goliath Hollybush**. Mrs. Hollybush's original name was Parthenia Rumbold; under that name she was sentenced in the eighteenth century to twenty years in prison for counterfeiting. She avoided serving out her term, however; a year later she gave birth to twin sons and changed her name to Hollybush. Discovered by Thanatopsis Grout*, Mrs. Hollybush is blackmailed by him into acting as housekeeper/cook at the orphanage he runs for profit. Mrs. Hollybush's cooking is excellent and so is her management of the orphanage, for little money is wasted by being spent on the orphans, and both Mrs. Hollybush and the Grouts are able to profit. Though Mrs. Hollybush raises her sons carefully, only David shows a flair for turning events to his own gain; when he discovers that the Grouts have been up to some shady dealings, he tricks them into leaving the orphanage and taking the Hollybushes with them. On the journey, Mrs. Hollybush has a terrible shock and retreats mentally into her childhood, though she does not lose her remarkable flair for cooking. Several years later she goes with the Grouts to Montreal.

HOMER ZUCKERMAN (*Charlotte's Web*). *See* Zuckerman, Homer L.

HOMILY CLOCK (the Borrower series). *See* Clock, Homily

HOOD, ROBIN. *See* Wood, Robin

HOOK, CAPTAIN JAS., a character in *Peter and Wendy**, by James M. Barrie*. This villainous pirate captain sails the seas of Neverland* in the *Jolly Roger*, lording it over a terrifying band of cutthroats. Hook is vain and wears the elegant clothes of an earlier time; for all his bravado, he is unhappy because he was educated at Eton and is insecure about the lack of ''good form'' of most of his actions. Hook's sworn enemy is Peter Pan*, who once cut off his hand and flung it to a passing crocodile*, so that now Hook bears a hook instead of a hand and lives in fear of the crocodile, who liked the taste and wants more. Hook is cruel and clever; his men live in terror of him. He captures Wendy Darling* and the lost boys* and poisons Peter's medicine; this leads to the final confrontation between Peter and Hook—which Peter and the crocodile win.

HOOKER, JAMES TOBIAS (DRIFTWAY JIM), a character in Penelope Lively's* *The Driftway**. His father is a gentleman in eighteenth-century Woodstock, Oxfordshire. Early in life, James discovered that each man must take care of himself; he also realized that he hated both poverty and hard work. As a result, James became a gambler, earning what he could by cardsharping and tampering with horse races. His skills were not as good as he might have wished, so James became a highwayman along a driftway*, and is soon called ''Driftway Jim.'' To keep the common folk of the country on his side, James is careful to rob only the rich. In his employ is Tom Winter, an orphan who spies for him. One day Black Gwyn, a Welsh drover, comes to James, asking for his help and offering part of a fortune in return. Gwyn's two partners are plotting to kill him after they sell the cattle, taking Gwyn's share of the profits and blaming James for the crime. With James, Gwyn plots to outwit them by sneaking off and leaving the drovers to be robbed by James in reality; Gwyn and James will split the money. All goes as planned, though James watches in astonishment as Jack Trip*, a quick-witted stableboy disguised as James, robs the two drovers; following Jack, James robs him and sends him on his way. Though he had planned to cheat Black Gwyn, the drover is too quick for him and makes off with half the money, about which James is philosophical. He starts north with his share, thinking to evade the law officers Sir Thomas Templar has brought into the country to get him, but Tom Winter betrays him and James is caught before he gets very far.

HOPKINS, MATTHEW, a seventeenth-century witch hunter (?–1647) who appears as a character in *The Devil on the Road**, by Robert Westall*. He is also known as Hobekinus. He is the fourth son of James and Marie Hopkins. Matthew was brought up as a devout Puritan. He was educated in the Low Countries, where witch hunting was rife at the time. Though educated in maritime law, Hopkins claims to be a lawyer. Declaring that he has bested the Devil and gotten from him a list of all the witches in England, Hopkins begins witch hunts that soon become very profitable for him. In reality, he does not believe in God or the Devil. In 1647 he comes to Besingtree and soon runs into trouble: Johanna Vavasour*, a young gentlewoman Hopkins accuses of witchcraft, brings from the twentieth century a young man named John Webster*. On the way to hang Johanna, Hopkins is suddenly confronted by what he thinks is the Devil, an awful figure in orange; it is John, in the clothes he wears motorcycling. When Johanna tells Hopkins that if he serves the Devil he will gain much money, Hopkins abases himself before John. Assured by Johanna that the Devil will come for him later and that orange-colored objects come from him, Hopkins spends the rest of his life in mortal and, finally, maddening terror. Haunting the woods at night, he begs the Devil to come to him and asks all he meets to tell him where witches hold their sabbaths, though he is more fervent than ever at church. The children begin to plague him, playing pranks on him. Finally he hits one, and after it dreams of Hopkins taking its soul away, he is swum to see if he is a witch. Always slight and dandyish, Hopkins may have tuberculosis; after his ordeal in the pond, where he floats as a witch should, he lies for two days on the bank, coughing, until he dies. Hopkins is buried in unhallowed ground, and his spirit seems to haunt the place.

HORACE, a Great Dane in *Mindy's Mysterious Miniature**, by Jane Louise Curry*. Horace belongs to the Hallam family, and when Arminta Hallam* is made miniature and accidentally kidnapped, Horace follows her trail, attracting the attention of the police. Because of his size, he is sometimes affectionately called ''Horse.''

HORN DANCE, a traditional dance in Hagworthy, England, in Penelope Lively's* *The Wild Hunt of Hagworthy**. Twelve dancers are needed, and all wear masks with antlers on them; two dancers dress as the Hobbyhorse and a Man-Woman. Early in its history, the dance was associated with the Wild Hunt*, the terrifying ghostly hunt that pursues whoever looks at it. The Dance grew out of that, starting as a dance, but ending as a Stag Hunt in which a person the dancers were against for some reason was pursued; when he was caught, he was usually ducked, though sometimes worse things happened. For this reason, the annual Dance was finally stopped in the early nineteenth century. It was also stopped, probably, because it seemed to bring the Wild Hunt to the village. In the twentieth century, the vicar at Hagworthy decides to revive the Dance as a tourist attraction, and as rehearsals go on, the Wild Hunt begins to ride at night. Kester Lang* finds himself making enemies among the local people and becomes the Stag in the Dance, pursued by the others until his friend, Lucy Clough*, stops them.

HORNED KING, a character in Lloyd Alexander's* *The Book of Three*. He is the champion of Arawn*, the Lord of Death. Who the king really is, few know, for he wears a mask of a human skull with a stag's antlers rising from it. He takes joy in death and torment. The Horned King rallies around him the kings of the southern cantrevs of Prydain*, and he leads them for his master against the Sons of Don*, Prydain's protectors. Hen Wen*, an oracular pig, knows the Horned King's real name; she tells it to Gwydion*, the war leader of Prydain's High King, and he uses it to destroy the man, for once one can name evil by its true name, it is powerless.

HORSE AND HIS BOY, THE. C[live] S[taples] Lewis. Illus. Pauline Baynes. London: Geoffrey Bles, 1954. 199 pp. British.

Shasta has lived all his life with a fisherman in Calormen*, but the old man has no compunction about selling the boy when a Calormene lord offers to buy him. Shasta discovers that the lord's horse—Breehy-hinny-brinny-hoohy-hah* (Bree)—is a talking horse from the barbaric land of Narnia* and learns from Bree that the lord is cruel. The two decide to run away, and they set off for Narnia.

One night, as they journey, they run from lions and find themselves galloping beside Aravis*, the proud daughter of a Calormene lord, on Hwin*, a modest talking mare from Narnia. They, too, are going to Narnia, for Aravis was promised in marriage to an ugly old man; drugging the slave set to watch her, she had run away to escape her fate. The four decide to journey together. Soon they come to Calormen's capital city, and they disguise themselves to get through it. The four agree to meet at the tombs of the ancient kings if they are separated.

At first they are unnoticed. When they come upon a group of visiting Narnians, however, Shasta, to his horror, is recognized by them as one of their number and is marched off to the palace where the Narnians are staying. Here he is fussed over and called "Prince Corin"*. The group includes Edmund and Susan Pevensie**, a king and queen of Narnia; Susan has come to Calormen to decide whether or not to marry Rabadash*, the son of the Tisroc*, the king of Calormen. She has decided to refuse him, but the Narnians fear Rabadash will not let them leave if Susan does not agree to marry him. After much discussion they come up with a plan of escape.

Shasta is not sure what to do, for he is afraid to reveal himself to the cheerful but awesome Narnians. He decides to go with them, if the real Corin does not show up. A few hours after he is left alone, the real Corin, who looks remarkably like Shasta, climbs in through the window. Shasta leaves the same way and makes his way to the tombs, where he waits for Aravis and the horses all that night and the next day, kept company by a black cat all night.

Aravis, meantime, is also having an adventure. Soon after Shasta is taken away, she is recognized by Lasaraleen*, an old friend, and she and the horses go with the girl to her house. Lasaraleen will help them get out of the city, but not until the next night, when she will have the horses taken to the tombs and will guide Aravis through the Tisroc's palace to a hidden gate. During the escape, the two girls get lost in the palace and, hiding in an empty room, are chagrined when Rabadash and the Tisroc enter it. They listen to Rabadash persuading his father to allow him to seize Anvard*, the capital of Archenland*, the land lying between Calormen and Narnia, and from there make a raid on Narnia to kidnap Susan, who has escaped. After Rabadash and the Tisroc leave, Lasaraleen leads Aravis to the gate and the girl escapes to meet the others at the tombs.

Following directions Shasta had overheard from the Narnians, the four travelers cross the desert between the city and Archenland, reaching a hidden river after a brutal ride. Though they do not meant to, they fall asleep and so get a late start the next day; by the time they reach Archenland Rabadash's army is in the desert behind them. The horses learn how furiously they can go when they are chased by a lion that tears Aravis's shoulders with its claws before the four reach the safety of the enclosure of the Hermit of the Southern March*. The hermit sends Shasta to find King Lune*, ruler of Archenland, to warn him of the invasion, and tends Aravis and the horses. After hard running, Shasta finds the king, who is hunting with his courtiers, and he is loaned a horse to ride back to Anvard with them. Shasta gets behind and, when a fog comes, he is separated from the others. Hearing Rabadash and his army go one way, Shasta rides another, traveling higher and higher in the mountains. Suddenly he is aware that something walks beside him in the fog—something which reveals that it had been the lion who chased him and Aravis and that it had been the cat at the tombs. When the fog melts, Shasta sees a golden lion: Aslan*, king over high kings in Narnia. Aslan vanishes.

Shasta comes upon some dwarves*, who send a stag to warn those at Cair Paravel*, capital of Narnia, and who see that he eats and rests. The next day an army led by Edmund and Lucy Pevensie*, a queen of Narnia, comes to fight at Anvard. Corin is with them, and he talks Shasta into dressing in armor so that they both can sneak into the battle. The army comes to Anvard, which is besieged by Rabadash's army, and after fierce fighting the Calormene army loses and Rabadash is captured.

Meanwhile, Aslan comes to the hermit's enclosure, frightening Bree—who had been pretending superior knowledge about the lion—into humbler behavior. Aslan reveals to Aravis that he had scratched her to show her how the beating given the slave she had drugged felt. Shasta comes after Aslan leaves; his real name, he tells Aravis, is Cor*, and he is the twin of Corin and the son of King Lune. When an unscrupulous courtier had heard a prophecy that baby Cor would grow up to save Archenland from great evil, he had kidnapped the baby to get rid of him. When the ship they were on had been chased by Lune's warships, Cor was put into an open boat with a knight who had starved himself to feed the child. Aslan had pushed the boat ashore, and Cor was found by a Calormene fisherman.

Cor and Aravis go to live in Anvard with King Lune and Corin and there witness a strange transformation: while the victors of the battle are deciding what to do with Rabadash, Aslan appears and changes him into a donkey. The Calormene lord can change himself back if he stands before the altar of Tash* in the capital city at the Autumn Feast, but if he goes more than ten miles from the altar he will become a donkey again, forever.

Rabadash goes back to Calormen and later becomes one of the most peaceable rulers that country has ever known, for he cannot himself lead invading armies and dares not trust anyone to do it for him. Cor grows up to be king of Archenland and marries Aravis.

HORT TOWN, a place in Ursula K. LeGuin's* Earthsea trilogy*. This town on the island of Wathort in Earthsea* is one of the Seven Great Ports of the Archipelago. Bright, noisy Hort Town has houses of clay plastered with white, orange, red, yellow, and purple, and gaudy awnings which shade its market-places. The port comes to have troubles, however, when its sorcerers and magicians lose their powers, leached out of the world by Cob*, a dead man seeking to pull the living world after him. Ged*, a mage, and Arren*, his young companion, come to Hort Town in search of the source of the strange leaching out of the world; here they find help, but Arren is captured by a slaver and Ged uses magic to save him, probably bewildering the citizens of the port, who no longer believe in magic.

HOUSE OF ARDEN, THE. E[dith] Nesbit Bland. Illus. H. R. Millar. London: T. Fisher Unwin, 1908, 349 pp. British.

When their aunt is called away one day, Edred and Elfrida Arden** take the chance to go to Arden Castle*, all that remains of the family estate. There they make some interesting discoveries: the old lord having died and Edred's father being lost, Edred is now Lord Arden, heir to a crumbling castle and a mysterious lost treasure which can be found only if Lord Arden says a long-lost spell while he is ten years old. After breaking into the library of the castle and searching it, Edred and Elfrida find the spell and say it, and suddenly the Mouldiwarp*, the white mole on the Arden crest, appears. This testy little creature will help them, but it will appear only when they call it by making up a rhyme. The two call it for the first time after they move into the castle, and the Mouldiwarp explains that if they do not quarrel for twenty-four hours, a door will appear in the house; if they go through it, they will get help in finding the treasure. Edred and Elfrida manage their difficult task and find a door leading to an attic containing old clothes. Trying them on, they find themselves in 1807.

Bewildered there by their new life, the two reveal to the cook that they cannot remember everything they once knew. Alarmed at their "bewitchment," the cook sends Edred and Elfrida to Betty Lovell*, the local witch, who is so touched by Elfrida's gifts to her that she begins to prophesy. When the Lord Arden of 1807 comes by the cottage, the witch informs him that the French, at war with the British, will land the next day. That night, a wind comes up, and the next morning a French ship, blown to land, floats helplessly toward the rocks. The villagers who had prepared the night before to repel the French prepare now to help them. Unwilling to see the shipwreck, Elfrida calls up the Mouldiwarp and it sends them to their own time.

The next time Edred and Elfrida call the Mouldiwarp, it explains that, in order for time in their own time to stand still while they are gone, they must "turn back the clock" by stopping the second hand, which Edred does symbolically by sitting on the second hand of a clock made of daisies. He is surprised when Elfrida, who had never moved, insists that she has had an adventure; but though no time passes for Edred, Elfrida has a long adventure in 1707.

Here she finds herself in Arden House*, in London, with her cousin Betty Arden*. On their journey to Arden Castle, they spend a night at an inn where Elfrida meets a very nice and handsome young man. The next day their coach is stopped by a highwayman, the handsome man of the inn, who carries off Betty's jewels and Elfrida. Leaving her at Arden Castle, he tells Elfrida to leave a parlor window ajar, and the jewels will be returned. That night through the window comes a letter in which is a request that the Ardens shelter and hide James the Third, the "rightful heir to the throne"—none other than the highwayman. Betty and Elfrida hide him in a secret room above the mantel and endure some breathless moments when men burst in, question them, and leave laughing. The next morning they discover the truth; the "king" is Edward Talbot*, who had made a bet that he could rob a coach of the Arden jewels and sleep all night in Arden Castle without anyone knowing his name.

Back in her own time, Elfrida explores the secret room where Edward had taken the jewels, but it is empty. In trying to follow her, Edred hurts himself and accidentally closes the secret door. The two endure an anxious afternoon, Elfrida in the dark chamber and Edred unable to help her because he has twisted his knee; he cannot leave the parlor because the door is locked and she has the key. The Mouldiwarp comes to the rescue by creating a clock that magically goes backward and leaves the key where it is found by their aunt, and the two are rescued.

The next time they travel in time, Edred and Elfrida take with them a camera; they will take pictures so that once they find the treasure they will be able to restore the castle to its former splendor. They find themselves in seventeenth-century Arden House. While Edred is taken to Court to meet the king, Elfrida plays with their cousin, Richard Arden*, reminding him that it is Guy Fawkes

Day and wondering why he knows nothing of it. Mr. Parados*, his tutor, hears and has the family arrested when the Gunpowder Plot is discovered later that day. After a time in prison, Edred and Lady Arden are freed, and Elfrida escapes while he and Richard are visiting, by disguising herself as one of the boys. Having read the Arden family history, she knows that Lord Arden will be released. The family servant who helps in the escape is, surprisingly, Betty Lovell, who helps them that night by calling the Mouldiwarp when soldiers come to Arden House, looking for Elfrida. The mole explains that they can escape only by jumping from a high place, and when Edred and Elfrida do, the falling snow becomes a carriage drawn by swans that take them to Arden Castle. The next morning they photograph the castle before calling the Mouldiwarp and leaving.

The photographs are developed and hung up to dry, and the two watch in astonishment as one becomes a window to the past through which they watch a treasure being hidden, but they do not see where. When they go through the strange door to try to find the clothes worn by the children in the picture, they cannot, and they lose a chance by not using the clothes they do find there. When they call the Mouldiwarp, he takes them back with Richard to meet Henry VIII* and Anne Boleyn*. Elfrida cannot help warning the doomed queen, and when Anne becomes upset, they hurry away to escape Henry's wrath. The Mouldiwarp takes the three into a hole with him.

From Richard, Edred and Elfrida learn that their father is alive; Richard has seen him. Though the Mouldiwarp explains that once the two travel to another place in their own time, they will never again be able to travel through time, Edred and Elfrida insist on going to their father. Richard goes, too, for if Edred and Elfrida appear to their father, they will have to explain the magic and it will no longer work. The Mouldiwarp grows as big as a bear and turns Edred and Elfrida into white cats to disguise them. They find their father and his partner in a mysterious South American city, where they are being held lest they tell the outside world about the rich place. The Mouldiwarp and the cats dig an entrance into a nearby cliff, entering to find themselves in a cave below Arden Castle. Richard is whirled away to his own time, never to be seen again. Edred and Elfrida become themselves, and their father and his friend go to the castle, where they tell a story of their escape and long journey across the sea back to Britain. Though he is no longer Lord Arden, Edred is content, and though the two have not found the treasure, they have found treasure enough.

Note: This work first appeared in *The Strand Magazine*, nos. 205–215 (Jan.– Nov., 1908).

HOUSE OF LLYR. *See* Llyr, House of

HOWSON, MR., a character in *The Twelve and the Genii**, by Pauline Clarke*. This parson is a great fan of the works of Anne, Emily, Branwell, and Charlotte Brontë. Max and Jane Morley** seek Mr. Howson's help during the journey of the twelve wooden soldiers, brought to life by the creative genius of the Brontës, to Haworth parsonage. He is delighted to meet the little soldiers. He becomes the Reverend Genie and helps them after their return to Haworth by convincing the museum officials that they are indeed the soldiers owned by the Brontë children.

HSU (PING), a character in Lucy Boston's* *The River at Green Knowe**, *A Stranger at Green Knowe*, and *An Enemy at Green Knowe**. He is the only child of a Chinese timber merchant. Ping and his father lived on the Burmese border until one day the six-year-old boy returned home to find his father gone and the house destroyed. He and another boy wandered in the forest until they were taken by a Buddhist monk to a mission. Ping spent the next five years being passed from camp to camp, until at last he came to England. Here he stays at the International Relief Society's Intermediate Hostel for Displaced Children. One summer he is sent to Green Knowe* at the request of Dr. Maud Biggin* for a summer holiday; here Ping and Ida*, Maud's great-niece, and Oskar Stanislawsky*, another displaced child, have many adventures on the river near Green Knowe. Reserved, polite Ping is the favorite of everyone but Sybilla Bun, Maud's friend, who does not like the fact that he eats so little when she loves to cook so much. When Ping goes back to school, he makes the acquaintance of Hanno*, a gorilla, at the zoo; he feels that they have something in common because both are displaced persons. The two meet again at Green Knowe, where Hanno, having escaped, has taken refuge and where Ping is staying at the invitation of Mrs. Linnet Oldknow*, the owner of the house. Here Ping has an enchanted summer, until Hanno is shot. Ping and Mrs. Oldknow get along so well that she makes arrangements for him to live with her. He and Toseland* (Tolly), her great-grandson, become close friends, eventually joining forces to protect Green Knowe from evil Dr. Melanie Delia Powers*. After this adventure, to Ping's unspeakable joy, his father is brought to Green Knowe by Tolly's father.

HUGH, a character in *The Tapestry Room**, by Mrs. Mary Molesworth*. He is the great-grandson of a woman named Jeanne and the cousin of a girl named Jeanne*; his parents are dead. After his parents died, Hugh lived with his grandfather in England. When he is eight years old, he is sent to live with Jeanne and her parents in France, taking along Nibble, his guinea pig. When he arrives, he is given the tapestry room to sleep in, and the room gives him a sense of déjà vu. Hugh is soon right at home, and he has several adventures in strange lands through the machinations of Dudu*, a raven, when on moonlit nights the tapestries in the room become real, and Hugh and Jeanne can enter the castle pictured on one.

HUGH LEWIS (*The Sleepers*). *See* Lewis, Hugh

HUNTER, THE, a character in Randall Jarrell's* *The Animal Family*. Because his parents died, the hunter lives by himself in the cabin he built between the forest and the sea. This large, fair-haired man who dresses in the skins of the animals he kills grows lonely, for there is no one with whom to share things. When he makes friends with a mermaid*, the hunter finds in her a delightful companion, though they are so different that at times he feels that they will never understand one another. Though the hunter teaches the mermaid his language and how to live in his world, he never succeeds in learning her language or develops any grace in swimming. They live contentedly together in the cabin, but he feels that something is missing, and in his dreams appears the trouble: he is longing for a child. Gradually he and the mermaid find "children": a bear*, a lynx*, and, later, a boy*. Though the family is made up of such disparate elements, the hunter loves them all equally; each is adopted for who he is. Because they are so different, the hunter and the mermaid come to believe they are alike, and they are alike in their love for each other and for their family.

HUNTING HORN, a magical object that appears in several works. In Lloyd Alexander's* *The Castle of Llyr** and *Taran Wanderer**, an ivory horn with a silver mouthpiece had been made by the Fair Folk*. Any who blow it in three distinctive blasts will get their aid as quickly as they can arrive. Somehow it becomes part of the treasure store of Caer Colur, on the Isle of Mona*. When that castle crumbles, the horn floats to shore and is given by Eilonwy* to Taran*, her sweetheart. By this time it has only one call left in it. Taran uses it to summon aid for himself and Craddoc*, a shepherd he thinks may be his father. In C[live] S[taples] Lewis's* *The Lion, the Witch, and the Wardrobe** and *Prince Caspian**, an ivory horn is also used to summon aid. It is given to Susan Pevensie* by Father Christmas in Narnia*, a magical land. When she leaves Narnia, she drops it, and centuries later the horn is found by Doctor Cornelius*. At his urging, Caspian X* uses the horn to summon Susan and her brothers and sister into Narnia to help him. In Susan Cooper's* *The Dark Is Rising** and *Silver on the Tree**, a battered old horn is given to Will Stanton* by Miss Mary Greythorne*, and he uses it to summon his friends to help in a final battle between good and evil. *See also* Anghalac

HUNTINGTON, HENRY PETER (H. P.), a character in Jane Louise Curry's* *The Sleepers**. His sister is Jennifer Huntington*. When his widowed mother remarries, H. P. and his sister go to Scotland with their archaeologist uncle, Gerald Rishanger*. There they discover and help save Artair*—King Arthur*—and his men and the *Brenhin Dlyseu**, the Thirteen Treasures of Prydein, from Margan*, Fata Morgana. Because he is blonde and blue-eyed, H. P. can open the door to the chamber where Artair and his men sleep until the time they are needed. Following a prophecy Myrddin*—Merlin—makes to Jennifer,

H. P. finds the Bell of Rhûn* under the remains of the Eildon Tree*. He proves himself to be a deft burglar when he breaks into a case in the British Museum to retrieve the Bell so that it may be rung to wake Artair and the sleeping knights.

HUNTINGTON, JENNIFER, a character in *The Sleepers**, by Jane Louise Curry*. Her brother is Henry Peter Huntington* (H. P.). Years after their father dies, their mother marries MacClure Mitchell, and the two children go with their archaeologist uncle, Gerald Rishanger*, to Scotland. There they discover and help save Artair*—King Arthur*—and his men and the *Brenhin Dlyseu**, the Thirteen Treasures of Prydein, from Margan*—Fata Morgana. Because she has an artistic bent, Jennifer is open and sensitive to the wonders of the world; it is to her that Myrddin*—Merlin—first appears as a prophesying boy and, later, as the old man he really is. He also trusts her enough to send her to help him break the spell binding him in the Eildon Tree*.

HUNTSMEN, a race of men in the Chronicles of Prydain* and *Coll and His White Pig*, by Lloyd Alexander*. These murderers for the joy of it and betrayers of comrades have sworn allegiance to Arawn*, the Lord of Death, in order to indulge their pleasures. Each is marked on the forehead with Arawn's brand, and he has given them swiftness and endurance, as well as a strange power: when any in their small company dies, the strength of the others in the band increases. These ruthless men are sent from Annuvin* several times, once to stop Taran* and his small band, who are searching for the Black Crochan* from which spring Arawn's deathless soldiers, and again during Arawn's last bid for control over Prydain*.

HUW HANNERHOB (*The Owl Service*). *See* Hannerhob, Huw

HUW THE FLITCH. *See* Hannerhob, Huw

HWIN, a character in *The Horse and His Boy** and *The Last Battle**, by C[live] S[taples] Lewis*. She is a gentle talking mare born in Narnia*, a land of talking beasts. Hwin was captured and sold to Aravis*, the daughter of a nobleman in Calormen*. She does not reveal herself as a talking beast until Aravis is prepared to kill herself rather than marry the elderly lord her stepmother has chosen for her. Then Hwin suggests that they go to Narnia, where both will be free. They are joined in their journey by Shasta (Cor*) and by Breehy-hinny-brinny-hoohy-hah* (Bree), another talking horse, and make their way north in time for Shasta to warn the king of Archenland* of the impending invasion by the Calormene army. Humble Hwin defers to Bree in many things, and she loves and believes in Aslan*, the great lion-protector of Narnia. She is one of those in Aslan's country when Narnia comes to an end.

I

ICELINGS, a race of beings in *The Wolves of Aam**, by Jane Louise Curry*. These giants are covered with dense hair that insulates them against the great winter that has covered their once-green land. Mistrustful of mortal men, the Icelings shun them but keep a constant watch on their doings. One, Ghagra*, joins the men commanded by power-hungry Lord Naghar* in order to keep close watch on that evil man's doings; Ghagra helps Runner-to-the-Sky's-Edge*—a Tiddi* captured because he might have information valuable to Naghar—to escape. Two Icelings wake the sleeping fires of the mountain of Gzel*, once part of their realm, and so complete the destruction of the fortress there.

ICHIGO, a character in *Time Cat**, by Lloyd Alexander*. His uncle is Fujiwara*, the regent and Ichigo's adviser. Ichigo is the boy-emperor of Japan in 998. Overawed by Fujiwara, Ichigo is completely under the man's control and knows little or nothing about the hardships his people suffer. When Jason*, a boy from the twentieth century, and Gareth*, his cat, accompany a gift of kittens to the Celestial Palace, Ichigo learns not only what a cat is, but a little about his people and, ultimately, how to deal as an emperor should with Fujiwara.

IDA, a character in Lucy Boston's* *The River at Green Knowe** and *A Stranger at Green Knowe*. She is the great-niece of Dr. Maud Biggin*. Self-reliant Ida is small for her age but very able to take care of herself. For this reason Maud invites her to Green Knowe* to be a companion for Oskar Stanislawsky* and Hsu* (Ping), two refugee orphans. Ida and the boys spend a fantastic summer, discovering the magic and the secrets of the river at Green Knowe. At one point she becomes the subject in one of Maud's experiments; convinced that giant prehistoric men once lived on the earth, Maud feeds Ida some of the seeds they might have eaten, to see if the seeds were the reason for their great size. The results of the experiment are inconclusive. The year after the summer spent at Green Knowe, Ida writes to its owner, Mrs. Linnet Oldknow*, and convinces her to invite Ping back for another summer.

ILLIGAN, THE, a character in *The Wolves of Aam**, by Jane Louise Curry*. He is one of the goblin-like Rokarrhuk*. One of Lord Naghar's* men, the Illigan commands the mountain fortress of Gzel*. He leads the party that captures Runner-to-the-Sky's-Edge* and is frightened to discover that the stone, Mirelidar*, which he has been ordered to seize, has vanished. The Illigan also questions Lek*, a conjuror, and captures Cathound*. He is killed by Ghagra*, an Iceling* posing as one of his men, just before the destruction of Gzel.

IMMÂNALA, THE, a beast in *The Three Mulla-mulgars**, by Walter de la Mare*. She is like no other beast ever born in the world: hence her name, which means "nameless, unknown." She is cruel, and ravenous, yet hungerless, and it may be that she is reborn each time she dies. The Immânala and her Jack-Alls, Jaccatrays, and leopards haunt the forest. Ummanodda* (Nod), a little Mulgar*, gets the better of the Immânala when she seeks the death of his friend, Andy Battle*; playing on her greed, he pretends that Andy's clothes are magical and, dressing her in them, tricks her Jack-Alls into thinking she is Andy. They kill her.

IMOGEN, a character in *The Story of the Amulet**, by E[dith] Nesbit Bland*. Imogen was born in England at the turn of the century. Her father was a carpenter who brought his family to London when he came looking for work. After he and Imogen's mother die, the girl is to be sent to the workhouse, until she meets Robert*, Anthea*, Cyril*, and Jane*. Saddened by her story, they take her to Jimmy*, a learned man who wishes they could find a place where someone would want her. The Psammead*, overhearing him, grants his wish, and a place is found in the Britain of 55 B.C. There, a woman Imogen recognizes as her mother identifies her as the daughter she had thought was lost. When Jimmy wishes Imogen could stay in that time, that wish is granted, too.

INAS EBHÉLIC, a place in Jane Louise Curry's* Abáloc novels*. It is an island in the river near what is in the twentieth century Apple Lock*, Ohio. It is "the Rock that reaches down to the root of things." Here the mysterious Aldar* formed the lovely Tree-Chamber—a cave with a pillar in the center that is carved like the trunk of an ammarn* tree; on the ceiling and walls are carved its branches, and around the circumference of the cave is carved a stream. The stream is the ring of time, the boundary of a lifetime; the tree is the fruitfulness a life can achieve. In the fourth century, Thiuclas*, the Keeper, lives on this island with Dalea*, his granddaughter. It is to this place that Tekla*, the queen of Kanhuan*, comes after she has freed Katóa*, a ravening, destructive force. After cutting down the last living ammarn on the island, she delves out below the Tree-Chamber a shrine for Katóa. This shrine stays intact until the twelfth century; an oracle here tells the people of Abáloc* to destroy their books, forcing them to rely on the knowledge of sometimes-unscrupulous wisemen. When Neolin* is thwarted in the twelfth century, he breaks the shrine and frees Katóa, which leaves the island. An ammarn tree sprouts from the stump of the one that had been felled; it is still alive in the twentieth century, when the island is called Apple Island*. In the twentieth century, the Tree-Chamber is sealed to protect it from curiosity-seekers.

INGELOW, JEAN (1820–1897), British writer. She was born 17 March 1820, at Boston, Lincolnshire. She was the oldest child of William and Jean Kilgour Ingelow. Jean was educated at home and spent her life in Lincolnshire, Ipswich, and London. At one time she was considered for the office of Poet Laureate of England. Ingelow died 20 July 1897.

*Mopsa the Fairy** is Ingelow's only book-length work for children; her other works are collections of short stories. *Mopsa* is a book about fairies that itself reflects the faery; though Ingelow's fair folk are sometimes downright precious, they still are true to their Celtic origins.

Ingelow's fairy world, like the traditional one, is just around the corner from our world. Jack*, the young hero, investigates the twittering noises in a hollow tree and finds fairies; he is pulled from the tree by a talking albatross and finds himself in a world where rivers run inland, abused horses become well and young again, and fairies are everywhere. It is his world with an enchantment on it.

Some of the fairy inhabitants are small, but some are as tall as mortal beings— the traditional height of Celtic fairies. Each race in Fairyland* is different. Like Celtic fairies, these good folk have no souls. They cannot cry, nor can they laugh, without seeing a mortal do it first. They are creatures with their own morality and their own thoughts. They are very close to nature, having sap running through their veins instead of blood and appearing in the shapes of animals as well as in human form. Like the traditional fairy folk, Ingelow's fairies seem to put a value on some of the objects mortals own: the gypsy asks for the use of a handkerchief woven "across the sea," for that kind she cannot see through; Jack's money has great value because it does not vanish, and one coin is enough to buy a slave. Because it is real money, Mopsa* can form Jack's fourpence into a magical wand.

In this fairy world, magic is recognized as a powerful force not to be lightly indulged in. When the old gypsy woman chants her spell to free the fairies, she has herself blindfolded because she dares not say the spell with her eyes open. Mopsa, too, has herself blindfolded when she uses the magical wand she has made from Jack's coins. Magic seems so powerful that to practice it with open eyes is to invite danger. This seems to be true only for the "mechanical" kind of magic, which depends on an enchanted object or a spoken charm to work. The fairies themselves possess some power to work magic, and when employing this power do not need to protect themselves; the queen of the fairies* relies on her own powers to stretch ribbon into a robe, to comb the gray from her hair, to remove the wrinkles from her face.

Violence is treated in this book with all the casualness one finds in traditional fairy tales. Fairies have their heads pulled off; Jack almost has a hole bored in the back of his head; the gypsy is set upon by parrots; the air fairy pulls off its wing so that Jack and Mopsa may travel on it. The violence is never lingered upon, and it is almost always for a purpose. Violence is as much a part of life as breathing.

Ingelow's fairy world, like the traditional one of the fair folk, is a place where there is little sadness or mental pain. In the land of people turned to stone, a mother sings to her baby of the mortal world she longs to see, but for the most part the inhabitants of Fairyland are content. Though the apple woman* is homesick for her own world, she stays in Fairyland because the mortal world has pain in it. As is traditional, though many days pass while Jack is in Fairyland, when he returns home no one seems to have noticed that he has gone. It is as if no time had passed between his leaving and his return.

But although Ingelow's fairy world reflects the traditional world of the fair folk, Jack's adventures there are filled with lessons about mercy. Cruel people are punished there: the bay at the back entrance to Fairyland is filled with the ships of those who did evil or were on evil missions; those who did a deed so cruel that their hearts seemed to be made of stone become stone in reality; for refusing a mortal beggar a handful of wheat, a fairy race is enchanted into deer, "a more gentle and innocent race." In this magical land, abused horses that die in our own world become strong and young again.

Though the books contains lessons, this didacticism is not overwhelming; the emphasis seems to be on entertaining rather than on teaching. It is an amusing book filled with strange stories and adventures. As in most fairy tales, character is not as important as plot; Jack and the other characters seem to be acted on rather than being actors, and few characters seem multidimensional. Ingelow's clear, descriptive style sets a mood of enchantment and reflection. A rather startling element in the book is the author's use of stream-of-consciousness, not in the narrative, as later writers have used it, but in the prophetic monologues Mopsa and the queen speak when they are in their trances. The queen looks into the future, but Mopsa speaks of the past and the future as well. Perhaps because it appeared soon after *Alice in Wonderland*, *Mopsa* seems a bit derivative; like Alice, Jack obeys his curiosity and finds himself adventuring in a strange land where he visits strange places and strange people. There are also touches of Carrollian logic and humor: as the fairies grow and change, their clothes change, too—from pinafores into aprons, for the girls—as Jack's jacket will turn into a tailcoat when he gets older. Ingelow surpasses mimicry, however.

Works

Juvenile fantasy: *Mopsa the Fairy* (1869).
Juvenile non-fantasy: *Tales of Orris* (1860); *Studies for Stories* (1864); *Stories Told to a Child* (1865) *Tales of Orris* reprinted with additions; *A Sister's Bye-Hours* (1868), stories; *The Little Wonder-Horn* (1872), stories; *The Little Wonder Box* (1887), stories.

Adult: *A Rhyming Chronicle of Incidents and Feelings* (1850); *Allerton and Dreux* (1851); *Poems* (1863); *Home Thoughts and Home Scenes* (1865); *A Story of Doom, and Other Poems* (1867); *Off the Skellings* (1872), novel; *Poems* (1874), second series; *Fated to Be Free* (1875), novel; *One Hundred Holy Songs, Carols, and Sacred Ballads* (1878); *Sarah de Berenger* (1879), novel; *Don Juan* (1881), novel; *The High-Tide on the Coast of Lincolnshire, 1571* (1883), poem; *Poems* (1885), third series; *Poems of the Old Days and the New* (1885); *John Jerome* (1886), novel; *Very Young and Quite Another Story* (1890).

Secondary Works

Peters, Maureen. *Jean Ingelow, Victorian Poetess.* Totowa, New Jersey: Rowman and Littlefield, 1972.

Some Recollections of Jean Ingelow and Her Early Friends. Reissued by Port Washington, N.Y., and London: Kennikat Press, 1972.

Stedman, Eustace A. *Jean Ingelow: An Appreciation.* London: Chiswick Press, 1935.

IRENE (THE GRANDMOTHER), a character in George MacDonald's* *The Princess and the Goblin** and *The Princess and Curdie**. She is the great-grandmother of a king* and the great-great-grandmother of Irene*, a princess. Another of her many names is Old Mother Wotherwop, which she is called by the miners of the area, who believe she is an evil witch intent only on doing bad. Just as she has several names, she can appear in several shapes, as a crabbed old woman or a young serving girl or a queen: a shape for her is only something in which to appear, and all the shapes she takes are true ones. Queen Irene has a house in the mountains, far from the capital, but she takes great interest in the king and helps him as best she can. Though she lives in rooms at the top of her house, few know she is there, for not all can see her, and even those who can cannot always find her. She is there, though, for those in desperate need: a light shines sometimes from her window to help the lost, and when an evil must be righted she can be counted upon to do it or send others to do it. When the Princess Irene is in danger from goblins*, her "grandmother" gives her a ring attached to a thread spun of spiders' silk which will lead her to safety; when the king is ill and in danger of dying, the woman sends Curdie Peterson*, a young miner, to help him. After he accompishes this mission, she goes to live at the palace, sometimes leaving to visit the strange creatures in a nearby wood. At the queen's command is a fire of roses which she can use to purify or to heal; she uses it to burn the calluses from Curdie's hands so that he can tell at a touch what kind of beast or human a person is inside; she also uses it to purge the despondent king of his bad dreams. The fire is also used to help Lina*, an odd, ugly creature. The old queen is always more than she appears to be and more than anyone else can comprehend.

IRENE (THE PRINCESS), a character in *The Princess and the Goblin** and *The Princess and Curdie**, by George MacDonald*. Her father is a king*, and her mother dies several years after her birth; she is the great-great-granddaughter of an ageless woman, also named Irene*. Soon after the princess's birth, she was sent to a house in the country, for her mother was not strong. Though no one has told her, Irene has been in danger from goblins* since her birth, for they hope to wreak revenge on her father through her. When she is about eight or nine, the goblins try to capture her to marry to their prince, but Irene is saved by her great-great-grandmother and by Curdie Peterson*, a young miner. Even at this young age Irene is a true princess, brave and honest and open-hearted. Over the next year she grows even more like a princess, maturing quickly, for her father becomes ill and she must care for him. Curdie again helps her and her father and stays on at the palace. Eventually they marry and rule together after the king dies, and under their rule the people are happy and good. The couple dies childless, however, and the succeeding king brings ruin.

ISABEL CHARLOTTE THEODORA FREDERICKA (ISABEL), a character in Lloyd Alexander's* *The Marvelous Misadventures of Sebastian**. She is the orphaned princess of Hamelin-Loring*; her parents, Prince Theodore and Princess Charlotte, were killed in an accident arranged by Count Grinssorg*, who became an oppressive Regent. Surrounded by his pompous minions, Isabel learns to speak in such complex sentences that sometimes she is hard to understand. When Isabel comes of age, Grinssorg announces their impending marriage, and the princess flees the palace, intending to use her cousin's army to regain her throne. Disguised as a boy, Isabel makes her way through Hamelin-Loring. On her travels, she meets Sebastian*, a young fiddler seeking his fortune, and the mysterious Nicholas*, who agree to help her. After adventures during which she learns much about the oppression her subjects suffer, Isabel regains her throne on the death of Grinssorg. She will not be ruler for life; once a more democratic government is firmly established, she can step down, and once Sebastian has explored his love of music, they will marry.

ISLAND-WHERE-YOU-MAYN'T-GO, a place in E[dith] Nesbit Bland's* *The Magic City**. It is a paradisiacal island in the land of Polistarchia*, which is made up of cities and places created by Philip Haldane*. Because the island was created by Philip and his sister, Helen, only they are allowed to land on it until Philip gives the island to the Dwellers by the Sea* as a permanent home. Philip comes to the island by accident; the Pretenderette* kidnaps him and flies to the island but cannot herself land. For a time Philip shares the island with Helen, who dreams herself onto it. When he gives the island to the Dwellers, Helen vanishes, for the island is her only link to Polistarchia. This little Eden has bushes on which grow all kinds of good things to eat, and houses that contain all anyone would ever need. Best of all, there is no fear here, which makes it perfect for the Dwellers. When Philip gives the island to them, he indirectly provides fruit for the city of Polistopolis*, for the island is the only place in the land where fruit grows.

ISLE OF MONA, a place in the Chronicles of Prydain*, by Lloyd Alexander*. This small island lies west of Prydain*. The king of Mona's castle is at Dinas Rhydnant; at the other end of the island lies Caer Colur, the ancient castle of the House of Llyr*. Rhuddlum rules Mona for a time; to his court comes Eilonwy*, a princess, to learn to be a lady. Rhuddlum is succeeded by Rhun*, who dies in Prydain during an attempt to rescue his friend, Taran*, and his companions from their enemies. The community projects left undone by Rhun's death are completed by Taran. On Mona Taran and his companions meet Glew*, a mean-spirited man greedy for greatness, and Llyan*, his gigantic cat.

IT, a monstrous power in Madeleine L'Engle's* *A Wrinkle in Time*. IT sometimes calls ITself the "Happiest Sadist." This phrase is apt, for IT seems to enjoy ITs position as vanquisher of the individual spirit through cruel means. IT is an oversized, disembodied brain residing in the capital city of Camazotz* and ruling that planet. All individual lives are given up to IT, all thinking is done by IT, and everything is done to the rhythm pulsing in IT. As a result, Camazotz has become a place of no individual initiative, where each person performs his or her actions in perfect synchronization; those who do not are dreadfully punished. The rhythm of IT is very easy to fall into, and for centuries no one has resisted IT. Mr. Murry*, a traveler from Earth, is the first, and he resists for some time, being rescued finally by his daughter, Meg Murry*. Meg must also help her little brother, Charles Wallace Murry*, who has allowed himself to succumb to IT; love is the one thing IT does not have, and her love vanquishes ITs hold on Charles.

JACK, a character in Jean Ingelow's* *Mopsa the Fairy**. Inquisitive Jack finds a nest full of fairies in a hollow tree and then embarks on an adventure-filled journey to Fairyland*, taking the fairies to meet the queen of the fairies*, whom he frees and accompanies to her palace. It is Jack's loving kiss that keeps Mopsa*, one of the fairies he is escorting, a child, for the love of mortals does strange things to a fairy. Jack later flees with Mopsa from the fairies who want to make her their queen and keep her prisoner; when Mopsa falls into their hands and unwittingly breaks their enchantment, Jack and a fairy prince help disenchant the fairy men. Though he loves Mopsa, Jack must return to his own world.

JACK GARLAND (*Poor Tom's Ghost*). *See* Garland, Jack

JACK-OF-THE-BEANSTALK, a character in *Are All the Giants Dead?**, by Mary Norton*. He lives in the Land of Cocklayne*, where characters from fairy tales live happily ever after. Try as he might, Jack is never able to grow another beanstalk as tall as the first one, but he becomes a very good gardener, quite an expert on composts. He runs a nameless inn with Jack-the-Giant-Killer* in Much-Belungen-under-Bluff*, growing much that appears on the menu. When James*, a visitor to Cockayne, brings Dulcibel*, a princess, to the inn and the two Jacks learn of the talisman that has kept Jack-the-Giant-Killer from killing the last giant* on the Bluff, Jack-of-the-Beanstalk takes a bean from the original stalk and plants it in the garbage the giant has thrown over the Bluff; in this rich matter the plant grows as tall as the Bluff and Jack-the-Giant-Killer climbs to the top and slays the giant.

JACK-THE-GIANT-KILLER, a character in Mary Norton's* *Are All the Giants Dead?**. He lives in the Land of Cockayne*, where characters from fairy tales live happily ever after. Jack has killed twelve of the thirteen giants living on the Bluff above Much-Belungen-under-Bluff*; because the last giant* has kept the frog with a jewel in its head, Jack is not able to kill it for several years. Because he has a reputation to uphold, Jack has destroyed the pass which the giant took into the valley and claims that he has killed the giant, though there is evidence to the contrary. Jack-the-Giant-Killer is cook at the nameless inn he runs with Jack-of-the-Beanstalk*; James* and Mildred* stay here during a visit to Cockayne. When James brings Dulcibel*, a princess, to the inn and it becomes clear why Jack was not able to kill the giant, he and Jack-of-the-Beanstalk do what they can to kill the giant and get the frog to help Dulcibel. Jack-of-the-Beanstalk grows a beanstalk as tall as the Bluff, and Jack-the-Giant-Killer climbs up and kills the last giant, cutting off a lock of its hair to hang with triumph with his trophies of the other twelve.

JACK TRIP (*The Driftway*). *See* Trip, Jack

JACOB, a character in Lucy Boston's* *The Chimneys of Green Knowe** and *The Stones of Green Knowe**. He is an orphan. Jacob was born into slavery in the West Indies, but when his master and father are killed during the slave uprising in 1795 and his mother is taken away, Jacob is left on his own. He is soon bought by Captain Oldknow*, to grow up free with the Captain's daughter, Susan Oldknow*. When he comes at last to Green Knowe*, Jacob is totally loyal to the Captain; he soon becomes just as devoted to blind Susan, leading her about, making up games, and bringing to her animals and objects to touch. With his companionship, Susan becomes strong and independent. Perhaps because he is not related to the Oldknows, Jacob cannot see the children who sometimes manifest themselves at Green Knowe; he can only hear them. Because he believes in Juju, however, he seems to accept them as part of the place. Jacob's nemesis is Sefton Oldknow*, Susan's older brother, who makes fun of him; when Sefton orders for Jacob a suit of clothes like that an organ grinder's monkey wears, Jacob wreaks subtle revenge on him by stealing small things from him. Jacob proves his courage and devotion to Susan when the new wing of Green Knowe burns down and he braves the fire to save her. As they grow up, they continue to be close, Jacob acting as Susan's groom after he is thirteen. When Susan marries, Captain Oldknow takes Jacob to Barbados, where he finds a wife who comes back to England with him. Jacob grows into a big, gentle man, and both his own children and Susan's love him very much.

JADIS, a character in *The Magician's Nephew**, by C[live] S[taples] Lewis*. She has a sister. Beautiful Jadis destroyed her world in order to destroy her sister and take the throne, by using the Deplorable Word that destroys all but the one who says it. After this Jadis put herself into a trance in a hall where sit images of her ancestors, in the city of Charn. She is wakened by Digory Kirke*, a boy from Earth, and is accidentally taken there by him and by Polly Plummer*, his companion. With her unearthly beauty she seems to enchant Andrew Ketterley*, Digory's uncle, and Jadis wreaks much havoc in London before Digory and Polly can get her away. Though they plan to leave her in the dreamy Wood between the Worlds*, which to her is a deadly place, Jadis follows them into

Narnia*, a magical land just being created. She immediately hates this world and its creator, a great lion called Aslan*, and she tries to kill him but fails. Having run away into the Western Wild, Jadis finds there a walled garden in which grows a tree with silver apples* that confer immortality on all who eat them; though she eats one and gains youth and immortality, it is a miserable kind of deathlessness, and the apples are henceforth an anathema to her. From one of the apples grows a tree that keeps her from Narnia for many generations. Jadis may be the White Witch* who comes from the north into Narnia after the tree falls; their names and personalities are similar.

JAMES, a character in *Are All the Giants Dead?**, by Mary Norton*. Practical, level-headed James dislikes anything saccharine or prettified and likes science fiction better than fairy tales, but he meets several fairytale figures during adventures in lands to which he is taken by Mildred*, a reporter of the fantastical. In the Land of Cockayne* James meets Sleeping Beauty, Cinderella, Beauty, and the Beast, all grown older and busily living happily ever after. James is a brave boy who seems to relish adventure. He meets and helps Dulcibel*, the daughter of Beauty and the Beast, who must marry a toad living in a well. Together they search for the frog with a jewel in its head, which may save Dulcibel from marrying a toad, and once the frog is found, James gives Dulcibel the advice she needs to bring her adventures to a happy ending.

JAMES (JIMMY), a character in E[dith] Nesbit Bland's* *The Enchanted Castle**. He is the brother of Gerald* and Kathleen*. When they cannot go home because their cousin has the measles, the three children spend the holidays at Kathleen's school. Exploring the grounds of nearby Yalding Castle*, they come upon what appears to be a sleeping princess, whom Jimmy wakes with a kiss. She is Mabel Prowse*, and together they have adventures with a magical wishing ring* that is what anyone says it is. At one point, excited by the prosperity of Mr. U. W. Ugli*, a dummy they have created which comes to life, Jimmy uses the ring to make himself rich. He becomes a pompous, stuffy, and rich adult whom the other children cannot abide, and Gerald must take some drastic steps to rectify matters.

JAMES BEALE (*Harding's Luck*). *See* Beale, James

JAMES HARRISON (*The Ghost of Thomas Kempe*). *See* Harrison, James

JAMES TOBIAS HOOKER (*The Driftway*). *See* Hooker, James Tobias

JANE, a character in E[dith] Nesbit Bland's* *Five Children and It**, *The Phoenix and the Carpet**, and *The Story of the Amulet**. She is the sister of Robert*, Anthea*, Cyril*, and the Lamb*. Her nickname is "Pussy." Like the others, Jane is not especially attractive, clever, or good, and she has a talent for getting into mischief without meaning to. Jane tries to be brave, but she sometimes does not succeed. She and the others have several adventures with magic when they find a Psammead* who grants wishes, a magic carpet* in which is rolled the egg of the Phoenix*, and half of an amulet* that takes them through time to find the other half. This amulet is Jane's special care, for she carries the half through their adventures into the past, using it to get them out of the trouble they get into. Jane's modicum of bravery is tested many times as the children hopelessly defend their house, which they have wished into a besieged castle; as she discovers a burglar* one night when the children are home alone; and as she wanders the streets of ancient Babylon, searching for the other children after they have become separated.

JANE, a character in *Peter and Wendy**, by James M. Barrie*. Her mother is Wendy Darling*; when Wendy grows too old to go to Neverland* to do Peter Pan's* spring cleaning, Jane takes her place. Jane grows up to have a daughter of her own who also cleans for Peter.

JANE CAROLINE BANKS (the Mary Poppins books). *See* Banks, Jane Caroline

JANE DREW (*Over Sea, Under Stone; Greenwitch; Silver on the Tree*). *See* Drew, Jane

JANE HARVEY (*The Revenge of Samuel Stokes*). *See* Harvey, Jane

JANE MORLEY (*The Twelve and the Genii*). *See* Morley, Jane

JARRELL, RANDALL (1914–1965), American writer. He was born on 6 May 1914, in Nashville, Tennessee, to Anna (Campbell) and Owen Jarrell. He was educated at Vanderbilt University, in Nashville, earning a B.A. in psychology and an M.A. in English. On 1 June 1939 he married Mackie Langham; they were divorced in 1952. On 8 November 1952 he married Mary Eloise von Schrader. Jarrell taught at Kenyon College, in Ohio; at the University of Texas, in Austin; at Sarah Lawrence College, in New York; and at the University of North Carolina at Greensboro. He was literary editor of *The Nation* and Consultant in Poetry at the Library of Congress. Jarrell died on 14 October 1965.

Jarrell was a poet, as is evident in his three short fantasies and one full-length fantasy for children, not only in the stress on the poet and his search for expression, as in *The Bat-Poet*, but in his lyrical style. *Fly by Night* is as much dream as it is fantasy, as a young boy travels the world in his dreams. These two works are especially quiet but full of meaning.

Central to Jarrell's fantasies—including *The Gingerbread Rabbit*, a short fantasy about a runaway gingerbread rabbit—is a sense of belonging. The bat of *The Bat-Poet* loves his art, but he is most content when he is with the other bats, snuggled up under the eaves. The gingerbread rabbit, running from those who would eat him, is safe and contented only when he finds other rabbits to live with. In *The Animal Family**, five disparate, separate beings—a hunter*, a mermaid*, a clumsy bear*, an effervescent lynx*, and a human boy*—come together and live contentedly in a little cabin by the sea.

Tied in several ways to the importance of belonging is the idea of family. David, the young dreamer in *Fly by Night*, hears the story of a family of owls and is reminded by the mother owl of his own mother; the bat-poet's final poem, the one he makes for the other bats, describes a mother bat and her baby. The gingerbread rabbit, running away from the woman baking him for her child, finds two rabbits with whom he forms a little family. The idea of family is especially important in *The Animal Family*. Here, the family is made up of opposites who come together and make up a family as whole as any in which the members are of the same species, from the same kind of life. Each member of the family seems to be loved as much for his or her differences as for anything else. The mermaid and the hunter are different from each other, for each is graceless and almost helpless in the other's element, and their languages are different, as is the way each looks at life; the mermaid does not understand the hunter's regret at the deaths of his parents, for sadness is foreign to her. When they live together in the hunter's cottage, he sleeps under the skin blanket, while she sleeps on top of it. Yet they are happy together, so different that they come to feel that they are the same. The bear is loved for its stolid stupidness and even for the way it fills the cottage with water when it is wet, or the lumbering way it runs. The lynx is loved for its beauty and its grace, and though it forgets to velvet its paws sometimes, this is tolerated too. The boy is loved for his humanness and for the qualities that make him different from the lynx and the bear. Though he learns from both the mermaid and the hunter, this makes him a wholly different person, one made up of both, and he is loved for this as well.

Landscape is important in several of Jarrell's works. The peaceful landscape above which David floats is as dreamlike as his own story. The bat finds the sun-filled daytime too fascinating to ignore and thus begins to make his poems, using as his subject the world around him. In *The Animal Family*, landscape serves to delineate the characters and to signal their integration. The hunter and the mermaid are described in terms of their environment: the hunter, dressed in deerskin, has hair as light as fire and his language has a "walnut" sound; the mermaid, silver blue-green as the sea, speaks a "watery" language. Born in the changeless sea, she must get used to the land, where things are always changing. Though the hunter's cabin has some things of the sea in it—crushed seashells on the floor and sealskin rugs on the seashells—the mermaid brings to it more things of the sea—shells, and a figurehead of a woman half human, half goat, as she is herself half human, half fish. The cabin becomes an environment suitable for both, made up of things each finds familiar. For the bear the cabin is also familiar, being, one supposes, a kind of cave; for the lynx, the cabin's rafters are the branches of a great tree. The bear is stolid as the land and the lynx as lively and variable as the sea. The boy is a land animal who comes to them in a boat; taught by the mermaid and the hunter, he combines the land and the sea, for he is at home in both, speaking both languages, and seeing nothing strange in either.

In all the works, the ultimate emotion is a sense of belonging. David wakes from his dream to his mother's face, the sleepy bat snuggles up to his fellows, the gingerbread rabbit is secure in his new home, and individuals so disparate that the only word to describe them all is "animal" become close enough to be described by another word: "family."

Jarrell's prose poems recreate with grace and liveliness the landscape and characters he describes. The nameless characters in *The Animal Family* especially become for the reader individuals who are also universal figures: each character seems right for the environment he or she inhabits. The artistic little bat-poet is the quintessential creator in love with his craft and forced to deal with almost every kind of criticism imaginable. These are quiet little books rich in theme and wholly engaging.

Works

Juvenile full-length fantasy: *The Animal Family* (1965).

Juvenile short fantasy: *The Gingerbread Rabbit* (1964); *The Bat-Poet* (1964); *Fly by Night* (1976).

Adult: *Blood for a Stranger* (1942), poems; *Little Friend, Little Friend* (1945), poems; *Losses* (1948), poems; *The Seven-League Crutches* (1951); *Poetry and the Age* (1953), essays; *Pictures from an Institution* (1954), novel; *The Woman at the Washington Zoo* (1960), poems; *A Sad Heart at the Supermarket* (1962), essays; *The Lost World* (1965), poems; *The Third Book of Criticism* (1969); *Kipling, Auden & Co.* (1980), essays.

Secondary Works

Jarrell, Mrs. Randall. "The Group of Two," in *Randall Jarrell: 1914–1965*, ed. Robert Lowell, Peter Taylor, and Robert Penn Warren (New York: Farrar, Straus and Giroux, 1967), pp. 274–98.

Neumeyer, Peter F. "Randall Jarrell's *The Animal Family*: New Land and Old," *Proceedings of the Seventh Annual Conference of the Children's Literature Association*, 1980, pp. 139–45.

Quinn, Sister Mary Bernetta. *Randall Jarrell*. Boston: Twayne Publishers, 1981.

Randall Jarrell, A Bibliography, comp. Charles M. Adams. Chapel Hill: University of North Carolina Press, 1958.

Travers, P. L. "A Kind of Visitation," in *Randall Jarrell: 1914–1965*, ed. Robert Lowell, Peter Taylor, and Robert Penn Warren (New York: Farrar, Straus and Giroux, 1967), pp. 253–56. [Reprinted from *New York Times Book Review* (21 Nov. 1965).]

Zander, Leo. "Randall Jarrell: About and for Children," *The Lion and the Unicorn*, 2 (Spring, 1978), pp. 73–93.

JASON, a character in *Time Cat**, by Lloyd Alexander*. This young boy owns Gareth*, a black cat who takes him on an incredible journey to nine different places in nine different time periods. Through his meetings with many different people, each of whom manages with Jason's help to solve his or her problem, Jason learns much about himself and others. Jason teaches Neter-Khet*, an Egyptian pharoah, that grandeur does not always bring respect and shows Cerdic Longtooth* how to tame cats to catch mice; he helps Sucat*, a Welsh slave, to achieve his destiny as St. Patrick and aids Ichigo*, a Japanese boy-emperor who needs to learn to rule and to consider the needs of his people; Jason helps Leonardo da Vinci* to prove to his father that he can become a great painter and makes Awin* realize that even though she looks different she can still be loved; he helps Don Diego Francisco Hernández del Gato Herrera y Robles* to escape his hated position as a conquistador and saves Mistress Ursulina* from being burned as a witch; and Jason carries the battle call to the Sons of Liberty at the beginning of the American War of Independence.

JASPER, a character in Ursula K. LeGuin's* *A Wizard of Earthsea**. He is an arrogant, self-assured student at the wizard's school on Roke* when impatient young Ged* begins his studies there. Because Ged feels slighted by Jasper, rivalry and hatred build between them that culminate in a challenge during which Ged summons the spirit of a dead heroine and unleashes a dark and dreadful shadow. Though by that time he is studying sorcery, Jason never wins his staff; he leaves that summer and becomes a sorcerer at O-tokne on the Island of O.

JEANNE, a character in Mrs. Mary Molesworth's* *The Tapestry Room**. Her great-grandmother was also named Jeanne; Jeanne lives with her parents in France; she is the cousin of Hugh*. Though she has several pets, including two chickens, a rooster named Houpet, and a tortoise called Grigna, she is a little lonely and thus is very glad when Hugh comes to stay with the family after he is orphaned. Like many seven-year-olds, Jeanne has a vivid imagination, and she believes implicitly in fairies. She does not like dolls much, though she has many. When Hugh comes, she and he have several adventures together in lands they enter through the machinations of Dudu*, a raven. To Hugh's dismay, Jeanne does not remember all their adventures during the daylight hours, because they happen only to her "moonlight" self and not to the self she is during the day.

JEFFERSON D. CONWAY (*The Enchanted Castle*). *See* Conway, Jefferson D.

JENKINS, MR., a character in Madeleine L'Engle's* *A Wrinkle in Time** and *A Wind in the Door**. He is a principal, first of Regional High School, then of an elementary school. Unpleasant in body and personality, Mr. Jenkins is not liked by many of his students; because he could not handle high school students, he has been given an elementary school and does not seem to be doing well here, either. He knows he is a failure and feels that he can do nothing about it. Abrasive as he is, Mr. Jenkins has been generous at least once in his life; noticing the poor shoes that are all Calvin O'Keefe* has to wear, Mr. Jenkins buys him a good pair, trying to make them look like castoffs. Inflexible of mind, Mr. Jenkins gets a shock one day when he is confronted by two replicas of himself in the school playground. Each is an Echthros*, a force of evil, which has taken on his form because he is the perfect host for it. Meg Murry*, a former student of Mr. Jenkins, is able to choose the real principal; and, utterly bewildered, Mr. Jenkins finds himself on a strange mission to help Charles Wallace Murry*, Meg's brother, who is suffering from mitochondritis. Having fought for Charles's life inside one of his cells, Mr. Jenkins realizes that upgrading the elementary school—and, perhaps, himself—might not be so impossible.

JENNIFER HUNTINGTON (*The Sleepers*). *See* Huntington, Jennifer

JENNY, a character in Jean Ingelow's* *Mopsa the Fairy*. Jenny is an albatross; she pulls Jack* from the hollow tree in which he has found a fairy nest and flies him and the fairies to the back way into Fairyland*. When Jack is ready to come back, all he needs to do is call her and she returns to fly him home. One of Jenny's eyes gleams green; the other shines red. This makes her visible at night.

JEREMY, a character in Robert O'Brien's* *Mrs. Frisby and the Rats of NIMH*. He is a not-too-bright crow. When Jeremy goes after a piece of silver string, he becomes tangled in it and cannot fly. Mrs. Frisby*, a field mouse, helps him, and Jeremy, in turn, helps her, flying her to the nest of a local owl so that she can ask advice of him.

JESSE TUCK (*Tuck Everlasting*). *See* Tuck, Jesse

JEWEL, a character in *The Last Battle*, by C[live] S[taples] Lewis*. This talking unicorn is the dear friend and good adviser of Tirian*, the king of Narnia*, a magical land. During Narnia's greatest need and her last battle against the oppressive forces of Calormen*, brave Jewel fights hard for his land. He is among those in the country of Aslan*, Narnia's mystical lion-protector, when Narnia comes to an end.

JILL POLE (*The Silver Chair; The Last Battle*). *See* Pole, Jill

JIMMY, a character in *The Story of the Amulet*, by; E[dith] Nesbit Bland*. This good and learned man is interested in ancient peoples and reads several of their languages. When Robert*, Anthea*, Cyril*, and Jane* bring him half of a powerful amulet*, he deciphers the writing on it for them and becomes fascinated by it. When the children take him to Atlantis* on their search for the amulet's missing half, he thinks the journey is a strange dream and barely escapes during the destruction of the island, because he wants to stay and see the end of his dream. Kind-hearted Jimmy is filled with sorrow when he hears Imogen's* story; he wishes that the orphan could be taken to where she would be wanted, and the Psammead* grants his wish. When Jimmy wishes Imogen could stay in what he thinks is a happy dream, reunited with her mother, the Psammead grants this, too, as it grants Jimmy's wish to meet Julius Caesar*. Caesar is so impressed by what Jimmy and Jane tell him about Britain that he decides to invade that country. Jimmy's thirst for knowledge is as great as that of Rekh-marā*, an Egyptian priest also searching for half of the amulet; and when the amulet is found, the Egyptian's soul joins with Jimmy's so that Rekh-marā can stay in this century. The children give Jimmy the whole amulet. His subsequent writings on Atlantis, ancient Britain, and ancient Egypt bring him fame and fortune.

JIMMY (*The Enchanted Castle*). *See* James (Jimmy)

JINGLE STONES, a circle of standing stones in William Mayne's* *Earthfasts*. In King Arthur's* time, these stones were eight giants twelve feet tall. When he died, time stopped for them, and they became standing stones, standing in a half circle. Here they stood through the Neolithic period to the twentieth century, though one was taken away to serve as a gatepost on a nearby farm. It is said that if several people visit the stones together, whoever gets there first can wish, if he touches the stones and walks around them widdershins. When the candle* that holds time still for the stones is taken from its place by an eighteenth-century soldier, the stones become pig-stealing giants again, who play ball with boulders in the twentieth century, until the candle is put back into its place by Keith Heseltine*.

JO NICHOLAS (*Poor Tom's Ghost*). *See* Nicholas, Jo

JOHANNA VAVASOUR (*The Devil on the Road*). *See* Vavasour, Johanna

JOHANNES, MASTER, a character in Lloyd Alexander's* *Time Cat*. He is a miller in Germany in 1600. During the witch hunts in his village, Johannes helps many who are accused of being witches. He himself is caught when he tries to help Mistress Ursulina* by tricking Master Speckfresser*, her accuser, into retracting his statement. With the help of Jason*, a boy from the twentieth century, and Gareth*, his cat, Johannes escapes with Ursulina and Speckfresser, who has been caught in his own web. The miller travels with them to a place where they can start anew.

JOHN BANKS (the Mary Poppins books). *See* Banks, John

JOHN CHERRY (*Earthfasts*). *See* Cherry, Nellie Jack John

JOHN DARLING (*Peter and Wendy*). *See* Darling, John

JOHN ROWLANDS (*The Grey King; Silver on the Tree*). *See* Rowlands, John

JOHN WEBSTER (*The Devil on the Road*). *See* Webster, John

JONATHAN FRISBY (*Mrs. Frisby and the Rats of NIMH*). *See* Frisby, Jonathan

JONES, EMELIUS, a character in Mary Norton's* *Bonfires and Broomsticks**. He becomes the husband of Eglantine Price*. Emelius was born in 1635 and was apprenticed to a necromancer. He worked hard as an apprentice, only to learn just before his master died that there is no such thing as magic and that all the man's potions and spells had been only so many props. When Emelius inherits the business, he does moderately well, but he has little nerve, knowing that none of his magic is real, and fearing that a dissatisfied customer will report him to the authorities and that he will be executed for witchcraft. On 27 August 1666, three children from the future visit Emelius, and for an awful moment he is afraid that his magic may actually work. Carey, Charles, and Paul Wilson***, however, have traveled to their past with the help of a magic bed-knob* enchanted by Eglantine Price in the twentieth century. Having become fast friends, Emelius and the children go to the twentieth century together, and Emelius is awed by Miss Price, whose magic actually works. He does not adjust well to technology-inundated twentieth-century life, but he does become fond of Miss Price and of the children. Emelius's return to his own century is traumatic, especially as he is taken into custody and charged with helping, through witchcraft, to cause the Fire of London, which had taken place during his absence. Failing the trial by water, Emelius is sentenced to be burned at the stake, but he is rescued at the eleventh hour by Miss Price and the children and taken back to the twentieth century. He does not remain here; he and Miss Price decide to marry, and they travel back to the seventeenth century, to live on the small farm on Tinker's Hill that Emelius has inherited from his aunt.

JONES, FISHEYE, a character in *The Fabulous Flight**, by Robert Lawson*. His parents are from Zargonia; their family name is Jonowkowski, but Fisheye takes the name Jones, that being easier. Originally from Chicago, Fisheye was drafted during World War II and did not try to dodge it, having had a "misunderstanding" with the police. He ended up in Zargonia, and here Fisheye deserted, stealing a jeep and a pinball machine and traveling around the country, bilking the natives. Finally he came to the castle of Doctor Professor Polopodsky*, a scientist who had developed an awful explosive. When the man died, Fisheye took his place, using the explosive to blackmail Zargonia into giving him gold. When Fisheye's pinball machine breaks down, Lumps Gallagher, an old crony, is brought to fix it, and the two enter into a partnership to get the gold into the United States. Lumps, however, decides to use the explosive to blackmail the world, and he tries to steal it. He is thwarted by Peter Peabody Pepperell III*, a tiny boy sent to steal the explosive. Fisheye and Lumps are handed over to the American Army by the Zargonian government, and the two are tried for desertion.

JONES, TIMOTHY (TIMMO), a character in Robert Westall's* *The Watch House*. His father is a doctor. Timmo has a very active mind, which examines subjects quite thoroughly. He is cynical and scientific and moves from one subject to another, going through phases when he is wholly involved in such things as astronomy, hypnotism, and mechanics, among others. Some nights he travels with a portable disco he calls Doctor Death's Disco. Timmo always needs someone to listen to him, and Pat Pierson* fits the bill nicely. Anne Melton*, whom Pat and Timmo meet at a disco, also proves to be a good listener. When Timmo hypnotizes Anne for fun, she has a vision of what Henry Cookson*, the ghost haunting the Watch House* on the cliff, had seen one night. Though Timmo thinks that anything having to do with the occult is nonsense, he becomes scientifically interested in Anne's problem, hypnotizing her to find out more about Cookson and finally helping to banish the ghost that has haunted him for years.

JUDE, a character in Alison Uttley's* *A Traveller in Time*. Perhaps because he is a deaf-mute, Jude is able to sense what others cannot; when first Penelope Taberner Cameron* meets the boy in Elizabethan Thackers*, he is afraid of her, for he can sense that she does not belong to the sixteenth century. Later he comes to accept her and carves her a bobbin boy* which she is able to use to contact him when she has been imprisoned under the old barn at Thackers. For his help in rescuing Penelope, Jude is given to Francis Babington* to be his personal servant.

JUDITHA CAKEBREAD (*Parsley Sage, Rosemary & Time*).   *See*   Cake-bread, Juditha

JULIUS CAESAR. *See* Caesar, Julius

JUNGLE BOOKS, THE. Rudyard Kipling. *The Jungle Book*. Illus. J. L. Kipling. London: W. H. Drake and P. Frenzeny, 1894. 212 pp. *The Second Jungle Book*. Illus. J. Lockwood Kipling. London: Macmillan and Co., 1895. 235 pp. [rev. Macmillan and Co., 1895]. British.

On a warm summer evening when Shere Khan*, the tiger, is hunting, a fat naked boy baby waddles into the cave of a family of wolves. When Shere Khan follows and demands the child, he is refused. The mother wolf names the baby Mowgli*, and accepts him as her own. At the proper time, Mowgli is ritually shown to the rest of the pack. Shere Khan is there and demands the child, but Baloo*, a wise old bear, and Bagheera*, a black panther, speak for Mowgli, Bagheera offering a bull for the boy. Mowgli is accepted. As the next ten or eleven years pass, Mowgli learns about the jungle and grows contemptuous of Shere Khan, though he is warned about the tiger. Shere Khan wins over the younger wolves of the pack, and they hate Mowgli because he is a man. Worried, Bagheera urges Mowgli to get some of the Red Flower—fire—and the boy brings it to one night's council meeting. Shere Khan shows up there also and, bold because there is no leader, demands Mowgli, backed up by the younger wolves. Disgusted by their betrayal, Mowgli declares that he will go to live with men, and he drives Shere Khan and the wolves from the council. He leaves; when he returns it will be with the tiger's hide.

While Mowgli is still growing up, he learns from wise Baloo. In spite of the bear's advice, Mowgli takes up with the monkeys, who flatter him and are good to him; the other people of the jungle have nothing to do with these foolish, vain chatterers. Because Mowgli has certain desirable skills, the monkeys kidnap him and take him to the ruined city where they live. Baloo and Bagheera go to Kaa*, the great snake, for help, and all follow to the city. Here Mowgli is miserable, having been mistreated by the monkeys and having lost all illusions about them. Bagheera and Baloo attack and try to rescue Mowgli, but things are going badly for them until Kaa comes and the monkeys flee. Mowgli is rescued from the building he has been imprisoned in, and he, Baloo, and Bagheera leave as Kaa dances his Dance of Hunger and hypnotizes the monkeys into becoming his prey.

After Mowgli leaves the council, renouncing the wolves, he goes to the village of men and here is taken in by Messua* and her husband. It is hard to learn to live with men, but Mowgli tries, herding buffalo as part of his responsibilities. He hears from a wolf that Shere Khan will seek his life; when the tiger comes, Mowgli has a plan ready. Having divided his herd in two, he and his wolf brothers drive the cattle from either end of the ravine where Shere Khan sleeps, and the tiger is trampled. When the chief hunter of the village comes and tries to claim the hide, Mowgli has one of the wolves keep him at bay until he has skinned Shere Khan. The man, when he gets to the village, makes the people think Mowgli is a sorcerer, so they drive him away. Mowgli goes back to the wolves and spreads Shere Khan's hide on the council rock. He is welcomed by his friends, but he will hunt alone in the jungle, with only his wolf brothers as companions.

One year, before he goes to live with men, the winter rains fail and a drought leads to hunger among the people of the jungle. A water truce is declared by Hathi*, the great elephant, who one night tells how fear came to the jungle: in the beginning, all had been perfect and peaceful, and all creatures ate grass. During a dispute, the first of the tigers had killed a buck, bringing death to the jungle. A monkey had later brought shame and, finally, a man had brought fear, making the people of the jungle afraid of him and of each other. The tiger had gone to kill the man for this but was too afraid. Because the tiger had once been the leader of the jungle, it had been decreed that for one night each year he would not be afraid of men. Because the tiger had shown man no mercy that first night, men show the tiger no mercy now.

After Mowgli leaves the village and the pack, a hunter comes into the jungle to hunt Mowgli. Following him, the boy learns that Messua and her husband are to be tortured and burned as witches for taking him in. Leaving the wolves to harry the man, Mowgli goes to the village and frees the woman and man, sending them through the jungle for safety and putting Bagheera in their place to frighten the villagers. Hathi and his three sons come; for Mowgli's sake they will let in the jungle where the village stands. A week later grazing animals invade the village gardens and grazing grounds, destroying all. The people stay until their food and hope are gone, and as the last ones leave, they see Hathi and his sons destroy the village. Six months later the jungle has taken over all.

Mowgli now lives in contentment in the jungle. When Kaa tells him what a cobra had told him of a wonderful thing, Mowgli goes with him to a ruined city and there meets an ancient, poisonless cobra who still guards a king's treasure. Mowgli thinks little of the treasure but takes a jeweled ankus to see it in the sun. It is pretty but disgusting because it has been used to hurt elephants, and Mowgli throws it away. Having slept and wakened, he thinks better of it and follows the trail of the man who had taken it, and of the man who had killed him for it, and of the men who had killed the latter. These men have killed each other, and Mowgli takes the deadly thing back to the cobra so that it will kill no more.

Many more things happen to Mowgli before a lone wolf reports the coming of the dholes, fierce red dogs, who have killed his family. Mowgli goes to Kaa, who makes a plan: Mowgli will lead the dholes over a cliff over a gorge where wild bees live; Kaa will help Mowgli, but those dholes not drowned in the river or stung to death by bees will be swept downstream to the waiting wolf pack. Mowgli glories in so insulting the dholes that they stay near him until sunset, when he leaps from tree to tree, leading them to their doom. Bees get many dholes, and others drown in the river; the rest die in the fight with the wolves. The head of the wolf pack also dies, telling Mowgli that he will eventually return to men.

Mowgli does not believe him, but two years later, in the spring, he is strangely unhappy and restless. That night he makes his annual spring running but finds only unhappiness. He comes upon a village and there finds Messua, who gives him milk and a place to sleep; when he leaves she asks him to return. Still tormented, Mowgli meets his friends, who advise him to live with his own kind, though the jungle will be at his command. Bagheera comes; he has killed a buck, and so all debts are paid. Mowgli is free. Heartbroken, he will leave the jungle.

Note: Mowgli's stories appear as chapters 1–3 of *The Jungle Book*, and as chapters 1, 3, 5, 7, and 8 of *The Second Jungle Book*. A related tale of Mowgli's adulthood is "In the Rukh," in *Many Inventions* (1893).

The contents of these works first appeared in various periodicals: "Mowgli's Brothers," in *St. Nicholas*, Jan. 1894; "Kaa's Hunting," in *To-Day*, April 7, 1894; "Tiger! Tiger!" in *St. Nicholas*, Feb. 1894; "How Fear Came," in *Pall Mall Budget*, June 7 and June 14, 1894; "Letting in the Jungle," in *Pall Mall Gazette*, Dec. 12 and Dec. 13, 1894; "The King's Ankus," in *St. Nicholas*, March, 1895; "Red Dog," in *Pall Mall Gazette*, July 29 and July 30, 1895; "The Spring Running," in *Pall Mall Gazette*, October, 1895.

The revised edition of *The Second Jungle Book* restores 514 words missing from the end of "The King's Ankus" in the first edition.

Those interested in more information should consult James McG. Stewart, *Rudyard Kipling: A Bibliographical Catalogue* (Toronto: Dalhousie University Press and University of Toronto Press, 1959), pp. 122–32.

JUSTIN, a character in *Mrs. Frisby and the Rats of NIMH**, by Robert O'Brien*. Justin was an ordinary rat until he was caught and taken to Nimh*, where he became part of an experiment. He was number A-9 of the experimental rats. As a result of the experiment, Justin's intelligence and lifespan became greater. Always bold, he was the first to figure out how to open the cages. Soon he, Nicodemus*, and the other experimental rats escaped and made their way to Mr. Fitzgibbon's* farm, where they formed a colony. Brave, handsome Justin is the idol of at least one young lady rat. When Mrs. Frisby* is captured by Billy Fitzgibbon, Justin rescues her. He also volunteers to be one of the handful of rats who stay behind to confuse the exterminators who come to wipe out the colony. He may be one of the two rats who are killed by the exterminators' gas.

KAA, a character in Rudyard Kipling's* Jungle books*. This python is about two hundred years old. Kaa is huge and powerful and whatever comes into his grip does not come out of it alive. One of his most potent weapons is his Dance of Hunger, which can hypnotize the unwary. Though he prefers goats, Kaa is the terror of the bandar-log, the monkeys of the jungle. When Mowgli*, a boy, is captured by the monkeys, Baloo*, a bear, and Bagheera*, a panther, call on Kaa to help rescue him. Kaa becomes Mowgli's good friend and adviser; he plans the extermination of the terrible red dogs that invade the area and helps Mowgli carry it out.

KALESSIN, a character in *The Farthest Shore**, by Ursula K. LeGuin*. He— or, perhaps, she—is a dragon, the oldest of his kind, and he lives on a great tower of rocks in the Dragon's Run*. Kalessin is the color of dark iron, with dark red wings and ancient yellow eyes. He goes to Selidor* and is there when Ged*, a sorcerer, and Arren*, his companion, return from the land of the dead; Kalessin wakes the unconscious Ged by calling to him. Kalessin carries Ged and Arren to Roke*, where he leaves Arren before taking Ged to his home, the island of Gont*.

KANHUAN, a place in Jane Louise Curry's* *The Watchers** and *The Bird-stones**. In the fourth century, Kanhuan is ruled by Tekla*, a power-hungry queen who seeks to extend her empire by conquering New Aztalán*.

KÁOLIN, a character in *Beneath the Hill**, by Jane Louise Curry*. He is one of *y Tylwyth Teg**, the Welsh Fair Folk*, who became lost in Elizabethan times during their journey to Tir na'nOg*, the Fortunate Isles, and landed in America. Though he looks like a boy, Káolin is much older. He is both wise and mischievous, taking things from the farms around Nūtayē (the City of the Moon Under the Mountain*) and leaving behind small presents. Káolin brings to Nūtayē Arthur Arthur*, Margaret Arthur*, and Stevie Griffith*, who help the Folk to resume their journey to Tir na'nOg.

KATE, a character in *The Borrowers**, *The Borrowers Afield**, and *The Borrowers Afloat**, by Mary Norton*. As a child, she listens to the stories Mrs. Ada May* tells her about the borrowers*, miniature human beings who "borrow" what they need from humans. A year later Kate meets Tom Goodenough*, who tells her more about the borrowers. When Kate becomes an adult with four children of her own, she puts together all she has been told and writes it up for her children, filling in gaps with her own imagination.

KATE (*Poor Tom's Ghost*). *See* Garland, Katherine Purfet

KATHLEEN, a character in *The Enchanted Castle**, by E[dith] Nesbit Bland*. She has two brothers, Gerald* and James* (Jimmy). When their cousin gets the measles and has to be quarantined one holiday, the three children spend the holidays at Kathleen's school. Exploring the surrounding area, they discover nearby Yalding Castle* and have several adventures with Mabel Prowse* and a magic wishing ring*. One day when she is very hot, Kathleen makes the ring into a ring that makes the wearer turn into a statue, and she becomes one. That night is unforgettable, for at sunset she becomes a living statue like the others at the castle and she and the other children—also turned into statues—feast and play with the gods and goddesses until dawn.

KATHLEEN, a character in E[dith] Nesbit Bland's* *Wet Magic**. She is the younger sister of Francis*, Mavis*, and Bernard*. Her nickname is "Cathay." When Freia*, a mermaid Francis and Mavis rescue from the circus, takes the children to Merland*, her home, Kathleen touches the bubble holding the sea back from the land; this lets in the sea and precipitates an attack on the Merpeople by the Under Folk*, their enemies. Kathleen also accidentally lets in the Book People* when she claims not to know a character she actually does know. When she and the others are captured by the Under Folk, Kathleen is so frightened that she does not take the antidote to the drink they give her to make her forget; she wants to forget all that has happened to her. Kathleen becomes the mindless pet of the doleful King and Queen of the Under Folk*, entertaining them with her antics. Her memory is restored at the banquet given to celebrate the end of the centuries-long war between the Merpeople and the Under Folk.

KATÓA, a ravening force of destruction in Jane Louise Curry's* Abáloc novels*, except *Beneath the Hill**. This power seems to take the form of a great snake. Katóa is the force of hunger, destruction, and fear, and it is often able to find power-hungry or money-hungry people to serve it. It is often represented as a snake with its tail in its mouth—the ring of time; those who follow Katóa see it as the ring of death. In the First Age of the world, Katóa had been bound beneath the mountains of Ebhélic* by Tion, the Wolf King, and Ravgal, one of the Wolves of Aam*. When it freed itself, it was bound again at Tûl Isgrun*. In the fourth century, Tekla*, the power-hungry queen of Kanhuan*, dedicates her people and herself to Katóa and frees it in order to use its power to conquer New Aztalán*. A new shrine to Katóa is dedicated at Inas Ebhélic*; this shrine lasts until the twelfth century. At the shrine is what is considered a great oracle. When the oracle tells the people of Abáloc* to leave the safety of the City of the Moon Under the Mountain* and destroy the ancient books and writings, they obey. By the twelfth century, the serpent is being worshipped in the form of the Sun Serpent by the people of Abáloc and Cibotlán*, the ever-growing empire to the south, though only those of Cibotlán believe that it requires blood sacrifices. When Neolin* breaks the shrine in the twelfth century, Katóa journeys back to Tûl Isgrun, only to be bound again by the Watchers there. In the twentieth century it is almost freed again by greedy Russell Boyd Moar*, who uses Ray Siler* to guide him, but the shrine there is destroyed by Ray and his cousins, Delano Mattick* and Bonethy Yanto*, and Katóa is sealed for good.

KAW, a character in Lloyd Alexander's* *The Black Cauldron*, The Castle of Llyr*, Taran Wanderer*,* and *The High King*. This large, ragged crow is the son of Kadwyr. He belongs to Gwystyl*, one of the Fair Folk*. Though he talks, it is in single words, not phrases, and the meaning is sometimes difficult to decipher. Kaw puts Taran*, a young man, and his companions on the right track to where the Black Crochan* they are seeking can be found, and as a reward for helping to destroy that dangerous cauldron Gwystyl gives Kaw to Taran. Kaw serves the young man well, helping him to find his sweetheart when she is kidnapped, leading him to the only object capable of causing the death of evil Morda*, and, during the final bid for power by Arawn*, an evil king, helping to rouse the animals of Prydain* against Arawn. With the passing of magic from Prydain, Kaw goes back to the realm of the Fair Folk.

KAY, a figure in Arthurian legend who appears as a character in T[erence] H[anbury] White's* *The Sword in the Stone*. He is the son of Sir Ector. Clever, proud, and ambitious, Kay is neither a leader nor a follower, but he has aspirations. He hates to be beaten at anything; though he hates haying and is not good at it, he labors away, probably because his foster brother, the Wart (Arthur*), is so good at it. Though Kay is two years older than the Wart and, consequently, bigger and stronger, Kay is a bad fighter, for he can imagine the blows that are about to fall on him, and this destroys his nerve. Kay and the Wart are tutored by Merlyn*, a magician. When the Wart seems to be getting extra attention from Merlyn, Kay becomes jealous, and Merlyn sends the two boys on an adventure in the Forest Sauvage*. Kay helps Robin Wood* and his men rescue Friar Tuck and two others from Morgan the Fay's* castle, and during the ensuing battle he kills a griffin; Sir Ector has its head mounted. As the years pass, Kay becomes difficult, insisting on using a bow too long for him, challenging people to fights, and becoming sarcastic, though he seems to get no pleasure out of it. As the time approaches for him to become a knight, he and the Wart drift apart, for the Wart is to be his squire and they must not be on equal terms. After Kay is knighted, he insists that they go to the tournament in London, where the best knight of all is to be chosen. When Kay leaves his sword at the inn, the Wart is forced to pull from a stone the sword that makes him king of Britain; though at first Kay claims to have done it, he soon confesses the truth. The Wart promises to make Kay the seneschal of all his lands.

KAYIM, a character in *The First Two Lives of Lukas-Kasha**, by Lloyd Alexander*. This versifier is almost executed for high crimes against Lukas-Kasha* (Lukas) and the Royal Court of Abadan* because he recites a poem satirizing them. Lukas, however, amused at the man's impudence, pardons him and makes him a personal servant. Kayim proves as much of a rascal as Lukas himself, but he also proves to be a good friend, helping Lukas flee the palace when Shugdad Mirza*, his Grand Vizier, tries to kill him. Traveling with Lukas to Bishangar*, Kayim teaches the young man to earn his living by telling stories and entertaining people. Kayim also helps rescue Lukas when Shugdad catches him and almost executes him. Because of Kayim's friendship and advice, Lukas makes him his Grand Vizier when he regains the throne.

KEHAAR, a character in Richard Adams's* *Watership Down**. He is a black-headed gull; his name is taken from the sound of the ocean waves. Like other gulls, Kehaar leaves the sea in the winter and moves inland until spring. One spring, however, he leaves for the sea a little late, for he has been injured, and during his journey he is attacked by a cat; he takes refuge near a rabbit warren on Watership Down. Though in his pain and desperation Kehaar at first attacks them, the rabbits, on the advice of their leader, Hazel*, feed the bird and make friends with him. They communicate by a common patois, which Kehaar speaks with a strange, guttural accent. Bigwig* is especially taken with the bird. In return, once he is well, Kehaar helps them by finding a warren with desperately needed does and by taking an active part in the subsequent raid. His part done, Kehaar resumes his journey to the sea.

KEITH HESELTINE (*Earthfasts*). *See* Heseltine, Keith

KEMPE, THOMAS, the title character in Penelope Lively's* *The Ghost of Thomas Kempe**. He was probably born in 1566. In life he was a sorcerer, astrologer, physician, and finder of lost goods and of witches. Thomas wore spectacles and smoked a pipe. He also had an apprentice, whom he thought lazy. Thomas died on 31 October 1629; despite his trade and his antagonism toward religion, he was buried in a vault beneath the local church. Thomas did not rest, however. He made his presence felt at least twice, once in 1856, and once in the twentieth century, in the house he had lived in. In 1856, Thomas was exorcised and bottled up. When the bottle was broken during renovations in the twentieth century, he is set free again and tries to resume his trade, with hapless James Harrison* as his unwilling apprentice. Probably opinionated and strong-willed in life, Thomas remains so after death, trying to arrange things to suit himself and causing trouble when they do not. He leaves notes to people to make his wishes understood. Major foci of his attacks are the local doctor, whom he sees as usurping his own place, the vicar, whom he seems to dislike just on principle, and Mrs. Verity*, who he claims is a witch. Thomas's activities range from chalking graffiti on fences and doors to vandalizing the doctor's office and setting Mrs. Verity's cottage on fire. The twentieth century, with its strange ways, proves too much even for Thomas, and he finally seeks rest. When his pipe and spectacles are put on his coffin, Thomas is put to rest.

KESTER LANG (*The Wild Hunt of Hagworthy*). *See* Lang, Kester

KETTERLEY, ANDREW, a character in C[live] S[taples] Lewis's* *The Magician's Nephew**. He is the brother of Letitia Ketterley and Mabel Ketterley Kirke; he is the uncle of Digory Kirke*; he has a cousin named Edward. Andrew is the godchild of Mrs. Lefay, a fairy godmother. From her he got a box of dust from another world; though she told him to destroy it, Andrew, a great scholar of magic, did not, realizing that he could do great things with the dust. After years of struggle and study that have turned his hair gray, Andrew has learned to make the dust into yellow and green rings*, though he has not learned to use them: being a great student and a learned man, he feels he is too valuable to risk and therefore gets others to take the risks for him. Andrew tricks Polly Plummer* and Digory into using the rings and is astonished when they bring back with them Jadis*, an evil enchantress who fascinates him even as she proves to be too much for him to handle. Andrew later has terrifying experiences in Narnia*, a magical land, for its talking beasts frighten him. He feels no better when the beasts, who have never before seen his like, decide that Andrew is a tree and plant him, watering him vigorously; they subsequently make a pet of him, calling him Brandy because that is what he continually calls for. When Andrew goes back to London, the beasts are very disappointed. Andrew is a changed man, for his experiences so shatter him that he never practices magic again, though he has warm memories of Jadis's beauty and spirit.

KEY, an object in *Beneath the Hill**, by Jane Louise Curry*. This star-shaped key made of *findruin* once belonged to Argána, who brought it out of her father's kingdom beneath the sea. The key's possessor can use it to control the waters of the land, binding them or setting them into new paths, if he can find the proper "lock." It was brought to America long ago and was lost, to be found again in the twentieth century by Margaret Arthur* (Miggle), who makes it the prize in a treasure hunt. Once the key is recognized for what it is, Miggle and her cousins use it to reseal an ancient evil force bound beneath the mountains of Pennsylvania and to allow *y Tylwyth Teg**, the Fair Folk* trapped in the caverns of Nūtayē (the City of the Moon Under the Mountain*), to resume their journey to Tir na'nOg*. Realizing that the key can be used for evil as well as for good, Miggle destroys it by melting it in her mother's kiln.

KING, THE, a character in *The Princess and the Goblin** and *The Princess and Curdie**, by George MacDonald*. He is the father of Irene (the princess)*; several years after Irene is born, her mother dies. The king's great-grandmother is also named Irene*, and she looks after him in many ways, though because he does not understand all he has seen and heard in her house, he has given up thinking about her. He is a good king who rules for the good of the country and his people. After his wife's death, though, he had begun to grow despondent over the wickedness of his people, who had been influenced by evil teachers and other figures. This despondency has affected his health, giving him bad dreams and making it impossible for him to trust anyone. Soon he takes to his bed, and wickedness reigns in the capital city. The king's daughter, Irene, nurses him, for the servants have become lazy, and he is in grave danger, for his doctor is slowly poisoning him. Curdie Peterson* is sent to help the king, and he manages to do so by finding him good food and bolstering his spirits. The king grows completely well when he is bathed by his great-grandmother in her healing, purifying rose fire; the next day he leads his army to defeat an invading enemy. Because his people could not govern themselves as free men, he rules them with an iron hand until his death, when he passes the government on to Curdie and the princess.

KING AND QUEEN OF THE UNDER FOLK, THE, two characters in E[dith] Nesbit Bland's* *Wet Magic**. They are Reuben's* parents. Once they were land people; the King was a magistrate who had sentenced a gypsy to prison. In revenge, the man had kidnapped Reuben. Because the couple were so handsome, they themselves were kidnapped by the Under Folk* and made the King and Queen of their kingdom beneath the sea. The Under Folk, having just dissolved their republic and established a monarchy, kidnapped the land people to rule them so that none of the Under Folk would be jealous. The couple were given a drink of oblivion, so they forgot their former lives, though they were always sad because they still felt Reuben's loss. After several years peace is made between the Under Folk and the people of Merland* and the King and Queen are allowed to go home. They take an antidote to the drink of oblivion and return to the land, where they are reunited with Reuben.

KINGDOM OF ASSASIMMON, a place in Walter de la Mare's* *The Three Mulla-mulgars.** The kingdom is in the Valleys of Tishnar*, a rich and lovely place. It is ruled by Assasimmon, the brother of Seelem*, who fathers the three Mulla-mulgars.

KINGSLEY, CHARLES (1819–1875), British writer. He was born on 12 July 1819, at Holne Vicarage, Devonshire, to the Reverend Charles Kingsley and his wife. Young Kingsley attended King's College, London, beginning in 1836, and Magdalene College, Cambridge, from 1838 to 1842. He was ordained in 1842 and was appointed curate at Eversley, Hampshire. In 1844 Kingsley became the rector at Eversley and married Fanny Grenfell; they had two sons and two daughters. Kingsley became one of the queen's chaplains in ordinary in 1859 and was appointed to the professorship of modern history at Cambridge in 1860; one of his pupils was the Prince of Wales. Ill-health forced him to resign this professorship in 1869. That year he was appointed canon of Chester; in 1873 he was appointed canon of Westminster. Kingsley died on 23 January 1875.

Kingsley wrote only a few books that are regarded as children's books, but one of these became a classic. *The Water-babies**, serialized in *Macmillan's Magazine*, was published in book form in 1863, and has been in print ever since.

Central to *The Water-babies* is the juxtaposition of fantasy and realism. Tom's* world is a world of fairies and strange transformations, but it is also the everyday world where poachers ply their trade and chimney sweeps are beaten and hungry. Kingsley was a keen observer of nature, and the creatures that Tom teases and talks with are true to their biological natures.

The Water-babies is a didactic book that makes light of its didacticism. Kingsley tells us that "we should learn thirty-seven or thirty-nine things" from his "parable." The most important message is that "hard work and cold water" are essential if one is to grow up "right." The story of young Tom bears this out: by "washing" himself, he expunges the sooty little chimney sweep and becomes a water-baby*; only through constant hard work and doing what he does not want to do is Tom able to transcend his animal-like nature. Mr. Grimes*, Tom's harsh master, must wash himself with his tears of repentance before he can be helped; the Doasyoulikes*, who do no work of any kind, gradually evolve into apes.

Though the message is implicit throughout the book, Kingsley tempers it with humor and adventure, for this is, after all, "all a fairy tale, and only fun and pretence." Exaggeration and humorous names and lists are the keys of Kingsley's humor. When Professor Ptthmllnsprt*, the Polish professor who causes Ellie's* accident, goes mad, over sixty remedies are tried and each is listed; they range from oil or wormwood and the Saturday Review to "antipathy, or using him like 'a man and a brother.' " Most of his humor is tongue-in-cheek, as Kingsley satirizes pedants, quacks, and evolutionists, spiritualists, and hypocrites—in fact, all those who take themselves too seriously to the detriment of their own common sense.

Kingsley is hard on those who hurt children: hard schoolmasters, authors of didactic books, doctors who hurt children and think they are healing them. This group is a major one in the book; most of those Kingsley puts down have offended children in some way and are presented as fools who do not recognize children as people. The real villain in the book is Grimes, the brutal master sweep who bullies and beats Tom and brutalizes him to get him to go up chimneys. His portrait is not softened by humor, for he knew what he was doing.

The Water-babies is not simply a fantasy; it is a Christian fantasy, and themes of baptism and repentance run through it. "Those that wish to be clean, clean they will be; and those that wish to be foul, foul they will be," says the washerwoman; much is made in the book of the cleansing power of water. Tom's tumble into the stream and Grimes's crying both have the needed baptismal effect. Each must repent, too: Tom repents of his dirtiness and tries to wash in order to go to church; and Grimes repents of his treatment of his mother and his subsequent tears wash him and free him from the chimney he is stuck in. Kingsley cannot help a bit of sermonizing, here and there, about Catholics and heathens and all those who are not English Protestants.

Kingsley's style is clear and fluid, if rambling. The book is full of digressions and requires much patience from the reader. Perhaps even in Kingsley's time it was a wise child who understood all the author's humor and allusions. But it is a rich book—rich in incident and humor—and is filled with memorable characters and races. Kingsley has reached into the allegorical tradition and the result affects characterization. Mrs. Doasyouwouldbedoneby* is sweet and loving; Mrs. Bedonebyasyoudid* rewards the good and punishes the bad. Grimes is as grimy as his name; the Doasyoulikes do exactly as they please. Characterization is almost nil, with the exception of Tom, who is both rascally and sweet. The rest of the characters are types and they act accordingly. Kingsley exalts the English and the English way to the disparagement of all others except for the Scotch; the Irish, the Welsh, and non-whites are spoken of in derogatory terms. Setting is richly evoked, and the irony and satire are skillfully handled.

Works

Juvenile fantasy: *The Water-babies* (1863).

Juvenile non-fantasy: *The Heroes* (1855); *Westward Ho!* (1855), novel; *Madam How and Lady Why* (1870).

Adult: *A Sermon Preached at Eversley, Hants* (1847); *The Saint's Tragedy* (1848); *A Sermon Preached at Hawley Church* (1848); *On English Composition* (1849); *Twenty-five Village Sermons* (1849); *Alton Locke* (1850), novel; *The Application of Associative Principles and Methods to Agriculture* (1851), lecture; *Cheap Clothes and Nasty* (1851), as Parson Lot; *The Message of the Church to the Labouring Man* (1851), sermon; *Phaethon* (1852); *Sermons on National Subjects* (1852); *Hypathia* (1853), novel; *Alexandria and Her Schools* (1854), lectures; *Who Causes Pestilence?* (1854), sermons; *The Country Parish* (1855), lectures; *Glaucus* (1855); *Sermons for the Times* (1855); *Two Years Ago* (1857), novel; *Andromeda, and Other Poems* (1858); *Esau and Jacob* (1858); *The Good News of God* (1859); *The Massacre of the Innocents* (1859), address; *Miscellanies* (1859); *Sir Walter Raleigh and His Time* (1859), essays; *The Two Breaths* (1859); *The Limits of Exact Science as Applied to History* (1860), lecture; *Why Should We Pray for Fair Weather?* (1860), sermon; *A Sermon on the Death of His Royal Highness the Prince Consort* (1861); *Town and Country Sermons* (1861); *Ode Performed in the Senate-House* (1862); *Speech of Lord Dundreary in Section D* (1862); *The Gospel of the Pentateuch* (1863); *Hints to Stammerers* (1864), as C. K.; *The Roman and the Teuton* (1864), lectures; *"What, Then, Does Dr. Newman Mean?"* (1864); *David* (1865), sermons; *A Game-Law Ballad* (1866); *Hereward the Wake* (1866), novel; *The Temple of Wisdom* (1866), sermon; *A Sermon Preached at the Volunteer Camp* (1867); *Three Lectures* (1867); *The Water of Life* (1867), sermons; *Discipline, and Other Sermons* (1868); *The Hermits* (1868), hagiography; *God's Feast* (1869), sermon; *Women and Politics* (1869); *At Last* (1871); *Songs and Etchings* (1871), poems; *The Study of Natural History* (1871; pub. 1874), lecture; *Poems* (1872); *Town Geology* (1872); *Frederick Denison Maurice* (1873), sermon; *Plays and Puritans, and Other Historical Essays* (1873); *Prose Idylls New and Old* (1873); *American Notes* (1874); *Health and Education* (1874); *South by West* (1874); *Westminster Sermons* (1874); *Lectures Delivered in America in 1874* (1875); *The Peace of God* (1875), sermon.

Secondary Works

Baldwin, Stanley E. *Charles Kingsley*. Ithaca, N.Y.: Cornell University Press, 1934.

Braybrooke, Patrick. "The Water Babies," in *Great Children in Literature* (London: Alston Rivers, 1929), pp. 244–56.

Chitty, Susan. *The Beast and the Monk: The Life of Charles Kingsley*. London: Hodder and Stoughton, 1974.

Coleman, Dorothy. "Rabelais and 'The Water-Babies,' " *Modern Language Review*, 66 (July, 1971), pp. 511–21.

Johnston, Arthur. "*The Water Babies*: Kingsley's Debt to Darwin," *English*, 12 (Autumn, 1959), pp. 215–19.

Leavis, Q. D. "*The Water Babies*," *Children's Literature in Education*, 23 (Winter, 1976), pp. 155–63.

Manlove, C. N. "Charles Kingsley (1819–1875) and *The Water Babies*," in *Modern Fantasy: Five Studies* (New York: Cambridge University Press, 1975), pp. 13–54.

Martin, Robert Bernard. *The Dust of Combat: A Life of Charles Kingsley*. London: Faber and Faber, 1960.

Pope-Hennessy, Dame Una. *Canon Charles Kingsley*. London: Chatto and Windus, 1948.

Prickett, Stephen. "Adults in Allegory Land: Kingsley and MacDonald," in *Victorian Fantasy* (Bloomington and London: Indiana University Press, 1979), pp. 150–97.

Thorp, Margaret Farrand. *Charles Kingsley: 1819–1875*. Princeton, N.J.: Princeton University Press, 1937.

Uffelman, Larry K. *Charles Kingsley*. Boston: Twayne Publishers, 1979.

KIPLING, RUDYARD (1865–1936), British writer. He was born in Bombay, India, on 30 December 1865, to John Lockwood and Alice MacDonald Kipling. He was educated at the United Services College, Westward Ho!, in Devon, England. Kipling worked on *The Civil and Military Gazette* and the *Pioneer*, in India; after 1896 he was a free-lance writer. In 1892 he married Caroline Walcott

Balestier; they had two daughters and a son. He received the Nobel Prize for Literature in 1907. In 1923 Kipling was elected Rector of St. Andrews University. He died on 18 January 1936.

Kipling's ten-odd works for children include short story collections, novels of adventure, and four highly episodic works involving fantasy. *Puck of Pook's Hill* and *Rewards and Fairies* are at heart collections of historical short stories whose narrators have been brought out of time by the ancient sprite, Puck. They chronicle the education of two British children, Dan and Una, in English history via meetings with various historical figures. In the course of the meetings the children learn what it is to be British. Mowgli's* story, which makes a more coherent whole, is sometimes scattered chapter by chapter among the animal stories in *The Jungle Book* and *The Second Jungle Book* (the Jungle books*), with a tale of Mowgli as an adult—actually the first to be written—appearing in a collection of adult short stories. But despite their episodic nature, Mowgli's tales form a single, moving story of a boy growing up at odds with himself and his environment, uncertain exactly where he truly belongs. He, too, is learning, but his lessons are in what it is to be a man.

In all the works, the learners accidentally discover a reality within the reality they normally inhabit. Dan and Una, acting out their play, accidentally call up Puck, the oldest Old Thing in England and the last of the People of the Hills. His world of magic and spells has almost vanished, but Puck uses his magic to teach the children their own heritage. Mowgli, as a baby, unconsciously waddles from the world of men into the world of the jungle animals, and he grows up in that world, secure in its values.

Duty and honor are the watchwords of the tales Dan and Una hear. Duty and honor are paramount in the jungle in which Mowgli grows up, though not in the world of the humans he must finally rejoin. Central to the animal society is the Law of the Jungle, a system of rules and admonitions that covers almost every aspect of life and provides for almost every occasion or emergency. This Law is absolute, but it is a code both reasonable and fair and is kept by most of the animals in the jungle, who believe in it implicitly. The only ones who do not keep the Law are the bandar-log—the monkey people—and, perhaps, the dholes—the savage red dogs of the north. The bandar-log have no Law and no leader and are scorned by the other jungle creatures; the dholes seem to recognize the rights of no creatures other than themselves, hunting where it suits them and living for slaughter. Shere Khan*, the tiger, seems to obey the Law as it suits him, for though it forbids the killing of man except under certain conditions, he kills men almost any time he wants to. Humans, for the most part, are contemptible. If they have a code, it is not apparent; logic and fairness do not seem to rule their lives. They are as foolish as the bandar-log, stealing, killing for wealth, killing or trying to kill all who are different, and believing in wild superstitions. As a result, Mowgli, though human, holds humans in contempt. Raised by jungle animals, like Adam before the Fall he is innocent, rational, and admirable in person and character; though he lives among humans for a time, he resists the urge to commit their lives among humans for a time, he resists the urge to commit their sins.

Sweet as it is, the magic cannot last. Once their meeting with a person of the past has ended, Dan and Una are made to forget it by Puck and his use of Oak, Ash, and Thorn. Lest they say too much, they must forget when they re-enter their own place. Mowgli, grown to be a man, cannot stay in the jungle, for it is always apparent to the animals and to himself that he is not really one of them. He is human. Thus, for all their admirable traits, and despite their physical superiority, the creatures of the jungle are somehow beneath him. Though he is not as strong physically as they are, his human abilities give him power they do not have; as he grows up, by sheer force of human will, Mowgli can make the creatures of the jungle submit to him. Mowgli becomes the master of the jungle, inspiring a loving devotion mixed with awe among his animal followers. Though he scorns humans, Mowgli must go back to them; although Kipling indicts humans for their frailties, it is ever clear that the jungle animals are not the answer to Mowgli's need of a family and a home. Back in his or her own place, it is up to Una, Dan, and Mowgli to use what he or she has learned in that brush with the other reality.

Kipling's style is rich and descriptive. He is especially successful in the Jungle books, recreating the jungle and its denizens with color and liveliness. His pithy indictments of human foibles are sometimes heavy-handed; the contrasting nobility of his good characters is occasionally overdone. But though their speech is sometimes more than grandiose, the animal characters are lively and well drawn. Puck is the essence of mischief and wisdom, and Mowgli is an appealing mixture of bravery and braggadocio.

Works

Juvenile full-length fantasies: The Jungle books: *The Jungle Book* (1894); *The Second Jungle Book* (1895); contents from each as *All the Mowgli Stories* (1933).

Juvenile short stories and novels: *Captains Courageous* (1896); *Stalky and Co.* (1899); *Kim* (1901); *Just So Stories for Little Children* (1902); *Puck of Pook's Hill* (1906); *Rewards and Fairies* (1910); *Land and Sea Tales* (1923); *Ham and the Porcupine* (1935).

Adult: *Schoolboy Lyrics* (1881); *Echoes* (1884), with Alice Kipling; *Quartette* (1885), with John Lockwood, Alice MacDonald, and Alice Kipling; *Departmental Ditties and Other Verses* (1886); *Plain Tales from the Hills* (1888); *Soldiers Three* (1888), stories; *The Story of the Gadsbys* (1888), stories; *In Black and White* (1888), stories; *Under the Deodars* (1888), stories; *The Phantom Rickshaw, and Other Tales* (1888); *Wee Willie Winkie, and Other Child Stories* (1888); *The Courting of Dinah Shadd, and Other Stories* (1890); *Departmental Ditties, Barrack-Room Ballads, and Other Verses* (1890); *The Light That Failed* (1890), novel; *The City of Dreadful Night and Other Sketches* (1890);*The City of Dreadful Night and Other Places* (1891), sketches; *The Smith Administration* (1891); *Letters of Marque* (1891) as *Out of India* (1895); *Mine Own People* (1891), stories; *Life's Handicap*

(1891), stories; *The Naulahka* (1892), stories, with Wolcott Balestier; *Barrack-room Ballads and Other Verses* (1892); *Many Inventions* (1893), stories; *The Seven Seas* (1896), verse; *Soldier Tales* (1896); *An Almanac of Twelve Sports* (1898); *The Day's Work* (1898), stories; *A Fleet in Being* (1898); *From Sea to Sea* (1899); *With Number Three* (1900), poems; *The Five Nations* (1903), verse; *The Muse Among the Motors* (1904), poems; *Traffics and Discoveries* (1904), stories; *Letters to the Family* (1908); *Abaft the Funnel* (1909), stories; *Actions and Reactions* (1909), stories; *A History of England* (1911), with C.R.L. Fletcher; *The Fringes of the East* (1915); *A Diversity of Creatures* (1917), stories; *Twenty Poems* (1918); *The Years Between* (1919), poems; *The Irish Guards in the Great War* (1923); *They and the Brushwood Boy* (1925), stories; *Debits and Credits* (1926), stories and poems; *A Book of Words* (1928), speeches; *Thy Servant a Dog* (1930), stories; *Limits and Renewals* (1932), stories and verse; *Souvenirs of France* (1933); *Something of Myself for My Friends Known and Unknown* (1937); *Uncollected Prose*, vol. 1 (1938); *Uncollected Prose*, vol. 2 (1938).

Secondary Works

Amis, Kingsley. *Rudyard Kipling and His World*. London: Thames and Hudson, 1975.

Avery, Gillian. "The Children's Writer," in *Rudyard Kipling: The Man, His Work, and His World*, ed. John Gross (London: Weidenfeld and Nicolson, 1972), pp. 114–18. [As *The Age of Kipling*. New York: Simon and Schuster, 1972.]

Beresford, G. C. *Schooldays with Kipling*. New York: G. P. Putnam's Sons, 1936.

Birkenhead, Lord. *Rudyard Kipling*. London: Weidenfeld and Nicolson, 1978.

Brown, Hilton. *Rudyard Kipling: A New Appreciation*. London: H. Hamilton, 1945.

Carrington, Charles E. *The Life of Rudyard Kipling*. Garden City, N.Y.: Doubleday, 1955.

Dobrée, Bonamy. *Rudyard Kipling: Realist and Fabulist*. London, New York, and Toronto: Oxford University Press, 1967.

Green, Roger Lancelyn. *Kipling and the Children*. London: Elek, 1965.

———. "Rudyard Kipling," in *Tellers of Tales* (Leicester, England: Edmund Ward, 1946), pp. 220–33.

Haines, Helen E. "The Wisdom of Baloo: Kipling and Childhood," *The Horn Book Magazine*, 12 (May-June, 1936), pp. 135–41.

Harrison, James. "Kipling's Jungle Eden," *Mosaic*, 7 (Winter, 1974), pp. 151–64.

Havholm, Peter. "Kipling and Fantasy," *Children's Literature*, 4 (1975), pp. 91–104.

Islam, Shamsul. "Education in the Law in Four Children's Books," in *Kipling's 'Law': A Study of His Philosophy of Life* (London: Macmillan Press, 1975), pp. 121–42.

Kipling, Rudyard. *Something of Myself*. London: Macmillan and Co., 1937.

The Kipling Index. Garden City, N.Y.: Doubleday, Page and Company, 1919.

Lesser, Margaret. "Kipling and His Publishers," *The Horn Book Magazine*, 12 (May-June, 1936), pp. 144–49.

Livingston, Flora. *Bibliography of the Works of Rudyard Kipling*. New York: Edgar H. Wells and Company, 1927.

———. *Supplement to Bibliography of the Works of Rudyard Kipling*. Cambridge, Mass.: Harvard University Press, 1938.

Manley, Seon. *Rudyard Kipling: Creative Adventurer*. New York: Vanguard Press, 1965.

Prickett, Stephen. "Worlds within Worlds: Kipling and Nesbit," in *Victorian Fantasy* (Bloomington and London: Indiana University Press, 1979), pp. 198–239.

Stewart, James. *Rudyard Kipling: A Bibliographical Catalogue*. Toronto: Dalhousie University Press and University of Toronto Press, 1959.

Stewart, J.I.M. *Rudyard Kipling*. London: Victor Gollancz, 1966.

Sutcliff, Rosemary. *Rudyard Kipling*. London: Bodley Head, 1960.

Tompkins, J.M.S. "Tales for Children," in *The Art of Rudyard Kipling* (London: Methuen and Co., 1959), pp. 55–84.

Wilson, Angus. *The Strange Ride of Rudyard Kipling*. New York: Viking Press, 1977.

KIRKE, DIGORY, a character in *The Lion, the Witch, and the Wardrobe**, *The Magician's Nephew**, and *The Last Battle**, by C[live] S[taples] Lewis*. He is the son of Mabel Ketterley Kirke; he is the nephew of Letitia and Andrew Ketterley*. Since his father is away in India, Digory and his mother come to London from the country when she falls ill; Digory is miserable here because of his mother's illness and because he thinks his uncle is mad. When he meets Polly Plummer* they become fast friends. The two run afoul of Andrew, who is studying magic; he tricks them into trying out two yellow and green rings* he has made that take their wearers to another world. The first place they visit is a dead planet, where Digory disobeys his heart and wakes Jadis*, an evil queen. Later the children accidentally take her and Andrew into Narnia*, a magical land only hours old, where they meet Aslan*, a great lion who has created it. Because Digory has brought evil into the land, he goes to the Western Wild and brings back a silver apple*, which, when planted, produces a tree that keeps the Witch out of Narnia as long as it stands. Aslan allows the boy to take an apple from that tree to his mother, and it cures her. Digory plants the seeds of this apple in Andrew's garden, and years later he makes from its wood a magical wardrobe*, which Edmund, Lucy, Peter, and Susan Pevensie****, staying at his house, use to travel between the worlds. During Narnia's final, greatest need, Digory tries to help it by getting the rings; he is killed in a railway accident and is whisked into Aslan's country, there to live in happiness forever.

KOSSIL, a character in Ursula K. LeGuin's* *The Tombs of Atuan**. She is the priestess of the Godking* on the island of Atuan*. After the One Priestess of the Nameless Ones* died, Kossil took over her duties until the successor, in whom the deathless and nameless Priestess is reborn, would be of age to take up her duties. Though Kossil is a priestess, she worships only power, and even the rites of the Godking are for her nothing but show. Thus, when the new One Priestess, Tenar*, starts to assert herself, demanding that the Nameless Ones be given the respect she feels they deserve, Kossil seems to have few qualms about doing away with her. Tenar at last begins to fear for her life, especially after she inexplicably helps instead of killing a stranger found wandering in the Labyrinth* beneath the temple grounds. When Kossil carries a torch into the Undertomb*, where light is forbidden, to make sure that the stranger is dead, Tenar realizes that the Nameless Ones must be dead, for they do not strike Kossil down. Kossil probably dies when the Nameless Ones destroy their temple trying to destroy Tenar and the stranger.

KOT. *See* de Lombre, Clovis Antoine

KURTZ, WILLIE (PROFESSOR), the name of two characters in Jane Louise Curry's* *Mindy's Mysterious Miniature*** and *The Lost Farm**. The first Professor Kurtz peddles spurious patent medicines and quack cures early in the twentieth century. By accident he builds a machine capable of reducing objects to a twelfth of their natural size. Angered by the rejection of Mary Buckle (now Mrs. Mary Buckle Bright*), he makes her house into a miniature; furious when no one in Dopple*, Pennsylvania, will back his research, he reduces that village and displays its tiny buildings in a traveling exhibit, unaware that the village has eight tiny inhabitants as well. When Donalbain MacCubbin* steals Kurtz's watch and a tiny car, the professor takes revenge by miniaturizing his farm and everyone on it. Kurtz's nephew, who shares his name, inherits the buildings and the reducing machine on his uncle's death; by tinkering he alters the machine to magnify what it has reduced. This Willie Kurtz is greedy and unscrupulous, and the tiny inhabitants of Dopple, with Arminta Hallam* and Mrs. Bright, play on his greed to hoax him into unshrinking them. He is so shocked at being caught that he goes a little mad. Ever spiteful, Kurtz stipulates in his will that his fortune is to go only to anyone then or later found to be miniaturized by his uncle; this excludes everyone, or so he thinks, but his money goes to Pete MacCubbin*, found miniaturized on his father's farm after Kurtz's death. Though uncle and nephew use the title "professor," neither has earned it.

KYTHING, a special form of communication in Madeleine L'Engle's* *A Wind in the Door** and *A Swiftly Tilting Planet**. It is like mental telepathy; but is much more; it is a way of perfect communion between individuals. Two kything individuals communicate without words, able to share everything without need of language. Kything is the way cherubim like Proginoskes* talk; it is also the way an adult farandola* moves and experiences things. Because he is good at kything, Charles Wallace Murry* is able to "go into" certain individuals in an attempt to change history and save the world. His sister, Meg Murry*, kythes to share his experiences and offer help.

LABYRINTH, THE, a place in *The Tombs of Atuan**, by Ursula K. LeGuin*.
This great, complicated maze was designed to confuse thieves seeking the Treasure of the Tombs on the island of Atuan*. Large as a city, it winds beneath the
Place of the Tombs of Atuan; its only entrance is from the Undertomb* which
lies beneath the Tombstones of the powerful Nameless Ones*. Several peepholes,
however, allow one to look into parts of the Labyrinth. Here, unlike in the
Undertomb, light is allowed, though there is not much to see but rock, dust,
and tunnels crossing and recrossing. Only the One Priestess of the Tombs can
successfully negotiate the Labyrinth, and she must relearn its twists and turnings
each time she is reborn. In the Labyrinth are the Room of Bones and the Six
Ways; here also is the Painted Room, where pictures of damned souls have been
painted, and the Great Treasure, where none but the One Priestess may enter.
Ged*, a sorcerer searching for half of the Ring of Erreth-Akbe*, comes to the
Labyrinth. He is discovered here by Tenar*, the One Priestess, who eventually
helps him and leaves with him.

LADY, THE, a character in *The Dark Is Rising** and *Silver on the Tree**, by
Susan Cooper*. She is very old; she has had many names. Though she usually
appears as an old woman, she can also seem young. The Lady is the greatest
of those of the Light, the forces of good; she alone can withstand the full force
of the Dark, though at great cost to herself. The Lady is beyond the power of
the Dark or any other power. She is the wren of the Hunting of the Wren, and
she may be associated with Jane or Juno. Without the Lady, the full power of
the Light cannot be reached. When Will Stanton*, another of the forces of the
Light, must find Eirias*, a crystal sword, the Lady comes to Jane Drew*, Will's
friend, and gives the girl the information needed to get the sword. The Lady is
present at the last battle between the Light and the Dark, and at the end of that
battle she sails with King Arthur* and the rest of the Old Ones beyond the world
of men.

LAKE-TOWN, a place in J[ohn] R[onald] R[euel] Tolkien's* *The Hobbit**. It is also called Esgaroth. As its name implies, the wooden town is literally built on Long Lake near the Lonely Mountain, on piles in the lake itself, connected to the shore by a great bridge. Once it was larger, when the men who lived here were more prosperous; though those times are gone, the lake men still make a good living from the trade up and down the river. So secure are they that they come to feel complacent about Smaug*, the dragon who lives on the Lonely Mountain, until he returns and burns Lake-town. He is killed by Bard, who becomes the leader of the town and rebuilds it.

LAMB, THE, a character in E[dith] Nesbit Bland's* *Five Children and It**, *The Phoenix and the Carpet**, and *The Story of the Amulet**. He is the much-beloved baby brother of Robert*, Anthea*, Cyril*, and Jane*. Among his names are Devereux, St. Maur, and Hilary. He is called "the Lamb" because "Baa" was the first thing he ever said. Though the others adore him, they sometimes find the Lamb a nuisance, for he makes messes, destroys things, and has to be taken everywhere. The Psammead*, a temperamental sand fairy the children find one holiday, is horrified by the baby because he is often wet. One day, exasperated by the Lamb's antics, Cyril wishes he would grow up immediately, and the Psammead grants his wish; the Lamb becomes an insufferable young man who wants to have nothing to do with the children, until sunset, when the magic ends. When the children hatch the egg of the Phoenix* and discover that they own a magic wishing carpet*, they take the Lamb to a tropical island where he can get over his whooping cough, accidentally taking along the cook*, who becomes queen of the island's natives. Though the Lamb's chatter seems to make no sense, his babytalk is a language understood by the carpet, which whisks him away one day to where he wants to go; the children spend some suspenseful minutes wondering if they will ever see him again, for the carpet is wearing thin and may not support his weight. After he returns, brought back by a wish of the Phoenix, the children put the carpet safely away. When the children's mother goes away to recover from an illness, the Lamb goes with her.

LAND OF COCKAYNE, THE, a place in *Are All the Giants Dead?**, by Mary Norton*. In this land, the characters from fairy tales live happily ever after. The people who live here wear whatever fashion they like, for they belong to no particular period. Here Beauty and the Beast—known as "Boofy" and "Beau"—live in a rich palace with their daughter, Dulcibel*; here, too, live Cinderella—known as "Pumpkin"—and Sleeping Beauty—nicknamed "Belle." In Much-Belungen-under-Bluff*, Jack-the-Giant-Killer* has killed twelve giants and finally gets the thirteenth after several years. All the witches but Hecubenna* are gone from Cockayne. To this land come James* and Mildred*, a reporter who reports on the happenings in high society and brings magazines and newspapers from London.

LANG, KESTER, a character in *The Wild Hunt of Hagworthy**, by Penelope Lively*. He lives with his parents; he is the nephew of Tom Hancock. Thirteen-year-old Kester enrages his family when he decides not to go into blacksmithing, the family business, like his uncle; they feel that he is setting himself above them. The summer that Lucy Clough* comes to stay with her aunt proves difficult for Kester in other ways, too, for he cannot keep himself from quarrelling with the other boys in the village of Hagworthy, and few people seem to take his side. One of these few is Lucy, who remembers the friendship they had had five years before; they are soon friends again, though Kester's bouts of quarrel-someness threaten to break up the relationship. When the vicar proposes res-urrecting the traditional Horn Dance* for a local fete, Kester is both fascinated and repulsed, for the antlered masks the dancers use remind him of a frightening experience he had had as a young child when someone wearing a similar mask had chased him. Fascination overcomes his fear when he sees the Wild Hunt*, the terrifying ghostly hunt that pursues whoever looks at it and that is somehow associated with the Dance. For reasons he cannot understand, Kester joins the Dance and is pursued by the other Dancers in the traditional chase in which the quarry is someone the others dislike for some reason. Lucy saves him from the Dancers, and then from the Hunt itself when it pursues him. Once the Hunt is gone, Kester feels as if he has just awakened and as if he has been made to do things he ordinarily would not have done.

LASARALEEN, a character in C[live] S[taples] Lewis's* *The Horse and His Boy**. She is married to a great lord in Calormen*. Lasaraleen has been the friend of Aravis*, another noble girl, since childhood. When she married, Las-araleen went to live in Tashbaan, the capital city of Calormen. Here Lasaraleen indulges her love of clothes, gossip, and parties, sometimes going to events at the palace of the Tisroc*. Silly and vain, she has trouble keeping her mind on one thing for very long. When Aravis runs away and, traveling through Tashbaan, is recognized by Lasaraleen, the girl takes her in, thinking that Aravis's running away is great fun. She helps Aravis escape from Tashbaan by showing her the gate in the city wall that opens onto the river, after being an unwilling eaves-dropper on the Tisroc and his son when she and Aravis take refuge in an empty room and overhear the two men.

LAST BATTLE, THE. C[live] S[taples] Lewis. Illus. Pauline Baynes. London: Bodley Head, 1956. 184 pp. British. Carnegie Award, 1956.

When Shift*, an ape, and Puzzle*, his patient donkey friend, find a lionskin, Shift makes it into a coat for Puzzle and talks him into pretending to be Aslan*, the great lion that protects Narnia*, the land where they live. Weeks later, Tirian*, the king, and Jewel*, his unicorn friend, discuss the fact that Aslan is making one of his infrequent visits to Narnia, but Roonwit*, a centaur, warns Tirian that Aslan is not really here, and that the stars are in disjunction. Suddenly a dryad appears; trees are being felled. Sending Roonwit to raise the army, Tirian and Jewel investigate and find men from Calormen*, Narnia's ancient enemy, laying waste to the woods and using Narnia's free talking beasts as slaves—all at Aslan's command. Enraged at their abuse of a talking horse, Tirian and Jewel slay two Calormenes; they give themselves up to the rest, willing to take whatever justice Aslan metes out to them, for this Aslan is not the one they have known and loved.

They are taken to Stable Hill*, for Aslan supposedly stays in the stable there. Shift comes out to speak for Aslan and says that the talking beasts are to work in Calormen as any other beast does, and that commerce with the Calormenes will continue, for their god, Tash*, is the same as Aslan; the two names are interchangeable. Tirian tries to protest, but he is knocked down and tied to a tree not far from the stable. That night he is cared for by the loyal talking beasts before a bonfire is lit and "Aslan" is shown to the animals. In despair at the state of things, Tirian cries out for Aslan to come or to send those who had helped Narnia in other times of dire need. Suddenly he seems to be in a room with strange people, and just as suddenly the vision fades; but two children, Jill Pole* and Eustace Clarence Scrubb*, who have had adventures in Narnia before, appear in front of him and untie him.

As they walk to a nearby guard tower, Tirian tells them his story and they tell him theirs: he had appeared during a dinner they were having with Digory Kirke*, Polly Plummer*, and Peter, Lucy, and Edmund Pevensie***, all of whom had had adventures of some kind in Narnia. Peter and Edmund had recovered four rings* used long ago to visit Narnia, and Jill and Eustace had gone in a train to meet them when suddenly the train had given a jerk and they had found themselves in Narnia. At the tower the three get weapons and disguise themselves as Calormenes. That night they go to Stable Hill and rescue Jewel, and Jill gets "Aslan": Puzzle, who is very tired by this time of the whole thing. Tirian's little band comes upon a party of dwarfs* being marched to mine in Calormen, and the Calormene guards are slain. But the dwarfs are unimpressed by Puzzle's disguise, for they no longer believe in Aslan, and they leave—all but one, who does believe and who joins Tirian.

The next day he tells Tirian and the others how Ginger*, a cat, and Rishda*, a Calormene, have taken charge of the plot. Suddenly they see a terrible shadow going north; it is Tash, whom Shift had called. Tirian starts to lead his band to meet the army Roonwit has called up, but an eagle tells them that Cair Paravel*, Tirian's castle, has fallen, and that Roonwit is dead. Back they all go to the stable, where they will show Puzzle to the animals there.

As they come up behind the stable after nightfall, they hear Shift explain to the animals assembled there that a donkey has dressed up as "Tashlan" and is wandering through Narnia—thus spoiling Tirian's plan. Shift further explains that anyone who wants to see "Tashlan" in the stable can go inside, but he is not pleased with them and might destroy them. Ginger offers to go in and does, but he soon streaks from the stable, terrified and speechless. Emeth*, a young Calormene, follows, and a man's body is flung out of the stable, though it is not his. Tirian and his band reveal themselves and call on the Narnians to help them. Then Tirian tosses Shift into the stable, and all see and hear a terrifying light and sound. Thus begins the last battle of the last king of Narnia. Some beasts come to Tirian's aid and fight with him; others fight with the Calormenes. The dwarfs fight for no one, though they kill the horses who decide to side with Tirian. It is a dreadful battle against impossible odds. Eustace is thrown into the stable, as are Jill and several dwarfs, and, at last, Tirian, fighting Rishda at the stable door, pulls him inside.

There is a bright light, and Tash appears. He takes Rishda and is about to take Tirian, but a king intervenes. For Peter, Digory, Polly, Lucy, Edmund, Eustace, and Jill are in the stable, dressed as kings and queens; and the stable door stands by itself in a wonderful landscape, though the fight in Narnia can be glimpsed through it. Digory, Polly, and Lucy had been on the same train as Jill and Eustace, and Edmund and Peter had been at the station; suddenly, all had been a jumble for them and they had come into Narnia. Here they had watched as a Calormene entered the stable and waited, as Ginger had come in and seen Tash appear, and as Emeth had entered, killed the guard, and wandered away. The dwarfs who were tossed in can see only a stable, and even Aslan himself cannot help them when he comes.

Aslan calls Father Time*, and the door flies open onto a dark Narnia. Time blows his horn, and the stars fall. Standing at the doorway, Tirian and the others watch as millions of creatures come from everywhere: those who hate Aslan go to the left, where his shadow stretches; those who love him come through the door. Then giant lizards eat the plants of Narnia and die themselves, and the sea rises and covers the barren world. The sun and the moon come together and are squeezed out of existence by Time. At Aslan's command, Peter shuts the door. Aslan runs westward, calling for them to follow, and as they do they meet Emeth, who tells him his story: he had served Tash as well as he could; when he had entered the stable and met Aslan, the lion accepted the good Emeth had done in Tash's name, and allowed him to stay. Puzzle also comes upon them, and they travel together through a Narnian landscape. At last they come to the walled garden where Digory had once picked a silver apple*; there they are met by all the good creatures and people in Narnia's history. They are in Aslan's country, of which the real England and Narnia are only spurs. When they meet Aslan, he whispers something to Puzzle that makes him feel better; and Aslan says something to the others that makes them feel glorious: Digory, Polly, and the others from Earth had been in a railway accident that had jolted them into Aslan's country, and they are to stay here forever.

LAWSON, ROBERT (1892–1957), American writer. He was born in New York, New York, on 4 October 1892, and was educated at the New York School of Fine and Applied Art. In 1922 he married Marie Abrams. Lawson was a free-lance magazine illustrator, a commercial artist, and a free-lance book illustrator; at one time he also designed Christmas cards. He died on 26 May 1957.

Lawson's seventeen works for children range from patriotic works to fictional biographies of famous Americans to fantasies, all illustrated by himself. All present the reader with a view of a warm and delightful world full of humor and hope. The heroes of Lawson's full-length fantasies have a wide range: from a young rabbit to a twenty-nine-year-old man, from Benjamin Franklin* to a boy who shrinks, not grows, as he gets older. His works take place in an equally wide choice of locales—from eighteenth-century Philadelphia to twentieth-century Zargonia—and their subjects range from the struggle of wild animals to survive during a terrible winter to the seeking out and destruction of a weapon that could destroy the world. Diverse as Lawson's works are, however, they have at least two things in common: a sense of great trust between their human and animal heroes, and a shining optimism. In Lawson's world, animals and humans respect and get along with each other; villains are made to be vanquished and heroes to win out and save the day.

In some, the animals and humans converse and interact with each other, and neither is surprised to find the other doing so. Typical of these is *Ben and Me**, one of four fictional biographies of famous men, as seen by the animals they knew. The others are *I Discover Columbus, Mr. Revere and I*, and *Captain Kidd's Cat*. Each tale concerns the friendship between animal and man—Columbus and his parrot, Paul Revere and his horse, and Captain Kidd and his cat—but only in *Ben and Me* do the two converse. When they meet, Benjamin Franklin is not at all surprised to discover that Amos*, a mouse, can talk; what catches his attention is Amos's ingenuity: Amos gives Ben the idea for the Franklin stove, though, of course, it is Franklin who gets all the credit. Their relationship has its ups and downs, once becoming quite literally stormy after Amos is tricked by Ben into accompanying the famous kite aloft as Ben seeks to learn the true nature of lightning during a thunderstorm. This is after he has played some tricks of his own on Ben: changing the tide tables and some of the proverbs in *Poor Richard's Almanack*, and electrifying the governor's chair during one of Ben's demonstrations of electricity. On the whole, they get on well with each other, and Amos is responsible for Ben's successes as ambassador to France—and for his downfall as well. In fact, were we to believe all that Amos writes, mice were instrumental in the affairs of eighteenth-century America, for Red Jefferson, a redheaded mouse who travels with redheaded Thomas Jefferson, writes the model for the Declaration of Independence. Women also take the advice of mice, for Sophia* travels in Madame Brillon's wig, giving her the benefit of her particular point of view.

Peter Peabody Pepperell III* also sees nothing strange in talking animals; in *The Fabulous Flight**, he becomes acquainted with the wild animals who live near his house and with Gus*, a traveling seagull. As a normal human boy, he has held no commerce with them, but once he begins to shrink after damage to his sacro-pitulian-phalangic gland, they are no longer afraid of him, and Peter finds them good companions, always ready to play. Even the adults in Peter's world, once they get past their astonishment, see little unusual in Peter's playing with his animal friends or even drilling them in military formation. Gus, a seagull, takes part in a top secret mission to save the world. Adults do not converse with the animals; only Peter does, and only after he has shrunk to a few inches high. William Wilmer*, in *Mr. Wilmer**, is also the only person in that book able to talk with animals. Unlike Peter, who seems to speak with them in his everyday voice, William communicates using a special little voice he discovers he possesses, and the animals' responses are inaudible to anyone but him. The animals are as willing to speak to William as Amos and Gus are to speak to their friends; to the animals it seems quite logical to communicate with humans, and most seem to feel relief at finally being able to do so. A Siberian bear who speaks no English politely communicates the fact. Once William has proved his unique talent, people are not so much interested in how he does it as in how it can be used.

In *Mr. Twigg's Mistake** and Lawson's better-known duo, *Rabbit Hill** and *The Tough Winter**, animals and humans do not communicate in words, but their respect for each other remains boundless. General de Gaulle*, the mole who grows to tremendous size in *Mr. Twigg's Mistake*, seems to begin his adventure as very much an everyday mole, biting whatever human finger comes near. As he begins to grow physically, so he grows in reason, understanding Arthur Amory Appleton's* games of adventure, and getting revenge on Mr. Snarple, the nasty next-door neighbor.

In *Rabbit Hill* and *The Tough Winter*, the relationship between animal and human is less intimate, but it is still based on mutual trust and respect. The New Folks in the house on Rabbit Hill seem to think of the animals who live on the Hill as their neighbors, even if these neighbors never speak. They seem assured of the reasonableness of the wildlife, convinced that if they leave the creatures to lead their peaceful lives and provide enough for them to eat, the animals will not ravage the garden or create havoc on the lawn. At the same time the Folks are well aware of the difference between themselves and the animals, and they think of the creatures who live on the Hill as wildlife to be cherished and protected. The animals, on their side, see the Folks mainly as providers of food, until they are convinced by the Folks' actions that these are humans to be trusted. Treated as reasonable beings, they react as reasonable beings, staying out of the vegetable garden and, in Mole's case, away from the lawn as well. The route to this trust is not a quick one, for when first Willie Fieldmouse* and, later, Little Georgie*, a rabbit, are nursed by the Folks after being injured, the animals on the Hill react with panic, certain that they are being tortured or killed. In *Rabbit Hill* and *The Tough Winter*, the villains are those who treat the animals like animals: Tim McGrath*, who sets out traps and poisons and has his garden ruined, and the caretaker, who shoots at animal trespassers in the garden.

Lawson's works may dip into satire—taking shots at the prepackaged food industry, as in *Mr. Twigg's Mistake*, and at the cult of celebrity, as in *Mr. Wilmer*—but they never lose sight of an essential optimism. People can get along with animals and with each other, if only they have trust and respect; once a pellet containing the terrible explosive is destroyed, all is well, and no other threat assails mankind.

Though his characters are essentially two-dimensional, they are lively enough to be memorable. Little Georgie's father is the quintessential Southern gentleman, as Uncle Analdas* is the soul of the crusty bachelor. Gus, the world-traveling seagull, is the essence of the unimpressed tourist. Perhaps one of the most unforgettable characters in *Mr. Twigg's Mistake* is Arthur's father, a unique specimen of the loving, sarcastic parent. Dialogue rings true, especially in the Rabbit Hill books. The works are brisk and full of incidents, and are narrated in an easy, colloquial style.

Works

Juvenile full-length fantasy: *Ben and Me* (1939); *Rabbit Hill* (1944); *Mr. Wilmer* (1945); *Mr. Twigg's Mistake* (1947); *The Fabulous Flight* (1949); *The Tough Winter* (1954).
Juvenile short fantasy, short stories, and novels: *They Were Strong and Good* (1940); *I Discover Columbus* (1941); *At That Time* (1947); *Robbut* (1948); *Dick Whittington and His Cat* (1949), retelling; *Smeller Martin* (1950); *McWhinney's Jaunt* (1951); *Edward, Hoppy, and Joe* (1952); *Mr. Revere and I* (1953); *Captain Kidd's Cat* (1956); *The Great Wheel* (1957).
Adult: *Country Colic* (1944).

Secondary Works

Burns, Mary Mehlman. " 'There Is Enough for All': Robert Lawson's America," Part I, *The Horn Book Magazine*, 48 (Feb., 1972), pp. 24–32.
———. "There Is Enough for All," Part II. *The Horn Book Magazine*, 48 (April, 1972), pp. 120–28.
———. "There Is Enough for All," Conclusion, *The Horn Book Magazine*, 48 (June, 1972), pp. 295–305.
Cornell, Robert W. "Robert Lawson: For All Children," *Elementary English*, 50 (May, 1973), pp. 719–25.
Lawson, Marie A. "Master of Rabbit Hill," *The Horn Book Magazine*, 21 (July-August, 1945), pp. 239–42.
Lawson, Robert. "The Newbery Medal Acceptance," *The Horn Book Magazine*, 21 (July-August, 1945), pp. 233–38.
Madsen, Valden J. "Classic Americana: Themes and Values in the Tales of Robert Lawson," *The Lion and the Unicorn*, 3 (Spring, 1979), pp. 89–106.
Robert Lawson, Illustrator. Introduction and comment by Helen L. Jones. Boston: Little, Brown and Company, 1972.
Sicherman, Ruth. "An Appreciation of Robert Lawson," *Elementary English*, 44 (Dec., 1967), pp. 866–69.
Weston, Annette H. "Robert Lawson: Author and Illustrator," *Elementary English*, 47 (Jan., 1970), pp. 74–84.

LEAF, MRS., a character in *The Magical Cupboard**, by Jane Louise Curry*. She is the grandmother of Gabriel Leaf. Mrs. Leaf was born into the Hollybush family; she is descended from Felicity Parmenter* and Goliath Hollybush* and has, therefore, been entrusted with the keeping of a magical cupboard* until its rightful owners come for it. In 1976 they do. William Wingard*, accompanied by Hepsibah Sagacity Walpole* and Rosemary Walpole*, comes to The Holly Bush, Mrs. Leaf's antique shop, to find the cupboard that was part of their adventures when they had been transported in time to the eighteenth century.

LEGUIN, URSULA K[ROEBER] (1929–), American writer. She was born in Berkeley, California, on 21 October 1929, to Alfred L. and Theodora (Kracaw) Kroeber. She was educated at Radcliffe College, in Cambridge, Massachusetts, where she earned a B.A., and at Columbia University, in New York, where she earned an M.A. On 25 December 1953 she married Charles A. LeGuin; they have two daughters and a son. She has worked at Mercer University, in Georgia, and at the University of Idaho, and has taught writing workshops in Oregon, Washington, England, and Australia.

LeGuin's five works primarily for children include a picture book, a realistic adolescent novel, and three high fantasies, her Earthsea trilogy*: *A Wizard of Earthsea**, *The Tombs of Atuan**, and *The Farthest Shore**. Each of these works concerns a young person becoming an adult, learning about himself and the world things that are sometimes painful, but that are essential to know.

Ged*, in *A Wizard of Earthsea*, grows from a careless boy full of pride in himself and his powers to a man who knows how to use his powers wisely and well. In the process he confronts his darker self and makes it part of him. Tenar*, in *The Tombs of Atuan*, has been raised as Arha, the One Priestess of the Tombs, whose spirit has gone from body to body down through time. Thus she has not really become aware of herself and who she really is, so long has she been forced into the mold of another nature. As Arha, Tenar has done things she can hardly face, and she must learn to face them and to accept that Arha and Tenar are not the same person. In *The Farthest Shore*, Arren* stands ready, eager, and untested on the threshold of his manhood; and as he helps Ged try to halt the leaching out of magic in Earthsea*, Arren sees more of the world than he ever has before, and learns much about himself that he has never known. In the process he learns how to love truly for the first time—a sometimes painful process. His first response to Ged is as a boy infatuated with a seemingly omnipotent man; when Arren realizes that the wizard is a man who is sometimes weak or seems to be wrong, like any other, he learns to love him despite his faults. In each work, the main character is tried in ways he or she would never have thought possible. Ged must face the shadow that seeks to swallow him and he goes beyond the known lands in eastern Earthsea to find it. Tenar comes to realize that the forces she has served and worshipped are powers of death and madness that she would not choose to worship were she given the choice, and that they try to destroy her; her journey to the world beyond the Tombs is as a journey to the ends of the earth, for her. Arren follows Ged past the known lands of Earthsea and into the very land of death itself. Ged, having confronted the shadow of his own dark side, is a whole person. Tenar is shattered by the realization of what she has done as Arha, but somehow she finds the strength to face those she must face, though she longs only to hide herself from all. Arren, having gone into the barren land of death, comes back from it over its Mountains of Pain, a journey of agony and hopelessness, but he does it, drawing on numb endurance to do what hope cannot. He is ready to be King of All the Isles, having faced death and overcome its terrors.

Knowing who one is is important in these works, where the true name of each object is essential. By knowing the true name of someone or something, one can command it: the mages on Roke* seek to know the names of everything, and by changing a thing's true name they can change its nature; by knowing the true name of his shadow, Ged conquers it. When an old silk dyer on Lorbanery* is given a new name by Ged, she forgets her son and becomes a new person. Cob*, who seeks immortality of the body while suffering a death of the spirit, forgets his true name. Changing a true name is an act of great consequence, since one also changes the object itself, for the world has an equilibrium that must be maintained.

Part of that balance is between death and life. The land of the dead is a dry land, barren and shadowy, where nothing grows and lovers do not know each other. It is a fearful place, full of shadows of those who have died. To Cob, a sorcerer, it is so terrifying that he tries to avoid it by becoming immortal. But the individual who will not accept his own death is not complete, for only by accepting death can he live life for its own sake. Cob, who does not accept his death and who tries to be immortal, loses himself in the attempt, becoming a great emptiness that seeks to pull the life of Earthsea after it. The life that refuses to accept its death cannot be creative. When Cob leaches Earthsea into the land of the dead, he takes from its people themselve and their skills, their songs, their imaginations, and their sense of wonder. He himself exists but does nothing else. The eternal life of ritual that is preserved at the Tombs of Atuan is just as static and as sterile. But, as Ged points out, those who die are not diminished by death; their shadows inhabit the land of death, but they still live in the world, in its sunlight and its beauty. Eternal life can be nothing but eternal existence: not doing, but being; not creating, but suffering to exist. Life is pain and change and wonder and creation, and we pay for this with death, which does not diminish us or life because we have lived.

LeGuin's works are epic in tone, with rich, descriptive prose. Though the reader is sometimes distanced from the characters, they seem three-dimensional, with all the nooks and crannies of real personalities. Earthsea is well realized, with a culture as rich and varied as any in our own world.

Works

Juvenile full-length fantasy: *A Wizard of Earthsea* (1968); *The Tombs of Atuan* (1971); *The Farthest Shore* (1972).

Juvenile non-fantasy: *Very Far Away from Anywhere Else* (1976), novel; *Leese Webster* (1979), picture book.

Adult: *Planet of Exile* (1966), novel; *Rocannon's World* (1966), novel; *City of Illusions* (1967), novel; *The Left Hand of Darkness* (1969), novel; *The Lathe of Heaven* (1971), novel; *The Word for World Is Forest* (1972), novel; *From Elfland to Poughkeepsie* (1973), speech; *The Dispossessed* (1974), novel; *The Wind's Twelve Quarters* (1975), stories; *Wild Angels* (1975), poems; *Orsinian Tales* (1976); *The Water Is Wide* (1976); *The Language of the Night* (1979), essays; *Malafrena* (1979), novel; *The Beginning Place* (1980), novel; *Hard Words, and Other Poems* (1981); *The Compass Rose* (1982).

Secondary Works

Attebery, Brian. "On a Far Shore: The Myth of Earthsea," *Extrapolation*, 21 (Fall, 1980), pp. 269–77.

Bailey, Edgar C., Jr. "Shadows in Earthsea: LeGuin's Use of a Jungian Archetype," *Extrapolation*, 21 (Fall, 1980), pp. 254–61.

Barbour, Douglas. "On Ursula LeGuin's 'A Wizard of Earthsea,' " *Riverside Quarterly*, 6 (April, 1974), pp. 119–23.

Cameron, Eleanor. "High Fantasy: *The Wizard of Earthsea*," *The Horn Book Magazine*, 47 (April, 1971), pp. 129–38.

Crow, John H., and Richard D. Erlich. "Words of Binding: Patterns of Integration in the Earthsea Trilogy," in *Ursula K. LeGuin*, ed. Joseph D. Olander and Martin Harry Greenberg (New York: Taplinger Publishing Company, 1979), pp. 200–224.

Dooley, Patricia. "Earthsea Patterns," *Children's Literature Association Quarterly*, 4 (Summer, 1979), pp. 1–4.

———. "Magic and Art in Ursula LeGuin's Earthsea Trilogy," *Children's Literature*, 8 (1979), pp. 103–10.

Esmonde, Margaret P. "The Master Pattern: The Psychological Journey in the Earthsea Trilogy," in *Ursula K. LeGuin*, ed. Joseph D. Olander and Martin Harry Greenberg (New York: Taplinger Publishing Company, 1979), pp. 15–35.

Galbreath, Robert. "Taoist Magic in the Earthsea Trilogy," *Extrapolation*, 21 (Fall, 1980), pp. 262–68.

Jago, Wendy. " 'A Wizard of Earthsea' and the Charge of Escapism," *Children's Literature in Education*, 8 (July, 1972), pp. 21–29.

Kemball-Cook, Jessica. "Earthsea and Others," *New Society*, 44 (11 Nov. 1976), pp. 314–15.

LeGuin, Ursula K. "The Child and the Shadow," *Quarterly Journal of the Library of Congress*, 32 (April, 1975), pp. 139–48.

———. "Dreams Must Explain Themselves," *Signal*, 19 (Jan., 1976), pp. 3–11.

———. *The Language of Night*. New York: G. P. Putnam's Sons, 1979.

———. "This Fear of Dragons," in *The Thorny Paradise: Writers on Writing for Children*, ed. Edward Blishen (Harmondsworth, England: Kestrel Books, Penguin Books, 1975), pp. 87–92.

Manlove, C. N. "Conservatism in the Fantasy of LeGuin," *Extrapolation*, 21 (Fall, 1980), pp. 287–98.

Rees, David. "Earthsea Revisited: Ursula K. LeGuin," in *The Marble in the Water* (Boston: The Horn Book, 1980), pp. 78–89.

Remington, Thomas J. "A Time to Live and a Time to Die: Cyclical Renewal in the Earthsea Trilogy," *Extrapolation*, 21 (Fall, 1980), pp. 278–86.

Scholes, Robert. "The Good Witch of the West," *The Hollins Critic*, 11 (April, 1974), pp. 2–12.

Shippey, T. A. "The Magic Art and the Evolution of Words: Ursula LeGuin's Earthsea Trilogy," *Mosaic*, 10 (Winter, 1977), pp. 147–63.

Slussen, George Edgar. *The Farthest Shores of Ursula K. LeGuin*. San Bernardino, Calif.: Borgo Press, 1976.

Ursula K. LeGuin: Voyager to Inner Lands and to Outer Space, ed. Jo De Bolt. Port Washington, N.Y.: Kennikat Press, 1979.

Walker, Jeanne Murray. "Rites of Passage Today: The Cultural Significance of *A Wizard of Earthsea*," *Mosaic*, 13 (Spring/Summer, 1980), pp. 179–91.

White, Virginia L. "Bright the Hawk's Flight: The Journey of the Hero in Ursula K. LeGuin's Earthsea Trilogy," *Ball State University Forum*, 20 (Autumn, 1979), pp. 34–45.

LEK, a character in Jane Louise Curry's* *The Wolves of Aam**. His real name is Kell, and he is from Uméar. At the age of eight, he was apprenticed to Azra, a sorcerer, who told him about the twelve magical skystones*. When the old man died, the boy was sent to Armon, the king's astronomer, keeper of Nirim, the Worldstone, and here tragedy befell the boy; the stone vanished from his hands during a ceremony, and he was banished from the kingdom. Under the name of Lek he has traveled as a conjuror. Knowing that the twelve stones were found in the caves under Uval Garath, the Opal Mountain, Lek searches for that place, hoping to find there a replacement for the stone he lost. Only an old seer knows the way, and that old man has gone to the City of the Moon Under the Mountain*, a place that was lost long ago. Lek's search for the way to that City brings him to Astarlind, a land forbidden to mortal men, and there he meets Runner-to-the-Sky's-Edge* (Runner), a Tiddi* who carries Mirelidar*, the Moonstone, which Lek takes from him and hides. Soon after their meeting, Lek is captured and brought to Gzel*, where he is forced by a magical mirror to reveal the stone's whereabouts to Lord Naghar*, who seeks Mirelidar for the power it contains. Lek is rescued by Runner and a little band that includes Icelings*, Tiddi, and Wolves of Aam*. After the destruction of Gzel, Lek resumes his search for the City of the Moon, guided by Findral*, one of the Wolves.

L'ENGLE, MADELEINE (1918–　　　), American writer. She was born Madeleine L'Engle Camp on 29 November 1918, to Charles Wadsworth and Madeleine (Barnett) Camp, in New York, New York. She graduated from Smith College, Northampton, Massachusetts, in 1941 with an A.B. with honors. On 26 January 1946 she married Hugh Franklin; they have two daughters and a son. L'Engle has worked in the theater in New York; has taught at St. Hilda's and St. Hugh's

School in New York; has been writer-in-residence at Ohio State University, Columbus, and the University of Rochester, New York; and has been librarian at the Cathedral of St. John the Divine, in New York.

L'Engle is the author of fifteen novels for children, including three high fantasies. Though *A Wrinkle in Time**, *A Wind in the Door**, and *A Swiftly Tilting Planet** are fantasies, some of the characters who appear here—and their descendants or friends—also appear in a handful of her realistic novels, such as *Dragons in the Waters* and *The Arm of the Starfish*, subtly interconnecting a portion of her works. L'Engle's three fantasies, her Time trilogy*, take place not only in America but in other worlds, not only in modern times but in other centuries as well. In her works, the humblest and shabbiest are often the most powerful, and love is a potent weapon; all things are essential, even the smallest, for all things augment the universe.

Conflict in the trilogy is essentially the never-ceasing war between evil and good in the cosmos. The evil forces are the Echthroi* and the Powers of Darkness, the un-Namers who seek to annihilate all creation. The forces of good are individuals like Meg and Charles Wallace Murry** and Calvin O'Keefe* or more celestial entities such as Gaudior*, a time-traveling unicorn, Proginoskes*, a cherubim, and Mrs Who*, Mrs Which*, and Mrs Whatsit*, angelic figures who appear as anything but that. The forces of evil have at their command hatred and the bewilderment of the soul that does not know exactly who it is; the forces of good have love, Naming—a force of love that makes the Named thing known and more particularly itself—and their own individuality. Though they may protest against who they are, still they know it and in time come to accept it.

In this war, the least likely have the most power. The balance of the universe can hang on a star, a planet, a child, or a farandola* so tiny that it cannot be seen through the most powerful microscope. Sporos*, a farandola, is part of a mitochondrion that is part of a cell that is part of the body of Charles Wallace; his refusal to mature and take up his true task results in the mitochondrion's inability to transport hydrogen and ultimately would result in Charles Wallace's death; his death would mean that he would not be able to travel in time and save the world from nuclear holocaust; the destruction of the world would alter the balance of the universe and be a victory for the Echthroi. The least likely candidate is often the one to bring victory for the forces of good. Homely Meg, full of faults and self-loathing, is an unlikely victor over powerful, self-confident IT*. Disagreeable, distasteful Mr. Jenkins* persuades the farandolae to take up their tasks when no one else can. Fifteen-year-old Charles Wallace, genius though he is, would hardly be expected to save the world. The humblest also has the best chance of triumphing over evil. Meg has no illusions about herself or her ability to defeat IT, but she succeeds; Mr. Jenkins does not understand what is going on and seems to feel that he is not an asset on the mission; Charles Wallace knows he has certain talents but feels that he is not special. Pride is downfall. Charles Wallace's pride at his own abilities when he is five years old gets him into trouble; Sporos's pride makes him easy prey for the Echthroi; it is a prideful star that becomes the first Echthros.

If the forces of good are humble and unlikely, they are also individuals who know, or come to know, who they are. The pressure to conform is hard on Meg, Calvin, and Charles Wallace, for they are very different from the others in the village; but conforming would mean denying their individual souls, and they resist. Being unique is painful sometimes, but the alternative is spiritual death, as they see on Camazotz*, where no one can think, act, or dream for himself or herself. The person who does not know who she or he really is is a person whom the Echthroi can use; knowledge of one's individuality is a defense against being taken in. Naming is an awesome force in L'Engle's cosmos, for it makes that which is Named more its particular self. The powers of evil seek to make everything alike, whether by annihilating the entity, as the Echthroi do, or by annihilating the individual soul, as does IT on Camazotz; but Naming makes all things individual, unique, and loved. For love is perhaps the most potent weapon the forces of good have against the forces of evil. It is the one thing IT does not have and which Meg can use to rescue Charles Wallace; love and Naming are and are not synonymous, for love, too, can make something more like itself. Love is deeper than a feeling, for it is not something you feel; it is something you do; it is at the core of all that you are. Through love Proginoskes makes the greatest sacrifice of all—himself—and through love Meg is able to Name Mr. Jenkins and bring him on a mission to save Charles Wallace.

The ultimate good in L'Engle's universe is to be unique but also one with the universe, to sing in the ancient, universal harmonies, but also to be Named. The beasts* on Ixchel, though blind, can hear the harmonies of the stars; the farandolae, though they cannot move, are one with the universe and sing with the stars; Charles Wallace, who belongs to the Old Music of the universe, hears and joins in the music of the spheres that keeps joy in the universe. All the entities in the universe swell this joyful harmony, but each sings with an individual voice; each of the harmonious stars is known by name.

L'Engle's works are uneven, but enthralling. Her evil forces are chilling; her human heroes have faults but they are imperturbably good: they may grouse, but they never seem to mean it. Still, they never become saccharine. They are individuals terribly earnest about being good. The stories are sometimes vague or confusing, but they are never dull. L'Engle's style is as sweeping as her works and is full of a sense of the wonder and terror of the universe.

Works

Juvenile fantasy: *A Wrinkle in Time* (1962); *A Wind in the Door* (1973); *A Swiftly Tilting Planet* (1978).

Juvenile non-fantasy: *And Both Were Young* (1946; rev. 1983); *Camilla Dickinson* (1951) as *Camilla* (1965); *Meet the Austins* (1960); *The Moon by Night* (1963); *The Twenty-four Days Before Christmas* (1964); *The Arm of the Starfish* (1965); *The*

Journey with Jonah (1967), play; *Prelude* (1968), adapted from *The Small Rain*; *The Young Unicorns* (1968); *Dance in the Desert* (1969); *The Summer of the Great-Grandmother* (1974); *Dragons in the Waters* (1976); *The Anti-muffins* (1980); *Ring of Endless Light* (1980).

Adult: *The Small Rain* (1945); *Ilsa* (1946); *The Love Letters* (1966); *Lines Scribbled on an Envelope* (1969), poems; *Intergalactic P. S. 3* (1970); *The Other Side of the Sun* (1971); *A Circle of Quiet* (1972), sketches; *Prayers for Sunday* (1974); *The Irrational Season* (1977); *The Weather of the Heart* (1978), poems; *Ladder of Angels* (1979); *Walking on Water* (1980); *A Severed Wasp* (1982), novel; *The Sphinx at Dawn* (1982), short stories.

Secondary Works

Edge, Peggy. "WLB Biography: Madeleine L'Engle," *Wilson Library Bulletin*, 36 (May, 1962), p. 766.

Franklin, Hugh. "Madeleine L'Engle," *The Horn Book Magazine*, 39 (Aug., 1963), pp. 356–60.

Glass, Rona. "*A Wrinkle in Time* and *The High King*: Two Couples, Two Perspectives," *Children's Literature Association Quarterly*, 6 (Fall, 1981), pp. 15–18.

L'Engle, Madeleine. "Childlike Wonder and the Truths of Science Fiction," *Children's Literature*, 10 (1982), pp. 102–10.

———. "The Expanding Universe: Newbery Acceptance Speech," *The Horn Book Magazine*, 39 (Aug., 1963), pp. 351–55.

———. "The Key, the Door, the Road," *The Horn Book Magazine*, 40 (June, 1964), pp. 260–68.

———. "What Is Real?" *Language Arts*, 55 (April, 1978), pp. 447–51.

Perry, Barbara. "Madeleine L'Engle: A Real Person," *Language Arts*, 54 (Oct., 1977), pp. 812–16.

Rausen, Ruth. "An Interview with Madeleine L'Engle," *Children's Literature in Education*, 19 (Winter, 1975), pp. 198–206.

Stott, Jon C. "Midsummer Night's Dreams: Fantasy and Self-Realization in Children's Fiction," *The Lion and the Unicorn*, 1 (Fall, 1977), pp. 25–39.

Townsend, John Rowe. "Madeleine L'Engle," in *A Sense of Story* (Boston: The Horn Book, 1971), pp. 120–29.

LEONARDO DA VINCI (*Time Cat*). *See* da Vinci, Leonardo

LETITIA HEPPLEWHITE (*The Whispering Knights*). *See* Hepplewhite, Letitia

LEWIS, C[LIVE] S[TAPLES] (1898–1963), British writer. He was born on 29 November 1898 to Albert and Flora Hamilton Lewis, in Belfast, Ireland. He was educated at University College, Oxford, and was a professor at Magdalene College, Cambridge. On 23 April 1956 he married Joy Davidman in a secret civil ceremony; on 21 March 1957 they held a church ceremony. Lewis died on 22 November 1963.

Most of Lewis's works for adults have a Christian outlook; this is also true of his seven books for children, the Chronicles of Narnia*, which can be read as Christian-oriented works or as high fantasy works of adventure. The order in which they were printed is not that of their interior chronology, and they should be read in the following order: *The Magician's Nephew**, *The Lion, the Witch, and the Wardrobe**, *The Horse and His Boy**, *Prince Caspian**, *The Voyage of the "Dawn Treader"**, *The Silver Chair**, and *The Last Battle**. Central to all is the choice between good and evil, which is continually being made by the characters in the works. Though sometimes acted upon by outside forces, each character has a choice between being good or not, and this choice is not always easy.

To be good one must first be honest, not only with others but also with oneself. Those who are bad are rarely honest with themselves. Andrew Ketterley*, in *The Magician's Nephew*, sees his selfishness and cowardice as evidence of his "high and lonely calling" as a scholar of magic; he excuses himself from thinking of others or trying out his experiments himself, because he feels that he is too valuable to thwart or risk. Jadis*, the evil queen in the same work, sees herself as the queen of her world, but she does not see it as the hollow honor it is, because her world is dead. Her "destiny" to be queen is not selfishness, she thinks, and it justifies her destruction of the world that she might gain it.

Being honest also means being willing to see oneself critically and to be aware of one's imperfections, and to try to be good. Edmund Pevensie*, in *The Lion, the Witch, and the Wardrobe*, sees how he has been taken in and how badly he has treated Lucy Pevensie*, and he resolves to try harder, after being forgiven by those he has hurt. In *The Voyage of the "Dawn Treader,"* Eustace Clarence Scrubb* realizes how obnoxious he has been and also tries to be better. Puzzle*, the donkey in *The Last Battle*, believes that he is not as clever as Shift*, the ape, and does what Shift tells him to do, despite his own conscience. Knowing fully how wrong he has been, he is received into Aslan's* country when Narnia* comes to an end.

Constant obedience to a higher good is essential. This good can be an ideal or it can be the commands of Aslan, the great protector and creator of Narnia, always mindful of its deepest needs and always working toward its salvation. It is not always easy to obey him or the demands of one's ideals. Shasta (Cor*), in *The Horse and His Boy*, exhausted from his travels, still must run on to warn the king of Archenland* of an impending invasion. Jill Pole*, in *The Silver Chair*, must remember and recognize four signs that will help her and her companions find a lost prince, though two are almost impossible to follow and one, if followed, might end in death. In *The Lion, the Witch, and the Wardrobe*, Mr. Tumnus* follows his heart and is turned into stone. Tirian*, in *The Last Battle*, fights on because he must, though he knows that he and his followers will lose. Aslan allows himself to be sacrificed by the White Witch* because the painful duty must be done. It is hard for Digory Kirke* to obey his instructions and pick only one apple from the tree of life, for his mother is dying, and he knows that an apple will save her.

Even if the act does not immediately result in something evil, disobedience to Aslan or to one's ideals ends badly. If Digory had taken an apple to his mother, Aslan tells him, she would have gotten well, but they both would have rued the act later. Jadis eats one in disobedience and becomes immortal, but it is an eternal life of loathing and misery. Because Jill and her companions do not obey the signs, their quest is made quite difficult.

One must depend on oneself and do what is right because it is right. Though help does not seem forthcoming, it is essential to depend on one's strength and win, or fail, on one's own power. Spells and enchantments may be easy, but they are not the way to do good. Using even the pleading chant they make up, Jill and Eustace cannot get into Narnia. The enchanters Nikabrik* finds to help Caspian* regain his throne are evil forces bent on bringing into Narnia an evil force, and all are killed in a fight. Jadis, the Queen of Underland*, and the White Witch all use enchantment to do their evil deeds; Andrew dabbles in magic and cannot control the results.

Because obedience to the demands of Aslan and the soul is hard, it is necessary to look beyond the immediate and see, as well as one can, what lies ahead of or just outside of what is right in front. Not to see truly is to deny oneself great joy. To Jadis and Andrew, even the talking beasts of Narnia are incomprehensible, because they will not hear. Eustace's early unimaginative vision keeps from him the wonder of Narnia; Trumpkin*, a dwarf, cannot believe Aslan could be real, because he has never seen a lion. Once Susan Pevensie* is in her own world, she cannot see beyond it, and she forgets Narnia. Though he is in a cave filled with the Queen of Underland's magic, Puddleglum* holds Narnia in his heart and prevails over her enchantment. Because he can see beyond the moment and knows of its ultimate result, Aslan goes through his painful sacrifice.

Being a good person is not always easy, but it has wonderful rewards. Those who are evil or untrue fall into darkness at the time of Narnia's end; Shift is gobbled up by the Calormene god he has called into Narnia. Aslan brings into his country to live in happiness forever all those who are or have been true to themselves, to each other, and to him, whether openly or in their own hearts. Emeth*, though a Calormene, has been true in the service of his god, and Aslan welcomes him, as he welcomes a dwarf who did what others think is a great wrong, while he was in Narnia. Puzzle, too, because of his upright heart, is allowed into Aslan's country. Those who are true to their better nature find happiness not only in Narnia but in the everlasting world beyond.

Lewis's works are well realized and full of the homely details that make Narnia seem a real place and not just a landscape of the imagination. His characters are full of life; Aslan, never stilted or smug, is one of the few truly good characters in fantasy literature.

Works

Juvenile fantasy: *The Lion, the Witch, and the Wardrobe* (1950); *Prince Caspian: The Return to Narnia* (1951); *The Voyage of the "Dawn Treader"* (1952); *The Silver*

Chair (1953); *The Horse and His Boy* (1954); *The Magician's Nephew* (1955); *The Last Battle* (1956).

Adult: *Spirits in Bondage* (1919), as Clive Hamilton; *Dymer* (1926), as Clive Hamilton; *The Pilgrim's Regress* (1933); *The Allegory of Love* (1936); *Out of the Silent Planet* (1938), novel; *Rehabilitations and Other Essays* (1939); *The Personal Heresy* (1939), with E.M.W. Tillyard; *The Problem of Pain* (1940); *The Screwtape Letters* (1942; rev. 1961); *A Preface to Paradise Lost* (1942); *Broadcast Talks* (1942) as *The Case for Christianity* (1943); *Christian Behaviour* (1943); *Perelandra* (1943), novel; *The Abolition of Man* (1943); *Beyond Personality* (1944); *That Hideous Strength* (1945), novel; *The Great Divorce* (1945); *Miracles* (1947); *Arthurian Torso* (1948); *Transposition and Other Addresses* (1949) as *The Weight of Glory and Other Addresses* (America); *Mere Christianity* (1952); *Surprised by Joy* (1955); *Till We Have Faces* (1956), novel; *Reflections on the Psalms* (1958); *The Four Loves* (1960); *Studies in Words* (1960); *The World's Last Night and Other Essays* (1960); *A Grief Observed* (1961), as N. W. Clerk; *An Experiment in Criticism* (1961); *They Asked for a Paper* (1962); *Letters to Malcolm: Chiefly on Prayer* (1964); *The Discarded Image* (1964); *Spenser's Images of Life* (1967); *Letters to an American Lady* (1967).

Secondary Works

Brady, Charles A. "Finding God in Narnia," *America*, 96 (27 Oct. 1956), pp. 103–5.

"C. S. Lewis," in *Chosen for Children*, rev. ed. (London: The Library Association, 1967), pp. 83–87.

Christopher, Joe R., and Joan K. Ostling. *C. S. Lewis: An Annotated Checklist of Writings About Him and His Works*. N.p.: Kent State University Press, n.d.

Colbath, Mary Lou. "Worlds as They Should Be: Middle-earth, Narnia, and Prydain," *Elementary English*, 48 (Dec., 1971), pp. 937–45.

Crouch, M. S. "Chronicles of Narnia," *Junior Bookshelf*, 20 (Nov., 1956), pp. 245–53.

Ford, Paul F. *Companion to Narnia*. San Francisco: Harper and Row, 1980.

Gibson, Evan K. *C. S. Lewis: Spinner of Tales*. N.p.: Christian University Press, 1980.

Glover, Donald E. *C. S. Lewis: The Art of Enchantment*. Athens, Ohio: Ohio University Press, 1980.

Gough, John. "C. S. Lewis and the Problem of David Holbrook," *Children's Literature in Education*, 25 (1977), pp. 51–62.

Green, Roger Lancelyn. *C. S. Lewis*. London: Bodley Head, 1963.

Green, Roger Lancelyn, and Walter Hooper. *C. S. Lewis: A Biography*. New York: Harcourt Brace Jovanovich, 1974.

Higgins, James E. "A Letter from C. S. Lewis," *The Horn Book Magazine*, 42 (Oct., 1966), pp. 533–39.

Holbrook, David. "The Problems of C. S. Lewis," *Children's Literature in Education*, 10 (March, 1973), pp. 3–25.

Hooper, Walter. "Narnia: The Author, the Critics, and the Tale," *Children's Literature: The Great Excluded*, 3 (1974), pp. 12–21.

———. *Past Watchful Dragons*. New York: Collier Books, 1979.

Howard, Thomas. *The Achievement of C. S. Lewis*. Wheaton, Ill.: Harold Shaw Publishers, 1980.

————. "The 'Moral Mythology' of C. S. Lewis," *Modern Age*, 22 (Fall, 1978), pp. 384–92.

Karkainen, Paul A. *Narnia Exposed*. Old Tappan, N.J.: Fleming H. Revell Company, 1979.

Kilby, Clyde. *The Christian World of C. S. Lewis*. Grand Rapids, Mich.: Wm. B. Eerdmans Publishing Company, 1964.

————. *Images of Salvation in the Fiction of C. S. Lewis*. Wheaton, Ill.: Harold Shaw Publishers, 1978.

Lewis, C. S. "On Three Ways of Writing for Children," *The Horn Book Magazine*, 39 (Oct., 1963), pp. 459–69.

Moorman, Charles. " 'Now Entertain Conjecture of a Time'—The Fictive Worlds of C. S. Lewis and J.R.R. Tolkien," in *Shadows of Imagination*, ed. Mark R. Hillegas (Carbondale and Edwardsville, Ill.: Southern Illinois University Press, 1969), pp. 59–69.

Poskanzer, Susan Cornell. "Thoughts on C. S. Lewis and the Chronicles of Narnia," *Language Arts*, 53 (May, 1976), pp. 523–26.

Schakel, Peter J. *Reading with the Heart: The Way into Narnia*. Grand Rapids, Mich.: William B. Eerdmans Publishing Company, 1979.

Smith, Lillian H. "News from Narnia," *The Horn Book Magazine*, 39 (Oct., 1963), pp. 470–73.

Smith, Robert Houston. *Patches of Godlight: The Pattern of Thought of C. S. Lewis*. Athens, Ga.: University of Georgia Press, 1981.

Stibbs, Andrew. " 'Honour' Be Blowed," *English in Education*, 14 (Autumn, 1980), pp. 27–30.

Walsh, Chad. *The Literary Legacy of C. S. Lewis*. New York: Harcourt Brace Jovanovich, 1979.

Wright, Marjorie Evelyn. "The Vision of Cosmic Order in the Oxford Mythmakers," in *Imagination and the Spirit*, ed. Charles A. Huttar (Grand Rapids, Mich.: William B. Eerdmans Publishing Company, 1971), pp. 259–76.

LEWIS, HUGH, a character in Jane Louise Curry's* *The Sleepers**. His father is an archaeologist at Edinburgh University. When Hugh's friend, Henry Peter Huntington*, visits with his sister and a colleague of Mr. Lewis's, Hugh and the others discover Artair*—Arthur*—and his men and help save them and the *Brenhin Dlyseu**, the Thirteen Treasures of Prydein, from Margan*, Artair's sister, and her son.

LILLIPUTIANS, a race of tiny beings in T[erence] H[anbury] White's* *Mistress Masham's Repose**. They were first described by Lemuel Gulliver, in Jonathan Swift's *Gulliver's Travels*. These tiny people are one-twelfth the size of humans, but they possess a dignity that belies their size. The Lilliputians had long been at war with the inhabitants of Blefuscu before Gulliver visited them, and when he left, the war was renewed; as a result, both nations were left desolate. Captain John Biddel, learning from Gulliver of the tiny people, had found Lilliput and managed to capture thirteen Lilliputians, of whom two had died on the voyage to England. Here they were taken around the country in a sideshow, with their cattle and sheep, bullied and beaten by Captain Biddel. When they came to the great house, Malplaquet*, the people escaped and took refuge on Mistress Masham's Repose, an island in one of the lakes. Here they have lived ever since, living off their cattle and sheep and insects, rising at dusk and sleeping during the day. They fish for "whales" in the lake and sometimes catch a rabbit. The people catch young rats and train them as we would horses, to ride and to pull plows. In spite of their difficult existence, their population grows to about five hundred. The Lilliputians have no revealed religion and few laws. Whatever an individual enjoys doing, that he does for a living, even if it means doing nothing. The tiny people are discovered by Maria*, a young girl, and once she gets over wanting to treat them as toys, they get on very well. When Maria comes into a fortune, she probably uses part of it to help the Lilliputians.

LINA, a character in George MacDonald's* *The Princess and Curdie*. She may once have been a woman who had done wrong; now she is a hideous furry beast, with a short body and long legs, a huge tail, and a head like a cross between a polar bear and a snake. The teeth in her lower jaw cover her upper lip, and Lina's green eyes shine with a light of their own in the dark. Curdie Peterson* discovers Lina's inner goodness when he touches her paw, for he feels inside the hand of a child; having done evil, Lina is becoming good. Because her fearsome appearance frightens everyone who sees her, Lina's greatest fear is that she may frighten others, and she quakes when someone who may be frightened is nearby. Lina accompanies Curdie when he goes to help his king*, protecting the boy along the way. When they pass through a wood, Lina fights and defeats many odd creatures who henceforth are loyal to Curdie. Not long after they accomplish their mission, Curdie watches as Irene (the grandmother)* kindles her magical, purifying rose fire and Lina leaps into it. Black smoke and dust billow up, and Lina is never seen again.

LINCOAS, a character in *The Daybreakers*￼* and *Over the Sea's Edge*, by Jane Louise Curry*. He is the younger son of Erilla* and Tepollomis* and a prince of ancient Abáloc*. Lincoas is one of the group of young people carried off by the Cibotlán* warriors. When he meets Harry Rivers* and his friends before the Cibotlán attack, Lincoas is intrigued by the Abalockian alphabet that the boys have recreated and demands that the letters be taught to him and the Abalockian youths. Thus Lincoas and the band are able to bring back to Abáloc the knowledge that will allow the people to read the ancient writings and rediscover lore and wisdom for themselves instead of being forced to rely on wisemen.

LINNET OLDKNOW (the Green Knowe books). *See* Oldknow, Linnet; Oldknow, Linnet (Mrs.)

LION, THE WITCH, AND THE WARDROBE, THE. C[live] S[taples]
Lewis. Illus. Pauline Baynes. London: Geoffrey Bles, 1950. 173 pp. British.

The time is World War II, and four children—Peter, Susan, Edmund, and
Lucy Pevensie****—are sent away from London to the safety of the country.
There they stay with an eccentric old professor, Digory Kirke*, who owns a
huge and ancient house. One wet day the children explore the house and discover
a room containing nothing but a wardrobe*. Disappointed, the others move on,
but Lucy investigates the wardrobe, gets inside, and finds herself in wintry
Narnia*. Here she finds an iron lamppost and, beside the lamppost, a faun named
Mr. Tumnus*, who takes Lucy to his house for a wonderful tea. Finding that
he has grown attached to the girl, Mr. Tumnus breaks down and confesses that
he has been ordered by the White Witch*—ruler of Narnia—to kidnap any human
children and take them to her. The Witch is so powerful that she has cast a spell
over Narnia, making it always winter; but despite this, Mr. Tumnus, having
learned what humans are really like, cannot obey her, and he helps Lucy to
escape back through the wardrobe.

Back in her own place, Lucy is distraught when the others do not believe in
her adventures. Edmund, especially, teases her unmercifully. One rainy day,
during a game of hide-and-seek, first Lucy, then Edmund, hide in the wardrobe,
and both find themselves in Narnia. Lucy visits Mr. Tumnus and has a lovely
lunch with him, but Edmund meets up with the Witch, who plays on his vanity
and feeds him enchanted Turkish Delight, thereby winning his loyalty. She is
strangely excited to learn of the other three children and exacts from him a
promise to bring them to her castle.

On their return to their own world, Lucy is ecstatic when she discovers that
Edmund, too, has been to Narnia, but she is devastated when he pretends to the
others that he and Lucy have been playing a game. Peter and Susan, however,
soon learn who is telling the truth when the four children take refuge in the
wardrobe to avoid visitors to the house and suddenly find themselves in Narnia.
There, Lucy leads them to the cave of Mr. Tumnus, only to discover that it has
been ransacked and that he has been arrested and taken to the Witch. The four
set out to rescue him. They follow a robin which leads them to Mr. Beaver*,
who proves he is a friend by showing the children the handkerchief Lucy gave
Mr. Tumnus. At the house of the Beavers, the children have a splendid supper
and learn of Aslan*, Narnia's true ruler. At the mention of his name, Lucy,
Peter, and Susan are thrilled, but Edmund feels only horror. The Beavers tell
the children that Aslan is coming back to Narnia and will soon take care of the
Witch and that when children of Adam—humans—rule from Cair Paravel*, the
evil times will be over. Creatures loyal to Aslan are to meet with him at the
Stone Table*. As they talk, Edmund slips out of the house and goes to the
Witch's castle. Here he finds a courtyard filled with strange statues: the Witch's
enemies, whom she has turned to stone with her wand. Edmund does not receive
a warm welcome, for he has come alone. When he tells the Witch all he has
heard, she dispatches her wolves to the Beavers' house, to kill all they find there.

No one is there, however, for the others, when they notice that Edmund is missing, realize that he is a traitor and leave for the Stone Table. They spend the night in a small cave and are cheered the next morning by a visit from Father Christmas, who is now able to enter Narnia, for now that Aslan is returning, the Witch's hold on the land is weakening. Father Christmas has gifts, of course: to Peter he gives a sword and a shield; to Susan he gives a bow and arrows and a hunting horn* to blow in time of need; to Lucy he gives a small dagger and a flask of a magically restorative cordial.

That afternoon, the Beavers and the three children reach the Stone Table. Their journey has been filled with wonder, for as they have traveled, spring has come back to Narnia, so that by the time they reach the camp at the Table, the weather is more like May than December. Here the children meet Aslan, a lion who fills them with awe. He shows Peter Cair Paravel, where the children are to reign. At this time, the camp is attacked by a wolf, which Peter slays. Another wolf is seen running away, and Aslan sends some of his people after it, for the wolf will probably go to the Witch. Aslan knights Peter for his exploit.

Meanwhile, Edmund is beginning to repent of his treachery. The Witch seems to have forgotten her promises and pays scarce attention to his wants. He rides with her in her sledge, driven by a dwarf*, until the melting snow forces them to abandon it and walk. Things get worse when the wolf running from Aslan's camp makes its report. After sending it to fetch her horrible minions, the Witch decides to thwart prophecy by sacrificing Edmund so that there are only three children to take the thrones at Cair Paravel. Just in time, Aslan's people arrive and Edmund is saved. The Witch is lost in the confusion, however, and gets away.

At the Stone Table the next morning, Edmund has a long, profitable talk with Aslan and apologizes to the others for his actions. The Witch arrives and parleys with Aslan; she invokes the Deep Magic, which states that all traitors belong to her; she has come to claim Edmund. After a long talk in private with Aslan, however, the lion announces that she has renounced her claim. Aslan's group breaks camp and moves to the Fords of Beruna*.

That night Susan and Lucy, unable to sleep, see Aslan steal out of camp. The girls follow and walk with him to the Stone Table. He is strangely sad and preoccupied. Leaving the girls in the safety of the trees, Aslan goes alone to the Table itself, where the Witch and her creatures are waiting. In tears and horror the girls watch as the lion is humiliated and sacrificed by the triumphant Witch, who then leads her army to Beruna. Lucy and Susan keep watch over Aslan's body the rest of that long and lonely night. At dawn, the Table splits and the girls are delighted and amazed to see Aslan alive again—fiercer and more glorious than before. Deeper magic than the Witch's Deep Magic has decreed that if an innocent and willing victim is killed in place of a traitor, death will work backward. After a wonderful frolic, the girls ride Aslan to the Witch's castle, where he melts her stone statues with his breath. The newly freed creatures follow Aslan to Beruna, where they join the battle. Aslan kills the Witch and the enemy is routed.

The four children are crowned in Cair Paravel and have a long and happy reign. They grow up to be wise and beautiful kings and queens. One day, while hunting the White Stag that grants wishes, they come across the iron lamppost. Passing it, they find themselves in the professor's wardrobe, themselves again in their own time and place, with the professor's visitors just outside the door.

LIONEL, a character in Lloyd Alexander's* *The Cat Who Wished to Be a Man*. Lionel begins life as the orange-tawny cat of Magister Stephanus*, a wizard who dislikes humans. Eager for conversation, Stephanus gives him human speech and is dismayed when the cat wants to become a man. Lionel pesters Stephanus into changing him into a young man, and the wizard sends him off to nearby Brightford*, with a magic wishbone* to get him out of trouble should he get into it. Full of innocence and wonder, Lionel makes his way in Brightford as best he can. He is enchanted by the people he meets there, especially by Gillian*, a lovely young innkeeper struggling to keep her inn from the grasp of greedy Mayor Pursewig*. In helping Gillian, Lionel endures dangerous adventures and feels the gamut of human emotions, from love to despair to murderous hate, and thus becomes human inside. At the same time, he loses some of his cat-like abilities. When he at last goes back to Stephanus, having vanquished Pursewig, Lionel discovers that he can never be a cat again unless he loses his human memories; though being human is sometimes uncomfortable, Lionel's love for Gillian cannot be denied, and he goes with her back to Brightford.

LISS MITCHELL (*The Daybreakers; The Birdstones*). *See* Mitchell, Melissa

LITTLE, MRS. FREDERICK C., a character in *Stuart Little*, by E[lwyn] B[rooks] White*. She is the wife of Frederick C. Little and the mother of George and Stuart Little*. Mrs. Little sometimes finds being Stuart's mother nerve-wracking, for he is only two inches high and many dangerous things can happen to such a tiny person. One day she accidentally shuts him in the refrigerator for half an hour, and he catches bronchitis. While he is sick, Mrs. Little finds Margalo*, a half-frozen bird, and brings it into the house. Stuart and Margalo become such close friends that when she leaves, he runs away to find her.

LITTLE, STUART, the title character in E[lwyn] B[rooks] White's* *Stuart Little*. He is the son of Mr. and Mrs. Frederick C. Little* and the brother of George Little. Though the rest of the family are normal humans, Stuart looks very like a mouse, having a mouse's head and tail and being only two inches tall. When he is only a few days old, Stuart walks and climbs and wears a hat and carries a cane. He is good-natured and helpful, rescuing Mrs. Little's ring when it goes down the drain and retrieving ping-pong balls that roll into tight places. Stuart is an early riser, and this leads to an unpleasant situation when he gets up one morning before anyone else is awake and, showing off for Snowbell*, the family cat, gets himself rolled up in a windowshade until lunchtime. Though Stuart's size presents some problems, it has its pleasures, as when Stuart navigates a toy boat belonging to Dr. Paul Carey* in a sailboat race. One day Mrs. Little brings a half-frozen bird into the house, and Stuart thus meets Margalo*, a sweet-natured bird who saves his life and whom he loves. When she leaves, he runs away to look for her, having adventures along the way as he substitutes for a schoolteacher and meets a girl as tall as himself. Stuart decides at last to go north, sure that someday he will find Margalo.

LITTLE FORDHAM, a place in *The Borrowers Afloat** and *The Borrowers Aloft**, by Mary Norton*. It is a model village in Fordham, built by Mr. Pott*, a retired railway man, and Miss Menzies*. Though Little Fordham started out simply as a model railway with a station, it has grown until finally it includes a church, several shops, many kinds of houses, a school, and a port. All are lovingly created by Mr. Pott, who patiently builds each with the same care and detail one would give to a full-sized building. The village becomes an attraction for tourists; it also becomes a legend for borrowers*, a race of miniature people just the right size for Little Fordham. Three borrowers, Pod, Homily, and Arrietty Clock***, even live here for a time. Little Fordham is the bane of Sidney Platter's* existence, for he is often hard put to make his own model village as detailed and complete and as popular with tourists.

LITTLE GEORGIE (GEORGIE), a character in Robert Lawson's* *Rabbit Hill** and *The Tough Winter**. He lives with his father, a Southern gentleman, and his mother, Molly; he has a sister named Hazel and an uncle named Analdas*; he was the uncle of eight deceased nieces and nephews. Georgie is a good runner and jumper; on the way to fetch Uncle Analdas, Georgie becomes the first rabbit in the history of the county to jump Deadman's Brook*. When New Folks come to Rabbit Hill, Georgie is hit by a car. The Folks take him in and care for him, and this cements the relationship between the Folks and the animals on the Hill. A subsequent winter tests Georgie's mettle, but tough as it is he and his friend, Willie Fieldmouse*, see it through together.

LIVELY, PENELOPE (1933–   ), British writer. She was born in Cairo, Egypt, on 17 March 1933, and was educated at St. Anne's College, Oxford; she earned a B.A. in history, with honors. On 27 June 1957 she married Jack Lively; they have a daughter and a son.

Six of Lively's fifteen works for children are fantasies; of the rest, one work is a collection of short stories, and the rest are realistic novels. Lively's fantasies range from tales of encounters with ghosts, such as *The Ghost of Thomas Kempe** and *The Revenge of Samuel Stokes**, to an animal story, *The Voyage of QV 66**. *The Whispering Knights**, is a high fantasy. Despite their wide range, all more or less share a common theme: that the past has played out its part, but it still exists and still can affect the present; the past is present with us, ready to be invoked.

This is readily apparent in *The Voyage of QV 66*, where the past is there to stumble over. Everywhere during their journey downriver to London, the animal voyagers come upon reminders and artifacts of England's past that were left behind when the humans fled to Mars to avoid a great flood. Some of the reminders, such as the menu at a restaurant, are unpleasant or uncomfortable, but for the most part the animals are uninterested, for either they do not understand them or do not need them. The exception is Stanley*, the monkey, who becomes enthralled with these things, tinkering, tampering, and becoming utterly fascinated with them. For Stanley the past—that is, man's past—is something to be used, to be adapted to present purposes. Other animals besides Stanley also seem to adapt the past for their own purposes, and parts of the book verge on becoming a satire on humans and human institutions. Manchester becomes a dictatorship of dogs as they overrun the city and set up their own form of government, excluding creatures not of their own kind. The monkeys at the London zoo also exclude other kinds of creatures and their society is fraught with rules and regulations, passes, and self-importance. They concern themselves with "thinking deep thoughts" and "making scientific discoveries," not caring or knowing that all they are doing is absurd. Left on their own, the animals also go back to a darker aspect of man's past when they seek to sacrifice an animal at Stonehenge at Midsummer.

In Lively's other works, it is humans who invoke the past—and not by design. The barrier between the present and the past seem very thin, and it can be pierced by accident. In *The Driftway**, Paul* feels shades of past events that have taken place on the ancient road because he is receptive, being tightly wound by events in his own life. The recreation of an ancient ritual releases the Wild Hunt* of Hagworthy; the witches' incantation from *Macbeth* does the same for Morgan le Fay* and, indirectly, for the Hampden Stones*, which become the knights that defeat her. In *The Ghost of Thomas Kempe*, Thomas Kempe's* ghost has been bottled up for many years before it is accidentally freed when the bottle is broken; all it takes is a housing project over his greatest masterpiece to bring landscaper Samuel Stokes* rampaging from his ghostly home in *The Revenge of Samuel Stokes*.

Once he has been summoned, the character from the past is mostly intent on continuing as he had been: Thomas Kempe seeks to resume his work as sorcerer, physician, and finder of lost goods, in spite of the fact that his services are no longer needed and that no one but James Harrison* believes that he exists; Samuel Stokes stubbornly restores his garden as well as he can, deaf and blind to the wishes of its twentieth-century owners; the Wild Hunt again seeks its victims; Morgan le Fay seeks power and evil. The shadows on the driftway* wish only to tell their stories to a willing heart, and they find one in Paul. The past is not dead; it is just waiting to resume its place in the world of the living.

On the whole, it does so with remarkable aplomb. Thomas Kempe finds the modern world difficult to deal with, for it does not believe in him, and his attempts to communicate and to affect events are written off as a young boy's pranks; finally it is too much for him to bear and he takes to his grave. But the other denizens of the past adjust remarkably well. Samuel Stokes appropriates television and radio waves to communicate, and he physically alters things to suit himself, with no compunction and little difficulty. He is not so much vanquished as directed elsewhere and carries out his mission undaunted by the modern age. Though unreceptive to new ideas, Morgan le Fay uses an automobile to further her schemes; when she is vanquished, it is by means of a power as ancient as herself. The Wild Hunt needs only the human mind to work with, and the mind of the twentieth century is just as susceptible as the mind of earlier ages; many modern people do not know how to deal with it. Modern arts have no power over it, but the ancient force of iron sends the Hunt back to where it had come from. The modern age is built on the past, and the past may lie waiting, but the two are not compatible, for they do not have the same goals. The past must give way to the present—that is, of course, except for Samuel, a granite will storming down the ages.

Lively's works are satisfying, for the most part; the encounters between present and past, especially in *The Ghost of Thomas Kempe* and *The Revenge of Samuel Stokes*, are full of gentle humor. Many of her child characters are not as well realized as her adult characters, but they are true to childhood: James longs not exactly to be rid of Thomas Kempe but to escape being blamed for his pranks; William* is embarrassed at being seen with girls; Jane Harvey* is a walking magnet for scratches, scrapes, and bruises. Thomas Kempe and Samuel Stokes are perhaps among the best realized of her characters, as are the shadows who tell their tales on the driftway. The books move briskly and surely to their ends, with nary a false step.

Works

Juvenile full-length fantasies: *The Whispering Knights* (1971); *The Wild Hunt of Hagworthy* (1971) as *The Wild Hunt of the Ghost Hounds* (1972); *The Driftway* (1972); *The Ghost of Thomas Kempe* (1973); *The Voyage of QV 66* (1978); *The Revenge of Samuel Stokes* (1981).

Juvenile non-fantasy: *Astercote* (1970); *The House in Norham Gardens* (1974); *Boy without a Name* (1975); *Going Back* (1975); *A Stitch in Time* (1976); *Fanny's Sister* (1977); *Nothing Missing but the Samovar, and Other Stories* (1978); *Fanny and the Monsters* (1979).

Adult: *The Presence of the Past* (1976); *The Road to Lichfield* (1977), novel; *Treasures of Time* (1979); *Judgment Day* (1981).

Secondary Works

Abbs, Peter. "Penelope Lively, Children's Fiction, and the Failure of Adult Culture," *Children's Literature in Education*, 18 (Fall, 1975), pp. 118–24.

Armstrong, Judith. "Ghosts as Rhetorical Devices in Children's Fiction," *Children's Literature in Education*, 29 (Summer, 1978), pp. 59–66.

Cleaver, Pamela. "Author by Accident," *Books and Bookmen*, 20 (Dec., 1974), pp. 66–68.

Lively, Penelope. "Bones in the Sand," *The Horn Book Magazine*, 57 (Dec., 1981), pp. 641–51.

———. "Children and Memory," *The Horn Book Magazine*, 49 (Aug., 1973), pp. 400–407.

———. "Children and the Art of Memory," Part I, *The Horn Book Magazine*, 54 (Feb., 1978), pp. 17–23.

———. "Children and the Art of Memory," Part II, *The Horn Book Magazine*, 54 (April, 1978), pp. 197–203.

———. "The Ghost of Thomas Kempe," *Junior Bookshelf*, 38 (June, 1974), pp. 143–45.

Rees, David. "The Narrative Art of Penelope Lively," *The Horn Book Magazine*, 51 (Feb., 1975), pp. 17–25.

———. "Time Present and Time Past: Penelope Lively," in *The Marble in the Water* (Boston: The Horn Book, 1980), pp. 185–98.

Townsend, John Rowe. "Penelope Lively," in *A Sounding of Storytellers* (New York: J. B. Lippincott, 1979), pp. 125–38.

LLAWCAE, BRANDON, a character in *A Swiftly Tilting Planet**, by Madeleine L'Engle.*. He is the son of Richard Llawcae and the younger brother of Ritchie Llawcae. Seventeenth-century Brandon's roots are in Wales; his family is among the early white settlers on the North American continent. Brandon has second sight: he sees visions of the future and the past. Until he is about twelve, life is good at his settlement, for the whites and the Wind People—who are descended from Madoc*, a twelfth-century Welsh prince who had come to North America—live together in peace. Brandon is a close friend of Maddok, one of the Wind People; Zylle Llawcae*, Ritchie's wife, is Maddok's sister. Now a minister filled with hate has separated the two races with suspicion and fear. Because she knows the healing herbs, Zylle is accused of witchcraft. The day she is to be executed, Brandon uses a rune* Zylle's father has taught him to call on heaven's lightning, which strikes the church and one of Zylle's accusers; the people decide that it is the wrath of God. When Zylle and Ritchie go back to Wales, Brandon is made one of the People of the Wind and eventually marries into the tribe. Among his descendants are Gwen, Matthew, and Bran Maddox***, Zillah Llawcae*, Branwen Zillah Maddox O'Keefe*, and Calvin O'Keefe*.

LLAWCAE, RICH, a character in Madeleine L'Engle's* *A Swiftly Tilting Planet**. He is the son of Richard Llawcae and his wife; he becomes the husband of Gwen Maddox* and the father of Zillah Maddox. Rich is from Wales; in 1865 he emigrates with his family to what is now Vespugia*, in South America. Gentle, good-hearted Rich quickly falls in love with Gwen Maddox, but she is attracted to Gedder*, a young native. One day Gedder provokes a fight with

Rich and, lunging for the knife Rich has taken from him, Gedder falls over a cliff. Upset by the experience, Gwen asks Rich to take her back home to America; he agrees, feeling that he cannot stay where he has been responsible for a death. In America Rich becomes a partner in the family grocery store. He and Gwen marry and lead fairly happy lives.

LLAWCAE, ZILLAH, a character in *A Swiftly Tilting Planet**, by Madeleine L'Engle*. She is descended from Madoc*, a twelfth-century Welsh prince who had come to the North American continent. Her father is a doctor. She becomes the wife of Bran Maddox* and the mother of Matthew and Rich Maddox. Zillah was born about 1847; she is seventeen in 1864. By this time she has become engaged to Bran. When Bran, wounded in body and soul during the Civil War, comes home, he cannot respond to her or to anyone; after Matthew Maddox*, his twin brother, helps Bran to heal, he goes to what is now Vespugia*, in South America, to make a new start, planning to send for Zillah later. Zillah's father is against her going until she is much older, though Bran's letters make it clear that a native girl, Zillie*, is being pressed on Bran by her power-hungry brother. Realizing that Bran must marry Zillah and not Zillie, Matthew sends Zillah to Vespugia against her father's wishes. She and Bran marry and have at least two children, one of whom is the ancestor of Madog Branzillo*.

LLAWCAE, ZYLLE, a character in Madeleine L'Engle's* *A Swiftly Tilting Planet**. She is descended from Madoc*, a twelfth-century Welsh prince who comes to North America. Zylle is the daughter of Zillo and the sister of Maddok; she is the wife of Ritchie Llawcae and becomes the mother of Bran Llawcae. Zylle is a blue-eyed native American living in the seventeenth century in what will become the United States. For love of Ritchie, she leaves her people to live with his family at the white settlement. For a time all is well, but Pastor Mortmain comes to the settlement and begins to spread suspicion and fear of Zylle's people. Because she knows the healing herbs, because she had not cried during labor, and because her baby stays well while others have died of a fever, Mortmain accuses Zylle of witchcraft. The day of her execution, Brandon Llawcae*, Zylle's brother-in-law, uses an ancient rune* to save her; it causes lightning to strike the church and one of her accusers, and Zylle is set free when people decide that it is the will of God. She and Ritchie and their son go back to Wales. From Zylle is descended Rich Llawcae* in the nineteenth century.

LLYAN, a character in Lloyd Alexander's* *The Castle of Llyr**, *Taran Wanderer**, and *The High King**. Once an ordinary house cat belonging to Glew*, a would-be sorcerer, Llyan becomes as big as a horse after he tries on her some potions that make her grow. Soon after this, Llyan chases Glew into a cave, where he is trapped after taking his own potion and growing too big to fit through the cave's small entrance. Llyan is reduced to scavenging. When Fflewddur Fflam*, a minstrel, and his companions come on Glew's cottage, Llyan traps them there. She becomes so enchanted with Fflewddur's music that she lets them escape, but she follows Fflewddur devotedly, rescuing him from danger and, eventually allowing him to ride her as he would a horse. Llyan can be ferocious in Fflewddur's defense, but she is gentle at heart and acts much like any cat would, though even her playful moods can be earthshaking because of her size. So devoted do the two become that when Fflewddur sails to the Summer Country*, where he will live forever, Llyan goes with him.

LLYR, HOUSE OF, a noble house in the Chronicles of Prydain*, by Lloyd Alexander*. Its members are of the blood of Llyr Half-Speech, King of the Sea; their fastness was at Caer Colur. The men of this house became great war leaders, and the women were among the most skilled enchantresses in Prydain*, handing down through generations a Golden Pelydryn* and a black book that held the secrets of their magic. Eilonwy* is the last princess of this noble line.

LLYWARCH AP LLEWELLYN, a twelfth-century Welsh bard who appears as a character in Jane Louise Curry's* *Over the Sea's Edge*. He is the friend of Madauc*, an unrecognized son of the king, and of Ithil, father of Dewi ap Ithil*. Though originally a pig-boy, Llywarch becomes a poet. It had been he who, while a boy, had discovered the seer who told the boys of the rich lands in the western sea; as a man, Llywarch helps Madauc escape his ambitious brothers and follow his dream across the sea.

LOBELIEZE, COUNT, a character in Lloyd Alexander's* *The Marvelous Misadventures of Sebastian*. This cruel, greedy, obese man is the Royal Treasurer and First Minister of Finance of Hamelin-Loring* under the Regent, Count Grinssorg*. His visit to Baron Purn-Hessel leads to the firing of Sebastian* when the young fiddler accidentally makes a fool of the count. When Isabel Charlotte Theodora Fredericka* regains her throne, Lobelieze is exiled.

LOCMAN, a character in *The First Two Lives of Lukas-Kasha*by Lloyd Alexander*. He is the court astrologer for the king of Abadan*. As court astrologer, Locman casts a daily horoscope for the king and, when the king dies, casts a horoscope to find the new one. Locman is continually surprised when his horoscopes are not completely right. After Lukas-Kasha* (Lukas), the new king, flees the palace, Locman refuses to cast a false horoscope proclaiming Shugdad Mirza* the new king and is himself forced to flee. During his subsequent travels, Locman realizes that life is full of chance and that the stars have no influence on what happens. Finally he comes to the village of Bayaz and becomes mayor of it. When Lukas, having taken up the life of a wandering storyteller, comes to Bayaz, Locman reminds him that he is still king of Abadan, and the young man decides to assert his kingship.

LONE ISLANDS, three islands in the Chronicles of Narnia*, by C[live] S[taples] Lewis*. Doorn, Felimath, and Avra lie in the Eastern Ocean and are the last known lands before the open sea. Most of the inhabitants live on Doorn; Felimath is where sheep are usually kept. During the reign of King Gale of Narnia*, the islands came under Narnian jurisdiction when Gale delivered the islanders from a dragon and they swore allegiance to him; the islands are ruled by a duke or governor responsible to the king of Narnia. During the reign of Caspian X*, the governor, Gumpas, is a man more interested in regulations and making money than in being a good leader, and he sanctions slavery on the islands. Caspian puts him out of office and appoints Lord Bern governor in his stead.

LONG, TOM, the main character in *Tom's Midnight Garden**, by Philippa Pearce*. He is the brother of Peter Long and the nephew of Gwen and Alan Kitson. When Peter catches the measles, Tom must go to stay with his uncle and aunt for the holidays, so he will not catch Peter's disease. Here he is kept inside, in case he has already caught the measles, and he soon becomes bored. Lack of exercise combines with the large, rich meals his aunt prepares to make Tom unable to sleep at night. Promising his uncle that he will stay in bed the ten hours he needs to sleep each night, Tom lies awake, listening to the grandfather clock* in the hall of the building strike every hour but the one on the dial. When it strikes thirteen one night, Tom reasons that there must be an hour he and his uncle had not thought of, and he goes downstairs to find himself in an earlier time. Each night that the clock strikes thirteen, Tom goes out of the house into the lovely garden it had once had. Here he meets and befriends Harriet Melbourne Bartholomew* (Hatty), a lonely Victorian girl, and they keep each other from being lonely. The day Tom is to leave, he meets the owner of the flats, Mrs. Bartholomew, who had been Hatty; his longing for companionship and her dreams of her youth had made it possible for Tom to go into that distant garden.

LONG DANCE, THE, a ceremony in the Earthsea trilogy*, by Ursula K. LeGuin*. This dance is held each midsummer eve all over Earthsea*, on both the islands and the sea, though steps and songs vary from place to place. The songs and dance celebrate the creation of the world by Segoy, and its sweetness, and probably ensures the world's fertility. The Children of the Open Sea* dance the Long Dance on their rafts, which are gathered into a circle; chanters sing of the creation of the world and of the inhabitants of the sea as the dancers leap from raft to raft and dance on each in turn, trying to dance on each before dawn. During one Long Dance, the chanters forget their songs; Arren*, the traveling companion of Ged*, a sorcerer, sings songs of his own land to finish out the night.

LONGTOOTH, CERDIC, a character in Lloyd Alexander's* *Time Cat**. He is a Briton in Gaul in 55 B.C. When Jason*, a twentieth-century boy, and Gareth*, his cat, travel to his century and live for a time with Cerdic and his family, he learns to enjoy having a cat so much that he decides to tame the kittens which a wild cat has in his storeroom. Until this time, there are no tamed cats in the village.

LORBANERY, a place in the Earthsea trilogy*, by Ursula K. LeGuin*. This island in southern Earthsea* has been famous for centuries for its fine silks, especially the blues and those of a spectacular crimson, the "dragon's fire." Lorbanery is a richly green island, for it is covered with hurbah trees on which feed the small worms that spin the silk. Little gray bats inhabit the island; they feed on the worms, and Lorbanery's citizens feel that it is unlucky to kill them. Trouble comes to rich Lorbanery when its magicians lose their powers, for neither the weather nor the skills of the craftsmen are right after that. The island becomes poor. Five years later, Ged*, a sorcerer seeking the source of the leaching of magic from Earthsea, comes to Lorbanery. Here he meets Sopli*, a madman who becomes his guide.

LORINGHOLD, a place in Lloyd Alexander's* *The Marvelous Misadventures of Sebastian**. The principal city of Hamelin-Loring*, it holds the Glorietta, the palace of the country's rulers.

LOST BOYS, several characters in *Peter and Wendy**, by James M. Barrie*. They are children who fall out of prams and are sent to Neverland* because no one claims them. The number of boys varies; when Wendy Darling* visits Neverland, there are six: Tootles, Nibs, Slightly, Curly, and the Twins. They long for mothers and are Wendy's devoted sons once she sets up housekeeping in Neverland. The boys follow Peter Pan* in everything, but they have the ability to grow up. They fly back with Wendy and her brothers and are adopted by the Darling family, gradually forgetting Neverland and finding a place in society.

LOST FARM, THE. Jane Louise Curry. Illus. Charles Robinson. New York: Atheneum, 1974. 137 pp. American.

It is 1922, and twelve-year-old Pete MacCubbin* is miserable, for his father, Donalbain MacCubbin* (Trashbin), the local scrap collector, is taking him out of school to teach him the family business. His father has always been hard on Pete, who lives with his father and grandmother, Granny MacCubbin*, on the family farm. On his last day, as he is going home, Pete stops at the deserted Sampson farm to sit in the shade and do some forbidden reading. Startled by what he thinks is a tiny voice talking to him, Pete investigates and discovers a van labelled "PROFESSOR LILLIPUT AND HIS MARVELOUS MUSEUM OF MINIATURES." Inside are several intriguingly small buildings. Pete settles down to read again, but he is interrupted by the owner of the tiny voice, Samantha Bostweiler*, a twelve-year-old girl about five inches tall. She explains that she and seven other citizens of Dopple*, Pennsylvania, had been miniaturized when

Professor Willie Kurtz* got his revenge on the village by reducing it with an invention for the development of which the village bank had refused to lend him money. Samantha asks Pete to fetch the authorities to help the villagers.

Knowing that no one will believe him, Pete hesitates, and, before he can do anything, his father brings down the wrath of Kurtz on them all. Trashbin had been looking for scrap metal on the Sampson place and had come away with a miniature car and Kurtz's gold pocketwatch. Realizing who the thief is but unwilling to bring in the authorities, who might become too curious about the miniatures, Kurtz miniaturizes the whole farm for revenge.

Pete tries various ways to get to town for help, but all fail. When he tries to ride one of the mules to town, the animal is spooked by a grass snake and sprains a leg; the other mule is lost when it and Pete meet a weasel. By the time Granny finds Pete and they return home, the farm is in chaos, for Trashbin, demoralized over what has happened to him and the others, is in a stupor from drinking all of Granny's arthritis medicine and has neglected the stock, and the farm is ravaged by bees and starlings.

Pete and his grandmother must use all their ingenuity to keep the farm safe from the weather and from foraging wild animals. Though they do not give up hope that they will find help, the two forage and store food for the coming winter. The snow that winter seems, of course, unusually deep, but they manage to survive it—except for Trashbin, who develops a cough and dies.

Time passes. Realizing that they may never get unshrunk, Granny writes down her recipes and household hints for Pete to use when she is dead. As the years pass, they get used to their situation, though Pete tries to find ways to get help. Among his father's scrap metal he finds an engine, which he fixes and attaches to a wagon, but it does not have enough power to get them anywhere. After the cover around the farm is burned away when Pete lights a fire to get the attention of the pilot of a plane passing overhead, the farm is in danger of being ravaged by flood or by wild creatures and they decide to leave, but cannot. The farm means too much.

Granny dies at age 105. Pete's life is pleasant, despite the Warneckis, who move into the Sampson place for a while and then move out. One day, Pete watches some hikers, who have come looking for a road George Washington is said to have surveyed. One of the hikers is a practical, older woman named Miss Bostweiler, who is a favorite with the children. One of the children finds Pete's lunch basket and shows Miss Bostweiler where it was. In dismay, Pete remembers that his rifle and his dog were nearby and hopes that the girl has tripped on the basket and not noticed the dog. Miss Bostweiler suddenly calls off the search for more tiny things and leads the children away. When Pete reaches the place where he left the basket, he finds the rifle, the dog, and the contents of the basket neatly hidden beneath a maple leaf. It is only after getting into bed that night that Pete associates Miss Bostweiler with the tiny girl, Samantha, he had met so long ago.

That night there is a vicious attack by a weasel, which tears a hole in the barn and almost kills Pete before he is saved by a huge boy, Ernie Goble*, who had been with the hikers. The next day Ernie tries to move the animals and Pete to his garage, where they will be safe from the people searching for Washington's road. But Pete refuses to be moved. The next day, the animals are uneasy. When Pete goes out to feed the barn animals, he notices that the places he had so carefully patched in the buildings now have gaping holes. He returns to the house to find Samantha Bostweiler fixing breakfast. The farm has been unshrunk. She explains to Pete how the tiny citizens of Professor Kurtz's little town managed, with the help of Arminta Hallam* and Mrs. Mary Buckle Bright*, to hoax Kurtz's nephew, who had inherited the exhibit, into unshrinking them. When Samantha saw the basket and Pete's dog, she realized what must have happened and had the farm unshrunk the night before. Because only what had already been shrunk could be unshrunk, anything used in the house or grounds that was not grown there would stay the size it already was—hence the holes where there should have been patches.

Pete is now a rich man, for Kurtz's nephew has made money from his uncle's invention and, out of spite, has stipulated in his will that it should go only to those reduced by his uncle who had not already been found. None of those from Dopple could get the money, but Pete could. A few months later, Pete and Samantha marry, and they market pickles and preserves made by using Granny's recipes at Found Again Farm.

LOUIS, a character in E[lwyn] B[rooks] White's* *The Trumpet of the Swan**. He is one of five cygnets hatched at the same time by a cob* and his mate. Though Louis is a trumpeter swan, he has no voice. Louis does not give up, however, for he seeks out Sam Beaver*, a friend of the swans, and learns to read and write at the boy's school. To Louis's chagrin, he still cannot communicate with the other swans because they cannot read. When Louis falls in love with Serena* but cannot express his love, the cob steals a trumpet for him so that Louis can make the sounds a swan should make. Conscience-stricken because the trumpet was stolen, Louis begins a quest to make money to pay for it. After bugling at a summer camp, he has the webbing on one foot slit so that he can play the keys on his trumpet. Louis's quest takes him to Boston and to Philadelphia, where he meets Serena again, and they fall in love. To leave the Philadelphia zoo, they agree with a head keeper to donate one of their cygnets when one is needed. Louis is very happy in his life with Serena, traveling and raising his families.

LOVELL, BETTY, a character in *The House of Arden** and *Harding's Luck**, by E[dith] Nesbit Bland*. She is a wisewoman skilled in the arts of magic, who has powers to prophesy and to transport herself through time. In the early seventeenth century, she acts as nurse to Richard Arden* and helps Dickie Harding*, the boy who takes Richard's place, to become accustomed to his new life. In 1605, Betty helps Elfrida Arden*, a time traveler, escape from the Tower of London, where the girl is imprisoned after she has revealed a too-intimate knowledge of the Gunpowder Plot. In 1807, Betty lives in a dilapidated hut near Arden Castle*; she foretells the landing of the Frenchmen who are shipwrecked while trying to invade England. When Elfrida and her brother, Edred Arden*, visit Betty in this existence, Betty can see the time from which they came by touching Elfrida.

LUCY, a character in *A Chance Child**, by Jill Paton Walsh*. She is a child worker in Britain in the early nineteenth century who works at forging chain for a "nailer." Her life is harsh and the working conditions brutal, but she retains her sensitivity. Because of an accident when she fell asleep and fell into the fire, she has a horrible black scar across one side of her face—hence her nickname, "Blackie." She runs away with Tom Moorhouse* and Creep* and journeys with them down the canal, finding work at a pottery plant. Here she gets the job of her dreams, painting china, but gives it up when Tom is dismissed after dropping a load of china. She has a crush on Tom and hopes to marry him eventually, but he scorns her and finally leaves. Lucy gets a job in a woolen mill and Creep goes with her. When Creep finally becomes part of the nineteenth century, he leaves her behind while he goes to find work, returning several years later to marry her. They have ten children.

LUCY, a character in Robert Lawson's* *Mr. Wilmer**. This elephant was born in the jungle of East Burma about 1867; in 1915, she had joined the herd of Dhingbat Dhong, attracted by a handsome elephant in his herd. Lucy still remembers fondly the labor she had done as a working elephant. On 27 March 1921, she arrived at a zoo in the United States. Lucy has never been really happy at the zoo, for she hates the city and the concrete at the zoo hurts her feet. All this she tells William Wilmer* when he comes to work at the zoo. William and Lucy become good friends, and she gets revenge for him on his boss when the man tries to make money from William's talent for talking with animals. When William buys a farm and decides to make it a rest farm for discontented animals, Lucy is one of the first to go there.

LUCY CLOUGH (*The Wild Hunt of Hagworthy*). *See* Clough, Lucy

LUCY GRAHAM (*The Magic City*). *See* Graham, Lucy

LUCY PEVENSIE (the Chronicles of Narnia). *See* Pevensie, Lucy

LUGAD, a character in *Time Cat**, by Lloyd Alexander*. This fat, bald, sour little man is magician to King Miliucc* in fifth-century Ireland. Because the country is plagued by rats and snakes, Lugad's task is to get rid of them. When he fails, the magician pretends that the vermin that are still around are actually ghosts of those he killed. After one of the "ghostly" vipers almost kills Diahan*, the king's daughter, Miliucc names Jason*, a boy from the twentieth century, and Gareth*, his cat, to be his sorcerers because Gareth kills the snake. Lugad regains his place as magician, but his jealousy is such that at Midsummer he demands that Jason and Gareth be killed, for the ghosts of a boy and a cat, he says, will be able to take care of the "ghosts" of the rats and snakes. He is thwarted when the two escape.

LUKAS-KASHA (LUKAS), the title character in Lloyd Alexander's* *The First Two Lives of Lukas-Kasha*. Lukas's first life is that of Zara-Petra's* village ne'er-do-well. Lazy and mischievous, Lukas harasses the town's sometimes-unscrupulous mayor and manages to live a satisfying and carefree life without working. When Battisto*, a traveling mountebank, comes to the town, Lukas, ever the performer, assists him and finds himself in the sea near Abadan* as the man plunges his head into a pot of water. Realizing that this is not a dream, Lukas decides to make the best of things in his second life, particularly after he is proclaimed king of Abadan. As King Kasha, he is at first interested only in entertaining himself, but, discovering the injustices in force in Abadan, Lukas tries to improve things. When he pardons Kayim*, a poet almost executed for reciting satiric verse, and does his best to delay preparations for an invasion of Bishangar*, Shugdad Mirza*, the Grand Vizier, tries to assassinate him. Escaping from the palace with Kayim and Nur-Jehan*, a Bishangari girl who irritates and fascinates Lukas, the young man eventually finds himself going to Bishangar to make peace with its king. After Shugdad is killed, Lukas is able to take control of his country and bargain with Nur-Jehan, queen of Bishangar. Realizing how much the young woman means to him, Lukas invites her to his palace and to unite their kingdoms. But before this can happen Lukas falls into the sea and finds himself again in Zara-Petra. Having learned in Abadan what it means to be responsible, Lukas has changed. Realizing that if he stays in Zara-Petra he will always be known as the town scamp, he leaves town, searching for Abadan and his friends or at least someone like them, telling tales to earn his keep.

LUNE, KING, a character in C[live] S[taples] Lewis's* *The Horse and His Boy** and *The Last Battle*. He is the father of Cor* and Corin*. Brave, hearty Lune is king of Archenland* during the Golden Age of Narnia*, a magical land. At his castle, Anvard*, he and his troops repulse the invasion of Archenland by Rabadash*, the prince of Calormen*, and his troops. Lune is a wise king and a fair one; he is succeeded by Cor. Lune is one of those in the country of Aslan*, Narnia's great lion-protector, at the end of Narnia.

LUPY, a character in Mary Norton's* *The Borrowers*, *The Borrowers Afield*, and *The Borrowers Afloat*. She is the wife of Hendreary* and the mother of Eggletina, Timmis*, and two other boys. She is a borrower*, one of the race of tiny people who "borrow" what they need from humans. Her maiden name was Rain-Pipe. Lupy's first husband was a Harpsichord; by him she had two children. As one of the elegant Harpsichord family, Lupy learned society ways, and she keeps these when she is widowed and marries Hendreary. A year after Eggletina disappeared, the rest of the family emigrated from the country manor where they lived to a badger's den in a nearby field. After a time, Lupy disappears, presumably "collected" by Tom Goodenough*; she, Eggletina, and the rest of the family get together again in the cottage where the boy lives. Lupy is proud of her home here, which is furnished with dollhouse furniture. When Homily, Pod, and Arrietty Clock*** come to stay, Lupy is very grand about helping them.

LYNX, THE, a character in *The Animal Family**, by Randall Jarrell*. As a kitten this bold, inquisitive creature strays too far from his den and is snatched up by the hunter* to become part of the family he and the mermaid* who shares his cabin are gathering together. Their family already includes a bear*. The lynx is graceful and grateful, loving all of them and not hesitating to show it by washing whomever is available—though not the bear, for the bear is too much for even the bear to wash. One morning the lynx finds a boy* who eventually becomes part of the family as well. Because the lynx is so lovely and graceful, he is well-loved by the hunter, the mermaid, and the boy.

LYON, MERRIMAN (MERRY), a figure in Arthurian lore who appears as a character in the Dark Is Rising series*, by Susan Cooper*. He is also known as Merlin. Merry is the first of the Old Ones, the forces of good, and he has been present in every age. In King Arthur's* time Merry is that king's trusted friend and adviser, and he helps Guinevere take her son, who becomes Bran Davies*, away from the mistrusting Arthur and into the twentieth century. In the thirteenth century, Merry is liege lord of Hawkin*, whom he has raised and whom he uses to keep safe a powerful book of knowledge and spells. In the twentieth century he is an archaeologist in Britain who teaches at a university and who makes amazing discoveries of ancient artifacts. Once he becomes the butler of Miss Mary Greythorne*, another Old One, for a time. Merry is well-loved by Hawkin and by his friends in the twentieth century: Will Stanton*, the youngest Old One, and Barnabas (Barney), Jane, and Simon Drew***, three children who call him Great-uncle Merry—"Gumerry," for short. To them he is mysterious and absolutely wonderful, a sturdy rock to cling to in the battle between evil and good. Merry helps Barney, Jane, and Simon find an ancient grail* and manuscript* necessary in the battle against the Dark, and he helps Will to learn the full extent of his own powers and gain the things that will help defeat the Dark. As one of the three Lords of High Magic, he keeps one, a golden harp*, though Merry is not permitted to help Will win it. At the defeat of the Dark, Merry's task is finished, and he leaves the world, to rest. *See also* Merlyn; Myrddin

M. E. DRAUT. *See* Medraut

MAB, QUEEN, queen of the fairies in *Peter Pan in Kensington Gardens**, by James M. Barrie*. Mab rules the fairies in Kensington Gardens. She gives Peter Pan* the two wishes he uses to fly home.

MABEL PROWSE *(The Enchanted Castle). See* Prowse, Mabel

MACCUBBIN, DONALBAIN (TRASHBIN), a character in Jane Louise Curry's* *The Lost Farm**. He is the son of Malcolm and "Granny" MacCubbin*, the widower husband of Maybelle, and the father of Pete MacCubbin*. He is called "Trashbin" bacause he collects and sells "valuable" trash. Trashbin is a mean-spirited man with little regard for his mother, his son, or the law, and it is his theft of Professor Willie Kurtz's* pocketwatch and miniature car that causes the professor to aim his reducing machine at the farm, miniaturizing it and everybody in it. Demoralized by what has happened, Trashbin never really recovers, finally dying of a consumptive condition the next winter.

MACCUBBIN, GRANNY, a character in *The Lost Farm**, by Jane Louise Curry*. She is the wife of Malcolm MacCubbin, the mother of Donalbain (Trashbin) MacCubbin*, and the grandmother of Pete MacCubbin*. Widowed when her husband died at Gettysburg during the Civil War, Granny struggled to raise their son, who, unfortunately, was greatly influenced by his ne'er-do-well grandfather. When Trashbin's son was born, Granny took care of both the farm and the child, putting up with her son's meanness for the sake of Pete. When they are miniaturized, Granny's knowledge of foraging and herbal medicine comes in handy. Granny dies at the age of 105, but her recipes and skills live after her, written in the little books she makes to help Pete.

MACCUBBIN, PETE, a character in Jane Louise Curry's* *The Lost Farm**. He is the son of Maybelle and Donalbain (Trashbin) MacCubbin* and the grandson of Granny MacCubbin*. Though his father is harsh to him, Pete's life is fairly normal until he turns twelve, in 1922. Then he meets Samantha Bostweiler*, a girl about five inches high, and is himself miniaturized when Trashbin steals from Professor Willie Kurtz* and Kurtz gets his revenge by miniaturizing the entire farm with his strange invention. Though ingenious Pete comes up with many ways to escape his predicament by getting help, all fail and he stays miniature most of his life, struggling, with Granny, to stay alive in a suddenly outsized world. Finally, long after Granny's death, when Pete himself is in his sixties, Samantha, now herself "unshrunk," finds him and brings him and the farm back to their normal size. Pete finds himself the heir to a large fortune because he is the only one of Kurtz's "victims" to be found after the man's nephew's will goes into effect. Pete marries Samantha and they live at the farm, selling pickles, syrups, and preserves made from Granny's recipes.

MACDONALD, GEORGE (1824–1905), Scottish writer. He was born on 10 December 1824, in Huntley, Aberdeenshire, Scotland. He was educated at King's College, University of Aberdeen, and at Highbury Theological College. In 1851 he married Louisa Powell; they had eleven children. MacDonald was a minister, a lecturer, and the editor of *Good Words for the Young*. He died on 18 September 1905.

Most of MacDonald's works for children are fantasies or fairy tales. His three full-length fantasies—*At the Back of the North Wind**, *The Princess and the Goblin**, and *The Princess and Curdie**—are works with a deep spiritual quality and an elusive, allegorical mood.

In *The Princess and the Goblin* and *The Princess and Curdie*, it becomes quite clear that appearances can be deceiving. Those who are of lowly birth can be just as noble and worthy as those higher on the social scale. Curdie Peterson*, despite the nobility in his background, is the poor son of a poor miner; his nobility and courage stem less from the strain of royalty in his family than from the influence of his parents, who are themselves noble is spirit, if not in station. When Curdie later is given the talent to discover what kind of person someone is inside, merely by touching that person's hand, he discovers that outside appearance has nothing to do with the person within the body. Touching the paw of Lina*, a misshapen beast, he feels the hand of a child; touching the work-gnarled hand of his own mother, Curdie finds the soft hand of a lady. When he touches the hands of the servants in the castle of the king*, he discovers that they are really the feet of beasts.

But, conversely, appearances can show what someone has become. Lina's outward appearance is the result of what she once had been inside; this seems true for the beasts she and Curdie meet in the wood. Having once been a human who had become inwardly foul, each of the beasts has taken on the appearance of that foulness. The same is true of the goblins* who haunt the mountains of Curdie's home: once humans who took refuge in the caves to escape a king they thought too severe, the goblins have become misshapen over the years as their grotesque natures became physical.

In the two works, obedience and severity may be painful, but they are necessary to life. Without a ruling power, people give in to their own selfish natures, and disaster results. Those who flee a king and seek to rule themselves become goblins. When the king of Curdie's country seeks to rule with a velvet hand, the inhabitants of his city become selfish, grasping, and cruel; his doctor poisons him. Because his people have proved that they cannot govern themselves as free men, the king then rules them with an iron hand, and all goes well. Later the man the people themselves choose to rule them ruins the city by mining so ruthlessly beneath it that it falls in when activity—at least part of it wrong—is at its height. Obedience to those wiser can keep one's selfish nature from taking control, but unless that higher authority sees to it that all commands are followed to the letter, disaster can still result.

Obedience is a factor in *At the Back of the North Wind*, where it can be the difference between happiness and unhappiness. Young Diamond*, who sometimes travels with the North Wind*, obeys without question the commands he receives from her and from his parents, and the outcome is always good. Nanny*, on the other hand, loses her wonderful dream when she does not obey the people she meets in it. Diamond's father learns that obedience can lead to happiness, when he takes in Mr. Raymond's* horse. He tries to do the best he can with the troublesome beast, working it only as long as Mr. Raymond has told him to, and caring for the horse at the expense of his own and of his family. He is rewarded when Mr. Raymond makes him his coachman. The North Wind, too, obediently does her work, for she knows that she must; when she does it she feels all right, but when she does not she feels all wrong. Even though she does not always understand why she is doing what she does, she obeys implicity.

But the main thrust of the story is a yearning for that which we cannot encounter except in dreams—that is, until we die. In dreams, Diamond and Nanny go to marvelous places: she to the moon, he to a land where little angels frolic and work, and to the country at the back of the north wind*. Nanny enjoys her dream because it is beautiful and there she is happy, until she makes her mistake; but she cannot believe that it has really happened, and she does not allow it to touch her. Diamond, too, is happy in the dream-lands he visits, but he believes in them and they touch his life.

Most of his dreams are quite vivid. The country at the back of the north wind is a beautiful place where a river sings its song as it flows over the grass, and the people are not sad, though they seem to wait to be gladder some day. It is a place of light and color, where no one wishes anything but good. Diamond visits this place in dreams when he is ill, and here he is quite happy until he sees the pain of those at home. In another land, he meets small boy angels and romps and works with them, helping them to dig up stars. Some nights he dreams of the country at the back of the north wind but does not remember. Yet each dream has an elusive quality about it; in each, there is a song of some kind that does not linger when he wakes. The song the little angels sing eludes Diamond as he hears it, so that he forgets each verse as it ends and has only an imperfect memory of the final stanza. The song of the river at the back of the north wind proves equally difficult to remember once he has wakened; on nights he does not remember his dreams, Diamond does recall hearing the river, though not what it sings. Even the poem his mother finds and reads to him at the seshore, though close to the song of the river, is something Diamond can remember only imperfectly, for when he hears it he is half asleep.

This elusive music is akin to the music the North Wind hears as she carries out her duties. Though it is still far-off and she cannot hear much of it, the music makes the North Wind able to bear her tasks, for it makes the promise to her that some greater good is coming. Though the song of the river makes no such promise, the echoes of it make it possible for Diamond to bear the troubles into which his family falls, for it reminds him of the beauty at the back of the north wind and helps him to be good.

MacDonald's works are skillfully crafted, and his prose is rich and descriptive. The children he writes about are fairly well realized; though Irene sometimes seems too good to be real, Curdie is the very picture of a rough-and-tumble boy, good-hearted and sharp; Nanny is convincing, and good as Diamond is, his goodness never cloys. The works themselves sometimes seem as elusive as the music in Diamond's dreams, for the reader is always aware that here there is more than meets the eye. The tales hold up well when one reads mainly for plot; the themes, though, are not always readily understood, at least not by the intellect, for there is always something that seems only half-explained. MacDonald's works are more readily understood by the heart.

Works

Juvenile full-length fantasy: *At the Back of the North Wind* (1871); *The Princess and the Goblin* (1872); *The Princess and Curdie* (1882).

Juvenile short stories, novels, etc.: *Dealings with the Fairies* (1867); *Ronald Bannerman's Boyhood* (1871); *Gutta-Percha Willie* (1873); *The Wise Woman* (1875) as *A Double Story* (1876); *A Rough Shaking* (1891).

Adult: *Within and Without* (1855), poem; *Poems* (1857); *Phantastes* (1858); *David Elginbrod* (1863); *Adela Cathcart* (1864); *The Portent* (1864); *Alec Forbes of Howglen* (1865); *Annals of a Quiet Neighborhood* (1867); *The Disciple and Other Poems* (1867); *Guild Court* (1867); *Unspoken Sermons*, vol. 1 (1867); *Robert Falconer* (1868); *The Seaboard Parish* (1868); *The Miracles of Our Lord* (1870); *The Vicar's Daughter* (1872); *Wilfrid Cumbermede* (1872); *Malcolm* (1875); *St. George and St. Michael* (1876); *Thomas Wingfold, Curate* (1876); *The Marquis of Lossie* (1877); *Sir Gibbie* (1879); *Paul Faber, Surgeon* (1879); *A Book of Strife, in the Form of the Diary of an Old Soul* (1880); *Mary Marston* (1881); *Castle Warlock* (1881); *Weighed and Wanting* (1882); *The Gifts of the Child Christ and Other Tales* (1882); *Orts* (1882), essays, as *The Imagination and Other Essays* (1883) and as *A Dish of Orts* (1893); *Donal Grant* (1883); *A Threefold Cord* (1883), poems, with John Hill MacDonald and Greville Matheson; *Unspoken Sermons*, vol. 2 (1885); *The Tragedie of Hamlet, Prince of Denmark* (1885); *What's Mine's Mine* (1886); *Home Again* (1887); *The Elect Lady* (1888); *Unspoken Sermons*, vol. 3 (1889); *There and Back* (1891); *The Flight of the Shadow* (1891); *The Hope of the Gospel* (1892), sermons; *Heather and Snow* (1893); *Lilith* (1895); *The Hope of the Universe* (1896); *Rampolli* (1897); *Salted With Fire* (1897).

Secondary Works

Blishen, Edward. "Maker of Fairy Tales," *Books and Bookmen*, 19 (May, 1974), pp. 92–95.

Douglass, Jane. "Dealings with the Fairies," *The Horn Book Magazine*, 37 (Aug., 1961), pp. 327–35.

Green, Roger Lancelyn. "George MacDonald," in *Tellers of Tales* (Leicester, England: Edmund Ward, 1946), pp. 51–63.

Kirkpatrick, Mary. "An Introduction to the Curdie Books by George MacDonald," *Bulletin of the New York C. S. Lewis Society*, 5 (1974), pp. 1–6.

MacDonald, George. "The Fantastic Imagination," *Signal*, 16 (Jan. 1975), pp. 51–63. [Reprinted from *A Dish of Orts: Chiefly Papers on the Imagination and on Shakespeare* (London: Edwin Dalton, 1908). Also in *A Peculiar Gift*, ed. Lance Salway (Harmondsworth, England: Penguin Books, Kestrel Books, 1976), pp. 162–67.]

McGillis, Roderick. "Language and Secret Knowledge in *At the Back of the North Wind*," *Proceedings of the Seventh Annual Conference of the Children's Literature Association*, (1980), pp. 120–27.

Manlove, C. N. "George MacDonald (1824–1905)," in *Modern Fantasy: Five Studies* (New York: Cambridge University Press, 1975), pp. 55–98.

Prickett, Stephen. "Adults in Allegory Land: Kingsley and MacDonald," in *Victorian Fantasy* (Bloomington and London: Indiana University Press, 1979), pp. 150-97.

Ragg, Laura M. "George MacDonald and His Household: Some Personal Recollections," *English*, 11 (Summer, 1956), pp. 59–63.

Reis, Richard H. *George MacDonald*. New York: Twayne Publishers, 1972.

Sadler, Glenn E. "At the Back of the North Wind: George MacDonald, a Centennial Appreciation," *Orcist*, 3 (1969), pp. 20–22.

Wolff, Robert Lee. *The Golden Key: A Study of the Fiction of George MacDonald*. New Haven, Conn.: Yale University Press, 1961.

Yates, Elizabeth. "George MacDonald," *The Horn Book Magazine*, 14 (Jan.-Feb., 1938), pp. 23–29.

MCGRATH, TIM, a character in Robert Lawson's* *Rabbit Hill** and *The Tough Winter** He lives with his wife near Danbury, Connecticut. This Irish Yankee becomes the gardener of the Folks who move into the house on Rabbit Hill, and at first he is a puzzled one, for the Folks will not allow him to trap or disturb the wildlife there. To his astonishment, though he traps and poisons, his own garden is ravaged, while that of the Folks is left untouched. Tim begins to wonder about himself during a subsequent winter, when the Folks go south; he finds himself defending the animals from the caretaker's dog and spreading food for them, like the Folks. The next thing he knows, he will be reading books, too. Seeking the bluegrass country, Uncle Analdas* finds it in Tim's barn, and Tim lets the old rabbit recover there.

MADAUC, a legendary Welsh prince who appears as a character in Jane Louise Curry's* *Over the Sea's Edge*. He is the son of Ywein Gwynet, a king in twelfth-century Wales; he is the brother of Hywel, Kynan, Rien, Rhirid, and Iorwerth. He becomes the husband of Coala* and the father of Rien. Madauc's mother had somehow displeased his father, so he was not raised as one of Gwynet's sons. Sent after his mother's death to the island of Lund, Madauc made friends with Ithil and with Llywarch Llewellyn*. Hearing tales of a wonderful land beyond the sea, Madauc had dreamed of finding it. Madauc becomes a great warrior, winning against King Henry of England, and Gwynet seems ready to acknowledge him. But Madauc is ambushed and almost killed by Hywel, and Gwynet dies while Madauc is recovering. Accompanied by Dewi ap Ithil* and a crew of men, Madauc sails in the *Gwennan Gorn* to the North American continent, searching for Antillia and its seven golden cities. He finds instead Cibotlán*, a bloody empire, and Abáloc*, a land of gentle people trying to remain free. Coala, a Cibotlán priestess, believes that Madauc is Matec, a sun-god who had left the world long ago, promising to return. Though disappointed at first to find that he is a man, Coala soon finds herself glad. Having helped the Abalockians defeat their enemy, and realizing that he loves Coala and the peace of Abáloc, Madauc sails back to Wales and then returns to Abáloc. He and his men, many of whom take Abalockian wives, form a peaceful community, wandering from place to place and raising their families. *See also* Madoc

MADDOX, BRAN, a character in *A Swiftly Tilting Planet*, by Madeleine L'Engle*. He is descended from Madoc*, a twelfth-century Welsh prince who had come to North America. Bran is the brother of Gwen and the twin of Matthew Maddox**; he becomes the husband of Zillah Llawcae* and the father of Matthew and Rich. Bran and Matthew have always been close, and they become closer after Matthew is crippled by a fall from a horse. Bran refuses to pity Matthew and forces him to become independent. Five years later, filled with idealism, Bran lies about his age and enlists on the Union side of the Civil War. He returns home wounded in body and spirit, for his experiences have been too terrible to tell. Bran withdraws from everyone, including Zillah, to whom he had become engaged before he had left. Finally Bran is able to pour out to Matthew his horrifying experiences and is at last healed. Recognizing a deep-rooted need for adventure without killing, Bran goes to settle in a Welsh settlement in Vespugia*, a small country in South America, leaving Zillah behind until he establishes himself. In Vespugia, Bran meets Gedder*, a native who tries to get Bran to marry his sister, Zillie*. In one time line he does, and one of his descendants is Madog Branzillo*, a Vespugian leader who almost destroys the world. But

Charles Wallace Murray*, a twentieth-century boy, travels through time to change events, and this time Bran marries Zillah. Branzillo is still their descendant, but he is a man of peace.

MADDOX, CHUCK, a character in Madeleine L'Engle's* *A Swiftly Tilting Planet**. He is descended from Madoc*, a twelth-century Welsh prince who had come to North America. Chuck is the younger brother of Branwen Zillah Maddox O'Keefe* (Beezie); he becomes the stepson of Duthbert Mortmain*. Like several of his ancestors, Chuck has a kind of sixth sense; he can "smell" whether a person is good or bad. Chuck's childhood is happy until his father dies and his mother marries Duthbert to keep the family store going. Duthbert is a brutal man who does not like his wife's children. When one night he tries to strike their grandmother, Chuck gets in the way and is knocked down a flight of stairs. The resulting skull fracture is almost fatal, but Gaudior*, a unicorn, keeps Chuck alive. His sense of time and space is drastically altered; Chuck lives as much in the past of nineteenth-century Bran and Matthew Maddox** as he does in the present, and he has visions of terrible past events. Gradually Chuck's eyesight worsens, and finally Duthbert finds an excuse to have him institutionalized; Chuck dies a few months later.

MADDOX, GWEN, a character in *A Swiftly Tilting Planet**, by Madeleine L'Engle*. She is a descendant of Madoc*, a twelfth-century Welsh prince who had come to North America. Gwen is the sister of Bran and Matthew Maddox**; she becomes the wife of Rich Llawcae* and the mother of Zillah. She was born about 1845. Sometimes silly and vain, Gwen is quickly enamored of flamboyant men. When she is caught kissing the hired hand, she is sent with Bran to a Welsh settlement in Vespugia*, a small South American nation. On the way, Gwen charms all the sailors on the ship. In Vespugia, she becomes infatuated with Gedder*, a strong, ambitious native who is attracted to her as well. During a fight he provokes with Rich, Gedder is accidentally killed. Upset and homesick, Gwen is taken back to the United States by Rich.

MADDOX, MATTHEW, a character in Madeleine L'Engle's* *A Swiftly Tilting Planet**. He is descended from Madoc*, a Welsh prince who had come to North America in the twelfth century. He is the brother of Gwen and the twin of Bran Maddox**. One day when he is riding, Matthew is crippled as his horse falls on him; the accident may have been arranged by an Echthros*, a force of evil in the universe. Any self-pitying Matthew might be inclined to do is cut short by Bran, who makes him become independent again. The two are very close, able to tell at a distance how the other is feeling. When he gets older, Matthew becomes a writer of short stories and, in 1865, a critically acclaimed novel. Intrigued by Madoc and his brother, Gwydry*, Matthew becomes obsessed with them after Bran settles in Vespugia*, a small South American country, and reports hearing their story there as well. About this time he begins to have visions of Bran and of twentieth-century Chuck Maddox*. Charles Wallace Murray*, a twentieth-century boy who has traveled through time and has gone "within" Matthew, influences him as he has Chuck. Matthew begins to trace the descendants of Madoc and Gwydyr and soon realizes that if Gwen, who is in Vespugia with Bran, marries Gedder*, a descendant of Gwydyr, the result will be disastrous, as it will be if Bran marries Gedder's sister. In his dreams, Matthew helps young Rich Llawcae* defeat Gedder, and in reality Matthew makes it possible for Bran's betrothed to join him in Vespugia. Matthew's investigations lead him to write his greatest novel, but he does not live to see it published in 1868; an Echthros causes him to die suddenly.

MADELEINE STUDDARD (*The Wind Eye*). *See* Studdard, Madeleine

MADELY, PIERS, a character mentioned in *The River at Green Knowe** who appears in *An Enemy at Green Knowe**, by Lucy Boston*. He is the vicar at Penny Sokey, near Green Knowe*, in the seventeenth century. This good and gentle man is well liked. He teaches Roger Oldknow until the boy has learned all Piers knows; in 1630, when the boy is nine years old, Dr. Wolfgang Vogel* comes to teach him. Dr. Vogel practices the black arts and finally becomes so afraid of these things that he confesses to Piers, who encourages him to burn his books. Piers is perhaps the last person to see Dr. Vogel alive, for the man vanishes that night. In 1647, Piers has another dreadful experience, this time involving Green Knowe itself; one night, when a full moon shines on it, he seems to see the house change into a prehistoric temple of the moon. So shocking is this experience that Piers wishes to confide it to someone but does not want to be thought mad; he describes it in Latin in a narrative that he puts into a bottle and throws into the river near Green Knowe. In the twentieth century, the narrative is found by Oskar Stanislawsky*, Ida*, and Hsu*, who are staying at Green Knowe, and they go out the next night of full moon to witness the transformation.

MADEMOISELLE, a character in E[dith] Nesbit Bland's* *The Enchanted Castle**. She becomes the wife of Lord Yalding*. After she fell in love with the poor young lord, Mademoiselle was put into a convent by well-meaning relatives; when she finally got out, she journeyed from France to England, taking a position as a French teacher at a girls' school near Yalding Castle*. Mademoiselle is reunited with her lover through the powers of a magic wishing ring*. On the night of the festival of harvest, Mademoiselle, standing in the Hall of Granted Wishes*, reveals the history of the ring and of Yalding Castle and makes the last wish the ring ever grants, undoing all the magic it has done and making it a charm to bind her and Lord Yalding. She and the lord are married with the ring and live contentedly at Yalding Castle.

MADOC, a legendary Welsh prince who appears as a character in Madeleine L'Engle's* *A Swiftly Tilting Planet**. He is the seventh son of Owain and the brother of Gwydyr*; he becomes the husband of Zyll*. Madoc was born in Gwynedd. When his brothers quarrelled over the throne after his father's death, Madoc had journeyed with Gwydyr to the legendary lands to the west—the North American continent. Here their ship was wrecked and their companions drowned. They came to a tribe living beside a lake. Afraid of these strange people, Gwydyr had run into the forest, and hunters reported that he had died of a snakebite. Searching for Gwydyr's grave, Madoc became lost; Zyll found him and brought him to the People of the Wind, where he was nursed back to health. Though they sought to worship him, he quickly put a stop to it. Now seventeen, Madoc feels that he has found his rightful place among these gentle people. He is married to Zyll, but on his wedding day Gwydyr returns; he had plotted to make Madoc think he was dead and now seeks to rule the People of the Wind as he rules the neighboring tribe. After a day-long fight, Madoc defeats Gwydyr and sends him in disgrace back to his tribe. Madoc's blue eyes are echoed in his descendants among the People of the Wind, and in every generation a blue-eyed baby is considered lucky. Among Madoc's descendants are Zylle Llawcae*, in the seventeenth century, and Matthew, Bran, and Gwen Maddox*** and Zillah Llawcae*, in the nineteenth. As long as Madoc's line is kept from Gwydyr's, all is well; Charles Wallace Murray* journeys through time to keep the two lines separate. *See also* Madauc

MADOC AB OWAIN GWYNEDD. *See* Madauc; Madoc

MADOG BRANZILLO (*A Swiftly Tilting Planet*). *See* Branzillo, Madog

MAE TUCK (*Tuck Everlasting*). *See* Tuck, Mae

MAGG, a character in *The Castle of Llyr** and *The High King**, by Lloyd Alexander*. Power-hungry Magg is the Chief Steward of King Rhuddlum, on the Isle of Mona*. Here he helps Achren*, an equally power-hungry queen, in her attempt to get Eilonwy*, a young sorceress, under her control. When that plot is thwarted by Eilonwy's friends, Magg escapes and makes his way to Annuvin*, the realm of the evil king, Arawn*, where he convinces Arawn that he is an asset in that king's bid to gain control of Prydain*. Arawn promises Magg the eventual rule of Annuvin in exchange for his services, and Magg gladly betrays the land of Prydain. At Arawn's defeat, Magg tries to take the iron crown of Annuvin, but when he places it on his head it burns with a white-hot heat and kills him.

MAGIC BED-KNOB, THE. Mary Norton. Illus. Waldo Peirce. New York: The Hyperion Press, 1943. Unpaged. British.
　　Carey, Charles, and Paul Wilson*** are sent to stay with their aunt during

the summer holidays. One morning they find Eglantine Price* sitting in the garden with a sprained ankle; she had fallen off her broomstick, Paul tells the others, revealing also that he has been watching her practice flying on it at night. When the children visit Miss Price later, they discover that she is learning to be a witch. To keep them from telling anyone, Miss Price enchants a bed-knob* Paul has unscrewed from his bed; if they twist it and wish, the bed will take them wherever they want to go, but if they tell anyone about her witchcraft, the bed-knob will stop working. The first time the children try it, the bed-knob does not work. Miss Price explains that this is because Paul must do the wishing, it being his bed-knob, and that, twisted one way, the bed will travel in the present, twisted the other way, into the past. Again one night the children try the magic bed-knob, wishing themselves at their parent's house, but to their dismay, no one is home. As they wait, a policeman comes and takes them to the station because the bed is obstructing traffic and they are talking nonsense about magic. The children spend the night in the police station and watch as, at dawn, the bed is brought to the station and left in the garden there. They escape when they are allowed into the garden.

Their next trip, they decide, will be to a place where it is light when it is dark in England, and Miss Price must go with them to help if things get dangerous. So it is that one night they go to Ueepe*, an island in the South Seas; Miss Price brings her broom, having flown on it to meet the children. Ueepe is delightful, and Carey and Charles explore, leaving Peter and Miss Price with the bed. When they return, Miss Price and Peter are gone, and the bed is cut off from them by high tide. Suddenly the two children are captured by cannibals and taken to a ritual dance, where they find Peter and Miss Price. All are going to be eaten. Miss Price, however, has a contest of magic with the cannibals' witch doctor, and wins. Turning the witch doctor into a frog, Miss Price barely escapes with the children on her broomstick, and they fly to the bed, which is about to be covered by the sea. Just in time they get away home.

Here, however, the children are in more trouble than they bargained for; their aunt, incensed at the mess they and the bed are in, plans to send them home. Before they leave, they visit Miss Price and learn some disheartening news. She has been having second thoughts about her magic and will give it up for a while. The children, though, are not ready to give up magic. When they leave, Paul brings the bed-knob.

MAGIC CITY, THE. E[dith] Nesbit Bland. Illus. H. R. Millar. London: Macmillan and Co., 1910. 333 pp. British.

Philip Haldane* was raised by his sister. When he is ten, she marries a widower with a daughter, Lucy Graham*, and Philip is left to stay alone in his new home. Miserable and bored, Philip builds a city out of books, toy blocks, and whatever else he can find, while Lucy's strict nurse is away. When she comes back, she threatens to tear it down. That night Philip goes downstairs to see how the city looks in the moonlight. Suddenly he seems to be on a large plain, which he crosses to a strange ladder that leads to a city on a great plateau. In the city, Philip is taken by soldiers, who are not sure what to do with him, for both the city's deliverer and destroyer, the prophets say, will come by that ladder, and they are not sure which he is. To Philip's dismay, Lucy is there, too.

After a night in the guardroom, Philip and Lucy are taken to Mr. Noah*, a judge. They are found guilty of trespass, and are sent to prison to await sentencing. Here Lucy convinces Philip that this is the city he himself had built and explains that she was in the room when he had come in and became changed when he did. Noah visits them, telling them about the city, Polistopolis*, and begging them to escape because keeping them prisoner is bad for his nerves; because the jailer echoes him, the children do escape. They are seen, however, and chased. Philip escapes by climbing down the ladder and sees a giant destroying the city. When he becomes his normal size, he sees that the giant is Lucy's nurse. Convinced that it had been a dream, Philip goes to bed.

The next morning, however, Lucy is missing, and a telegram is sent to her honeymooning father and stepmother. The city is gone and all Philip finds of it is the little toy figure of Noah he had put into the city. Desolate with guilt because he left Lucy behind, Philip wets Noah with his tears and the little figure comes to life, for tears have strong magic. Noah tells Philip that Lucy is still in the city, which is gone in this world but still exists in another. Philip can go there by building something and going through it. He builds a building, rubs a tear on one of the pillars, and, now made tiny, goes inside. Here he meets the carpenter who made Philip's first wooden blocks, and the man explains that if Philip wants to be the deliverer, he must accomplish seven deeds and become king. The first deed is to slay a dragon.

Philip is taken to see Noah, who knights him. At the ceremony a veiled lady, the Pretenderette*, appears; she claims to be the deliverer, but Philip already has that position. Should he fail his tasks, she will have her chance. Killing the dragon becomes complicated: Philip must first make his plans, then a princess is tied to a pillar, and Philip must carry out the slaying. When Philip sees the dragon, he realizes that it is a clockwork lizard he had once owned. Because dragons sleep for an hour after sunset, Philip has a chance to tie it by the key to one of the buildings; when the dragon wakes, it pulls out the key in its struggle and runs itself down trying to get the princess. The princess turns out to be Lucy, who had been captured and kept as a princess until the deliverer king should come.

Philip's second task is to remove a frustrating carpet by unravelling it, which he is able to do only with Lucy's help after she recognizes it as a crocheted mat she once made. Lucy helps Philip after he agrees to let her help him with the other tasks, too. The third task is to slay the fear of the Dwellers by the Sea*, who live three days' ride from the city. On the way Philip, Lucy, and the two dogs who go with them kill two lions. The Dwellers by the Sea live in what Philip recognizes as a sand castle he once built, and their fear is that the sea will wash it away. Philip and Lucy spend several delightful days with the Dwellers, until Philip decides to have an ark made and put on top of the castle so that the people can get away if the sea ever rises. Noah, of course, oversees the work.

At its completion, the Pretenderette seizes Philip and flies away with him on a winged horse. That night there is a storm and the tide washes away the castle. Lucy, Noah, and the Dwellers are safe in the ark and soon come to land. When Lucy and Noah visit an oracle, it tells them to take the ark to the Island-where-you-mayn't-go*, a lush place where only two people can land. Philip, meanwhile, is taken to the Island by the Pretenderette; he tumbles off as she flies over, but she cannot land, so she goes away. Philip has recognized her as Lucy's nurse. To his joy, Philip discovers his sister on the Island; because they had created it, only they can live there. They spend a happy time together until the ark comes, when, because there is no fear on the Island, Philip gives it to the Dwellers to live on forever.

In doing so, he has completed the fifth task—that of supplying Polistopolis with fruit, for the Island is the only place where fruit grows in all the country of Polistarchia*. Because the slaying of the lions was to be another task, only two deeds are left for Philip to accomplish. He must go to Somnolentia*, a town to the north, which the Great Sloth* has taken over, and keep him awake and busy, so that the inhabitants can help themselves; for whenever the Sloth sleeps, they sleep, and the place has fallen into ruin.

Philip, Lucy, and the dogs sail in a magic yacht up a river. Suddenly the river dips into a tunnel and comes out into an underground lake Lucy recognizes from one of her books: someone is opening the books Philip had used to build the city, and images are coming out. As they watch, a bucket is lowered from a hole in the ceiling of the cave. Seeing no other way out, Lucy and one of the dogs get into it and are pulled up. She finds herself in Somnolentia and is dismayed when the well she is pulled out of is shut; the Sloth has made a rule that the bucket can only be lowered forty times a day, and that was the fortieth. She carves the word "WAIT" into a pineapple and throws it down to Philip. The next day, he and the other dog are brought up.

While Philip tries to rally the citizens to revolt against the Sloth, Lucy talks that creature into wishing for a machine to draw water eight hours a day, leaving the people free to sing to the Sloth. Because this kind of wish is always granted, the machine appears, but the Sloth has to operate it, because the one wishing for the machine must be the one to use it. Philip organizes the roused citizens to take care of themselves.

The two children travel back to Polistopolis, only to discover that the Pretenderette has made herself queen and taken over, using warriors from one of the books Philip had used to build the city. Philip opens another book and calls on Julius Caesar*, who sends his legions to chase the other warriors back into their book. Caesar sends the Pretenderette to Somnolentia to make the Sloth enjoy his work and to make people love her; once that is accomplished, she can go back to her world. Philip is crowned, having delivered Polistopolis as his seventh task. He and Lucy return to their home by building a model of it. The model complete, they find themselves home.

Note: This work first appeared in *The Strand Magazine*, nos. 229–238 (Jan.-Nov., 1910).

MAGICAL CUPBOARD, THE. Jane Louise Curry. Illus. Charles Robinson. New York: Atheneum, 1976. 138 pp. American.

During a Christmas visit in 1976 with her aunt and uncle, Sagacity Hepsibah Walpole* (Sibby) and William Wingard* (Bill), Rosemary Walpole* is eager to search for the magical cupboard* that played a large role in an adventure she had in eighteenth-century New England the summer before.

In 1722, Thanatopsis and Sufferana Grout** steal the cupboard and take it with them when they flee the wrath of Thomas Cakebread*, whose mother spent time in their jail. Safely back at the orphanage they run, the Grouts try out the cupboard, which magically transforms objects put inside it—if the cupboard wants to. For the Grouts it refuses to work, but when Felicity Parmenter* (Fissy), one of the orphans, hides in it a small piece of gingerbread given her by Goliath Hollybush* (Golly), son of the housekeeper, the cupboard changes it into a gingerbread cake, which she shares with the other hungry orphans. Mrs. Hollybush's* other son, David Hollybush* (Davvy), begins to suspect that the Grouts are not who they pretend to be, and drops hints that someone is after them. Alarmed, they close the orphanage and give away all the orphans but Fissy. Fissy, according to a letter, is heir to a fur-trading company in New Hampshire, so the Grouts set out for there, taking Fissy, the cupboard, and the Hollybushes with them. Having collected furs in New Hampshire, they will go to Montreal to sell them and live in style.

Before they get far, Mrs. Grout and Golly leave the group to go to Boston, to sell some valuables. That night the other travelers stop at an inn and Fissy is left in the stable to guard the wagon all night. It is cold, and, hoping for shelter, she crawls into the cupboard—and finds herself on a bed in a cozy little room. Delighted, Fissy realizes that the cupboard is really enchanted. When she looks out the window, she sees a disturbing sight: it is the tavern but it is greatly changed, and as Fissy watches, two oddly dressed people emerge, discussing a cupboard, and get into a horrible metal monster, which leaves. A sign on the inn gives its name, with the dates 1676–1976. Puzzled, Fissy sleeps.

When she awakes the next morning, Fissy tries to get into that other time, where she might be happy, but she cannot. Suddenly, outside the cupboard she hears Mr. Grout telling Davvy about her inheritance; when Davvy opens the cupboard door, Fissy finds the room gone and herself in a cramped cupboard. As they travel a few days later, the group is attacked by robbers, who are frightened off when Golly rides up. He brings several well-laden horses, but Mrs. Grout is not with him; she has been recognized and arrested in Boston. Shaken by the news and the robbery, Mr. Grout seems to lose his reason. Mrs. Hollybush, bruised when the wagon fell almost on top of her as she hid beneath it, also loses part of her reason. Though Davvy wants to leave them behind, Golly will not let him.

The group travels on and at last reaches Fissy's inheritance, only to find that the house there has burned and that the fur trade is gone. Enraged at the turn of events, Davvy puts the strongbox containing their money into the cupboard, demanding that the cupboard increase it. When the door is opened, however, the strongbox is gone. Soon after that, Davvy leaves, never to be seen by them again. Golly and the others rebuild the farm and, when Fissy turns seventeen, he marries her. That day, Mrs. Grout, having been released from jail, finds them; overjoyed at his wife's return, Mr. Grout makes plans to go on to Montreal. When the cupboard is opened, the strongbox is there—filled with gold coins.

In the twentieth century, Rosemary, Sibby, and Bill visit an out-of-the-way antique store and are puzzled to find themselves expected. The old woman who owns it, Mrs. Leaf*, was born a Hollybush, and the store is in the old Hollybush house. The cupboard has been kept for over two hundred years, according to Fissy's instructions; learning that the cupboard was stolen, she had it kept for the "Sebby" and "Bill" she saw looking for it that long ago night at the inn. Mrs. Leaf tells them the rest of Fissy's story: on the way to Montreal, the cupboard had reached its present place and would not go further, so, after seeing the Grouts and Mrs. Hollybush safely to Montreal, Golly and Fissy sold their farm and built a new house on the present site. Stolen from Bill's ancestors long ago, the cupboard finally returns to its rightful owners.

MAGICIAN'S NEPHEW, THE. Clive Staples Lewis. Illus. Pauline Baynes. London: Bodley Head, 1955. 183 pp. British.

One very wet summer some time ago, Polly Plummer* and Digory Kirke* meet and became friends. Digory is miserable, for his mother is very ill and he and she have been sent to live with his uncle, Andrew Ketterley*, who seems to be mad. The children discover a passage behind Polly's attic that runs down the row of houses where they live. Trying for the empty house beyond, they come out instead into Uncle Andrew's study. He wants to use them in an experiment. They want no part of it, but Polly takes one of two yellow rings* he offers her and vanishes. Andrew has used dust from a distant world and created a yellow ring to take there all who touch it; the green rings he had created bring one back. To rescue Polly, Digory takes both green rings and the other yellow one and suddenly finds himself in the Wood Between the Worlds*, a lovely, peaceful wood in which lie many small pools. After Digory finds Polly, they start to return but realize that each pool must lead to another world. They make sure that they can actually get back to their own world and then they go off to another pool to have an adventure.

The pool leads Digory and Polly to an empty city on a blasted world. They explore a palace and come to a hall in which sit tall, richly dressed figures of men and women. In the middle of the hall hangs a bell; when Digory strikes it, part of the hall crumbles and the last figure, a woman, comes to life and leads them out of the palace as it collapses. She is Jadis*, who had destroyed her world to make herself queen of it and who then slept among the figures of her ancestors. Now she wants to go to Polly and Digory's younger world to rule it. The children try to get away from her, but Jadis has Polly by the hair and thus comes with them into the Wood. Here they again try to escape into their own world, but the queen comes with them, for she grabs Digory.

Andrew is overawed and frightened by Jadis and so obeys her commands. They go out to get what Jadis desires, and Digory waits for a chance to use the ring to take her out of the world. Suddenly Jadis drives up in a cab, followed by a crowd of people, including Frank*, the cab's owner. When the people make fun of Jadis, she attacks them with the cross-bar of a nearby lamppost, having cut the cabhorse free and jumped onto its back. Digory grabs her and, with Polly touching her ring, takes Jadis to the Wood between the Worlds. The horse, Strawberry, naturally comes as well, as do Frank and Uncle Andrew, who had hold of it. When Strawberry goes to drink at a nearby pool, they follow, still holding on, and the children use their rings to take them into whatever world the pool leads to.

It is dark, but they hear a voice singing beautiful music. Stars appear, and a sun, and in its light they see that the singer is a great lion. As he sings, grass and trees grow in the empty land. Hating the lion, Jadis throws the iron bar at him, but the lion pays no attention, and Jadis runs away. Before their eyes a lamppost grows where the bar had landed. Polly and Digory approach the lion after Digory decides to ask it if there is anything in this young, richly kindled place to heal his mother, and watches as, at the lion's song, animals come from the earth. The lion chooses some, including Strawberry, and sends the others away; the animals he chooses change size. The lion calls on Narnia* to wake and speak and understand, and fauns, dryads, and dwarfs* come from the woods; they and the animals the lion had chosen answer him. The lion is Aslan*, and he charges them with the keeping of Narnia. Some he calls to a council because evil has already entered the world. Strawberry takes Digory to Aslan, to ask his help. Andrew, meanwhile, is afraid of the lion and afraid of the place, and faints under the strain. The animals decide that he is a tree, and they plant him in the earth.

Digory asks Aslan for some sort of fruit to give his mother and must admit that he is responsible for Jadis's being there. Frank likes Narnia very well, and after calling Frank's wife, Aslan makes them its king and queen. Digory must undo the evil he has done by going west into the wilds there and bringing a silver apple* from a certain tree. To help him and Polly, Aslan turns Strawberry into Fledge*, a winged horse, who flies Digory and Polly west. When they rest that night and repeat their instructions, they hear something moving but see nothing. The next day they come to a beautiful garden surrounded by a wall; on the gate is an injunction to take the fruit only for others. Inside Digory finds the tree of silver apples and takes one. Jadis is there, having come ahead of them, and has eaten an apple. Though she tempts him to eat an apple or take one to his mother, Digory resists. Fledge takes him and Polly back to Aslan.

At his order Digory throws the apple. Andrew, who, the animals have realized, is not a tree, is freed and sent into a merciful sleep by Aslan. Out of the gold and silver coins Andrew had had, gold and silver trees have grown, and their branches are used by the dwarfs to make crowns for their new king and queen. From the seeds of the apple grows a beautiful tree that will shield Narnia, and from this tree Digory is allowed an apple to take to his mother. Aslan takes Andrew and the children back to the Wood between the Worlds and sends them home.

Digory gives the apple to his mother and it seems to help her. He buries the core in the back garden and, the next day, buries the rings around the seedling that has come up. His mother gets well. Digory grows up to become a professor, and he and Polly stay close friends. When the apple tree falls because of a storm, Digory has it made into a wardrobe* with certain properties. Uncle Andrew never tries magic again, but he has awed memories of Jadis.

MAGISTER STEPHANUS (*The Cat Who Wished to Be a Man*). *See* Stephanus, Magister

MAIA, a character from Greek mythology who appears in P[amela] L[yndon] Travers's* *Mary Poppins**. She is one of the Pleiades, the sister of Electra, Tagete, Alcyone, Celaeno, Sterope, and little Merope, the baby. With her sisters, Maia goes hunting with Orion and makes and stores the spring rains. One Christmas the sisters cast lots to see who will do the Christmas shopping, and Maia wins; during her brief visit to London, she meets Mary Poppins* and Jane Caroline and Michael George Banks** in the department store where she gets her gifts. Maia brings out the kindness in people; the clerks treat her like a queen and, because she has no money, the gifts are free. Maia gets nothing for herself, so Mary Poppins gives her her cherished new gloves.

MAIMIE MANNERING (*Peter Pan in Kensington Gardens*). *See* Mannering, Maimie

MAITLAND POPE (*An Enemy at Green Knowe*). *See* Pope, Maitland

MALEBRON, a character in Alan Garner's* *Elidor**. He is a king in Elidor*, a magical land. This lame man recognized *The Lay of the Starved Fool*, an ancient book read for its nonsense, as confused prophecy, and, when the power of evil began to take over Elidor, he struggled to discover the truth of it. Finally he finds the one musical note that opens a gate between Elidor and the London of David, Helen, Nicholas, and Roland Watson****, four figures of the prophecy, and brings them one by one into his world, sending them into a mound to retrieve three of four Treasures* essential to Elidor; he himself bears the fourth, the Spear of Ildana, until he gives it to Roland. Once the Treasures have been found, Malebron sends them with the children back to their world, for safe-keeping. He then takes up the search for Findhorn*, whose song will bring Elidor back to life. From Gorias, a castle, Malebron witnesses the reburgeoning of Elidor at Findhorn's death. Though he appears in London as on old beggar, in his own land Malebron is tall and yellow-haired and dressed in gold, shining like sunlight.

MALLORY, a character in Lloyd Alexander's* *The Wizard in the Tree**. Young Mallory is an orphan; her mother and her carpenter father died of a fever. Now she lives as maid-of-all-work with Mr. and Mrs. Parsel**, who run the village cookshop. Cruel Mrs. Parsel works her mercilessly, but Mallory keeps up her spirits by thinking of the fairy tales her mother used to tell her. When she finds Arbican*, an enchanter, in a felled oak, Mallory thinks she has found her fairy godparent. but Arbican soon sets her straight. The girl helps him get out of the scrapes his erratic powers get him into, and together they expose the murderer of Squire Sorrel. On his exposure as the murderer, Squire Scrupnor's* fortune goes to Mallory. As a result of her adventures Mallory learns to rely less on fairy tales and more on herself, for fairy tales are not about what has actually happened but about the possibilities of the human spirit.

MALPLAQUET, a place in *Mistress Masham's Repose**, by T[erence] H[anbury] White*. Parts of this justly famous palace are very old: the infamous dungeons were built in William the Conqueror's time. The castle that once stood above the dungeons was blown up by Cromwell, and on the site the present house was erected. Malplaquet is huge, about four times longer than Buckingham Palace, and it has 365 windows, fifty two state bedrooms, and twelve company rooms, besides a kitchen a little too small for an airplane hangar and innumerable stairways and corridors; the cook, Mrs. Noakes*, bicycles down the corridor when she is wanted. The grounds are equally spacious, being twenty-five miles in circumference and including two lakes, several avenues, many monuments and temples, and acres of gardens. Some of the world's most famous people have visited here, including the two princes King Richard shut up in the Tower of London, Guy Fawkes, Alexander Pope, Charles I, Sir Francis Bacon, Edward Gibbon, Jonathan Swift, Dr. Johnson, the Empress Amelia, Lola Montez, the King of Bavaria, and Queen Victoria, who held a Drawing Room here. Secret inhabitants include Lilliputians*, who had escaped from a travelling show in the eighteenth century. Once splendid—having been designed by Christopher Wren, Capability Brown, and others; plastered by Adam among others; and furnished by Sheraton, Hepplewhite, and Chippendale—by the time it comes to Maria*, Malplaquet is in sorry shape. Most of its more valuable pieces have been sold to keep up the place, but it is a ruin, its gardens overgrown. When Maria comes into an unexpected inheritance, she restores Malplaquet to its former glory, hiring 365.2564 men to keep up the estate.

MAMGU, a character in *The Change-Child**, by Jane Louise Curry*. She is the maternal grandmother of Eilian Roberts* and the mother of Emrys*. This redoubtable old woman is the "Queen" of the Red Fairies*, a band of thieves and con artists living near the Great Dark Wood, and she is an absolute ruler. When Eilian comes under her protection, Mamgu tries to send the girl to Simon Rastall*, the nobleman's son she is fleeing; the old woman hopes to thereby win the safety of the Red Fairies. She is thwarted when Emrys comes to Eilian's rescue.

MANAN, a character in *The Tombs of Atuan**, by Ursula K. LeGuin*. This eunuch is dedicated to the Nameless Ones* on Atuan*; he guards and serves the nameless Priestess of these gods. Manan was born on Atuan, in the green hills of the northern part of that island. He helped search for the reborn Priestess of the Nameless Ones and was there when Tenar*, believed to be the deathless Priestess reborn, was found. Manan also plays a part in the ceremony which takes away the girl's identity. As she grows, Manan is the only person to give Tenar affection. When the girl, now the One Priestess of the Tombs, finds Ged*, a sorcerer, in the Labyrinth* beneath the temple grounds, Manan counsels her to kill him and is disturbed when she does not. He never ceases to obey her, however, though he finally tries to kill Ged by pushing him into a pit. It is Manan himself, however, who falls and is killed.

MANNERING, MAIMIE, a character in James M. Barrie's* *Peter Pan in Kensington Gardens**. Four-year-old Maimie has an older brother, Tony Mannering*, whom she terrifies at night with an imaginary goat. When Tony breaks his promise to spend a night in Kensington Gardens, brave Maimie takes his place and has many adventures. She gives encouragement to Brownie* and follows the little fairy to the ball. Chased by the angry fairies, Maimie falls and sleeps in the snow; the fairies build a house around her so that she will not freeze. When Maimie meets Peter Pan*, he is so taken with her that he askes her to marry him, but Maimie goes back to her mother. The girl later gives Peter her imaginary goat as an Easter present.

MANNERING, TONY, a character in *Peter Pan in Kensington Gardens** by James M. Barrie*. Tony is the six year old brother of Maimie Mannering*. A brave boy in the daytime, Tony is afraid at night, especially when his little sister terrorizes him with an imaginary goat. When Tony breaks a promise to stay the night in Kensington Gardens, Maimie takes his place.

MANUSCRIPT, THE, an object in *Over Sea, Under Stone** and *Greenwitch**, by Susan Cooper*. It was written long ago, on parchment, in an ancient, difficult alphabet. The writing on the manuscript explains the inscription on a golden grail* that holds a prophecy concerning the final coming of King Arthur*; neither piece of writing is readable without the other. When the grail was hidden centuries ago in Cornwall, the manuscript was put into it, safely rolled up, in a lead case. Here it stayed until the twentieth century, when Barnabas, Jane, and Simon Drew*** find it. In a struggle with evil people who seek to get the grail and the manuscript, the parchment, in its case, falls into the sea. Here it is found by the Greenwitch*, a sacrificial figure thrown into the sea, and the witch keeps it for its own, finally giving it up to Jane, who had pitied the figure. Once Will Stanton*, Merriman Lyon*, and Captain Toms*, three of the forces of good, use the manuscript to translate the cup's inscription, the manuscript is destroyed.

MARA, a type of creature in Alan Garner's* *The Weirdstone of Brisingamen**. These troll-women come from rock, and to rock they return if the light of day touches them. They are grotesque, vaguely woman-shaped but misshapen. Physically powerful, the mara have very little intelligence and seem to be unable to think at all; when they are sent to track Cadellin Silverbrow* and his companions, they do literally that, following his tracks in the snow but losing those who have made them once the tracks stop. When one of the mara accidentally touches the Mark of Fohla*, a powerful bracelet, the troll-woman melts into a boulder. The mara are swallowed up with the rest of his forces by Fenrir of Ragnarok, sent by Nastrond, their evil lord, in his fury.

MARCELLINE, a character in *The Tapestry Room**, by Mrs. Mary Molesworth*. This old lady is the nurse of Jeanne*; she had been the nurse of Jeanne's mother, too. Where Marcelline's childhood was spent, she will not tell; though she never leaves Jeanne's house in France, Marcelline claims to visit her childhood home often. She knows things she does not tell and is often mysterious. When Hugh*, Jeanne's cousin, comes to stay with the family, he feels that she understands many things he cannot put into words. She is very good at telling stories and may be the beautiful lady dressed in white who spins stories; Hugh and Jeanne meet her during a magical adventure they have one night. If she is, she is well over four hundred years old and is possibly as old as man, for the white lady spins all the stories that have been told in the world.

MARGALO, a character in *Stuart Little**, by E[lwyn] B[rooks] White*. This sweet little brown bird with yellow on her breast is from "fields once tall with wheat, from pastures deep in fern and thistle...from vales of meadowsweet" and she loves to whistle. In New York City, she is overcome with the cold and is taken in by Mrs. Frederick C. Little*. Here Margalo becomes friends with Stuart Little*, Mrs. Little's tiny, mouse-like son. The family cat, Snowbell*, reacts to Margalo as a cat would, and Stuart must defend her. When Snowbell plots with another cat to help the other eat Margalo, the bird is warned by a pigeon, and she leaves, flying north, for winter is over. Heartbroken, Stuart runs away to look for her.

MARGAN, a character in Jane Louise Curry's* *The Sleepers**. She is the sister of Artair* and the mother of Medraut*. Margan is also known as Fata Morgana. Intent on the destruction of Artair, Margan persuaded Nimiane* into imprisoning Myrddin*, the king's adviser, in the Eildon Tree*. The lady later slept away the ages until the twentieth century, when she and her son wake and set into motion her plans for Artair's final destruction. Assuming the guise of an archaeological research committee, Margan's group excavates to discover the chamber where Artair and his men lie sleeping amid the *Brenhin Dlyseu**, the Thirteen Treasures of Prydein. Margan plans to kill the men and take the Treasures, which will give her control over Britain. She is thwarted, however, when Henry Peter Huntington* discovers and rings the Bell of Rhûn*, waking Artain and his men, who defeat Margan before they sail to safety beyond the seas, taking the Treasures with them. *See also* Fay, Morgan le; Fay, Morgan the; Morrigan, the

MARGARET ARTHUR *(Beneath the Hill)*. *See* Arthur, Margaret

MARGARET BASSUMTYTE *(The Bassumtyte Treasure)*. *See* Bassumtyte, Margaret

MARIA, the main character in T[erence] H[anbury] White's* *Mistress Masham's Repose**. She is an orphan. Maria lives at the ancient family home of Malplaquet*, a place rich in history but now quite in ruins, for the family fortunes have fallen. She is looked after by Mrs. Noakes*, the cook, and by Miss Brown*, the governess. Friendly and possessing a loving heart, Maria is the kind of person who does things first and thinks about them later. Though bold, she is afraid of cows and of Miss Brown, with good reason, for the woman torments her in subtle ways, making her life as miserable as possible. When she is ten years old, Maria wears glasses, though she will not have to wear them always. When she is ten, she also meets the Lilliputians* who have been living in Mistress Masham's Repose, an island in the Quincunx, a lake. Maria's first temptation is to treat these tiny people as she would toys, taking them from their work and homes and playing games of adventure with them, despite the advice of her friend, the Professor*. The Lilliputians, who had begun to trust Maria, soon avoid her whenever possible. Finally, when a young Lilliputian farmer is hurt in the crash of a tiny airplane Maria has decided the Lilliputians need, she realizes that they are not toys, but people, and she treats them with the dignity they deserve. They in turn help her when she is imprisoned by Miss Brown and the vicar, Mr. Hater*, who want the Lilliputians, to sell to a circus. Since an ancient parchment has been found that makes it possible for Maria to inherit a fortune, she becomes rich enough to renovate Malplaquet and hire the Professor to be her tutor, replacing Miss Brown, who is now in prison.

MARIA OLDKNOW (the Green Knowe books). *See* Oldknow, Maria

MARK OF FOHLA, a bracelet in Alan Garner's* *The Weirdstone of Brisingamen** and *The Moon of Gomrath**. There are at least three Marks, and all are from the early magic of the world. Engraved exactly alike, of silver and black enamel, they differ in which of the two colors predominates. The Marks are associated with the moon, and those who wear them can have magical powers that wax or wane according to the moon: Angharad Goldenhand's* powers are at their full force when the moon is full; those of the Morrigan* are greatest during the old moon; Susan* comes into her fullest power when the moon is new. She receives her Mark from Angharad, and it protects her, for evil cannot abide it. When she loans it to Atlendor, king of the elves*, the girl is almost destroyed by the Morrigan. Susan knows little of how to use the Mark, but special knowledge is not necessary, for certain words of power engraved on the bracelet glow and give her power when she speaks them. When they go against the Morrigan, Atlendor and his warriors touch their spears and arrows to the Mark, so that the weapons will make wounds that gall evil. Because Susan wears the Mark, Garanhir*, the lord of the Wild Hunt*, treats her with respect.

MAROONER'S ROCK, a place in *Peter and Wendy**, by James M. Barrie*. This rock is in the middle of the Mermaid's Lagoon* in Neverland*. It is completely covered at high tide and got its name because pirates leave their prisoners here to drown. After Peter Pan* rescues Tiger Lily* from the rock, the Indians become his friends. Trapped on the rock, Peter experiences perhaps the only moment of fear in his life.

MARSH-WIGGLE, a race of beings in the Chronicles of Narnia*, by C[live] S[taples] Lewis*. They live in the marshes in the northern part of Narnia*, dwelling in reed huts and fishing for their food. The Marsh-wiggles are perfectly adapted for their life, for they have long, thin arms and legs and their hands and feet are webbed. The Marsh-wiggles have long, somber faces and a sober outlook on life. Though they enjoy good food and good drink and good times, they always see the dark side of everything. The Marsh-wiggles usually take charge of the jobs in Narnia requiring one to be around water; they are ferrymen, for the most part. One, Puddleglum*, goes on a journey to the mountains of the north to rescue Rilian*, a lost prince.

MARTHA, a character in *Five Children and It**, by E[dith] Nesbit Bland*. She is a servant in the house where Cyril*, Jane*, Anthea*, Robert*, and the Lamb* spend one of their summer holidays. Martha has a lot to put up with when the children discover a Psammead* who grants their wishes—particularly since everyone but her can see the effects of the wishes, the children having wished that the servants not notice anything different, no matter what they wish. At least once this wish stands them in good stead, when Martha almost convinces two men that they are mad because they see money the children have wished up, and she does not. Martha becomes engaged to a gamekeeper.

MARTHA TIMMS (*The Whispering Knights*). *See* Timms, Martha

MARVELOUS ADVENTURES OF SEBASTIAN, THE. Lloyd Alexander. New York: E. P. Dutton and Co., 1970. 204 pp. National Book Award, 1971. American.

After he accidentally insults Count Lobelieze*, Royal Treasurer of Hamelin-Loring*, Sebastian* is dismissed from his position as violinist in a baron's orchestra. Sebastian is unused to the ways of the world, but he is ready for adventure, and he finds it when he resuces a white cat from some superstitious villagers who are going to hang it as a disguised witch. In the melee, Sebastian's fiddle is smashed, but he finds the cat a good companion and names him Presto*. They come to a town where hungry Sebastian is caught stealing eggs and is rescued by Nicholas*, a mysterious little man who informs Sebastian that he could have been hanged for stealing, according to the new laws of Count Grinssorg*, the Regent. They travel together, meeting roadmenders who complain of Grinssorg's tyranny and speak of "Captain Freeling," a Robin Hood figure who fires Sebastian's imagination.

Nicholas and Sebastian come to an inn and there meet Isabel Charlotte Theodora Fredericka* (Isabel), the orphaned princess of Hamelin-Loring, who, disguised as a boy, is fleeing her betrothed, the Regent. She is going to seek the help of her uncle, who rules the kingdom to the north. Nicholas and Sebastian decide to help her and realize that they would be safer away from the inn, particularly after they discover that the innkeeper has been murdered by a mysterious barber* who tries to kill Sebastian. On the road they come again upon the roadmenders, who are seeking to join Captain Freeling. When they come upon soldiers and a fight breaks out, Nicholas sends Sebastian and Isabel on ahead. The two stay the night in a deserted farmhouse.

The next day, they meet Quicksilver* and his troupe, Quicksilver's Gallimaufry-Theatricus, which they join because it is going north and Nicholas has not come. Among the troupe's shabby props Sebastian finds a lovely violin* which, Quicksilver tells him, is cursed: it will play only for a true musician and then seems to pull the life from him. Sebastian finds that he can play the violin, which has a lovely voice. The troupe comes to a village, where it sets up a stage and inflates the huge balloon used for balloon rides. At the performance that day, Sebastian sees the murderous barber. The Gallimaufry-Theatricus acrobat, jealous of the attention paid to Sebastian and his violin, brings constables who try to arrest Sebastian for the murder of the innkeeper. As the rest of the troupe fights to defend him, he and Isabel escape in the balloon, cheered when it drifts north toward their goal. During the night, however, a storm comes up, and the next morning they come down off course—in the middle of Loringhold*, where Grinssorg's palace is located.

Frantically trying to escape the city, Sebastian and Isabel literally run into Count Lobelieze, the Treasurer, and they take refuge with a washerwoman, who goes for help. Alarmed when an obviously fake beggar approaches the house, the two run and make their way through the town gate. There they accept a ride in a coach, only to find that it is occupied by the murderous barber, who takes them back into town. When the coach is suddenly stopped, Sebastian and Isabel are rescued by the fake beggar, who takes them to a safe place where they wait and meet Captain Freeling. To their astonishment, the captain turns out to be Nicholas.

He arranges for Isabel to escape by ship to her uncle, and at the appointed time the disguised travelers go to the wharf. Here they are stopped by port officials, who, thinking Sebastian has stolen the violin he carries, try to arrest him. In the resulting melee, Sebastian, Nicholas, and Isabel are cut off from the others. Sebastian runs and, after a brief and ugly struggle with the murderous barber, Sebastian is captured and flung into the prison under the palace.

The young man shares his cell with Quicksilver, who has lost his fight with the constables. They are rescued by Presto, who brings a skeleton key, which was tied around his neck by an enemy of the Regent. Quickly the lock is picked and their belongings found, but in trying to escape, Sebastian finds himself in the palace ballroom. Here he is mistaken for a member of the orchestra and ordered to play. The magical music of the violin forces all who hear it to dance, and Sebastian feels the strength gradually being drawn from him into the music. Grinssorg, the Regent, who hates music, draws his sword to kill Sebastian. Suddenly the young man is knocked down by Presto, who leaps to his shoulder, and when Sebastian comes to himself, he finds the Regent dead and the violin broken.

Isabel retakes the throne and makes Nicholas First Minister of State. The princess would gladly share her rule with Sebastian, but the young man has discovered that music is his life and he wants to learn more about it. Then he will come back and marry Isabel.

MARY, QUEEN OF SCOTS. *See* Stuart, Mary

MARY BUCKLE BRIGHT (*Mindy's Mysterious Miniature*). *See* Bright, Mrs. Mary Buckle

MARY GREYTHORNE (*The Dark Is Rising*; *Silver on the Tree*). *See* Greythorne, Mary

MARY POPPINS. *See* Poppins, Mary

MARY POPPINS. P[amela] L[yndon] Travers. Illus. Mary Shepard. N.p.: Gerald Howe, 1934. 206 pp. British.

One day their nanny quits without warning, and that evening a startled Jane Caroline and Michael George Banks** watch as Mary Poppins* arrives literally on the east wind. Engaged to be their nanny, she slides up the banister to the nursery, brings her things out of an apparently empty carpetbag, and makes herself at home. She will stay until the wind changes. In the meantime, the Banks children have many adventures with magical, sometimes caustic Mary Poppins.

On her day out, Mary Poppins meets Herbert Alfred* (Bert), the match-man/sidewalk artist, but he has no money to take her to tea. Instead, they go into one of his pictures and have a wonderful time. One Friday Jane, Michael, and Mary Poppins visit Albert Wigg*. Because it is a Friday and his birthday besides, he is filled with laughing gas, so they find him floating near the ceiling. Jane and Michael, laughing at him, find themselves floating, too; when Mary Poppins joins them, they have a lovely tea. Later the thought of having to go home is so sad that it deflates them and they come down. On the way home, Mary Poppins is very offended when they speak of Mr. Wiggs's floating.

One day, in the park, they all meet Andrew*, a pampered lapdog, who converses with Mary Poppins, though she will not tell the children what the conversation is about. They soon find out, for Andrew returns to his finicky owner with his mongrel friend. As Mary Poppins translates, he insists that the mongrel live with him and his owner and that Andrew not be made to wear overcoats or go to the hairdresser again. His flustered owner agrees. One day when Jane is in bed with an earache, a cow comes down the street, and Mary Poppins tells her and Michael about it: it is Red Cow*, who had been most respectable until one night she had begun to dance and could not stop. Learning that she had a star stuck on her horn, Red Cow had jumped over the moon, and when she came to earth, she danced no more. Dissatisfied because she misses the dancing, now she travels from place to place on the advice of Mary Poppins's mother, hoping to catch another star on her horn.

Not long after this, Michael wakes and is naughty all day. That afternoon he finds a compass in the park; Mary Poppins uses it to take them all to visit friends in the North, the South, the East, and the West before they go home. So naughty is Michael that he is sent to bed early, and he takes the compass and tries to use it. The people they had met on their earlier trip appear and menace him before he calls for Mary Poppins and they vanish; having been very bad, now he feels very good. The children also visit the Bird Woman* who Jane thinks cares for the birds as a hen does her chicks.

One day, while shopping, Mary Poppins takes the children to a strange little sweetshop, where they meet Mrs. Clara Corry*, a spry little woman whose fingers are sweets and who is old enough to remember the world being made. Here they buy gingerbread stars with gilt paper on them. That night, Mary Poppins leaves the nursery, and Jane and Michael watch as she joins Mrs. Corry and her daughters to glue the gilt stars from the gingerbread to the sky. On an afternoon when Jane and Michael are at a party, their younger sister and brother, Barbara and John Banks**, discover that they will forget how to speak the language of sunlight and of birds as they grow up; though they declare that they will not, they do.

On the evening of a day when Mary Poppins has been very impatient, a voice calls to Jane and Michael after they are put to bed, and they follow it to the zoo. Because they are special guests, they are allowed in. Here they find the animals loose and the people who had been left in the zoo after it had closed in cages, because it is Mary Poppins's birthday, which has fallen on a full moon. A Hamadryad* gives Mary Poppins its cast-off skin as a gift, and Jane and Michael watch as the animals dance around Mary Poppins. All creation, the Hamadryad tells them, is one. The next morning Mary Poppins denies all the nights events, but she is wearing a lovely snakeskin belt.

Christmas shopping, the children meet Maia*, one of the Pleiades, come down from her constellation to do Christmas shopping. She selects presents for all her sisters, but there is none for her, so Mary Poppins gives her her cherished new gloves, and the children watch Maia walk back into the sky. On the first day of spring, the wind is in the west. Mary Poppins is oddly quiet that day, and she gives Michael her compass. That evening, the children watch as she opens her umbrella and is carried away by the wind. Beneath Jane's pillow is a package containing Mary's picture, with a note reading "au revoir"—to meet again.

Note: This work seems to have had at least two revisions (P. L. Travers. Letter to the Editor. *The Horn Book Magazine*, 58 [June, 1982], p. 243.), most of them to chapter 6, "Bad Tuesday," because of alleged racism in the chapter. The eskimo family living in the north has been changed to a polar bear friend; instead of an African family in the south, the travelers meet a macaw friend named Heather; in the east, they meet a panda in place of a mandarin; and in the west, in place of a native American, they meet a family of dolphins.

MARY POPPINS BOOKS, three episodic novels having as their central character Mary Poppins*. *See Mary Poppins*; *Mary Poppins Comes Back*; *Mary Poppins Opens the Door*. Four related works are *Mary Poppins in the Park*, *Mary Poppins from A to Z*, *Mary Poppins in the Kitchen*, and *Mary Poppins in Cherry Tree Lane*.

MARY POPPINS COMES BACK. P[amela] L[yndon] Travers. Illus. Mary Shepard. London: Lovat Dickson and Thompson, 1935. 303 pp. British.

Ever since Mary Poppins* had left the family, nothing has gone right at the Banks's house. One day Jane Caroline and Michael George Banks** are sent to the park. Here they fly a kite, which disappears behind a cloud for a moment; when they bring it down they find, not the kite, but Mary Poppins at the end of the string. She will stay and be their nanny until the chain of her locket breaks, and she is very offended that they think she has come to them on the end of a kite string, though the kite tail hangs from her coat pocket. So begin adventures for the Banks children with loving, sharp-tongued Mary Poppins.

One afternoon Euphemia Andrew*, who had been the children's father's governess, sends word that she is coming. When she arrives, she proves herself a true holy terror, unafraid to criticize everything and everyone, including Mary Poppins. Mary Poppins discovers the caged lark Miss Andrew keeps and sets it free; when Miss Andrew finds out, she is angry, but Mary Poppins gives her a look and Miss Andrew scurries into the cage, which the lark picks up and flies up with before dropping it and heading south. When Miss Andrew lands, she is terrified of Mary Poppins; she apologizes and begs to be allowed to go, and then does. Mary Poppins denies having done anything.

Jane wakes early one morning and is annoyed at being routed out of bed first, annoyed at being the eldest, and so naughty that she is not allowed to go to tea at the neighbor's. Left alone, in anger she cracks the Royal Doulton bowl* on the mantel and is chidden by one of the three boys pictured on it, whose knee has been hurt by the crack. The three bring Jane into the bowl and play, finally taking her deeper into the bowl and introducing Jane to the rest of their family. Now in the past, Jane cannot go home, but when she calls for Mary Poppins, the nanny appears and pulls her out of the bowl. In doing so, Mary Poppins loses her scarf. The children later see it lying on the grass in the bowl's picture, and they see that Jane's handkerchief is where she had left it, wrapped around the boy's hurt knee.

On a rainy day, they take the bowl to be mended by Arthur Turvey*, Mary Poppins's cousin. When they arrive, he is hanging out the window and must be hauled in; it is the second Monday of the month, when everything goes wrong for him from three to six in the afternoon. Because he is so busy and wants to be in, he has been automatically out. Now, wanting to be rightside up, he goes upside down. Jane and Michael do, too, as do the buildings outside the window. Mr. Turvey fixes the bowl, Marry Poppins turns upside down, and they all have tea; Topsy Tartlet*, his unfriendly landlady, comes up and is suddenly upside down, too, and very cheerful. They all have a happy time until six o'clock, when all goes back to normal but Miss Tartlet; she is so happy that Mr. Turvey asks her to marry him and she agrees. When they leave, Mary Poppins is quite put out that the children say her cousin is odd.

Annabel Banks* is born one day and is convinced that she will always remember the long, dark journey she has come on. She forgets it in a week, becoming concerned with the things of this world. One day, in the park, Mary Poppins and the children meet the devil-may-care Dirty Rascal, whose clothes are fringed with bells, and Mary Poppins tells his story: once there was a king who could not learn, until the Rascal came and taught him true wisdom. When the two climbed a rainbow together, the king stayed on it, but the Rascal came over and now wanders the world, bringing good luck to those he works for. As the children leave the park, they see the Rascal ahead of them, going to their home. He is not there when they arrive, but Robertson Ay*, their lazy servant, is; they hear the tinkle of bells when he moves in sleep, and Mary Poppins is oddly gentle with him.

Many shooting stars appear on Mary Poppins's night out; one comes in and takes Jane and Michael into the sky, where they watch a circus of the stars and see the performers hail Mary Poppins. When it is time to leave, she is kissed by the sun. The next day, Mary Poppins denies everything, but the mark of the kiss burns on her cheek. After they run their errands one day, Mary Poppins buys balloons for the children with the leftover money. Having chosen their balloons carefully, the children are delighted to find their names on their choices. The balloons lift them into the air, where they are joined by many people with balloons, and they go home, wondering what would have happened had Mary Poppins not been with them.

One snowy day when it seems that spring will never come, Mary Poppins takes the children to the park. Jane and Michael follow her to a large, ark-like house, where they meet Nellie-Rubina Noah*, who, with her uncle, is making trees, flowers, and birds out of wood. That night, the children watch as Mary Poppins leaves. The ark is nearby, and she and Nellie-Rubina place the wooden things in the park before the ark sails away through the air. The next morning, spring has come.

On a quiet day, Robertson Ay tells the children of the merry-go-round in the park, and Mary Poppins takes them to it. Jane is oddly sad, and people seem to be saying goodbye to Mary Poppins. After the children take a long, lovely ride, Mary Poppins gets on, with her carpetbag. The merry-go-round moves faster and faster, until suddenly the chain breaks on Mary Poppins's locket and it flies off. The picture in the locket is of all the Banks children. They watch as the merry-go-round rises off the ground and spins off into the sky. When they go home, the children believe that Mary Poppins will return. That night a new star shines in the sky—it is the merry-go-round.

MARY POPPINS OPENS THE DOOR. P[amela] L[yndon] Travers. Illus. Mary Shepard. London: Peter Davies, 1944. 219 pp. British.

As has been usual since Mary Poppins* left the Banks house, things have been going wrong this November 5. Jane Caroline and Michael George Banks** go off with Herbert Alfred* (Bert) and a chimney sweep to set off their fireworks in the park. One rocket goes off but does not explode; a spark that drifts toward them turns out to be Mary Poppins, who goes home with the children to be their nanny. She will stay until the door opens. True to form, Mary Poppins is offended that the children think she has come from a rocket, though on her umbrella are the rocket's stars. The children have several adventures with acid but loving Mary Poppins.

One day they go to Fred Twigley*, Mary Poppins's cousin, to get the piano tuned. Because he gets seven wishes on certain days, his greedy landlady, Mrs. Sarah Clump*, wants to marry him. When she comes in, Mr. Twigley wishes himself in a nice, safe place and is suddenly a figure on a music box, as are the children and Mary Poppins. To get rid of Mrs. Clump, Mr. Twigley wishes for her what she wants—but his way: she becomes tiny and goes to live in a tiny golden palace. When Mary Poppins and the children leave, Mr. Twigley's house and the street it is on vanish, and Mary Poppins is offended that the children think she had stood on a music box. The piano is tuned when they get home, for Mr. Twigley has done it with a wish, and outside sings a nightingale he had been fixing when they left.

The day after his birthday Michael has a toothache from too many sweets. Suddenly the flowery china cat* he had gotten as a gift comes to life and goes to see the queen; Mary Poppins tells the children why: King Cole*, very fond of facts, had had everyone thinking and thinking, while the palace had become dull and mouse-infested and the queen had grown lonely. When a cat came and was insolent to him, Cole made a bargain with it; each would ask three questions of the other, and the winner would rule the kingdom. The cat had won. Cole realized that he was not the cleverest man in the world but he was quite merry, so he had concentrated on that. The cat gave back the kingdom, receiving the queen's flower necklace and permission to come and look at her. Suddenly there are shouts from downstairs, for the children's father has seen a strange animal. It is the cat, returning.

On a lovely day, the children go with Mary Poppins to the park. Here a marble statue, Neleus*, comes off his pedestal. Though she is angry with him, Mary Poppins allows him to stay down the rest of the afternoon. He explains to the children how lonely he is for the rest of his family, who are far away over the sea. People remark on Neleus's nakedness, so Mary Poppins gives him her new jacket; when he sadly goes back onto his pedestal, the jacket becomes marble. This, the city officials decide, is a vast improvement over the naked statues. That night the children think of Neleus dreaming of home.

Jane and Michael have longed for horses. When one day they go out shopping with Mary Poppins they go to Miss Calico*, who sells peppermint walking sticks for a pin. Each child buys one, and they soon discover that they can ride the walking sticks through the air; Mary Poppins rides her umbrella. Hundreds of people are also riding peppermint sticks as the children ride home. That night, they hear a whistle and see Miss Calico ride by, calling to her all her peppermint steeds.

It is the second Thursday, Mary Poppins's night out. That evening, when Jane and Michael listen to a shell and hear a voice inviting them to dive into it, they do. They find themselves in the sea, going to a High-Tide party. Mary Poppins arrives at the party and is given a starfish pin. After a dance, the children are suddenly home and it is morning, and Mary Poppins is wearing a starfish-shaped pin. On New Year's Eve, when she puts the children to bed, Mary Poppins shuts their toy animals into a cupboard with their books. At midnight Jane and Michael wake. The toys have come alive and lead them into the park, where they meet the people form the storybooks, who are all friendly with one another; in the crack between the old year and the new, all live happily ever after. When Mary Poppins comes, there is a dance. At the last stroke of twelve, all run away and vanish; Jane and Michael find themselves in bed, and it is morning. Though Mary Poppins denies all that has happened, the feet of the toys are wet, and so are the children's slippers.

On a chilly morning, Jane and Michael watch their reflections in the nursery window. Mary Poppins is very busy that day, and Jane feels as if she is going to lose something, especially after Mary Poppins gives them her precious dominoes. On the way back from the park, many old friends come and say goodbye: Nellie-Rubina Noah*, Mrs. Clara Corry*, Albert Wigg*, Mr. Twigley, Miss Calico, Bert, and many others. Mary Poppins goes into the house, and all watch as a reflection of the nursery appears on the wall of the house, including the door into the nursery. Realizing that Mary Poppins is leaving, the children rush into the house, but she is not there. In the reflection of the room, they see Mary Poppins go through the nursery door and float off under her umbrella into darkness, a glowing figure like a shooting star. Jane and Michael wish on it that they will always remember Mary Poppins and all she has shown them.

MARY SWEENEY (*Mr. Wilmer*). *See* Sweeney, Mary

MATTHEW COBHAM (*The Driftway*). *See* Cobham, Matthew

MATTHEW HOPKINS (*The Devil on the Road*). *See* Hopkins, Mathew

MATTHEW MADDOX (*A Swiftly Tilting Planet*). *See* Maddox, Matthew

MATTICK, DELANO (DELLY), a character in Jane Louise Curry's *The Watchers**. He is the son of Harry and Luce Mattick. Delly had a twin brother who was killed in Vietnam; Delly himself spent over a year in a Veterans Administration hospital. Though shy and sometimes uncertain, Delly gains a kind of strength through his compulsion to protect Twilly's Green Hollow* and the people who live there. He is perhaps the only person living there who understands something of what the Hollow contains; Penn Dreego's* father taught him about Tûl Isgrun* and what lies there, seeing, perhaps, that the boy would become the Watcher of his generation. Delly successfully defends the Hollow and its people, watching over the children as they go to and from school, keeping an eye on what is happening in surrounding areas, and endangering his own life to keep intruders from finding Tûl Isgrun. Finally he sets fire to the mine, effectively sealing the shrine forever. He plans to marry Bonethy Yanto* and move back Up Top*, above the Hollow, where their ancestors lived for so long.

MAUD BIGGIN (*The River at Green Knowe*). *See* Biggin, Maud

MAVIS, a character in E[dith] Nesbit Bland's* *Wet Magic**. She is the sister of Francis*, Bernard*, and Kathleen*. Mavis and the others have many adventures after she and Francis rescue Freia*, a mermaid, from the circus people who have captured her. When Freia invites the children to visit her home, Merland*, Mavis helps defend it against the Under Folk*; she also helps bring about peace by aiding in the rescue of Freia's father, who convinces the King and Queen of the Under Folk* to make peace.

MAX MORLEY (*The Twelve and the Genii*). *See* Morley, Max

MAY, ADA (MRS.), a character in Mary Norton's* *The Borrowers**, *The Borrowers Afield**, and *The Borrowers Aloft**. When she was a child, Mrs. May's brother* told her of the miniature people called borrowers* whom he saw at Firbanks, the home of their great-aunt. When she visited Firbanks not long after he said the borrowers were driven from the place, she collected things for them to use and left them there. Though she did not see the borrowers herself and though her brother was known for his teasing, Mrs. May grew up almost believing in the tiny people. When she becomes an old woman and goes to live with Kate's* parents, Mrs. May tells the little girl about the borrowers. She later moves to a small cottage she has inherited at Leighton Buzzard, Bedfordshire.

MAYNE, WILLIAM (1928–   ), British writer. He was born on 16 March 1928, to William and Dorothy (Fea) Mayne, in Hull, Yorkshire. Mayne was educated at the Choir School, Canterbury. He has been a lecturer at Deakin University, Geelong, as well as a free-lance writer.

Most of Mayne's many works for children are realistic novels, some of them dealing with the nature of reality and unreality. *Earthfasts**, Mayne's fantasy, deals with time. Here time is fluid, like the wind or the flame of a candle.

In Mayne's world, time is not a straight path from the past to the future; it is, if anything, like an onion, with several layers, all individual but connected. David Wix* and Keith Heseltine* are on one layer, in one time frame, in twentieth-century England. Another time frame is that of King Arthur* and his knights, sleeping as stone in a cave beneath a castle; they seem to share this layer with various denizens of a world normally unseen by us; the giants and wild boars who also sleep as stones. Other invisible forces seem to occupy other layers of time. Though normally one cannot step from one layer to another, Nellie Jack John Cherry* (John) does exactly that, starting out in his own layer— the eighteenth century—and marching through time to the twentieth.

He bears in his hand a strange candle* that does not burn as candles should; it burns cold, not hot, and it does not use oxygen. This candle, taken from its place in Arthur's chamber, seems to contain within its flame all time and as a result it sheds light on all time at once. Carrying this candle, John can march from one century to another; without it he cannot get back to his own century. Looking into its flame, David seems to see everywhere at once, at every time. Those who look into its flame seem to continue to see other layers even after they stop looking. David sees a spinning force Keith can see only the effects of, and he walks around objects that are not there for Keith; once he himself has looked into the candle, Keith sees shadows of objects and people that are not really there. When the candle burns in its socket in the middle of a round stone table, Arthur and his knights are stone, as are the giants who once roamed England, and certain strange forces sleep. The cave seems a kind of bubble where time does not operate as we know it: though David thinks he is there only a few moments, he comes out about five months after he has gone in; Keith spends a moment or two in the cave and he, too, comes out months later. In the cave, the candle is in its own layer, its own present, and it burns hot, though slowly. When John takes the candle from its socket and brings it to the twentieth century, it is out of its own time, a fossil, and thus it acts as a fossil candle should.

Like a pivot holding together the blades of a fan, the candle seems to hold time in place. In its own place, the candle stops time for Arthur, his knights, and the giants and other forces, and they become as stones, with the centuries whistling around them like the wind, for their time has not yet come. When the candle is taken from its socket, time resumes for them, and they can move in the twentieth century. A boggart* that had plagued a family on and off for years and then gone to sleep wakes again to resume his pranks. Arthur and his knights are still on a layer different from that of Keith, whom they seek because he has the candle, but as he walks with them back to the castle, they meet gradually on the same layer of time. When he puts the candle back, time stops again for the king and those who sleep as he does, and in the twentieth century things return to normal. Perhaps because it is somehow a little independent of the candle, the boggart takes more time to settle down and sleep, and even then if anyone knocks on the floorboard above it, it knocks back.

Earthfasts is a fascinating, frustrating book. Wonderfully imaginative, it is obscure in places, sometimes to a maddening extent. David and Keith are fairly three-dimensional, though at times they seem curiously uninvolved in what is going on all around them, and the reader is not always able to tell just how they feel at a given moment. In a way this is probably caused by their pragmatism; in the face of the inexplicable, more than one logically minded individual has retreated into science. But it makes them seem curiously lacking. Mayne's style is descriptive, and the tone is never moody. The book has moments of humor—especially when the boggart is around—and these brightly offset the moments of unease, when powers beyond our control are at work.

Works

Juvenile full-length fantasy: *Earthfasts* (1966).
Juvenile non-fantasy: *Follow the Footprints* (1953); *The World Upside Down* (1954); *A Swarm in May* (1955); *The Member for the Marsh* (1956); *Choristers' Cake* (1956); *The Blue Boat* (1957); *A Grass Rope* (1957); *The Long Night* (1957); *Underground Alley* (1958); *The Gobbling Billy* (1959), with Dick Caesar; *The Thumbstick* (1959); *Thirteen O'Clock* (1960); *The Rolling Season* (1960); *Cathedral Wednesday* (1960); *The Fishing Party* (1960); *Summer Visitors* (1961); *The Changeling* (1961); *The Glass Ball* (1961); *The Last Bus* (1962); *The Twelve Dancers* (1962); *The Man from the North Pole* (1963); *On the Stepping Stones* (1963); *Words and Music* (1963); *Plot Night* (1963); *A Parcel of Trees* (1963); *Water Boatman* (1964); *Whistling Rufus* (1964); *Sand* (1964); *A Day Without Wind* (1964); *The Big Wheel and the Little Wheel* (1965); *Pig in the Middle* (1965); *No More School* (1965);

Rooftops (1966); *The Old Zion* (1966); *The Battlefield* (1967); *The Big Egg* (1967); *The Toffee Join* (1968); *Over the Hills and Far Away* (1968) as *The Hill Road* (1969); *The Yellow Aeroplane* (1968); *The House on Fairmont* (1968), with Fritz Wegner; *Ravensgill* (1970); *Royal Harry* (1971); *A Game of Dark* (1971), psychofantasy; *The Incline* (1972); *Robin's Real Engine* (1972); *Skiffy* (1972); *The Jersey Shore* (1973); *A Year and a Day* (1976); *Party Pants* (1977); *Max's Dream* (1977); *It* (1977); *The Patchwork Cat* (1982); *All the King's Men* (1982); *Skiffy and the Twin Planets* (1982).

Secondary Works

Townsend, John Rowe. "William Mayne," in *A Sense of Story* (Boston: The Horn Book, 1971), pp. 130–42. [Revised in *A Sounding of Storytellers* (New York: J. B. Lippincott, 1979), pp. 139–52.]

Whitaker, Muriel A. " 'The Hollow Hills': A Celtic Motif in Modern Fantasy," *Mosaic*, 13 (Spring/Summer, 1980), pp. 165–78.

MEDRAUT, a character in *The Sleepers**, by Jane Louise Curry*. He is the son of Margan* and the nephew of Artair*—King Arthur*. Medraut is also known as "Mordred." In Artair's last battle, Medraut fought against him and killed his son, Anir, taking from him the Ring of Luned*. Medraut wore this ring as he slept through the ages beside his mother. In the twentieth century he wakes and, assuming the name "M. E. Draut," sets into motion a plan for Artair's final destruction. Medraut hopes to gain possession of the *Brenhin Dlyseu**, the Thirteen Treasures of Prydein, which will give him dominion over Britain, but he is thwarted when Artair and his men are wakened and regain the Ring, bearing it with the other Treasures to safety beyond the seas.

MEDWYN, a character in *The Book of Three**, *The High King**, and *The Foundling, and Other Tales of Prydain*, by Lloyd Alexander*. He also may be named Nevvid Nav Neivion. If so, he is a legendary figure who built a boat to save two of every kind of creature in Prydain* when that land flooded. The animals have never forgotten him or the place where the boat had come to rest, though men have. Medwyn is an ancient-looking man with white hair and a long beard. He lives in a valley at the foothills of the Eagle Mountains, alone except for the animals who come to him for help in time of need. Medwyn understands and helps them, healing their hurts or simply giving them a place to rest. He often has trouble remembering a human's name, but he has no such trouble with animals. His valley is a lovely place where all animals live side by side in peace and the land itself seems to have restorative powers. To this valley come Taran* and his companions, led by their horse, when one of them is injured. During the final bid of Arawn*, an evil king, for control of Prydain, Medwyn sends word to his animals to help in the battle, for if Arawn were to gain control, their freedom and happiness would be destroyed. Once Arawn is vanquished, Medwyn closes his valley to men, allowing none but animals to enter.

MEERMUT, a word referring to "spirit" in Walter de la Mare's* *The Three Mulla-mulgars**. This word also refers to a shadow or even a memory. Each creature has a Meermut, which belongs to Tishnar*; in certain contexts, however, another type of spirit seems to be implied by the author. A row of ghoulish Meermuts guards a valley through which Ummanodda* and the other Mulgars* must travel in order to reach the Valleys of Tishnar*; because he has the Wonderstone*, Ummanodda sees them for what they really are—trees.

MEG MURRY (the Time trilogy). *See* Murry, Meg

MELANIE DELIA POWERS (*An Enemy at Green Knowe*). *See* Powers, Melanie Delia

MELBOURNE, HARRIET. *See* Bartholomew, Harriet Melbourne

MELISSA MITCHELL (*The Daybreakers*). *See* Mitchell, Melissa

MELTON, ANNE, a character in Robert Westall's* *The Watch House**. Her father is in the automotive trade; her mother is Fiona Melton. She has a pony called Toby. Anne loves her easy-going father more than she does her insensitive, aggressive mother, though the first time Fiona left her father, she was given custody of Anne. When her mother leaves a second time, Anne is taken to live with Fiona's old nanny, whose brother caretakes the Watch House*, from which generations of rescuers have gone out to rescue shipwrecked men. Lonely and eager for something to cherish, Anne proves to be a good audience for Henry Cookson's* ghostly activities, and she soon becomes his ally against the spirit of Major Scobie Hague*, who had haunted him in life and now haunts him in death. As she tries to help Henry and works to save the Watch House, Anne finds courage enough to defy her mother and attempt to live her own life.

MENZIES, MISS, a character in *The Borrowers Aloft** and *The Borrowers Avenged**, by Mary Norton*. Her family home was Gadstone, and her best childhood friend was her cousin, Aubrey. Though they were close, he married someone else, and Miss Menzies was heartbroken. She comes to live in Fordham, designing Christmas cards and writing children's books for a living. When Mr. Pott* begins to build his model village, Little Fordham*, Miss Menzies helps him by making tiny inhabitants out of barbola. Patient, laconic Mr. Pott soon learns not to listen completely to Miss Menzies, who often talks on and on without really needing an audience. Miss Menzies believes in fairies and is sure three have moved into Little Fordham when she sees Pod, Homily, and Arrietty Clock***, three miniature people. Arrietty soon makes friends with Miss Menzies, and the woman often provides things for the tiny people to use. When they disappear, she and Mr. Pott refurnish their house for their return, and she goes to the local constable but is unable to persuade him that the tiny people actually exist. When Miss Menzies helps Lady Mullings arrange flowers in the church, she discovers that Sidney Platter* had taken the borrowers*, who had subsequently escaped. She is present when the Platters are caught breaking into the church, trying to capture another borrower.

MERLAND, a kingdom in *Wet Magic**, by E[dith] Nesbit Bland*. This lovely place beneath the sea is separated from the water by a thin bubble made strong enough to hold back the sea by the concentrated thought of the Merpeople. Its atmosphere is not air or water, but something both land and water people can breath. The seawater which once inundated Merland was blown out of the place by whales and is now held back by the sky which sits like a blue dome over the kingdom. This thin bubble can be broken, however, by a touch, as Kathleen*, a land child, proves when she accidentally touches the sky and lets in the sea. The inhabitants of Merland are beautiful people who wear fish tails when they go out of the kingdom into the water. Their servants are fish. In Merland is the source of all the rivers of the world; it is the responsibility of the high-born to see to the wind, rain, snow, tides, and whirlpools of the world. The Merpeople have many enemies: the treacherous "Thin-Skins," frivolous but deceitful creatures, like flying fish, who live near the surface of the sea; the Book People*, who lurk in the rocks of the Cave of Learning*; and the Under Folk*, ugly creatures of the cool, deep waters who have been at war with the Merpeople for 3,579,308 years. When Freia*, a Merprincess, is rescued from a circus sideshow by Francis*, Mavis*, and Reuben*, she invites them and their brother and sister, Bernard* and Kathleen, to Merland. These children help bring about peace between the Merpeople and the Under Folk when they rescue the king of Merland from captivity and the man makes peace.

MERLIN. *See* Lyon, Merriman; Merlyn; Myrddin

MERLYN, a figure in Arthurian legend who appears as a character in T[erence] H[anbury] White's* *The Sword in the Stone**. He is a wizard, educated by Bleise. Unlike other people, Merlyn lives backwards: he was born at the wrong end of time and has been living backwards ever since, growing constantly younger and making his way back to the beginning of time. For this reason, he is sometimes confused, not knowing whether he has done a thing or not, or whether he has told someone a thing or is just about to tell them. Merlyn lives with his owl, Archimedes*, in a cottage in the Forest Sauvage* that is filled with wonderful things, some of which have not yet been invented. One day the Wart (Arthur*), comes upon Merlyn, and the wizard goes to Sir Ector's castle to be the tutor of the Wart and Kay*, Ector's son. Though he has testimonials from everyone from Hecate to the Master of Trinity, Merlyn's spells do not always go right. He is a good enough wizard to win a duel with Madame Mim* and to change the Wart into several kinds of animals to teach the boy about responsibility and about life. Testy Merlyn has few illusions about life, and he tries to help the Wart abandon his own romanticism, but fails. Once Kay is knighted, Merlyn leaves, his task finished, for his lessons are over. But when the Wart pulls from the stone the sword that makes him king of all Britain, Merlyn returns to him to be his adviser. *See also* Myrddin; Lyon, Merriman

MERMAID, THE, a character in *The Animal Family**, by Randall Jarrell*. Like others of her kind, the mermaid lives in perpetual contentment in the sea, regretting nothing—not even the death of her sister. Because nothing ever changes beneath the surface of the water, the mermaid's life there never changes its tenor. One night, however, a hunter* hears her singing in the sea and comes to her. Night after night she sings and he comes, and gradually she comes to trust him. They become close. The mermaid is amazed at the differences the land provides; the hunter's world is constantly changing. This is attractive to her, so she accustoms herself to living on the land, and finally goes to live in the hunter's cabin. They are happy there; they are so different that they feel they are alike. Gradually they gather a family: a bear*, a lynx*, and a boy* whose mother has died in a shipwreck. Each is loved as much for his difference from the rest as for any other reason. Slowly the mermaid realizes that the land has made her different, for while she had forgotten her sister's death the next day, the mermaid feels that her heart would break if the hunter or the boy were to die. For this reason, to her the land is better.

MERMAID'S LAGOON, a place in James M. Barrie's* *Peter and Wendy**. This lagoon in Neverland* is where the mermaids live; the lost boys* come here to try to catch them. The Never bird* floats in her nest in this lagoon. Marooner's Rock* is located here.

MERRIMAN LYON (the Dark Is Rising series). *See* Lyon, Merriman

MERRY LYON (the Dark Is Rising series). *See* Lyon, Merriman

MESSUA, a character in the Jungle books*, by Rudyard Kipling*. She is a wife and the mother of two sons, one of them named Nathoo. The boy was carried off by a lame tiger, so when Mowgli*, a boy raised in the jungle, comes to her village, Messua takes him in, thinking he may be her son, and she calls him Nathoo. She is a good woman and Mowgli loves her dearly. After the village people drive Mowgli away because they think he is a sorcerer, Messua and her rich husband are declared witches and are almost burned, but Mowgli rescues them. The couple goes to Khanhiwara, to get justice from the English, but by the time they return, their village is gone, taken over by the jungle. Messua's husband gets a job in the fields and they buy a little land; a year before her husband dies, Messua's second son is born. She lives in a village near a marsh; when Mowgli leaves the jungle for good, he probably goes to live with her.

METRON ARISTON, a postulatum in Madeleine L'Engle's* *A Wind in the Door**. It is not a place, but an idea; thus, it can appear visually any way one chooses. In Metron Ariston, nothing is anywhere, and all size can become relative; an individual can seem as big as a galaxy or as tiny as a part of a cell. Blajeny*, a Teacher, brings Meg Murry*, Mr. Jenkins*, Calvin O'Keefe*, and Proginoskes* here when it is time for them to enter one of Charles Wallace Murry's* cells so that they can save him from mitochondritis.

MICHAEL DARLING (*Peter and Wendy*). *See* Darling, Michael

MICHAEL GEORGE BANKS (the Mary Poppins books). *See* Banks, Michael George

MICHAEL STUDDARD (*The Wind Eye*). *See* Studdard, Michael

MICHAELANGELO PUCCI (*The Daybreakers*; *The Birdstones*). *See* Pucci, Michaelangelo

MIDSUMMER TREE, a tree in *Silver on the Tree**, by Susan Cooper*. This giant oak in the Chiltern Hills of England is the pillar of the world, the tree of life. It can be seen only once every seven hundred years, and on that day the mistletoe twined in its branches comes into flower. When each flower on the branch of mistletoe opens, whoever cuts it can command Wild Magic and High Magic and drive rival powers from the land. The final battle between the Dark and the Light, the forces of evil and of good, takes place around the tree; Bran Davies* uses Eirias*, a crystal sword, to cut the flowering branch, and the Dark is driven out of the world and out of time.

MIGGLE. *See* Arthur, Margaret

MILD EYE, a character in Mary Norton's* *The Borrowers Afield** and *The Borrowers Afloat**. This gypsy has one normal eye and one hazel colored eye with a drooping lid. He helps support himself by poaching and stealing; he takes at least one pair of the gentleman's boots and loses one of them by throwing it at his cat. This boot is dragged away by Dreadful Spiller* (Spiller), a borrower*, one of the race of tiny people who live by "borrowing" what they need. Mild Eye makes a potent elderflower wine; Pod, Homily, and Arrietty Clock***, a family of borrowers who lives inside the boot, drink some wine which Spiller has borrowed for them and sleep so deeply that they do not wake when Mild Eye finds the boot and takes it home with him. He is most surprised to find little people inside and spends most of a day trying to catch them. They are rescued by Tom Goodenough*. Mild Eye gets another chance at the little people when he finds them at the stream from which he is poaching. After spending hours trying to catch the Clocks, Mild Eye is arrested for poaching by a passing policeman.

MILDRED, a character in Mary Norton's* *Are All the Giants Dead?*. She seems to be a magical sort of journalist who reports on the exploits of people in society—whether in London or in the land of fairy tales. Sometimes she takes James*, a young boy, with her. Slender, elegant Mildred is popular wherever she goes, whether it is to the palace of Beauty and the Beast or the nameless inn run by Jack-the-Giant-Killer* and Jack-of-the-Beanstalk* in Much-Belungen-under-Bluff*. When Mildred takes James with her, she manipulates his environment so as to make their journeys from his world to her fantastic ones possible, leaving behind a replica of James so that his mother will not worry at his absence. At least one of their trips is to the Land of Cockayne*, where characters from fairy tales live happily ever after; Mildred brings to these people the latest magazines and papers from London. When she goes to report on a royal wedding, James is free to get into an adventure during which he helps Dulcibel*, the daughter of Beauty and the Beast.

MILES TUCK (*Tuck Everlasting*). *See* Tuck, Miles

MILIUCC, a character in Lloyd Alexander's* *Time Cat*. His daughter is Diahan*. This big, hearty, red-bearded man is a king in Ireland in A.D. 411. He induces jealousy in his court magician, Lugad*, by naming Jason*, a boy from the twentieth century, and Gareth*, his cat, the new court sorcerers after they save Diahan from a snake. Among Miliucc's slaves is a Welshman, Sucat*, who is known in later ages as St. Patrick.

MIM, MADAME, a character in *The Sword in the Stone*, by T[erence] H[anbury] White*. This beautiful, evil witch earned a bachelor's degree from the College of Witches and Warlocks under the sea at Dom-Daniel and set herself up in the Forest Sauvage*, to teach pianoforte, needlework, and necromancy. She keeps an owl, which she forgets to feed, and a gore-crow named Grizzle Greediguts. Madame Mim is very fond of small boys, finding them very tasty if roasted or stewed. When Kay* and his foster brother, the Wart (Arthur*), come to her cottage to retrieve an arrow the crow has taken, Madame Mim catches them and plans to eat them. Their tutor, a wizard named Merlyn*, comes to their rescue, and the two have a wizards' duel refereed by Hecate. Merlyn wins by turning into the microbes of hiccups, scarlet fever, mumps, whooping cough, measles, and heat spots, and infecting Madame Mim with them; she immediately dies.

MINDY HALLAM (*Mindy's Mysterious Miniature*). *See* Hallam, Arminta

MINDY'S MYSTERIOUS MINIATURE. Jane Louise Curry. Illus. Charles Robinson. New York: Harcourt Brace Jovanovich, 1970. 157 pp. American.

Arminta Hallam* (Mindy) is at a country auction with her parents when, exploring the old barn, she comes upon a dollhouse. Because it is so grimy, she buys it for only sixty-eight cents and two cartons of pop bottles. When the house is cleaned up, even Mindy's mother, who runs an antique store from the house, is impressed: everything in the house is a perfect miniature and many of the pieces are antiques. Mindy is so pleased with her find that she displays some of the furniture in the window of her mother's shop—carefully marked NFS. When Mindy comes home from school, the furniture is gone from the window; her father had called and told her mother to hide it. Mindy's mother tells her of a strange television repairman who came to fix their unbroken set and seemed interested in doll furniture. They are interrupted by the arrival of a customer— Mr. Putt, the repairman—who seems interested in prying into things he shouldn't. Mindy's father comes home, full of excitement; he has looked at the wood from a piece of the furniture under a microscope and has discovered that either the furniture has once been full-sized and mysteriously shrunk or it is made of "miniature wood."

That night Mindy visits Mrs. Mary Buckle Bright*, the next-door neighbor, who recognized Mr. Putt as someone very like an old suitor of hers—Willie Kurtz*— and who also recognized the doll furniture in the shop window as very like the furniture in the house she was raised in, since torn down. As Mrs. Bright describes the house, Mindy recognizes the dollhouse in her description. They decide that perhaps Mrs. Bright's grandfather made a model of the old house, and Mindy takes Mrs. Bright to the barn to show her the dollhouse. It is exactly like her old home. Suddenly there is an explosion of sorts and Mindy and Mrs. Bright are the right size to enter the house. The back of it is gone, for Mr. Hallam had removed the back of the dollhouse. Mrs. Bright admits that the house mysteriously vanished fifty-five years before, in 1915, and here it is, back again. She tells Mindy of growing up in the house and of Willie Kurtz, her rejected suitor, who sold patent medicines and invented strange devices. The house vanished the summer she rejected him.

Sudenly there is a commotion, and Mindy has a strange sensation. As the house lurches, she realizes that it and they have been made small and are being loaded onto a truck. All they can do is stay quiet, so they go to bed, waking when the house is unloaded. The next morning they find themselves in a strange place: part of an indoor village which Mindy recognizes as a museum of miniatures she once visited. They smell coffee, but the man who brought them is not eating. Mindy and Mrs. Bright follow the smell to the inn, where they meet eight timid, elderly people, who are having breakfast. They are citizens of Dopple*, a little town which vanished in 1915. Professor Kurtz had come to town and tried to get money to use in his experiments; enraged at the refusal, he waited until the day of the country fair, when the town was deserted, and miniaturized the town, intending to use it as a traveling exhibit and make some money. Mrs. Bright's house was once part of the exhibit; it was left behind when the professor had had to leave quickly the place where he had stopped for repairs. When the professor died, his nephew—also called Willie Kurtz—took over the exhibit.

The eight citizens of Dopple who had stayed home that day and had been miniaturized have lived by their wits, and the professor does not know they are living in his little town. Having tried and failed many times before to escape, they have given up. Samantha Bostweiler*, the youngest, steals what they need to live on.

On the television news, the disappearances of Mindy, Mrs. Bright, and Horace*, the Hallams's huge dog, are reported. Suspicious, Kurtz searches the house, finding nothing. After reading a newspaper article describing Horace's apparent search for the two, Kurtz is more thorough in his search, but he is interrupted when the television newsman reports that the police are following Horace, who evidently knows where he is going. Kurtz roars off in his van.

Knowing the strong hold greed has on Kurtz, the miniature people come up with and execute a plan. They will hoax him into unshrinking the bank—with them inside—and there they will capture him. A rope is tied to a tree and left to dangle over the edge of the table, to make it appear that Mindy and Mrs. Bright have escaped. A note, written in letters as large as they can manage, which appears to be someone's jottings about the supposed fortune in stock certificates in the bank, is dropped on the floor beside the table. Kurtz, who has returned in the rented truck he will use to transport the village to somewhere Horace cannot find, takes the bait and hauls the little bank to a nearby field, but when he tries to magnify it, nothing happens. The people inside the bank endure a bruising journey to the site where Dopple used to be. Because conditions are like those when the building was shrunk, Kurtz's attempt to magnify it works, and he rushes inside, unlocks the vault, and becomes a prisoner when Mindy shuts the door on him.

By the time the police arrive with Horace, the rest of the village has been unshrunk. In the shock that follows his capture, Kurtz becomes hysterical and finally goes mad. The stock certificates really are worth a fortune, and the eight elderly citizens of Dopple use the money to fix up the town before the return of the other citizens. They invite Mrs. Bright, whose house, were it unshrunk, would be too close to the highway for comfort, to live in Dopple. And at Mindy's next birthday, a great celebration is held and she is presented with a dollhouse that is "GUARANTEED UNSHRUNK."

MINIMULS, a race of beings in Walter de la Mare's* *The Three Mulla-mulgars*. These fierce, cunning little creatures are the enemies of the Mulgars* and will eat them if they get a chance. The mouse-faced Minimuls are gray or sand-colored, and their glassy gray eyes glow in the dark. They wear slippers made of silver grass, which they also plait into belts. Minimuls live in long tunnels underground. They hold feasts at full moon. When the three Mulla-mulgars are captured by Minimuls, Thumma* and Thimbulla* are fattened to be slaughtered, but because he carries the Wonderstone* Ummanodda* is not slated to be eaten.

MIRAZ, a character in C[live] S[taples] Lewis's* *Prince Caspian**. He is the husband of Prunaprismia and the father of a son; he is the uncle of Caspian X*. Miraz murdered Caspian's father, the ruler of Narnia*, and became Lord Protector; after the queen's death, Miraz got rid of the old king's friends and took the throne from his nephew when his own flatterers begged him to become king. Miraz's rule is oppressive, and he is not popular. He raises Caspian at his court, intending to give him the throne, but changes his mind when Prunaprismia gives birth to a son; he wants to leave the throne to his own child and decides to kill Caspian. Before he can do this, the boy escapes, going into hiding and gathering around him the talking beasts and other magical creatures that had gone into hiding during the reign of Miraz and of the other conquerors from Telmar*. Miraz, who is not the best of captains but who is a tough fighter, leads his army against Caspian. When Peter Pevensie*, Caspian's champion, offers to meet Miraz in single combat, the winner to have won the war, Miraz is goaded by two of his lords into accepting, for the lords think that Miraz will lose and that they can seize the throne of Narnia. After a tough fight Miraz does lose, but only after he stumbles and one of the lords kills him.

MIRELIDAR, the name of a stone in *The Wolves of Aam**, by Jane Louise Curry*. This milky stone is one of the twelve powerful skystones* found beneath the Opal Mountain at the beginning of the world. Mirelidar represents the moon, and once it lay in the City of the Moon Under the Mountain*. Somehow it vanished from there and came into the possession of Lord Naghar*, who coveted its power. Then it came into the hands of the Tiddi* child who grew up to become Runner-to-the-Sky's-Edge* (Runner) and who treasures it as the ''dream-stone'' that sends him prophetic dreams. When Runner is injured, he is tended by Lek*, a conjuror who recognizes the stone and hides it so that Lord Naghar will not find it. Finally Mirelidar is carried to Werrik, a city where it will be safe.

MIRROR, an object in Lucy Boston's* *An Enemy at Green Knowe**. This very old Persian glass was owned by the wife of Aubrey Oldknow in the seventeenth century; it is one of a few of her looking glasses that survive at Green Knowe* into the twentieth century. This small mirror is set in a wide red lacquer frame in which are embedded smaller bits of mirror. Though it reflects objects as any other mirror would, it also reflects the past, the future, or what may be happening elsewhere. In the mirror Toseland* and Hsu* catch their first glimpse of Dr. Melanie Delia Powers* and can sometimes see what she is doing.

MIRROR OF LLUNET, a small body of water in Lloyd Alexander's* *Taran Wanderer*. It lies in a shallow cave at the head of Lake Llunet, in the Llawgadarn Mountains north of the Free Commots* of Prydain*. Having been fed over countless years by a trickle of water, the Mirror is still only a finger deep, but it seems depthless and full of light. Those who look into the Mirror, it is said, can see themselves as they truly are. Taran*, a young man seeking to find himself, travels hard and long in search of the Mirror; when he looks into it, he sees himself, with all his frailties and strengths and his own individuality. The Mirror is destroyed by Dorath*, an outlaw leader who had thought Taran had hidden a treasure in the pool and who stamps out the water in his rage.

MIRZA, SHUGDAD, a character in Lloyd Alexander's* *The First Two Lives of Lukas-Kasha*. He is the Grand Vizier of the king of Abadan*. When the king dies and the court astrologer predicts where the new king will be found, Shugdad has the prospective monarch killed—as he does the next prospective king. The third candidate, Lukas-Kasha* (Lukas), escapes death and is proclaimed king. For a time Lukas shows no inclination to exercise his prerogatives as king and Shugdad rules the country as he likes. When Lukas becomes interested in affairs of state and the well-being of Abadan's citizens, Shugdad tries to kill him and, after Lukas flees the palace, has him declared dead and himself proclaimed king. When Lukas is captured by Abadani troops and is about to be executed, Shugdad tries to force him to sign a confession that he has betrayed his country and killed himself. Lukas, however, escapes. Shugdad prepares to invade the nearby province of Bishangar*, but the invasion is cut short when Shugdad is killed trying to kill Lukas, and the young man takes charge of the Abadani forces.

MISHCHA, a character in *The Three Mulla-mulgars*, by Walter de la Mare*. This old Quatta hare and her sister, Môha, live in the forest, about which Mishcha is fiercely proprietary. She and her sister grumpily nurse Ummanodda* (Nod) after his escape from the cannibalistic Minimuls*; though she hates Mulgars* as a rule, Mishcha finds herself liking Nod. She later warns him that the Immânala* is stalking Andy Battle* and tells Nod that his brothers are near.

MISS HICKORY. Carolyn Sherwin Bailey. Illus. Ruth Gannett. New York: Viking Press, 1946. 123 pp. American. Newbery Award, 1947.
　　Miss Hickory* is a little woman of mixed parentage: her body is a twig from an apple tree and her head is a hickory nut. Having spent last winter in the warm farmhouse near her home, she feels despair when the people who live in the house go to Boston for the winter and her little corncob house is taken over by a chipmunk. Crow*, however, finds her an empty robins' nest in the old apple tree, and here she makes her little home, though she is disconcerted when Squirrel*, who has his hole at the foot of the tree, takes a rather uncomfortable interest in her—especially in her head.

Life in the nest suits Miss Hickory, who gathers food and makes a smart new wardrobe for the coming winter. She helps the hen pheasants, forlorn because their mates ignore them, to form a "Ladies Aid Society" in a comfortable niche; she watches a venturesome heifer calf and a motherless fawn, who have found each other in their loneliness, eat together in the barn. Because of her hard-headed nature, however, Miss Hickory misses the exciting events of Christmas Eve, for she does not believe Squirrel when he tells her that at midnight the imprint of a baby appears in one of the mangers in the barn. When the woodland animals and beasts from exotic lands gather at the barn, Miss Hickory follows but is too late to see the miracle.

In February, when grumpy, fearful Ground Hog* runs away from his shadow, Miss Hickory organizes the hen pheasant Ladies Aid Society and sends them to him with food, so, she reasons, he will no longer be afraid because he steals food from the farmers. When Ground Hog does not run from his shadow—because it is not there—it means that spring is on the way.

Spring is filled with adventures. In March comes Old Crow Week, when the crows return to the wood and Crow takes Miss Hickory flying with him. Miss Hickory also saves Bull Frog*, who has been frozen into the ice. But the greatest adventure occurs after her spring cleaning, when she leaves the nest for a week to make her new spring outfit. Miss Hickory returns to find that the robins have moved back into the nest, and they chase her away. Not having heard Squirrel in his hole for some time, she decides that he must be away and starts to move into his home. Squirrel *is* there, however, weak with hunger because he has eaten his small store of nuts and cannot find the ones he buried. Bitter at her treatment of him, Squirrel takes her hickory-nut head and eats it.

While he is eating her head, Miss Hickory realizes that the hardness of her head has made her stubborn. Her headless body, feeling the sap running through it, happily finds its way up the old apple tree, resting, finally, in a crotch. In May, the children come back to the house and, climbing the tree, find her; Miss Hickory's apple-twig body has joined with the tree and she has become a scion, a graft that will help the old tree to produce again. She has found a permanent home, where she will have to do no more "hard thinking," and she will produce apples.

MR. TWIGG'S MISTAKE. Robert Lawson. Illus. Robert Lawson. Boston: Little, Brown and Company, 1947. 141 pp. American.

One day an employee at the company that makes Bita-Vita Breakfast Food* makes a mistake, and as a result one box of the cereal is packed to the brim with the vitamin X that gives the cereal its nutrition. This box is ultimately delivered to the house of Arthur Amory Appleton*. Arthur finds a mole, which he names General de Gaulle*, and feeds some Bita-Vita to it, for lack of anything else. He eats a flake or two himself, and by that evening, both have grown an astonishing amount. Over the next week, de Gaulle grows bigger and bigger, and he and Arthur become close. Arthur teaches de Gaulle several tricks and skills. De Gaulle proves useful when Arthur accidentally shoots an arrow into a neighbor's yard and the neighbor will not allow him to get it; de Gaulle digs under the wall and fetches it for him.

The neighbor decides that de Gaulle is a dog and complains to the authorities; the family is badgered by the police and the dog warden, and Arthur's father becomes less than thrilled with the mole. De Gaulle exhibits a new, useful talent, however, for spading up the flower beds, and Arthur's father, in gratitude, gets him a new box of Bita-Vita, to replace the old, stale one. De Gaulle refuses to eat the new cereal, though, and Arthur digs the old box out of the trash. His uncle has it analyzed and realizes what the contents really are, and that after this box is gone there may be no more, for the company will not give any out. Meanwhile the cellar floods and de Gaulle performs a new trick, that of digging a drain in the cellar floor, leading directly into the neighbor's garden.

The mole grows bigger and bigger, until he is as large as Arthur. When fall comes, de Gaulle roams farther and farther from home, until one day he does not come back. A day and a half later, the family is outside when suddenly the ground rumbles and a geyser of oil shoots up, bearing with it de Gaulle, who swims upward and becomes lost in the clouds. The well makes Arthur rich, but he would rather have de Gaulle, whom he will never see again.

MR. WILMER. Robert Lawson. Illus. Robert Lawson. Boston: Little, Brown and Company, 1945. 218 pp. American.

On his twenty-ninth birthday, William Wilmer* discovers that he can understand and talk with animals. His life until this time has been quiet, regular, and rather dull. This particular morning is so upsetting that William changes his routine and goes to the zoo in the afternoon, though normally he does not go on Saturday. Here he talks to a sick lion, who tells him that it has a toothache. No one will believe William, though. The zoo authorities discover that he is right, and when William visits the zoo again the next day, they ask him to help. Later that day he proves that he really can talk to animals. On Monday, disaster strikes; the publicity he has gotten results in William losing his job at the insurance company. Anxious at being out of work for the first time in his life, William seeks solace at the zoo and is offered a job there, as ombudsman for the animals. William also finds himself deluged with other offers, but the only one he takes is one from a rich woman whose dog is ill. After helping, he agrees to come each week and help the two talk with each other.

William finds his new job—and life—much more interesting, happier, and more profitable than his old one. One day he helps a policeman during a parade when his horse starts a lie-down strike because people are no longer allowed to give sugar to the horses. As a result, William becomes liaison between the horses and the police. William's sudden popularity has an unforeseen result; the paperwork begins piling up and William gets anxious. He hires Mary Sweeney*, the woman of his dreams, who had worked at the insurance office, and she even moves into his boarding house. Now starts a lovely time for William, as he does something he loves to do and gets revenge on his former boss through Lucy*, a zoo elephant. He even helps a trumpet-playing circus seal who is having a nervous breakdown.

Because he has always wanted a country place and because the seal's trumpet-playing disturbs the neighbors, William decides to buy a farm, which his landlady and her husband will work, and make it a rest farm for discontented animals like Lucy, who is unhappy in the city. William makes a long-promised tour of the country while Miss Sweeney finds the perfect place.

When William returns, he finds that people are acting strangely toward him. The day they are all to move to the farm, Miss Sweeney leaves him because of a vicious gossip columnist's intimations about their relationship. Lucy, who is supposed to walk to the farm, refuses to budge, though the police have been sent to find Miss Sweeney; William searches for her himself, finds her at the zoo, and asks her to marry him. After her ready acceptance, they are married in City Hall. The couple rides in a howdah on Lucy's back to their beautiful new home.

MISTRESS MASHAM'S REPOSE. T[erence] H[anbury] White. Illus. Fritz Eichenberg. New York: G. P. Putnam's Sons, 1946. 255 pp. British.

Maria*, an orphan, lives in the huge, historic, now dilapidated house of Malplaquet* with Mrs. Noakes*, the cook, and Miss Brown*, Maria's frightening governess. One day Maria visits an overgrown island in one of the estate's lakes and there finds a tiny baby in a cradle made of a walnut shell. She is attacked by its mother and takes both, on impulse. Maria takes care to hide them from Miss Brown but is disappointed because the woman will not respond to her. The next day she takes the mother and child to the Professor*, who has a cottage on the estate. He recognizes them as Lilliputians* and persuades her to take them back to the island. Maria does and becomes curious about the tiny people; she tries to learn their language from a book and goes to visit them, bringing gifts. The understandably shy Lilliputians have hidden themselves, but one speaks with her, in English; realizing that since she already knows about them they should make the best of things, the Lilliputians show themselves. They are very pleased with her gifts.

On Maria's next visit, she eats a dinner they have prepared for her and receives a handkerchief they have embroidered. She also hears their history: how their ancestors, with their cattle and sheep, had been captured by a ship captain after civil war had decimated the population; and how after being shown in a traveling show, they had escaped at Malplaquet. Now the people are free, even if their lives are hard. Maria begins to visit them at night, when Miss Brown is safely in bed and when they are usually abroad. One night she is present when they harpoon and kill a pike, but Maria cannot help interfering and the fish is lost.

After this, despite the Professor's warnings, Maria seeks to control the Lilliputians—to play with them—and they begin to avoid her. Finally Maria gets a toy plane for her Lilliputian favorite to fly, and the trip ends in disaster; the plane crashes and the young man breaks his leg. Heartbroken, Maria goes to the Professor, who lectures her and advises her to apologize. After two days she does, in a letter, and finally the apology is accepted. Maria makes her visits at night and successfully controls her impulses to interfere, becoming quite popular with the Lilliputians. One night, Miss Brown catches her returning. The governess has found the presents the Lilliputians have given Maria and thinks the girl has gotten them from a secret room that may hold a parchment she and Mr. Hater*, the vicar, are searching for; Miss Brown will alter the parchment to get an inheritance which is supposed to go to Maria. Realizing that Miss Brown would sell the Lilliputians if she knew about them, Maria refuses to tell her anything and is sent to her room without supper. The spying Lilliputians learn of this and bring her food; just as they are leaving, Miss Brown storms in and manages to grab a Lilliputian during the melee. The next morning she takes the man to Mr. Hater and they decide to follow Maria on her excursions to find the rest of the tiny people. After they leave, a Lilliputian hunter rescues the tiny man.

With all the cunning she is capable of, Maria gets Miss Brown and Mr. Hater well lost that night and the next day. The next time, she locks them in a tower. Meanwhile, the Lilliputians, thinking that Maria is in danger and not knowing that the captive Lilliputian is free, gather an army and march on the house. Maria warns them before Miss Brown and Mr. Hater can capture them, but she herself is locked in Malplaquet's famous dungeon. Mrs. Noakes goes to the Professor because she is worried, and he bravely searches the house, finding nothing before he is ignominiously chased out by Miss Brown. He goes to the Lilliputians and they agree to search for Maria. At last they find her and break into her prison, only to be locked into the cellar by Mr. Hater and Miss Brown. Breaking a pane of glass, the Lilliputians escape and get Mrs. Noakes—much amazed—to open the cellar door. The Professor finds the parchment Miss Brown and the vicar have been searching for, and takes it with him. Maria is taken to his cottage and gently tucked into bed.

When Mr. Hater and Miss Brown discover that their captives are gone, they start after them, with the Lilliputians hampering them along the way as best as they can manage. The Professor, trying to get help, is not believed by the authorities until they read a note from Mrs. Noakes. By the time they arrive at the cottage, the two villains have been locked into a shed by Maria. Mr. Hater and Miss Brown are arrested, tried, and sent to jail. The Professor is hired to teach Maria, and she gets her inheritance, which allows her to restore Malplaquet to indescribable splendor; and on their island the Lilliputians live happily.

MITCHELL, MELISSA (LISS), a character in *The Daybreakers**, by Jane Louise Curry*. She is the daughter of Nan and Bill Mitchell, the granddaughter of Senator Tapp, and the cousin of Conway Tapp* (Sonny). Though a member of a distinguished family, Liss does not feel that she is better than anyone else in Apple Lock*, Ohio, and she enrages her grandfather when she plays with

Callista Lee (Callie) and Harry Rivers**, who are black. Liss does not really like her grandfather or her cousin, Sonny, whom she calls "the Drip." Her rejection of Sonny intensifies his longing to be stronger than everyone else and therefore makes him easy prey for the seven priest-kings of ancient Cibotlán*. Liss is with Callie when the latter finds the blue-green stone* that takes them to ancient Abáloc*; there, she is hailed as a child of the moon because of her fair skin, and she is almost sacrificed. Liss is also among the group of girls who rescue Lincoas* and his band. When Sonny disappears, Liss realizes that she loves the boy, and she feels his fear and his yearning for her, which are strong enough to pull Liss and her friends back to Abáloc in time to rescue the child from the sacrificial altar of the sun.

MOAR, RUSSELL BOYD (ARBIE), a character in *The Watchers**, by Jane Louise Curry*. He is married to Jenny Moar. His nickname comes from the initial letters of his first and middle names. Arbie is a wealthy man bent on getting wealthier; he owns the local grocery store and his wife owns Deep Run Coal Mining Company. He seems to come under the power of Katóa*, an evil force bound in Twilly's Green Hollow*; Arbie is instrumental in initiating snake-handling in the local church, and he resorts to unscrupulous methods to start mining operations in the Hollow. When Delano Mattick* and Ray Siler* try to destroy the shrine above the place where Katóa is sealed, Arbie tries to stop them and almost loses his life.

MOLE, THE, a character in Kenneth Grahame's* *The Wind in the Willows**. Naive and innocent in the ways of the world, the Mole finds adventure when he responds to the call of spring and tunnels his way to the surface. There he learns the ways of the River and gains wisdom and confidence through his escapades with Toad*, the Badger*, and the Water Rat*. The Mole becomes a highly respected citizen of the River, and the tales of his exploits are told and retold by the parents of Riverbank families to their children.

MOLESWORTH, MARY [LOUISA] (1839–1921), British writer. She was born on 29 May 1839 in Rotterdam, the Netherlands, to Major-General Stewart and his wife, and was educated in Switzerland. In 1861 she married Richard Molesworth; they had seven children; they were separated in 1879. She died on 20 July 1921.

Of Molesworth's thirty-two books for children, four are fantasies. *The Carved Lions*, though it has one incident of fantasy in it, is primarily a realistic novel. Of *Four Winds Farm*, *Christmas-Tree Land*, *The Cuckoo Clock**, and *The Tapestry Room**, the latter are her most popular. In these works, Molesworth blends reality and fantasy to give the everyday world of the child richness beyond reality.

The Tapestry Room and *The Cuckoo Clock* are full of the details of ordinary life. Griselda*, the little girl in *The Cuckoo Clock*, minds her great-aunts and prepares her lessons, nurses colds, and feels sulky sometimes, just as any little girl would. Jeanne* and Hugh*, in *The Tapestry Room*, play at being cooks, whipping up an egg and creating a "ragout" of cocoa, squashed prunes, and bread crumbs which only a child would find edible; having heard the story of a juggling princess, they teach themselves to juggle, though they cannot get the golden balls she uses.

The books are full of ordinary objects which become the doors into a world of faery and imagination. Even as themselves, the objects seem quite wonderful. The cuckoo clock* with its mechanical inhabitant is a thing of wonder as the bird pops out to give the time. The Chinese cabinet in the next room is a "delicious" thing in the shape of a temple or palace, and the nodding mandarins inside its doors are astonishing. The tapestries in the tapestry room are fascinating, filled with wonderful figures and stories. The raven, Dudu*, seems to know more than he can tell; Marcelline*, the nurse of Jeanne, a little French girl, also seems to know more than she tells. These everyday things have a fascination a child would understand and find believable. But they are even more magical than this, for things are never quite what they seem. The cuckoo clock harbors a "fairyfied" cuckoo* who confers good luck on the house where the clock hangs and who can take a little girl, Griselda, to places far from her everday world. A tapestry on which the moon shines becomes real enough for Hugh, a young boy, to enter. Inside the Chinese cabinet is a wonderful place of bright colors, where the inhabitants accomplish their tasks by nodding; in dressing Griselda, her attendants simply nod to a piece of clothing and it immediately fits itself onto her. Butterflies, which seem so gay and desultory, are revealed to have a purpose in life that no one would guess, for they paint all the flowers in the world with colors from a beautiful garden. Dudu really does know more than he tells, for he is three or four hundred years old and is responsible for the adventures Hugh and Jeanne have in the tapestries. Marcelline, too, is more than she seems, for she may be a woman in white who has spun all the stories ever told in the world. The pets Hugh and Jeanne have never speak, as Dudu does, but they appear in the magical land which Jeanne and Hugh visit. The effect is not only to make the magical seem less threatening—for how comforting it is to be near something or someone from one's ordinary life!—but to make the ordinary wonderful, to imbue every-day objects with a richness they do not ordinarily have.

Though the fantasy world has elements of our own, familiar world in it, it still has mystery. The cuckoo explains to Griselda that not only are there things she will never understand, but that there are things it is intended she never understand. Hugh and Jeanne are never quite sure that Marcelline and the lady in white are really one and the same, and Dudu is full of secrets he never will reveal. Both the cuckoo and Dudu go off to mysterious places they say nothing of to the children; they only stop to say goodbye.

Though written for entertainment, there is an air of didacticism about the books, especially about *The Cuckoo Clock*. The cuckoo has ulterior motives for taking Griselda on her adventures, for some have a moral attached. Griselda's trip to butterfly-land* is a result of her sulky wish to be there, where, she feels, no one has to prepare lessons or do work of any kind; the trip soon changes her mind. As she speculates about what lies at the back of the moon, the bird has several reproving suggestions that she immediately rejects: that at the back of the moon are all the unfinished projects in the world, such as the many things Griselda has started and never gone back to; and that at the back of the moon are all the "little black dogs" of ill temper that children nurture in this world and must carry on their backs on the moon. Griselda prefers what they actually find: Phil*, her young friend, sailing his boat on a sea. When the cuckoo leaves Griselda at the end, it is because she now has friends who will help her, as it has been doing. This didacticism is not as apparent in *The Tapestry Room*; though Jeanne is downright rude to Dudu at times, he never reproves her. However didactic the works are, they are works of delight, to read for pleasure.

Molesworth's prose sometimes plods, but her works do not. The episodic stories are very entertaining. Perhaps the best thing about the books is the way they blend realism and fantasy, never straining the reader's disbelief. On the whole, the children in the works are wonderfully life-like, reacting to events as one would expect. Griselda, especially, is a skillfully drawn, three-dimensional character, sweet but plaguing at times, and very human in her cantankerous reactions to her stodgy, well-meaning great-aunts. Phil, however, is the prattling Victorian tot, earnestly cute and mauling the English language in a way that makes the modern reader wince.

Works

Juvenile full-length fantasy: *The Cuckoo Clock* (1877), as Ennis Graham; *The Tapestry Room* (1879); *Christmas-Tree Land* (1884) [not included]; *Four Winds Farm* (1886) [not included].

Juvenile novels, short stories, etc.: *Tell Me a Story* (1875), as Ennis Graham; *Carrots: Just a Little Boy* (1876), as Ennis Graham; *Grandmother Dear* (1878); *A Christmas Child* (1880); *Hermy* (1880); *The Adventures of Herr Baby* (1881); *Hoodie* (1881); *Rosy* (1882); *The Boys and I* (1882); *Summer Stories for Boys and Girls* (1882); *Two Little Waifs* (1883); *The Little Old Portrait* (1884), as *Edmee* (1915); *Lettice* (1884); *Us: An Old-Fashioned Tale* (1885); *A Charge Fulfilled* (1886); *Silverthorns* (1886); *The Palace in the Garden* (1887); *Little Miss Peggy* (1887); *The Abbey by the Sea* (1887); *A Christmas Posy* (1888); *Five Minute Stories* (1888); *The Third Miss St. Quentin* (1888); *Neighbours* (1889); *A House to Let* (1889); *The Rectory Children* (1889); *Nesta* (1889); *Great Uncle Hoot-Toot* (1889); *Twelve Tiny Tales* (1890); *Family Troubles* (1890); *The Children of the Castle* (1890); *Little Mother Bunch* (1890); *The Green Casket and Other Stories* (1890); *The Story of a Spring Morning and Other Tales* (1890); *The Red Grange* (1891); *The Bewitched Lamp* (1891); *The Lucky Ducks and Other Stories* (1891); *Nurse Heatherdale's Story* (1891); *Sweet Content* (1891); *Imogen* (1892); *An Enchanted Garden* (1892); *The Girls and I* (1892); *Farthings* (1892); *The Man with the Pan-Pipes and Other Stories* (1892); *Robin Redbreast* (1892); *The Next-Door House* (1892); *Stories of the Saints for Children* (1892); *Studies and Stories* (1892); *The Thirteen Little Black Pigs and Other Stories* (1893); *Mary* (1893); *Blanche* (1893);

Olivia (1894); *My New Home* (1894); *The Carved Lions* (1894); *Opposite Neighbors and Other Stories* (1895); *Sheila's Mystery* (1895); *White Turrets* (1895); *Friendly Joey and Other Stories* (1896); *The Oriel Window* (1896); *Philippa* (1896); *Stories for Children in Illustration of the Lord's Prayer* (1897); *Meg Langholme* (1897); *Miss Mouse and Her Boys* (1897); *Greyling Towers* (1898); *The Magic Nuts* (1898); *The Grim House* (1899); *This and That* (1899); *The Children's Hour* (1899); *The Three Witches* (1900); *The House That Grew* (1900); *The Wood-Pigeons and Mary* (1901); *"My Pretty" and Her Little Brother "Too,"* *and Other Stories* (1901); *The Blue Baby and Other Stories* (1901); *Peterkin* (1902); *The Mystery of the Pinewood, and Hollow Tree House* (1903); *The Ruby Ring* (1904); *The Bolted Door and Other Stories* (1906); *Jasper* (1906); *The Little Guest* (1907); *Fairies—of Sorts* (1908); *The February Boys* (1909); *The Story of a Year* (1910); *Fairies Afield* (1911).

Adult: *Lover and Husband* (1869); *She Was Young and He Was Old* (1872); *Not without Thorns* (1873); *Cicely* (1874); *Hathercourt Rectory* (1878); *Miss Bouverie* (1880); *Marrying and Giving in Marriage* (1887); *Four Ghost Stories* (1888); *That Girl in Black, and Bronzie* (1889); *Leona* (1892); *Uncanny Tales* (1896); *The Laurel Walk* (1898); *The Wrong Envelope, and Other Stories* (1906).

Secondary Works

Baker, Margaret J. "Mary Louisa Molesworth," *Junior Bookshelf*, 12 (March, 1948), pp. 19–26.

Green, R. L. "Mrs. Molesworth," *Junior Bookshelf*, 21 (July, 1957), pp. 101–8.

———."Mrs. Molesworth," in *Tellers of Tales* (Leicester, England: Edmund Ward, 1946), pp. 102–15.

———. *Mrs. Molesworth*. London: Bodley Head, 1961.

Laski, Margharita. *Mrs. Ewing, Mrs. Molesworth, and Mrs. Hodgson Burnett*. London: Arthur Barker, 1950.

Molesworth, Mrs. "On the Art of Writing Fiction for Children," in *A Peculiar Gift: Nineteenth Century Writings on Books for Children*, ed. Lance Salway (Harmondsworth, England: Penguin Books, Kestrel Books, 1976), pp. 340–46. [Reprinted from *Atalanta*, 6 (May, 1893), pp. 583–86.]

MOON OF GOMRATH, THE. Alan Garner. London: Collins, 1963. 160 pp. British.

An odd well is found, and Susan* and Colin* go with Gowther Mossock*, with whom they are staying, to see it. On the way home, Colin and Susan walk through the woods and see a strange black shape with fiery red eyes. Soon after, they are stopped by an elf* and a dwarf*, Uthecar Hornskin*. Uthecar and Albanac*, a man clothed in black, take the children to Fundindelve*, a cave where 140 knights lie sleeping until England's greatest need. The children's help is needed, for the elves are disappearing and they must use the Mark of Fohla*, the silver bracelet given to Susan by Angharad Goldenhand* not long ago. Though reluctant, for the Morrigan*, a witch Colin and Susan had helped thwart, may be seeking revenge on them, Susan gives the Mark to Albanac, with the promise that she will get it back quickly. Evil is abroad that night, for the Brollachan*, long imprisoned in the earth, is free; the elves and Cadellin Silverbrow*, a wizard, are seeking it. The children get home safely.

Two days later, alone at a nearby quarry, Susan rides a black pony that plunges into the water. When she goes home, she seems in a trance. That night Colin wakes and finds that Susan has gone. He follows and loses her and comes to the quarry, where he meets something that has Susan's shape but is not her, and it chases Colin to the farmhouse, where he falls on the doorstep, shouting a strange word. He wakes at dawn, on the doorstep of the house. Susan is still in bed. While all but Susan and Colin are out that day, Albanac comes, with the bracelet. When he hears what has happened, he forces the Mark onto Susan's arm, and the Brollachan emerges from her. Albanac fails to control it with a spell and tries his sword; at a stab, the Brollachan vanishes, destroying the sword. Susan is sleeping. Albanac brings Cadellin, but the wizard cannot wake her, for she is beyond his magic. Uthecar realizes that the only thing that will help is the Mothan*, a magical flower that grows only in certain places and blooms only at full moon. The next night there is a full moon and Colin gets the Mothan. As he walks home, he is followed by something, then Albanac comes on his horse and takes Colin back home.

As they give Susan the Mothan, they hear the baying of hounds and Susan wakes. She runs to the window, begging "Celemon"* to stay, and Colin, following, sees nine young women riding with hawks and hounds in the sky. Susan remembers going into the water; she had been pulled out by Celemon, who has a bracelet like hers, and Susan had ridden with her and her maidens until she had tasted the bitter Mothan and come back. Cadellin explains that she has been riding with the daughters of the moon; many things long sleeping have been quickened that night.

Days pass and Colin and Susan decide to watch the moon rise on the mound where Colin had found the Mothan. Cold, they build a fire and thus wake three of the Einheriar of the Herlathing, the Wild Hunt*, who capture them and take them along as the rest of the riders are wakened. Finally the riders call Garanhir*, the lord of the Hunt. He is a great man with a stag's antlers, but he bows to Susan's Mark before the Hunt rides away, leaving the children. Colin realizes that Garanhir had followed him the night he had picked the Mothan. A dwarf comes upon the children and sends Susan to find Cadellin, for the Hunt must be laid to rest again. But when the wizard, Albanac, and Uthecar go to find Colin and the dwarf, they are gone. From Susan's description, Uthecar recognizes the dwarf as Pelis the False*. While Cadellin and Uthecar search, Susan is to stay with Albanac in Fundindelve, but when the man sleeps, she leaves.

Colin has been driven by wildcats and by Pelis to the house where the Morrigan is. Wildcats also drive Susan toward an unknown destination, but the Mark seems to deter them. When Susan drops it, it bounces and becomes a tunnel that takes her to Angharad, who explains that the Morrigan's power is waxing because she is of the old moon, which shines now; Susan's power is of the new moon, and she can defeat the Morrigan at that time if she will, if she uses the Mark. Susan is given a horn, Anghalac*, to blow only if all is lost. She comes to herself beside a river and eventually comes to the Morrigan's house, where Uthecar saves her from a guard. A night and a day have passed, and the Morrigan is holding Colin ransom for the Mark. Susan and the dwarf are attacked by wildcats and grotesque creatures; Uthecar holds them off, but suddenly Susan reads aloud a word of power on the bracelet and the Herlathing come, driving and slaughtering the Morrigan's creatures.

As Uthecar and Susan hurry toward Fundindelve, they come upon Morrigan, but Susan manages to deflect her spell and the witch vanishes. Albanac goes with Susan to the Morrigan's house; it is a ruin. When they report this to Cadellin at Fundindelve, he realizes that the Morrigan had rebuilt her ruined house with moon magic and that it appears whole only when the old moon shines on it. Because the witch is not inside it now, Colin is probably safe there. That afternoon Susan, Uthecar, and Albanac clear brush from around the house and ring it with fires at twilight. They themselves leave the place to wait for the army of elves, not daring to risk a confrontation with the Morrigan's minions. But when they return with the army, the fires are out, and the Morrigan is somewhere near. They manage to relight the fires and all wait for moonrise.

When the moon appears, so does the house. Susan and Uthecar search it for Colin, finding the Brollachan imprisoned in a bottle, and Pelis, who fights Uthecar. Susan finds Colin, and they leave the house with Uthecar after Pelis escapes. Outside a battle rages against the Morrigan's creatures. They are beaten back, but in saving Uthecar from an attack, Albanac is wounded by Pelis, who is slain by Uthecar. Albanac goes to heal his wound, for it is the destiny of his people never to be at the end of what they begin, but he will return. When the elves leave, Susan goes back to the house, for the Morrigan still has the Brollachan. Seeing a word of power on the Mark, Susan speaks it, and she and the Morrigan have a battle of magic, which Susan loses. When the Morrigan sends the Brollachan after the elves, Susan blows the horn as the creature overtakes her. Suddenly Celemon and her maidens and the Herlathing are there, all around her. Before Colin's eyes, silver lightning flashes inside the Brollachan, and it breaks into the riders of the Herlathing and of Celemon. One, Susan, is left behind, but the rest ride across the night, free for ever.

MOONA-MULGARS, a race of beings in Walter de la Mare's* *The Three Mulla-mulgars*. These black and white Mulgars*—or monkeys—live in the mountains. Most have pink eyes—some have eyes that are turquoise—and all are nearsighted. Because their eyes are weak, they prefer to go abroad in the evenings. They have sad-looking faces. These Mulgars prefer their Ukka-nuts and cheese moldy. The Moona-mulgars are perfectly adapted to their mountain habitat, living in villages of mushroom-shaped huts on inaccessible ledges and creeping along the narrowest ledges with no fear of falling, climbing up and down by holding onto one another to form "ropes." When Thumma*, Thimbulla*, and Ummanodda*, the three Mulla-mulgars, are trapped on a ledge on a mountain, some Moona-mulgars rescue them and take them to the end of their domain; there the Moona-mulgars agree to accompany the three to the Valleys of Tishnar*.

MOONFLOWER, an object in E[dith] Nesbit Bland's* *Harding's Luck**. This flower is grown by Dickie Harding* from a seed found in Perrokett's Artistic Bird Seed. Tall as a sunflower, the moonflower has blooms as white as water-lilies, with a gold center, and its seeds are silvery. Dickie uses some of the flowers to claim his silver rattle* after his aunt has pawned it; when he arranges the seeds in a pattern around the rattle and a sealing ring, he is transported back in time to the seventeenth century, where he lives as Richard Arden*.

MOORHOUSE, TOM, a historical character in Jill Paton Walsh's* *A Chance Child**. Tom is a nineteenty-century apprentice coal miner who, helped by Creep*, a boy from the twentieth century, escapes from his brutal master. Tom later finds work at a chain-maker's, where he meets Lucy*. When the two run away and find work at a pottery plant, Tom gets them dismissed when he drops a load of china. He later gets a job with a coal miner and leaves Creep and Lucy, who is disappointed, for she had hoped that she and Tom would eventually marry. Though Creep had rescued Tom from his first master, down-to-earth Tom is forced to admit that the ghostly Creep looks even more ghostly when Tom has had enough to eat—a charge Lucy emphatically denies. He is also insensitive enough to tell Lucy that the scar on her face makes her too ugly for him to marry. Tom seems to have been based on a real boy whose testimony about his working conditions is in the Parliamentary Papers.

MOPSA, the title character in Jean Ingelow's* *Mopsa the Fairy**. Mopsa is one of four baby fairies Jack* finds in a nest in a hollow tree and takes to Fairyland*. Because she is so sweet, Jack kisses her and therefore she stays a child, not growing older but growing taller. When they reach Fairyland, Mopsa learns that she is the sister of the queen of the fairies*, but because there can be only one queen, Mopsa must leave. Fairies in the shape of deer offer Mopsa the rule of their kingdom, but when she learns that they keep their queen shut away from the sun, the girl flees with Jack, only to find herself in the power of the strange fairies. These fairies had been enchanted into deer, and the enchantment is now at an end, for only by bringing an alien queen to rule them against her will could their disenchantment be accomplished. Mopsa becomes their queen.

MOPSA THE FAIRY. Jean Ingelow. London: Longmans, Green, and Co., 1869. 248 pp. British.
On a lovely day Jack* sits with his little sister and their nurse in the meadow. Hearing a twitter from a nearby hollow tree, Jack climbs into the tree and

discovers a nest of four baby fairies. When the hole through which Jack entered the tree vanishes, he is trapped. When, at the suggestion of the rapidly growing fairies, Jack whistles, something grabs his legs and flies off with him. It is Jenny*, an albatross, who is taking Jack and his little companions to the back way into Fairyland*.

They come to a bay filled with rotting ships which were involved in some way with evil; here Jack is set on a small boat that sails itself up a river guarded by flamingoes. Jack lands at a sort of horse paradise where people are clockwork and abused horses come to ''get right again.'' Finding that Jack has no hole in which to place a key, the clockwork people are greatly distressed and offer to make one. Jack objects, and he barely gets away to his boat.

Here a tragedy occurs. Ravens land on the boat and plan to eat the four young fairies Jack has in his pocket. But when Jack explains that in his world there is only one moon, instead of three in Fairyland, the ravens think he is mocking them and leave—all but one, who tricks Jack into taking one of the fairies from his pocket, and snatches it away from him, gobbling it down before his horrified eyes.

The next day is hot and Jack lands at a cool spot where a fair is being held. Everywhere he sees parrots in cages. Two tell him that they are actually fairies enchanted by an old gypsy woman. The gypsy soon comes on the scene, carrying what appears to be a baby with a handkerchief over its face, but when the gypsy throws the ''baby'' at the mocking parrot, it turns out to be a bundle of rags. Snatching the gypsy's handkerchief inside his cage, the parrot forces her to free the rest of the parrots by threatening to pick out the embroidery in the handkerchief, where the gypsy's life-power is hidden. The gypsy frees all but two of the parrots. Jack frees these by pulling off their heads, revealing the fairy imprisoned in each parrot skin. The freed parrots cover the gypsy and force her to take the form of a condor, which flaps away to the gypsy camp for protection; the woman's clothes and handkerchief are burned so that she will not be able to ''put herself together again.'' Fear-stricken at the fight which ensues between the gypsies and the other folk, Jack flees to his boat.

He next lands at a large, empty city. Unable to find anyone, Jack swims in the river and, coming out, discovers that his stockings have been thrown into the river by an old woman knitting nearby. The stockings she is knitting for Jack will give her power over him. She is a slave whose master will sell her if she is late once more; she begs Jack to buy her and hurries off when he agrees. When Jack goes into town, he finds it busy and bustling and is puzzled by the actions of the town dogs, who sniff everyone's feet and sometimes gnaw them. One dog explains that people had feuded with the fairies and one night decided to steal their wheat. Forgetting that they would not be able to become visible until the next moon, the people had crept into the wheatfield and made themselves invisible. They were not able to move, either, and when the fairies came to cut the wheat the next morning, the people among the wheat were cut off at the ankles. So they make their feet of wood.

The old slave has been sold to another master, who sells her to Jack. Jack sends her into town to buy new clothes and she returns with a piece of purple and gold ribbon, which they stretch into a gown, and a comb, which she uses to comb the gray from her hair; the hair erases her wrinkles. She is the queen of the fairies* and the three fairies come out of Jack's pocket to greet her. Two have grown up and wear splendid clothes, but the third, Mopsa*, looks and acts like a child, for Jack had kissed her earlier. Still Jack's slave, the queen buys herself from him with a piece of her robe and is thereby able to enter her kingdom again.

Hundreds of fairies come to tow the boat through a tunnel into the kingdom. The queen tells Jack how she had grown bored with her kingdom and decided to travel with a retinue, and how they had all been caught and sold as slaves. Jack and the others come into Fairyland, where they meet the apple woman*, a mortal woman valued because she can make the fairies cry. She becomes Mopsa's nurse. After breakfast the next morning, the queen reveals to Jack that she is Mopsa's sister, but because there cannot be two queens in the kingdom, one must leave. That day a fairy in the shape of a deer comes from another kingdom to ask Mopsa to be their queen, for their queen must be of alien birth. Frightened by the apple woman's story that the queen of these people is always shut away from the sun, Mopsa and Jack run away in the boat. Following them, the apple woman advises them to cross the mountains to the next kingdom.

Jack and Mopsa cross a strange desert land where the people, who are stone during the day, come alive at evening. Once they had done a deed so cruel that they were told their hearts were like stones, and stone they became, except for the two hours of twilight every day. Tiring as they trudge along, Jack and Mopsa are helped by the gleaming, bat-like air fairies, who seat the two on a wing which one fairy nips off itself, and carry them across the mountains into a beautiful country.

The two come to a lovely castle. When Mopsa enters, she is surrounded by deer and Jack is closed out; he breaks in and finds people there. One of them, the prince, looks exactly like Jack. Mopsa explains that the deer were fairies who had been enchanted and could be unenchanted only if a queen of alien birth came to rule them against her will. Once three fairies had come to teach these fairies but were turned out. When harvest came, the ignorant fairies wasted what the three would have taught them to use, refusing to give it to the needy. The three fairies set a spell on them, hiding the fairy knights and men and directly enchanting those in the castle.

Mopsa melts Jack's money by holding it in her hand and shapes it into a rod, which Jack must name and state the use of. He calls it a "wand" and says it is to be used to point at things, and the others are overjoyed, for Mopsa can use the wand to point to anything hidden or lost. She uses it in the manner of a dowsing rod to find the fairy men. At a certain rock the three fairies of the story appear and tell Jack and the prince to dig. The boys come to a stone, under which is a tunnel which the boys follow to a stable sheltering a herd of stags that run away at their approach. As the stags run, they turn into men, and all eventually arrive at a door that leads them out of the rock. During the succeeding jubilation, Jack is sad. Reminded by one of the three fairies of Jenny, Jack calls her and Jenny flies him home, where none are surprised to see him. He goes to bed.

MORDA, a character in Lloyd Alexander's* *Taran Wanderer**. Born a human, Morda sought power and everlasting life and made himself into a powerful sorcerer. When one winter night Angharad*, an enchantress of the House of Llyr*, finds refuge at his cottage, he takes from her on her death a jeweled emblem possessing powers to lighten labor. Realizing that it is one of the powerful stones of the Fair Folk*, Morda uses it for his own purposes, discovering that it can enchant even the Fair Folk themselves. By magical arts Morda concentrates his life-power in the bone of his little finger, cuts it off, and hides it, that he may never die or weaken. Now he seeks to rule Prydain*. Taran*, a young warrior, and his companions find the finger bone and, later, Morda himself, and are almost enchanted by him. Taran destroys the man by breaking the bone.

MORDRED. *See* Medraut

MORGAN LE FAY. *See* Fay, Morgan le; Fay, Morgan the; Margan; Morrigan, the

MORGANT, a character in *The Black Cauldron**, by Lloyd Alexander*. He is king of Madoc. A ruthless, fearless warrior, Morgant is second only to Gwydion*, the war leader of the High King of Prydain*, and he has even saved Gwydion's life. Ambitious for power, Morgant sees his chance when Gwydion and his followers seek to destroy the Black Crochan*, a cauldron in which dead warriors can become living, heartless warriors who cannot be killed. Morgant captures Ellidyr*, a young warrior, with the cauldron, and plans to use it to create his own army. Gwydion and his men come upon Morgant's camp, however, and in the ensuing battle Morgant is killed by King Smoit*.

MORLEY, JANE, a character in Pauline Clarke's* *The Twelve and the Genii**. She is the sister of Max and Philip Morley**. Jane is enchanted when the Twelves*, the wooden soldiers Max finds in the attic of their house, come to life, and she becomes a genie for them just as Max does. She helps him to watch over the soldiers as they journey back to their old home, Haworth parsonage, where they first came to life through the creative genius of Charlotte, Emily, Anne, and Branwell Brontë.

MORLEY, MAX, a character in *The Twelve and the Genii**, by Pauline Clarke*. He is the younger brother of Jane and Philip Morley**. When his family moves into a house near Haworth, where the Brontës lived, eight-year-old Max finds twelve old wooden soldiers hidden in the attic; these are the Twelves*, toy soldiers the four Brontë children loved and brought to life through their creative genius. Max is delighted when the soldiers come alive for him; they call him the Genie Maxii. His pleasure is short-lived, though, for an American professor looking for the Brontës' soldiers hears about these from Philip. When the soldiers decide to run away to Haworth, Max, Jane, and Philip watch over them during their night marches. Though he loves the little soldiers, Max knows that they will be safer at Haworth, and he visits them often.

MORLEY, PHILIP, a character in Pauline Clarke's* *The Twelve and the Genii**. He is the fourteen-year-old brother of Max and Jane Morley**. When practical Philip hears that an American professor is offering a large sum of money for the wooden soldiers Charlotte, Emily, Anne, and Branwell Brontë played with and wrote about, he writes a letter to the man about the twelve soldiers Max has found in the attic of their house. To Philip's amazement, the Twelves*, as the soldiers are called, have been given life through the creative genius of the four Brontës, and Philip becomes one of their protectors—or genii. He helps Max and Jane watch over the soldiers as they journey to their old home, Haworth parsonage, and gets himself locked inside the Brontë house so that he can open a window from the inside and help the little soldiers in.

MORRIGAN, THE, a character in Alan Garner's* *The Weirdstone of Brisingamen** and *The Moon of Gomrath**. She is the Third Bane of Logris, and an ancient witch-queen of great power, especially when the moon is old, for then her power waxes. The Morrigan has powers as a shape-shifter, taking on any form that will help her; once she becomes Selina Place, who lives in a house in Alderley, England. She is one of the minions of Nastrond, the Great Spirit of Darkness, and with Grimnir*, a wizard, seeks to gain more power than their master. The Morrigan fails, only just escaping Fenrir, the great wolf Nastrond sends to destroy them. For a time she regains her strength and then makes another bid for power, at the same time seeking revenge on those who had helped to defeat her. The Morrigan captures and imprisons the Brollachan*, a mighty force, and she seeks to destroy Susan* and Colin*, two human children who had helped to defeat her. Though Susan uses the Mark of Fohla*, a bracelet, to fight the Morrigan in a contest of magic, the witch defeats her, only to be defeated, in turn, when Susan uses Anghalac*, a magic horn, to summon the powers of Wild Magic and destroy the Brollachan. *See also* Margan; Fay, Morgan le; Fay, Morgan the

MORTMAIN, DUTHBERT, a character in *A Swiftly Tilting Planet**, by Madeleine L'Engle*. He is perhaps descended from a seventeenth-century minister; he becomes the second husband of Mrs. Maddox and the stepfather of Chuck Maddox* and Branwen Zillah Maddox O'Keefe* (Beezie). Brutal and loutish, Duthbert has a good head for business, and Mrs. Maddox marries him to keep the family grocery store going. Though Duthbert tries to make her love him, she does not. At first things are peaceful in the house, but soon Duthbert begins to show his resentment of his stepchildren, boxing Chuck on the ears at the slightest provocation, and pinching Beezie whenever he can. When one night the children's grandmother protests, Duthbert tries to strike her, but Chuck gets in the way and is knocked down the stairs. The boy's skull is fractured, and the grandmother suffers a fatal heart attack. After this Duthbert is gentler, but he has Chuck institutionalized as soon as he can.

MOSSOCK, GOWTHER, a character in the *Weirdstone of Brisingamen** and *The Moon of Gomrath**, by Alan Garner*. He is the husband of Bess Mossock. Gowther is a farmer, working Highmost Redmanhey, near Alderley, like three centuries of Mossocks before him. Not overly tall, he is solid and steady and sees no need to change his way of life just because it is thirty years behind the world around him. Pragmatic Gowther has had no dealings with the magical creatures that sometimes haunt Alderley Edge, near his farm, but when they show themselves he is not one to quibble, and he accepts and helps Cadellin Silverbrow*, an ancient wizard, as well as he can.

MOTHAN, THE, a flower in Alan Garner's* *The Moon of Gomrath**. It is part of the Old Magic and a strong charm to use in evil times. Red-rooted and having five petals to the flower, the Mothan glows with the light of the moon; it flowers only during full moon and can thus be found only at that time, growing by itself on the highest part of the ancient straight tracks that cross Britain. Colin*, a young boy, finds and plucks a flower of it to give to his sister, Susan*, who is under an enchantment of Old Magic.

MOULDIERWARP, a magical creature in *Harding's Luck**, by E[dith] Nesbit Bland*. This white mole is one of three Mouldiwarps; it is more refined than the Mouldiwarp* and is controlled by the Mouldiestwarp*. The Mouldierwarp is the crest of the house of Arden; it has power over the magic of space.

MOULDIESTWARP, a magical creature in E[dith] Nesbit Bland's* *Harding's Luck**. It is the largest and most powerful of three Mouldiwarps and controls the Mouldiwarp* and the Mouldierwarp*. This white mole is the creature on the shield of arms of the house of Arden. Edred and Elfrida Arden** call on the Mouldiestwarp when Dickie Harding* is kidnapped; it tells Edred how to find Dickie and gives him the courage to do what he must.

MOULDIWARP, a magical creature in E[dith] Nesbit Bland's* *The House of Arden** and *Harding's Luck**. This white mole is from Sussex County, England; it speaks with the accent of the country people, though it can speak and has spoken other languages, including French. It is the badge of the house of Arden, and it has power over time and all things white. It is one of three Mouldiwarps;

the Mouldiestwarp* controls it. The Mouldiwarp can be called by Lord Arden at sunset the day before he turns ten years old, if he speaks the correct rhyme; it can also be called by verse. This testy little creature is called by Edred Arden* in the twentieth century and is asked to help him and his sister, Elfrida Arden*, in their search for the treasure of the Ardens. Despite the Mouldiwarp's occasional scorn of them, it helps Edred and Elfrida by telling them how to travel back in time to see the treasure being hidden and, sometimes, by rescuing them when they have gotten into trouble. The Mouldiwarp goes with them when the two travel to South America to rescue their father; it grows and takes on the semblance of a dancing bear and helps the children escape with their father and Richard Arden*, another time traveler. The mole later rescues Richard when he is captured in a battle at the time that the treasure of Arden was hidden.

MOUNT DRAGON, a place in Lloyd Alexander's* Chronicles of Prydain*. This mountain stands in the western part of Prydain*. Sheer on one side, Mount Dragon slopes gently on the other side, where Annuvin*, the stronghold of Arawn*, the Lord of Death, stands at the mountain's foot. Atop Mount Dragon is a great boulder around which the wind whistles. When Arawn steals Dyrnwyn*, a powerful sword, he hides it under the rock. Here it is found by Taran*, a young warrior, who uses it to turn the tide of battle against Arawn.

MOWGLI, a character in the Jungle books*, by Rudyard Kipling*. He may be Nathoo, the son of Messua*, who was carried off by a lame tiger; eventually he marries and fathers a child. He is called Mowgli because he resembles a naked frog. When he is still a baby, Shere Khan*, a tiger, attacks Mowgli's family, and the boy escapes, toddling into the den of a wolf. These wolves adopt and raise him, and Mowgli grows up wise in the ways of the jungle, taught by Baloo*, a bear, and Bagheera*, a panther. Mowgli is as bold, boastful, and beloved as any boy, and he cares nothing that Shere Khan still seeks his life. When he is eleven or twelve years old, the tiger tries again, and Mowgli meets him with fire. Disgusted at the betrayal of the wolves who have sided with the tiger, Mowgli leaves the jungle, to live in the village of men. Here he does not belong, for he is too much a creature of the jungle, and when the people take him for a sorcerer after he kills Shere Khan, Mowgli leaves the village. He returns only once, to rescue Messua, who had taken him in, and he causes Hathi*, the elephant, to destroy the village. Henceforth, Mowgli lives in the jungle apart from the wolves, hunting with the wolves he had been raised with. He has many adventures during these years and becomes master of the jungle. Mowgli delights in "pulling Death's whiskers," and he does it whenever he can. Thus things stand until he is about seventeen, when one spring he is more restless and unhappy than usual; it is time, his friends tell him, that he go to live with his own, and though it breaks his heart, he does so. Mowgli remains the master of the jungle.

MRS. FRISBY AND THE RATS OF NIMH. Robert O'Brien. Illus. Zena
Bernstein. New York: Atheneum, 1971. 233 pp. American. Newbery Award,
1972.

Mrs. Frisby*, a widowed mouse, lives with her children in a cinderblock in
Mr. Fitzgibbon's* garden. Every spring they move from the garden to a nearby
creek, to be safe when the farmer tills his garden, but this year is different; one
of her children has been sick with pneumonia and must not be moved until the
ground is warmer. Desperate, Mrs. Frisby asks Jeremy*, a crow she once helped,
to take her to the owl that lives nearby to ask for advice. Hearing that she is the
widow of Jonathan Frisby*, the owl sends her to a group of rats for help,
suggesting that they move her house to the lee of a large boulder in the garden.
Puzzled, Mrs. Frisby goes to the entrance of the rats' burrow, under a rosebush,
but she is not let in.

She gets help from an unexpected source: Mr. Ages*, a white mouse skilled
in the art of healing, who takes her into the burrow. Here Mrs. Frisby is astonished
by what she sees, for the rats have set up electric lights and an elevator and
have accomplished amazing feats of engineering. She meets Nicodemus*, their
leader, and Justin*, who is highly respected, and learns of their plan to move
all the rats to a secluded valley, where they will be safe from man. The rats
agree to move Mrs. Frisby's house behind a boulder in the garden, where Mr.
Fitzgibbon will miss it when plowing, but someone must put sleeping powder
into the food of Dragon*, the family cat, to keep him out of the way. Only Mrs.
Frisby is small enough to get through the hole into the house, and she volunteers
to do the job.

Because her husband was killed accomplishing the same task, Nicodemus tells
Mrs. Frisby their story: he and Justin were ordinary rats captured and taken to
Nimh*, where they were subjected to experiments which altered their DNA and
made them more intelligent, and were taught to read. When the rats escaped,
they helped a group of experimental mice to escape, too; Jonathan Frisby and
Mr. Ages were the only two mice to make it out. The group of rats and mice
spent the winter in a closed-up house, reading and practicing their writing.
Learning that humans have hated rats for centuries because they steal, the rats
decided the build their own civilization and not live by taking from humans. In
spring they left the house, coming upon the body of a traveling toy mender and
salvaging his tools and toy engines. Digging out a cave near Mr. Fitzgibbon's
house, they tapped into his electrical cable and created the wonderful things
Mrs. Frisby saw. The rats are still stealing power, however, and they have
decided to go to a secluded valley nearby where they can build a civilization of
their own, independent of man. Because this means leaving behind the luxuries
of electricity, some rats have protested, and a small group has left to set up its
own colony.

That evening Mrs. Frisby enters the Fitzgibbons' house and puts the sleeping
powder into Dragon's food. As she tries to leave, however, she is caught by
one of the Fitzgibbon children and put into a cage. Here she listens to their

conversation and learns that a group of rats were electrocuted while trying to take a small motor from a local hardware store; she realizes that they must have been the group that left the larger colony. The health department, worried that they might have had rabies, is sending out a team to exterminate the colony near the Fitzgibbon house.

After the family goes to bed, Justin rescues Mrs. Frisby and she warns him of the danger. The rats move her house and then make plans to move to the valley, dismantling their machinery so as to leave behind no evidence. Justin and a small group of rats will stay behind, running from the burrow when the extermination begins to make it look as though the rat colony were still there. The next day, Mrs. Frisby watches as the rosebush protecting the burrow is pushed over and gas is pumped through the burrow. Of the rats who stayed behind, all but three come out; they make it look as if many rats were running from the burrow before they vanish into the landscape. Another rat finally crawls out of the burrow and Mr. Ages helps it. When the burrow is opened, the men find two dead rats in it; Mrs. Frisby does not see whether or not one is Justin.

The garden is plowed around the Frisby home and warm weather comes. The family goes to its summer home, where Mrs. Frisby tells the children about their father, and one of her sons vows to visit the rats in their valley.

MRS. MAY'S BROTHER, a nameless character in Mary Norton's* *The Borrowers*. Like his older sister, who becomes Mrs. Ada May*, he grows up in India. Never strong, when he comes to England at age nine he catches rheumatic fever and is sent to Firbanks, the house belonging to his great-aunt, to get well. Here he has a miserable time, bullied by Mrs. Driver*, the housekeeper, and grouched at by his great-aunt. One evening the boy helps Pod Clock*, one of the miniature people called "borrowers"*, and after that things change. Though Pod is frantic to keep the boy out of their lives, the boy meets the rest of Pod's family: Homily Clock*, Pod's wife, and Arrietty Clock*, their daughter. The boy helps them by bringing them furniture from a dolls' house until he is caught by Mrs. Driver. When she brings in a rat catcher, the boy manages to help the Clocks escape. When he tells his sister of the tiny people, she is not sure whether to believe him or not, for he loves to tease her. The boy grows into a man and becomes a colonel in the army; he dies a hero's death on the North-West Frontier.

MUCH-BELUNGEN-UNDER-BLUFF, a place in *Are All the Giants Dead?*, by Mary Norton*. This little village in the Land of Cockayne* is one of several named Much-Belungen; two others are Much-Belungen-in-the-Marsh and Belungen-on-the-Hill. Much-Belungen-under-Bluff lies at the base of a great bluff where thirteen giants once lived; all but one were killed by Jack-the-Giant-Killer*. Once the thirteenth loses his talisman, he is killed, too. In the village live several people from fairy tales, including Big Hans and Little Hans. Jack-the-Giant-Killer and Jack-of-the-Beanstalk* own a nameless inn here.

MULDOON, MR., a character in *Rabbit Hill** and *The Tough Winter**, by Robert Lawson*. This old tiger-striped gray cat belongs to the Folks on Rabbit Hill. He is not threat to any of the animals that live there, being too old and having bad teeth. His hunting instincts come into play, though, when Willie Fieldmouse* is taken into the Folks' home to recover after a dunking, but Willie is rescued. So unafraid of him do the field mice become that when Mr. Muldoon is trapped beneath the snow and ice after a snowfall followed by an ice storm, the mice bring him food. He is finally freed by Red Buck, who smashes through the ice.

MULGARS, a race of beings in Walter de la Mare's* *The Three Mulla-mulgars**. The word means "monkey." There are many kinds of Mulgars: Gungamulgars*, the great gorillas; and Moona-mulgars*, who live in the mountains, among others. The Mulla-mulgars are those of royal descent. Nearly all the Mulgars are sentient, each type having a language and culture of its own, though some types are more advanced than others; some Mulgars use fire and know the making of it, while others do not. All Mulgars share common enemies, such as Roses, which is what they call the leopard.

MURRY, CHARLES WALLACE, a character in Madeleine L'Engle's* Time trilogy*. Mr. Murry* is a physicist and Mrs. Murry is a scientist; Charles is the youngest brother of Meg Murry* and of Sandy and Dennys Murry. Charles' parents are brilliant, but he is something more, with an IQ so high that it cannot be tested and an innate ability to kythe*—to communicate with people in a language deeper than words. He can tell what is troubling Meg or his mother and gather knowledge from them. Charles does not learn to talk until he is several years old, and then he speaks in clear, complete sentences, using words most young children do not know. Because he does not talk much to anyone besides his own family and because he is different, the people in the town where the Murrys live think he is stupid. When Charles had been about three, his father disappeared; two years later Charles meets Mrs Whatsit*, Mrs Which*, and Mrs Who*, and they send him, Meg, and Calvin O'Keefe* to rescue Mr. Murry. Overconfident of his own strength, Charles is subsumed by IT*, a monstrous brain, and is rescued by Meg's love. When he is six, Charles starts school. This is a miserable time, for he is bullied and beaten up by the other children, who think he is showing off when he talks about things they cannot understand. Charles also suffers from mitochondritis and almost dies; Meg saves him by going into one of his cells. Charles learns to adapt, to live with those who cannot understand his abilities, though he is not always completely accepted. When he is fifteen, he is still small for his age, appearing to be about twelve. Now he is called to use his talents to the utmost, to travel through time and alter the course of events, in order to keep Madog Branzillo* from destroying the world.

MURRY, MEG, a character in the Time trilogy*, *Dragons in the Waters*, and *The Arm of the Starfish*, by Madeleine L'Engle*. she is the only daughter of Mrs. and Mr. Murry*; she is the sister of Sandy, Dennys, and Charles Wallace Murry*; she becomes the wife of Calvin O'Keefe* and the mother of Polyhymnia, Charles, Sandy, Dennys, Peggy, Johnny, and Mary O'Keefe. Meg's adolescence is troubled, for, with her braces, glasses, and uncontrollable hair, she feels homely; despite her high IQ, Meg does not do well in school. Though she understands math very well, Meg resents having to do the problems the way she is told and becomes a trial to her teachers. Meg wishes she could be like her mother, able to control her emotions and carry on despite the gossipy neighbors and despite Mr. Murry's disappearance, but Meg cannot hold everything in; she feels too strongly to control her emotions and lashes out at those who hurt her, especially Mr. Jenkins*, the hostile principal of her school. Meg's faults stand her in good stead when she is sent with Charles and Calvin to rescue Mr. Murry, for they keep her from being completely subsumed by IT*, a monstrous brain. Meg's great capacity for love helps her to rescue Charles from IT's power, for love is something that IT does not possess and cannot understand. A year later, Meg learns more about love when she learns to accept and even to love Mr. Jenkins, in spite of all his faults. She also goes inside one of Charles's cells to help heal it and thereby save his life. The relationship between Calvin and Meg has been special from the very start, and it deepens, resulting in their marriage. Though she has grown out of her awkward stage to become a lovely woman, Meg has not left behind her tendencies toward strong emotions; but she does control them better. As she awaits the birth of Polyhymnia, Meg kythes* with Charles, sharing his adventures as he alters history to keep the world from nuclear holocaust.

MURRY, MR., a character in Madeleine L'Engle's* Time trilogy*. He and Mrs. Murry are the parents of Sandy, Dennys, Meg, and Charles Wallace Murry**. Mr. Murry is a physicist and a Ph.D. several times over. Though he prefers to work alone, he has worked at the Institute for Higher Learning at Princeton, and for the United States government as well. Mr. Murry is part of a government team working to learn about time and space and how to travel through them by tessering—"wrinkling"—them. During this top secret project, he tries to tesser to Mars but ends up, instead, on Camazotz*, a planet which has given in to the powers of evil and has done away with individuality. Here Mr. Murry resists IT*, the gigantic brain that controls Camazotz. IT offers him peace, for IT will make all his decisions for him and take care of all his thinking. Mr. Murry resists as long as he can, but he is about to give in when Meg, Charles, and Calvin O'Keefe* rescue him and take him home. Because Mr. Murry has no special project of his own to espouse, he later becomes a special adviser on physics and science to the president of the United States. As time passes, Mr. Murry becomes very aware of the evil that is trying to take over the universe, though there is little he can do to stop it. A call to him from the president warning that Madog

Branzillo* is threatening atomic war sends Charles on a journey through time to alter events and halt the threat of war. Mr. Murry becomes a special consultant on the uses of space for peace.

MYRDDIN, a character in *The Sleepers**, by Jane Louise Curry*. He is an ancient figure who knows how to use the powers of the earth. By some he is called Merlin. Long ago, while he was adviser to Artair*—King Arthur*—Myrddin was tricked by Nimiane* and imprisoned in the Eildon Tree*. There he has remained for several centuries. In the twentieth century, once or twice he is able to project Jennifer Huntington* into that long ago time where he is able to speak with her; Myrddin first appears as a boy to speak a prophecy about her brother, Henry Peter Huntington* (H.P.); later he appears as a crusty old man beneath the Eildon Tree. When Jennifer, H. P., Hugh Lewis*, and Gillian Peresby* discover Artair and his knights sleeping amid the *Brenhin Dlyseu**, the Thirteen Treasures of Prydein, Myrddin helps them to save the treasures and the men. By tricking Ellen Peresby*, a descendant of Nimiane's family, into saying a spell, Myrddin is freed from the tree. He accompanies his king, the men, and the Thirteen Treasures to a place of safety beyond the sea, where they will stay until they are needed. *See also* Lyon, Merriman; Merlyn

MYSTERIOUS SHRINKING HOUSE, THE. See Mindy's Mysterious Miniature

NAGHAR, LORD, a character in Jane Louise Curry's* *The Wolves of Aam**. This lord lusts for power and seeks Mirelidar*, one of twelve powerful sky-stones*, in order to gain its power. He may have destroyed the Worldstone, Nirim, containing power over the quickening of life, as part of his plot. Though he learns, through a magical mirror, where Lek*, a conjuror, has hidden Mirelidar, he does not solve the riddle before the stone is taken to safety.

NAGHAROT, a place in *The Wolves of Aam**, by Jane Louise Curry*. It is the fastness from which Lord Naghar* commands his forces.

NAHDIR AGA (*The First Two Lives of Lukas-Kasha*). *See* Aga, Nahdir

NAMASH, a character in Lloyd Alexander's* *The First Two Lives of Lukas-Kasha**. When this poor waterseller in the capital of Abadan* is kind to Lukas-Kasha* (Lukas), the king, Lukas rewards him with a bag of gold. Namash travels to Jannat al-Khuld, in Bishangar*, where he sets himself up as a merchant and buys a house. When Lukas is imprisoned in Namash's house by his political enemies, Namash burns the place to the ground in an effort to rescue him. This sacrifice of all he owns ends favorably for Namash, for under the house he discovers a large underground stream which, in dry Bishangar, is the greatest treasure of all.

NAMELESS ONES, nine nameless powers in *The Tombs of Atuan**, by Ursula K. LeGuin*. They are powers of death, madness, and destruction—the cruelty of the Earth—and they are older than man. The Nameless Ones ruled Earthsea* before the world of men was created, and they died before that world came to be; their Tombstones stand on the island of Atuan*, where they have been worshipped since men were created. Their Priestess is as nameless as they are and, it is believed, as deathless; her spirit is constantly reborn into a new body when her old body dies. The perfect girl child born when the old Priestess dies is taken to the Tombs and consecrated there; her own identity is "eaten" by the

Nameless Ones and she is called Arha, "the Eaten One." Dressed constantly in black, she perfoms ceremonies at the dark of the moon and "feeds" two of the Tombstones with blood at the full moons nearest the spring and fall equinoxes. For centuries the Nameless Ones were consulted by the kings of the Kargad Lands, but since the rise of the Godking* their temple has been more or less neglected and is falling into ruin when Tenar* becomes Arha and helps a sorcerer, Ged*, retrieve the Ring of Erreth-Akbe* from the Treasure of the Tombs. Trying to destroy the two, the Nameless Ones destroy their temple and their tombs.

NANA, a character in James M. Barrie's* *Peter and Wendy**. Though a Newfoundland dog, Nana acts as a nurse to Wendy, John, and Michael Darling***.

NANCY, a character in Alan Garner's* *The Owl Service**. She is the mother of Gwyn*. When she was twelve, Nancy became one of the staff at a cottage that Bertram* owned. So pretty was Nancy that she eventually attracted his attentions and those of Huw Hannerhob*, another servant. The valley where the cottage stood had been the site of the tragic story of Blodeuwedd*—a mythical woman made of flowers—her husband, and her lover, and in the centuries since then the tragedy of love and jealousy has been replayed in every generation. Nancy, Bertram, and Huw were the participants this time, and again it ended tragically, with Bertram's death. Bitter at losing the rank and wealth she would have had as Bertram's wife and hating Huw because he inadvertenely caused Bertram's death, Nancy left the valley and went to the city. Though Huw had fathered her son, she never spoke of him to Gwyn, though she told the boy much about the valley, which she both hated and loved. Nancy's hard life has made her a bitter woman seemingly intent on hurting Gwyn however she can; though he longs to go on the college in order to make something of himself, she wants him to quit school and get a job in a shop. When Alison Bradley*, who has inherited the house, comes with her family to vacation at the cottage, Nancy comes back, with Gwyn, to be their cook. She has nothing but scorn and hatred for the Bradleys and for Huw, who still tends the grounds; she refuses to allow Gwyn to speak to him. Suddenly the past catches up with her as Gwyn, Alison, and Roger Bradley*, Alison's stepbrother, are caught up in the the old triangle. Though she does what she can to stop it, Nancy cannot; finally she leaves Gwyn and the valley, walking over a dangerous pass in a storm to get away.

NANNY, a character in *At the Back of the North Wind**, by George MacDonald*. She is an orphan; she has a grandmother named Sal. Nanny lives with her grandmother and sweeps crossings for a living. The old woman is cruel, locking the girl out some nights when she comes home late. As a result, Nanny has learned to be tough and self-sufficient. She encounters kindness when she meets Diamond*, a little boy who wanders the streets of London with her one night. Nanny later meets Jim, a lame boy, and she saves things for him to eat.

When she falls ill, Nanny is taken to a hospital and there is kindly cared for for the first time. Mr. Raymond*, a poet, takes an interest in Nanny and gets her a place with Diamond's family, where she learns to take care of the baby and learns some gentleness; she later goes with the family to serve Mr. Raymond. Because Nanny is uncomfortable at the thought of leaving Jim behind, he comes too. Though Nanny has had a strange dream in the hospital that Diamond tells her had really been true, she scoffs at him, being a literalist. Though they are fond of Diamond, Nanny and Jim ignore him unless he can help them have fun or keep them from getting into trouble.

NARNIA, the setting of the Chronicles of Narnia*, by C[live] S[taples] Lewis*. It is bounded on the north by the Wild Lands of the North; on the south lie Archenland* and Calormen*. A great ocean lies to the east; to the west lie marvelous unknown lands, among them Telmar*. Narnia is created by and lies under the protection of Aslan*, a great, omniscient lion. It is a land of talking beasts and dumb ones, of spirits inhabiting rivers and trees, of fauns and satyrs, and of Bacchus* and his "wild girls." Unicorns live here, as do giants, beavers, apes, and kangaroos. This beautiful land has a long, rich history. Aslan creates it, and immediately evil enters the land, in the person of Jadis*, an evil queen brought by Digory Kirke* and Polly Plummer*, two human children. At Aslan's command, Digory plants a magical tree to keep Jadis out of the land. The first king is Frank*, a former London cabbie. Many generations later the White Witch* rules Narnia and makes it a wintry land, until Aslan, aided by Edmund, Lucy, Peter, and Susan Pevensie****, defeats her. The children take the throne until they return to their own land. Many years later, warriors from Telmar take Narnia, and under their rule the talking beasts and magical creatures are killed or imprisoned. Aslan again returns and Caspian X*, who is sympathetic to the old Narnia, takes the throne from his usurping uncle. Eight generations later Tirian* is king, and, at Aslan's command, Father Time* blows his horn and Narnia comes to an end. It is, however, but a shadow of the real Narnia in Aslan's country, and those who have defended it live in Aslan's country forever.

NATHANIEL CREEP (*A Chance Child*). *See* Creep, Nathaniel

NED, a character in Penelope Lively's* *The Voyage of QV 66*. He is a horse who calls himself Flying Warrior, though his friends just call him Ned. Ned is descended from a Derby winner and is proud of his ancestry, though the other animals do not understand why. When the world floods and all the humans go to Mars, Ned is among the animals left behind, and he joins the small group that accompanies Stanley*, a monkey, to London to find others like him. Normally staid and steady, Ned indulges himself when the group comes to a racetrack by galloping through a pretend race—winning, of course, by a length and a half.

NELEUS, a figure in Greek mythology who appears as a character in P[amela] L[yndon] Travers's* *Mary Poppins Opens the Door**. He is the son of the King of the Sea and his wife; he is the older brother of Pelias. Neleus is a statue from a family of statues by a famous sculptor. He was bought and brought to London, where he stands in a park, with his dolphin. Though he is lonely, Neleus tries not to think about it, entertaining himself by talking with the birds and reading over the shoulders of park visitors; he knows *Alice in Wonderland* and *Robinson Crusoe* by heart. One day he is so disappointed at not being able to finish the end of a story that his feet twitch him off his pedestal, and for the first time he runs with Jane Caroline and Michael George Banks**. Because people are appalled at his nakedness, Mary Poppins* gives Neleus her new jacket to wear. He is still wearing it when after a lovely afternoon, he remounts the pedestal; the Lord Mayor compliments the Park Keeper on the marble jacket he thinks the Keeper has given to Neleus, for the Mayor has never approved of naked statues.

NELLIE JACK JOHN CHERRY *(Earthfasts)*. *See* Cherry, Nellie Jack John

NELLIE-RUBINA NOAH *(Mary Poppins Comes Back)*. *See* Noah, Nellie-Rubina

NEOLIN, a character in *The Daybreakers** and *Over the Sea's Edge**, by Jane Lousie Curry*. He is the wiseman in Abáloc* around A. D. 1100. His grandfather was an earlier sage in Abáloc; Neolin's mother was of a different people who lived in the west. As sole source of ancient wisdom and tradition, learned from his grandfather, Neolin is respected and feared by the people of Abáloc. No one dares challenge him for no one knows the old traditions as well as he, and he uses his wisdom to further his own ends; though apparently trying to buy time and propitiate the Cibotlán* empire, Neolin works instead to bring the people of Abáloc to the Cibotlán way of thought. He demands that a sacrifice be made to the Sun Serpent (Katóa*), and he arranges for Callista Lee and Harry Rivers** and Melissa Mitchell* to be taken to Quanatilcó*. Neolin almost sacrifices Conway Tapp* but is thwarted by the children of Apple Lock* and by the untimely return of Lincoas*. After this Neolin goes mad, speaking, he thinks, to the Sun Serpent in an underground shrine. When he realizes that he is really talking to himself, Neolin breaks the shrine and is killed by a falling rock.

NESBIT, E. *See* Bland, E[dith] Nesbit

NETER-KHET, a character in *Time Cat**, by Lloyd Alexander*. He is a pharoah in Egypt in 2700 B.C. When he was young, he had several cats, but after he became Pharoah, cats did not like him because of the pomp surrounding him and because he expected them to obey his commands. When Jason*, a twentieth-century boy, and Gareth*, his cat, visit Neter-Khet, he learns from them how to make cats like him again and feels happier.

NEVER BIRD, a creature in *Peter and Wendy**, by James M. Barrie*. The Never bird once nested in a tree like other birds; when its nest fell into the water, it stayed on the eggs and became quite adept at paddling around the Mermaids' Lagoon*. When Peter Pan*, wounded in a fight with Captain Jas. Hook*, is trapped on Marooner's Rock* by the rising tide, the bird offers him its nest to sail away in. Grateful, Peter puts the eggs into a pirate's hat and the bird nests there instead. The hat proves so practical that its shape becomes the shape all future nests are built in.

NEVERLAND, an island of enchantment in *Peter and Wendy**, by James M. Barrie*. Each child has his personal Neverland full of adventures by day but a little frightening at night. Neverland is not a large island; it is small enough to be nicely crammed with adventures and supports a surprisingly large population of Indians, pirates, mermaids, wild beasts, fairies, and lost boys*. Here lives Peter Pan*, lord of all he surveys and leader of the lost boys, who are sent here after they fall out of their prams and are not claimed. Wendy, John, and Michael Darling*** fly to Neverland and have many adventures, but once they grow up they stop believing they can fly and can never again visit the island.

NEW AZTALÁN, a place in fourth-century America in *The Watchers** and *The Birdstones**, by Jane Louise Curry*. This land had at least seven great cities. It is conquered by Kanhuan*.

NEWS, a cat in Robert Westall's* *The Devil on the Road**. This black and ginger cat was born in seventeenth-century England and became the familiar of Johanna Vavasour*; its portrait appears as one of several familiars in a picture of Matthew Hopkins*, witch hunter, in his *Discoverie of Witchcraft*. When News is still a kitten, Johanna sends her through time to John Webster*, a twentieth-century student. He cares for the scrawny, sick little kitten, feeding and medicating her, though even he is amazed at the progress she makes. News wanders from century to century, hunting and playing, and occasionally she brings to John souvenirs of her trips into the past: a quillpen, a plague rat. By following News, John goes back and forth through time, and helps Johanna, who is accused of withcraft by Hopkins. In John's final struggle with Hopkins's troops, News is killed. When, in the twentieth century, Johanna wants to please John, however, she brings, from a forgotten fold of time, News as she would have been had she never met John; she is an older cat which has had many kittens and knows Johanna but not John.

NICHOLAS, a character in Lloyd Alexander's* *The Marvelous Misadventures of Sebastian*. He is a small, unprepossessing man who has many varied skills. When Sebastian*, a young fiddler seeking his fortune, is almost caught and hanged for stealing food, Nicholas rescues him from the crowd and helps him. When the two find Isabel Charlotte Theodora Fredericka* (Isabel), the runaway princess of Hamelin-Loring*, at an inn, Nicholas helps her, too. Both Sebasian and Isabel are astonished to learn that this quiet little man is the bold rebel Captain Freeling, a heroic figure to the oppressed citizens of Hamelin-Loring. Isabel appoints Nicholas her First Minister of State when she regains her throne.

NICHOLAS, JO, a character in Jane Louise Curry's* *Poor Tom's Ghost*. She is the mother of Pippa Nicholas*; her second husband is Tony Nicholas*; she is the stepmother of Roger John Nicholas*. Jo is an actress. After she is divorced from her first husband, she marries Tony. For a time their marriage seems to be dissolving, but the family finds new strength after weathering a crisis in Castle Cox*, the house Tony has inherited. Jo's research uncovers information that Roger uses to lay a ghost that has haunted the house since the sixteenth century.

NICHOLAS, PIPPA, a character in *Poor Tom's Ghost*, by Jane Louise Curry*. She is the daughter of Jo and Tony Nicholas** and the stepsister of Roger John Nicholas*. Ten-year-old Pippa, who has a special rapport with animals, shares some of Roger's adventures during the haunting of Castle Cox* by Tom Garland*, its original owner. She keeps him from drowning when he somehow falls into the Thames River.

NICHOLAS, ROGER JOHN, a character in *Poor Tom's Ghost*, by Jane Louise Curry*. He is the son of Jo and Tony Nicholas** and the brother of Pippa Nicholas*. Thirteen-year-old Roger has led a haphazard life. The son of a widowed actor, he was first raised by his grandmother; then he traveled with his father, dealing with erratic schooling, far-flung travel, and loneliness. He has developed a desperate sense of rootlessness. After Tony's marriage to Jo, things do not change much, but at least Roger has Pippa's companionship. He is elated when his father inherits Castle Cox*, for at last it seems that his family will settle down. When Tom Garland*, an Elizabethan actor, haunts the house, however, Roger finds himself drawn with his father into an old tragedy. Tony identifies more and more with the Elizabethan who is using him to wander through the past, searching for the supposed lover of Tom's wife; Roger himself begins to "remember" the actions of Jack Garland*, Tom's brother, who—jealous of his sister-in-law—had sought to break up the marriage by making Tom think she had deserted him. Roger finds himself drawn into the past and uses Jack to set things right, discovering himself how to trust in the security of his family's love.

NICHOLAS, TONY, a character in Jane Louise Curry's* *Poor Tom's Ghost*.
He is the husband of Jo Nicholas* and the father of Pippa and Roger Nicholas**.
Tony is a widowed twentieth-century actor who marries Jo and adopts her daughter, Pippa. He is a warm, generous, loving man who thrives on his haphazard
lifestyle. After inheriting Castle Cox*, Tony is drawn into the story of Tom
Garland*, its Elizabethan owner, who was an actor in his own day and who
now haunts the house, reliving his misery over what he believes to be his wife's
unfaithfulness. Tony, Tom's descendant, acts as catalyst, causing the ghost to
walk. Tom uses Tony's body to wander into the past, searching for the man he
believes stole away his wife. Tony becomes Tom, reliving Tom's memories,
playing one of Tom's old roles as he would have done, and wandering through
Elizabethan England as Tom himself. After Tony contracts the plague, which
is raging through Elizabethan England, Roger undertakes to set things in the
past right and thus to keep Tom's ghost from walking.

NICHOLAS WATSON (*Elidor*). *See* Watson, Nicholas

NICODEMUS, a character in Robert O'Brien's* *Mrs. Frisby and the Rats of
NIMH*. An ordinary rat who lives with his family near a farmer's market, young
Nicodemus was captured one night and taken to Nimh*, where he became part
of an experiment. He was number A-10 of the experimental rats. As a result of
the experiment, his intelligence and lifespan were greatened. Soon Nicodemus
and the other experimental rats escaped and made their way to Mr. Fitzgibbon's*
farm, where they set up a colony with Nicodemus as its leader. Chagrined because
they are taking food and electrical power from the Fitzgibbons, Nicodemus comes
up with a plan whereby the rats will move to a secluded valley and there develop
their own civilization. When Mrs. Frisby* needs their help, Nicodemus and the
others come to her aid before moving to their valley.

NIKABRIK, a character in *Prince Caspian**, by C[live] S[taples] Lewis*. He
is a black dwarf* in Narnia*. Because of the persecutions that conquerors from
Telmar* have inflicted on the magical creatures of Narnia, Nikabrik is suspicious
of all humans. When Caspian X*, the young prince whose throne has been
usurped by his uncle, Miraz*, flees the castle and is found by Nikabrik, a badger
named Trufflehunter*, and a red dwarf named Trumpkin*, Nikabrik wants to
kill the boy. Though Caspian loves the old Narnians and longs for the days when
they had ruled their own land, the dwarf cannot trust him, having gone sour
from hating and being tormented. Reluctantly he agrees to help Caspian gain
the throne, but Nikabrik tries to use sorcery to call up the White Witch*, an
ancient evil, and defeat Miraz and his army. Nikabrik is killed in the struggle
when Caspian and the others object to the hag and the werewolf he has brought,
and the evil creatures attack.

NIMH, a place in *Mrs. Frisby and the Rats of NIMH**, by Robert O'Brien*. "Nimh" may stand for "National Institute for Mental Health." In this large, white building Justin*, Nicomedus*, Jonathan Frisby*, Mr. Ages*, and other rats and mice became part of an experiment performed by Dr. Schulz. In this experiment, the animals' intelligence and lifespans were increased as their DNA was altered. These experimental animals became so intelligent that they escaped.

NIMIANE, a character mentioned in Jane Louise Curry's* *The Sleepers**. Her father was Tark-of-the-Perys, one of King Lot's men in the time of Artair*— King Arthur*. Nimiane is also known as "Viviane" and "Nimue." This flighty, erratic girl, influenced perhaps by Margan*, Artair's sister and enemy, imprisoned Myrddin*—Merlin—in the Eildon Tree* with one of his own spells.

NIMUE. *See* Nimiane

NINA HARMSWORTH (*The Court of the Stone Children*). *See* Harmsworth, Nina

NISROCH, a character in E[dith] Nesbit Bland's* *The Story of Amulet**. This eagle-headed, eagle-winged being is the servant of the gods of ancient Babylonia. When Robert*, Anthea*, and Cyril* are imprisoned in the King of Babylon's dungeon, they call on Nisroch to help them escape; he opens a way for them out of the prison.

NOAH, a Biblical personage who appears as a character in E[dith] Nesbit Bland. Bland's* *The Magic City**. Noah is actually a small wooden figure that Philip Haldane* places in the toy city he builds; but in the city, Polistopolis*, Noah becomes a person of great importance as a judge. When Philip and Lucy Graham* enter the city, Noah finds them guilty of trespass, but he begs them to escape because he is not sure what to do with them. Noah also informs Philip about the seven deeds the boy must accomplish to deliver the city from evil, and he oversees, of course, the building of an ark for the Dwellers by the Sea*. In Philip's world, the figure of Noah comes to life for a time after Philip sheds tears on it, for tears are strong magic. Because the figure stands on a small piece of wood, in Polistopolis Noah carries a little mat on which he stands when he stops.

NOAH, NELLIE-RUBINA, a character in P[amela] L[yndon] Travers's* *Mary Poppins Comes Back** and *Mary Poppins Opens the Door**. She is the daughter of Noah* and the niece of Uncle Dodger. Round, solid Nellie-Rubina seems to be made of wood, and she moves with a rolling gait because she has no legs, having instead a large, flat disc where her feet should be. She lives in an ark-like house with Uncle Dodger—whom she bosses—making flowers, green tree branches, birds, and sheep from wood. When she, Uncle Dodger, and their friend, Mary Poppins*, set these up in the night, they bring the spring. Nellie-Rubina is fond of conversation sweets, which she sometimes uses as messages to people.

NOAKES, MRS., a character in T[erence] H[anbury] White's* *Mistress Masham's Repose*. She is a widow. Mrs. Noakes has for many years been the cook at the great house, Malplaquet*, and she is famous for her quail in aspic and her oyster soufflé. Now that the family fortunes have fallen, Mrs. Noakes remains at Malplaquet, despite tempting offers to go elsewhere, because of Maria*, the last of the family. Mrs. Noakes lives in Malplaquet's famous kitchen, with Captain, her loving dog, as company; when she is needed, she bicycles down the corridor, ringing her bell at every intersection. She is a good friend of the Professor* and often takes him tea, leaving behind a special treat for that impoverished scholar. When Maria and the Professor are locked in Malplaquet's famous dungeon by Miss Brown*, Maria's governess, and Mr. Hater*, the vicar, Mrs. Noakes is called upon by some Lilliputians*, friends of Maria and the Professor, to help get them out. Though at first she thinks the Lilliputians are fairies or ghosts, Mrs. Noakes soon complies, to save Maria.

NOD. *See* Ummanodda

NORMAN WITHERS. (*Over Sea, Under Stone*). *See* Withers, Norman

NORTH WIND, a force in *At the Back of the North Wind**, by George MacDonald*. She has many names, among them Ruin, Bad Fortune, Evil Chance, and Death. Though she can appear as a lovely woman with flowing dark hair, as small as a bee or as large as a house, the Wind can also take on fearsome shapes; she appears once as a wolf, to frighten a nurse who has been mistreating a child. The Wind is kept busy sweeping the world. Her work also includes more unpleasant things, such as sinking ships, but she does this—as she sweeps the cobwebs from the sky or helps a bee out of a tulip—because it is her work. It is what she has been made for, and she can bear hearing the cries of those she drowns because through them she hears far-off music coming closer and closer—music that will swallow up all cries and make everything all right. Behind the Wind, where she cannot see it, is the country at the back of the north wind*. She cannot enter it, but she can sit on its doorstep and hear the voices of those inside. The Wind sometimes takes Diamond*, a little boy, with her as she works. Once she allows him into the country at her back; he enters by going through her and finds the journey very cold.

NORTON, MARY (1903–   ), British writer. She was born in London on 10 December 1903, to Mary Seville Hughes and Reginald Spenser Pearson, and was educated at a convent school. In 1927 she married Robert Charles Norton;

they have two daughters and two sons. She has been an actress and has worked in the British Purchasing Company in New York.

Norton has written eight works, all for children, seven of them full-length fantasies, and one, *Poor Stainless*, a short fantasy about a character mentioned in one of the books in her Borrower series*. Her fantasies deal with things familiar to us all: with yearnings, with dreams, with fears of the unknown. Though they are fantastic, the works are never far from our own world and our own experiences of it.

Often elements of our own world are given a little twist that makes them like and unlike what we see every day. Miss Eglantine Price*, of *The Magic Bed-Knob** and *Bonfires and Broomsticks**, is the picture of the country spinster, prim, sharp-nosed, and genteelly poor; but she also has a surprising talent for witchcraft. What is more, she has a secret desire to become a *wicked* witch— not what one would expect from a well-bred lady who comforts the sick and teaches piano. In the four Borrower books, it is the whole world that gets this twist, for few of us are accustomed to looking at the world as if we were only a few inches high, and ordinary objects so familiar to us take on new aspects. Who would think, for example, that a boot could become a house, outside of a nursery rhyme? Or that blotting paper makes lovely, practical carpeting? Or that half a ping-pong ball, packed with wool, becomes a comfortable, if wobbly, seat?

If that twist makes our own world familiar but changed, so can it make the fantastic in Norton's works homely and familiar. It is no surprise that Miss Price learns her witchcraft through a correspondence course, or that her practice runs on her broomstick are much like those of someone learning to ride a bicycle. That she treats the ingredients of her magical potions as nonchalantly as one treats something from the corner store is no surprise, either. Though they are fantastic, the improbable characters in Norton's works have very human feelings and motives, which they sometimes must transcend. The only fantastic elements in the Borrower series are the borrowers* themselves: tiny people one-twelfth our size but with familiar passions, hopes, and fears. It is only logical that they should come to view humans as nothing more than a meal ticket and a threat, that they should show tremendous ingenuity in using the odd objects they find, or that they should have the same hopes and fears for their offspring that humans have. Arrietty Clock*, a young borrower raised in safety and in ignorance of the dangerous world outside her tiny home, feels imprisoned in her place beneath the floor of the large house her family lives in, longing for the freedom of the outdoors as does any human child who has been kept in for a long time. Her parents are as solicitous of her safety as any human parents ever were. In *Are All the Giants Dead?** it is a given that there should be a journalist who acts as social reporter for the fairytale royalty who live happily ever after in the Land of Cockayne*, just as it is logical that Cinderella be nicknamed ''Pumpkin,'' or that Jack, of beanstalk fame, should be an expert on composts as well as beanstalks. That Dulcibel*, a princess fated to marry a toad, is nervous about her fate, despite assurances that the toad will turn into a prince, is understandable. For people associated with magic or fantasy, the world can be as daunting a place as it is for those who are not.

Norton's works are light and good-humored. Meticulous attention is paid to detail and to characterization; the Borrower series, especially, is made more plausible by the details of life for those only five or six inches high and of their particular view of the world. On the whole, characters are very well realized and three-dimensional: Emelius Jones* is unforgettably pathetic but earnest; Miss Price is conventional, with a streak of eccentricity; Homily Clock*, though hysterical at the thought of living roughly in the dangerous world outdoors, bears up for the sake of her family, as many human women would. The plots of the works are equally plausible, for they grow out of the actions of the characters themselves. Norton's style is descriptive without being dull, and her works are rich and rewarding without being ponderous.

Works

Juvenile full-length fantasy: *The Magic Bed-Knob* (1943); *Bonfires and Broomsticks* (1947); *The Borrowers* (1952); *The Borrowers Afield* (1955); *The Borrowers Afloat* (1959); *The Borrowers Aloft* (1961); *Are All the Giants Dead?* (1975); *The Borrowers Avenged* (1982).
Juvenile short fantasy: *Poor Stainless* (1971).

Secondary Works

Hand, Nigel. "Mary Norton and 'The Borrowers,' " *Children's Literature in Education*, 7 (March 1972), pp. 38–55.
"Mary Norton," in *Chosen for Children*, rev. ed. (London: The Library Association, 1967), pp. 66–69.
Olson, Barbara V. "Mary Norton and the Borrowers," *Elementary English*, 47 (Feb., 1970), pp. 185–89.
Toomey, Philippa. "Writing a Timeless 200 Words Forever and a Day," *The Times* (1 Aug. 1975), p. 12.
Ulman, Ruth. "WLB Biography: Mary Norton," *Wilson Library Bulletin*, 36 (May, 1962), p. 767.

NUR-JEHAN, a character in *The First Two Lives of Lukas-Kasha**, by Lloyd Alexander*. Her father was Ardashir*, king of Bishangar*. This fierce young warrior-maiden became Queen of Bishangar at her father's death. After she is captured by Abadanis, she is made a slave in Shirazan, the capital of Abadan*. When she runs away with Rakush, her horse, Nur-Jehan meets Lukas-Kasha* (Lukas) on the beach where he has just washed ashore. Recaptured and sent back to the Abadani palace, Nur-Jehan does not believe the young man when he explains that he would like to help her, and it is only after they both escape from the palace and are on their way to Bishangar that she begins to accept and trust Lukas, though she has little respect for him as a king. Dismayed by Nur-Jehan's direct and bloody-minded way of dealing with many situations, Lukas proves to her that there are ways of dealing with these situations that do not involve bloodshed, and she develops a grudging respect for his talents as a rascal and a swindler. At the first opportunity, however, Nur-Jehan leaves Lukas and rejoins her people, organizing them against the impending Abadani invasion. After Lukas regains control of the Abadani forces, he bargains with Nur-Jehan before leaving to go back to his palace. As soon as she can, Nur-Jehan visits him, not as Queen of Bishangar but as a close friend, but their meeting is thwarted when Lukas falls into the sea and vanishes into his own world.

NŪTAYĒ. *See* City of the Moon Under the Mountain

OBEHOL, a place in *The Farthest Shore**, by Ursula K. LeGuin*. This large island in the southeastern part of Earthsea* has tree-covered mountains. To Obehol come Ged*, a sorcerer, and Arren*, his companion, to find the source of the leaching of magic from Earthsea. They are guided by Sopli*, a madman seeking eternal life, who is sure that he will find it on Obehol. When they try to land, however, they are attacked by the island's spear-wielding natives and Ged is injured. Frantic to reach the island, Sopli leaps into the water and drowns.

O'BRIEN, ROBERT C. (1918–1973), American writer. His real name was Robert Leslie Conly, and he was born on 11 January 1918. In 1943 he married Sally McCaslin; they had three daughters and a son. He worked in an advertising agency, was a researcher and writer for *Newsweek*, a reporter and a member of the staff of *National Geographic* magazine, where he became senior assistant editor. He died on 5 March 1973.

O'Brien's works for children include two science fiction works and a fantasy that has elements of science fiction and of the animal story. In *Mrs. Frisby and the Rats of NIMH**, O'Brien presents the reader with animals who have their own society but are still animals; though they are of a species man has been taught to hate, they become heroic as they fight not only to survive but to survive with dignity.

The idea of an organized society of creatures is as new to the animals as it is to the reader. For Mrs. Frisby* and the others, life means getting by and making do as best one can by oneself. The creatures of the fields and forest do not help one another except, sometimes, against Dragon*, the cat. When Mrs. Frisby helps untangle Jeremy*, it is as much a surprise to them both as when the owl agrees to help Mrs. Frisby. Neighborliness the creatures do have—one can always count on Mr. Ages* to solve medical problems, and the lady shrew gets very agitated when she thinks that the rats are destroying Mrs. Frisby's house; but a sense of purpose and cooperation is lacking—that and the urge to change the environment for the better, which seem to be important to O'Brien's definition of society.

For purpose, cooperation, and a desire to change their environment to suit their needs are exactly what the rats themselves have. They manipulate their environment by tapping into Mr. Fitzgibbon's* power line to work motors and provide light for their tunnels. They plan to plant and harvest their own crops to provide food for themselves. The rats make and execute plans to benefit themselves later on, and they write and read.

Though experimentation by humans is responsible for the high intelligence of the rats, they feel that they must get as far away from human civilization as possible to form their own society. The society-less creatures—Mrs. Frisby, the shrew, Jeremy, the owl—use, yet do not depend on, humans; but the social rats do, taking not food but electrical power. While they stay near humans, they are not only in danger of being discovered and destroyed but are forced to depend on humans as their new society stagnates. Only by getting away from people can they build a true society built to their own proportions and reflecting their own values and ideals. Away from the shadow of man, the creatures can find their true potential.

This is true, however, only of those creatures who have been radically altered by the experiments, or of their descendants. Though Mrs. Frisby tries, she cannot learn to read well, but her children, who inherit their father's traits, can and do. The rats, whose lifespans as well as intelligence have been made greater, have the time needed to develop their society. The creatures of the wood have neither.

Though O'Brien presents creatures who talk to one another and are forming their own society, they are not anthropomorphized; they are still animals. O'Brien's style is descriptive. Characterization is almost nonexistent, though Mrs. Frisby's anxiety comes through very well. Suspense is skillfully handled, especially the touch of doubt at the end of the book.

Works

Juvenile full-length fantasy: *Mrs. Frisby and the Rats of NIMH* (1971) as *The Secret of NIMH* (1982).
Juvenile science fiction: *The Silver Crown* (1968); *Z for Zachariah* (1975).
Adult: *A Report from Group 17* (1972).

Secondary Works

O'Brien, Robert C. "Newbery Award Acceptance Speech," *The Horn Book Magazine*, 48 (Aug., 1972), pp. 343–48.
O'Brien, Sally. "Robert C. O'Brien," *The Horn Book Magazine*, 48 (Aug., 1972), pp. 349–51.

ODILE CHRYSOSTOME (*The Court of the Stone Children*). *See* Chrysostome, Odile

OFFA, a character in *The Voyage of QV 66**, by Penelope Lively*. He is a pigeon and is one of the creatures left on Earth after all the humans go to Mars to avoid a world-wide flood. Because Offa was raised on the right shoulder of a statue of King Offa, he takes his name from the statue. Offa can read; he has memorized the Bible and often quotes from it. He is part of the small group that accompanies Stanley*, a monkey, to London to find others like him. Offa proves a valuable companion, helping Stanley when he is locked in Barclay Bank, and scouting ahead for the voyagers.

OGION, a character in the Earthsea trilogy*, by Ursula K. LeGuin*. He is a respected wizard on the island of Gont* when he helps young Duny (Ged*) recover from the effects of a spell the boy has cast. Ogion names the boy Ged when he comes of age and accepts him as an apprentice. Ogion's slow and subtle teaching methods do not satisfy impatient Ged, and once the wizard has to protect the boy from an evil spirit he conjures up. Though Ged leaves the wizard to study at the school on Roke*, Ogion is always available to help him; he disenchants Ged when the young man remains too long in the form of a hawk and makes him realize that he must hunt down and destroy the shadow he has brought into the world. Ogion accepts into his keeping Tenar*, the former Priestess of the Nameless Ones*, when she seeks refuge and a place to learn about herself.

O'KEEFE, BRANWEN ZILLAH MADDOX (BEEZIE), a character in the Time trilogy*, by Madeleine L'Engle*. She is descended from Madoc*, a twelfth-century Welsh prince; she is the granddaughter of a woman named Branwen and a man named Pat; she is the older sister of Chuck Maddox*; she becomes the wife of Paddy O'Keefe and the mother of eleven children, among them Calvin O'Keefe*. Beezie is a bright, happy child until her father dies and her mother marries Duthbert Mortmain*, a brutal man, to keep their small store going. Mortmain is soon after Beezie, pinching her, in the beginning; when her grandmother protests this treatment and Chuck protects the woman, Mortmain knocks him down some stairs, fracturing his skull. Beezie's world closes in on her, for Chuck is never the same as before and is finally institutionalized; Paddy O'Keefe, whom she dislikes, begins to help out at the store. Finally she marries him, probably so that there will be someone to provide for her. As Mrs. O'Keefe, she learns not to feel, not to care about anyone, not even her children, and they in turn do not care for her—except for Calvin. Mrs. O'Keefe comes to look much older than she is and to distrust and resent everyone. She rarely speaks, and when she does it is in incomplete sentences. When Madog Branzillo* threatens to destroy the world, however, Mrs. O'Keefe teaches Charles Wallace Murry* a rune* her grandmother taught her, and tells him to use it to stop Branzillo. With the rune and the help of a unicorn, Charles does so. Mrs. O'Keefe's heart is bad and she may not live long after that.

O'KEEFE, CALVIN, a character in Madeleine L'Engle's* Time trilogy* and *The Arm of the Starfish*. He is the third of eleven children of Paddy and Branwen Zillah Maddox O'Keefe*; he becomes the husband of Meg Murry* and the father of Polyhymnia, Charles, Sandy, Dennys, Peggy, Johnny, and Mary O'Keefe. Calvin is different from the rest of his family, being more open and intelligent. By virtue of this, he rises above the extreme financial and emotional poverty of his family. Despite the fact that they do not seem to love him, Calvin loves his family deeply. Nevertheless, when he meets the Murry family, he feels that he has found his true home. He is enormously curious about everything and does well in school, where he is popular because he gives no indication of his vast intelligence. By the time he is fourteen, he is a junior in high school. At this time Calvin meets Meg and her brother, Charles Wallace Murry*, and is sent with them to rescue their father from Camazotz*, a planet where the forces of evil have triumphed. Calvin is better with words and feelings than with numbers, and on Camazotz he uses his intuitions to try to keep the three out of danger. He and Meg have a special relationship from the very start, and this relationship soon deepens into love. At sixteen, Calvin helps Meg save Charles's life by going into one of his cells and combatting his mitochondritis. Calvin and Meg eventually marry, and he earns an M.D./Ph.D.

O'KEEFE, MEG MURRY. *See* Murry, Meg

OLD BILL (BILL), a character in *The Driftway**, by Penelope Lively*. He was married for twenty-five years. Bill has always been a restless man, taking off from time to time even when he had been married. He has always liked being outdoors and prefers to work there when he can. Money and material things do not matter as much to Bill as being his own boss does, and he will not work for someone he does not respect, just for the money. Once, when times were tough, he refused to work for a vain, wealthy man who treated him as an object. Since his wife's death, Bill has made his living on the road, traveling in ancient driftways* in an old horse-drawn cart and earning his keep by sharpening knives and giving donkey rides. He is a popular figure. Bill understands and accepts the strange goings-on of the driftway, where ancient dramas sometimes become real again for certain people. One night he picks up two young runaways, Paul* and Sandra*, and helps Paul understand the visions the boy has as he travels the road; Bill also helps make him realize how unfairly he has acted toward the children's new stepmother.

OLD FELLER. *See* Cookson, Henry

OLDKNOW, ALEXANDER, a character in *The Children of Green Knowe**, *The Chimneys of Green Knowe**, and *The Stones of Green Knowe**. He is the third son of Captain Oldknow and his wife; his brothers are Aubrey and Toseland Oldknow* (Toby), and his sister is Linnet Oldknow*. Alexander had a white pony named Bucephalus and lived in Green Knowe* in the seventeenth century. Well educated, Alexander could read Latin. His ambition was to be a poet, but Alexander loved music, too; so sweetly could he sing that Gabrieli McTavish took him to court to sing the part of Cupid in *Cupid and Death*, and the king gave him a flute, which he cherished. Through the magic of the Stones*, Alexander several times meets Roger d'Aulneaux*, the Norman boy whose father built Green Knowe. Though he died, with Toby and Linnet, during the Great Plague, Alexander has not really left Green Knowe; he and his brother and sister show themselves or allow people to hear them at least into the twentieth century, when they drive Toseland* nearly to distraction before they accept him.

OLDKNOW, CAPTAIN, a character in Lucy Boston's* *The Chimney's of Green Knowe*. He is the husband of Maria Oldknow* and the father of Sefton and Susan Oldknow**. He is master of Green Knowe* in the eighteenth century. Descended from sea captains, he himself takes to the sea, and his journeys on the *Woodpecker* take him to many faraway places. In Barbados, he finds Jacob*, an orphaned slave child, whom he brings home for Susan. The Captain loves his family very much, sometimes overindulging them; at Maria's insistence, he has an addition to Green Knowe built that encloses the house in red brick. When the gardener's son is caught poaching for Caxton*, the butler, Captain Oldknow dismisses the man and takes the boy on as one of his crew; in revenge Caxton steals Maria's jewels the day a fire destroys the additions to Green Knowe.

OLDKNOW, LINNET, a character in *The Children of Green Knowe*, *The Chimneys of Green Knowe*, and *The Stones of Green Knowe*, by Lucy Boston*. She is the youngest child of Captain Oldknow and his wife; her older brothers are Aubrey, Toseland (Toby), and Alexander Oldknow**. Linnet had a little curly-haired dog named Orlando. She lived in Green Knowe* in the seventeenth century. Bouncy and irrepressible, six-year-old Linnet was good with animals, which she loved. Through the magic of the Stones*, she several times visited Roger d'Aulneaux*, the Norman boy whose father built Green Knowe. One Christmas Eve, Linnet watched as the statue of St. Christopher* that stands beside the house took the Christ Child on his shoulder across the snowy fields to Midnight Mass. Though Linnet died in the Great Plague, she has not really left Green Knowe; she and Toby and Alexander show themselves or allow certain people to hear them at least into the twentieth century, when they tease Toseland* before finally accepting him.

OLDKNOW, LINNET (MRS.), a character in Lucy Boston's* Green Knowe books*. She is the daughter of Alexander Oldknow and the granddaughter of Sir Toseland Oldknow; she is the great-grandmother of Toseland* (Tolly). When her parents died, she was brought up by her uncle at Green Knowe*. A lonely child, she pretended that Toseland (Toby), Alexander, and Linnet Oldknow***, her seventeenth-century ancestors, were her brothers and sisters. Through the magic of Green Knowe and of the Stones*, she one day meets Roger d'Aulneaux*, the Norman boy whose father built Green Knowe, and swears to him to keep the house safe, giving to him a ring that will be handed down through the generations until it again comes to her. Long after she becomes Mrs. Oldknow, she inherits the house, living there alone with only a gardener who comes each day. Sensitive to the old house, she sometimes sees and hears those of her ancestors who manifest themselves here, especially Toby, Alexander, and Linnet. Keeping her promise to Roger is often difficult, for some seem to feel that because Green Knowe is old and different, it should be torn down. Money to keep up the place is also a problem, until Tolly finds the long-lost treasure of Green Knowe. Mrs. Oldknow, however, manages to keep Green Knowe safe, even bringing to it those objects she can afford that seem to belong there. She also collects bits of old gossip and legend about the people who lived there; she loves to tell these stories to Tolly and, eventually, to Hsu*, a Chinese refugee who stays at Green Knowe for a time. Mrs. Oldknow lives at peace with the house, guarding its treasures and treasuring its secrets, which she will eventually hand down to Tolly.

OLDKNOW, MARIA, a character in *The Chimneys of Green Knowe* and *The Stones of Green Knowe*, by Lucy Boston*. She is the wife of Captain Oldknow* and the mother of Sefton and Susan Oldknow**. Maria lives at Green Knowe* in the eighteenth century. Very vain and often insensitive, she is interested only in being fashionable in her dress, her manners, and her opinions. In this she is indulged by Captain Oldknow, who before their marriage had added a brick addition to Green Knowe that enclosed the house, for her. Maria has some regard for her husband but almost none for Susan, for since the girl is blind it is no fun dressing her and Maria regards her mostly as a little animal, to tolerate but not to love. Perhaps the greatest tragedy of Maria's life occurs when Caxton*, the butler, is dismissed; the day before he leaves he steals Maria's jewels and that night dies in the fire that destroys the addition to the house. On the advice of an old gypsy, Maria stitches a picture of the house as it stood, using hair from all who lived there, in order to recover the jewels. The picture still hangs in Green Knowe, but the jewels are not recovered until the twentieth century.

OLDKNOW, MRS. *See* Oldknow, Linnet (Mrs.)

OLDKNOW, SEFTON, a character in Lucy Boston's* *The Chimneys of Green Knowe*. He is the son of Captain and Maria Oldknow** and the older brother of Susan Oldknow*. Irresponsible, inconsiderate, and arrogant, Sefton looks down on nearly everyone, including his father and Susan. Sefton sometimes plays cruel tricks, as when he orders for Jacob*, the black child Captain Oldknow brings to Susan, a suit of clothes like those an organ-grinder's monkey wears. Sefton gets himself deeply in debt and gambles to try to get out of it; Caxton*, the butler, loans him money, planning to use this later as a hold over the young man. Sefton helps Caxton to sell some of the local young men into press gangs until Caxton is found out. Then, in order to get away before his father finds out about the debts and the press gangs, Sefton starts his studies at Oxford early.

OLDKNOW, SUSAN, a character in *The Chimneys of Green Knowe**, *An Enemy at Green Knowe**, and *The Stones of Green Knowe**, by Lucy Boston*. She is the daughter of Captain and Maria Oldknow** and the sister of Sefton Oldknow*; she becomes the wife of Jonathan Morley. Susan lives at Green Knowe* in the eighteenth century. She is born blind, and therefore is kept almost a prisoner in the house as she grows up, always in the care of someone. Though she tries to be independent, Susan's nanny does not allow her to be, for fear she will hurt herself. Because she is blind, Susan is thought to be an idiot as well. Captain Oldknow, who loves her deeply, discovers that she is not and engages Jonathan Morley to tutor her. In 1795, during a voyage to the West Indies, the Captain meets and buys Jacob*, a young black orphan, and brings him to take care of Susan. A new life begins for the girl. Jacob takes her everywhere and helps her to do many things, and Susan is happy. When Green Knowe catches fire, Jacob saves Susan's life. During some point in her early life, Susan is pulled out of her century into the twentieth when Dr. Melanie Delia Powers* works magic on a piece of Susan's nightdress, hoping to get someone in the house under her power. Toseland* (Tolly), a young boy living in Green Knowe, manages to break the spell. Because of the magic in Green Knowe itself, Susan visits and is visited by Tolly several times, and once feels the topiary deer in the garden come alive at the instigation of Toseland Oldknow*. She grows up to marry Jonathan Morley and live happily, having many children, all of whom can see; she and Jacob are always devoted to each other.

OLDKNOW, TOSELAND (TOBY), a character in Lucy Boston's* *The Children of Green Knowe**, *The Chimneys of Green Knowe**, and *The Stones of Green Knowe**. He is the second son of Captain Oldknow and his wife; his older brother is Aubrey, his younger brother is Alexander Oldknow*, and his younger sister is Linnet Oldknow*. Toby lived at Green Knowe* in the seventeenth century. He had a magnificent chestnut horse named Feste*. Well educated, Toby could speak Latin; he used the language to call Neptune, one of the carp that lived in the garden pool. Toby also had a pet deer. He was to become a soldier, so his father gave him a sword when he was thirteen. Feste was his pride and joy. Toby rode him one perilous night to get the doctor for Linnet, and he rides Feste with Roger d'Aulneaux*, the Norman boy whose father built Green Knowe, when Roger uses the magic of the Stones* to visit the seventeenth century. Though Toby died during the Great Plague, he does not really leave Green Knowe, for he, Alexander, and Linnet show themselves or allow themselves to be heard there into the twentieth century. Once, Toby calls his deer and thus brings to life the topiary deer that stands in the garden so that Susan Oldknow*, the blind girl living at Green Knowe in the eighteenth century, can touch it.

ORDDU, a character in Lloyd Alexander's* *The Black Cauldron*, Taran Wanderer*, The High King*,* and *The Foundling, and Other Tales of Prydain.* She is the sister of Orgoch* and Orwen*. Like her sisters, Orddu is neither evil nor good, "simply interested in things as they are." Though heartbreakingly beautiful, Orddu often appears as an old hag with jeweled pins and vines in her hair. At least once she also appears as a lovely maiden. Orddu and her sisters are weavers, weaving on their loom the pattern of lives, not controlling them but recording them. The sisters are untouched by events around them; they loan to Arawn*, the Lord of Death, their Black Crochan*, knowing that he will probably use it for evil but feeling that he must be given a chance. Those who get favors from the three pay dearly for them, for they give nothing away. Orddu, Orwen, and Orgoch seem to alternate personalities, each being all three, one after another. They find and raise Dallben*, an enchanter, until he learns as much as they know. Orddu and her sisters live in the Marshes of Morva in southwestern Prydain* until the passing of magic from that land. After that they are anywhere and everywhere.

ORGOCH, a character in *The Black Cauldron*, Taran Wanderer*, The High King*,* and *The Foundling, and Other Tales of Prydain,* by Lloyd Alexander*. She is the sister of Orddu* and Orwen*. Like her sisters, Orgoch is neither evil nor good, being only "interested in things as they are," though in Orgoch's mind, things as they are should be served up on a platter. She will eat nearly anything and has terrible indigestion as a result. When the sisters raise Dallben*, a foundling, Orgoch can scarcely control her appetite for the boy. Orgoch's face is always nearly hidden by the black hood she wears, but, like her sisters, she appears as an old hag or a lovely maiden, though she is really a beautiful woman. The three women seem to alternate personalities, each taking a turn at being one of the others, though no one likes to be Orgoch because of her nature. Weavers in the Marshes of Morva, they weave the patterns of people's lives, though they do not control them. They are also something greater, untouched by the events around them and caring only in a way humans would not see as caring. When magic passes from the land of Prydain*, the three leave with it, going anywhere and everywhere.

ORLANDO, a dog in *The Children of Green Knowe** and *The Chimneys of Green Knowe**, by Lucy Boston*. This little white curly-haired dog with a black face is given to Toseland* (Tolly), a young boy living at Green Knowe*, as a Christmas present. He names him after the dog Linnet Oldknow* owned in the seventeenth century. Orlando is a little bundle of energy. He calls Tolly's attention to a certain tree at Green Knowe by barking up at it; Tolly thus makes the acquaintance of Jacob*, the black child who lived at Green Knowe in the eighteenth century and whom Orlando could see, even of Tolly could not.

ORM EMBAR, a character in Ursula K. LeGuin's* *The Farthest Shore**. He is a dragon on Earthsea* and is related to Orm, the great dragon who killed Erreth-Akbe*. Orm Embar is a magnificent dragon, the mightiest of his kind; he is the color of steel glinting with gold, and is so strong and powerful that he does not hide his name, not fearing that anyone will gain power over him. He meets and spares Ged*, a sorcerer, on Selidor*, and there tells him how to find the lost Bond-Rune*, which is engraved on the broken Ring of Erreth-Akbe*. When Cob,* a dead man, returns from the land of the dead and leaches the magic from Earthsea, Orm Embar seeks out Ged to help him against this powerful man who does not die. Like all dragons, Orm Embar speaks the words of Making, the oldest tongue, but this power is taken from him by Cob. When Cob tries to kill Ged with an enchanted sword, Orm Embar saves him by coming between them; he dies among the bones of Orm, his great ancestor.

ORWEN, a character in Lloyd Alexander's* *The Back Cauldron**, *Taran Wanderer**, *The High King**, and *The Foundling, and Other Tales of Prydain*. She is the sister of Orddu* and Orgoch*. Incredibly beautiful, Orwen often appears as an old hag and, once, as a lovely maiden, but always she has a necklace of milky stones. She is giggly and girlish, always ready for a game. Like her sisters, Orwen is neither evil nor good, only "interested in things as they are"; she, like them, is untouched by the events around them, seeming somehow above them. They live in the Marshes of Morva, weaving on their loom the pattern of people's lives, over which they have no control. Though they care about things, it is not in a way humans would recogize as caring. With her sisters, Orwen leaves Prydain* when the magic passes from that land, going anywhere and everywhere.

OSKAR STANISLAWSKY (*The River at Green Knowe*). *See* Stanislawsky, Oskar

OSMAN, a character in Lloyd Alexander's* *The First Two Lives of Lukas-Kasha**. He is one of the guards who protect Lukas-Kasha* (Lukas) while he is king of Abadan*. Under Shugdad Mirza's* command, and believing that Shugdad has the best interests of the nation at heart, Osman tries to garrot Lukas. When the guard fails and Lukas escapes, Osman is brutally beaten and put into an army punishment troop made up of soldiers who have committed crimes punishable by death. Heartsick because he has betrayed the king, Osman welcomes the troop's suicidal missions and is dismayed that he himself is not killed;

when the troop's commander dies, Osman takes his place. When Lukas is put into the troop, Osman turns the command over to him and helps him lead, saving Lukas from Shugdad and proclaiming Lukas king before the Abadani forces.

OSSKIL, an island in *A Wizard of Earthsea**, by Ursula K. LeGuin*. On this bleak island in the northern part of the Archipelago of Earthsea* is the Terrenon*, a stone in which is imprisoned an evil spirit.

OTAK, a type of creature in Ursula K. LeGuin's* *A Wizard of Earthsea**. The true name of the otaks is "hoeg." These rare, sleek little brown creatures are found on only four islands of the Archipelago of Earthsea*. They have no voice. Though they are untameable, one becomes the pet of Ged* when he is a young student at the wizard's school on Roke.* When the young sorcerer lies in a trance, having traveled too far into the land of the dead, the otak wakes him with its touch. It is killed on Osskil* when Ged comes up against a man possessed by the evil spirit the sorcerer accidentally loosed upon the world.

OTHER-END-OF-NOWHERE, a place in Charles Kingsley's* *The Water-babies**. The Other-end-of-Nowhere consists of many different lands, each stranger than the last. Tom*, a water-baby*, reaches this place via a hole in the bottom of the sea; he has come here to find Grimes*, his old master in his earlier life.

OVER SEA, UNDER STONE. Susan Cooper. Illus. Margery Gill. New York: Harcourt, Brace and World, 1966. 252 pp. American.

Barnabas (Barney), Simon, and Jane Drew*** and their parents go to Cornwall to visit Merriman Lyon* (Merry), a mysterious friend of the family, staying in the house of Captain Toms*. On their arrival, they see a white yacht, of which Merry seems oddly frightened. The next day is rainy, and, bored, the children explore the house, finding in the attic an ancient manuscript with a map; in the writing on the scroll, they recongnize the names of King Arthur* and one of his knights. That night at supper, Norman and Polly Withers**, a brother and sister, visit the Drews and invite them onto their yacht. Simon and Barney go the next day, but Jane stays home. Studying the strange map, she matches it to a map in a book about the area, and she goes to the vicar, Mr. Hastings (the Black Rider*), to learn more. He is strangely interested in the book and her questions.

The next day the house is ransacked, and the children realize that someone has been searching for the manuscript. They tell Merry, who recogizes it; the manuscript tells where to find the hidden grail* which, when found, will presage the coming of Arthur. Those allied with evil want it, and the Witherses have been watching Merry closely. The children will follow the map as he acts as decoy. The next day they begin at a ring of standing stones, but Polly Withers comes upon them and sees the map. Simon takes it and runs, and is rescued by Merry after a terrifying chase. But the children have discovered the key to the map, which consists of lining up certain land marks which then point the way to a certain place.

Because the next clue involves the full moon, Merry takes Simon and Jane out the next night, leaving Barney with the map. The children learn that the next point is a clump of rocks off the headland. Suddenly Merry is gone, and when the two look for him they come across Mr. Hastings, one of several threatening figures in the dark. They also find Merry, and he gets them home. Barney, meanwhile, has slept and wakened to find the housekeeper searching his room, though she leaves when he questions her.

The next morning the three children go to the rocks. Here they find a hole in the ground, through which they hear the sea. They go back to the house to get Merry, but he has been sent elsewhere by the housekeeper, so the children go to the carnival which is being held, to find him. Simon and Jane are swept up into a dance by the dancers, and Barney, separated, is kidnapped by the Witherses. They take him to Mr. Hastings, who asks him where the grail is and tries to persuade him to tell him. When Barney replies with a phrase that suddenly comes to him, unbidden, Mr. Hastings stops and makes plans to set out to sea, taking Barney. Simon and Jane go home and are found here by Rufus*, Captain Toms's dog, who has been trying to find Barney and who leads them to a cliff overlooking the sea. Barney, below them, is being trundled along by his captors, drugged and apathetic, but when Rufus howls, he comes out of his trance and manages to get away to Simon and Jane.

They must get the grail now, for the low tide has uncovered the entrance to the cave beneath the rocks. Barney and Simon follow a passageway in the rocks until they come to a rockfall; Barney crawls through and discovers the beautiful grail, which holds a lead cylinder containing a manuscript*. When he comes out, he and Simon put the cylinder into a spyglass case they have kept the map in. They leave to find the tide coming. Mr. Hastings and his people are also drawing near in small boat, and the three children run, but are soon trapped by the approaching tide. Rather than give up, Barney threatens to throw the manuscript and grail into the sea. Mr. Hastings gets ashore, grabs Simon, and threatens to break his arm unless Barney hands over what he has found. Merry, however, comes upon them in a boat, and Simon is released. He tosses the grail to Merry and then throws the case, but it opens in madair, and the cylinder falls into the sea. Mr. Hastings dives to get it but cannot, and he climbs into his boat. Merry speaks strange words which cow him, and he and his followers leave.

The grail is put into a museum. The children are disappointed that they may never know what the manuscript in the cylinder says or whether it holds the key to the ciphers on the grail, but Barney, who has made a connection between Merry and Merlin, thinks that they might yet find out, some day.

OVER THE SEA'S EDGE. Jane Louis Curry. Illus. Charles Robinson. New York: Harcourt Brace Jovanovich, 1971. 182 pp. American.

David Reese* has seen several times that week a long-haired boy in a tunic and boots, wearing a silver pendant* that matches the one Dave had found in a cave by the river. Dave envies the boy his apparent freedom, for he himself feels stifled and longs for adventure. One night Dave dreams that the other boy gives Dave his pendant, and Dave wakes into a dream that he is the other—a boy named Dewi ap Ithil*—in a noisy castle in twelfth-century Wales. The dream is reality, as Dave soon discovers. Though he is confused, some names and phrases seem to come naturally to the boy. He meets Llywarch ap Llewellyn*, a poet, who speaks to him of the squabble between the princes for the throne new that the king is ill. One of the illegitimate contenders is Madauc*, whom the king has summoned, perhaps to recognize as legitimate. When he reaches the castle, Madauc is set upon and almost killed by fighting men commanded by the two legitimate princes; because one cannot allow him to be killed, Madauc is taken prisoner and blinded.

That night Dave—now Dewi—realizes that the silver medallion he wears seems to have the same pattern as Madauc's banner. Wanting to learn more, he starts to the dungeon but instead meets two figures leading Madauc from the castle. One is the castle priest, who asks Dewi to take Madauc to a hermit, who will heal him; the other is Llywarch, who urges Madauc to "go on pilgrimage." Dewi and Madauc do not get far that night; they spend the next day hiding from pursuers. The day after, they reach the hermit, who cares for Madauc. Madauc has not been blinded after all; it was a trick. Gradually Dewi forgets his former life, though once he dreams of that other boy, who tells Dewi to leave him alone. Madauc talks to Dewi about his father, a friend of Madauc's and Llywarch's. When he was a boy, he had been given the pendant by a seer who claimed to have taken it from the body of a strangely dark man who washed ashore with a richly dressed woman; the woman spoke a riddling poem in a language like Welsh before she died. The seer had told the three of Avallach and Antillia, rich lands that lie far to the west, and Madauc now longs to go there. While Dewi and Madauc are with the hermit, the king dies and so do the young man's chances to be king. Madauc gathers his men and builds a boat to sail for the western lands.

They are many weeks at sea, and when they finally come to land there is no sign of golden Antillia, with its seven cities. The men become disgruntled. One evening Madauc leaves the camp and Dewi follows with a dog, finding the man in a moonlit clearing. The boy watches as a young, dark girl comes into the clearing, seemingly fascinated by Madauc's pale hair. She is captured. She carries a baby and a bundle which holds rich gold jewelry. Her name is Coala*, and she makes the men understand that they are in Cibotlán*, a place with seven cities. The men make her understand that they want gold, and, though seemingly disappointed, Coala tells them they will find it, especially in Abáloc*, a land to the north.

To Abáloc they go, finding little gold along the way. At last they reach a great river, where they stop to build boats. One day Dewi is keeping lookout from above the camp when a band of Cibotlán warriors comes upon it; sharp-tongued Coala speaks to them and they leave abruptly. Just as abruptly Dewi is captured by Lincoas*, one of several youths from Abáloc who have escaped from warriors from Cibotlán and are making their way home. In a language very like Welsh they tell Dewi how Abáloc was once a great kingdom but has been forced to rely on its wisemen for knowledge and is now beset by Cibotlán, which seeks to conquer it. Coala is a princess of Cibotlán and a priestess of a snake oracle; she seeks the oracle that had led Abáloc long ago, hoping to use its power.

Using Dewi as bait, the Abalockians ambush Madauc's boats as they come by and capture Coala. They are set upon by Cibotlán warriors, and in the fracas Madauc is hurt. Coala is shocked and disappointed; because of his light hair, she had thought that he was the god who sailed away long ago, promising to return. She herself had fled Cibotlán with the baby—her brother—because the priests had sought to sacrifice the child in place of Lincoas and the others after they had escaped.

The Abalockians and Welshmen come to Abáloc by boat on the day Neolin*, the wiseman, has tried to sacrifice a foreign child to the sun, only to have it spirited away. Reading the words on a pendant his mother wears, Lincoas proves that he and the others have regained the art of reading and can therefore read the one ancient book that survives, so that they will not have to depend on unscrupulous Neolin for knowledge. They also will be able to find the City of the Moon Under the Mountain*, an ancient haven. But this is the day Cibotlán has chosen to attack Abáloc, and armies from five of the cities have gathered near the village. Neolin, who has been advancing the Cibotlán cause in Abáloc, goes to meet the priest-kings who lead the army and to talk his way out of trouble.

Suddenly, to the the bewilderment of the Cibotlán warriors, Madauc appears like the god he is supposed to be. Coala, speaking for him, says he is offended and has sent a fever that is raging in the land; if the warriors try to take Abáloc, they will die. The Cibotlán warriors panic and flee, and a confused Neolin, who had not seen Madauc before this, takes refuge with his god, who he is convinced has been speaking to him. Dewi and Siona*, an Abalockian girl, follow Neolin to an island with apple trees, where they find a richly carved cave. In an alcove, steps lead down to another chamber from which they feel evil radiating. Neolin is there, talking to himself, speaking, he thinks, to the Sun Serpent (Katóa*), but answering his own questions. Dewi and Siona listen as he asks a question which he cannot answer, and they hear stone striking stone and watch as a dark shape swims from the island as a snake swims; Neolin has attacked the carved stone snake in the lower chamber and has been killed by falling rock. In the chamber they find treasures: books and rich objects, some carved with the device Dewi has finally traced on his medallion.

The time has come for the Welshmen to go, but Dewi wants to stay, happy with what he has found here. Some of the men stay, too, but Madauc sails home with pearls from Abáloc, promising the others, especially Coala, that he will return.

In the twentieth century, David Reese—once Dewi—is staying with his aunt and uncle. Exploring by the river, he finds a cave, in which he discovers a parchment on which Dewi ap Ithil has written his adventures. In that other time Madauc had returned. They found the City of the Moon but did not stay there long. Dewi has married Siona and is happy in his new life. Tucked between the last, illegible pages is Dewi's medallion, which Dave's young cousin abruptly claims. She has refurbished a boat she has found, and when they take it out, Dave begins to think of adventures. On the shore, a breeze blows the parchment into the river, but Dave writes down as much of it as he can remember.

OVERMANTEL, PEREGRINE (PEAGREEN), a character in Mary Norton's* *The Borrowers Avenged**. Though his name is spelled "Peregrine," it is pronounced "Peagreen." He is a borrower*, one of a race of tiny people who live by "borrowing" what they need from humans. Until he was five or six, Peagreen lived with the rest of his family over the mantel in the library of the Old Rectory in Fordham. Here he received his education by eavesdropping on the rector's children as they took their lessons. When the mantelpiece was to be taken down during renovations, the Overmantels were forced to move, and in the confusion Peagreen fell from the mantelpiece and was not missed until it was too late. Having broken his leg in the fall, Peagreen was cared for by the Wainscot family living behind the wainscot, until they too moved, and he was left to care for himself. The quiet rectory suits Peagreen, who likes to read and write, especially poetry (though he is writing the story of his family), and also likes to paint. Lamed by the fall, he does not walk or run well, but Peagreen is a good climber. He is also a good borrower, using equipment left by the Wainscots. Because the outside entrance of his home is inconvenient and his home is so far from the rectory kitchen, Peagreen relocates in the nesting boxes of the rectory's aviary. About this time he befriends Arrietty, Homily, and Pod Clock***, who have come to live in the rectory. Peagreen likes his quiet, but he agrees to teach Timmis*, a lively younger borrower, and this arrangement suits both of them.

OWL SERVICE, THE. Alan Garner. London: Collins, 1967. 157 pp. British. Carnegie Award, 1967.

Alison Bradley*, sick in bed in the house she has inherited from her cousin, Bertram*, hears scratching from the ceiling above. Investigating, Gwyn*, son of the Bradleys' temporary cook, finds a set of oddly patterned plates* in the attic; touching one, he feels faint for a moment. On the other side of the valley, Roger Bradley*, Alison's stepbrother, sees something shoot past him as he stands near an odd stone with a hole in it, and he hears a scream but sees no one nearby. Alison learns that, by tracing the flower pattern on the plates in a certain way, she can make little paper owls. Nancy*, Gwyn's mother, is strangely upset, and she demands the plate Alison has been using, from which the pattern has mysteriously vanished.

Soon events prove even stranger. Roger realizes that the scratching above Alison's bed is getting louder, and the owls Alison has made keep disappearing. She insists that tracing the pattern seems to make it disappear. A plate is thrown at Nancy, and another at a wall in the house, which is cracking for no reason. Huw Hannerhob*, who works at the house, warns Gwyn that "she" is coming and explains that the stone Roger had found is a stone where one man threw a spear that passed through it and his wife's lover on the other side. Gwyn realizes that Roger had heard the man's death when he himself touched the plates. Picking the cracked plaster off the wall, he exposes the painting of a lovely woman with a background of clover heads formed of petals like owls' claws; whatever is happening is dangerous.

On a trip to the store, Gwyn and Roger overhear women saying that "she" is coming and "is owls." When the boys go home, Alison, who was supposed to hide the plates from Nancy, denies knowledge of them. When Gwyn remonstrates with her, a whirlwind of objects flings itself at him and drives him away. One of the objects is a book Alison has been reading, and here Gwyn reads the story of Blodeuwedd*, a woman made of flowers by Gwydion*, an enchanter. She had betrayed her husband, who killed her lover with a spear that passed through a stone; in punishment, Blodeuwedd was made into an owl. Gwyn realizes that what may be at work here is not ghosts but the old story going on and on.

That night, having failed to find the plates, he follows Alison as she leaves the house. For a time he is lost, having followed a light that turns out to be methane gas. Finally he finds Alison and the plates in an old hut; she is feverishly tracing owls. Though he wants to stop her, he cannot. Alison feels tension building inside her, which is released only when she makes the owls or causes objects to fling themselves. She makes the last owl and they start to leave, but Alison is frightened by a flame that is vaguely woman-shaped, and they stay till morning. When they return to the house, Huw tells them that "she" has come. She has wanted to be flowers but they have made her owls; Huw confuses himself with Gwydion. After breakfast Gwyn finds that the flower plates are all clear and have been smashed.

Roger, who has taken some pictures through the hole in the stone, sees on some of the prints what appears to be a long haired man on a horse—or a man on a motorcycle. He discovers that the picture of Blodeuwedd has disappeared and blames Gwyn for scraping it off. That day Gwyn learns from Nancy that she was to have married Bertram, but somehow Huw had spoiled it. When Alison goes up the mountain that afternoon, Gwyn, who is not supposed to talk to her, follows. Looking out her window, Alison has seen her reflection in a tank, from an impossible angle; Gwyn realizes that the reflection had been of Blodeuwedd. The valley they live in is like a reservoir where the power Gwydion had used to make the woman builds up and must be let loose. The force in the painting and the plates is now in them; Huw is trying to deal with it, but they must watch out and learn what they can about Nancy and Bertram and Huw.

Days later Nancy decides to leave. Gwyn is having a miserable time; Roger scoffs at his story and Alison has been avoiding him. Finally he confronts her. She has learned that Bertram was killed in a motorcycle accident. When Roger makes jokes about Gwyn's attempts at self-improvement, about which only Alison had known, Gwyn, betrayed, runs to the mountain. He thinks he will never go back, but he does, for farm dogs drive him like a sheep back to the house. That evening, however, having taken food and clothing, he tries to leave again, only to be chased by a sow into a tree. Here he is found by Huw. This, Huw tells him, is the place which is always used, and he has Gwyn explore a small hole in the roots of the tree, where the boy finds the spearhead Blodeu-wedd's husband had used, with other things on which appear an owl's face. Many have been here before him, for the powers in the valley—the powers of the plants Gwydion had used to create Blodeuwedd—have built themselves up and have been unleashed through people many times. Only the creators of the plates and of the portrait of Blodeuwedd sought to imprison the power and thwart it instead—as had Huw, for Gwyn finds the brake blocks Huw had removed from Bertram's motorbike to teach him a lesson. Gwyn, the son of Huw and Nancy, must not fail the valley as his father had. Gwyn goes back to the house, taking from the roots of the tree a stone pendant for Huw to give to Alison for him.

The next day Roger manages to break into a long-locked stable where strange noises have been heard, and he finds Bertram's motorbike and Alison's owls, with owl tracks patterning the dust in the place. In furious fear, Nancy wrecks the room. When she and Gwyn try to leave, they cannot, for the road has been blocked by a tree felled by a storm. Gwyn goes back to the house to be met by Roger, who has been sent by Huw to find him; when Huw had given the pendant to Alision, she had fainted, and scratches from a bird's claws had marked her face. Gwyn finds Alison lying in Huw's room, with feathers falling all around her, for the power is in her. Gwyn can help her, but so badly hurt has he been by Roger and Alison that he cannot. "She" has always been made owls, Huw says, and so she has hunted; always there has been destruction. Because Gwyn cannot comfort Alison, Roger does, persuading the girl that Blodeuwedd is flowers, that it had been flowers on the plate, not owls. As he watches, the marks on Alison's skin fade, and the feathers swirling in the room become petals of the flowers from which Blodeuwedd was created.

PAFF, ANGELA, a character in *The Daybreakers** and *The Birdstones**, by Jane Louise Curry*. Because she is bossy and self-centered, the other children of Apple Lock*, Ohio, tend to be wary of Angela, though they tolerate her. Angela is part of the group that travels back in time to twelfth-century Abáloc* to rescue Conway Tapp*; she also organizes much of the "Dayla Jones" hoax the next year. On Halloween night on Apple Island*, Angela keeps an eye on Mrs. Buttery, the librarian, who has been possessed by Tekla*, the queen of fourth-century Kanhuan*. When Angela is captured by Tekla's men, she provides the diversion Dalea* and Thiuclas* need to get back to ancient Abáloc. Angela's exploits earn her a lovely black eye and the grudging respect of the other children.

PAINTER, THE, a nameless character in Susan Cooper's* *Greenwitch**. He is one of the minions of the Dark, sent to steal from the British Museum a grail* necessary in the battle between the Dark and the Light. Thinking to make himself one of the lords of the Dark, he also tries to get the manuscript* that translates a prophetic inscription on the grail itself. Toward this end he tries to control the Greenwitch*, a sacrificial figure that has the manuscript, but the Greenwitch refuses his hold and causes the painter to be taken aboard a strange ship of Wild Magic, to sail out of time.

PAL, the narrator of *The Voyage of QV 66**, by Penelope Lively*. He is a dog who got his name from a dogfood can that bore a picture of a dog like him and the word "pal." When the world floods and all the humans go to Mars, Pal is one of the animals left behind. After he and Freda*, a cow, find a monkey, Stanley*, Pal's troubles and adventures begin; soon he is part of a small group traveling to London to find other creatures like Stanley. Pal is sensible and steady and, though he is sometimes exasperated with Stanley, he sticks by him.

PAN, PETER, the title character of *Peter and Wendy** and *Peter Pan in Kensington Gardens**, by James M. Barrie*. Peter is old but forever young; when he is a week old, he flies away from his mother and goes to live in Kensington

Gardens. When he at last decides to return to his mother, he is too late, for she has another little boy. Peter has the run of the Gardens after the gates are locked, and he is the only human who does, for he is not really human. In the Gardens he meets Maimie Mannering*, whom he asks to marry him, but she goes back to her parents. Peter takes up residence in Neverland*, lording it over the lost boys* and having many adventures. Ageless, Peter is the perfect age for every child he meets. Time means little to him; all time is the present as far as he is concerned and he forgets what is past almost immediately, as Wendy, Michael, and John Darling*** discover when he forgets them as they fly to Neverland. Once his arch-enemy, Captian Jas. Hook*, and Tinker Bell*, Peter's fairy companion, are dead, the boy forgets them completely. Peter is as conceited, overbearing, and unthinkingly cruel as any young boy, but there is something about him that makes the females around him want to be something other than his mother—something he does not understand. Peter is the best at everything he tries. He is an accomplished flier and fighter and is sometimes overwhelmed by his own cleverness, and he is the undisputed lord of Neverland. At night, however, he sometimes has bad dreams. Peter still has his baby teeth and his first laugh; he is childhood and freedom personified and, no matter what the temptation, he resolutely refuses to grow up.

PANSY, a character in Penelope Lively's* *The Voyage of QV 66*. She is an orange cat with black and gray markings. Pansy is one of the animals left on Earth after the humans go to Mars to avoid a world-wide flood. She becomes part of a small group accompanying Stanley*, a monkey, to London, to find others like himself. Pansy has a great curiosity that gets her into trouble when she gets into the basket Stanley has tied to some inflated balloons and sails across England. Pansy finally comes down near Stonehenge and, because she is alone, is almost sacrificed there at Midsummer before the others manage to rescue her.

PARADOS, MR., a character in *The House of Arden** and *Harding's Luck**, by E[dith] Nesbit Bland*. Mr. Parados's large nose has earned him the nickname "Parrotnose." He is the tutor of Richard Arden* in 1605. Parados is particularly nasty, being a strict tutor who has the habit of creeping up behind people and eavesdropping. On 5 November 1605 he overhears Elfrida Arden*, a young time traveler from the twentieth century, telling Richard about the Gunpowder Plot. When the plot is discovered later that day, Parados has her and most of the family arrested for high treason. After they get out of the Tower of London, Elfrida and her brother, Edred Arden*, get revenge on Parados by shovelling snow into his room and then locking him out on the roof of Arden House*.

PARKER, PROFESSOR PETER PERSEVERANCE, a character in *Time Cat,** by Lloyd Alexander*. He is a traveling peddlar in America in 1775. This lanky patriot travels across New England in a wagon, selling kittens and spreading the news of the colonial rebellion. He picks up Jason*, a boy from the twentieth century, and Gareth*, his cat, and allows them to accompany him on his rounds. When they come too close to a battle between the Minutemen and the British near Boston, the professor is wounded in the chest, leaving Jason to spread word of the battle to the colonists Parker served.

PARMENTER, FELICITY (FISSY), a character in Jane Louise Curry's* *The Magical Cupboard*. Her grandfather was John Parmenter; she comes to marry Goliath Hollybush* (Golly). When Fissy was orphaned, she came under the care of Sufferana and Thanatopsis Grout**, who kept her in their orphanage, also keeping what little she inherited, including land and a fur trade along the Connecticut River. Fissy grew up pinched and hungry in the orphanage, dreaming of luxuries and enough to eat. When the Grouts close down the orphanage, they take Fissy with them to claim her inheritance, accompanied by Golly and his family. During the journey, Fissy one night is set to guard the wagon in the stable of the inn where they are staying; because she is cold, she climbs inside the magical cupboard* they are carrying and is astonished to find that inside is a cosy little room with a warm bed. Even more surprising is the room's window, through which Fissy sees into the twentieth century and watches William Wingard* and Hepsibah Sagacity Walpole*, who are searching in that century for the cupboard. Fissy's inheritance proves to be long gone, but Golly rebuilds the house and starts a farm on the property. On her seventeenth birthday, Fissy marries him. During a trip to Montreal with the Grouts, the cupboard refuses to leave a certain spot, so Golly sells the farm and builds a new house. Remembering the twentenieth-century couple she saw searching for the cupboard, Fissy leaves instructions to future generations of Hollybushes that the cupboard is to be kept for them.

PARSEL, MR., a character in *The Wizard in the Tree*, by Lloyd Alexander*. He and Mrs. Parsel* own a cookshop. Though not as rapacious as his wife, Mr. Parsel generally goes along with what she want in order to keep the peace. When Mallory*, his servant, and Arbican*, a wizard, are captured by Squire Scrupnor*, who plans to frame them for a murder he committed, Mr. Parsel helps them to escape by slipping Mallory a knife to use on her bonds.

PARSEL, MRS., a character in Lloyd Alexander's* *The Wizard in the Tree*. She and Mr. Parsel* own a cookshop; Mrs. Parsel makes a bargain with greedy Squire Scrupnor* that would make the shop into the only inn in the village. Greed and cruelty are the basis of Mrs. Parsel's nature. She abuses Mallory*, the orphaned maid-of-all-work, and even turns the girl over to Scrupnor for a reward when the squire tries to frame Mallory and Arbican*, an enchanter, for a murder he himself has committed.

PARSLEY SAGE(*Parsley Sage, Rosemary & Time*). *See* Sage, Parsley

PARSLEY SAGE, ROSEMARY & TIME. Jane Louise Curry. Illus. Charles Robinson. New York: Atheneum, 1975. 108 pp. American.

Because her parents must go to China, staid, level-headed ten-year-old Rosemary Walpole* stays with her eccentric aunt, Hepsibah Sagacity Walpole* (Sibby). Behind Sibby's centuries-old house lies a secret garden, to which Rosemary is led by Parsley Sage*, Sibby's ancient tomcat. Here Rosemary finds a small herb garden that includes a patch of "time"*. When the girl picks the herb, time stops for everything but her. Investigating further, Rosemary nibbles some of the plant near the little garden's strange sundial and suddenly things speed up and the dial and everything else vanish. Rosemary finds herself not in the June garden but in a forest where the trees have changed for fall. Sibby's house has been replaced by a low, dark house where an old woman, disturbed at the visit of "another one," shooes Rosemary away. On a nearby beach, Rosemary meets Baba, a small girl dressed in jeans, like Rosemary, who assures her that this is not the twentieth century and who tells her that the old woman is Goody Cakebread* and has the reputation of being a witch. With the child is Goody Cakebread's cat, which looks like a younger version of Parsley Sage. Baba had come the day before, and Goody Cakebread had not been at all pleased to see her and was less pleased when two-year-old Wim appeared the next morning. Goody Cakebread kept the little boy with her, however. Rosemary and Baba go and get the little boy, learning from Goody Cakebread that they should know how to get home—all her other visitors had.

The three wander into the little village, where they hear Parson Thanatopsis Grout* preaching that Goody Cakebread is a witch, for Carolanna*, his Indian slavegirl, had seen her work magic. He incites the people against the woman, so the children go back to warn her. Goody Cakebread decides to live with some nearby Indians, taking with her the children, dressed in the proper clothes provided by a magical cupboard* she owns. They are caught, however, and taken to jail. The cupboard is locked up too, in another room. This wedding present from her husband's grandmother has been very useful to Goody Cakebread, providing its owner with whatever she needs. It helps even more when Carolanna, repenting her part in Goody Cakebread's incarceration, comes to help her. The cupboard gives her a bottle of apple wine that intoxicates the jailer and his wife so that they sleep while Carolanna steals the keys to the cell.

Freed, they go to the Indians. Here Rosemary learns how to get home; she must walk between two elms called the Dreaming Trees*, which stand between one time period and another. Wim goes first and Baba follows, and as she walks between the trees, Goody Cakebread's cat jumps into her arms and is taken into her time. Just as Rosemary steps through, Goody Cakebread's long-lost son, Thomas Cakebread*, rides up, accompanied by a young woman.

Rosemary finds herself in the little garden, now tidied up and spaded. The patch of "time" is gone. A young man—William Wingard*—has arrived; he used to live in the old house and wants to buy it, but Sibby will not sell. Suddenly Rosemary realizes that Baba was Sibby as a child, and both are delighted and amazed. William, who has read the old family diaries, tells them the end of Goody Cakebread's story: Thomas, having made his furtune in the tropics, took a wife and came to live with Goody Cakebread. His wife, Juditha Cakebread*, was a real witch and planted the "time" in the little garden. William suggests that they look for the cupboard; he believes Rosemary's story, for once as a baby he was lost for a time and, when found, was dressed in old-fashioned clothes: Wim was himself, as a baby.

PAT PIERSON (*The Watch House*). *See* Pierson, Pat

PATON WALSH, GILLIAN BLISS (1939–   ), British writer. She was born 29 April 1939 to John Llewellyn and Patricia (Dubern) Bliss, in London, England. Paton Walsh was educated at St. Anne's College, Oxford, from which she graduated in 1959 with a degree in English (with honors). She was a teacher of English in London from 1959 to 1962 and married Antony Paton Walsh on 12 August 1961; they have two daughters and a son.

Most of the works of Jill Paton Walsh for children are historical fiction. *A Chance Child**, her fantasy, is a time fantasy rich in historical detail.

The nineteenth-century England Creep* finds himself in the England of the Industrial Revolution, when cottage industry is giving way to mechanization and children are cruelly exploited. Paton Walsh evokes this era with great skill through direct description as Creep makes his way through the landscape and through a kind of flashback as his brother, Chris*, reads the Parliamentary Papers in an effort to find him. Paton Walsh's nineteenth-century England is a place of contrast: the quiet, green countryside differs sharply from the harsh and raucous factories the children work in. The reader becomes aware of the deadening effect of such labor and watches as not only the jobs but the people become mechanized.

Traveling through this world is Creep, a child abused in the twentieth century who tries to help children abused in the nineteenth. Creep is innocent in every sense of the word. It does not seem wonderful to him that he suddenly finds himself in another century; he has not had experience enough to notice the difference or to realize that movement between the two is unusual. Nor does it seem outrageous to him that children should be worked as if they were machines and beaten if they fail to perform; this is the way life is, and he tries to help them as much as he can. Creep seems to find himself in a century and a place not out of keeping with his own experience of the world.

For a time, in his journey, Creep seems to belong to neither century. In the nineteenth he is a ghostly figure—unseen by adults but perfectly visible to the abused child workers. He seems to be visible only to those who need him; when Tom is well-fed, Creep seems to him to fade a little. Creep does not need to eat; he does not laugh or cry. When he finds joy in a mother championing her son, he laughs out loud; then he is wholly engaged by something out of his experience and he suddenly becomes part of the world around him, faint with hunger and visible to all.

426 PATON WALSH, JILL

Creep's innocence may play a part in his time travel; he does not believe he cannot travel into the past, so he does. The man who tells him about the small boat he has taken refuge in explains that the canal goes on or back from where they are; "I'll go back," Creep says, and he does—back in time as well as place. Creep's small boat seems to have a mind of its own, taking him to the coal mines, where he finds Tom and carrying them to freedom; taking the children to the place from which they disembark and find Lucy*; taking them to the china factory, to the mines where Tom gets work, to the cotton mills. Once Creep becomes part of his new century, the boat does not move again of its own accord.

Paton Walsh handles well the parallel aspects of her story, alternating the chapter between Creep's adventures and his brother's attempts to find him. Her characters, especially the children, are life-like and three-dimensional. Historical information is skillfully presented and details of the day-to-day life of that earlier age are convincing. Paton Walsh's prose is rich and descriptive and it successfully evokes both the present and the past.

Works

Juvenile fantasy: *A Chance Child* (1978).
Juvenile non-fantasy: *Hengest's Tale* (1966); *The Dolphin Crossing* (1967); *Fireweed* (1969); *Wordhoard* (1969), with Kevin Crossley-Holland; *Goldengrove* (1972); *The Dawnstone* (1973); *Toolmaker* (1973); *The Emperor's Winding Sheet* (1974); *The Butty Boy* (1975), in America as *The Huffler; The Island Sunrise* (1975); *Unleaving* (1976); *Crossing to Salamis* (1977); *The Walls of Athens* (1977); *Children of the Fox* (1978); *Persian Gold* (1979); *The Green Book* (1982); *Babylon* (1982).
Adult: *Farewell, Great King* (1972), novel.

Secondary Works

Rees, David. "Types of Ambiguity: Jill Paton Walsh," in *The Marble in the Water* (Boston: The Horn Book, 1979), pp. 141-54.
Townsend, John Rowe. "Jill Paton Walsh," in *A Sounding of Storytellers* (New York: J. B. Lippincott, 1979), pp. 153-65.

PATON WALSH, JILL. *See* Paton Walsh, Gillian Bliss

PATRICK, ST. *See* Sucat

PAUL, the main character in Penelope Lively's* *The Driftway**. After his mother dies, he becomes the stepson of Christine*; he is the older brother of Sandra*. Paul feels that his one-parent life is as complete as it needs to be, with his grandmother helping him and his father to take care of Sandra and the house. When his father remarries, Paul bitterly resents Christine and tries to ignore her. Finally deciding to make the room he shares with Sandra absolutely out of

Christine's realm, Paul shops for a padlock and is caught accidentally shoplifting a chain. He and Sandra escape and start for their grandmother's house, trusting that she will hide them and take care of them. One th way they hitch a ride with Old Bill* on a driftway*, and as they travel, Paul experiences the lives of those who have traveled this ancient road before him. Jolted out of himself by these experiences, Paul comes to see how selfish he is, and how he has hurt Christine and his father, and by the time they come to the end of their journey, Paul has resolved to let Christine into his life.

PAUL CAREY (*Stuart Little*). *See* Carey, Paul (Dr.)

PAUL WILSON (*The Magic Bed-Knob; Bonfires and Broomsticks*). *See* Wilson, Paul

PAULINE, a character in *A Chance Child*, by Jill Paton Walsh*. She is the sister of Chris* and the half-sister of Creep*. She goes with Chris on his search for their younger brother. Pauline later denies Creep ever existed, but Chris tricks her into admitting her denial.

PEAGREEN OVERMANTEL (*The Borrowers Avenged*). *See* Overmantel, Peregrine

PEARCE, [ANN] PHILIPPA (1920-   ), British writer. She was born in Great Shelford, Cambridgeshire, England, in 1920, to Ernest Alexander and Gertrude Alice (Ramsden) Pearce. She was educated at Girton College, Cambridge, where she received a B.A. and an M.A. On 9 May 1963 she married Martin Christie (died 1965); they have one daughter. Pearce has been a civil servant, a scriptwriter and producer for BBC Radio in London, an assistant editor in the educational department of Oxford University Press, and the children's editor at André Deutsch Ltd., as well as being a reviewer and lecturer.

Pearce's eleven works for children include novels, short stories, and one fantasy, *Tom's Midnight Garden*. This quiet fantasy is unforgettable in its setting and its theme.

In this time fantasy time is not a straight path but a twisted circle. On the pendulum of the grandfather clock* that makes it possible for Tom* to step out of the flats where he is staying and into a Victorian garden, are written the words "Time no longer," and, in the novel, time as we perceive it means very little.

At the center of this time fantasy is a conundrum. Tom, sent to stay with his aunt and uncle in a small flat with no place for the boy to play, discovers that he can go each night, when the grandfather clock in the hall strikes thirteen, to a wonderful garden behind the flats where he is staying; here he meets a Victorian girl, Hatty, whom he plays with and who has grown up to be Mrs. Harriet Melbourne Bartholomew*, the owner of the flats. Tom's visits to the past are linked to Mrs. Bartholomew's dreams of her childhood and of Tom, for when she dreams of him, his way to the garden is open, but when she does not dream of him or of the garden, he cannot get into it. Tom thus not only affects Mrs. Bartholomew's past, but his own present, for by playing with Hatty and providing memories for Mrs. Bartholomew, he is able to go into the past to play with Hatty. Because of Mrs. Bartholomew's dreams, the past events Tom takes part in are not always in strict chronological succession; once, Tom goes into the garden and witnesses a fir tree being struck by lightning, but the next time he looks out, it is whole again. After a scene in which Hatty is woefully humiliated by her aunt, Tom wanders through the garden to find the girl as a small child who has just come to live at the house after the deaths of her parents. "Time no longer" means that chronological time in the garden itself is changed, for time means nothing in dreams, and dreams pattern what Tom experiences.

Exactly how the time shifts are accomplished is never quite clear, but longing seems to have something to do with it. Mrs. Bartholomew's dreams of the past and Tom's yearning for a companion and a place to play seem to combine and make it possible for him to travel through time, but only when the eccentric grandfather clock strickes a thirteenth hour that does not exist. This hour symbolizes the fact that time no longer means anything, but it also serves as an impetus for Tom, who needs that extra hour to justify his getting out of bed and going into the garden.

Once he is in the garden, Tom seems to exist as a ghost there. He is seen by only two people and by some animals. Abel, the gardener, can see Tom, perhaps because as a Fundamentalist he is ready to believe in things outside his ken. At first he thinks Tom is a demon, but later, when he sees Tom reading from the Bible, Abel changes his mind. Animals have traditionally been thought to sense things beyond men's understanding, and their behavior to Tom is understandable. Hatty seems to see Tom only when she needs him, for as she grows older and finds other companions, the boy seems more and more transparent each time she sees him. On her wedding day she does not need or think of Tom at all, and when Mrs. Bartholomew dreams of that day, Tom cannot get into the garden. As he remains unseen by most in the garden, so is Tom unable to touch the garden itself, again, just as a ghost. Tom cannot move anything himself and in fact can go through solid objects at will. He can affect the past in nonphysical ways by affecting Hatty, but he cannot affect it physically, perhaps because Mrs. Bartholomew's dreams will not let him.

For, because of Mrs. Bartholomew's dreams, the garden is already a place wonderful both for Tom and for herself. Like anyone's nostalgic dreams, Mrs. Bartholomew's dwell on the happy times when she had been with Tom or with her husband, and as a result the weather is always good—if not for playing, as in the warm months, then for ice-skating, in the winter. The beautiful garden is a place where there are many things to do, where there are trees to climb, games to play, and places to hide. Though it belongs to Hatty's aunt and is the scene of some humiliations, the garden is a place where Hatty can be secure and happy, and she enjoys it until she has grown up and it is time to leave the garden for the outside world.

Pearce's novel is believable throughout because of her attention to detail in her characters and in the landscape itself. The garden becomes so real for the reader that one can almost hear it and smell it. Most characters are well realized and three-dimensional, though some, like Hatty's aunt, seem more like types than people. The shifts in time are well handled. Pearce's prose is fluid and descriptive, and though there is little overt action in the novel, it is exciting and suspenseful.

Works

Juvenile full-length fantasy: *Tom's Midnight Garden* (1958).

Juvenile short stories, novels, etc.: *Minnow on the Say* (1955) as *The Minnow Leads to Treasure* (1958); *Still Jim and Silent Jim* (1959); *Mrs. Cockle's Cat* (1961); *A Dog So Small* (1962); *From Inside Scotland Yard* (1963), with Sir Harold Scott; *The Strange Sunflower* (1966); *The Children of the House* (1968), with Brian Fairfax-Lucy; *The Squirrel-Wife* (1971); *Beauty and the Beast* (1972), retelling; *What the Neighbours Did, and Other Stories* (1972); *The Shadow-Cage, and Other Tales of the Supernatural* (1977); *The Battle of Bubble and Squeak* (1978).

Secondary Works

Ayers, Lesley. "The Treatment of Time in Four Children's Books," *Children's Literature in Education*, 2 (July, 1970), pp. 69-81.

Pearce, Philippa. "The Writer's View of Childhood," *The Horn Book Magazine*, 37 (Feb., 1962), pp. 74-78.

Philip, Neil, "'Tom's Midnight Garden' and the Vision of Eden," *Signal*, 37 (Jan., 1982), pp. 21-25.

Rees, David, "Achieving One's Heart's Desires: Philippa Pearce," in *The Marble in the Water* (Boston: The Horn Book, 1980), pp. 36-55.

———. "The Novels of Philippa Pearce," *Children's Literature in Education*, 4 (March, 1971), pp. 40-53.

Townsend, John Rowe. "Philippa Pearce," in *A Sense of Story* (Boston: The Horn Book, 1971), pp. 163-71.

PELIS THE FALSE, a character in *The Moon of Gomarth**, by Alan Garner*. He is the son of Argad. This dwarf* dresses all in black and has a gold-hilted sword. He is false-hearted and becomes the minion of the Morrigan*, an evil witch. As Uthecar Hornskin* helps rescue Colin*, a boy Pelis had kidnapped for the Morrigan, he fights Pelis and, though wounded, finally kills him after a terrible battle.

PELLINORE, KING, a figure in Arthurian legend who appears as a character in *The Sword in the Stone**, by T[erence] H[anbury] White*. Like all his family, Pellinore has been trained for one thing only: to chase the Questing Beast*, which only a Pellinore can catch. One Michaelmas he starts out after it, and he chases the Beast for seventeen years. Both keep regular hours, rising at the same time in the morning, chasing about, and going to bed at half past ten. Pellinore is aided in his chase by a white brachet, a friendly dog which shows absolutely no interest in the Beast and has a remarkable talent for tangling itself and everyone else in its leash. Chasing the Beast is difficult for Pellinore, what with the brachet, and his visor always falling, and his glasses always steaming up, and the armor getting rusty; and what the king would like best would be to live in a nice castle, with a featherbed all his own. After a joust with Sir Grummore Grummursum*, that knight invites Pellinore to stay with him, and the king jumps at the chance. He soon repents, for the Questing Beast, with no one to care about it, pines away, and Pellinore must nurse it back to health and resume his questing. Once he is captured by a giant, Galapas*, and the Beast helps save him. Pellinore takes part in the ritual that makes Kay*, Sir Ector's son, into a knight. When the Wart (Arthur*), Ector's foster son, becomes king of Britain, Pellinore and the Beast send him as a coronation present their best fewmets, beautifully wrapped.

PENDANT, SILVER, an object in Jane Louise Curry's* *Over the Sea's Edge*. It was originally found by Diermit, an Irish seer, who took it from the body of a strangely dressed man who washed ashore on the island of Lund in the twelfth century. He gave it to Ithil, who gave it to his son, Dewi ap Ithil*, asking the boy to search for the magical land from which it had come. In the twentieth century, it is found by David Reese*, an adventurous boy who feels stifled in his own time. When the two boys dream of one another, Dewi uses the pendant to trade places with Dave, who carries it to America. It is found again in the twentieth century by the new Dave Reese, who gives it to his cousin, Alice. The silver pendant bears a design of either a bird or a tree surrounded by a ring or a snake with its tail in its mouth. It can be interpreted several ways: the inner figure is freedom or fruitfulness, surrounded by time or eternity. One can see the eternal loop of the snake as eternity itself, as the Abalockians do, or as death, as do the people of Cibotlán*. Within eternity, we are free to be fruitful as the tree or free as the bird.

PENDOR, a place in *A Wizard of Earthsea*, by Ursula K. LeGuin*. This island lies just west of the Ninety Isles on Earthsea*. The lords of the island were pirates and slave traders, feared and hated by all, until a great dragon killed them and drove the townspeople away because of the great riches collected here. On Pendor the dragon raised its young, and to Pendor it and its surviving young are bound by Ged*, a sorcerer who knows the dragon's true name and who makes it swear not to leave the island.

PENELOPE TABERNER CAMERON (*A Traveller in Time*). *See* Cameron, Penelope Taberner

PENN DREEGO (*The Watchers*). *See* Dreego, Penn

PEPPERELL, PETER PEABODY, III, a character in Robert Lawson's* *The Fabulous Flight*. He is the son of Mary and Peter Peabody Pepperell II; he is the nephew of Dora and the cousin of Barbara. Until he is seven, Peter is a normal little boy. Shortly after his seventh birthday, he falls from a tree and lands on his chest; this affects his sacro-pitulian-phalangic gland, causing him to grow smaller, not larger, as he gets older. On the other hand, Peter's brain seems to develop faster than usual, which leads to embarrassment on the part of his schoolmates. Eventually Peter is taken out of school and is tutored at home by Barbara. As Peter shrinks, he makes friends with the small wild animals in the area, riding a rabbit as one would a horse, and training his new friends in military exercises. By the time Peter is thirteen, he is four inches high, and when he meet Gus*, a seagull, Peter can ride on his back. Peter and Gus are soon sent on a mission to steal a powerful explosive developed by Doctor Professor Polopodsky*; on its successful completion, Peter receives a medal from the president of the United States and the Grand Cross of St. Filbert, the Supreme Exalted Star of Zang, and several other honors from Zargonia, the country he had helped. Best of all, Peter learns that as a result of a shock he has gotten, he will start growing larger again.

PEREGRINE OVERMANTEL (*The Borrowers Avenged*). *See* Overmantel, Peregrine

PERESBY, ELLEN, a character in Jane Louise Curry's* *The Sleepers*. She is the sister of Gillian Peresby* and the grandaughter of Sir Daniel Persesby, a famous archaelogist. Ellen is probably descended from Nimiane*, who imprisoned Myrddin*—Merlin—inside the Eildon Tree* long ago. Ellen is a student at the University of London. This bright, flighty, absent-minded young woman comes under the power of Margan*, the fey sister of Artair*—King Arthur*— who sometimes seems to possess Ellen, making her do thing she ordinarily would not do. Because of the strange Peresby prophecy Ellen discovers, she tries to halt Gerald Rishanger's* archaelogical dig near the Eildon Tree by appearing to him as the Queen of Elfland, who supposedly met Thomas the Rhymer at the same spot. Under Margan's influence, Ellen also tries to talk Gerald into joining Margan's minions. Because of Ellen's ancestry, Myrddin uses her to disenchant him by tricking her into saying the spell to free him. Though Gerald is often aggravated by Ellen, he comes to enjoy her company very much.

PERESBY, GILLIAN, a character in *The Sleepers*, by Jane Lousie Curry*. She is the sister of Ellen Peresby* and the granddaughter of Sir Daniel Peresby, a noted British archaeologist. Gillian may be descended from the family of Nimiane*, who imprisoned Myrddin*—Merlin—in the Eildon Tree* long ago. When Gillian's friend, Jennifer Huntington*, and her brother come with their archaeologist uncle to visit one of his colleagues, Gillian and the others help to discover and save Artair*—King Arthur*—and the *Brenhin Dlyseu**, the Thirteen Treasures of Prydein, from Margan*, Artair's sister and enemy. Gillian proves her mettle when she helps Henry Peter Huntington* to retrieve the Bell of Rhûn* from a locked case in the British Museum.

PETE MACCUBBIN (*The Lost Farm*). *See* MacCubbin, Pete

PETER AND WENDY. James M. Barrie. Illus. F. D. Bedford. London: Hodder and Stoughton, 1911. 267 pp. British.

Wendy Moira Angela Darling* has known from the age of two that someday she would grow up. She is the oldest child of Mr. and Mrs. Darling**, who are so poor that they have recruited Nana*, a Newfoundland dog, to be the nurse for Wendy and her brothers, John and Michael Darling**. The Darling family is happy, though sometimes Mrs. Darling is afraid; in tidying her children's minds at night, she has come upon Peter Pan*, who sometimes flies into the nursery at night and plays his pipes for Wendy as she sleeps. One night Mrs. Darling dreams of Peter and wakes to find him in the room. Though he escapes, he leaves his shadow, which Mrs. Darling rolls up and tucks into a drawer.

One night, as Mr. and Mrs. Darling dress to go to a party, there is an altercation in the nursery and Mr. Darling ties Nana outside. He and Mrs. Darling go next door to the party, leaving the children asleep in the nursery. They are not alone for long: Tinker Bell*, a fairy, comes into the room to find Peter's shadow; she is followed by Peter, who finds his shadow but cries when it will not reattach itself to him. Wakened by the crying, Wendy sews the shadow to his foot. Peter gets conceited about having his shadow again, and Wendy is miffed, but they make up and she offers him a kiss. When Peter holds out his hand, she gives him a thimble, so as not to embarrass him. In return, Peter gives Wendy an acorn button which she threads onto a chain around her neck.

Peter tells Wendy how, as a baby, he had heard his parents talking of what he would be when he grew up, and he escaped. Now he lives with the lost boys* in Neverland*. Peter likes Mrs. Darling's stories, and when Wendy reveals that she, too, knows stories, Peter teaches her and Michael and John to fly so that they can all go to Neverland. Nana breaks her chain to fetch Mr. and Mrs. Darling from the party, but they arrive just too late to stop the children.

The flight to Neverland is not much fun, for Peter is easily bored and sometimes flies off and forgets them. Flying over Neverland after dark is frightening. When, to the children's horror, the pirates aim a cannon at them, using Tinker Bell's light as a target, she agrees to travel in John's hat so that her light will not be seen. Wendy carries the hat in her hands, and when the gun goes off, John and Michael are blown in one direction, and Peter and Wendy in two others. Wendy must rely on jealous Tinker Bell to guide her.

On the ground, the lost boys are looking for Peter, the pirates are looking for the boys, the Indians are looking for the pirates, and the wild beasts are looking for the Indians. Vicious Captain Jas. Hook*, captain of the pirates, discovers the underground home of the lost boys, but he is interrupted in his nefarious plotting by the approach of his nemesis, the crocodile* with the clock in its belly, which had so enjoyed the taste of Hook's hand, flung to it by Peter, that it longs for more.

When the lost boys come out of their house, they see what they think is a great white bird, flying their way, and shoot it at Tinker Bell's urging. All are horrified to discover that the bird is a girl. Peter arrives and is wild with grief, but Wendy is not dead; the arrow hit the "kiss" he had given her and she has only fainted. The boys, joined now by Michael and John, build a little house around the girl. When they knock at the door, Wendy opens it and agrees to be their mother. Housekeeping for Peter and the boys becomes a game for Wendy and she is quite happy at it.

One day the children are at the Mermaids' Lagoon*, on Marooner's Rock*, and Peter rescues Tiger Lily*, the daughter of the Indian chief, by imitating the voice of Captain Hook and ordering her pirate captors to set her free. Hook himself swims to the rock, sad because the lost boys have found a mother; he decides to capture Wendy and make her the pirates' mother instead. Hearing his men's story, Hook discovers whose the voice really was, and a great and bloody fight ensues in the waters of the lagoon. Peter and Hook meet on the rock, and Peter is wounded before the ticking crocodile comes and chases Hook away. Peter and Wendy are left behind on the rock by the lost boys, who think the two have gone home. Neither is strong enough to fly and escape the rising tide. When Michael's kite, which had gotten away from him, drifts past, Peter uses it to get Wendy to safety, and he is left alone to face death. But the Never bird*, which floats in its nest on the lagoon, paddles up and offers the nest to Peter. He puts the bird's eggs in a pirate's hat and sails to safety in the nest.

Because of this adventure, the children and the Indians become friends, and the Indians are guarding the house one night when Wendy tells how Mrs. Darling leaves the nursery window open for her children's return. Hearing from Peter that when he had tried to return to his mother he found the window barred, Wendy, Michael, and John decide to go home while they have a chance. The lost boys will go with them. Peter is staying; he does not want any part of growing up or of mothers, though he agrees to take the "medicine" Wendy pours out for him.

Suddenly the pirates attack the Indians on guard above the house and defeat them. The children wait breathlessly to hear who the victors are; if the Indians have won, they will beat a tom-tom. The pirates beat the tom-tom and capture the children when they emerge, taking them away to the ship. Only Peter escapes, for he has stayed and is now asleep. Hook creeps down to the house but is too large to get in, so he poisons the medicine. When Peter wakes, Tinker Bell tells him of the capture and drinks the poisoned medicine before he can. Peter saves her from death by appealing to the sleeping children of the world to clap their hands if they believe in fairies. Then he is off for the pirate ship to save Wendy and the others.

At the ship, Hook is preparing to have his prisoners walk the plank when the ticking crocodile is heard. Hiding Hook, the pirates are not watching when Peter, ticking like the crocodile, slips onto the ship and into the cabin. When the pirates who are sent into the cabin are killed, the panicked pirates decide that the ship is cursed and send in the boys, whom Peter releases and arms. When Hook decides to throw Wendy overboard, the boys attack. The pirate crew is routed and Peter finally forces Hook overboard and into the jaws of the waiting crocodile, which is no longer ticking because the clock has run down. On the ship, the children play pirate.

At home, Mr. and Mrs. Darling are still waiting. One night Peter and Tinker Bell fly into the nursery. Peter would close the window against Wendy and her brothers, but he cannot once he sees Mrs. Darling, so he leaves. There is a touching and happy reunion after John, Michael, and Wendy return, and the lost boys are adopted into the family. Mrs. Darling agrees to let Wendy go to Neverland every year to spring-clean.

But to Peter Pan, all time is the present, and though he does come for Wendy the very next year, in subsequent years he is erratic and finally does not come until Wendy is a grown woman with a daughter of her own, Jane*, whom she has told about Peter. When at last Peter comes for Wendy, he is upset to find her grown. Peter's crying wakes Jane and he teaches her to fly; Wendy watches as Jane leaves with Peter to do the spring cleaning. In time, Jane grows up, too, and her daughter does spring cleaning for Peter as well, and her daughter after her, and so it will go on.

PETER PAN. *See* Pan, Peter

PETER PAN. *See Peter and Wendy*

PETER PAN IN KENSINGTON GARDENS. James M. Barrie. Illus. Arthur Rackham. London: Hodder and Stoughton, 1906. 126 pp. British.

Peter Pan* is old, but his age is only one week, because when he is one week old, he flies out the window and back to Kensington Gardens, thinking himself still a bird, for all babies were once birds. Not understanding why the fairies in the Gardens run away from him, Peter flies to the island in the Serpentine to consult Solomon Caw*, the old bird in charge of sending babies to human mothers. Solomon proves to Peter that he is human and Peter decides to go back to his mother, but he cannot; having lost his belief that he can fly, he has lost the power to do so as well. Peter must stay on the island, fed and laughed at and taught by the birds. He learns many of the birds' ways, including how to have a glad heart, and, being unable to sing like the birds, Peter makes himself panpipes of reed and plays to express his happiness and his sorrow because he cannot swim or fly and thereby reach the Gardens across the Serpentine.

One evening a poet with an extra five pound note makes a boat of it and sends it off on the Serpentine. Peter knows what it is, having, after all, been a baby for a week, and he uses it to hire some thrushes to build him a large waterproof nest for him to boat in. Using his nightgown as a sail, Peter makes the difficult journey across the Serpentine, only to be met by the fairies of the Gardens, who try to make him go away. Peter explains to them that he is no ordinary human, and all the female fairies are smitten by him, for they can tell by his nightgown that he is a baby. Peter is given the run of the Gardens after Lock-out Time.

His new life is full of fun; Peter plays by himself with the toys that are left behind, and he plays his pipes for the fairy balls. When the princess comes of age, Queen Mab* gives Peter a wish—a big one that he trades for two small ones. One wish Peter holds in reserve; the other he uses to get the power to fly home. There, he finds the window open and his mother asleep, and Peter watches her, knowing that he could wake her but not really sure he wants to. Finally Peter decides that he will have one last sail in his boat before he goes back to being her boy. One last sail leads to more last sails and it is quite a while before Peter makes up his mind to go home. When he makes his second wish and goes back, he finds that his mother has a new little boy, and the window is locked and barred.

Meanwhile Maimie Mannering* is growing up in London. Maimie is four years old and seems perfectly ordinary during the day but is terrible at night, terrorizing her older brother, Tony Mannering*, with an imaginary goat. Frightened as he is at night, Tony is boastful during the day and claims that he will spend the night in the Gardens, despite the fierce fairies. One winter day seems the perfect chance, but to Maimie's dismay Tony runs away home instead of hiding and waiting for nightfall, so Maimie decides to spend the night for him and hides until the gates are locked.

That night Maimie makes the acquaintance of the plants and trees who come awake at night and they warn her that the fairies will be angry with her for staying. The entire fairy court is in a bad temper, for the exotic Duke of Christmas Daisies*, having failed to fall in love, has sought a bride in the Gardens and has so far found no one. Maimie starts toward the fairy ball and comes upon Brownie*, a plain street singer fairy, who will try her luck with the Duke. Maimie follows Brownie to the ball and hides herself from the fairies. Brownie causes much laughter from the others until the Duke falls instantly in love and marries her, fairy-style, by jumping into her arms. In excitement, Maimie reveals her presence and is chased by the angry fairies until she stumbles and falls asleep in the snow.

When the fairies come upon her, they are not quite so angry, for Brownie has begged Queen Mab for a boon and has been granted one—that Maimie will not be harmed. But the child will die of cold, for the fairies cannot wake her, nor can they carry her to a warm spot. So they build a little house around her and thus shelter her for the night. When Maimie wakes the next morning, she leaves the house through the roof, which is hinged like a lid, and she watches as the little house shrinks into nothing. Turning, she meets Peter Pan and they have a chat during which he reveals how he plays with the toys left behind in the Gardens. When Maimie tells him that his way of playing is all wrong, Peter becomes upset and, to comfort him, Maimie offers Peter a kiss. Misunderstanding, he holds out his hand and Maimie gives him a thimble so as not to offend.

The two get along so well that Peter asks Maimie to marry him, but she wants to visit her mother occasionally and he is forced to reveal what happened between him and his mother. Afraid that her mother has found someone new, Maimie leaves as the gates to the Gardens are unlocked, promising to return that night if she is not wanted. But Maimie is in time. With her mother's help, Maimie gives her imaginary goat to Peter as an Easter present.

Now, every night but ball nights, the fairies build a little house for the children who are lost. Peter rides his goat, looking for lost children, and when he finds them he takes them to the house, where they are safe. Sometimes he is too late and then he must bury them and mark the spot with a stone, as he did for Walter Stephen Matthews and Phoebe Phelps, who lie under initialed stones at the place where Westminster St. Mary's and the parish of Paddington meet.

Note: The contents of this volume first appeared as Chapters 13–18 of *The Little White Bird* (London: Hodder and Stoughton, 1902).

PETER PEABODY PEPPERELL III (*The Fabulous Flight*). *See* Pepperell, Peter Peabody, III

PETER PERSEVERANCE PARKER (*Time Cat*). *See* Parker, Professor Peter Perseverance

PETER PEVENSIE (the Chronicles of Narnia). *See* Pevensie, Peter

PETERSON, CURDIE, a character in *The Princess and the Goblin** and *The Princess and Curdie**, by George MacDonald*. He is the son of Peter and Joan and there is royalty in his ancestry. Like his father, Curdie is a miner in the silver mines. Bright and bold, Curdie is the nemesis of the goblins* who live in the mountains, for he is quick-witted enough to make up songs, which they hate, and he is equally quick with his pickax. When he is about twelve, Curdie meets Irene*, a young princess, and he thwarts the evil plans the goblins have for her and for the miners. In the next year, however, Curdie's body grows faster than his mind, and he begins to believe less in what he has never seen; his growing up becomes more a continual dying than a continual rebirth. One night he wounds a pigeon probably belonging to Irene's "grandmother," who is also named Irene*, and—though he has never seen her and cannot believe in her—Curdie takes the bird to the old woman. She welcomes him and sends him on a mission to help Irene and the king*, her father. To prepare him for his task, she makes his hands so sensitive that they can tell at a touch what sort of beast or human the person he touches really is. He travels with an odd and ugly creature named Lina*, whom Curdie gradually learns to love and trust. Having accomplished his task, Curdie stays on at the palace, and the people call him Prince Conrad. Eventually he marries the princess, and when the king dies, they rule for a very happy time. The couple dies childless, and the king who succeeds them brings ruin on the capital city.

PEVENSIE, EDMUND, a character is C[live] S[taples] Lewis's* *The Lion, the Witch, and the Wardrobe*, Prince Caspian*, The Voyage of the "Dawn Treader"*, The Horse and His Boy*,* and *The Last Battle*. He is the brother of Lucy, Peter, and Susan Pevensie***. Edmund tends to be spiteful sometimes, teasing his sisters, especially, as mercilessly as he can. When Lucy announces that she has found a way through a wardrobe* in the house where they are staying, into another world, Edmund makes fun of her, even after he himself goes into the wardrobe and comes out in Narnia*, a magical land. Here he meets and comes under the spell of the evil White Witch* who rules Narnia; at her orders, Edmund tries to take his brother and sisters to her, not knowing that she plans to kill them all. When Aslan*, Narnia's true ruler, comes back to his land, the Witch demands Edmund's life, for all traitors belong to her. Aslan shoulders Edmund's blame and is killed in his place, to come alive again because he himself is blameless. By this time Edmund has realized what he has done, and he does all he can to rectify it. He is a changed boy and tries hard not to be spiteful. After the Witch is defeated, the children rule Narnia; Edmund is called Edmund the Just. During their reign Edmund accompanies Susan to Calormen*, when the prince of that country wants to woo her, and he helps repulse the Calormene invasion into Archenland*. Now an adult, he becomes a child again when he and the others find their way from Narnia back through the wardrobe. On subsequent journeys he helps Caspian X* regain the throne of Narnia, and accompanies the king on a voyage beyond the known lands. After this Edmund can make no more journeys to the magical land. When Narnia later needs her heroes, though, Edmund tries to help. He is killed in a train accident, and is whisked to Aslan's country, to live there in happiness forever.

PEVENSIE, LUCY, a character in *The Lion, the Witch, and the Wardrobe*, Prince Caspian*, The Voyage of the "Dawn Treader"*, The Horse and His Boy*,* and *The Last Battle*, by C[live] S[taples] Lewis*. She is the younger sister of Edmund, Peter, and Susan Pevensie***. When the children stay with Digory Kirke*, an old professor, Lucy discovers that she can go through a certain wardrobe* in his house and come out in the magical land of Narnia*. Though the others do not believe her, she soon proves it by taking them into it as well. Here they take part in the war between Aslan*, Narnia's omniscient lion ruler, and the evil White Witch* who wants to rule it. During this war, Lucy watches with Susan, in despair, as the White Witch slays Aslan; but she is overjoyed when he is resurrected because he is blameless. After the battle, Lucy uses a magic cordial she has been given to heal the wounded. Lucy and the others rule in Narnia until they are adults; Lucy is called Queen Lucy the Valiant, for she does not hesitate to help in the battles sometimes necessary to perserve Narnia. When she and the others find their way back home, through the wardrobe, Lucy becomes, like them, a child again. During subsequent journeys to Narnia, she helps Caspian X* gain his throne and accompanies him on a voyage beyond the known lands. Because she must learn to know Aslan in her own world, after this Lucy can have no more adventures in Narnia. Of the four children, she is the one best able to believe in Aslan and what he has to say. When the Pevensies and their friends try to help the land in its greatest need, Lucy is killed with them in a train accident and is whisked to Aslan's country, to be happy there forever.

PEVENSIE, PETER, a character in *The Lion, the Witch, and the Wardrobe*, *Prince Caspian*, and *The Last Battle*, by C[live] S[taples] Lewis*. He is the older brother of Edmund, Lucy, and Susan Pevensie***. When Peter and his brother and sisters find their way into Narnia*, a magical land, through an old wardrobe* in the house of Digory Kirke*, Peter proves himself equal to the adventures they find there. He and the others join in the battle of Aslan*, Narnia's mystical lion-protector, against the evil White Witch*. Before this battle he slays with a sword a wolf that menaces his sisters and is knighted by Aslan, who calls him Sir Peter Fenris-bane; after the battle, Peter rules Narnia as High King over all the kings of Narnia but under Aslan himself. His reign is one of the golden ages of Narnia. Peter becomes an adult in Narnia, but when he and the others find their way back home, through the wardrobe, he becomes a child again. Peter has one more adventure in Narnia when he helps Caspian X* gain the throne; after this, because of his age, Peter can no longer go to the magical land, for he must learn to know Aslan in his own world. Years later, when Narnia is in great need, Peter tries to help, getting the green and yellow rings* Digory and Polly Plummer* had used long ago to come to this world, so that they can be used again. Before they can be used, a train accident kills him and his friends, and he is whisked into Aslan's country, to live happily there forever.

PEVENSIE, SUSAN, a character in C[live] S[taples] Lewis's* *The Lion, the Witch, and the Wardrobe*ics* and *Prince Caspian*. She is the sister of Edmund, Lucy, and Peter Pevensie***. During World War II, when the Pevensies are sent to stay with Digory Kirke* in the safety of the country, Susan and the others discover that by going through a certain wardrobe* in the large house, they can come out in the magical land of Narnia*. There they take part in the battle between the evil White Witch* and Aslan*, Narnia's mystical lion-protector. When the Witch is defeated, Susan and the other children rule Narnia for several years; Susan becomes known as Queen Susan the Gentle. She grows into a lovely woman who is a good swimmer and archer. She has many suitors but accepts none, though one, Rabadash*, prince of Calormen*, tries to take Narnia in order to get her. When Susan and the others find their way back through the wardrobe into their own world, she becomes a child again. But, using the hunting horn* Susan had dropped during her last hunt, Caspian X*, a young prince whose uncle has usurped his throne, calls the Pevensies into Narnia to help him. This is Susan's last adventure in Narnia, for, Aslan tells her, she must learn to know him in her own world. Instead Susan becomes interested only in parties and all the accoutrements of adulthood, and she no longer believes in Narnia.

PHIL, a character in Mrs. Mary Molesworth's* *The Cuckoo Clock**. Five-year-old Phil usually lives with his parents, but when his mother falls ill, he is taken by his nurse to a farm. Here he is lonely until he follows the call of a cuckoo* and meets Griselda*, who is staying at a nearby house. Phil is well acquainted with the cuckoo's ways. This well-mannered little boy learns much about the local flowers in his loneliness and in his searches for the door into fairyland. When his mother recovers, Phil's family goes to live at the White House, not far from the house where Griselda is staying.

PHILIP HALDANE (*The Magic City*). *See* Haldane, Philip

PHILIP MORLEY (*The Twelve and the Genii*). *See* Morley, Philip

PHOENIX, the title character in *The Phoenix and the Carpet**, by E[dith] Nesbit Bland*. This golden bird lays one egg before it immolates itself on a fire of sweet gums; it then hatches from the egg and thus lives on, dying and hatching again every five hundred years. Wearied by this routine, the Phoenix once laid its egg on a magic wishing carpet* and sent the carpet to where the egg would not be discovered for two thousand years. In the twentieth century, the carpet is bought by the parents of Robert*, Anthea*, Jane*, and Cyril*, and the egg is hatched on a sweet-smelling fire. With the admiring children the vain Phoenix has a hectic time, advising them on how to use the carpet and getting wishes from the Psammead* to get them out of trouble. Because it can talk, it is sometimes taken for a parrot, but in its infinite superiority, it is infinitely forgiving. At one point, the Phoenix visits the Phoenix Fire Insurance office, convinced that it is its temple, and it is gratified when the men who work there honor it in a ceremony. The children are sometimes dazzled by but most often patient with the Phoenix, humoring it in its vanities until it sets a theater on fire and upsets their mother. After that they do not feel quite the same about it. Because of all the excitement it has endured, the Phoenix is more than ready to rest for a while. It lays an egg and sends it, wrapped in the carpet, to a place where it will be undisturbed for two thousand years, before the bird immolates itself. Its last action is to get a wish from the Psammead that the family be sent everything it has ever wanted.

PHOENIX AND THE CARPET, THE. E[dith] Nesbit Bland.   Illus. H. R. Millar. London: George Newnes, 1904. 236 pp. British.

Because Robert*, Anthea*, Jane*, and Cyril* accidentally ruin the nursery carpet, their mother buys another one—a Persian rug with an egg rolled up in it. One day, while the children are trying magic, the egg is knocked into a fire and they are astonished when a Phoenix* hatches from it. This vain but forgiving bird informs them that the carpet is a wishing carpet*. The next day, when the house is empty, the children try out their carpet, letting it choose where to go. It takes them to France, where Jane wishes it would land on top of a square tower. To their alarm, the children discover that the tower has no roof, and they soon find themselves inside the doorless tower, with Robert, who got off the carpet to investigate a bird's nest, far above them. After wishing Robert safely down, the children learn from the Phoenix that the carpet obeys only three wishes a day—and they have used their third wish. While the Phoenix goes for help, the children explore a tunnel and discover some gold coins. Suddenly they find themselves home; the Phoenix has gone to the Psammead*, a magical creature who has granted its wish that they be home. Because the carpet is filthy after the trip it is taken away from the children for a week.

The next Saturday the children wish to take their sick baby brother, Lamb*, somewhere where he won't have whooping cough. When the cook* interferes, the carpet takes her along, and they find themselves on a warm tropical island in what the cook insists is a lovely dream. Exploring, the children find natives, and they run back to the beach, where they find the cook up to her neck in the ocean. The astonished natives ask her to be their queen; an old prophecy states that their queen would wear a white crown and arise from the sea, and the cook's white cap appears to be a crown. Still thinking this is a dream, she happily agrees, and the children leave her there, feeling better about it when Anthea checks back on the woman and learns how happy she is.

When the Lamb is taken to the seaside with the children's mother to get over his cough, the other children miss him and wish to be taken to see him, stipulating that only the Lamb should see them. Discovering how horrible it is being invisible to their mother, the children leave. Because she is to provide Indian things for the church bazaar, the children go to India, where they tell their story to a queen who rewards them with things for the bazaar. From India they go to the bazaar, and there they have a terrible experience; the young lady they are helping accidentally sells the carpet to mean-tempered Mrs. Biddle*, who will not sell it back. They follow her home where, standing on the carpet, they wish she were in a good mood. Suddenly Mrs. Biddle changes her manner and gives them the carpet.

The Phoenix longs to see more of the city, so the children take it to the Phoenix Fire Insurance office, where—unbelievably—the men who work there hold a ceremony honoring it. When the Phoenix leaves, the men decide that they have been dreaming. Christmas comes, and the children's next wish is to go where they can do a good action; and when the carpet does not move, they are forced to specify a place outside their home. They find themselves in the tunnel in the tower and decide to find the owner of the gold coins they had found on their first trip. Leaving via a trapdoor, the children go to a nearby cottage, where they meet an old woman and a little boy. Both are sad because the boy's father, a marquis, has spent all his inheritance and must sell the castle and lands; when the children show them the hidden gold, they are overjoyed.

After the Christmas holidays, which the children spend away from home, they are not met at the station because a letter has been mislaid. Undaunted, they go home by themselves and find the house empty of all but the Phoenix, who helps them get in. After dinner, because the children do not feel that they should go anywhere, they send the carpet to where it was made to fetch something for them. It brings back 199 hungry Persian cats. When they send it for food for them, the carpet brings 398 muskrats, which the cats cannot eat, so the children send the carpet for milk. It brings a cow, which the children cannot milk. Because they have used their wishes and have to get rid of the cats, the boys start to take them away, leaving the girls in the house. Having fallen asleep, Jane wakes to find in the house a burglar* who does not like cats but who does milk the cow to quiet them down. He is a likable man who entered the house only because someone stole his money; he does not plan to do it again. He calls on a friend who can sell the cats, and they take them all away. Realizing that it is after midnight, the children wish away the cow and go to bed.

The next morning they mend the worn-out carpet with ordinary yarn. Discovering that the burglar has been arrested on suspicion of stealing the cats, the children wish themselves to his cell and take him to the island where they had left the cook. These two are quite taken with one another and want to marry, so the carpet is sent for a clergyman. Because Reverend Septimus Blenkinsop* is standing on the darned place, he is only half on the island, but the marriage is performed and the celebrations last past midnight in London, when the children go home.

Because their mother is coming home, the children wish themselves to a place where they can get money for presents. On the way the darning tears, and Robert and Jane fall through onto a roof. Cyril and Anthea go on to a road where they meet an uncle who gives them a sovereign, and they go home to mend the carpet. Robert and Jane, meanwhile, have dropped into the attic of Reverend Blenkinsop. Remembering them from what he thinks has been a dream, he wonders if he has gone mad, especially after they vanish from in front of him; the Phoenix has gone to the Psammead and wished them back home.

When the children take the Phoenix to the theater, it is the beginning of the end. Exicted by what it thinks are rites in its own temple, the bird starts a fire and the children are trapped in their box, rescued only when the carpet is sent for them. Though the Phoenix restores the theater that night, the children cannot forgive it for frightening their parents, and they wish that it would leave. After the Lamb gets on the carpet and makes a wish that is counteracted only by a wish the Phoenix gets from the Psammead, the children realize how dangerous the worn carpet could be and put it away.

At last, the Phoenix does leave. After laying an egg on the carpet, the Phoenix sends the carpet first to the Psammead to get a wish, and then to a place where the egg will not be found for two thousand years. Then the Phoenix burns itself in a sweet-smelling fire. The next day there is delivered a huge box filled with everything the family ever wanted, sent by the wish of the Phoenix.

Note: This work first appeared in *The Strand Magazine*, nos. 151–161 (July, 1903–May, 1904).

PIERS MADELY (*The River at Green Knowe*; *An Enemy at Green Knowe*). *See* Madely, Piers

PIERSON, PAT, a character in *The Watch House**, by Robert Westall*. Though she calls herself "Fat Pat" and is certainly not thin, she is not fat, either. Pat is well liked, for she is easy to get along with. This trait holds her in good stead when she is around Timothy Jones* (Timmo), who likes to talk and talk on the many subjects that hold his imagination. Pat simply takes his quirks and sudden enthusiasms in stride, sometimes smoothing the people Timmo has left ruffled. When she meets Anne Melton*, Pat gratefully relinquishes some of the burden Timmo represents. Pat is very interested in the occult, having, her spiritualist aunt tells her, certain gifts. These gifts come into play when Pat tries to help Anne learn about Henry Cookson*, who is haunting the Watch House*. Though terrified, Pat helps Father da Souza* exorcise the spirit that has been haunting Cookson for many years.

PILIPALA, a character in *The Change-Child**, by Jane Louise Curry*. She becomes the wife of Emrys*. Pilipala is one of the Red Fairies* who live by stealing what they need. Quiet, unobtrusive Pilipala is in love with Emrys and he with her, though they dare not show it for fear of what Mamgu*, his mother, would do; finally, however, they leave the Red Fairies and marry.

PING. *See* Hsu

PIPPA NICHOLAS (*Poor Tom's Ghost*). *See* Nicholas, Pippa

PLATES, a set of objects in *The Owl Service**, by Alan Garner*. These thick china dishes are decorated in green and gold in a stylized pattern that, looked at one way, resembles clumps of flowers but, looked at another, seems to be three owls. They were made by the grandfather of Huw Hannerhob*, after the Welshman "went mad" and was forced by his English employers to leave their service. The man had seen Blodeuwedd*—a mythical woman made of flowers who was later changed into an owl—and had gone mad because she had changed into something else; he did not like to speak of it. Later the plates were to be part of Nancy's* hope chest, but after the man she was to marry died, the plates were put into the attic of his house. Here they stay until Alison Bradley* and her family come to the house. Hearing scratching from above Alison's room,

Gwyn*, Nancy's son, climbs into the attic to investigate and finds the plates. In the pattern Alison recognizes the figures of owls, and she begins to trace them, making them into little paper owls. This tracing becomes a compulsion for her, and she gradually works her way through the entire set. As she finishes tracing the pattern on each plate, the pattern fades and the plate becomes white; the plate is subsequently smashed in some way. Blodeuwedd's tragic story has been replayed in subsequent generations ever since, and the outcome has always been tragic, for only her destructive tendencies have been recognized each time; as Alison sees only the owls in the pattern and not the flowers, so earlier generations have seen Blodeuwedd as the owl she becomes instead of as the flowers she once was. In Alison's time it is no different; as soon as the girl traces the last owl, the power of Blodeuwedd is unleashed, and the results will be tragic unless she is persuaded that the pattern on the plates was flowers, not owls.

PLATTER, SIDNEY, a character in Mary Norton's* *The Borrower's Aloft** and *The Borrowers Avenged**. He is the husband of Mabel Platter. Once an undertaker and builder, Mr. Platter experiences harder times when the industry of Went-le-Cray, where he lives, slows. He helps his wife run her tea garden in as profitable a way as possible. When Mr. Pott's* model village, Little Fordham*, begins to draw visitors from Mrs. Platter's tea garden, Mr. Platter puts in a tiny village of his own and finds himself in a one-sided race to keep Ballyhoggin more complete and attractive to visitors than is Little Fordham. When borrowers*, miniature people who live by "borrowing" from humans, move into Little Fordham, Mr. Platter becomes so hysterical that he kidnaps them and keeps them in his attic. The tiny people, Pod, Homily, and Arrietty Clock***, spend the winter in the attic, escaping, finally, in the spring. Maddened at the escape of such treasures, Mr. Platter and his wife search for them, and are finally caught breaking into a church in an attempt to capture Timmis*, a young borrower. Whether the Platters go to prison or simply pay a fine is unknown, but they finally sell their house and go to Australia, where Mr. Platter has a brother.

PLUMMER, POLLY, a character in *The Magician's Nephew** and *The Last Battle**, by C[live] S[taples] Lewis*. she and her parents live in London at the turn of the century. Polly is a brave girl who enjoys adventure, though she hates to be made afraid and has no interest in finding out things no one has ever heard of before. Polly has more adventures than she bargains for when she and Digory Kirke* are sent by Andrew Ketterley* to a different world, via certain yellow and green rings*. She is present with Digory, Andrew, and Jadis*, an evil enchantress, at the creation of Narnia*, a magical land, by Aslan*, its great lion-protector. Polly accompanies Digory on his journey to the garden there. Back on Earth, Polly probably leads a fairly normal life, but she never forgets her journey to Narnia and sometimes gets together with Digory and others who have gone there to talk about it. At the time of Narnia's greatest need, Polly tries to help. She is killed in a railway accident and is whisked to Aslan's country, to live there in joy forever.

PLUMTREE. *See* Grout, Sufferana; Grout, Thanatopsis

POD CLOCK (the Borrower series). *See* Clock, Pod

POEM, a verse which acts as a magic charm in *Wet Magic**, by E[dith] Nesbit Bland*. Its lines appear beneath a picture of water nymphs; the poem, lines 859–863 of John Milton's *Comus*, concern Sabrina, a water nymph. This poem acts as a charm to call people from the sea. When Francis* says them near his aquarium he gets a sudden vision of a water nymph; when he says them near the sea, he calls up Maia, the sister of Freia*, a captured mermaid. It is only when someone on land says this verse that Francis and his brother and sisters can come back when they visit Merland*, Freia's home beneath the sea. The verse works beneath the ocean, too; by saying it, Francis calls Freia to him when he and the other children are captured by the Under Folk*.

POLE, JILL, a character in *The Silver Chair** and *The Last Battle**, by C[live] S[taples] Lewis*. She is a student at Experiment House, with Eustace Clarence Scrubb*. Jill is often bullied by the bigger students and has therefore developed the science of getting away into an art. She and Eustace are called into Narnia*, a magical land, by Aslan*, its mystical lion-protector, to find Rilian*, a long-lost prince. Here she makes mistakes, endangering Eustace's life and forgetting, once, the four signs Aslan has taught her that she might know how to find the prince. Jill's experiences in Narnia are a bit overwhelming at first, but she soon begins to love the land and its people. With Eustace and Puddleglum*, a Marsh-wiggle*, Jill travels to Harfang*, a place of giants, in the mountains to the north of Narnia. Here they find and release Rilian and defeat the Queen of Underland*, who plans to invade Narnia and rule it through Rilian. On their return to Experiment House, Jill and Eustace get revenge on the bullies and, after the ensuing scandal, the school becomes a better place to learn. In Narnia's time of final, desperate need, Jill and Eustace again visit it, helping Tirian*, its king, withstand the Calormenes who are exploiting it. Though they lose their battle, they win the war, for Aslan brings Narnia to an end and Jill is one of those who go to his country, to be happy there forever.

POLISTARCHIA, a place in E[dith] Nesbit Bland's* *The Magic City**. This country contains all the cities, buildings, and places ever created by Philip Haldane*, from the first crude building he made of wooden blocks to the Island-where-you-mayn't-go*, which he and his sister create, and the model city he builds. That city, Polistopolis*, is the country's capital. Two types of people live in this country: the ones Philip put in his cities to begin with, such as Noah*, and those who appear by magic, whether from books used in its construction or from Philip's world. Sometimes when books used to build the place fall open, images come out and take their places in Polistarchia; the Dwellers by the Sea* are such. People from Philip's world can also enter when they sleep too deep for dreams, but only if they have somehow helped to create part of the place; the creators of actual building pieces and their assistants are among these. The citizens of Polistarchia must be careful when they wish for machinery, for when they do, they receive it and must use it and keep on using it. Polistarchia is an eclectic country, for here lives the Great Sloth* in the city of Somnolentia*, to the north, and here also live the gentle, happy Dwellers by the Sea. When Philip enters Polistarchia, he accomplishes seven tasks and is at last crowned king.

POLISTOPOLIS, a place in *The Magic City**, by E[dith] Nesbit Bland*. This city in Polistarchia* exists in two worlds: the world where Philip Haldane* builds it as a toy city, and the world where it lasts forever, though the model city is torn down. Polistopolis is an eclectic city, for it is built of everything from books to dominoes to Oriental vases, and its inhabitants reflect its materials. Some of the citizens had been placed there by Philip himself; others appeared by magic. Some inhabitants are the people who created the building materials Philip used— from those who made the actual materials to those who helped only a little. Only those who build or rebuild all or part of the city can come from Philip's world into Polistopolis; in this way Lucy Graham* and the Pretenderette* enter. Soon after the city was created, a prophecy was made that both the deliverer and the destroyer of Polistopolis would enter by a ladder which leads from the plateau the city is on to a grassy plain, so the ladder is always guarded. The destroyer who comes is the Pretenderette, who sets herself up as Queen of Polistarchia; the deliverer is Philip, who overthrows her and is crowned king. The citizens of Polistarchia have no fruit to eat until Philip provides it as one of his seven tasks.

POLLY PLUMMER (*The Magician's Nephew*; *The Last Battle*). *See* Plummer, Polly

POLLY WITHERS (*Over Sea, Under Stone*). *See* Withers, Polly

POLOPODSKY, DOCTOR PROFESSOR, , a character mentioned in Robert Lawson's* *The Fabulous Flight**. This Zargonian scientist developed an explosive many times more powerful than the atomic bomb, finally managing to make three grains of the stuff in his castle. One summer Fisheye Jones* came to the castle with a pinball machine, with which the professor became fascinated. A man with no relatives or friends, Polopodsky came to treat Fisheye as his own son. That summer Polopodsky died; Fisheye, realizing that he could make a lot of money, impersonates the man to blackmail Zargonia.

POOCH. *See* Pucci, Michaelangelo

POOLEY, DEREK, a character in *The Devil on the Road**, by Robert Westall*. He is the husband of Susan Pooley; he is descended from Sir William Pooley. Derek was a major at twenty-five, in World War II, and he won the M.C. in Korea. Now he lives in what had been the inn of Old Besingtree, part of the family's old holdings. Derek is very old-fashioned, believing in a kind of morality which seems to be disappearing. After a problem with the Income Tax, Derek withdrew into the past, enjoying his position as Squire. Perhaps in an attempt to hold onto the past, Derek helps John Webster*, a young man who takes refuge from a storm in a barn on Derek's estate; he insists that the young man stay in the barn and is very pleased when John brings into the twentieth century Johanna Vavasour*, a seventeenth-century witch whom the local people hold in awe.

POOR TOM'S GHOST. Jane Louise Curry. New York: Atheneum, 1977. 177 pp. American.

Roger John Nicholas*, age thirteen, is the only son of widowed actor Tony Nicholas*. The boy has led a haphazard life, traveling with his father and coping with erratic meals, far-flung travel, and a sense of homelessness that verges on the desperate. Though Tony has since married Jo Nicholas*, an actress and the mother of Pippa Nicholas*, life has not changed much; the family still has no permanent home and seems to be drifting apart. Roger is thrilled when Tony inherits Castle Cox*, for perhaps the house will pull them together; but the house in an architectural nightmare filthy with the refuse of previous occupants. Still, the Nicholas family decides to spend the weekend there.

The first night, Roger is disturbed by crying from the empty room next to his. It is a man, mourning for someone named Kitten. When Roger sleeps, he dreams of oddly laden boats sailing from the house's water stairs on the nearby Thames. The next morning Pippa and Jo admit that they, too, heard someone crying. Later the family uncovers the original stonework of the house, which is dated 1603, and, intrigued, decide to strip the house to its original state. That night Roger does not dream but sees this time his own room superimposed over a seventeenth-century hallway, through which bursts an angry, grief-stricken man dressed in doublet and hose. Pippa hears but does not see the apparition. When friends of the family, Alan Collet* and his wife, arrive, the house begins to yield its secrets, including a staircase in what is now Roger's room.

That night the police bring home Tony, whom they had found in a rowboat on the river, apparently sleepwalking. Roger begins to worry about his father, especially when the two go alone to London, where Tony is appearing in *Hamlet*. During rehearsal, Tony cuts a passage, insisting that it had been cut before, then he makes a cryptic remark and Roger sees in him a disturbing resemblance to the man he had seen in Castle Cox. Later Alan tells Roger how Tony had tried to take him to a pub that does not exist, seeming to walk through a landscape

Alan could not see. Tony's performance in *Hamlet* is amazingly good, full of such subtle nuances as the strange, soft accent he uses.

Roger becomes more and more anxious. One night he wakes to find Tony laying wet clothes on his head, calling him "Jack," and speaking of Kitten. Strange, bitter words about "Katherine" sometimes slip into Roger's mind. One night Roger follows Tony as he sleepwalks through a landscape that is at once the city and a forest, as Tony is at once himself and the man Roger had seen at Castle Cox. Something in Roger recognizes the forest. When Tony walks through the wall of a shop and disappears into that other world, Roger wants to follow, but he stops himself. The next morning Tony—who has hurt his hand grappling with an assailant a nearby constable did not see—insists in his accented voice that he had to find and kill someone named "Cliffe." His performances are getting bad: he appropriates lines, confusing his fellow actors, and his accent contrasts sharply with that of the others.

The weekend Tony and Roger go home, Tony seems to be suffering from the flu. Jo has discovered that Castle Cox was built by Tom Garland*, an Elizabethan actor, husband of Katherine Purfet Garland* and brother of Jack Garland*. Jo has traced him fairly easily up to 1603, after which time there are no records of him; there are hints that he died that year. That night Roger realizes that he and his father have been drawn into an old tale, a blurring of the past and present. He "remembers" that Jack had hated Katherine, who he felt had taken Tom away from him. And Roger remembers more:

Jack had gone home from London to find Katherine gone. The plague is ravaging England and Kate has taken refuge with her family in the country. She has left a letter for Tom, the last page of which—in which she says goodbye— could be incriminating if read by itself, for Tom has been made jealous before by Harry Cliffe*, who had made advances toward Kate. Realizing that Cliffe will pay for information on where Kate is, Jack concocts a plot. He dresses as Kate and, just as Tom arrives at the house, Jack rides off with Cliffe, knowing that his brother will think he sees Kate riding off, and that Tom's suspicions will be confirmed when he reads the single page Jack has sealed and left for him.

Roger comes to himself. In the ensuing hours, he realizes that Tony acts as a catalyst, causing Tom to haunt the house, and that Tom uses Tony in his search for Kate. As Tony is bundled off to the hospital, Roger realizes that somehow he must lay the ghost to rest. He is asleep when time shifts and Tom storms into the house and reads Kate's letter, but Roger wakes when Tom slams out.

He is in the seventeenth-century house. Roger feels light and oddly insub-stantial; when he tries to pick up the letter to take it and go after Tom, he finds that he cannot, for he is as much of a ghost in this century as Tom is in the twentieth. When Jack comes into the house, Roger sees his chance, and Pippa watches as the two boys merge into one figure who opens a hiding place in the newel post and takes out some folded papers there before running after Tom.

Roger, in Jack's body, is not in time to catch Tom, but the trail leads to

London, where the two have lodgings. There, Roger discovers that the pouch he carries contains the gold Cliffe had paid Jack for information on Kate's whereabouts. He stuffs into the pouch the first three pages of Kate's letter. After spending the rest of the night in the lodgings, Roger sets out to search for Tom. He soon discovers that a confession he had meant to leave at the lodgings has somehow appeared in Jack's purse, for Jack would not let him leave it. In that day of searching, the boy falls ill. Tom hears from the landlady at the lodgings that the boy is at a nearby inn, and he goes to care for him.

Roger, meanwhile, has cut himself from Jack, but, trapped and helpless in the wrong century, he can only plead with Jack to tell Tom before it is too late and the man catches the plague from him. The boy refuses. Circumstances work in Roger's favor, however, for Tom finds the first pages of Kate's letter and the confession Roger had meant to leave, and he realizes what Jack has done.

Roger finds himself suddenly in his own century, half in the river, being held by Pippa, who has found him there. When the two go back to the house, they discover that the fireplace is bricked up again and all is as it was when they first came to the house. Roger realizes that, since what he had done in the seventeenth century had meant that Tom's ghost did not walk, the times when it did walk must be redone, so the next morning is a repeat of the family's first morning in Castle Cox. Roger and Pippa tell their puzzled but dimly remembering parents of the events of the past days and prove their story by uncovering Jack's secret hoard in the newel post. In later research, the family discovers records of Jack's death in 1603, of the christening of the children of Tom and Kate later that year, of the couple's deaths in 1642, and of their daughter's marriage to one of Tony's ancestors.

POPE, MAITLAND, a character in Lucy Boston's* *An Enemy at Green Knowe**. He is a scholar interested in ninth-century manuscripts; he comes to Green Knowe* to work because it is quiet and old. Mr. Pope rents from Mrs. Linnet Oldknow* the modernized vaults under the ruined chapel at Green Knowe. When Toseland* (Tolly) and Hsu* (Ping) find an ancient copy of *Decem Potentiae Mosio*, a book of spells of which no other copy has ever been found, Mr. Pope has the pleasure of working with it. His translation and speaking aloud of certain of its spells are instrumental in the protection of Green Knowe; when he speaks "The Invocation of Power" as the masonry of the house is being crumbled by bodiless fingers called up by the evil Dr. Melanie Delia Powers*, the fingers vanish; Tolly and Ping use a spell he has read to them to send away Melanie's demon and leave her powerless.

POPPINS, MARY, the title character in the Mary Poppins books*, by P[amela] L[yndon] Travers*. She is related to only the Very Best People: she is the niece of Mr. Wigg* and the cousin of Arthur Turvey*, the Hamadryad*, Fred Twigley*, and the Terrapin, the oldest and wisest creature in the world. By a native American friend, she is called "Morning-Star-Mary." Though Mary Poppins looks quite ordinary, with shiny black hair, small blue eyes, and a turned up nose, she is anything but; she is the Great Exception, a "fairy-tale come true." She remembers all that has ever happened to her, including the long, dark journey of her birth, and unlike other humans she can still talk to animals, sunlight, and the wind, though she is grown up. On her birthday all creatures are safe from one another and the great protect the small. She knows everything but never tells anything. She has a difficult side, too; Mary is her own greatest admirer, especially when she is wearing something new, and she always gets what she wants the way she wants it; she never wastes time being nice and has a look that can kill laughter. What she calls speaking her mind, others call crossness. You never argue with Mary Poppins. Yet, as the Banks family finds when she comes to be their nanny, everything goes right when she is around. Strange adventures happen, too; peppermint sticks turn into flying hobby horses, statues step down from their pedestals, a compass can take one around the world. Her days and nights off might be spent at a circus of the constellations or at tea in a chalk picture drawn by Herbert Alfred*, Mary's dear friend. Jane and Michael Banks** find Mary Poppin's relatives very strange, and her friends just as odd, but Mary is the soul of propriety and always denies everything, highly offended that anyone would think she or her friends or relations should be anything but proper. Though caustic, she can be kind, giving even her cherished new things to those in need of them. Without lectures she teaches the Banks children many things before she leaves them for the better.

POTT, MR., a character in *The Borrowers Aloft**, by Mary Norton*. He was once a railway man; after a badger he was trying to help bit him and caused him to lose his balance, Mr. Pott lost his leg to a passing train and was forced to retire. When he sees a model train for sale, Mr. Pott buys it and sets it up in his backyard. Before long he is hard at work on a signal box and a station for it, and a village soon follows. Mr. Pott is patient and pays close attention to detail; buildings are built of tiny bricks, and interiors are as detailed as the exteriors. Little Fordham*, as the village is called, soon becomes a tourist attraction, exciting the envy of Sidney Platter*. Mr. Pott, however, does not care whether people come or not, for he is building his little village for the joy of it. He is helped by Miss Menzies*, whose chatter Mr. Pott usually ignores. Thus it is that she has a difficult time convincing him that little people called "borrowers"* have moved into Little Fordham. Once he is convinced, however, Mr. Pott helps Miss Menzies furnish a house as comfortably as possible. Because Mr. Pott is so good at "making do" with what she has, the borrowers come to think of him as a "human borrower."

POULTER, SUSAN, a character in Penelope Lively's* *The Whispering Knights**. Her parents run a small shop in the village where they live; she has a baby brother. To Martha Timms*, her friend, plump Susan seems very sure of herself, helping around the shop, and unafraid of spiders and dead mice. She is practical and competent, providing the practical suggestions for the sometimes-wild schemes of William*, Susan and Martha's friend. If Susan dreams, it is only after she has eaten too much, and then they are not really dreams. Susan's ingenuity gets a workout when she, William, and Martha recreate the witches' spell from *Macbeth* and must improvise the ingredients. When the spell calls up Morgan le Fay*, who wants to get the children, Susan's love of food is almost her undoing, for she nearly eats a cake left for her by Morgan—discovering in time that it could kill her. Even fearless Susan has some shaky moments as the children try to defeat Morgan, and she does not look during the final, terrible battle between Morgan and the Hampden Stones*, when Morgan is defeated.

POWERS, MELANIE DELIA (DR.), a character in Lucy Boston's* *An Enemy at Green Knowe**. Her true secret name is Melusine Demogorgona Phospher; she is a witch. Seeking certain ancient books of spells, she comes to Green Knowe*, where she hopes to find the library of Dr. Wolfgang Vogel*, a seventeenth-century alchemist who once lived here. Though Melanie pretends to be only a scholar, her behavior is strange, and Mrs. Linnet Oldknow*, her great grandson, Toseland*, and his friend, Hsu*, are suspicious of her from the beginning. Melanie tries trickery and spells to get what she wants, even, at one point, accidentally calling Susan Oldknow*, a past inhabitant of the house, in an attempt to get someone who lives in the house under her power. She is thwarted at every turn, however. When the boys chant a spell for the diminishing of a demon, using Melanie's true secret name, her demon lord leaves her, and she is powerless and empty, a confused woman who runs away.

PRESTO, a cat in *The Marvelous Misadventures of Sebastian**, by Lloyd Alexander*. It is a white cat with blue eyes. When superstitious villagers decide that Presto is a wizard in disguise and try to hang it, it is rescued by Sebastian*, a young fiddler seeking his fortune. He names it Presto because of its quickness; he also calls it the Duke of Gauli-Mauli. Presto rewards Sebastian several times, bringing to him a skeleton key so that he can unlock his prison door, and stopping Sebastian's playing when the violin* he plays threatens to kill him by drawing out his life strength.

PRETENDERETTE, a character in E[dith] Nesbit Bland's* *The Magic City**. She is actually the strict and capricious nurse of Lucy Graham*; her brother is a sailor. Hating Philip Haldane*, who comes under her care, she carries this dislike with her when she magically shrinks and enters Polistopolis*, a city he builds out of odds and ends. Because she wants to try her hand at the seven tasks Philip must perform and thereby take the throne, she is called the Pretenderette. The Pretenderette tries to be at hand every time Philip attempts a task, so as to step in should he fail, but she is thwarted in this. She also kidnaps him to keep him from accomplishing his deeds, but this fails also. Finally the Pretenderette lays claim to the throne and takes over Polistopolis, using soldiers from a book. Her reign is harsh but brief, for Philip retakes the city, using soldiers he calls from *De Bello Gallico*, by Julius Caesar*. Caesar sends the Pretenderette to Somnolentia*, to teach the Great Sloth* there to enjoy its work and, because no one loves her in Philip's world, she must make the people of Somnolentia love her before she can go free.

PRICE, EGLANTINE, a character in *The Magic Bed-Knob** and *Bonfires and Broomsticks**, by Mary Norton*. She is a spinster living in Much Frensham, in England; she becomes the wife of Emelius Jones*. As a child, Miss Price had a talent for witchcraft, but was never able to develop it. As an adult, she takes up the study and progresses well, though, to her sorrow, she has started too late to become a wicked witch. Broomstick-riding gets Miss Price into trouble, for one night she falls and hurts her ankle and is discovered the next morning by Carey, Charles, and Paul Wilson***, three children spending the holidays in Much Frensham. To bribe them to keep quiet, Miss Price enchants a bed-knob* which, when twisted, will take the children anywhere they wish in the present or past, but will lose its power if they tell anyone about her witchcraft. After she accompanies the children on a trip to a South Sea island where she must use her magic to rescue them from cannibals, Miss Price is unnerved by the experience, as she is by the realization that she has been using magic for the wrong ends. Miss Price gives up magic for two years, but at the end of this time, the cost of living causes her to advertise in the London *Times*, offering bed and board for two children. Carey, Charles, and Paul get their parents to send them to her, and again Miss Price dabbles in magic, allowing the children to journey into the past. When they bring Emelius Jones back with them, Miss Price is attracted by the idea that he is a professional magician, but repulsed by his seventeenth-century personal habits. She enjoys his company, however—so much so that a few days after she sends him back to his own time, she goes after him to make sure all is well and must use her magical powers to save his life. Miss Price and Emelius decide to marry, and they move back to the seventeenth century permanently, taking with them some twentieth-century luxuries and living on the small farm Emelius has inherited from his aunt.

PRICHARD, CARADOG, a character in *The Grey King**, by Susan Cooper*. He is the husband of Betty Prichard. When Caradog was young, he wanted to become a great bard, so he spent the night on Cader Idris; instead, it seems, he went mad. He is a violent, passionate man. When Caradog found a young woman, Guinevere, at the cottage of Owen Davies, one of Caradog's workers, he tried to rape her but was stopped by Owen; since then he has hated Bran Davies*, Guinevere's son. Later Caradog sees his chance to hurt the boy by shooting his dog after accusing it of killing his sheep. Caradog is so full of ill-will that he finally becomes possessed by the Grey King*, a force of evil, who uses the man to try to keep Will Stanton*, one of the forces of good, from rousing six warriors of the Light. When this fails and the Grey King withdraws, Caradog's mind is broken.

PRINCE CASPIAN. C[live] S[taples] Lewis. Illus. Pauline Baynes. London: Geoffrey Bles, 1951. 195 pp. British.

It is the end of the holidays and Lucy, Susan, Edmund, and Peter Pevensie**** are traveling from London to school. While waiting in a train station, however, they are suddenly transported from their own world to a thickly wooded island. On the island they find the ruins of a castle and soon realize that it is the remains of Cair Paravel*, the castle from which they once had ruled as kings and queens of Narnia*. In the castle treasure room the children recover all the gifts once given them by Father Christmas but a magical hunting horn* Susan had lost the last time she was in Narnia.

After a very uncomfortable night, the children wake in time to rescue Trumpkin*, a dwarf*, who is about to be executed by two Telmarines. During breakfast, Trumpkin tells the children of the troubles Narnia faces:

In the centuries since the rule of the Pevensies Narnia had been conquered by Telmarines, who came from the drought-stricken land to the west. Telmar's* domination of Narnia has been cruel, and the magical creatures and talking beasts have gone into hiding to keep from being killed. Even the trees hate the Telmarines. Narnia's capital has been moved inland from Cair Paravel because the Telmarines have heard that Aslan* comes from over the sea to help his people, and for that reason they avoid any contact with water except for drowning their enemies. An unscrupulous king, Miraz*, has usurped the throne, having taken advantage of the youth of his nephew, Caspian X*, the real king. The boy lives at the castle and expects to take the throne at Miraz's death, for the king has no heirs. Caspian is not like the other Telmarines, for he loves the stories his nurse has told him of Old Narnia, before the Telmarine invasion.

Miraz's queen is delivered of a son whom Miraz would like to see on the throne, so Caspian flees the palace to keep from being killed. His escape is engineered by his tutor, Cornelius*, who is half dwarf. Cornelius gives the boy Susan's ivory hunting horn, which the tutor had found with the help of magic and which he hopes will summon powerful aid. Caspian escapes from the castle but is knocked off his horse when the creature bolts, and he wakes to find himself being cared for by Trumpkin, Nikabrik*, an eternally suspicious dwarf, and Trufflehunter*, a talking badger. After hearing the boy's story, Trufflehunter thinks that they should help him, for he is the rightful king, and Caspian is introduced to the other creatures hiding from the Telmarines. During a meeting of Old Narnians to see what they should do, Cornelius appears and tells Caspian that Miraz has called out his army against him and the Old Narnians.

Caspian and the Narnians take refuge at a huge mound built over the remains of the Stone Table*. There they battle Miraz's army. Caspian's side fares badly and he blows Susan's magical horn after sending Trumpkin to Cair Paravel to guide whomever the horn summons. Trumpkin had been caught and was about to be executed when the Pevensies rescued him.

Trumpkin is less than impressed with them, having expected someone more impressive. An exhibition of their skills soon sets him right and the five set off for the mound. Narnia's landscape has changed greatly over the centuries and the party has difficulty finding its way. At the gorge that now contains the River Rush, Lucy sees Aslan, who beckons them upriver. The others do not see him, however, and they vote to go downstream, where they eventually come in sight of Beruna*. Here the party is driven back by some of Miraz's archers, and they must follow the gorge upstream, anyway.

That night Lucy wakes to Aslan's call. He rebukes her for giving in to the others and not following him; then Aslan tells her to wake the rest and tell them that she saw him and that he wants them to follow. Follow they do, sleepily and reluctantly, Trumpkin voicing his disbelief in Aslan. As Aslan leads the group to the mound, one by one they begin to see him: Edmund first, for he had believed Lucy in the beginning, Peter next, and Susan last, for she believed but would not allow herself to believe. Trumpkin, however, believes only after Aslan snatches him up and shakes him; then he believes very much, indeed.

Aslan sends Peter, Edmund, and Trumpkin to the mound, where they find an argument going on. Nikabrik, distrusting Caspian's methods and resentful of the way he thinks his people are being treated, has brought a hag and a werewolf to call up the White Witch*, whose powers he hopes to use in aid of the dwarfs, if of no one else. When Caspian refuses, the creatures attack, and Edmund, Peter, and Trumpkin enter just in time to kill them and Nikabrik. Meanwhile the girls, who are with Aslan, watch as the rest of the Old Narnians come out of hiding at his roar. Bacchus* and his maenads provide a marvelous grapey breakfast. Aslan then leads them all on a wild riot, during which they destroy the bridge at Beruna, wade the liberated river, and liberate the town, terrifying the terrifiable and carrying with them those who have secretly longed for Old Narnia.

Peter, meanwhile, challenges Miraz to single combat. The king is talked into accepting by two treacherous Telmarine lords who think that he will lose, clearing the way for them to rule in his place. During the combat, Miraz trips, is stunned, and then is killed by one of the lords as they cry foul and attack Peter. Suddenly there is full battle between the Telmarines and the Narnians. But the Telmarines panic as Narnian trees awakened by Aslan enter the battle. The Telmarines are routed and surrender when they discover that the bridge to Beruna is gone and that Aslan is in the land. With the Telmarines safely locked up in Beruna, the Narnians indulge in a great feast magically danced up by Bacchus and his followers.

The next day a general proclamation goes forth: that Caspian is to be king, that the Old Narnians are to prevail, and that those Telmarines who object must meet with Aslan. On the appointed day, the Telmarines gather and Aslan creates a door into the world where they really belong. The first Telmarines, he tells them, were pirates on Earth and were stranded on a tropical island, where they stumbled upon an entrance into Telmar, which was at that time unpopulated. These violent men and their native wives were the ancestors of the Telmarines. Now Aslan will send them back to the island from whence they came.

It is time, too, for the Pevensies to go home. Peter and Susan are too old ever to come back, but Edmund and Lucy might. After a Telmarine soldier swallows his fear and goes through the doorway, the four children follow; they have a startling vision of Narnia, their train station, and a tropical island, all at once, and find themselves in the station, where they were before their adventures began.

PRINCESS AND CURDIE, THE. George MacDonald. Illus. James Allen. London: Chatto and Windus, 1882. 255 pp. British.

As he grows up, Curdie Peterson*, an honest boy who once saved a princess, believes less and less in things he has never seen and loses the brightness he once had. One day he shoots a pigeon and is instantly ashamed; seeing a light in the house where Irene*, the princess, once lived, he recognizes it as the light in the room of her "grandmother," also named Irene*. Curdie carries the pigeon to her. When she asks him what he has done wrong besides hurting the pigeon, Curdie realizes that he has been doing wrong for some time. The grandmother will help the bird, and Curdie, too; to see if he will obey her, she makes him promise not to laugh or make fun of her if any speak of her, before she sends him away.

The next day the men in the mines where Curdie works speak slightingly of "Old Mother Wotherwop," who sounds like the grandmother. Curdie resists speaking and endures their jeers. That evening he and his father, the last to leave the mine, see and follow a great light in the tunnels. They come upon the grandmother, who tells them that there is royal blood in their family and leads them out of the mine. Curdie is to come to her the next night. When he does, the housekeeper refuses to let Curdie in until she sees behind him a strange creature which follows him to the grandmother's room. Here Curdie is made to thrust his hands into the grandmother's rose fire, and his calluses are burned off; now his hands are sensitive enough to tell, by touching a person's hand, if that person is becoming a beast inside. When he touches the paw of the odd creature, Lina*, Curdie feels a child's hand. Curdie is to go to the court of the king*.

The next day Curdie sets out. He walks all day and, as he rests under a tree, Lina comes to him. Birds come and dance around the tree, and Curdie falls asleep; he wakes when they attack him. Lina rescues Curdie and leads the birds away, and Curdie realizes that odd, ugly Lina is to be his companion. When she returns, he washes her wounds and is kind to her. They journey seven days, coming to a wood. Here, as they travel through it, strange creatures come one by one to Lina, are defeated in a fight, and come along behind Lina and Curdie, until forty-nine creatures follow them. At the edge of the wood, Lina speaks to the creatures and they hide in the wood.

Curdie and Lina go on, coming to the city where the king's palace lies. The city is full of complacent people who hate strangers; the dogs and their masters attack Curdie and Lina but become frightened of the creature. The two are sheltered for the night by an old woman, but they wake the next morning to find themselves shut into the house. Curdie and Lina are to be tried by the townspeople for killing one of the dogs, among other things. Lina escapes and Curdie is put into a dungeon, where Lina soon joins him. They dig through the dungeon floor until they break into a cave with a river and follow a cleft in a cave wall to a door into the wine cellar of the palace. As Curdie and Lina watch, a man comes into the cellar and drinks from a cask, tampering with another before he fills a flagon from it. Lina's howl makes the man run, and Curdie gets his keys.

After the palace is quiet that night, Curdie and Lina explore it. Everywhere is filth, and the servants are drunk. The hands of all feel like the feet of beasts. Curdie and Lina find Irene in the king's chamber, where he has lain ill for a year. Beside the bed sits a table bearing the flagon Curdie had seen filled from the tampered-with cask. When the doctor comes in, his hand feels to Curdie like the belly of a crawling thing. Curdie manages to get rid of the wine and refills the flagon from the good cask, realizing that he has been sent to help the king. He manages to get good bread for him. The next day the king is almost tricked into signing his will, but refuses. Irene nurses him, and he seems to get better.

That evening Curdie finds an honest servant and tells her to warn the others that they will be driven from the palace if they do not mend their ways. He also warns the king about the doctor, who tries to kill the king but is stopped by Lina. That night Curdie sends Lina out of the town. The next day the other servants mock the honest servingmaid, but they change their tune when Lina comes back that evening leading the creatures from the wood, who drive them from the palace. The creatures clean the place and the treacherous courtiers are sent away.

This causes great consternation among the townspeople, who decide that the strange creatures are evil spirits, and when a former courtier talks the nation's enemy into invading, the people welcome the foreign army. Though the king is better, he is not quite well. The night the enemy army comes near, Curdie wakes to see Irene's grandmother bathing the king in her rose fire. The next morning the king is well, and he leads the good servant, Irene, Curdie, and the beasts into battle. Aided by pigeons seemingly guided by the good servant, they defeat the enemy, and the treacherous courtiers are bound to the strange beasts and taken away. The king will now rule with an iron hand. All discover that the good servant is actually the grandmother, disguised.

Financed with gold dug from beneath the city, a new government is formed. Curdie stays in the city, and his parents join him there. One day the boy watches as the grandmother kindles her fire of rose and Lina leaps into it, vanishing.

Irene and Curdie eventually marry and rule the country; when they die childless, the people choose a king who ruthlessly mines the gold beneath the city, reducing the pillars in the mine so that finally the mines collapse and the city falls into them. Now a river rushes where it had stood, and the city's name is forgotten.

PRINCESS AND THE GOBLIN, THE. George MacDonald. London: Strahan, 1871. 249 pp. British.

Irene*, a princess, lives away from her parents, with country people, near the mountains. The mountains harbor goblins* which would like nothing better than to harass her, though she does not know this. One day, bored and miserable, Irene wanders up a stairway in her great house and gets lost, eventually finding an old woman whose name also is Irene*; she is the princess's great-great-grandmother, though the girl calls the old woman her grandmother. She shows the girl the way back to her nurse, who does not believe Irene's story. When Irene finds her grandmother the next day and asks to bring her nurse, she is refused.

When Irene and her nurse go out walking the next afternoon, they go too far and sunset comes while they are still on the mountain. Goblins find the two but are dispersed by Curdie Peterson*, a cheerful young miner who keeps the goblins at bay with his songs, for goblins hate song. Curdie sees the princess home. That night his house is visited by goblins, but he chases them away. The next evening Curdie works late and suddenly hears goblins on the other side of the mine wall; it is a family moving to get away from the miners. Eavesdropping, Curdie learns that the only weak spot on a goblin is his feet—very useful knowledge—and that the goblins are planning some disaster for the miners. Gently breaking through the wall, Curdie follows the father goblin to a large meeting; here, though he does not discover the whole plan, Curdie realizes that one part of it calls for the flooding of the mines, if another part goes awry. He goes home and warns his parents.

Autumn passes and winter comes. One day Irene stabs her hand with a pin. So much does it hurt that she wakes that night and finds her grandmother, busily spinning, who cares for Irene's hand and tucks her into the old woman's bed, telling the girl to come again a week later. Irene wakes the next morning in her own bed, her hand healed. Meanwhile, each night Irene's guards have seen strange creatures playing near the house; they are the goblin's pets, which have found where the goblins have broken through near the house. The night Irene is to go to her grandmother, one of the creatures climbs through the girl's window. Frightened, Irene first runs out of the house and up the mountain, but she comes back, guided by the light in her grandmother's window, and goes to the old woman's room. Irene's grandmother, young and richly dressed this time, gives the girls a ring and a ball of thread; the end of the thread is attached to the ring, and the ball stays in the grandmother's cabinet; if Irene is in danger, she is to follow the thread wherever it leads her. Irene sleeps and wakes in her room, and the guard is doubled around the house because of the creature.

Spring comes. Curdie, who has been exploring the goblins' cave in hope of discovering their plan, one night becomes lost because the goblins' pets tamper with the string he has been unwinding behind him to mark his path. Curdie wanders to the palace of the goblin king and queen, where he is discovered and imprisoned in a hole; he will be fed to the goblins' pets later. Irene wakes, frightened, and follows her thread up the mountain. Day breaks as she follows the thread into a cave and to a heap of stones. Because the thread seems to go into the heap, Irene begins to remove the stones and finds Curdie on the other side. Together they leave the goblins' cave, Irene following the thread and Curdie following Irene, for he cannot feel the thread. He cannot see Irene's grandmother, either, when Irene takes him to meet her, and he leaves, feeling that he is being made a fool of. Irene's grandmother tells the girl that she could not show herself to Curdie because he had not been ready to believe. She tucks Irene into bed.

Curdie goes home and tells his parents, feeling sorry he had not believed Irene, after his mother tells him of the night she had been upset by goblins on the mountain, to have them driven away by the light from the grandmother's room and by pigeons sent by the old woman. From what he has overheard from the king and queen of the goblins, Curdie is convinced that they are digging a tunnel to Irene's house, to carry her off and marry her to the goblin prince. The direction the goblins' digging has taken confirms his theory.

For a time all is quiet. Curdie checks every night on the goblins' tunnel. One night he comes too close to Irene's house and is wounded by the guards. They carry him to an empty room in the house and do not believe his story. The next night Curdie hears the goblins break through into the wine cellar, but he is too weak and feverish to do anything. A lady comes and anoints Curdie's wound, and he sleeps, waking to hear goblins in the house. Curdie rises, healed, and attacks, helping the guards to drive the goblins away. In the cellar, Curdie finds the servants, who had been herded there; it seems evident to him that Irene has been carried off. As he prepares to follow, Curdie feels a thread which he follows home. There he finds Irene, who had followed the thread attached to her ring to this safe place.

Realizing that, because the plan has failed, the goblins are probably flooding the mine, Curdie and his father shore up the weak places in the mine with masonry. The next day they take Irene home. During a feast that night, the revellers hear water coming and take refuge on the mountain. As they watch, water rushes from the house into the valley; instead of flooding the mines, the water has flooded the goblins' tunnels, coming out, finally, through the outlet in the wine cellar. Curdie and Irene watch as a white bird flies from the grandmother's room and vanishes. The king offers to take Curdie to his palace, but the boy refuses, wishing to stay with his parents. Irene goes with her father. A few days later, the men of the valley dig an outlet to drain the waters, and they shore up the house. Though many goblins have drowned, many others have escaped and left the valley; of those who have stayed, most become friendlier and cause no more trouble.

PROFESSOR, THE (*The Lion, the Witch, and the Wardrobe*). *See* Kirke, Digory

PROFESSOR, THE, a character in *Mistress Masham's Repose**, by T[erence] H[anbury] White*. This very erudite scholar lives on the grounds of the great house of Malplaquet*, in what had been the gamekeeper's cottage. He is a failure, for he can write nothing but a twelfth-century Latin hand with abbreviations. He does not always get enough to eat but has thousands of books (among them some first-folio Shakespeares, a first edition of *Gulliver's Travels*, and—somewhere—Du Cange's dictionary of medieval Latin), and he does not tyrannize anyone, preferring to let them go their own way, leaving him to his. When Maria* comes to him with a Lilliputian* she has found on Malplaquet's grounds, the Professor warns her against being a dictator and does not himself visit the tiny people until he must, for fear he might accidentally tyrannize them himself. The Professor lives mostly on bread and butter and the wine he makes himself, besides the sausages and bloaters Mrs. Noakes*, Malplaquet's cook, tactfully supplies him with. He may seem incompetent, but the Professor has his practical side; he knows how to open a locked door, and he is instrumental in getting Maria's inheritance restored to her. He then becomes her tutor.

PROGINOSKES, a character in Madeleine L'Engle's* *A Wind in the Door**. He is a cherubim, which is not a higher order than humans—only different. "Cherubim" is plural, but so is Proginoskes, with his many eyes and wings. Proginoskes is a Star Namer, and thus he has memorized the names of all the stars in all the galaxies in order to make each star more particularly itself. Like all cherubim, Proginoskes has no feelings, but he does have love, because love is what an individual does, not how he feels. Proginoskes is one of several pupils of Blajeny*, a Teacher; he finds himself the partner of Meg Murry*, a girl from Earth. Because she finds it easier to converse with a visible entity, Proginoskes materializes as a cherubim does, with hundreds of eyes and hundreds of wings, spouting small jets of flame. Much of the time he would rather be off somewhere quiet, reciting the names of the stars, but Proginoskes works hard with Meg, helping her pass their tests, knowing that if she fails, he must choose between becoming an Echthros*, one of the forces of uncreation, or Xing himself, "giving himself completely away," as one does with love. When Meg faces her final test, to fill the void that is an Echthros, Proginoskes flings himself into the void to help her, Xing himself as he does so. Because he had made this sacrifice himself, wherever he is Meg feels he is all right.

PROWSE, MABEL, a character in *The Enchanted Garden**, by E[dith] Nesbit Bland*. This young orphan lives with her aunt, the housekeeper at Yalding Castle*. Bored one day when everyone is out, Mabel pretends to be an enchanted princess asleep in the castle maze and is surprised to be wakened by a kiss from James*, who has wandered onto the grounds with his brother and sister, Gerald*

and Kathleen*. Undaunted, Mabel maintains her game and shows the children through the castle. She is distressed, however, when a ring* that she says makes the wearer invisible actually does so, and she confesses who she really is. Mabel and the other children become fast friends and share many adventures with the ring. Imaginative Mabel changes the purpose of the ring several times, making it into a ring to make the wearer bigger, and making it a wishing ring. Mabel endures invisibility, being twelve feet high, and being a stone statue before the magic of the ring is wished away.

PRYDAIN, the title place of Lloyd Alexander's* Chronicle of Prydain* and the setting of *Coll and His White Pig, The Truthful Harp,* and *The Foundling, and Other Tales of Prydain*. The largest river in the land is the Great Avren, which is fed by the Small Avren, the River Ystrad, and the River Tevvyn. To the east of Prydain is the Isle of Mona*. Caer Dathyl*, from which the High King rules, is almost in the center of Prydain, beside the River Ystrad. Prydain is split into many small kingdoms; Pryderi's* realm is in the west, north of Annuvin*, which is the realm of the evil king Arawn*, the lord of death; King Smoit's* cantrev, Cadiffor, is in the south. To the east are the Free Commots*. South, across the Great Avren, lies Caer Dallben*, the small farm where Dallben*, an enchanter, lives and raises Taran*, an orphan who becomes High King. Before the coming of men, Prydain belonged to the Fair Folk*; as men spread over the land, the Folk retreated to their mines and to their realm among the mountains in the east. For a time Achren*, the Queen of Annuvin, ruled Prydain, but her power was usurped by Arawn. The Sons of Don*, sailing from the far-off Summer Country*, helped men to resist him and stayed as guardians at Caer Dathyl. For many years Arawn has struggled to control Prydain, but finally he is defeated. With Arawn's defeat, the Sons of Don and their relatives sail back to the Summer Country, their task finished. All magic leaves Prydain, and the Fair Folk close their realm to men. Taran rules for a time as High King, seeking to mend the ravages of war, and long after his death only the bards remember the truth about him.

PRYDERI, a character in *The High King*, by Lloyd Alexander*. He is one of the sons of Pwyll. Pryderi is king of lands in the northwestern part of Prydain*, and he is a great warrior who never sheathes his sword until the battle is won. The handsome king is full of pride and ambition; as Arawn*, an evil lord, seeks to rule Prydain, Pryderi casts his lot with him, for under Arawn the small kingdoms of the land will cease to fight among themselves, and Pryderi believes that he can win the land from Arawn. Pryderi's army destroys Caer Dathyl*, the palace from which the High King of Prydain rules; he then leads his men to Caer Dallben*, to kill Dallben*, the wizard who lives there, and take *The Book of Three*, a book of prophecy. Pryderi dies when he seizes the powerful book and it destroys him with lightning.

PSAMMEAD, THE, a character in *Five Children and It**, *The Phoenix and the Carpet**, and *The Story of the Amulet**, by E[dith] Nesbit Bland*. This sand-fairy has a body shaped like a spider's and ears like a bat's; its eyes are on stalks, like a snail's. It is covered all over with thick, soft fur. It and many other sand-fairies lived on the seashore thousands of years ago, granting wishes to the children who played there. Because the children built sand castles with moats for the fairies to live in, many got wet and, catching cold, died; because this Psammead once got the end of a whisker wet, it dug a hole high up on the beach and stayed there into the twentieth century, after the sea receded and the beach became a sand-pit. Here it is discovered by Robert*, Jane*, Anthea*, and Cyril*, who are on their summer holidays. Because the Psammead is very old, rather lazy, and extremely temperamental, it can no longer grant them innumerable wishes; it allows one wish a day among them. Because these wishes are so esoteric, what the children wish for does not turn to stone at the end of the day as used to happen thousands of years ago; instead, the enchantment ends at sunset. Still, the children find one day plenty of time to get themselves into more trouble than they ever thought they could. Finally one wish causes such an uproar that the only way to manage matters is by magic, and the Psammead agrees to give Jane and Anthea as many wishes as they need if they promise to make no more wishes after that day. For a time the Psammead has peace, broken only when it is visited by the Phoenix* who comes to ask for wishes that will get the children out of the trouble they get into using a magic wishing carpet*. Then the Psammead is caught and sold to a London pet shop owner, who is glad to sell it to the children because it bites everyone else who comes near it. Because the children are miserable at having the rest of their family far away, the Psammead tells them about the amulet* which will give them their heart's desire. Finding only half of the amulet, the children search through time for the other half, taking the Psammead with them. Though it can no longer grant the children's wishes, the Psammead can and does grant the wishes of other people: the Queen of Babylon*, who wishes to visit London, and Jimmy*, who wishes to find a place where Imogen*, an orphan, will be wanted. Hearing the Psammead complain about its lot, Jimmy absent-mindedly wishes it safe in the past, in the warm sand of a temple in ancient Egypt, and the Psammead grants his wish.

PSAMMEAD, THE. See *Five Children and It*

PSYCHE, a character in E[dith] Nesbit Bland's *The Enchanted Castle**. She is one of the statues on the grounds of Yalding Castle* that come alive after sunset. Psyche's statue stands in the Hall of Granted Wishes* beneath an island in the lake; light from the statue radiates through the Hall. When Mademoiselle* uses a magic wishing ring* to undo the magic it has made, the statue reveals itself as the stone on the grave of the wife of the man who built the castle—the woman whose life was the price he had to pay for using the ring.

PTTHMLLNSPRT, PROFESSOR, a character in Charles Kingsley's* *The Water-Babies**. A learned man whose mother was Dutch and whose father was Polish, he is a naturalist and the chief professor of Necrobioneopalaeonthy-drochthonanthropopithekology at a university in the Cannibal Isles. Walking with Ellie* by the sea, the professor catches Tom*, a water-baby*, but lets him go because, of course, water-babies do not exist. When Ellie, trying to catch Tom, slips and falls on some rocks and subsequently dies, the professor is overcome with guilt and a fairy teaches him a lesson in humility by making him believe in all kinds of impossible creatures. Doctors try to cure the professor through methods both ancient and modern, but he is only cured when he writes a book proving that there are babies on the moon. The rest of his life, he is a much humbler man.

PUCCI, MICHAELANGELO (POOCH), a character in Jane Louise Curry's* *The Daybreakers** and *The Birdstones**. His parents own Pucci's Grocery Store. Mike is called "Pooch" by his friends. Pooch helps Harry Rivers* "translate" the alphabet of twelfth-century Abáloc* and is part of the group that travels there in time to save Conway Tapp*. Later, going to Apple Island* to weed the family garden, Pooch discovers there Dalea*, a girl from fourth-century Abáloc, and her birdstones*. He takes her to live with Mr. Douglass, the eccentric owner of the local plant nursery, and helps Dalea to assume her role as "Dayla Jones." Pooch and Anna Maria D'Agostino* are the only witnesses when Dalea and Mr. Douglass—who is really Thiuclas*, Dalea's grandfather—travel back to their own place in time. Because he has always been intrigued by codes and languages, Pooch vows to learn to translate the Abalockian language someday and to read the *Book of the Kings of Abáloc**.

PUDDLEGLUM, a character in C[live] S[taples] Lewis's* *The Silver Chair** and *The Last Battle**. He is a Marsh-wiggle* living in the marshes in the northern part of Narnia*. Like all Marsh-wiggles, Puddleglum has long legs and webbed feet and hands, and an amazingly somber outlook on life; though the other Marsh-wiggles consider him flighty, Puddleglum has a remarkable ability to see the dark side of everything. Though he points out how likely everything is to go wrong, he is good-hearted underneath and is a good companion. Puddleglum accompanies Jill Pole* and Eustace Clarence Scrubb*, two children from Earth, on a quest north to the mountains where the giants live, there to find Rilian*, a Narnian prince who has been missing for ten years. Though Puddleglum prophesies doom, the questers find the prince, who is a captive of the Queen of Underland*. She tries to get them under her spell, but Puddleglum manages to stop her; though she has tried to persuade them that Narnia is only a dream, Puddleglum keeps his head long enough to step on her magic fire with his webbed foot. He recovers from his burns three weeks later and lives a happy—to a Marsh-wiggle—life. Puddleglum is one of those in the country of Aslan*, Narnia's mystical lion-protector, when the land comes to an end.

PURSEWIG, MAYOR, a character in Lloyd Alexander's* *The Cat Who Wished to Be a Man**. This wizened little man is mayor of Brightford*. Though he exacts a heavy toll from those who cross his bridge, it is not enough; he owns as much of Brightford as he can and intends to own The Crowned Swan, the inn belonging to Gillian*, as well. To do this, Pursewig has Swaggart*, his hired bully, damage the inn beyond Gillian's ability to repair it so that he may buy it from her cheaply. Gillian does not give up easily, however, and Pursewig meets his match when she is joined by Lionel*, a young man who was once a cat. Pursewig loses claim to his tollgate when Lionel informs the town council that the bridge had been built by his master, Magister Stephanus*, for the good of all the town; the mayor loses his wealth and his mayorship when, trapped by a fire he has ordered set, he promises anything if Lionel will save him. Stripped of his power and his wealth, Pursewig becomes the scullery boy in Gillian's inn.

PUZZLE, a character in C[live] S[taples] Lewis's* *The Last Battle**. He lives near Cauldron Pool in western Narnia*. Puzzle is a talking donkey, but he does not think himself at all clever. He has great respect for his friend Shift*, a talking ape, and generally gives in and does whatever Shift wants him to do. When the ape finds a lion skin in Cauldron Pool and makes it into a coat for Puzzle, the donkey wears it and pretends to be Aslan*, Narnia's great lion-protector, though he feels that it is disrespectful; Shift persuades him that it is Aslan's wish that he pretend to be Aslan and "make things right" in Narnia. Being Aslan is a miserable job, for Shift is kept in the stable on Stable Hill*, lest those who see him realize that he is not a lion at all. Sometimes no one brings him any water; he is not allowed out except at night, and then only for a moment. Thus when Jill Pole*, a girl from Earth, finds him, Puzzle is willing to go with her, her friend, Eustace Clarence Scrubb*, and Tirian*, the king of Narnia. Puzzle is very aware of the wrongs he has committed and seeks to repair them. When Aslan brings Narnia to an end, Puzzle is brought into Aslan's country. Though miserable, he faces Aslan and is forgiven. Puzzle stays in the country forever and is happy.

QUANATILCÓ, a place in Jane Louise Curry's* Abáloc novels*. In the fourth century, this city is known as Kaouanatl'ico. In the twelfth century, it is the home of the seven priests of the sun in Cibotlán*. It is here that Callista Lee and Harry Rivers** and Melissa Mitchell* are brought when they first journey back in time.

QUEEN OF BABYLON, a character in *The Story of the Amulet*, by E[dith] Nesbit Bland*. Though the king of ancient Babylon has thirteen other wives, she is the only one who is the Queen. This sometimes-foolish woman is very vain; when she metes out justice in the palace, those who play on her vanity sometimes get off. The Queen is charmed when Robert*, Anthea*, and Cyril* visit her during their trip to ancient Babylon in search of the missing half of a powerful amulet*. Much impressed by what they tell her about twentiety-century England, she makes a wish to visit them there, and the Psammead* grants it. The visit is disastrous, for London does not suit her nor she it, and the Psammead is kept busy granting wishes for her. Upset at seeing her things on display at the British Museum, she wishes they would come to her, and this nearly causes a riot; sorry for the working poor, whom she calls slaves, the Queen wishes they had what they like best to eat and drink; thinking to improve the looks of the Stock Exchange members, she wishes they were dressed like Babylonians and is so frightened by their anger at her that she calls her guards to kill them. Horrified at the slaughter, the children can do nothing, but an onlooker wishes it were all a dream, and the Psammead grants his wish, sending the Queen back to Babylon.

QUEEN OF THE FAIRIES, a character in *Mopsa the Fairy*, by Jean Ingelow*. This unnamed ruler of Fairyland* becomes bored and goes traveling with her retinue. Coming to a lovely tower, they climb it, only to be cast into the river, for the tower is made of water. The fairies, out of their element, are easily captured and sold into slavery. The others escape; their queen remains a slave until Jack*, a boy seeking Fairyland, frees her. Mopsa*, a fairy child whom Jack escorts, is the queen's sister.

QUEEN OF UNDERLAND, a character in *The Silver Chair*, by C[live] S[taples] Lewis*. She is also called the Lady of the Green Kirtle. This enchantress rules Underland*, a gloomy land beneath the surface of Narnia*, a magical place. She has arts which can make one forget his past as he listens to her beautiful music and breathes the smoke of her magical fire. The Queen always dresses in green and can sometimes appear in the shape of a green serpent. She is friendly with the giants who live at Harfang* and visits them sometimes. The Queen has great ambitions: she hopes to rule Narnia. To this end she calls from Bism* the Earthmen*, to dig a passage to the surface; she kills the mother of Rilian*, prince of Narnia, and gets him under her spell, kidnapping him and taking him to Underland, where he is her slave and her devoted champion, as long as the sun does not shine on him, and except for an hour each evening, when her enchantments fail. She hopes to use him to take over Narnia and rule through him. The Queen is thwarted when Jill Pole*, Eustace Clarence Scrubb*, and Puddleglum* come to Underland to rescue the prince. When she turns into a huge serpent and tries to kill him, he, Eustace, and Puddleglum kill her. At the Queen's death, the city falls and Underland is flooded.

QUESTING BEAST, THE, a legendary creature that appears in T[erence] H[anbury] White's* *The Sword in the Stone*. It is also called the Beast Glatisant. The Beast has the head of a serpent, the body of a libbard (leopard), the haunches of a lion, and feet like a hart. It makes a noise in its belly like thirty pair of hounds, except, of course, when it drinks. The Questing Beast can only be caught by someone of the Pellinore family; King Pellinore* has been hunting it for seventeen years when young Wart (Arthur*) meets him in the Forest Sauvage*. Pellinore and the Beast keep regular hours over the years, getting up at the same time and going to bed at half-past ten, until the king goes to live at Sir Grummore Grummursum's* castle. After this the Beast pines away, with no one to care about it. But Pellinore finds it and nurses it back to health and they start off again. The Questing Beast later saves Pellinore from Galapas*, a cruel giant. When the Wart is crowned king of Britain, Pellinore and the Questing Beast get together and send him a coronation present of fewmets, tastefully wrapped.

QUICKSILVER, a character in Lloyd Alexander's* *The Marvelous Misadventures of Sebastian*. He is the husband of Madame Sophie, the Thornless Rose, and the head of Quicksilver's Gallimaufry-Theatricus, which travels from village to village in Hamelin-Loring*, providing entertainment of many kinds. This theatrical man helps Sebastian*, a young fiddler, and Isabel Charlotte

Theodora Fredericka* (Isabel), the princess of Hamelin-Loring, in their journey out of the country. This help lands Quicksilver in jail, but he gets his reward when Isabel ascends the throne and appoints his troupe the Royal Gallimaufry-Theatricus.

R

RABADASH, a character in C[live] S[taples] Lewis's* *The Horse and His Boy**. He is the son of the Tisroc*. Rabadash is also known as Rabadash the Peacemaker (to his face) and Rabadash the Ridiculous (behind his back). This prince of Calormen* is as spoiled as any prince of Calormen has ever been, and as selfish and cruel. He woos Susan Pevensie*, a queen of Narnia*, but is rejected; furious, he mounts a campaign to take Archenland*, the land between Calormen and Narnia, and from there to invade Narnia itself, to carry off Susan. His invasion plans come to naught, however, for Aravis*, a young girl, and her companions learn of them and warn the Archenlanders. Rabadash's army is decimated and he is changed by Aslan*, Narnia's great lion-protector, into a donkey. Rabadash changes himself back into a man by standing before a temple of Tash* at the time of the Autumn Feast. When he takes the throne, his reign is the most peaceful in Calormene history, for if he goes more than ten miles from Tashbaan, the capital, he will become a donkey forever, and Rabadash does not trust his officers to make conquests without toppling him from the throne. His name becomes a synonym for asininity.

RABBIT HILL. Robert Lawson. Illus. Robert Lawson. New York: Viking Press, 1944. 127 pp. American. Newbery Award, 1945.

New folks are coming to the house on the Hill, and all the animals for miles around are looking forward to it, hoping for better times. Little Georgie*, a young rabbit, is sent, after many warnings and instructions, to ask his Uncle Analdas*, an old bachelor rabbit, to come stay with the family. Full of the importance of the errand, Little Georgie sets off, singing a song about the new folks coming. When he is chased by a crafty old hound, Georgie runs beautifully, but gradually he is steered toward the legendary, unjumpable Deadman's Brook*. In a burst of fear and energy, however, Little Georgie leaps it. Crusty old Analdas is quite willing to come to the Hill, and the next day they go there, finding all the animals singing Georgie's song.

In the next days, much happens: a garden is plowed, and the house and chicken coop are repaired. When the new Folks come, they seem nice, though they own an old cat, Mr. Muldoon*. Georgie's father proves how mannerly they are by running in front of the car as it goes down the driveway; the Folks put up a sign warning drivers to be careful "on account of small animals." And when Willie Fieldmouse*, listening at a window to hear what the Folks are planning, falls into a rain barrel, the folks fish him out and care for him, protecting him from Mr. Muldoon and setting Willie free. In joyful anticipation, the animals watch the large garden grow.

Then, on the night the animals decide what part of the garden goes to whom, Little Georgie is hit by a car, and the folks take him in. All the animals are sorrowful, for Georgie is a great favorite. One night Willie catches a glimpse of Little Georgie and he seems happy. All feel better, but still they worry. Uncle Analdas decides that Georgie is being held hostage and is being tortured, and the idea spreads; when, as Midsummer Eve approaches, the animals see something being built near the garden, they decide that it is a dungeon or a gallows for Little Georgie. At last the Eve arrives, and the animals gather at the garden as is traditional. The Folks are there, as is Georgie, bright and well, and he rejoins his family. The mysterious thing is a statue of St. Francis, with food spread at its base, and the Folks watch as the animals eat. The garden is declared forbidden to all animals, by the animals themsleves. And every night, food is spread at the statue, and all are fed; the garden is not touched.

RAMANDU, a character in C[live] S[taples] Lewis's* The Voyage of the "Dawn Treader"*. He has a daughter. Ramandu was a star in the sky, but he grew old and came to a small island at the end of the world. Here he and his daughter tend a great table put there for the refreshment of travelers by Aslan*, the great lion-protector of Narnia*. Each morning a bird brings from the valleys of the sun a fire-berry that takes away a bit of Ramandu's age; when he is as young as a day-old child he will take his place among the stars. Caspian X* and his companions meet Ramandu when they sail in the Dawn Treader* to the edge of the world; Caspian later married Ramandu's daughter.

RASTALL, SIMON, a character in Jane Louise Curry's* The Change-Child*. He is the unscrupulous son of Sir Edmund Rastall. Because he covets the manor that Eilian Roberts* will inherit, Simon uses treachery and guile in an attempt to kidnap the girl and force her to marry him. He dies in a fall from his horse, and his father uses a curse put on Simon by Mamgu*, one of the Red Fairies*, as an excuse to destroy the Great Dark Wood that shelters them, thereby also driving away y Tylwyth Teg*, the Fair Folk*, who live at the center of the Wood.

RAT. See Water Rat, the

RATTLE, SILVER, an object in Harding's Luck*, by E[dith] Nesbit Bland*. This old silver "coral and bells" once belonged to a child of the house of Arden; handed down three generations, it becomes the property of Dickie Harding* in the early twentieth century. The rattle is a stick about five inches long with small round bells on it and a piece of whitish coral attached to it. On the side of the rattle is drawn the Arden crest—a white mole. By arranging moonflower* seeds in a pattern around the rattle and an old sealing ring with the Arden crest, Dickie learns by accident that he can travel back into time, living in the seventeenth century as Richard Arden*.

RAY SILER (*The Watchers*). *See* Siler, Ray

RAYMOND, MR., a character in George MacDonald's* *At the Back of the North Wind*. He becomes the husband of a very kind woman. Mr. Raymond seems to like children; he often visits the children in the hospital and tells them stories. When he meets Diamond*, a little boy, Mr. Raymond encourages him to learn to read and takes an interest in Diamond and his family. The man seems to test Diamond's father by giving him the use of his horse, Ruby; later he hires the man as his coachman and the family moves to Mr. Raymond's house in the country. Diamond becomes the Raymonds' page. Mr. Raymond is a poet and writer of stories, and he has Diamond read his stories to see if they are good or not.

RED COW, a character in P[amela] L[yndon] Travers's* *Mary Poppins*. She is the mother of Red Calf. Red Cow has spent all her life in a large field filled with buttercups and dandelions. A model cow, she has always known What was What and behaved like a perfect lady, until one night she gets a fallen star stuck on her horn and therefore begins to dance. She has always thought dancing improper, but Red Cow enjoys it until she discovers that she cannot stop. The king of the country advises Red Cow to jump over the moon and see if that helps; she does, though jumping is improper, and dislodges the star. Her return to her quiet life is refreshing for a time, but Red Cow begins to miss the happy feeling the star had given her. On the advice of Mary Poppins's* mother, Red Cow now wanders the world, looking for a fallen star to catch on her horn.

RED FAIRIES, a band of people in Jane Louise Curry's* *The Change Child*. These golden-haired people are all related to one another and to Eilian Roberts*; they are descended from the offspring of a woman of *y Tylwyth Teg*—the Fair Folk*—and a mortal. Doomed to wander, they make their living by hook and crook, stealing what they need. Under the iron rule of Mamgu*, their "Queen," the Red Fairies live on the edge of the Great Dark Wood, taking advantage of the old tales of fairies who are supposed to live there to ensure that no one will come after them. When the Wood is destroyed, they are free to wander again. The Red Fairies are fond of music and dancing and bright clothing; they take life lightly and as it comes.

REEPICHEEP, a character in C[live] S[taples] Lewis's* *Prince Caspian**, *The Voyage of the "Dawn Treader"**, and *The Last Battle**. He is a talking mouse in Narnia*, a land of talking beasts and marvelous creatures. Not long after Reepicheep's birth, a dryad spoke over his cradle the prophecy that he would find all he would seek in the utter East, where the salt water grows sweet. Reepicheep grew into a mouse famed for his noble bearing, careful of his honor, and dreaming of glory charges and courageous last stands; he is a bad chess player because he sometimes forgets it is chess and makes his pieces behave as they would were it a real battle. Serious as Reepicheep is about his honor, it is difficult for others to see him as anything but a bit comic, because of his small stature. During the War of Deliverance, Reepicheep leads the talking mice in the battle against Miraz* and his army, and here he loses his tail; so woeful are he and his followers that Aslan*, the mystical lion-protector of Narnia, causes him to grow another when the mice prepare to cut their tails off in sympathy. Reepicheep goes with Caspian X*, the king of Narnia, in a voyage to the end of the world, and here he finds his heart's desire—Aslan's country. Riding in a small coracle, Reepicheep vanishes over a great wave into that country, not to be seen again until Narnia comes to an end.

REESE, DAVID (DAVE), a name shared in the twentieth century by two personalities in Jane Louise Curry's* *Over the Sea's Edge**. The original Dave was born in twentieth-century America. Longing for adventure and freedom, but pressured by his ambitious father to achieve intellectually, Dave feels stifled and resentful. By means of a strange silver pendant*, he trades places with Dewi ap Ithil*, a timid Welsh boy in the twelfth century who longs to get away from his rough life and become a scholar. This second Dave Reese is almost too intellectually eager, burying himself in intellectual pursuits because of his timidity. He gets more of a taste for adventure, however, when he reads the parchment manuscript left behind by Dewi, and is persuaded by Alice, his cousin, to help her with her boat, which she wants to use to travel down the river. Dave promises himself to someday sail down the Mississippi River.

REGENT, THE. *See* Grinssorg, Count

REKH-MARĀ, a character in *The Story of the Amulet**, by E[dith] Nesbit Bland*. He is the Divine Father of the Temple of Amen-Rā in ancient Egypt. When half of a powerful amulet* comes into his possession, Rekh-marā searches through time and space for the other half, having learned of its existence from Robert*, Anthea*, Cyril*, and Jane* during their visit to his time in their search for the matching half of the amulet they have. Rekh-marā travels to ancient Tyre and there poses as a sailor; when the children come to the ancient city in their search, he claims to have brought them and shares their fate when they are sold into slavery. His half of the amulet is taken from him by a ship captain, and he gets it back when he and the children use their half of the amulet to follow the man. Rekh-Mara comes to twentieth-century London in his search, and there he and the children discover that the half of the amulet each has is actually the same half. At the suggestion of Jimmy*, a learned man, Rekh-mara and the children journey back to where the amulet was whole and unguarded and take it. Because Rekh-mara's heart's desire is to stay in the twentieth century and gain wisdom, and the only way he can stay is by joining with a kindred spirit, Rekh-mara joins with Jimmy. The evil in his soul takes the form of a centipede during the exchange.

RENGA, a character in *The Wolves of Aam**, by Jane Louise Curry*. Her mate is Rovanng, and one of her pups is Findral*. Renga is one of the magical Wolves of Aam*, who have the ability to communicate with beings who are not of their kind. When Runner-to-the-Sky's-Edge* tells Renga of his lovely "dreamstone," she realizes that it is Mirelidar*, one of twelve powerful skystones*, and that it must be kept from the grasp of power-hungry Lord Naghar*. Renga and the other Wolves help to rescue Lek*, a conjuror, from the fortress of Gzel* and take Mirelidar to a place of safety.

RETURN OF THE TWELVES, THE. See *Twelve and the Genii, The*

REUBEN, a character in *Wet Magic**, by E[dith] Nesbit Bland*. His parents become the King and Queen of the Under Folk*. His last name starts with "V." Reuben grows up not knowing his parents, for when he was a year and a half old, he was stolen for revenge by a gypsy who had been sent to prison by Reuben's father. Reuben leads the harum-scarum life of gypsy circus folk, doing an "Infant Prodigious Act on the Horse with the Tambourines" and watching for a chance to run away and find his parents, who will recognize him by one shoe and a shirt he was wearing when he was kidnapped. When he is ten and a half, Reuben gets his chance. He helps Mavis* and Francis* rescue Freia*, a mermaid captured by the gypsies, and takes this opportunity to run away. When Freia brings the children to Merland*, her home beneath the sea, Reuben helps defend it from the Under Folk* by joining the Sea urchins—the Boy Scouts of Merland—and spying on the enemy. He is then made the general of the Sea urchins. Reuben finds his parents in an unexpected way; when he returns to land after peace is made between the warring Merfolk and Under Folk, he is told that the first people he meets will be his parents. The first people he meets are the King and Queen of the Under Folk, who have returned to the land from which they had been taken years ago, and who are very happy at last to find their son.

REVENGE OF SAMUEL STOKES, THE. Penelope Lively. London: Heinemann, 1981. 122 pp. British.

During the building of houses in a development on an old estate, geometric figures appear on the ground near one house, but they melt away and building goes on. Eleven-year-old Tim Thornton* and his parents move into the house, Jane Harvey* and her parents move in next door, and the residential area begins to establish itself. Strange things begin to happen, however. A hedge begins to grow where none was planted, and a nearby shop mysteriously floods. The Thorntons' washing machine gives out the smell of roasting venison. A neighbor's greenhouse turns into a Greek temple overnight, and brick walls begin to grow from the ground. Television reception gets worse and worse, and sometimes there seems to appear on the screen the figure of a man.

When Tim and Jane go to a museum with Tim's Grandpa*, they see a painting of the old estate, and Grandpa begins to get ideas, realizing that Samuel Stokes*, who had planned the estate's gardens in the eighteenth century, might have a hand in what is happening now. This belief is confirmed one night when Stokes suddenly appears on the television screen as Grandpa, Jane, and Tim are watching it, and vows to get rid of the houses. Immediately there is a small earthquake. A few days later, Stokes again appears on the television screen, this time to complain about the houses marring his greatest achievement and to again vow to get rid of them. Another tremor follows.

Stokes bides his time for a while; then a new house is destroyed by a tremor. That night, Stokes speaks to Tim on the telephone, but they are interrupted before he can give the boy his instructions. During a local garden competition, Stokes makes some changes of his own in one entry, giving it a grotto with statues including a plaque attributing the grotto to him in 1795. To his fury, the entry does not win, and Stokes gets his revenge by putting back an eighteenth-century lake—stocked with fish—that once lay where the houses are now. Though the area is flooded, the houses are not, and though the lake is pumped, it shows no sign of leaving.

The inhabitants of the area not unnaturally begin to believe that the old estate is returning. They get used to the lake but are still so angry that the city council starts work on a nearby park ahead of schedule to placate them. Tim realizes that if Stokes could become interested in the park, he might leave them all alone. In order to attract Stokes's attention, he, Jane, and Grandpa cook up a banquet modelled on eighteenth-century fare. Stokes communicates with them over the radio, and, after a few nasty remarks about the cooking, he becomes involved with the idea of the new park. Grandpa suggests that Stokes clear away his other manifestations so as not to spoil the effect, and Stokes complies. The next day the lake is gone, and the grotto and Greek temple crumble. The residential area is at peace, but all kinds of havoc are being raised in the new park.

RHUN, a character in Lloyd Alexander's* *The Castle of Llyr** and *The High King**. His father is Rhuddlum, King of the Isle of Mona*; his mother is Teleria. This clumsy, good-natured prince is sent to escort Eilonwy*, a princess, to Mona, to learn to be a lady; it is hoped that she will eventually marry Rhun. His father, aware that the young man probably will not make a good king, asks Taran*, the orphaned ward of an enchanter, to teach him and to keep an eye on him. When Eilonwy is kidnapped, Rhun joins Taran and his companions in their search for her, exasperating Taran by his clumsiness and sometimes managing to do things right. Though through Rhun's foolishness the search nearly ends tragically, Taran finds himself quite fond of the prince. At Rhuddlum's death, Rhun becomes King of Mona and tries to do the best for his people, though his intentions sometimes outreach his skills. When he accompanies Eilonwy back to Caer Dallben*, Rhun becomes part of the party searching for Dyrnwyn*, a sword of great power stolen by the evil lord Arawn*. After Taran and Gwydion*, the war leader of the High King of Prydain*, are captured and held prisoner in King Smoit's* castle, Rhun helps plan their rescue; a clever ploy on his part makes the rescue a success. But in the battle Rhun is killed, and he is buried near Caer Cadarn.

RHYS, DAVYT. *See* Dewi ap Ithil; Reese, David

RICH LLAWCAE (*A Swiftly Tilting Planet*). *See* Llawcae, Rich

RICHARD ARDEN (*Harding's Luck: The House of Arden*). *See* Arden, Richard

RILIAN, a character in C[live] S[taples] Lewis's* *The Silver Chair** and *The Last Battle**. He is the son of Caspian X* and his wife. When Rilian's mother is killed by a great, green serpent, Rilian searches for it every day, hoping to find it and slay it. After a month, he searches no more, having discovered in the place where his mother had died a lovely lady dressed in green, who appears each day and is so beautiful that all he longs to do is gaze upon her. She is the Queen of Underland* and one day she kidnaps Rilian and takes him to her kingdom under Narnia*. Here Rilian is enchanted, so that each day he forgets who he really is and thinks only of loving the Queen and being her champion; each night for an hour he remembers his real nature, but she binds him in a silver chair and he cannot escape. The evil Queen plans to invade Narnia from below, digging to the surface and overwhelming the unsuspecting Narnians, and putting Rilian on the throne; she will rule through him. For ten years Rilian lives in Underland*, to be rescued at last by Jill Pole* and Eustace Clarence Scrubb*, two children from Earth, and Puddleglum*, a Marsh-wiggle* from Narnia. Rilian comes back home just in time to see his father before Caspian dies. The prince becomes king of Narnia and rules well, and the land is happy and prosperous under his reign. Rilian is one of those in the country of Aslan*, Narnia's lion-protector, when the land is brought to an end.

RING, a magical object in several works. In *The Magician's Nephew** and *The Last Battle**, by C[live] S[taples] Lewis*, there are four rings, two yellow and two green. They are made of dust from the Wood between the Worlds* that somehow was brought from the Wood by scholars of Atlantis*; the dust eventually came to Mrs. Lefay, a woman with fairy blood in her, and then to Andrew

Ketterley*. He makes the rings and tricks his nephew, Digory Kirke*, and Polly Plummer* into trying them. The yellow rings take their wearers into the Wood; the green rings take them out of it. Anyone or anything touching the wearer also goes when the rings are used. Digory and Polly use the rings to go to a dead planet, where they meet Jadis*, an evil queen. They accidentally take her, a cabbie named Frank*, his horse, and Andrew to Narnia* in time for the creation of that land. When they are safely back in London, Digory buries the rings around the core of a magic apple that he plants in the garden behind Andrew's house. Years later his friends, Edmund and Peter Pevensie**, dig up the rings so that they can be used again to go to Narnia, but they are never used.

In E[dith] Nesbit Bland's* *The Enchanted Castle*, a plain ring made of dull metal belies its looks by possessing great magical powers. It is whatever the bearer says it is: a ring to make one invisible or to grant wishes, among other things. The ring must be used precisely and a time limit set on its enchantments or they will be erratic in the length of time they last. While he wears the ring, the bearer feels no fear; at sunset he can see the marble statues on the grounds of Yalding Castle* come alive. Except for children, those who use the ring must pay a price for every wish but the last one ever made. Given to a mortal long ago, the ring came to the family of Lord Yalding* when one of his ancestors married its owner; he used it to help build Yalding Castle for his wife, whose death was the price the ring exacted. It lay forgotten for centuries among hidden treasures in a tower room, to be found in the twentieth century by Mabel Prowse* and her friends, Gerald*, James*, and Kathleen*. Unaware of the ring's powers, they get into difficulties as a result of its use. Finally, the day after the festival of harvest, the children go with Lord Yalding and Mademoiselle*, his long-lost lover, to the Hall of Granted Wishes*, where Mademoiselle wishes that all the magic the ring has done be undone, and that the ring become a charm to bind her and the lord forever. The ring becomes a plain gold ring that is used in their wedding ceremony.

In the Chronicles of Prydain*, by Lloyd Alexander*, a gold ring, set with an ancient stone carved by the craftsmen of the Fair Folk*, is given to Eilonwy* by Gwydion*, war leader of the High King of Prydain*, in token of their friendship. She wears it through all her subsequent adventures. Though Eilonwy does not know it, the ring will grant her one wish, and that one the deepest wish of her heart. When Eilonwy realizes that the one thing she truly wishes is to be rid of her magic powers so that she can marry Taran*, her sweetheart, she uses the ring to accomplish this.

In J[ohn] R[onald] R[euel] Tolkien's* *The Hobbit* and *The Lord of the Rings*, it is an ancient ring, made many ages ago by a great evil lord, Sauron, to control nineteen other rings he had given to elves*, dwarves*, and men. Much of his own power has passed into the ring. When Sauron was defeated, the ring came to Isildur. Falling from his finger into a river, it finally came to Gollum*, who killed his friend for it. For many years Gollum has treasured the gold ring as his most precious thing. It makes its wearer invisible, and he finds this very useful, using the ring to spy and, after he goes to live by himself beneath the mountains, to grab the little goblins* he so enjoys eating. One day Gollum loses the ring and it is found by Bilbo Baggins*, a hobbit*, who uses it to get out of the caves he is wandering in, unnoticed by Gollum. The ring casts a kind of enchantment over those who wear it, making them covet it and lie to keep it; Bilbo later lies about how he had gotten the ring. After using it in a quest to recover a treasure from a dragon, Bilbo finds the ring useful when he wants to avoid unwanted callers. After many years Sauron again seeks his ring, and after a difficult journey it is melted in the fires of Mount Doom, carried there by Frodo Baggins.

RING OF ERRETH-AKBE, an object in Ursula K. LeGuin's* *The Tombs of Atuan**. This silver ring is small enough to fit only the arm of a woman or a child. A wave pattern decorates the outside; inside are inscribed nine Runes of Power, among them Pirr—which protects against fire, wind, and madness—Ges—which gives endurance—and the Bond-Rune*—which is the sign of peace and dominion. Nine holes pierce the Ring. For whom it was made no one knows, but it was worn by Elfarran the Fair centuries before Erreth-Akbe*, a sorcerer, came to possess it. The Ring was broken in his battle with the High Priest of the Inmost Temples of the Twin Gods in the Kargad Lands; when it was broken, the Bond-Rune was, too, and after that time there were no great kings in Havnor* to rule all Earthsea*. The Priest-Kings of Kargad became powerful and the Kargish Empire was formed under the Kargish Godking*. The Ring and his staff broken, Erreth-Akbe lost his power and was defeated. He gave half the ring to Thoreg of Hupun, a Kargish king; the other half remained with the High Priest, who put it among the Treasures of the Tombs of Atuan*. Thoreg and his descendants kept their half of the ring and were constantly in rebellion against the reigning Kargish power. When they were finally defeated, their half of the Ring was lost; it went with a brother and sister, the last of their line, who were marooned on a tiny island. Years later Ged*, a sorcerer, finds them and is given the half, which he learns the importance of from a dragon. He comes to Atuan to find the other half and join them, succeeding only with the help of Tenar*, the One Priestess of the Tombs. She wears the Ring into Havnor, but it is almost twenty years before a king, Arren*, rules all of Earthsea.

RING OF LUNED, an object in *The Sleepers**, by Jane Louise Curry*. This gold ring with a red stone was meant to be worn by Artair*—King Arthur*—as one of his signs. During the king's last battle, however, it was taken from his son, Anir, by Artair's nephew, Medraut*, who wears it into the twentieth century. When Artair regains the Ring, he takes it, with the other *Brenhin Dlyseu**, the Thirteen Treasures of Prydein, to a place of safety beyond the seas.

RISHANGER, GERALD, a character in *The Sleepers**, by Jane Louise Curry*. His niece and nephew are Jennifer and Henry Peter Huntington*. Gerald is an archaeologist at Stanford University in California and an expert in prehistoric tombs and mound dwellings. When he comes to Great Britain to visit a colleague and stay with his niece and nephew, Gerald gets more than he bargained for as he and the children uncover the chamber where Artair*—King Arthur*—and his men sleep until the time Britain has need of them. Practical Gerald never quite understands the actions of Ellen Peresby*, a flighty girl sometimes "possessed" by Margan*, Artair's sister and enemy. He does come to understand, however, that he likes the girl very much.

RISHDA, a character in *The Last Battle**, by C[live] S[taples] Lewis*. Originally from Calormen*, Rishda comes to Narnia*, the land to the north, to help Shift*, a talking ape, exploit the land. He and Shift claim to be advised by "Tashlan," a great power whose name is made of the names of Aslan*, Narnia's great lion-protector, and Tash*, Calormen's great bloody god. Rishda believes in neither. Tiring of Shift's temperament, Rishda leagues himself with Ginger*, a talking cat who does not believe in Aslan but who does believe in reaping as much profit as he can out of the situation. During a great battle between Rishda's forces and those of Tirian*, Narnia's king, Tirian and Rishda fight each other, and Tirian drags the Calormene into the stable on Stable Hill*, where Tashlan is supposed to appear. Tash is here, called by Rishda and Shift, and to his horror Tash claims Rishda for his own before vanishing at Aslan's command.

RIVER AT GREEN KNOWE, THE. Lucy Boston. Illus. Peter Boston. London: Faber and Faber, 1959. 144 pp. British.

One summer Dr. Maud Biggin*, an archaeologist, and a friend rent Green Knowe*, a large old house in the country, and invite Ida*, Dr. Biggin's eleven-year-old niece, and two displaced children, Oskar Stanislawsky* and nine-year-old Hsu* (Ping), to the house for a summer holiday. From the first day, the children are enthralled by the river that flows past Green Knowe and decide to explore it and the many islands it contains, using a canoe they find. Because the river is full of people on holiday during the day, the children decide to go out early in the morning.

During their first trip, they find an old house and explore a nearby channel, coming upon a hermit* living off the river. He tells them of a vision he had of the river teeming with wildlife and of wild, long-haired men in canoes. Then he sends the children away, telling them not to return, for others would follow. Because they have rested so much after their early-morning trip, the children decide to stay up all night, and that night they cross the river to an island where there are horses; after Ping says a word of power that the river gives him, they see that the horses are winged and spend a lovely time with them until the horses are frightened away and the children go to bed.

The next day, an equally wonderful thing happens: trying to build a mouse nest from the inside, Oskar succeeds, growing smaller and smaller in the process, until he is two inches high. The next morning, however, after spending the night in Green Knowe, he is the right size again. Because it has rained in the night, the river is flooded, but the children canoe on it anyway, going far downstream. Here they meet Terak*, a giant boy of a race of giants, who tells them about his parents and his life; Terak's mother says that his father died of laughter, but discovering from the children how wonderful laughter and producing it can be, Terak decides that he wants to be a clown. He gives Ping a tooth he has lost before searchers find the children and take them home.

Because Dr. Biggin believes that giant men once walked the earth and would be interested in the tooth, the children leave Terak's tooth for her to find. She is quite excited by it, and when the children return from another expedition on the river, the archaeologists' meeting she has called is in an uproar over the tooth. The children have found an old glass bottle; in it are a narrative and map by Piers Madely*, who was a vicar in 1647. The narrative is in Latin, because the story is so strange, but Piers's adventure seems to have taken place near Green Knowe, when the moon rose over the house. They go out that night, hoping to see what so frightened Piers, and watch in wonder as hunters wearing deer antlers dance around the house, which has become a building made of rushes. When the hunters rush off into the night, the building becomes Green Knowe again and the awed children go to bed.

The circus comes, and in it is Terak. The children go, of course, taking Dr. Biggin. Terak is a clown and a very good one, but Dr. Biggin, though she has a giant before her eyes, does not believe it; like many grownups, she cannot believe that what is wonderful can exist now and not only in the past.

RIVERS, CALLISTA LEE (CALLIE), a character in *The Birdstones** and *The Daybreakers**, by Jane Louise Curry*. She is the twin sister of Harry Rivers*. Originally from Daingerfield, Texas, Callie is unhappy when her family moves to Apple Lock*, Ohio. The Riverses are black, and Callie is uncomfortable in her new school and unable to make friends. However, she becomes friendly with Melissa Mitchell* (Liss) and then with a large group of children with whom she shares adventures in ancient Abáloc*. Callie makes the seven snowmen inhabited by the seven priests of Cibotlán*, and she and Liss are the first from Apple Lock to make the journey to Abáloc, where she is hailed as a child of the sun and almost sacrificed. Later Callie leads the other girls back into Abáloc in time to rescue Lincoas* and his party. She is also part of the group that rescues Conway Tapp* when he is about to be sacrificed. Later, with Anna Maria D'Agostino*, Angela Paff*, and other girls, Callie helps create Dayla Jones, an imaginary student whose persona is filled by Dalea*, a fugitive from Abáloc.

RIVERS, HARRY, a character in Jane Louise Curry's* *The Daybreaker** and *The Birdstones**. He is the twin brother of Callista Lee Rivers* (Callie). Originally from Daingerfield, Texas, easy-going Harry is not particularly bothered when his family moves to Apple Lock*, Ohio. Harry is pulled into twelfth-century Abáloc* by the force of Callie's need for him; she and Melissa Mitchell* are in danger of being sacrificed to the Sun Serpent (Katóa*). Back in Apple Lock, Harry and his friends "translate" the ancient Abalockian alphabet, which they take back to Abáloc and teach to Lincoas* and his group before the band is captured by warriors of Cibotlán*. Harry is one of the group that rescues Conway Tapp* from Neolin's* knife; during the rescue, Harry eloquently points out the returning Lincoas and his band, calling them the "daybreakers" bringing the light of knowledge to Abáloc.

ROBERT, a character in *Five Children and It**, *The Phoenix and the Carpet**, and *The Story of the Amulet**, by E[dith] Nesbit Bland*. He is the brother of Anthea*, Jane*, Cyril*, and the Lamb*. Robert and the others have many adventures with magic, discovering a Psammead* who grants wishes, a wishing carpet* in which is rolled the egg of the Phoenix*, and half of an amulet* which takes them back through time to find its other half. Robert's ingenuity and patience are sometimes tested to the utmost, for he endures being a giant, as well as being held in the enemy camp when the other children wish that their house was a besieged castle. The Phoenix hatches when Robert accidentally knocks its egg into the fire, for which the bird is duly grateful and allows itself to be hidden in Robert's coat whenever it and the children go out. Like his brothers and sisters, Robert is not particularly clever, attractive, or good, and, also like them, he has an infinite capacity for getting into mischief without meaning to.

ROBERTS, EILIAN, a character in *The Change-Child**, by Jane Louise Curry*. She is the daughter of Ifan ap Robert and the sister of Elizabeth and Angharad Roberts. Her grandmother is Mamgu*; she becomes the wife of Goronwy*. Because of twelve-year-old Eilian's lame foot and her golden hair, the superstitious folk of Elizabethan Wales think that she is a changeling, a child of *y Tylwyth Teg**, the Fair Folk*, left in exchange for a mortal baby, and they make Eilian's life miserable. The girl dreams of becoming a famous poetess. When it is discovered that she is an heiress, due to inherit a great manor at her father's death, Eilian is sent with Mamgu to the Great Dark Wood to be safe from Simon Rastall*, an unscrupulous young nobleman who seeks to marry her in order to get the manor. In the Wood, Eilian meets the true *Tylwyth Teg* and acts as the catalyst for events that drive them from their sanctuary to the uncertain seas that will take them to Tir na'nOg*. Eilian realizes that she has not the skill to manipulate the complex rhyme schemes of Welsh poetry and will not become the great poetess she dreamed of being, but by this time she has found a place with people who love her, and it does not matter. She later marries Goronwy.

ROBERTSON AY (the Mary Poppins books). *See* Ay, Robertson

ROBIN WOOD (*The Sword in the Stone*). *See* Wood, Robin

ROBLES, DON DIEGO FRANCISCO HERNÁNDEZ DEL GATO HER-RERA Y (*Time Cat*). *See* del Gato Herrera y Robles, Don Diego Francisco Hernández

ROGER BRADLEY (*The Owl Service*). *See* Bradley, Roger

ROGER D'AULNEAUX (*The Stones of Green Knowe*). *See* d'Aulneaux, Roger

ROGER JOHN NICHOLAS (*Poor Tom's Ghost*). *See* Nicholas, Roger John

ROKARRHUK, a race of beings in Jane Louise Curry's* *The Wolves of Aam*.
These evil, goblin-like creatures have yellow eyes and tails and are horrifying
to look at. They ride huge wolves, called Dread Ones, and they obey the commands of power-hungry Lord Naghar*. The Illigan*, one of their number, commands the fortress of Gzel*.

ROKE, an island in the Earthsea trilogy*, by Ursula K. LeGuin*. This island,
in the Archipelago on Earthsea*, is famous for its school for wizards. Sorcerers
from the school are eagerly sought and command high prices. Because of the
school, the people of Roke are hard to startle, being used to schoolboys' prankish
illusions. Roke is protected from evil by a strong wall of spells woven by the
great masters of sorcery who live there. On the island is Roke Knoll, which was
the first hill of Earthsea to stand above the sea when the First Word was spoken
by Segoy, the world's creator, and will be the last to sink when the world comes
to an end.

ROLAND WATSON (*Elidor*). *See* Watson, Roland

ROONWIT, a character in *The Last Battle*, by C[live] S[taples] Lewis*. He
is a mighty centaur who is a great astrologer. When it is rumored that Aslan*,
the great lion-protector of Narnia*, is in the land, Roonwit consults the stars
and finds them in disjunction, presaging disaster. His warnings to Tirian*, Narnia's king, are of little help, for already events have gone too far to be halted.
Tirian sends the centaur to Cair Paravel*, the king's castle, to call up a small
army to help him, but Roonwit is felled by an arrow shot by a warrior of
Calormen*, Narnia's traditional enemy, before he gets to the castle. His last
words, heard and repeated by Farsight, an eagle, make Tirian realize that Narnia
is coming to an end. Roonwit is among those in Aslan's country when the land
does come to an end.

ROSEMARY WALPOLE (*Parsley Sage, Rosemary & Time*; *The Magical
Cupboard*). *See* Walpole, Rosemary

ROWLANDS, JOHN, a character in Susan Cooper's* *The Grey King* and
Silver on the Tree. He has several brothers; he is the husband of Blodwen

Rowlands. Though John is of a long line of sailing men, he is a shepherd on the farm of David Evans, at Tywyn, Wales. When his father died when John was six, his mother took her family far from the sea. At about eleven or twelve, John saw Merriman Lyon*, one of the lords of the Light, riding the wind above the hills. John knows much and remembers much about the lore of the place where he lives; he is a good harpist and has two harps in his cottage. John is happy in his life with Blodwen until the time comes for the last battle between the Dark and the Light, when he discovers that she is the White Rider*, one of the great forces of the Dark. This knowledge so shocks him that he can help neither the Dark nor the Light, though he does make the final decision on whether or not Bran Davies* should be allowed to fight for the Light in the battle. But when the battle is raging around him, John helps the forces of the Light to defeat the Dark, by taking one of the six powerful Signs of the Light*, so that Bran can do what he must. John goes home, where "Blodwen" has died; the Light saves him pain by making him forget her true nature and making it seem that she had died some time before.

ROYAL DOULTON BOWL, an object in the Mary Poppins books*, by P[amela] L[yndon] Travers*. It sits on the mantel in the nursery of Annabel, Barbara, Jane Caroline, John, and Michael George Banks*****. On it are pictured three boys—Valentine, William, and Everard—who are playing horses. When one day Jane, in a fit of temper, throws her paintbox at the bowl, she cracks it, hurting Valentine's knee in the process. The boys invite her into the bowl, and here Jane has a lovely time until they take her to their house to meet their sister, Christina, and their great-grandfather. Here Jane learns that she is in the past and must stay here forever, sixty years from those she loves. Mary Poppins*, her nanny, rescues her, and when Jane again looks at the bowl, she sees her own handkerchief wrapped around Valentine's knee, and Mary Poppins's scarf lying in the painted grass. The bowl is later mended by Arthur Turvy*.

RUAN, a character in *The Watchers*, by Jane Louise Curry*. He was born in the fourth century, in what is now West Virginia, near what is now called Twilly's Green Hollow*. Ruan is descended from the Aldar* and his people keep watch over Tûl Isgrun*, the Dark Shrine, and the evil force that lies bound there. When Ruan is captured and taken to Kanhuan* to be sacrificed, he is forced by Tekla*, the power-hungry queen, to betray his people. In an effort to buy his freedom, he leads Tekla and her men to the shrine, where she frees the power that will help her to conquer her enemies. Ruan has a counterpart in the twentieth century: Ray Siler*, who, after sharing Ruan's experiences by sharing his body, learns enough to keep himself from betraying his people in his own century.

RUFUS, a character in *Over Sea, Under Stone** and *Greenwitch*, by Susan Cooper*. This beautiful Irish setter belongs to Captain Toms*, one of the Old Ones, the forces of good who seek to defeat the forces of evil. Friendly and enthusiastic, Rufus quickly makes friends with Barnabas (Barney), Jane, and Simon Drew***, who stay at the Captain's house. He proves useful in the battle between good and evil because of his good tracking abilities and his love for Barney; when the boy is under the spell of the evil Black Rider*, Rufus's howl wakes him; Rufus also leads the way to the caravan of a mysterious, evil painter* who has used the boy to find out the future.

RUNE, a thirteen-line poem in Madeleine L'Engle's* *A Swiftly Tilting Planet*. It was once used by Branwen, an Irish queen, to save herself from her abusive husband. The rune calls on Heaven, the sun, snow, fire, lightning, wind, sea, rocks, and earth and puts them between the chanter and the powers of darkness. It has been used several times since Branwen's age and has been passed down from generation to generation: Madoc*, a twelfth-century Welsh prince who flees to the North American continent, uses the rune to help him vanquish his brother; seventeenth-century Brandon Llawcae* uses it to save his sister-in-law from hanging; in the twentieth century, Branwen Zillah Maddox O'Keefe* teaches the rune to Charles Wallace Murry*, who uses it to call upon Gaudior*, a unicorn. With Gaudior, Charles travels back in time, altering it to keep Madog Branzillo* from destroying the world. As she shares his adventures by kything*, a kind of telepathy, Meg Murry*, Charles's sister, uses the rune to save him from danger.

RUNNER-TO-THE-SKY'S-EDGE (RUNNER), a character in *The Wolves of Aam**, by Jane Louise Curry*. His parents were Oona and Olf; his real name is Arl. Runner is one of the Tiddi*, a nomadic race of small folk who wander in the land of Astarlind. Fleeing with his parents from Nagharot*, where power-hungry Lord Naghar* rules, the child found a lovely stone and kept it, not knowing that it was Mirelidar*, one of the twelve powerful skystones*. Soon after that, his parents died and he was found by a band of Tiddi and raised as one of them. As Runner, he is the scout for the small band. When Runner is injured one day while fleeing from two wolves, he meets Lek*, a conjuror, who tends his wounds and takes his beautiful stone before leaving him. After Runner is found by his people, he is kidnapped by Lord Naghar's men, who think he might be able to tell them where Lek and the stone are. When Lek is captured, however, Runner is to be executed by Ghagra*, an Iceling*, who sets the Tiddi free instead. Runner meets the Wolves of Aam* and through them is reunited with Fith* and Cathound*, two Tiddi who followed him. Together the Tiddi, the Wolves, and two Icelings befriended by Fith and Cat travel to Gzel* and rescue Lek, destroying the fortress there as well. His adventures over, Runner gives up his lovely stone and he and the other Tiddi return to their little band of people.

RUSSELL BOYD MOAR (*The Watchers*). *See* Moar, Russell Boyd.

SAGE, PARSLEY, a tortoiseshell cat in *Parsley Sage, Rosemary & Time** and *The Magical Cupboard**, by Jane Louise Curry*. Originally his name is Oliver Tolliver, and he belongs to Goody Cakebread* in New England in 1722. When she is visited by three children from the twentieth century, the cat travels with one, Hepsibah Sagacity Walpole* (Sibby), back to her own time, where he is named Parsley Sage. Parsley lives to be at least twenty years old. When Rosemary Walpole* visits Sibby one summer, Parsley leads her to a tiny, secret garden where she tastes an herb called "time"* and is transported into the eighteenth century to have an adventure with Sibby and make sure that the girl gets back into her own century.

ST. PATRICK. *See* Sucat

SALLY STUDDARD (*The Wind Eye*). *See* Studdard, Sally

SAM BEAVER (*The Trumpet of the Swan*). *See* Beaver, Sam

SAMANTHA BOSTWEILER (*Mindy's Mysterious Miniature; The Lost Farm*). *See* Bostweiler, Samantha

SAMUEL STOKES (*The Revenge of Samuel Stokes*). *See* Stokes, Samuel

SANDRA, a character in Penelope Lively's* *The Driftway**. She is the younger sister of Paul* and the stepdaughter of Christine*. Seven-year-old Sandra does not share Paul's resentment of their new stepmother, though she goes along with his suggestions that they fix up the room they share so that Christine will not have to go into it. Sandra loves fixing up their room, and it is strewn with the toys, pictures, cigarette cards, and bits of fabric she has collected like a little nesting bird. Though she does not always understand what Paul is doing or why he does it, Sandra goes along with him, running away to their grandmother's when he decides to, and happily going home when he decides to give Christine a chance.

SARAH CLUMP (*Mary Poppins Opens the Door*). *See* Clump, Sarah

SCOBIE HAGUE (*The Watch House*). *See* Hague, Scobie (Major)

SCRUBB, EUSTACE CLARENCE, a character in C[live] S[taples] Lewis's* *The Voyage of the "Dawn Treader"*, The Silver Chair*,* and *The Last Battle*.* He is the son of Harold and Alberta Scrubb; he is the cousin of Edmund, Lucy, Peter, and Susan Pevensie****. Eustace almost deserves his name, for his is sulky, annoying, and completely distasteful. He has been raised by his parents to be up-to-date, unimaginative, and soulless. When Lucy and Edmund come to stay with the Scrubbs, Eustace takes every chance he can to tease them about their visits to Narnia*, a land of talking beasts and marvelous creatures; when he and they are pulled into the land he makes himself quite unpopular on board the *Dawn Treader*, the ship that picks them up. Eustace insults everyone and everything and complains when things do not go his way. When the ship puts in at Dragon Island to reprovision, Eustace comes upon a dragon's hoard and, putting on one of the bracelets and sleeping on the treasure, he becomes a dragon himself. So lonely does Eustace become, cut off from the human race, that he does all he can to make himself popular among those he travels with, and he so enjoys the result that when Aslan*, Narnia's mystical lion-protector, changes him back into a boy, Eustace is a changed person. He becomes well liked during his adventures in Narnia and has subsequent adventures there. With Jill Pole*, a fellow student at the progressive school Eustace attends, he finds Rilian*, a lost prince; he later is whisked into Narnia after he is killed in a railway accident, and helps Tirian*, its king, in the last battle of that land. When the battle is over, Eustace goes into Aslan's country to be happy there forever.

SCRUPNOR, SQUIRE, a character in *The Wizard in the Tree*, by Lloyd Alexander*. This rapacious man stops at nothing to gain power and wealth; he murders Squire Sorrel so as to inherit his lands, and then decides to turn the tenants out of their homes so that he can mine the coal beneath the land. Scrupnor's plans go awry, however, after a notary tests the sincerity of his efforts to find Sorrel's killer by having the squire sign an agreement to give his inheritance to the person who hands over the murderer. Scrupnor tries to keep the inheritance by framing Arbican*, an enchanter, for the murder; when Arbican escapes and is recaptured by Bolt*, Scrupnor's gamekeeper, the squire murders Bolt to keep him from claiming the reward. Scrupnor is finally annihilated when he tries to grab Arbican when the wizard's powers are at their peak; he vanishes, and all that are left are one boot and his waistcoat, still smouldering.

SEA RAT, THE, a character in Kenneth Grahame's* *The Wind in the Willows*. He is an adventurous animal who journeys up and down the coast from Europe to Africa, enjoying the exotic ports along the way. Though he tries to settle down, he cannot. The Sea Rat has a fey quality; when he meets the Water Rat*, he seems to enchant the latter with his stories of exotic lands and, literally entranced, the Water Rat agrees to follow him. Only forcible restraint by the Mole* keeps the Rat from following the wanderer.

SEARCH FOR DELICIOUS, THE. Natalie Babbitt. Illus. Natalie Babbitt. New York: Farrar, Straus and Giroux, 1969. 167 pp. American.

Long, long ago, when the earth was a lovelier place, a dwarf*, digging, finds a spring. He and the other dwarfs build a rockhouse over the spring, with a door that opens or closes whenever a whistle* is blown. As the spring floods the valley and it becomes a lake, Ardis*, a little mermaid, comes to it; she is given the whistle and a doll and plays happily with both. One day a man finds the whistle and blows it, shutting the doll in the rockhouse, and he takes the whistle away. Unable to get her doll, Ardis haunts the lake and weeps for it. Years pass and people no longer believe in her or the dwarfs.

The king's prime minister is writing a dictionary but cannot find a definition for "delicious" that all can agree on. His naive assistant, twelve-year-old Vaungaylen* (Gaylen) is sent to poll the kingdom. At the first town, a free-for-all erupts, for Hemlock*, the queen's brother, is riding through the kingdom, talking against the king, and the people are excited. After the poll is done, Gaylen hears of the legendary woldweller* living in the forest and seeks him out. The old man reveals that Hemlock visits him, trying to discover how to find Ardis and the dwarfs. Hemlock rides up and sends Gaylen away. Night is coming, and Gaylen shares a fire with a minstrel who sings of Ardis and gives to him a key before they part the next day. Pressing on, Gaylen comes to a farm, where he learns that Hemlock has been spreading the story that the poll will be used by the king to make new laws about eating. Gaylen is growing disillusioned about the world and its inhabitants when he comes to a neat little cottage where a widow gives him food and a place to sleep that night; her crow talks of whistles and keys and Ardis's lost doll. Comforted by the woman's warmth, Gaylen sleeps well that night.

At the next town, though, Gaylen finds the people unhappy because of the riot at the first town, and during the polling a fight breaks out, forcing Gaylen to leave. He gets a message via a messenger bird from the palace; the kingdom is splitting. Gaylen rides hard for the next town, hoping to get there before Hemlock, but his horse goes down because of a patch of loose stones. It is raining, and Gaylen take refuge in a cave, and when Hemlock rides into the cave and into its dark recesses, Gaylen follows. Hemlock has come to see the dwarfs who live here; he wants them to make him a new whistle so that he can lock Ardis in the rockhouse, where she cannot interfere with him and he can take over the kingdom. But the dwarfs cannot make another whistle, so he leaves. Discovered by the three dwarfs, Gaylen trades them his last three apples for a new shoe for his horse. The walls of their cave are beautifully carved with scenes of the new-formed world, among them a figure of Ardis with her whistle; Gaylen recognizes it as his key and decides to give it back to her.

When he leaves the dwarfs, Gaylen meets a shepherd, from whom he learns about the war among the people in the kingdom. When Gaylen is driven out of the next town, he decides that he has had enough of everyone; he will live in the woods and mountains and see no one again. The next day, feeling very alone, Gaylen comes upon the winds, which tell him that the streams are drying up. He soon discovers that it is true. That night Gaylen overhears two men sent by Hemlock to build a dam across Ardis's lake and thus dry up the streams flowing from it, making the people fight out of fear. Though he has given up on humans, Gaylen feels that he must help; he rides to the lake and watches helplessly as it is dammed. He does not know what to do and feels even more helpless when he receives a message that the king is coming to the lake, where Hemlock and his men are waiting. Exhausted, Gaylen sleeps.

When he wakes it is night, and Ardis is there. She tells him about her doll and Gaylen makes her promise to destroy the dam if he gives her the key. At dawn, however, the dam is still intact. The king and the people of the kingdom come, and Hemlock exhorts them to kill the king; if they do so, he will open the dam. Suddenly, though, the dam breaks and collapses, and Hemlock is hurt. The thirsty people drink and agree that the water is delicious—the best definition of the word. Safely home, Gaylen decides that he will go out into the world again sometimes, though he likes it at home, and when he grows up he keeps that promise.

SEBASTIAN, the title character in Lloyd Alexander's* *The Marvelous Misadventures of Sebastian**. This young man is Fourth Fiddle in Baron Purn-Hessel's orchestra until he accidentally makes a fool of Count Lobelieze*, the Royal Treasurer of Hamelin-Loring*. Lobelieze demands that Sebastiain be sent away. Reluctantly, Sebastian leaves his sheltered life and makes his way through a sometimes hostile world. Here he finds friends and adventure as he helps a runaway princess, Isabel Charlotte Theodora Fredericka* (Isabel), to regain her rightful place as ruler of Hamelin-Loring. Along the way Sebastian discovers as he plays a magical violin* that music is very important to him. He also fall in love with Isabel. Though she wants him to share her throne, Sebastian goes on his own journey to learn more about music and how to write down the tunes he hears in his heart. Once he has proved himself, he will come back to Isabel.

SECOND JUNGLE BOOK, THE. *See* Jungle books, the

SECRET OF NIMH, THE. *See Mrs. Frisby and the Rats of NIMH*

SEELEM a character in *The Three Mulla-mulgars**, by Walter de la Mare*. He is the brother of Assasimmon, Prince of the Valleys of Tishnar*; he is the mate of Mutta-matutta and the father of Thumma*, Thimbulla*, and Umman-odda*. Seelem is a Mulla-mulgar, or monkey of royal blood. Having grown up in luxury, he wearies of this and leaves the Valleys of Tishnar with his servant. Eventually he comes to the Forest of Munza-mulgar and, falling ill, is nursed back to health by Mutta-matutta, by whom he has three sons. They live together contentedly for thirteen years, but Seelem comes to miss his brother, the Prince, and sets off again for the Valleys of Tishnar. Behind him he leaves several objects of value, among them the Wonderstone* of Tishnar*, with instructions that his sons are to take these things and follow him if he does not return. Seelem does not go back to the Forest. Painfully he makes his way to the Valleys, startling the Moona-mulgars* with his strange disappearance and leaving the Fishing-mulgars a fire that they keep alive to cook their fish on. When his sons come to the Valleys of Tishnar, they find there the gun he had taken away with him and know that he has arrived there before them.

SEFTON OLDKNOW (the Green Knowe books). *See* Oldknow, Sefton

SELIDOR, a place in the Earthsea trilogy*, by Ursula K. LeGuin*. This large island lies in the westernmost part of Earthsea*; so far is it that it has become a catchphrase for something so far away as to be almost mythical. Lovely, desolate Selidor was the site of the great battle between Orm and Erreth-Akbe*. Orm's descendant, Orm Embar*, a great dragon, lives here. To Selidor comes Ged*, a mage, with his companion, Arren*, to seek the source of the leaching out of magic and vitality from Earthsea.

SEPTIMUS BLENKINSOP (*The Phoenix and the Carpet*). *See* Blenkinsop, Septimus

SERENA, a character in *The Trumpet of the Swan**, by E[lwyn] B[rooks] White*. She becomes the wife of Louis*. Serena is a beautiful trumpeter swan. Though she likes Louis's looks, Serena cannot fall in love with him because he cannot talk. They meet again some time later in a Philadelphia zoo, and here Louis wins her heart, for he has acquired a trumpet with which to communicate. So that the head keeper in charge of birds will let them leave, Louis and Serena agree to donate a cygnet whenever the zoo needs one. Louis and Serena live happily together, traveling and raising their cygnets.

SERRET, a character in *A Wizard of Earthsea**, by Ursula K. LeGuin*. She is the daughter of the Lord of Re Albi and an enchantress from Osskil*, and the wife of Benderesk, Lord of the Court of the Terrenon. On Gont* she meets Ged*, the young apprentice of Ogion*, a sorcerer, and teases him into learning the spell to summon the dead, which later has dire consequences for the young man. Serret grows up to marry the Lord of the Court of the Terrenon on Osskil and becomes enslaved to the Terrenon*, a stone in which an evil spirit is imprisoned. In trying to tempt Ged into using the stone, Serret provokes her husband's jealousy and must flee the castle. She is killed by the Terrenon's creatures, which her husband sends after her.

SHASTA. *See* Cor

SHERE KHAN, a tiger in Rudyard Kipling's* Jungle books*. He is also called Lungri, the Lame One, for he has been lame in one foot from birth. Therefore he goes after only the easier game: cattle and man. Usually Shere Khan hunts near the Waingunga River, but when he angers the villagers there, he changes his hunting ground. That night he attacks a woodcutter's family, and the child toddles away and into a wolf's den; enraged that the wolves will not give the baby to him, Shere Khan swears to have it eventually. But he is thwarted at every turn. Ingratiating himself with the easily flattered young wolves, Shere Khan brings them over to his side and again makes his bid when Mowgli* is eleven or twelve. But the boy has fire and he singes Shere Khan's coat, driving the tiger away. After his coat regrows, when Mowgli has gone to the village to live with men, Shere Khan again seeks to kill the boy, but Mowgli uses the village cattle to trample him to death. He spreads Shere Khan's hide on the wolves' council rock, as he had promised he would.

SHIFT, a character in *The Last Battle**, by C[live] S[taples] Lewis*. This clever talking ape lives near Cauldron Pool in the western part of Narnia*. So clever is Shift that he has his neighbor, a donkey named Puzzle*, completely under his thumb; Puzzle will do anything for Shift, for he believes that the ape always knows what is best. Shift is very clever with his hands, as he proves when he finds a lion skin in Cauldron Pool and makes it into a coat for Puzzle. Persuading Puzzle that he must wear the skin and pretend to be Aslan*, Narnia's great lion-protector, Shift very soon has all he wants and milks the situation for all it is worth. He brings into his scheme Rishda*, a man from Calormen*, and together they exploit Narnia as best they can, paving the way for a Calormene invasion. Shift tries to become a man, of sorts, dressing like one and learning to drink like one; such a drunkard does he become that Rishda soon has Shift completely under his control. Claiming that Aslan and Tash*, the god of the Calormenes, are one and the same, Shift slurs their names into Tashlan and incidentally calls Tash himself into Narnia. He is one of Tash's first victims, for the god snaps him up.

SHINY WALL, a place in *The Water-babies**, by Charles Kingsley*. Shiny Wall is a great ice floe with no gaps in it. Tom*, a water-baby* trying to get to the Other-end-of-Nowhere*, must dive under the floe. Beyond Shiny Wall is Peacepool, where the whales go to hide from men; in this pool sits Mother Carey*, causing the creatures of the sea to create themselves.

SHIR KHAN, a character in *The First Two Lives of Lukas-Kasha**, by Lloyd Alexander*. This robber chief and his band pillage towns and caravans in Abadan* and prey on solitary travelers, selling some into slavery. When Shir Khan's men capture Lukas-Kasha*, the young man tricks them into thinking that their chief is holding back for himself a valuable ruby captured in an earlier raid. Furious, one of the robbers kills Shir Khan.

SHUGDAD MIRZA (*The First Two Lives of Lukas-Kasha*). See Mirza, Shugdad

SIBBY. *See* Walpole, Hepsibah Sagacity

SIDNEY PLATTER (*The Borrowers Aloft; The Borrowers Avenged*). *See* Platter, Sidney

SIGNS OF THE LIGHT, six objects in *The Dark Is Rising** and *Silver on the Tree**, by Susan Cooper*. They are in the shape of a quartered circle. In each of the six ages of the history of men, a Sign has been shaped and hidden. Each is of and for a different element or material: the Sign of Iron is of non-rusting iron; the Sign of Bronze is of bronze; the Sign of Wood is also called the Sign of Learning and is of rowan, which must be renewed each century; the Sign of Fire is of seven colors of gold, twisted together and set with gems, and on it is engraved "Liht Mec Heht Gewyrcan," or "The Light ordered that I should be made"; the Sign of Stone is of flint, formed in its pattern naturally, not carved; and the Sign of Water is of translucent glass, engraved with water creatures and waves and gleaming like mother-of-pearl. In the twentieth century the Signs are found by Will Stanton*, one of the Old Ones, the forces of the Light. They are linked in a great circle by John Wayland Smith. Later Merriman Lyon*, another Old One, takes them into the past to help King Arthur*, but Arthur does not have them long enough to help. In the final struggle between the Dark and the Light, Barnabas, Jane, and Simon Drew***, Merriman, Will, and John Rowlands* each take a Sign and hold it against the Dark, forming a barrier around the midsummer tree* until it blossoms and its flowers can be used to banish the Dark. This done, the Signs burn into nothing and vanish.

SILER, RAY, a character in *The Watchers**, by Jane Louise Curry*. When his mother dies and his father remarries, Ray cannot get along with his step-mother, so he is sent to his aunt and uncle in Twilly's Green Hollow*. Bitter and alienated, Ray is intent only on getting back home, so when Russell Boyd Moar* (Arbie) tells him that it might prove profitable for the boy if he keeps his eyes open for anything unusual about the Hollow or those who live there, Ray obliges. When he finds what seems to be a huge fossil snake in the family mine, this seems to be just what he is looking for. Ray finds more than he bargained for, however, for he is soon caught up in an ancient drama; in fourth-century America, Ruan*, a young boy, betrays his people and leads Tekla*, the queen of Kanhuan*, to Tûl Isgrun*, where she sets free an ancient evil that is bound there. Ray realizes that he shares not only blood ties with Ruan but situational ties as well; Ruan brought Tekla to Tûl Isgrun in an attempt to buy his freedom, just as Ray hopes to use Arbie Moar to buy his way home. In Twilly's Green, Ray finds the love and sense of belonging that he needs, and he helps Delano Mattick* to protect the Hollow from Arbie and his men. Finally Ray helps to seal the evil force bound in the mine by destroying the shrine above it. Though his father has sent him a bus ticket home, Ray sends it back; he has found a place in Twilly's Green and he will stay here.

SILVER CHAIR, THE. C[live] S[taples] Lewis. Illus. Pauline Baynes. London: Geoffrey Bles, 1953. 217 pp. British.

On a dull autumn day Jill Pole* is crying behind the gym, having been bullied by some of the others at the experimental school she is attending. Eustace Clarence Scrubb*, another pupil, comes upon her and, in the course of the conversation, tells her of Narnia*, the magical land he had visited during the holidays. Interrupted by bullies, they run away along a stone wall and there find a door that opens into a rich, sun-filled landscape. Here Jill and Eustace wander, coming eventually to a cliff that seems miles high. Showing off because she has little fear of heights, Jill freezes on the edge of the cliff and Eustace, trying to rescue her, falls over the edge. Suddenly a bright lion is there, and it begins to blow. Eustace stops falling and floats away, borne by the lion's breath.

Upset, Jill does not notice when the lion leaves. She is thirsty, however, and when she finds a stream, discovers the lion, Aslan*, in the way. He invites her to drink and, though frightened, she does. She also admits to Aslan that she was the cause of Eustace's fall and learns that the lion has blown him to Narnia. Aslan has called them to find the prince, Rilian*, who has disappeared; Jill is given four signs to remember and follow: that Eustace is to greet the old friend he meets in Narnia; that they are to journey north to an ancient ruined city; that they are to do what the writing on a stone in that city tells them to; and that they will know the prince because he will be the one to ask them to do something in Aslan's name. The lion blows Jill to Narnia; it is a pleasant journey.

She lands at sunset at a castle by the sea and watches as an old king boards a ship and sails away. Eustace learns from Glimfeather*, an owl, that the king was Caspian X*, a friend of Eustace's, and the boy is upset to find him so old. Jill is upset because they have muffed the first sign. They are taken to the castle. That night Glimfeather flies Jill and Eustace to a meeting of owls in an abandoned tower, where the two learn that Rilian vanished after becoming enchanted with a lady dressed in green, whom he met while hunting the green serpent that killed his mother. Many champions have sought him, but none have returned. Now Caspian has gone to find Aslan, hoping for his help. The owls fly Jill and Eustace north to the marshes, there to meet Puddleglum*, the Marsh-wiggle* who will accompany them.

Sober, steady Puddleglum is comforting to be with as the children journey north into the country of the giants, just missing, once, becoming casualties in a giants' game of cock-shies. They come to rugged country and follow an ancient road across the bridge, on the other side of which they meet a knight in black armor and a lady dressed in green, who are riding toward them. She tells the three that the road leads to Harfang*, where gentle giants live, and that they should stay there, telling the giants that "She of the Green Kirtle" has sent them for the Autumn Feast. Eager for warmth and good food after their days of hard, cold travel, Jill and Eustace persuade Puddleglum to go to Harfang. When they arrive, a blizzard is raging and the three make their way across a strangely flat landscape crisscrossed with deep ditches; exhausted, they reach the castle, where they are warmly welcomed. That night Jill dreams of Aslan, who, finding that she cannot repeat the four signs, shows her, from the window, the words "UNDER ME."

The next day the three see from her window that the flat land they had crossed the night before was a pavement in the ruined city, with the words "UNDER ME" carved into it. Realizing that they have missed the third sign, the three know that they must go under the pavement but must first get out of the castle. By acting like the children the giants think they are—an art which Puddleglum completely lacks—they learn that a door from the scullery to the outside is always left open. Waiting for a chance to escape, Jill discovers that she, Eustace, and Puddleglum are to form the main course for the Autumn Feast. Sobered, they slip out and are forced to hide in a hole when they are spotted. Groping in the dark tunnel, the three slide to a lower level, where they are found by the Earthmen*, somber, odd-looking gnomes who take them across a dark sea to an underground city.

Here they meet a handsome young man, the knight in black armor. The knight admits that he remembers nothing of what his life was like before he came to Underland* and knows nothing of Narnia or of Rilian. Every night, he tells them, he goes mad because of a spell, which will be broken when he is made king of a land in Overland, the lands that lie above the surface. This time will be soon, for the tunnel they are digging to the surface is almost done. Unwilling to be taken to a prison, Jill, Eustace, and Puddleglum talk the knight into letting them stay while his mad fit is upon him and agree to promise not to free him, no matter what he says. Hidden from the Earthmen, they watch as he is bound to a strange silver chair and are horrified at the awful fit that comes upon him. Despite his entreaties, they do not free him until he asks them in Aslan's name, for this is the fourth sign. Immediately he destroys the chair. He is Rilian, and he remembers everything.

Suddenly, in comes the Queen of Underland*, the lady in green who sent them to Harfang. Using a magic powder and enchanting music, she works to convince them that Narnia is only a dream. But stubborn Puddleglum stamps his foot on the magic fire, troubling the enchantment, and he breaks the spell with some well-chosen words. The enraged queen turns into a serpent and tries to kill Rilian, but is killed instead. Having dressed Puddleglum's foot, they slip out to the stables for the horses. The sea is rising; without the queen's spell Underland is being destroyed. They will ride to the tunnel and escape that way.

As they go through the city, the Earthmen try to keep out of the way, for all they want to do is get back to Bism*, their homeland, and they are afraid that Rilian will stop them. Overjoyed that he will let them go home, the Earthmen guide the party to the road leading to the tunnel. On the way they pass a chasm into glorious, tempting Bism. The ecstatic Earthmen hurl themselves into it and it closes. The travelers are left alone to follow the lamplit tunnel, until the lamps go out and they reach the end. They come out in Narnia.

The next day Jill and Eustace follow Rilian to the king's castle to meet the returning Caspian. Just after he greets his son, Caspian dies. Jill and Eustace are blown by Aslan to his mountain, near a stream where Caspian lies in the water, to be revived and rejuvenated by a drop of Aslan's blood. He leaps from the water, hale and healthy. It is time for Jill and Eustace to go home. Caspian, who wants a glimpse of their world, gets it, for Aslan breaks through the wall near the school, and lies with his back to England as Caspian, Jill, and Eustace chastise the school bullies. Then Caspian leaves, the gap is closed, and Jill and Eustace quietly take their places in school.

In England, the school is investigated because the head of it seems to be crazy, insisting that she saw a great lion and three strange figures, and she loses her position. School becomes much better. In Narnia, Rilian buries his father and the people of Narnia go down into the cool caves on hot days and sail on Underland's sea.

SILVER ON THE TREE. Susan Cooper. New York: Atheneum, 1977. 269 pp. American.

Warning visions come to Will Stanton*, the youngest of the Old Ones, the forces of good—visions of ancient terrors that mean that the Dark is gathering strength. His older brother, who has been abroad in the military, has been entrusted with messages from the Old Ones in the south and the Caribbean— they are ready. That night Will suddenly finds himself in the past, with King Arthur* and Merriman Lyon* (Merry), his trusted adviser. Will is to help Arthur as well as his own world by getting the six Signs of the Light*, which he had gathered in an earlier adventure, and using them to call the Old Ones together. Back in his own time, Will is not sure how to get to where the Signs are hidden and get them. Going into a picture, he experiences the hiding of the Signs in Roman times and manages to transport himself to the twentieth century, when the place is being excavated. Here he gets the Signs. Using them, Will calls the Old Ones. The Lady*, however, the most powerful, is too weak; when the mountains sing she will come. The Old Ones fade away, Merry takes the Signs to help Arthur in his battle, and Will goes home.

When Will goes to the mountains in Wales, he uses a hunting horn* to call Simon, Barnabas (Barney), and Jane Drew***, who, though not Old Ones, have been instrumental before in the fight against the Dark. Bran Davies*, Arthur's son, also comes. Will explains what they must do, and they decide to start their search for the Lady at a lake where Arthur is supposed to have routed a water monster. This lake has an echo, and when Will sings here it seems as if the mountains are singing. To Jane, who is apart from the rest, the Lady comes, and she gives the girl a final message, about a crystal sword to be found in a lost land, before she fades. Suddenly a monster comes from the lake and tries to get the Lady's message from Jane, but Bran sends it back. As a result, Will is forced to reveal Bran's parentage.

As they sit on the hill above it, they realize that the lost land of the message must refer to the place flooded centuries ago when the dykes had burst. Suddenly the city appears, with a road leading to it. Bran and Will go down to the road, and before the Drews' eyes, they, the city, and the road fade. The three children find themselves driven by polecats to meet Blodwen and John Rowlands*, who are to take them back to where they are staying. They stop in the village, and here John reveals to them events that had taken place a year ago, that had involved Will, Bran, and the Grey King*, a force of the Dark. As they stand on the old wharf, they find themselves in the nineteenth century. A returning ship reports the sinking of another ship, and the people confront its builder, who had built other ships that have sunk. In the resulting struggle, Simon is thrown into the water and is saved by Merry, who sends the shipbuilder back to the Dark before he and the children go back to the twentieth century. The Dark had put Simon in peril so that Merry would save him; now Merry goes to help Will and Bran.

Bran and Will are in the strange, empty city. Here they meet a man who sends them on in a coach. They are followed and passed by the Black Rider*, a lord of the Dark, riding with others; the boys follow the riders into a park, and after confrontation the Black Rider leaves with another, the White Rider*. In the waters of a fountain the boys see a king with Eirias*, the crystal sword. The king has taken refuge in a castle by the sea, and the boys journey there, losing their horses when the beasts are frightened by the skeleton of a horned horse; the petals of a may tree make the living skeleton fall apart. Encouraged by a vision Will has of Merry in a mirror, the boys walk toward the castle, meeting along the way the White Rider, who fails to tempt them to go back. Coming to the castle, they manage to get past the wheel that bars the door. The despairing king does not give Bran the sword until he realizes that he has seen the boy in a dream. When they take Eirias, the dykes break and the sea floods in, bringing a small boat that takes them back to the beach in their own time.

Jane and Simon, in the meantime, have found a railroad track and are surprised when the train stops before them and they are taken on by Merry. John and Blodwen Rowlands are there, too; the train is filled with people from all lands and all centuries. Dark riders keep pace with it, unable to attack it because one of their kind is on board. After the train stops for Will, Barney, and Bran, it plunges into darkness, and Merry, Will and Bran confront Blodwen, their hostage of the Dark, who is the White Rider. She is sent off the train.

The train becomes a fleet of boats, and they sail down a river. On the shore Arthur's battle is being won. The king comes to Will and gives him the Signs of the Light. They sail on. Suddenly the Black Rider appears and challenges Bran's right to be there. When the Lady appears and declares that the challenge holds, John Rowlands is chosen to judge. Though the Dark tries to use his love of Blodwen to influence him, John judges that Bran belongs in the twentieth century, with those he loves, not the earlier century where he had been born and where the Dark wants him to be.

Suddenly they come to their objective, the midsummer tree*, where whoever plucks a blooming branch can drive out rival powers. As the first bud opens, the Dark comes, as do the six Sleepers*, with Herne*, the leader of the Wild Hunt*. As the Sleepers chase away part of the Dark's forces, Herne waits. Simon, Barney, Jane, Merry, Bran, and Will stand in a circle around the tree, each holding a Sign against the Dark. As the last flower on the tree opens, John takes Bran's Sign so that the boy can cut a branch. Merry catches the branch and flings it into the air, where it becomes a bird vanishing into the sky. The Riders fall out of time and vanish; the six Signs burn themselves into nothing. Arthur's boat sails down from the sky for the Lady and the Old Ones. The Lady sends John home, where he will forget Blodwen's true nature and mourn for her, for she has died in his world. Their task done, the Lady and the Old Ones get onto the boat. Will and Merry will join them in time. Though Arthur asks him, Bran declines the offer to be with his father; he will stay in his own world and time because he belongs here, though it means that he will be mortal. The ship leaves and Merry brings the children back to their own world. Good and evil things will happen here, he tells them, but they are on their own and must have the courage to combat evil themselves. He leaves them, following Arthur's ship, and as he does he makes all but Will forget what has happened to them; no hint of their dealings with the Light and the Dark will come to them except in their dreams.

SIMON DREW (*Over Sea, Under Stone; Greenwitch; Silver on the Tree*). *See* Drew, Simon

SIMON RASTALL (*The Change-Child*). *See* Rastall, Simon

SIONA, a character in *Over the Sea's Edge**, by Jane Louise Curry*. She lives in twelfth-century Abáloc* and is among those captured and taken to Cibotlán* to be sacrificed to the Sun Serpent (Katóa*). After their escape, Siona and the others make their way home, encountering along the way Madauc* and his men. Siona later marries Dewi ap Ithil*; they have one daughter.

SKYSTONES, twelve powerful stones in Jane Louise Curry's* *The Wolves of Aam**. These stones were found at the beginning of the world under Uval Garath, the Opal Mountain. Each stone represents a power and each was given to a prince of the Aldar*, representatives of the twelve Aldarin peoples in the Great Dance that celebrated the first rising of the sun. The twelve stones are Lisar, the Sunstone; Nirim, the Worldstone; Mirelidar*, the Moonstone; Lurizel; Oniyel; Tionel; Otalidar; Aturil; Aalenor; Hammurel; Almiron; and Azilar. Nirim holds the power of the quickening of life. Lisar holds the power of the sun, and when it was stolen the glaciers in the north slowly crept south. The theft of Lisar also caused the Aldar to take nine of the other stones beyond the reach of men: Nirim was left, only to vanish during a ceremony from the hands of Kell, later known as Lek*, a conjuror; Mirelidar, which once lay in the City of the Moon Under the Mountain*, came first into the possession of power-hungry Lord Naghar* and then to Runner-to-the-Sky's-Edge*. The twelve stones give their names to twelve stars and the twelve months.

SLEEPERS, six warriors in Susan Cooper's* *The Grey King** and *Silver on the Tree**. They sleep in an enchanted sleep beside Lake Tal y Llyn, in Wales. These six warriors of the Light, the forces of good, are awakened in the twentieth century by Will Stanton*, one of the forces of the Light, who plays a golden harp* near the lake. When the warriors ride their horses through the air, they meet and salute Bran Davies*, the son of King Arthur*, before they ride away. The Sleepers are joined by the Wild Hunt* at the last battle between the Dark and the Light, and together they harry the Dark until its final defeat.

SLEEPERS, THE. Jane Louise Curry. Illus. Gareth Floyd. New York: Harcourt, Brace and World, 1968. 255 pp. American.

When their mother remarries, Jennifer and Henry Peter (H. P.) Huntington** take a trip to Scotland with their archaeologist uncle, Gerald Rishanger*. There they meet old friends—Hugh Lewis* and Gillian Peresby*—and help their uncle and his colleague try out a new sonic probe that will reveal buried objects. According to legend, Arthur* and his knights sleep near the area where they are searching. There, too, was the place where Thomas the Rhymer met the Queen of Elfland beneath the Eildon Tree*. Jennifer is especially interested, because once, while she was painting on a bridge, a mysterious boy came up to her and told her that when her brother stood beneath the Eildon Tree, he should listen for the ringing. The brooch the boy wore was identical to an ancient one found at a nearby dig.

The sonic probe locates a mysterious spot and the group decides to dig. Before they do they break for lunch, and Uncle Gerald has a strange encounter with a dark lady dressed in green and riding a white horse. It is, Gillian tells Jennifer, her sister, Ellen Peresby*, who is trying to get Gerald to leave because his digging may set into motion an old, tragic family prophecy. Undaunted, Gerald and the others dig and find a broken, inscribed stone beneath the roots of an ancient tree. Standing in the pit, H. P. hears a bell ringing and, digging, finds a lovely bronze bell. Taking it to the house, he cleans it up and discovers the words "RING ME" inscribed on it in Latin. When he does, the sound is too lovely to bear. It is sent to the British Museum to be studied.

Because the area is due to be quarried, any artifacts will have to be discovered quickly, but the digging waits for a month while the children go back to London for school. During this time, they discover an old tradition that if a certain bell is rung at an abbey near the dig, Arthur and his warriors will wake. The school holidays find the children back at the dig in Scotland, eager to find what lies there. They have competition; a research committee ostensibly looking for the remains of a Roman villa has established itself nearby and is using heavy machinery to go after its prize.

One day, while others are in town, Jennifer looks up from a drawing she is making while sitting beside the remains of the tree, to discover herself beneath the tree that was, and here she meets Myrddin*—Merlin—the boy she met on the bridge now grown into an old man. Though she is just as suddenly back in her own time, Jennifer finds that Myrddin is still with her; the Eildon Tree was the tree in which he was imprisoned by Nimiane* so long ago. He wants Jennifer to ring the bell to wake Arthur and, finding that she does not have it, commands her to dig in the pit instead. She breaks through into a passage and is understandably alarmed when Binky*, the dog, falls into the cave. When the others return, they go into the passage to rescue Binky, while Hugh's mother stands off M. E. Draut, one of the members of the research committee, who is just a little too curious about what the group might have discovered.

The children find Binky at the end of the passage, scratching at a wooden door that only H. P. can open. In the chamber beyond they come upon a scene that is both awesome and touching; a motley group of small, shabby men in battle-stained gear sits sleeping around a table on which are eleven glorious objects and a guttering candle. Nearby sleep their shaggy, pony-sized horses. Here Artair* and his warriors sleep until they are needed. The children realize that the treasures are what the research committee is after; they hear above them the sound of the drill it is using.

When they return through the passage, Myrddin explains that the treasures they saw are the *Brenhin Dlyseu**, the Thirteen Treasures of Prydein, which should have been carried to safety long ago. The bell they had found is the Bell of Rhûn*, one of the treasures, and because they must wake the sleepers to save them, H. P. and Gillian go to London to steal it out of the British Museum. Myrddin is a bit suspicious of Gillian and her sister, Ellen, for they are descended from Nimiane's family, but he senses that Ellen is not malicious, that someone is using her. He sends Jennifer to use the Treasures to trick Ellen into saying the spell that disenchants him. An examination reveals that Artair's ring, the Ring of Luned*, is missing.

At the museum, H. P. and Gillian get themselves locked in after closing and have little trouble stealing the Bell and leaving with the museum staff. Meanwhile, Myrddin and some of the others spy on the research committee, and Myrddin discovers there an old enemy: Margan*—Fata Morgana—who plans to kill Artair and his men and take the Treasures which will give her power over Britain. Her son, Medraut*—M. E. Draut—already wears the Ring.

When H. P. and Gillian return to the dig, they ring the Bell and the sleepers wake. Artair explains how Medraut had gotten the Ring in the last battle they fought; Medraut and his mother must have slept somewhere out of time, as Artair and his men did. Now they will ride again into the battle, bearing certain of the Treasures with them, and regain the Ring. Jennifer and H. P. offer them the venerable family houseboat in London so that the men and the Thirteen Treasures can sail to a place of safety to wait until they are truly needed. The children take the rest of the Treasures to London as Artair and his men prepare for battle.

In London, the children put the Treasures safely aboard the boat and wait through the night for Artair and his warriors. At last they come, riding soundlessly and triumphantly through an unearthly fog. Past and present merge as the children watch the ghostly procession; they see the men reach their boat and set sail on a long-ago morning. Then the time becomes the present again. They know that Britain's greatest treasures are all safe.

SMAUG, a character in *The Hobbit**, by J[ohn] R[onald] R[euel] Tolkien*. This red-gold dragon is greedier and wickeder than most, and when gold became scarce in the north, he had flown south and taken the treasure beneath the Lonely Mountain, killing all the dwarves* who had lived there. For centuries Smaug had lain in his lair, guarding his treasure and making a few forays in search of food; maidens from a nearby village seem to have been a particular favorite. His years of sleeping on his hoard have made him knowledgeable about it and he knows each and every piece. It has also given him particularly fine armor for his underbelly, which has become encrusted with gold and jewels over the years, except for one tiny spot. When Thorin Oakenshield* brings his dwarves to the Lonely Mountain to recover their treasure, Smaug suspects that the inhabitants of nearby Lake-town* are behind the quest. He attacks and burns Lake-town but is himself killed by Bard, who shoots an arrow into Smaug's unprotected patch. The dragon and, later, his bones, lie in Long Lake for many years, with the jewels that fall from his body.

SMOIT, a character in Lloyd Alexander's* *The Black Cauldron**, *Taran Wanderer**, and *The High King**. He is the king of Cantrev Cadiffor, one of the small kingdoms in the southern part of Prydain*. Huge, red-haired Smoit is a hearty warrior always ready for battle, if battle is needed. Though he tries to be a good king, Smoit feels better when he has a sword in his hand than he does without one, and he is not much of a thinking man but is wise enough to know it. Smoit takes part in several ventures to thwart Arawn*, an evil lord, in his bid to control Prydain. During one adventure Smoit's castle is taken over for a time by Magg*, one of Arawn's minions. Smoit is also forced to kill Morgant*, a king who seeks power himself.

SNOWBELL, a character in *Stuart Little**, by E[lwyn] B[rooks] White*. He is the white cat living with the Little family. Being a cat, Snowbell has difficulty liking Stuart Little*, a member of the family who looks like a mouse. When Stuart, trying to prove his strength to Snowbell, gets rolled up in a windowshade, Snowbell tries to make it look as if he crawled down a mousehole, greatly upsetting the Littles. Later Margalo*, a bird the Littles take in, proves a great temptation for Snowbell, who one night tries to eat her and is thwarted by Stuart. Though Snowbell comes to feel that he should not harm Margalo, who is a guest of the Littles, he does help another cat plot to get Margalo, who flees to save her life.

SOLOMON CAW (*Peter Pan in Kensington Gardens*). *See* Caw, Solomon

SOMNOLENTIA, a place in *The Magic City**, by E[dith] Nesbit Bland*. This city in northern Polistarchia* was once called Briskford because its people were always bustling. Through the town ran a river which the citizens worked hard to keep clear of the gold that choked it, so that they could use the water to irrigate their fields. One day, however, the Great Sloth* came to the city, and the citizens were so impressed by it that they built the temple of gold it asked for and held it in great honor, singing choric songs to it. Because of their neglect of the river, it became choked and the fields grew so dry that only pineapples could be grown in them. Water had to be drawn from a well. The Sloth's influence was so great that all the citizens slept when it did (which was almost all the time). Such is the state of affairs when Philip Haldane* and Lucy Graham* enter the city to force the Sloth to keep busy all day. By tricking the Sloth into wishing for machinery it must then use all day long and rousing the citizens by reminding them of Halma, a great leader of their race, Philip and Lucy turn things around. The water the Sloth pumps with its machine is diverted into a channel and used to water the fields and wash the people (who had been washing in pineapple juice). The name of the town is changed back to Briskford, and those who call it by its old name are not allowed to wash with water for a week.

SONNY TAPP (*The Daybreakers*). *See* Tapp, Conway

SONS OF DON, THE, a race of men in the Chronicles of Prydain*, by Lloyd Alexander*. They are descended from the Children of Don, the sons of Lady Don and Belin, the King of the Sun. Early in Prydain's* history, the Sons of Don sailed to this land from the Summer Country* and helped the people of Prydain to withstand Arawn*, an evil lord. Now their descendants rule and protect Prydain from its capital of Caer Dathyl*. Math, the High King, is of the

House of Don, as is Gwydion*, his war leader. When Arawn is finally slain, the Sons of Don and their descendants leave Prydain and sail back to the Summer Country.

SOPHIA, a character in *Ben and Me** by Robert Lawson*. This mouse is married and has seven children. In the late eighteenth century, she lives with her family at the court at Versailles. But when her husband, through a conspiracy by the white mice of the court, is exiled to America, Sophia is forced to flee from the court, leaving her children, who are held captive beneath the queen's throne. Sophia takes refuge with Madame Brillon, a kind woman to whom Sophia acts as close friend and adviser. When she meets Amos*, a mouse-friend and adviser of Benjamin Franklin*, Sophia dazzles him with her brilliant mind and manners, and he leads an army of mice to rescue her children. Sophia and the children go to America, where Sophia's husband has made a success of himself, and they soon delight all with their charm and wit. Three of Sophia's children marry three of Amos's siblings.

SOPLI, a character in Ursula K. LeGuin's* *The Farthest Shore**. He is the son of Akanen. Sopli is the Dyer of Lorbanery*, an island in the south of Earthsea*, and is famous for his skills. Terrified of death, Sopli gives up his skill and goes mad seeking the way to eternal life that he sees offered by Cob*, a dead man seeking to pull the living world after him into the land of the dead. When his mother is given a new name and subsequently does not know him, Sopli leads Ged*, a mage seeking the source of the leaching of magic from Earthsea, and Arren*, his companion, to Obehol*. During the journey he manages to convince Arren that Ged is seeking their deaths. When they reach Obehol and are attacked while trying to land, Sopli becomes so frantic to land that he leaps into the water, an element he fears, and is drowned.

SPARROWHAWK. *See* Ged

SPECKFRESSER, MASTER, a character in *Time Cat**, by Lloyd Alexander*. This sharp-nosed, turkey-faced little man lives in Germany in 1600. Though witch-hunters are everywhere, Speckfresser tries to practice sorcery, longing to do the things sorcerers are said to do. After Mistress Ursulina* refuses to sell her land to him, Speckfresser denounces her as a witch, and Jason*, a boy who travels from the twentieth century with Gareth*, his cat, tries to blackmail him into retracting his statement. Speckfresser discovers how uncomfortable being denounced can be when he is arrested for his ''experiments'' and sentenced to die. With Ursulina, Jason, Gareth, and the town miller, Speckfresser escapes, and he travels with the miller and the old woman to a place where they can start anew.

SPILLER, DREADFUL (SPILLER), a character in Mary Norton's* *The Borrowers Afield*, *The Borrowers Afloat*, *The Borrowers Aloft*, and *The Borrowers Avenged*. He is a borrower*, one of the tiny people who live by "borrowing" what they need from humans. Of Spiller's background, little is known; all he remembers of his mother is that she once called him a "Dreadful Spiller," and he assumes that this is his name. He grows up in the outdoors, living off the land and becoming skillful at borrowing. Spiller is a fine hunter, using a bow with arrows made of pine needles and black-thorn. His clothes are made for him by Lupy*, another borrower; she makes for him a spring suit and a winter suit, and both become so stained and rubbed that they blend with the landscape, providing Spiller with camouflage. Spiller supplies several families of borrowers with food and other things. When Pod, Homily, and Arrietty Clock*** are forced to leave their home and take to the wilds, he brings them meat and helps them find safe places to live. Spiller is, like many country men, quiet and fairly unrefined, and he does not answer questions gracefully. Though he is secretive and concerned about staying near cover, Spiller is so taken with Arrietty that he offers to tell one of her human friends that she and the others have gone, so that the woman will not be upset, though he will do so only when it suits him.

SPOROS, a farandola* in *A Wind in the Door*, by Madeleine L'Engle*. His parent is Senex. Sporos is born in Yadah, a mitochondrion in one of the cells of Charles Wallace Murry's* body. Like all young farandolae, Sporos is a silver-blue, mouse-like creature able to move freely about the mitochondrion. And like all farandolae he eventually must Deepen, become mature, and add his voice to the song of creation that fills the universe. Because many of the farandolae of his generation are refusing to Deepen, Sporos becomes an unwilling pupil of Blajeny*, a Teacher. He is partnered with Calvin O'Keefe*, a human boy whom Sporos feels is beneath him; they accompany Meg Murry*, Charles's sister, Mr. Jenkins*, a human adult, and Proginoskes*, a cherubim, on a journey into Yadah. Desiring to be only a free-moving, pleasure-seeking farandola all his life, Sporos refuses to Deepen, for this would mean that he must stay rooted in one place all his life, unable to move as freely as he likes. In this decision he is backed by an Echthros*, a force of uncreation in the universe; by refusing to Deepen, Sporos and his generation of farandolae are interfering with the energy transfer taking place within the mitochondrion, and Charles is slowly dying from energy lack. Awed, however, when Mr. Jenkins almost sacrifices his own life to save Meg, Sporos and his friends Deepen to try to help Mr. Jenkins.

SPRING, a place in Natalie Babbitt's* *Tuck Everlasting*. This tiny spring may be a remnant of the way the earth was earlier intended to be; it confers on all who drink of its waters everlasting life. A great tree grows above it. In the late eighteenth century Angus, Mae, Jesse, and Miles Tuck**** and their horse drink from the spring and soon discover that not only do they not grow older, but that they cannot be hurt, either. Around 1881 a stranger* learns of the spring and obtains ownership of the woods where it lies, but he is killed before he can sell the waters of the spring. Sometime before 1950, the tree above the spring catches fire when lightning hits it, and the woods are bulldozed out.

SQUIRREL, a character in *Miss Hickory**, by Carolyn Sherwin Bailey*. Unable to plan ahead and incredibly absent-minded, Squirrel blames the overindulgence of his parents for his scatter-brained ways. He alarms Miss Hickory* by paying too close attention to her hickory-nut head. Having devoured his winter stores and forgotten where he buried the rest of the nuts he gathered in the fall, Squirrel is so hungry in the spring that he pulls off and eats Miss Hickory's head.

STABLE HILL, a place in *The Last Battle**, by C[live] S[taples] Lewis*. This hill stands in the Lantern Waste, near the Great River in Narnia*, a magical land. On it is a wooden stable; here Puzzle*, a donkey pretending to be Aslan*, the great lion-protector of Narnia, is kept, and here are held the councils at which he is shown and in which the Narnians get their instructions from Shift*, an ape pretending to be his mouthpiece. Stable Hill is the site of the last battle ever fought in Narnia. Its stable becomes much bigger on the inside than it is on the outside; its door is the entrance into Aslan's country. Through it come all who are allowed to stay in the country forever.

STANISLAWSKY, OSKAR, a character in Lucy Boston's* *The River at Green Knowe**. His father was shot by the Russians for his ideas. Orphaned, eleven-year-old Oskar became a refugee at the International Relief Society's Intermediate Hostel for Displaced Children, in England. When he spends the summer with Ida* and Hsu*, another orphaned refugee, at Green Knowe*, Oskar has many fantastic adventures on the river at Green Knowe. During the course of one adventure, he grows smaller and smaller as he builds a mouse nest, until he is two inches high; the next day Oskar is his normal height again. After that summer, Oskar is adopted by a family in Canada.

STANLEY, a character in Penelope Lively's* *The Voyage of QV 66**. He is a monkey. Quite full of himself and his own brilliance, when Stanley is disappointed he does not stay down for long. He enjoys his emotions by giving vent to them at all times. Being with Stanley can be exhausting but exhilirating. Stanley is one of the animals on Earth after all the humans have gone to Mars to avoid a world-wide flood. Because there are no other monkeys around, the other animals chase him or make remarks about him. Stanley is not quite sure, himself, what kind of animal he really is. When he meets Pal*, a dog, and Freda*, a cow, he talks them and three other animals into joining him on a trip to London, to find others like him. The trip is eventful and sometimes dangerous. Stanley, curious and irrespressible, discovers and improves upon Milton, invents music by playing a Stradivarius, and invents flying without wings by blowing up balloons and attaching them to a basket. This experiment endangers Pansy*, a kitten, who climbs into the basket and sails away, to be rescued only after much trouble. Once Stanley gets himself locked into a cage in the vaults of Barclay Bank and must himself be rescued. When he finally gets to London and meets other monkeys, Stanley is disappointed in them, for he finds them silly creatures, and he decides to stay with his friends, planning a journey to see what lies beyond the ocean.

STANTON, WILL, a character in Susan Cooper's* *The Dark Is Rising*, *Greenwitch*, *The Grey King*, and *Silver on the Tree*. He is the seventh son of a seventh son. Will is the son of Roger Stanton and his wife and the youngest brother of Tom, Stephen, Max, Gwen, Robin, Paul, Barbara, Mary, and James Stanton. Will is the last of the Old Ones, the forces of good, and the first to be born since the fifteenth century. He comes into his power on his eleventh birthday, which falls on Midwinter Day; on that day Will speaks as an Old One and has an Old One's power, but he does not know all that he should until he reads the magical *Book of Gramarye*. Will is the Sign-Seeker, whose quest is to gather and guard the six Signs of the Light*, to be used in the battle of the Light against the Dark. He accomplishes this task over the days after he comes into power. Other tasks await Will, too, and these tasks he also accomplishes: he helps his friend and mentor, Merriman Lyon* (Merry), to find a grail* with a prophetic inscription; he is friend and adviser to Bran Davies*, the son of King Arthur*, as Merry had advised Bran's father; Will plays a golden harp* that wakes the Sleepers* who defeat the Grey King*; and he enters the Lost Land to find Eirias*, a magical sword used in the final battle against the Dark. After this battle Will remains in the world when the other Old Ones leave it, but he will join them after many years.

STAYNES, HELENA HAMPTON (MRS.), a character in *The Court of the Stone Children*, by Eleanor Cameron*. She is the registrar at the French Museum in San Francisco, California. Fascinated by the de Lombre family, Mrs. Staynes has been working for some time on a biography of Clovis Antoine de Lombre* (Kot), executed by Napoleon in 1804. As part of her research, Mrs. Staynes had gone to his home in France, where, discovering many of the old furnishings for sale, she purchased them, with some of the wall panels and fireplaces, for the museum. She also bought a ring that once belonged to Kot's wife and to his daughter, Dominque de Lombre*. Though her research is thorough, Mrs. Staynes is convinced that Kot was guilty of the murder for which he had been executed, and she cannot capture his true character. When Nina Harmsworth* discovers a painting that sheds light on a journal kept by Odile Chrysostome*, Kot's unknown bethrothed, Mrs. Staynes revises both her feelings about Kot and her research.

STEPHANUS, MAGISTER, a character in *The Cat Who Wished to Be a Man**, by Lloyd Alexander*. Though once he tried to help humans, this wizard now has nothing to do with them, for they have perverted everything he taught them. Now he lives quietly in Dunstan Forest, tilling his garden and living simply in a little cottage. When he longs for conversation, Stephanus gives his cat, Lionel*, human speech and is dismayed when Lionel wants to be changed into a man. Pestered nearly out of his wits by Lionel's insistence, Stephanus changes the cat and sends him off to Brightford* to learn what being human is really like. When Lionel returns as human on the inside as he is on the outside, Stephanus cannot change him back into a cat and sends him off; the wizard will still have nothing to do with humans, even if they once were animals.

STEVIE GRIFFITH (*Beneath the Hill*). *See* Griffith, Stevie

STOKES, SAMUEL, the title character in *The Revenge of Samuel Stokes**, by Penelope Lively*. He was a landscape gardener in eighteenth-century England. Highly creative, he had a temperament to match, allowing nothing to stand in his way; once he removed an entire village in order to improve a view. His greatest achievement was the landscape at Charstock House. When, in the twentieth century, the old estate, now in ruins, becomes the site of a housing development, Stokes takes action, replacing various features of the old landscape and frightening the inhabitants of the houses with small earthquakes in an attempt to drive them away. Stokes's presence is usually heralded by the smell of the pipe tobacco he often smoked in life. When Tim Thornton*, Tim's Grandpa*, and Jane Harvey* realize what is happening, they persuade Stokes to leave the housing development alone and turn his attentions to a nearby park, where he continues to wreak havoc by changing the landscape to suit his own design.

STONE, BLUE-GREEN, an object in Jane Louise Curry's* *The Daybreakers**. Two blue-green stones make it possible for children from Apple Lock*, Ohio, to travel through time to twelfth-century Abáloc*. The stones themselves seem not to contain all the real power; those holding them somehow become attuned to the needs and wishes of the person to whom the stones belonged in another time. The power of the stones can be drained, however, by too much use. One of the two stones was buried with Erilla*, an Abalockian, and the other with Tepollomis*, her husband, in the twelfth century.

STONE OF POWER, an object in *An Enemy at Green Knowe**, by Lucy Boston*. This black, lovely, pear-shaped stone has a star-shaped figure on it and a hole at its top. It may have belonged to the Chief Druid of the last Druids in England; in the twentieth century it is found at Fydlyn Bay, where the last Druids were driven by the Romans into the sea. It is found by Hsu*, while on holiday, and he gives it to Mrs. Linnet Oldknow*, who wears it on a horsehair ribbon he has made. This stone has powers of protection against evil; when Mrs.

Oldknow one day leaves it off, she almost comes under the power of Dr. Melanie Delia Powers*, but that influence stops when she resumes wearing the stone. The only time Melanie touches the stone it hurts her.

STONE TABLE, a place in the Chronicles of Narnia*, by C[live] S[taples] Lewis*. This huge gray table stands atop a hill in the heart of Narnia*, a magical land. On it are carved strange lines and figures which seem to be an ancient alphabet; at least some of them deal with the law of Deep Magic, which states that traitors in Narnia must be given to the White Witch*, lest the land perish in flood and flame. Presumably this is where traitors are sacrificed by her. When Aslan*, Narnia's omniscient lion-protector, returns to his land to vanquish the White Witch, who is ruling here, he comes to the Table to gather his armies; here he meets four human children, Edmund, Lucy, Peter, and Susan Pevensie****. Because Edmund is a traitor, he must die, but Aslan takes his place. Since he is a willing substitute who has done no treachery, the Table cracks after he is sacrificed and he is resurrected. The Table is not used again. Aslan's How, a mound, is later raised over the remains of the Table, which stands in the How's central cavern. It is from here that Caspian X* directs his campaign to gain the throne of Narnia, which his uncle has usurped.

STONES, two objects in *The Stones of Green Knowe*, by Lucy Boston*. They were created some time before the year 580. The Stones stand on a small hill that comes to be called "Roger's Island," after Roger d'Aulneaux*, who owned the land in the twelfth century. These Stones are shaped like small thrones; the bigger is four feet tall at the back, but its seat is very low. They were shaped from two blocks of stone, but not by tools of iron. Before Roger's time, many tales are told of them: that the Devil and his wife sat on them at times of full moon, and that they were the thrones of the King and Queen of the Little People. Offerings of flowers were brought to them, until an abbot who went to exorcise them was killed by wolves, and the people were too afraid to go back to them. Roger finds the Stones one day when he is hawking and learns that the larger Stone can take a person forward in time; the smaller can take him back. Via the Stones, he travels through time, meeting his descendants, who will live in the great manor house, Green Knowe*. In the middle of the twentieth century, the Stones are uprooted and taken to a museum.

STONES OF GREEN KNOWE, THE. Lucy Boston. Illus. Peter Boston. London: Bodley Head, 1976. 118 pp. British.

In 1120, eleven-year-old Roger d'Aulneaux* watches in fascination as his family's new manor house is built. When it is done, the huge stone manor is something to be proud of. One day when he is out hawking, Roger finds the Stones*, two stone thrones, on a nearby hill. He clears away the brush that has grown up around them and sits in one. From here Roger can see the manor, and he longs to see who will live there five centuries later. Suddenly he finds himself walking toward the manor, which has subtly changed. On the way he saves eight-year-old Linnet Oldknow* from a man who is trying to kidnap her. Though they are grateful, the Oldknow family is just as puzzled by him as he is by them. Linnet, however, realizes that he is one of "the others" who step through time to visit Green Knowe*, as the manor has come to be called, and as she says this, Roger finds himself back in his own time, on the throne.

The next days are spent learning to be a lord and a knight. Roger finally gets away, however, and rides to the Stones, where he wishes that both he and his horse could go to Linnet's oldest brother, Toseland Oldknow* (Toby). Suddenly Roger is riding to meet Toby, and they ride together for a while before Roger suddenly finds himself back in his own time. A few weeks later, Roger again visits the Stones and sits playing his flageolet, becoming aware that someone is playing with him. It is Alexander Oldknow*, who is with his young sister Linnet, but they fade into their own time before they can speak with Roger. Realizing that one Stone seems to take one forward in time and the other to take him back, Roger asks to be taken back in time 540 years and is horrified to see a settlement burning and its inhabitants being slaughtered as his Saxon ancestors invade the place. He is glad to return to his own time.

It is autumn before Roger tries to use the Stones again; this time he wishes to go to the year 1800 and is puzzled and enraged to find the manor enclosed in a house of red brick. He comes upon Susan Oldknow*, the blind daughter of the master of Green Knowe, and Jacob*, her black friend. Susan tells Roger about the children who haunt the house, among them Toseland* (Tolly), before Roger returns to his century. Wondering how to find Tolly, he goes back to the Stones the next day and finds there a strange boy—Tolly himself—who had sat on the Stone and wished to see the first boy to live in the manor. Roger and Tolly explore part of the great forest surrounding the area before Tolly vanishes into his own time.

Roger uses the Stones to visit Tolly's time and is amazed and terrified by the strangeness of that century. He is pleased, however, to find that the manor is still there, though changed. Here he finds friends: an old woman, Mrs. Linnet Oldknow*, who is pleased to see him, and, in the garden, Tolly, with Susan and Jacob, then Alexander, Toby, and Linnet. Finally there comes a slim young girl—Mrs. Oldknow when she was young—who gives Roger a ring to keep for her; it will be handed down through the generations until it comes to her again. She, and Tolly after her, will keep the manor safe. Relieved by her promise, Roger suddenly finds himself in his own century.

During the next days, Roger learns to joust. Finally he uses the Stones to go to Tolly and arrives just in time to watch with horror as the Stones are wrenched from the earth to be taken to a museum. Tolly is sad because he cannot use the Stones again to visit Roger, but Roger can still visit him, for in his time the Stones still stand.

STORY OF THE AMULET, THE. E[dith] Nesbit Bland. Illus. H. R. Millar. London: T. Fisher Unwin, 1906. 374 pp. British.

Because their parents and baby brother are away, Robert*, Anthea*, Cyril*, and Jane* must stay in London with their old nurse for the holidays. One day, at a pet shop, they find an old friend, the Psammead*, an odd creature capable of granting wishes. They buy it. Because it can no longer grant the children's wishes, the Psammead tells them about an amulet* which will grant their heart's desire: to have the rest of their family safely home again. When the children buy the amulet, they discover that they have only half; but the Psammead assures them that, if they read the name on their half, the amulet will take them to find the other half. Discovering from a learned gentleman who lives upstairs how to read the name, the children try it, and the voice of the amulet tells them that the other half was ground into dust long ago; they must travel to when the amulet was whole and try to get it.

The children travel into the past, taking the Psammead with them, and find themselves in Egypt in 6000 B.C. Here lives a race of fair people who keep the amulet in a sacred place in their wattle-and-daub village. When the village is attacked, the children try to get away, but they cannot find the Psammead, nor can they find the East, which they must face for their ritual to work. They spend the night in the village. At dawn, the raiders overrun the place, and before the children can get the amulet, one of the raiders grabs it. The children escape with the Psammead—who had spent the night near the amulet—and find themselves home an instant after they left.

Their next visit is to Babylon, and again they take the Psammead. One of the guards at the city gate takes them to his wife, who takes them to see the Queen of Babylon.* Because the Psammead does not care to see her, Jane carries it and the amulet back to the guard's house. The vain and flighty Queen enjoys her visit with the foreign children and sends for Jane, but the girl cannot be found; she has left the house and is looking for the palace. That night, Robert, Cyril, and Anthea meet the king at a banquet. He is so enthralled by their singing that he offers to give them whatever they like as a reward. Robert asks for the amulet, and the children are thrown into prison to be questioned, for half of the amulet has been taken. In despair, they call on Nisroch*, a Babylonian power, who sends them to Jane, now in the Queen's quarters with the Psammead. The amulet takes them safely home.

Here they have a problem. The queen had wished to visit the children's world "soon," so they stay home for fear she will come and find them gone. When the Queen does come, the children and the Psammead have a most trying day, for the Queen and London do not suit one another. Taken to the museum, she wishes out of their cases the things that once belonged to her and then has to wish them back to unmuddle the situation. When she visits the poor end of London, the Queen wishes the people would have what they like best to eat and drink; when a surly cabby leaves the group near the Stock Exchange, the Queen wishes the men into Babylonian clothing; and when the crowd gets angry, she wishes guards would kill them. The slaughter and the Queen's visit end when one man wishes it were all a dream.

Having overheard Jimmy*, the man upstairs, express a wish to see Atlantis*, the children take him there with them as they search for the amulet. In Atlantis the children witness a huge tidal wave which wrecks the lower part of the island, and they narrowly escape death, for Jimmy thinks it is a dream and wants to see it to the end. With difficulty they escape before the island is destroyed.

Days later, the children meet Imogen*, a poor orphan, and take her to see Jimmy. When the man wishes they could find a place where someone would want her, the Psammead transports all of them to the Britain of 55 B.C. There a woman recognizes Imogen as her lost daughter, and the reunion is permanent when Jimmy wishes she could stay. Realizing that Julius Caesar* will soon invade, Jimmy wishes to see him and manages, before his return to London, to arouse the Roman's curiosity and ensure the invasion.

The children next journey to ancient Egypt, where Rekh-marā*, a priest, takes them to Pharoah. When the king takes a liking to the Psammead and tries to take *it*, the children protest and are thrown into prison. Bribing the guards with a small gift from the future, they manage to get the Psammead and leave.

Realizing that in the future they might have found the amulet's other half and might remember where they found it, the children go forward in time. In the utopian future, they find the whole amulet in a museum but do not know how they got it. During a second trip into the future, they talk with Jimmy, who tells them that they gave him the complete amulet on 3 December 1905, but did not tell him how they found it.

The children use the amulet to go where it wants to take them and find themselves in ancient Tyre. Here they find Rekh-marā, who seems to have the other half of the amulet. He loses it to an unscrupulous ship captain. Using their half, the children take Rekh-marā with them on board the ship, which is bound for the rich, valuable Tin Islands*. Near the Islands, the captain discovers an enemy ship behind his and wrecks his ship on rocks rather than inadvertently show the other ship the way to the Islands. Rekh-marā grabs his half of the amulet, and all escape before the ship goes down. The Psammead explains to the children that the Egyptian's half is actually the same half they have; Rekh-marā is looking for the same thing they are.

One day, at a magic show, the Egyptian suddenly joins the children, and they take him home. Here they watch as both halves of the amulet merge. Rekh-marā reluctantly agrees to help them find the whole amulet. He meets Jimmy, who thinks it is all a dream but who advises them to pick a time when the amulet was unguarded and go there. The children and the priest journey to the beginning of time and finally gain the whole amulet. They return home to find that the children's parents are returning. In Jimmy's room, the half amulet merges with the whole amulet. The children have got their heart's desire; now Rekh-marā wants his: to gain wisdom and stay in their world. They consult the amulet, which tells them that he can stay if he joins with a kindred spirit, and he joins with Jimmy. Both sought wisdom, and both had what the other wanted. Hearing the Psammead complain about its hard lot, Jimmy wishes it safe in the past, and it happily grants the wish. To grant his heart's desire, Anthea gives Jimmy the amulet before the children run downstairs to find their parents at the door.

Note: This work first appeared as "The Amulet" in *The Strand Magazine*, nos. 173-184 (May, 1905-April, 1906).

STRANGER, THE, a nameless character in *Tuck Everlasting**, by Natalie Babbitt*. When he was a boy, he was fascinated by stories his grandmother told of a family of people who never grew older. Obsessed with the idea, he studied to learn whether everlasting life could be possible. Finally he set out to find the family. A few months later he does find Angus and Mae Tuck** and their sons, and learns their story when he eavesdrops as they explain it to Winifred Foster* (Winnie). The stranger follows as Winnie is taken to the Tucks' cabin to stay until they can make her promise to keep their secret. Offering to guide the constable to the child, he strikes a bargain for a wood the Fosters own, where a tiny spring*, the waters of which confer everlasting life, bubbles. He plans to sell the water of the spring, using Winnie to demonstrate its qualities after the Tucks refuse to help him. When he tries to force Winnie to drink from the spring, Mae hits him so hard with the butt of a shotgun that he dies.

STRAWBERRY. *See* Fledge

STUART, MARY, Scottish queen (1542-1587) who appears as a character or is mentioned in several works. In Alison Uttley's* *A Traveller in Time**, she is a brave, doomed queen who has suffered much but is still able to make others love her and be loyal to her. Among those who come to love her is Penelope Taberner Cameron*, a twentieth-century girl who slips into Elizabethan times. Anthony Babington*, Mary's admirer, tries to help her to escape when she visits Wingfield Manor*, but he fails. In Jane Louise Curry's* *The Bassumtyte Treasure**, Mary is the mother of a baby, Thomas Bassumtyte* (Small Thomas), who is taken to Boxleton House* to be raised by the Bassumtyte family. When Small Thomas's "father," also named Thomas Bassumtyte, had tried to help Mary gain the throne of England, he had been executed. Not until the twentieth century does this story become known. Then the owners of Boxleton discover a doctored portrait of Mary that, when sold, will bring them enough money to restore the old house.

STUART LITTLE (*Stuart Little*). *See* Little, Stuart

STUART LITTLE. E[lwyn] B[rooks] White. Illus. Garth Williams. New York: Harper and Brothers, 1945. 131 pp. American.

To Mrs. Frederick C. Little* is born a son who looks very like a mouse. He is named Stuart Little*, and he soon proves to be good-natured and helpful, though, because he is about two inches high, life is sometimes difficult for him. Because of his size, Stuart gets into many adventures. One day when he is three years old, he gets up very early and, showing off his athletic skills to the family cat, Snowbell*, Stuart gets himself rolled up in a windowshade and is not found until lunch. Another day he goes to Central Park and there navigates Dr. Paul Carey's* toy boat across the sailboat pond in a race. Despite a collision between the boats after Stuart accidentally sails into a paper bag, he wins, to Dr. Carey's satisfaction. When Stuart is seven, he is accidentally shut in the refrigerator for half an hour and catches bronchitis.

While Stuart is sick in bed, Mrs. Little finds a half-frozen bird and brings it into the house to get warm. The bird's name is Margalo*, and Stuart loves her at once. That night he protects her from Snowbell. As the days pass, Stuart and Margalo become fast friends. One day, when Stuart goes for a walk and is forced to hide from a dog by jumping into a garbage can, he finds himself being hauled out to sea in a garbage scow after the can is dumped. Margalo, who had followed him, rescues Stuart and flies him home. Then, one night a pigeon overhears Snowbell plotting with one of his friends to help the friend eat Margalo. The pigeon warns Margalo by writing her a note, and Margalo flies away.

Stuart is heartbroken, and he runs away to find her. He goes to Dr. Carey for help, and the man gives Stuart a miniature car to travel in. Stuart does not start out until the next day, for the car becomes damaged while he is trying out its modern conveniences and it must be repaired. Stuart's adventures on the road are varied. The first day, he meets the superintendent of schools of a small town, who is dismayed because the regular teacher is sick and there is no substitute. Stuart volunteers to substitute and is a very popular teacher after he makes drastic changes in the curriculum. Stuart's next stop is in another small town, where he sees Harriet Ames*, a beautiful girl just two inches tall. Taken with her, he invites her to canoe with him and then buys a canoe to take her out in. Stuart looks forward eagerly to their boating, and he is thrilled when Harriet comes. They discover, however, that the canoe had been spoilt by someone when Stuart was away. So disappointed is Stuart that he cannot even fix the canoe to take Harriet boating, and she goes home. The next day, as Stuart leaves town in his car, he meets a telephone repairman who agrees he should go north, which is a fine direction in which to seek Margalo. Stuart goes north, pleased with his decision.

STUDDARD, BERTRAND, a character in Robert Westall's* *The Wind Eye*. He is the second husband of Madeleine Studdard*, the father of Beth and Sally Studdard**, and the stepfather of Michael Studdard*. A university scholar, Bertrand is calm, logical, and atheistic, denying everything he cannot see, touch, or measure, and he tries to instill these qualities in his children. After his first wife died, leaving him with Beth and Sally, Bertrand became involved with Madeleine, marrying her after people in the town where they lived had begun to talk. Tensions rise between them, for she is vastly different from him. During a holiday during which the family visits an old house Bertrand has inherited from his uncle, things come to a crisis for Bertrand when St. Cuthbert* (Cuddy) makes his powers felt across thirteen centuries. Bertrand cannot accept Cuddy as a saint, and his miracles offend him, especially when the saint cures Sally's hand, horribly burned in an accident Bertrand blames himself for. Bertrand uses a boat* to sail back in time and try to thwart Cuddy, only to shatter his own cherished illusions about himself. He realizes that he cannot go back to his old life as it was, for that world of things one can only touch, see, and measure has become a prison. He will sail the boat back in time, seeking the answer to his questions—perhaps, like his uncle and grandfather before him, finding a place to stay far from the twentieth century.

STUDDARD, BETH, a character in *The Wind Eye**, by Robert Westall*. She is the daughter of Bertrand and the stepdaughter of Madeleine Studdard**; she is the sister of Sally and the stepsister of Michael Studdard**. After her mother's death, Beth seems to have concentrated her efforts on pleasing her father, whom she loves because he is clever and strong and protects her. Beth wants all around her to be happy, even if it means denying the person she is inside. Despite Bertrand's atheism, she is a religious person and has often thought of becoming a nun. After her father remarries, Beth is miserable when the marriage seems to be breaking apart and tries every way she can to keep things going well. When the family vacations near the island where St. Cuthbert* (Cuddy) had once lived, the saint makes his power felt across thirteen centuries, affecting each of the Studdards. Beth comes to love her father for who he is, not just because he protects her; Cuddy helps her realize that she must live for herself as much as for others and that her dreams of becoming a nun has been just a way of running away.

STUDDARD, MADELEINE, a character in Robert Westall's* *The Wind Eye**. She is the second wife of Bertrand Studdard*, the mother of Michael Studdard*, and the stepmother of Beth and Sally Studdard**. After the death of her first husband, anger kept Madeleine going and, using it, she managed to surmount the problems of a single parent. Now this can be hard on those around her, for she does not hesitate to speak her mind. Madeleine drives with great drama, as if doing battle on the road. Madeleine can charm, too, for she is bright and witty, with a mind that dances over every subject. Though she had wanted only an affair with Bertrand, they had gotten married after the people in the town where they live had begun to talk. Bertrand tries to remake her, to imbue Madeleine with his own rationality; in defense, she becomes more fascinated by the unknown, something Bertrand regards with distaste. The tension between them comes to a crisis when the family vacations near the island where St. Cuthbert* (Cuddy) had lived. On the way there, the family stops in the village where Cuddy is buried, and Madeleine deliberately steps on his tomb in a kind of defiance of Bertrand. Cuddy somehow feels Madeleine's unspoken need;

across thirteen centuries he makes his power felt and brings her the peace she has not had in years. It is shattering, for it incapacitates her until she learns to live with it as she had her anger.

STUDDARD, MICHAEL, a character in *The Wind Eye**, by Robert Westall*. He is the son of Madeleine and the stepson of Bertrand Studdard**; he is the stepbrother of Beth and Sally Studdard**. After his father died, Michael grew up tough and self-sufficient, both traits useful for anyone living with mercurial Madeleine. When she remarries, Mike finds himself coming to care for Beth, who is a teenager like him. When the family vacations near the island where St. Cuthbert* (Cuddy) had lived in the seventh century, tensions in the family seem to come to a crisis. Michael and the other children discover an ancient boat* that takes those who sail in it back to Cuddy's time. Because Beth and Sally have needs only Cuddy can fulfill, they meet the saint. But Michael is contented with his lot, and Cuddy does nothing for him beyond indirectly forcing him to deal with things he has always tried to run away from before.

STUDDARD, SALLY, a character in Robert Westall's* *The Wind Eye**. She is the daughter of Bertrand and the stepdaughter of Madeleine Studdard**; she is the sister of Beth and the stepsister of Michael Studdard**. When Sally was two, she had burned her hand badly on an electric heater; it is crippled and she wears a glove on it to keep people from staring at it. In stressful times, Sally sucks the thumb of her bad hand. The burned hand makes her miserable, though her family does not realize how deeply she is affected. When Sally is six, the Studdards vacation near the island where St. Cuthbert* (Cuddy) had lived in the seventh century. Sally uses an ancient boat* to travel back in time and meet Cuddy; during the ten days they spend together, she comes to love and trust him so completely that he is able to heal her hand.

STUMPS, a character in *The Twelve and the Genii**, by Pauline Clarke*. He is one of the Twelves*, a dozen wooden soldiers once owned by Branwell Brontë, who come to life through the creative genius of Branwell and his sisters, Charlotte, Emily, and Anne. Stumps becomes the favorite of Max Morley*, the twentieth-century boy who finds the soldiers hidden in the attic of his house, after the boy imagines the soldier's escape from the kitchen where he is lost. Stumps was once Frederic Guelph, Duke of York, and was elected king; after Frederic I "died," he came back to life and was again made king. As Frederic II, he gave up his throne to the Duke of Wellington and became simple, adventurous Stumps again.

SUCAT, a character in Lloyd Alexander's* *Time Cat**. This quiet, black-haired young Welshman is the slave of the Irish King Miliucc* in A.D. 411. Sucat's name means "Good Cat" or "Good Warrior"; in Britain he is called "Patrick." Because he helps Jason*, a boy from the twentieth century, and Gareth*, his cat, escape when Miliucc's sorcerer seeks their deaths, Sucat goes with them so that he will not be killed. He longs to go out into the world and become educated, so that he can return to Ireland and drive out ignorance and fear. He also plans to bring back cats to deal with the snakes and rats that plague Ireland. Later he becomes a saint.

SUFFERANA GROUT (*The Magical Cupboard*). *See* Grout, Sufferana

SUMMER COUNTRY, a place mentioned in *The Book of Three** and *The High King**, by Lloyd Alexander*. This land lies outside the ken of men. It is rich land where all heart's desires are granted and all live happily forever. The Sons of Don* sail from this country early in the history of Prydain*, and to it they and their kindred return when Arawn*, the Lord of Death, is defeated. Gwydion* and Fflewddur Fflam* are among these, as are Dallben*, an enchanter, and Gurgi*, a creature of undefinable ancestry. Taran*, a young warrior, and Eilonwy*, his sweetheart, are to accompany them, but he stays behind to rebuild war-ravaged Prydain, and she gives up her magic to stay with and marry him.

SUN SERPENT. *See* Katóa

SUSAN, a character in Alan Garner's* *The Weirdstone of Brisingamen** and *The Moon of Gomrath**. She is the sister of Colin*. When their parents have to go abroad for six months, Susan and Colin stay with Bess and Gowther Mossock* at Alderley Edge. Here they have adventures in a world previously unknown to them, of magic and dwarfs* and wizards. Susan discovers that the crystal her mother had given her is the powerful stone, Firefrost*, meant to keep the warriors sleeping in Fundindelve* from waking until the proper time, and she gives it back to Cadellin Silverbrow*, the wizard entrusted with its keeping. During this adventure Susan is given the Mark of Fohla*, a bracelet that keeps her safe but leads her from the ways of humans; she is taken even farther from human life when the powerful Brollachan* takes her spirit out of the world and thrusts it into Abred, a level of darkness and unformed life, from which she rises and rides with Celemon*, the daughter of the moon, among the stars. Susan uses the Mark to gain her own power, which waxes when the moon is new, and fights the evil Morrigan*. Defeated, Susan uses a magic hunting horn* to call Celemon and the riders of the Wild Hunt* and to destroy the Brollachan. Though she longs to go with the riders, she cannot—not yet, though one day she will.

SUSAN OLDKNOW (the Green Knowe books). *See* Oldknow, Susan

SUSAN PEVENSIE (the Chronicles of Narnia). *See* Pevensie, Susan

SUSAN POULTER (*The Whispering Knights*). *See* Poulter, Susan

SVART, a type of creature in Alan Garner's* *The Weirdstone of Brisingamen*.
The svarts call themselves the svart-alfar. They stand about three feet high and
have wiry bodies and large hands, feet, and heads. Hating the sun, they live in
mines, rarely coming out, and then only under the cover of darkness. They are
fairly cowardly, though they can fight fiercely when they must for Nastrond,
their powerful, evil master. The svarts cannot bear bright light, but they can
look on the firedrake, a red, glaring flame, and it prepares them for brighter
light. Iron dissolves the flesh of the svarts, and when it touches them they crumble
into dust. Nastrond uses svarts to try to find Fundindelve*, where warriors sleep
until they are needed to slay a great evil. The svarts vanish with the rest of his
forces when, in rage, he sends Fenrir, the wolf of Ragnarok, to swallow up
those who have betrayed him.

SWAGGART, a character in Lloyd Alexander's *The Cat Who Wished to Be
a Man*. He is the bullying right hand man of Pursewig*, the greedy mayor of
Brightford*. When Lionel*, a young cat changed into a man, visits Brightford,
Swaggart swindles him out of his money; this violent man later tries several
times to kill Lionel. When the villagers in Brightford finally get the better of
Pursewig, Swaggart escapes into nearby Dunstan Forest and tries again to kill
Lionel. In a murderous rage, Lionel discovers that he, too, could kill, as he
longs to kill Swaggart. The bully more than meets his match in Magister Ste-
phanus*, Lionel's wizard master, who changes Swaggart into a skunk.

SWEENEY, MARY, a character in Robert Lawson's* *Mr.Wilmer*. She becomes the wife of William Wilmer*. When they first meet, Miss Sweeney is
secretary for Arthur Wellington Twitch, at the Safe, Sane, and Colossal Insurance
Company. Lovely Miss Sweeney, with her red hair, blue eyes, and pert nose,
is the most wonderful person William knows, and greeting her is the high point
of each day. When William, who has discovered a talent for talking with animals,
gets a job at the zoo and needs a secretary, Miss Sweeney takes the job. She
even moves her canary and everything else she owns into a room in William's
boarding house, to be close by in case he needs to do some work at home. Miss
Sweeney has no trouble charming everyone she meets, and she is a great help
to William, taking care of his correspondence, his business, and his finances for
him. When William buys a farm and plans to move there with Miss Sweeney
and the Keelers, their landlords, Wally Wencher, a vicious gossip columnist,
makes some offensive hints about their relationship, and Miss Sweeney leaves
William to protect her reputation. He finds her, though, and they marry, honeymooning at the farm.

SWIFTLY TILTING PLANET, A. Madeleine L'Engle. New York: Farrar,
Straus and Giroux, 1978. 278 pp. American.
It is Thanksgiving, and Mr. Murry* receives a phone call from the President
of the United States; Madog Branzillo*, dictator of Vespugia*, a South American

country, will start a nuclear war with the United States in twenty-four hours. Mrs. Branwen Zillah O'Keefe*, the mother-in-law of Meg Murry* O'Keefe, says a rune* taught to her by her grandmother. This rune mentions sun, snow, fire, lightning, wind, and sea and is a protection against danger. Mrs. O'Keefe tells Meg's fifteen-year-old brother, Charles Wallace Murry*, that he is to use the rune to stop Branzillo.

That night Charles goes to the Murrys' meadow. Meg shares his experience through kything*, a type of empathy. Charles calls the first two lines of the rune and Gaudior*, a winged unicorn, appears and takes Charles on his back. They ride the wind and watch the Earth being created, and land. Charles is to travel in and out of time and people, finding a Might-Have-Been that has led to the present evil and changing it. They must trust the wind to take them where they must go, for the Echthroi (Echthros*), evil forces, ride it too. Again they ride the wind, coming down at the place they had started from, but centuries before, when there had been a lake. Here Charles goes within a young Indian boy, merging consciousness with him, and he shares the boy's joyful life before he leaves with Gaudior.

This time as they ride the wind, the Echthroi throw them into a Projection, a poisonous future the Echthroi want to make real. Charles calls the rune, calling on snow, and it snows. The wind comes and they ride it to safety. This time, they land at the lake centuries after their first visit. Charles goes within Madoc*, a Welsh prince who had come across the sea with his brother, Gwydyr*, to escape the quarrelling over their father's throne. Today Madoc is to marry Zyll*, a native girl, but suddenly Gwydyr, whom Madoc had thought dead, comes from across the lake and claims Zyll for his own. He will be king and god here and exact tribute from Zyll's people. Gwydyr and Madoc agree to fight, each to create fire and the strongest fire to win. Suddenly, in a small pool of water Madoc sees a vision of a bad-tempered baby who grows up to consume the world with flame: this is Gwydyr's fire. Madoc builds a pyre of flowers, and in the puddle appears another, happy baby; Madoc calls the rune and calls on fire, and the sun kindles the flowers: this is Madoc's fire. The brothers wrestle all day and into the night, Madoc finally winning. Gwydyr leaves him; he eventually ends up in South America, in what is now Vespugia. Charles leaves Madoc, going to Gaudior.

Meg learns from another brother that there had been Welsh settlements in Vespugia in 1865, and she also learns of Matthew Maddox*, who had written of the Welsh princes. Kything, she gets this information to Charles. When he and Gaudior try to go to 1865, however, the Echthroi attack and Charles is nearly lost; Gaudior saves him and they manage to land again. The lake is gone. Charles this time goes within Brandon Llawcae*, a boy of the seventeenth century. His sister-in-law is Zylle Llawcae*, one of Madoc's descendants. The local people think she is a witch because she has skills with healing herbs, and after a baby dies of sickness not long after her own child is born, she is condemned as a witch. The night before she is to be hung, Zylle's father teaches Brandon the rune. At the hanging, the boy uses it to call the lightning, and when lightning strikes the church and one of her accusers, the people decide that it is the wrath of God and the hanging is stopped. Zylle, her husband, and their child go back to Wales, and Brandon becomes one of Zylle's people.

When Charles comes out of Brandon, he realizes that Madog is the Welsh spelling of Madoc, and he and Gaudior try to get to Vespugia in 1865. Instead they crash into a freezing sea. They are almost drowned when Meg uses the rune to call on the wind, and it pushes Charles and Gaudior to land. To give them a chance to recover, Gaudior takes Charles to his home world, with its healing snow, an experience which exhilirates the youth.

Again they ride the wind, and this time Charles goes within Chuck Maddox*, who learns the rune with his younger sister, Beezie. Meg realizes that Beezie is Mrs. O'Keefe. Chuck and Beezie are happy children until one day their father dies. Suddenly Meg is recalled to her own world; Mrs. O'Keefe has come back to the house, bringing old letters from Matthew Maddox's brother, Bran Maddox*, to him. Bran had landed in Vespugia and met Gedder* and Zillie*, descendants of Gwydyr. Mrs. O'Keefe had realized that the names Bran and Zillie sound close to Branzillo. When Meg kythes again with Charles, he has found the diary of Zillah Llawcae*, who loves Bran. Things are not going well for Chuck's family, and his mother marries vicious Duthbert Mortmain* to keep from going into debt. One night the man tries to hit Chuck's grandmother, and the boy himself takes the blow, falling downstairs and fracturing his skull. His brain is damaged, but though a voice tempts Charles to leave the boy, he does not. From now on, Chuck's world is warped, and the past of Gedder, Bran, and Zillie is as real as Chuck's present. Finally Duthbert has him institutionalized, and Charles is brought out of Chuck.

He and Gaudior ride the wind, and Charles is pushed within crippled Matthew Maddox. Bran has just come back from war, wounded and sick in spirit. Gwen Maddox*, their sister, is in love with a cruel hired hand. After months, Bran talks with Matthew about his pain and finally feels healed; he goes to Vespugia, taking Gwen with him after she is caught kissing the hired hand. He will send for Zillah later, though her father does not want her to go. Bran settles in Vespugia, where Gedder seems to push Zillie on him; Gedder himself wants Gwen. Sensing his brother's weakening, Matthew saves enough money to send Zillah to be his wife. In dreams, Matthew sees Gwen toying with ambitious Gedder and with Rich Llawcae*, descended from seventeenth-century Zylle Llawcae. When he sees Gedder and Rich finally fighting on a cliff, he helps as best he can, and Gedder goes over the edge. Zillah marries Bran; Gwen and Rich set out for America, but before they arrive Matthew dies.

Meg and Mrs. O'Keefe hurry to the meadow, where they find Charles lying very still. The women say the rune and Charles wakes. Gaudior leaves, making them forget his presence. When they go home, there is a call from the President;

Madog, always a man of peace, is setting up a congress to work out peace. The joy is tinged with sadness, for Mrs. O'Keefe's heart is failing. But in the hour of need, she had put herself between them and the powers of darkness.

SWORD IN THE STONE, THE. T[erence] H[anbury] White. London: Collins, 1938. 338 pp. British.

After their governess leaves them, young Kay* and the Wart need a tutor. One afternoon they go hawking near the Forest Sauvage*; when they lose the hawk, the Wart follows it deep into the terrible forest. He is shot at and, escaping, loses the hawk and gets lost himself. Once he meets King Pellinore*, out after the great Questing Beast*, but the king gallops off after the Beast. The Wart sleeps that night in the forest, and the next morning he finds Merlyn*, a wizard, who takes the Wart home, stopping on the way to get the hawk. Merlyn is engaged as tutor to the Wart and Kay.

His lessons are not like any the Wart has ever had before. One hot day Merlyn turns the boy and himself into fish and they swim in the cool, lovely moat; Merlyn takes the Wart to meet a pike, so that the boy will see what it is like to be a king. The pike believes in power to rend and destroy, and he almost destroys the Wart before he escapes and finds himself a boy again, on dry land. The Wart's next adventure is entirely his own doing. One day when he and Kay are shooting arrows, the Wart shoots one into the air and a crow catches it; Kay and the Wart follow the crow into the Forest, to the cottage of Madame Mim*, a witch, who catches them to eat. The Wart helps a goat she has caged to escape and get help. Just as Madame Mim is about to kill the Wart, Merlyn appears and there ensues a contest of magic, which Merlyn wins by becoming a new virus and infecting Mim.

The Wart longs to be a knight, so Merlyn takes him to see a joust between King Pellinore and Sir Grummore Grummursum*. It is a ridiculous affair that leaves both knights stunned; and King Pellinore goes home with Sir Grummore to recover. The Wart learns about courage one wet night when he is bored. Merlyn changes him into a merlin and puts him with the other hawks to stay the night, and here he is sworn in by the others, proving his courage by an ordeal.

The next day Kay is jealous because the Wart is changed into animals and he is not. Merlyn cannot transform Kay, but he does send Kay and the Wart into the Forest Sauvage to have an adventure. Here they meet Robin Wood*— otherwise known as Robin Hood. One of his men and two other people have been captured and are in the castle of Morgan the Fay*, and Robin takes the boys on the rescue mission because only boys can enter the castle. After dark they enter it, carrying iron to break the enchantment. Resisting all temptations, the boys find the prisoners, disguised by magic, and release them with the touch of iron. The ordeal is not yet over, for the boys and Robin's men must fight the creatures that guard Morgan's castle, but all goes well and Kay's adventure is finished safely, though the Wart breaks his collarbone.

Autumn comes. One day Merlyn changes the Wart into a snake and he learns from another snake the history of their kind; he also hears a legend about killing and one dealing with responsibility and the power to kill, before he sleeps and wakes as a boy. That Christmas the king of England sends his hunstmen and hounds to hunt boar in the Forest Sauvage. Robin leads them because he knows where they are. The hunters kill a boar and find something else—the Questing Beast, pining away because King Pellinore has left it to live with Sir Grummore. Tearful, Pellinore nurses the Beast back to health, and the two resume their quest.

In spring, Merlyn turns the Wart into an owl one night, and he flies with Archimedes*, Merlyn's owl, to Athene*; there he sees and listens to the trees and the stones, watching the creation of the earth and the ultimate violence man is capable of. One night in summer Merlyn takes the Wart to see Galapas*, a giant. The two are invisible for safety's sake, for he keeps and torments several captives. One of these is Pellinore, who is being held for ransom. Merlyn and the Wart are almost captured, too, but just in time the Questing Beast comes and chases Galapas away. The giant's captives and slaves are all freed.

Six years pass, and as the time when Kay is to be made a knight grows near, the Wart becomes a little disconsolate. Merlyn changes him, for the last time, into a badger and sends him off to visit another badger. Instead, the Wart, feeling cross and defiant, goes into the woods. Here he finds, and offers to eat, a hedgehog, but so pathetic is the urchin that he relents, especially after its miserable monologue on the powerful and the helpless. The Wart then goes to visit the badger, which tells him a story of how man had come to be above the animals, though defenseless compared with them, because he had chosen to be what God had made him.

The King of England dies, leaving no heir, though a sword in a stone has appeared outside a church; whoever draws the sword will be king of England. Because none have been able to draw it, a tournament has been arranged to find the best knight. Merlyn leaves the Wart and Kay the day before Kay is knighted. Sir Kay, his father, the Wart, and others go to London for the tournament. The day of the tournament, they arrive at the field and find that Kay has left his sword at the inn, and when he goes back for it, the Wart finds the inn closed. Seeing the sword in the stone, he takes it for a war memorial and decides to borrow the sword. The Wart's first attempts to draw it fail, but he takes the advice he has learned in his transformations and finally succeeds in drawing the sword from the stone. Sir Kay's first instinct is to take credit for the feat, but he confesses the truth. It is painful for the Wart to see those he loves kneel before him, but he cannot help but become king. To his joy, Merlyn returns to advise him, and the boy at last learns his true heritage and is called by his true name, Arthur*.

Note: This work was extensively altered to fit into White's five-part epic, *The Once and Future King*. The greatest alterations are the following: In Chapter 6, Madame Mim is cut out entirely; in Chapter 11, the adventure with Morgan the

Fay is considerably altered; the Wart's adventure as a snake in Chapter 13 is changed to an adventure as an ant; his transformation into an owl in Chapter 18 becomes a transformation into a wild goose, which encompasses two chapters (18 and 19); Chapter 19, the Wart's adventure with Galapas, is removed; and Chapter 21 has been extended a page or so after the badger's story.

TABERNER, BARNABAS, a name shared by two characters in Alison Uttley's* *A Traveller in Time**. The first Barnabas was the brother of Cicely Taberner* of Thackers* in the sixteenth century. He was killed in the wars in the Netherlands. The second Barnabas is the farmer at Thackers in the twentieth century. Penelope Taberner Cameron* is his great-niece and Cicely Ann Taberner* his sister. He is a stolid, quiet, practical man who loves Thackers dearly.

TABERNER, CICELY, a character in *A Traveller in Time**, by Alison Uttley*. She lives at Thackers* in Elizabethan times and works for the Babington family as cook. For Penelope Taberner Cameron*, a twentieth-century girl who visits the Elizabethan age, Cicely bears a striking resemblance to Cicely Ann Taberner*, who lives at twentieth-century Thackers. Cicely is warm and loving and proud of Thackers and those she serves. Her brother, Barnabas Taberner*, was killed in the wars in the Netherlands.

TABERNER, CICELY ANN (TISSIE), a character in *A Traveller in Time**, by Alison Uttley*. She helps her brother, Barnabas Taberner*, work the twentieth-century farm at Thackers*. ''Aunt Tissie'' is warm, practical, and loving. She is Penelope Taberner Cameron's* great-aunt.

TALBOT, EDWARD, a character in E[dith] Nesbit Bland's* *The House of Arden**. This daring and handsome young baronet lives in England in 1707. Having made a bet with his friends that he can rob a coach of the Arden jewels and sleep all night in Arden Castle* without anyone's knowing his name, Edward poses as a highwayman. He makes friends at a roadside inn with Elfrida Arden*, who is journeying with Betty Arden* to Arden Castle, and learns from her what time the two will resume their journey the next day. As their coach nears the castle, Edward robs it and carries Elfrida off to the castle, promising her that if she leaves a window open that night, he will return the jewels. Through the open window Edward tosses a letter in which, posing as James III, the ''rightful'' heir to the throne, he asks them to shelter him. Elfrida and Betty hide Edward in a secret room behind the mantelpiece, and there he stays all night, winning his bet.

TALBOT, LADY, a character in *Harding's Luck**, by E[dith] Nesbit Bland*. She is married to Edward, Lord Talbot; they live at Talbot Court. When Dickie Harding* is caught acting as accomplice for two burglars, Lady Talbot feels compassion for the boy and takes care of him. She recognizes in Dickie a resemblance to members of the Arden family and is gratified when it is proven he is of that line.

TAPESTRY ROOM, THE. Mary Louisa Molesworth. Illus. Walter Crane. London: Macmillan and Co., 1879. 237 pp. British.

One cold day, Jeanne*, a little French girl, is bored and makes a wish, as her nurse, Marcelline*, bids her to do. Sent to her mother, Jeanne stops for a moment in a room hung all with tapestries, and to her surprise Dudu*, an old raven, speaks to her from outside. Jeanne's mother has received a letter; Hugh*, Jeanne's cousin, is coming from England, so Jeanne's wish is fulfillled. When Hugh comes, he sleeps in the tapestry room. The first night he dreams that Dudu comes and talks to him.

It is several more nights before Hugh wakes to find the room flooded with moonlight, and before his eyes the figures on the tapestries become real. Dudu hops out of a pictured castle and out of the tapestry itself. Hugh and Jeanne have both wished to visit the castle, but Dudu will send only Hugh, alone, into it. Dudu will come at Hugh's call, if he needs him. Hugh enters the castle and follows an endless corridor. When the lights suddenly go out, he stumbles on to the end, where he finds a door into a garden. There Jeanne sits in a carriage attended by the children's pets. They drive off through a wonderful land, through a forest of rainbows to a fountain-filled plain, and here the animals lead the children to a trapdoor. When Jeanne and Hugh go through it, the pets do not follow. Jeanne and Hugh eventually come to a small door opening into a landscape, where they find a boat in a small stream. They take the boat down the stream until they can go no further, then Hugh whistles and hundreds of little frogs come and pull the boat to a lovely lake. Here the frogs sing for them, and with their chorus comes also the lovely death song of a swan. After the concert, the children feel sleepy, but before he falls asleep, Hugh sees Dudu and one of the pets rowing the boat. He wakes in the tapestry room. The next day, to Hugh's dismay, Jeanne does not remember their adventure.

Several nights later Hugh wakes to find Jeanne in the moonlit room. Dudu is perched on her head and she is wearing a pair of wings; she gives another pair to Hugh, and together they fly to the tapestry castle. There is no corridor this time, but a hall, which they fly through, coming to a spiral staircase. Here Dudu leaves them, as do the wings, and the children climb the stairs. Jeanne now remembers their other adventure because she is the Jeanne of moonlight, as she had been that night, not the Jeanne of daylight Hugh sees every day. The children come to a white room where sits a white lady who spins stories, and she tells them the tale of a princess who helps a prince disenchant himself and then marries him. The story over, the children are surprised to find the lady changed into Marcelline, who puts them to bed.

Jeanne and Hugh get some balls and teach themselves to juggle like the princess in the story. One day, looking for a ball, they find some stairs behind a tapestry and climb them. At the top they meet Dudu. He tells them a story about their great-grandmother, whom he had known, expressing sadness that so many things can change. He also tells them goodbye. The children are not surprised to hear later that he has disapppeared, and they feel that he will not come back.

TAPP, CONWAY (SONNY), a character in *The Daybreakers**, by Jane Louise Curry*. He is the son of Gwen and Conway Tapp, the grandson of Senator Tapp, and the cousin of Melissa Mitchell* (Liss). Seven-year-old Sonny hates those around him, especially Liss. After he was orphaned, he went to live with his grandfather and has been so babied and smothered by those around him that he has become a bitter, sickly child who feels like a prisoner. Sonny is promised by the seven priest-kings of ancient Cibotlán* that he will be made stronger than everybody else, able to pay back all those he hates. When Sonny goes to get his reward, however, he is nearly sacrificed to the Sun Serpent (Katóa*). Sonny's terror makes him yearn for Liss, and his emotion is strong enough to pull her and her friends back into Abáloc* in time to save him.

TARAN, the main character in Lloyd Alexander's* Chronicles of Prydain*. He is an orphan; as a baby, he was found beside a battlefield by Dallben*, an enchanter searching for the one who would become the High King of Prydain*. Realizing that this child was, as the future king would be, of no station in life, Dallben took the child, named him Taran, and raised him at Caer Dallben*. As a youth, Taran is impetuous and sometimes headstrong, yearning for a life filled with glory and chafing at the quiet and peace of Caer Dallben. At last he gets a taste of adventure when, with Gwydion*, the war leader of Prydain's present High King, he seeks to end the threat against Prydain by slaying the Horned King*, the champion of the evil lord, Arawn*. Taran later attempts to destroy the Black Crochan*, a huge cauldron in which are created the deathless Cauldron-Born*. Throughout Taran's adventures, he learns more about his weaknesses and strengths and grows closer to his trusted companions: Fflewddur Fflam*, Gurgi*, and, especially, the fiery-tempered princess Eilonwy*, whom he helps rescue when Achren* attempts to take control of her magical powers. Taran's orphaned state becomes increasingly irksome to him, as he longs to marry Eilonwy but feels he has nothing to offer her. During a journey through Prydain, searching for his parents, Taran learns to love the people and the land and also discovers much about himself. Though Taran does not find his parents and learns much that is unpleasant about his own character, he realizes that he is what he makes himself and finds the courage to speak frankly to Eilonwy about his love for her. He does not get a chance to do so, however, until a final great battle, when he draws Dyrnwyn*, a powerful sword, and slays Arawn. After the death of the evil lord, the job of the Sons of Don* is finished and they must journey to the Summer Country*, taking with them those who possess magical powers. Because of what he has achieved, Taran can go with them and live forever among the people he loves, wedded to Eilonwy. The young man chooses not to, for there remains much to be done in Prydain, and, hearing his decision, Dallben joyfully reveals that Taran is the true High King of Prydain. Prophecy has it that the High King would win and lose a powerful sword—as Taran has won and lost Dyrnwyn—would slay a serpent—as Taran has slain Arawn—and choose a kingdom of sorrow over one of happiness—as Taran has chosen to stay in Prydain. Eilonwy is freed of her magical powers and marries Taran. He rules Prydain, accomplishing much during his reign.

TARAN WANDERER. Lloyd Alexander. New York: Holt, Rinehart and Winston, 1967. 254 pp. American.

When spring comes to Prydain*, Taran*, the orphan ward of Dallben*, grows restless; wanting to ask Eilonwy*, a princess, to marry him, he feels that he cannot because he does not know who he is or who his parents are. So Taran sets off from Caer Dallben* with Gurgi*, his hairy companion of uncertain ancestry, to the marshes to ask the three hags who live there. Orwen*, Orddu*, and Orgoch* could tell the young man what he wants to know, but he has nothing to trade for the knowledge, so they tell him of the Mirror of Llunet*, which lies in the Free Commots* to the east and which may hold the answer to his quest for identity.

During his journey across the cantrev of King Smoit*, thieves steal Taran's horse; his life is saved by Aeddan*, a farmer eking out a bare existence on a harsh plot of land. Taran helps the man till his single field before going to Lord Goryon's* stronghold, where he plays on the man's pride to get back his horse. That night he and Gurgi seek shelter in the stronghold of Lord Gast*, where they meet an old friend: Fflewddur Fflam*, a wandering bard/king, who, disgusted with Gast's miserly table, leaves with them and accompanies them to Smoit's castle. Here they learn that Gast and Goryon have begun another war over a herd of cows each claims to own, and, furious, Smoit rides out to stop them. When the king is hurt fording a river, Taran takes him to the closest cottage, Aeddan's farm, where the young man is dismayed to find that the battle has destroyed the farmer's crop. Advised by Taran, Smoit gives the best cow in the disputed herd to Aeddan and, splitting the rest of the herd between them, commands Gast and Goryon to work beside the farmer to raise another crop. Despite Smoit's offer to make him heir to the throne, Taran moves on with Gurgi and Fflewddur.

They are joined by Kaw*, Taran's mischievous talking crow, who steals Fflewddur's harp key and drops it into a hole in a tree. Retrieving the key, Gurgi finds a little box containing a dried bone; realizing that magic may be a factor here, the companions hastily put it back in the tree. That night Llyan*, a huge cat Fflewddur rides as a horse, brings him a frog as a present. It is another old friend—Doli*, one of the Fair Folk*—who was bewitched by Morda*, a wizard who has found a source of great power. Because Doli must learn more before he reports to his king, the companions take him back to Morda's stronghold, and on the way Kaw finds the dried bone and brings it to Taran; under Doli's advice, Taran keeps it. They come to a great barrier of thorns and when Taran and Gurgi try to climb it, they are caught by hidden nooses and flung inside.

Taran wakes, bound and helpless, in Morda's clutches. The wizard wears a necklace with the emblem of the House of Llyr*, which he got from Angharad*, Eilonwy's mother, before she died; it helps him get the better of the Fair Folk. When Fflewddur is also caught in Morda's snares, the wizard uses the emblem to change him into a rabbit and Gurgi into a mouse who chews Taran's bonds while he stalls for time. Free, Taran tries to kill Morda, only to learn that the wizard's life is safely hidden away so that he cannot be killed. When Morda tries and fails to transform Taran, the young man realizes that Morda's life is in the bone Gurgi found, and, after a terrible struggle, the bone is broken, Morda dies, and his enchantments are broken. Because the jewel in the emblem once belonged to the Fair Folk, Taran gives it to Doli, who identifies the hunting horn* the young man carries as one that will call the Fair Folk if blown. It holds one call.

Having left Doli, the companions come across Dorath* and his band of brigands, who become convinced that the trio are seeking a great treasure. When Dorath demands Taran's sword in payment for the food and security he has given the three, Taran fights him and is beaten when Dorath cheats; the outlaw takes Taran's sword. Taran and his commpanions travel on deeper into the hills and there meet Craddoc*, a crippled shepherd struggling against the harsh land he lives on. The man once had a son whom he was forced to send to a place less harsh so that the boy would survive. A healer named Dallben took the boy; Taran must have been that child. Though this is not the parentage Taran hoped for, he feels obliged to stay and help his father and this he does, sending Fflewddur to Dallben to tell him. Taran and Gurgi work hard that summer and into the winter, though the young man's yearning for a better life galls him. One day Craddoc falls into a gorge and Taran, after a struggle to overcome a sudden urge to leave the man to die, is hurt trying to save him. Realizing why Taran will not save himself at the expense of the shepherd, Craddoc confesses that Taran is not his son, for the child died at its birth. He had lied because he needed Taran's help. Desperate and close to death, Taran blows the hunting horn and the Fair Folk come, though not in time to save Craddoc. By the time Taran gets well, Fflewddur has returned; Dallben sent him back to tell Taran that Craddoc was not his father.

Spring comes, but, ashamed at his pride, Taran will not continue his quest. Instead, with only Gurgi, he wanders the Free Commots, meeting its people and making friends. He meets a man who feeds, clothes, and houses his large family by using what he finds and making his own luck. Taran serves as apprentice to a blacksmith who teaches him metal-forging by having him make a sword, and a weaver who teaches him weaving by having him make a new cloak. Then he comes to meet the greatest potter in Prydain, and tries his craft, but this is not for Taran, either. When Taran one day takes a load of pots to a nearby village, he stays to help the villagers defend their homes against Dorath and his band. During the fight Dorath escapes, though his men do not.

Realizing Taran's agony at not knowing himself, the potter tells him of the nearby Mirror of Llunet, which is supposed to reflect the truth of what is reflected in it. Taran finds this lovely little pool and looks into it. Suddenly Dorath is there and attacks Taran, furious because there is no treasure. When the man's sword shatters against Taran's, the young man is able to get away. In the Mirror Taran has seen reflected himself. Realizing that his life is what he makes of it, Taran rides back with Gurgi to Caer Dallben, for his life is there.

TARTLET, TOPSY, a character in *Mary Poppins Comes Back** and *Mary Poppins Opens the Door**, by P[amela] L[yndon] Travers*. She becomes the wife of Arthur Turvey*, and they call themselves the Topsy-Turvies. When Jane Caroline and Michael George Banks** first meet this portly woman, she is very peevish and has straight hair and a perpetually sour expression. She is Mr. Turvey's landlady. When one second Monday of the month Mr.Turvey has one of his usual everything-gone-wrong days, Topsy has one, too, turning upside down, as he has done, when she enters his room. Her personality goes upside down, too; she becomes cheerful all the time and her hair curls. After their marriage, she thoroughly enjoys Arthur's second Mondays.

TASH, a character mentioned in C[live] S[taples] Lewis's* *The Horse and His Boy**, who appears in *The Last Battle**. This great god of Calormen* has a temple in Tashbaan, the capital city. Though roughly the shape of a man, Tash has the head of a bird of prey, and four arms with sharp claws. He withers the grasses he touches and carries with him the smell of putrefaction. No service that is not evil can be done for him; those who do good in his name are really doing it to Aslan*, his opposite, Narnia's* great lion-protector. To Tash the Calormenes make human sacrifices. Rabadash*, a Calormene prince who has been changed by Aslan into a donkey, is transformed back into a man when he stands before the temple of Tash during the time of the Autumn Feast. Tash is called into Narnia by Shift*, an ape, and by Rishda*, a Calormene, who do not believe in the god. Though Tash is Aslan's oppposite, Shift and Rishda slur their names together into one in an attempt to legitimize their exploitation of Narnia. When Tash comes at their command, he takes Shift and Rishda for his own. Tash seems to recognize Aslan's power; he vanishes when Aslan commands him to.

TEENY. *See* D'Agostino, Anna Maria

TEKLA, the queen of fourth-century Kanhuan* in *The Watchers** and *The Birdstones**, by Jane Louise Curry*. Tekla seeks the power to conquer New Aztalán*, and therefore she dedicates her cause to Katóa*, a hungering power of evil. When Ruan*, a boy captured for sacrifice, speaks of Tûl Isgrun*, the place where Katóa has been bound under the earth, Tekla forces him to take her there, and she sets free the evil force. Seeking to dedicate a shrine to Katóa, she comes to Inas Ebhélic*, where the power had lain before the coming of the Aldar*, and, laying waste the small village there, Tekla creates an underground shrine for Katóa. Finding that Dalea*, who lives on the island with her grandfather, Thiuclas*, has escaped with the birdstones*, Tekla tries to find the girl. She inhabits the body of Mrs. Buttery, the librarian of twentieth-century Apple Lock*, Ohio, and thereby recognizes Dalea, who has taken refuge there. Tekla's plans are foiled, and Dalea and her grandfather escape her.

TELMAR, a place in *Prince Caspian**, by C[live] S[taples] Lewis*. This land beyond the western mountains has no talking beasts or marvelous creatures. Originally unpopulated, Telmar was peopled by six pirates and their native wives from Earth. The pirates were shipwrecked on a small island in the South Seas and had taken native wives; when they fought among themselves, six couples fled into a cave which opened into Telmar. The population of Telmar grew and, finally, famine in that land incited them to invade Narnia*, a rich place with talking beasts, dwarfs*, unicorns, and other fantastic creatures. Caspian the Conqueror led his people into Narnia and waged war against the marvelous creatures they found there, killing many and driving others into hiding. During Telmarine rule, even the memory of the Old Narnians is covered up. Because Aslan*, Narnia's great lion-protector, is said to come from beyond the Eastern Ocean in times of great need, the Telmarines are afraid of the ocean and of any body of open water; they do not rule from Cair Paravel*, the traditional capital, because it is on an island off the coast of Narnia. The Telmarines wage ceaseless war against the Old Narnians, killing any they happen to find and fearing greatly the return of Aslan, though some long for the marvels of the old days to return. One of these is Caspian X*, who, when he finally takes the throne, brings the Old Narnians into their own again.

TEMPLE OF FLORA, a small building in E[dith] Nesbit Bland's* *The Enchanted Castle**. This temple on the grounds of Yalding Castle* has a secret passage which leads to the Hall of Granted Wishes*. When the dummies they create come to life, Mabel Prowse*, Gerald*, James*, and Kathleen* imprison these Ugly-Wuglies* in the passage; one of the dummies becomes human when he finds his way to the Hall of Granted Wishes. When Mademoiselle* undoes the magic done by a magic ring*, the passage at the back of the temple disappears.

TEMPLE OF STRANGE STONES, a place in *The Enchanted Castle**, by E[dith] Nesbit Bland*. This Stonehenge-type temple is on the grounds of Yalding Castle*. It is one of several temples onto the altar of which falls one beam of perfect light from the moon on the night of the festival of the harvest. On that night, living statues gather here, and any question asked by a mortal must be answered.

TEMPLETON, a character in E[lwyn] B[rooks] White's* *Charlotte's Web**. He is a rat living in Homer L. Zuckerman's* barn, a rat in both body and spirit, having no morals, kindness, conscience, manners, or decency. Templeton is out for himself and helps no one, though he can be bribed with food, for he is a tremendous glutton. He collects odd objects and pieces of refuse and stashes them in the vast tunnel system he has dug under Mr. Zuckerman's farmyard. Here Templeton stores a goose egg that did not hatch and thereby saves Charlotte A. Cavatica*, a spider who also lives in the barn; when Avery Arable tries to catch her, he accidentally breaks the rotten egg and is driven away by the smell. Templeton also helps save Wilbur*, a pig, from being slaughtered by bringing to Charlotte words to weave into her web, which so impress Mr. Zuckerman that he lets Wilbur live. The high point of Templeton's life is probably the night he spends at the county fair, for here he stuffs himself beyond belief with garbage. On the last day of the fair, Templeton helps Wilbur rescue Charlotte's egg sac after the pig promises to let Templeton eat first at his trough. Wilbur keeps his word and Templeton becomes as big as a young woodchuck from overeating.

TENAR, a character in *The Tombs of Atuan**, by Ursula K. LeGuin*. Her father is a poor man who tends another's orchards; she is one of five children. Because Tenar is born the night the Priestess of the Tombs of Atuan* dies, she is believed to be the reincarnation of the Priestess, who does not die but is continually reborn. At age five, Tenar is taken to her temple and at six is rededicated to the nine Nameless Ones* she has served down through the centuries. She becomes Arha, the Eaten One, who is as nameless as her gods. Arha's upbringing is strict and loveless, and sometimes she is not happy with her life. When she is fourteen, Arha comes fully into the priesshood, and a year later she is shown the caves which are her domain when Kossil*, the Priestess of the Godking*, takes her there to arrange for the sacrifice of three men. This sacrifice upsets Arha greatly, so that when she finds Ged*, who is searching for half of the Ring of Erreth-Akbe*, which lies among the treasures of the tombs, she cannot let him die but cares for him. Arha vacillates, unable to let Ged die, but fearing the wrath of her gods, until Ged forces her to choose between Tenar and Arha. She chooses to be Tenar, and Ged takes her from Atuan. At first the world is a delightful place, but Tenar cannot forget what she has done as Arha. Ged promises her a quiet place to find her own way, but first she must bear the Ring of Erreth-Akbe into Havnor*, Earthsea's* capital. Then he takes her to Ogion*, an old wiseman.

TENCH, BURDICK, a character in Lloyd Alexander's* *The Wizard in the Tree**. Burdick's father is a farmer. This slow-witted lad quickly realizes that he can make money by exhibiting Arbican*, an enchanter who has changed into a pig, as a talking pig. He is thwarted when Arbican refuses to talk and then escapes.

TEPOLLOMIS, a character in Jane Louise Curry's* *The Daybreakers**. He is the king of Abáloc* around A.D. 1170, and is the husband of Erilla* and the father of Lincoas*. Tepollomis dies defending himself and his band of young people from attack by Cibotlán* warriors. His burial mound contains the blue-green stone* Harry Rivers* and his friends use to travel back into ancient Abáloc.

TERAK, a character in Lucy Boston's* *The River at Green Knowe**. His father is dead. Terak is a 150 year-old giant; his parents wandered away from the land in the east where the giants live and eventually were brought to England as part of a circus. Terak's father had been told he was to be king, and when people laughed at him at the circus, he lost his temper. Trying to get at one of the clowns on the tightrope, he fell and broke his neck. Terak's mother took her son and ran away; they have been hiding ever since, moving from place to place to avoid humans. Though his mother has tried to instill in Terak a fear of laughter and of being seen, he is too bold and inquisitive to stay hidden. Most people, however, do not notice him, and he is often mistaken for a tree or other inanimate object. When Terak meets Oskar Stanislawsky*, Ida*, and Hsu*, he learns that laughter is pleasant and that creating it can be pleasant too. He decides to become a clown at the circus and becomes a very successful one. Terak gives a tooth to the children, who leave it for Dr. Maud Biggin*, an archaeologist who believes that giant prehistoric men once existed, to find.. Even she, however, does not believe that Terak is real.

TERRENON, a stone on the island of Osskil* in Ursula K. LeGuin's* *A Wizard of Earthsea**. In this ancient stone an equally ancient evil spirit is imprisoned; over the stone has been raised a great castle. The Terrenon enslaves those who touch it. Ged*, a powerful young sorcerer, is lured to it so that it can enslave his will and use him. Though he escapes both the stone and its hideous creatures, Serret*, the lady of the castle, does not.

TERWILLIGER (WILLY), a dog in Jane Louise Curry's* *Beneath the Hill**. He belongs to Margaret Arthur* (Miggle). This motley, light-eyed dog is men-tioned in an old song of *y Tylwyth Teg**, the Fair Folk*; its coming will herald the freeing of the Folk trapped in the City of the Moon Under the Mountain*. Willy leads Arthur Arthur* to Káolin*, one of the Folk; and Miggle, Arthur, and the others are thereby plunged into a strange adventure. When the children are lost in a mysterious fog created by an evil force bound beneath the mountain, Willy finds them and leads them home.

THACKERS, a manor in Alison Uttley's* *A Traveller in Time**. In Elizabethan times, Thackers is the manor of Anthony Babington*, supporter of Mary Stuart*, Queen of Scots. In an effort to free the queen from nearby Wingfield Manor* he partially clears a tunnel connecting this place and Wingfield. Though the plot is not discovered, Anthony later is convicted of high treason, and after his death part of the house is pulled down. By the twentieth century, the house and some of the surrounding land have become the property of the Taberner family, descendants of some of the Babington servants. The land is farmed by Barnabas Taberner*, great-uncle of Penelope Taberner Cameron*. She can slip from twentieth-century Thackers to Elizabethan Thackers and become involved with those who live there. Twentieth-century Thackers is filled with reminders of its past; many of the furnishings date from the Elizabethan time. Thus Penelope is able to recognize that she is but one in a long line of those who have loved Thackers and that she holds her own place in its history.

THANATOPSIS GROUT *(The Magical Cupboard)*. *See* Grout, Thanatopsis

THIMBLE. *See* Thimbulla

THIMBULLA, a character in Walter de la Mare's* *The Three Mulla-mulgars**. He is the son of Seelem* and Mutta-matutta; his brothers are Thumma* and Ummanodda*. He is called ''Thimble'' for short. Because his uncle is Prince of the Valleys of Tishnar*, Thimble is a Mulla-mulgar, or monkey of royal blood. When their mother dies years after their father has returned to the Valleys of Tishnar, Thimble and his brothers make a long, perilous journey to the Valleys.

THIRTEEN TREASURES OF BRITAIN. *See* Brenhin Dlyseu

THIRTEEN TREASURES OF PRYDAIN. *See* Brenhin Dlyseu

THIUCLAS, a character in Jane Louise Curry's* *The Daybreakers** and *The Birdstones**. He is the grandfather of Dalea*. Though born in fourth-century Abáloc*, where he is the Keeper on Inas Ebhélic*, he travels—via the birdstones*—to twentieth-century Apple Lock*, Ohio, and is trapped there. As Keeper, Thiuclas takes care of the books kept at Inas Ebhélic, among other things. When the people of fourth-century Abáloc take refuge in the City of the Moon Under the Mountain*, he sends the books with them—all but the five *Books of the Kings of Abáloc**, which Thiuclas takes to the twentieth century to hide. He is trapped in this century when Dalea follows him into this time and brings away the birdstones. Thiuclas takes the name ''Mr. Douglass'' and runs a plant nursery in Apple Lock. A vegetarian who pretends to dislike children, he is nonetheless a great favorite with them. Thiuclas finally travels back to his own time when Dalea comes to the twentieth century and brings the birdstones. He and Dalea take refuge in the City of the Moon.

THOMAS BASSUMTYTE (*The Bassumtyte Treasure*). *See* Bassumtyte, Thomas

THOMAS CAKEBREAD (*Parsley Sage, Rosemary & Time*). *See* Cakebread, Thomas

THOMAS KEMPE (*The Ghost of Thomas Kempe*). *See* Kempe, Thomas

THORIN OAKENSHIELD, a character in J[ohn] R[onald] R[euel] Tolkien's* *The Hobbit**. He is the son of Thrain and the grandson of Thror; he is the uncle of Fili and Kili. This dwarf* was born and raised in his grandfather's great palace beneath the Lonely Mountain. Always adventurous and given to wandering, Thorin was outside the day Smaug*, a great dragon, attacked the place and took it over, killing all those inside but Thorin's father and his grandfather. After this, years passed, during which Thorin eked out a living doing whatever metal-forging and mining there was to do. Finally he is found by Gandalf*, a wizard, who bears a map of the secret way into the mountain. Thorin gathers a group of twelve dwarves and a hobbit* and leads them to the Lonely Mountain, enduring many dangers along the way. For a time he bears the sword Orcrist, the Goblin-cleaver; it is taken from him when he is held prisoner by the Elvenking. The vast treasure beneath the mountain stirs the greed in Thorin's soul, and when he refuses to share it with men and elves* who have claim on some of it, they march against him. The battle is cut short when goblins* and wild wolves attack all the armies, and Thorin falls in that battle. He is buried beneath the mountain, with the fabulous Arkenstone*, which he had coveted, on his breast; on his tomb is laid Orcrist, which gleams in the dark when foes approach.

THORNTON, TIM, a character in Penelope Lively's* *The Revenge of Samuel Stokes**. He is the son of Mary and Ted Thornton and the grandson of Grandpa*. Eleven-year-old Tim and his family move into what seems to be a perfectly normal house in a new residential area, but strange things begin to happen, for Samuel Stokes*, who had planned the garden for the eighteenth-century estate where the new houses are built, is trying to drive everyone away. Tim, Grandpa, and Jane Harvey*, Tim's friend, realize what is going on and are able, finally, to steer Stokes's attention away from the residential area and onto a nearby park.

THREE MULLA-MULGARS, THE. Walter de la Mare. Illus. E. A. Monsell. London: Duckworth and Co., 1910. 312 pp. British.

Thumma* (Thumb), Thimbulla* (Thimble), and Ummanodda* (Nod) live with their mother in the forest in a hut built by a Portuguese sailor. These Mulgars*— or monkeys—are the sons of Seelem*, a Mulla-mulgar—or royal monkey—who came originally from the Kingdom of Assasimmon* in the Valleys of Tishnar*. He taught his sons to walk upright, to never eat meat, and to never—unless in danger or despair—climb trees or grow tails. Then he had gone back to his old home, promising to return. Years have passed without a trace of him. As she lies dying, the mother tells her sons to follow their father and gives them presents; to Nod, because he is a Nizza-neela, she gives the powerful Wonderstone*, showing him how to use it and warning him not to give it up. After she dies, the snows come and the brothers put off their journey until Nod accidentally burns down the hut and they have no choice.

Their journey is long and hard. Traveling north to the Valleys of Tishnar, the three come to a river, where they also find a boat belonging to a Gunga-mulgar*— or gorilla—who catches Nod in the act of borrowing the boat. Nod convinces the Gunga that he knows the secret of catching big fish, which involves rowing halfway across the river and using various chants and nets. The next morning the Gunga allows him to demonstrate, first promising not to watch. Nod and his brothers are almost across before the Gunga breaks his word; enraged, he fires arrows at the three, and one of them strikes Nod. Near the opposite shore, the three wreck the boat and, after struggling to land, Nod faints.

He wakes in the caves of the Minimuls*, who have captured Thimble and Thumb to eat; because of the Wonderstone, Nod will be spared. After regaining his strength, Nod uses the Wonderstone, which produces a flame that leads him to his brothers and then to the outside. In their escape, Nod puts the Wonderstone in his mouth for safekeeping and accidentally swallows it. The three flee on Zevveras—zebras—and are separated. Nod, found by Mishcha* and her sister Quatta hare, is nursed completely back to health. When he leaves them, he is caught in a snare set by Andy Battle*, an Oomgar—man—who is astonished by Nod's ability to imitate his speech and who teaches him English. The two become friends. But the Immânala*, the ravenous beast like no other beast, is stalking Battle. Mishcha warns Nod and also tells him that his brothers are nearby. Nod goes out at night to meet the Immânala, and when he does so, the Wonderstone slips up his throat and puts it in his pocket. Greedy to possess Battle's coat and hat, which she thinks are magic, the Immânala agrees to bring her Jack-Alls and leopards to the hut the next night to kill Battle, if Nod will betray the man. At the appointed time Nod meets the Immânala and dresses her in the "magic" clothes which he has weighted with rocks so that she cannot get away. Her Jack-Alls kill her in mistake for Battle. Sadly, Nod leaves Battle to travel north with his two brothers.

They reach the mountains, and after some quarrelling out of weariness and frustration, set out to cross them, though no one they meet can tell them the way. When they are trapped on a narrow ledge, the three are rescued by Moona-mulgars* who live in the mountains and who agree to take the travelers to the end of their domain, though they do not know the way to the Valleys of Tishnar. This journey is long and perilous; they are attacked by eagles and wolves and pestered by witless Mulgars called Obobbomans. When they reach the end of the Moona-mulgars' country, Ghibba* and the rest of his Mulgars decide to continue with Thimble, Thumb, and Nod and are rewarded with a vision of one of the middens (maidens) of Tishnar*. Ghibba reveals that Seelem journeyed through the country of the Moona-mulgars, but he vanished. As they journey through the night, the group hears music, and they come to a valley to find huge Meermuts*, or spirits, guarding the opposite ridge. When Nod consults his Wonderstone to find a way around, the stone makes him a dazzle of light, and Nod guides Thumb through the Meermuts, which Thumb sees as ghoulish spirits and which Nod sees as trees. On the other side, Thumb sees only darkness until the Wonderstone makes him see the orchards of Tishnar that Nod sees. Using the stone, Nod brings the others into the orchard and they feast and sleep, to wake refreshed in the snow.

As they push on, they come to a village of Fishing-mulgars by a river, who tell of an old Mulgar who came to their village and left behind a campfire when he journeyed on. Confident that Seelem has gone before them, the Mulgars follow the river until it forks; one branch falls in a cataract, and the other glides into underground caverns. As Ghibba and five Mulgars explore beyond the cataract, the others camp beside the river. Unable to sleep that night, Nod goes to the river and meets a sad and lovely Water-midden*. To lessen her sadness, he shows her the Wonderstone, then lets her hold it and is chagrined when she says she will not give it back until the next night. The next morning Ghibba and three of his followers return and rafts are built; there is no way past the cataract and they must journey through the caverns. That evening Nod calls the water-midden and tricks the Wonderstone away from her. She has been trying to wish on it but could not get it to work. Nod promises to obey her wish—that he not forget her—anyway, and she knots around his wrist a strand of her hair.

The Mulgars put off and drift through the caverns. On this long journey, those who get thirsty and drink from the river fall into a deep sleep. Torches gutter out, the air gets thick and hard to breathe, and Nod finally is so parched that he drinks from the river and sleeps. He wakes in the Valleys of Tishnar, and there he and the others find the rusted gun Seelem brought with him on his journey, and meet an inhabitant of the Kingdom of Assasimmon.

THREE ROYAL MONKEYS, THE. *See Three Mulla-mulgars, The*

THUMB. *See* Thumma

THUMMA, a character in *The Three Mulla-mulgars**, by Walter de la Mare*. He is the son of Seelem* and Mutta-matutta; his younger brothers are Thimbulla* and Ummanodda*. He is called "Thumb." Thumb is a Mulla-mulgar, or royal monkey, for his uncle is the Prince of the Valleys of Tishnar*. When their father, bound on a journey to the Valleys of Tishnar, does not return, and their mother dies, Thumb and his brothers make a long and perilous journey to the Valleys.

TIDDI, a race of beings in Jane Louise Curry's* *The Wolves of Aam**. They are the oldest mortal race. The Tiddi are a small people, standing half the size of men. Their broad feet have long toes for gripping the earth and the soles of their feet are tough as leather, for they go barefoot. Since the fall of the last age in the land of Astarlind, the Tiddi have been nomads, following a circular route around the boundaries of the land that was laid out long ago by Lobb the Singer. They were great hunters of the small horses that once ranged Astarlind; by the time Runner-to-the-Sky's Edge* (Runner), Fith*, and Cathound* are born, the numbers of both horses and Tiddi have decreased drastically. These nomadic people are fond of songs, which are usually sung at feasts and celebrations. Special dances that celebrate the rising and setting of the sun and the moon are also a part of their lore. Each Tiddi is born with a name and can earn another; Runner had earned his name when he was appointed scout for the tribe.

TIGER LILY, a character in James M. Barrie's* *Peter and Wendy**. Tiger Lily is the lovely daughter of the Piccaninny tribe of Indians in Neverland*. Many braves want to marry her, but Tiger Lily will have none of them, though she hints that she wants to be something other than a mother to Peter Pan*. When Peter rescues her from drowning on Marooner's Rock*, Tiger Lily and the rest become friends with Peter and the lost boys*.

TIM, a character in *The Ghost of Thomas Kempe**, by Penelope Lively*. He is a dog of uncertain parentage. Tim is independent and good-natured, staying with anyone who treats him well, and he becomes the unofficial pet of James Harrison* when the boy moves into town with his family. Here Tim proves himself a great appreciator of television, particularly westerns. His strange behavior when the spirit of Thomas Kempe*, a seventeeth-century sorcerer, is around alerts James to Thomas's presence.

TIM MCGRATH (*Rabbit Hill; The Tough Winter*). *See* McGrath, Tim

TIM THORNTON (*The Revenge of Samuel Stokes*). *See* Thornton, Tim

TIME, an herb in Jane Louise Curry's* *Parsley Sage, Rosemary & Time**. It was planted in the eighteenth century by Juditha Cakebread*, the wife of Thomas Cakebread*, in a little garden at Wychwood. This short herb with leaves like crows' feet thrives in the garden, growing thickly there into the twentieth century. Though it looks ordinary, "time" has strange properties; held in the hand, it stops time for all but the one who holds it, and, when eaten, it opens a gap in the wall around the Dreaming Trees*, thereby allowing one to travel through time. William Wingard*, Hepsibah Sagacity Walpole*, and Rosemary Walpole* all use it accidentally at different times in the twentieth century and find themselves in 1722. Late in the twentieth century the bed of "time" is spaded up.

TIME, FATHER, an entity in C[live] S[taples] Lewis's* *The Silver Chair** and *The Last Battle**. Once a king above ground in Narnia*, a magical land, this gigantic, noble-faced man lies sleeping in a cave in Underland*, dreaming of what is happening in the world above him, until he is awakened by Aslan*, Narnia's great lion-protector, at the end of the world. Once awake, Time blows his horn, signalling the end, and squeezes out the sun, bringing darkness over the land. Now that he is awake, he has a new name.

TIME CAT. Lloyd Alexander. Illus. Bill Sokol. New York: Holt, Rinehart and Winston, 1963. 191 pp. American.

One day when he has caused more than a little trouble at home, Jason* wishes aloud to his cat, Gareth*, that *he* had nine lives like the cat. Gareth informs him that cats have not got nine lives, but they do have the ability to visit nine different lives, in any country in any time period. Because it is a special occasion, Gareth can take Jason with him, and so begins their journey.

They start out in ancient Egypt. Jason has no trouble fitting in, for he is wearing the proper clothes and understands the language. Because Gareth bears the sign of the sacred ankh on his chest, he is taken to entertain the pharoah, Neter-Khet*, and Jason is imprisoned to get him out of the way. Because Gareth will not entertain the pharoah on command, Jason is brought into the court, and he teaches Neter-Khet a valuable lesson in the independence of cats. The pharoah gives Jason a golden ankh before Gareth winks his eye and transports the two to Imperial Rome.

Here Jason and Gareth contact a legion wanting a cat as a mascot and accompany them to Gaul, where Jason is separated from the troops during a battle and becomes the captive of a Briton—Cerdic Longtooth*. Like other Britons, Cerdic and his family are wary of Gareth, for they have never seen a tame cat. When Jason pretends to have tamed Gareth, all are much impressed. Slowly Cerdic and his family come to love Gareth and are delighted when a wild cat has her kittens in their storeroom and they can tame them. Jason and Gareth leave and find themselves in fifth-century Ireland.

Here they meet Diahan*, the daughter of King Miliucc*. They have had much trouble with rats and snakes, but Lugad*, the king's magician, explains that he has taken care of that problem and that the rats and snakes they see now are only the ghosts of the real ones. When Gareth saves Diahan from a "ghostly" viper, Miliucc makes the boy and the cat his sorcerers and then, as usual, forgets about the appointment. But Lugad does not; jealous, he seeks to sacrifice them at the next Midsummer. They escape with Sucat*, a Welsh slave who is also called "Patrick." He longs to go and become wise so that he may come back to Ireland and drive out ignorance and fear, and also bring cats to deal with the serpents and the rats.

Gareth winks and suddenly he and Jason are in tenth-century Japan, traveling with a merchant who has promised to bring the boy-emperor Ichigo* something unique. He has brought five kittens, and Jason stays to care for them. Though Ichigo is emperor, he is afraid of his overbearing uncle, Fujiwara*. Slowly Jason teaches Ichigo about cats; and Gareth teaches the kittens what they need to know, taking them outside the palace each night to hunt rats. One night they are caught leaving, and Jason is almost executed. Hearing how the cats have helped his people, Ichigo forgives Jason and decides that the kittens should be free to come and go, but Fujiwara, enraged, demands that they all die. Emboldened, Ichigo remembers he is emperor and humbles his uncle.

Jason and Gareth leave and find themselves in Renaissance Italy, where they meet a copper-haired boy named Leonardo, of the Vinci family, who is fascinated by everything. Leonardo da Vinci* wants to be a painter, though his father wants him to be a notary. When a farmer wanting a picture painted leaves a board for Leonardo's father to take to an artist, the boy paints on it a picture of an angry Gareth that so startles his father that the man decides to apprentice Leonardo to a painter. Gareth whisks Jason to sixteenth-century Peru.

Here they meet Don Diego Francisco Hernández del Gato Herrera y Robles* (Don Diego), a conquistador who hates being in the army and fighting Incas. Fascinated by the Indian culture, he is writing a history and a dictionary. One day Jason and Gareth, walking outside the fortification, are captured by the Incas and held for ransom. Don Diego secures their freedom by promising that he will try to help the Indians; he gains a position as adviser to the Viceroy at Lima and at last is free of the hated army.

In a wink, Gareth and Jason find themselves on the Isle of Man in the sixteenth century. One of the ships in the Spanish Armada has broken up and Dulcinea*, a tailless cat, and her kittens have come ashore. Jason and Gareth go with her to a nearby village, where they meet Awin*, a girl convinced that she is ugly because one of her eyes is brown and the other is blue. Because of this, she refuses to marry Baetan*, who seems to think she is lovely. When Jason points out that some would think Dulcinea ugly because she, too, looks different, Awin defends the cat hotly, then seems to see herself in a new light. When the men go fishing, Awin makes clear her love for Baetan, and Dulcinea overcomes her fear of the sea and goes out in the boat for luck.

Suddenly Jason and Gareth are in seventeenth-century Germany, where they are chased by superstitious villagers convinced that Gareth is a demon. They take refuge with Mistress Ursulina*, an old woman having trouble with Master Speckfresser* because she will not sell her land. He threatens to denounce her as a witch, and she sends the two to the miller, Master Johannnes*, before she is arrested. Realizing that Speckfresser is a sorcerer they saw as they ran through the village, Jason helps Johannes come up with a plan; while Speckfresser conjures that night, Jason and Gareth, disguised as demons, come down the chimney and try to bluff the man into setting Ursulina free. The plan backfires, however, when guards break in and arrest them all as witches. They are tried, found guilty, and sentenced. Speckfresser, Johannes, Ursulina, Jason, and Gareth manage to escape; they will go to another place and try to start over again. Jason and Gareth leave the three and their century and find themselves in America in 1775.

Professor Peter Perseverance Parker*, traveling with kittens and news of rebellion, picks up Gareth and Jason and takes them along as he sells his kittens and spreads the word. Turning back to Boston, they are in time to watch as Minutemen fight British soldiers, galvanized by that morning's battle at Lexington. Gravely wounded, the professor sends the boy and the cat to warn the Sons of Liberty in a nearby town. After doing this, Jason walks with Gareth through a shifting landscape. Having taken Jason on this journey to teach him things he needs to know about himself and others to be an adult, Gareth will not be able to speak to him any more. When they come home, Jason thinks it has all been a dream, until he reaches into his pocket and finds the ankh Neter-Khet gave him.

TIME TRILOGY, three novels by Madeleine L'Engle* that chronicle the adventures of the Murry family in time and space. *See A Wrinkle in Time; A Wind in the Door; A Swiftly Tilting Planet*

TIMMIS, a character in *The Borrowers Afloat* and *The Borrowers Avenged*, by Mary Norton*. He is the youngest son of Hendreary* and Lupy*; he has two older brothers and a sister named Eggletina. Timmis's name appears as "Timmus" in *The Borrowers Avenged*. He is a borrower*, one of a race of tiny people who live by "borrowing" what they need from humans. Timmis is irrepressible, loving to climb and to scamper about, especially if he can show off for Arrietty Clock*, his beloved cousin. Early in his life, Timmis does not get a chance to do much scampering, for he and his family live in the wall of a small cottage and he must be quiet. When the family is forced to move and takes up lodgings in the vestry of a small church, Timmis, too young to go borrowing with Hendreary, uses the church as his playground and quickly becomes adept at running and at climbing up the bell rope in the bell chamber. A favorite pasttime is painting his face brown and pretending to be one of the tiny figures in the church's heavily carved rood screen, from which he can watch humans. When Arrietty and her family move into the nearby rectory, Timmis is very pleased, for he likes Arrietty and her stories and, accompanied by her, helps borrow food for his family. He also begins to take enjoyable lessons from Peregrine Overmantel*, another young borrower. Timmis's liveliness almost gets him caught by Sidney Platter* and his wife, but the young borrower escapes and indirectly causes the Platters to be caught breaking into the church.

TIMMO. *See* Jones, Timothy

TIMMS, MARTHA, a character in *The Whispering Knights*, by Penelope Lively*. She is the daughter of Tom Timms and his wife and the older sister of two brothers, the youngest of whom is Tommy. Martha is not good at concealing things. She fears witches and goblins and giants, who people her dreams. Thus when she, Susan Poulter*, and William* try the witches' spell from *Macbeth* in a barn where a witch once lived, Martha is fearful of the consequences. Things turn out worse than she had feared, for Morgan le Fay* is called and tries hard to get the children into her power. She succeeds with Martha, perhaps by playing on her fear, putting the girl into a trance in which she obeys Morgan's wishes until at last the spell ends. After a final struggle the children run from Morgan to the Hampden Stones*, where Morgan is defeated.

TIMMUS. *See* Timmis

TIMOTHY JONES (*The Watch House*). *See* Jones, Timothy

TIN ISLANDS, a place in E[dith] Nesbit Bland's* *The Story of the Amulet*. The location of these islands is a secret known only to the navigators of ancient Tyre; a journey to them takes six months to a year. Robert*, Anthea*, Cyril*, and Jane* find themselves on a ship going to these islands when they search through time for half of an ancient amulet*. To keep the location of the islands secret, the men wreck their ship on the rocks when a ship from another land follows them, rather than show the other sailors where the islands are.

TINKER BELL, a fairy from Neverland* in James M. Barrie's* *Peter and Wendy*. She gets her name because she acts as the fairies' tinker. Tinker Bell is Peter Pan's* companion and is very jealous when he becomes acquainted with Wendy Moira Darling*. Tinker Bell tries to get Wendy killed by telling the lost boys* that Peter wants them to shoot her; she later saves Peter's life by drinking his poisoned medicine, from which she recovers. Tinker Bell's attachment seems more than motherly, but Peter soon forgets her after she eventually dies.

TIR NA'NOG, a place of peace and safety in *Beneath the Hill** and *The Change-Child**, by Jane Louise Curry*. This land lies beyond the sea and is the last place of sanctuary for *y Tylwyth Teg**, the Fair Folk*.

TIRIAN, a character in C[live] S[taples] Lewis's* *The Last Battle**. He is the son of Erlian. Tirian is the last king of Narnia*, a magical land. During his rule, while he is yet in his twenties, word comes that Aslan*, Narnia's great lion-protector, is in the land, but he soon discovers that it is not true. When Tirian and his good friend, Jewel*, a unicorn, come on talking beasts of Narnia being treated as slaves by warriors from her enemy, Calormen*, Tirian and Jewel slay them; because the warriors had been weaponless, Tirian gives himself up to the rest, for his honor is gone. In despair at what he has seen as the prisoner of the Calormenes and of Shift*, the talking ape who pretends to be the mouthpiece of Aslan, Tirian calls on the great lion's help and appears, briefly, to seven people from Earth who have helped Narnia in the past. Two of them, Jill Pole* and Eustace Clarence Scrubb*, come to Narnia to help Tirian, but the forces against them are too great and their battle is lost. It is ultimately won, for Tirian and his companions are taken into Aslan's country and live there in joy forever after Aslan brings Narnia to an end.

TISHNAR, a power in Walter de la Mare's* *The Three Mulla-mulgars**. Her name refers to that which cannot be thought about or expressed. She is the Beautiful One of the Mountains and wanders the mountain snows. From her will come the last sleep of all the World. Beautiful Tishnar is represented veiled. The lovely Water-middens* are among her maidens, who ride on Zevveras, or "the Little Horses of Tishnar." The wind that blows in the first twilight is her wind, and the valleys that flank the Mountains of Arakkaboa are her valleys. The spirit and beauty of each creature are also hers. Ummanodda*, who carries the Wonderstone* of Tishnar, is under her special care.

TISROC, a character in *The Horse and His Boy**, by C[live] S[taples] Lewis*. He is the father of Rabadash*. "Tisroc" is actually a term for the ruler of Calormen*. This nameless Tisroc gives in to his son's demand to conquer Narnia*, a magical land to the north. That Narnia is still free is a sorry affair, in the Tisroc's eyes, but he does not try to conquer it himself for fear of the great kings who rule it. He allows Rabadash to make the attempt, which fails.

TISSIE. *See* Taberner, Cicely Ann

TOAD, a character in Kenneth Grahame's* *The Wind in the Willows**. Wealthy Toad is good-hearted and will do anything for his friends, but he is also conceited, erratic, and a little overbearing. Toad's all-consuming interests vary as the mood strikes him; he becomes enchanted by boats, caravans, and motorcars in turn. His love of automobiles is nearly his undoing, for Toad smashes up six and is imprisoned for "borrowing" another and cheeking a policeman. Toad's escape from jail is as dramatic as he could wish, and he returns home to discover that weasels and stoats from the Wild Wood have taken over Toad Hall; he and his friends—the Mole*, the Water Rat*, and the Badger*—take back the Hall. At the subsequent celebration, Toad's boastfulness is quelled by the others, and he seems to find humility as heady an experience as boastfulness was.

TOBY OLDKNOW (the Green Knowe books). *See* Oldknow, Toseland

TOLKIEN, J[OHN] R[ONALD] R[EUEL] (1892-1973), British writer. He was born on 3 January 1892, in Bloemfontein, South Africa, to Arthur and Mabel Suffield Tolkien. He was educated at Exeter College, Oxford University. In 1916 he married Edith Bratt; they had three sons and a daughter. Tolkien taught at Leeds University and at Oxford. He died on 2 September 1973.

Tolkien's works specifically for children include a collection of poems, a collection of illustrated letters, a picture book, two short fantasies, and a full-length fantasy, *The Hobbit**, a precursor to his high fantasy trilogy more generally read by adults, *The Lord of the Rings*. In most of Tolkien's work, the hero is unexpected: a clever farmer in *Farmer Giles of Ham* defeats a dragon and saves the day. In *The Hobbit*, the hero is a hobbit* who seeks out a great treasure and finds something more: a self-confidence and a sense of a world richer than he could have imagined. In *The Lord of the Rings*, a mysterious, tattered figure is really a king, and a small, stay-at-home hobbit is instrumental in the defeat of a powerful, evil lord.

None of the heroes begins as a truly heroic figure. Farmer Giles is slow and complacent, caught up in his own concerns and going after the dragon only after getting a little drunk and learning that the sword he has been given is magic. Little Bilbo Baggins*, of *The Hobbit*, is anyone but the person one would take on a long and difficult quest when first we meet him; fond of house, hearth, and larder, he loves to smoke his pipe, take his walks, and eat at least two breakfasts in his neat and comfortable little home. When he meets Gandalf*, the legendary wizard, Bilbo's response is to wish he would go away, for Gandalf is "not his sort"; when fourteen dwarves* descend on him for tea, Bilbo is understandably flummoxed, and when they sing of dragon fire he is frightened; when, as they begin to plan their journey, he realizes that not only do the dwarves plan to include him but that they may never return, he shrieks in terror and has a fit. Bilbo is late for his own quest, for he has overslept and does not get the dwarves' message in time to pack. Smaller than the dwarves and sometimes unable to keep up with them, unhandy at his burgling, longing for his hearth and his soft, warm bed, Bilbo is not the traditional hero even on the journey. Frodo, in *The Lord of the Rings*, is not quite as unhandy as Bilbo is, on his quest. He does, however, have a hobbit's natural reluctance to roam, until he inherits the mighty ring* of power that he must destroy, and even then, small and innocent of warfare, magic, and the world, Frodo has little about him of the traditional hero.

But adventure soon brings out the best in each, calling forth from each hero qualities he may not have known he had and leaving each changed. Giles, the clever, hard-bargaining farmer, becomes even cleverer and learns to drive even harder bargains after dealing with a wily dragon; finally he outwits the king and becomes so fabulously rich and popular that he himself is crowned. Though Bilbo tries to deny his adventurous, imaginative side, for adventure and poetry are not "respectable" for a hobbit, it burns within him and, ultimately, will not be denied. Thus he finds, during his adventure, that though much of it is uncomfortable, and that some of the time it is downright dangerous and he is afraid, still it is an exhilirating experience. Tried by the fire of the quest, he finds that he has resources he had not known of, and makes resources he had not had. Bilbo learns or uses cleverness and nerve, quick thinking and perservance, and he wins through, but he is changed; at the Battle of Five Armies, he prepares to lay down his life for the king of the elves*. Though Bilbo will never have the thirst for adventure of his ancestors, he allows the hidden aspects of his own nature to come to the fore; he writes poetry and visits elves and loses his reputation among the hobbits forever. Frodo's adventures call forth his bravery and endurance, but they leave him weary to the heart and longing for peace; he has seen the world and held great power, and finally he must go far beyond his world to gain the peace he seeks.

For, having had adventure, no hero can go back and be what he was before. Giles, having defeated a giant, must defeat a dragon, and, having done that and vanquished a king besides, finally becomes king himself. Sheltered in Hobbiton, Bilbo has not had experience of the world outside his peaceful place, and he does not think about it much. On the quest he meets dwarves and elves and trolls*, dragons and spiders and men, and he sees a world where there are greed and war, hatred and mistrust, where thinking beings of one kind kill thinking beings of another for food or out of malice. But it is a world of beauty and peace, too, as he finds at the last Homely House of the elves. Though at the end he is glad to be home, among familiar things, he cannot quite shut out the rest of the world; he visits elves and welcomes Gandalf and one of the dwarves warmly when they visit. Having carried to its destruction a great ring of power, Frodo returns to the Shire, but his happiness there is lost, and finally, with Bilbo, he must leave his beloved home and travel far into the West, to sweet lands beyond the High Sea.

Tolkien's works are rich in incident and in a sense of place; the worlds of his tales are wonderfully detailed, and his descriptive prose creates them vividly for the reader. Though some of the characters seem more like types than anything else—all but two of the dwarves in *The Hobbit*, for example, are little more than names—all are interesting and lively, and Bilbo is very believable.

Works

Juvenile full-length fantasy: *The Hobbit* (1937; rev. 1951).

Juvenile short fantasy, poetry, letters: *Farmer Giles of Ham* (1949); *The Adventures of Tom Bombadil* (1962); *Smith of Wootton Major* (1967); *The Father Christmas Letters* (1976); *Mr. Bliss* (1983), picture book.

Adult: *A Middle English Vocabulary* (1921); *The Fellowship of the Ring* (1954); *The Two Towers* (1954); *The Return of the King* (1955); *Tree and Leaf* (1964), essays; *The Tolkien Reader* (1966), essays and short pieces; *The Road Goes Ever On* (1967), songs; *The Silmarillion* (1977), stories; *Unfinished Tales* (1980).

Secondary Works

Carpenter, Humphrey. *J. R. R. Tolkien*. London: Allen and Unwin, 1977.

Carter, Lin. *Tolkien: A Look Behind "The Lord of the Rings."* New York: Ballantine, 1969.

Chant, Joy. "Niggle and Númenor," *Children's Literature in Education*, 19 (Winter, 1975), pp. 161-71.

Christensen, Bonniejean. "Gollum's Character Transformation in *The Hobbit*," in *A Tolkien Compass*, ed. Jared Lobdell (La Salle, Ill.: Open Court, 1975), pp. 9-28.

Colbath, Mary Lou. "Worlds as They Should Be: Middle-earth, Narnia and Prydain," *Elementary English*, 48 (Dec., 1971), pp. 937-45.

Crouch, M. S. "Another Don in Wonderland," *Junior Bookshelf*, 14 (March, 1950), pp. 50-53.

Evans, Robley. *J. R. R. Tolkien*. New York: Thomas Y. Crowell Company, 1972.

Foster, Robert. *The Complete Guide to Middle-earth*, rev. ed. London and Boston: George Allen and Unwin, 1978.

Grotta-Kurska, Daniel. *J. R. R. Tolkien: Architect of Middle Earth*. Philadelphia: Running Press, 1976. [Re-issued as *The Biography of J. R. R. Tolkien: Architect of Middle-Earth*, by Daniel Grotta, 1978.]

Helms, Randel. *Tolkien's World*. London: Thames and Hudson, 1974.

Kocher, Paul. *Master of Middle-Earth*. Boston: Houghton Mifflin Company, 1972.

The Letters of J. R. R. Tolkien, ed. Humphrey Carpenter. Boston: Houghton Mifflin Company, 1981.

Matthews, Dorothy. "The Psychological Journey of Bilbo Baggins," in *A Tolkien Compass*, ed. Jared Lobdell (La Salle, Ill.: Open Court, 1975), pp. 29-42.

Noel, Ruth S. *The Mythology of Middle-Earth*. Boston: Houghton Mifflin Company, 1977.

Ready, William. *The Tolkien Relation: A Personal Inquiry*. Chicago: Henry Regnery Company, 1968. [Reprinted as *Understanding Tolkien and "The Lord of the Rings."* New York: Paperback Library, 1969.]

Rogers, Deborah Webster, and Ivor A. Rogers. *J. R. R. Tolkien*. Boston: Twayne Publishers, 1980.

Ryan, J. S. "German Mythology Applied—The Extension of the Literary Folk Memory," *Folklore*, 77 (Spring, 1966), pp. 45-59.

Shippey, T. A. "Creation from Philology in *The Lord of the Rings*," in *J. R. R. Tolkien, Scholar and Storyteller: Essays in Memoriam*, ed. Mary Salu and Robert T. Farrell (Ithaca, N.Y.: Cornell University Press, 1979), pp. 286-316.

Stein, Ruth M. "The Changing Styles in Dragons—from Fáfnir to Smaug," *Elementary English*, 45 (Feb., 1968), pp. 179-83.

Stevens, C. D. "High Fantasy Versus Low Comedy: Humor in J. R. R. Tolkien," *Extrapolation*, 24 (Summer, 1980), pp. 122-29.

Stimpson, Catherine. *J. R. R. Tolkien*. New York: Columbia University Press, 1969.

Tolkien, J. R. R. "On Fairy Stories," in *Essays Presented to Charles Williams* (London and New York: Oxford University Press, 1947), pp. 38-89.

Tolkien and the Critics, ed. N. D. Isaacs and R. A. Zimbardo. Notre Dame, Ind.: University of Notre Dame Press, 1968.

Tyler, J. E. A. *The New Tolkien Companion*. New York: St. Martin's Press, 1979.

West, Richard C., comp. *Tolkien Criticism: An Annotated Checklist*, The Serif Series: Bibliographies and Checklists, Number 11. N.p.: Kent State University Press, 1970.

Wood, Michael. "Tolkien's Fictions," in *Suitable for Children?: Controversies in Children's Literature*, ed. Nicholas Tucker (Berkeley and Los Angeles: University of California Press, 1976), pp. 165-72. [Reprinted from *New Society*, 27 March 1969.]

TOLLY. *See* Toseland

TOM, the main character in Charles Kingsley's* *The Water-babies**. He is an orphan, the uneducated young apprentice of Mr. Grimes*, a brutal chimney sweep. Tom is never ashamed of his unlettered, unwashed state until he gets lost in the maze of chimneys in a country manor and comes out in the clean, white bedroom of Ellie*. Chased by the household, who think he must have stolen something, he flees across the moor and, while feverishly trying to wash himself, drowns and becomes a water-baby*. Impulsive and mischievous while on dry land, Tom is just as impulsive and mischievous in the water, teasing the water creatures until he learns forbearance. Tom meets other water-babies in the sea and comes under the care and tutelage of Mrs. Doasyouwouldbedoneby* and Mrs. Bedonebyasyoudid* and, finally, of Ellie, who does not teach him on Sunday, for that day she must go somewhere else. So that he might go to this wonderful, indescribable place, Tom goes to the Other-end-of-Nowhere*—a place he does not like—to help Mr. Grimes—something he does not want to do. By the time Tom succeeds, he and Ellie have grown up and when they meet again they fall in love. Tom becomes a man of science, wise with the things he has learned as a water-baby.

TOM GARLAND (*Poor Tom's Ghost*). *See* Garland, Tom

TOM GOODENOUGH (the Borrower series). *See* Goodenough, Tom

TOM LONG (*Tom's Midnight Garden*). *See* Long, Tom

TOM MOORHOUSE (*A Chance Child*). *See* Moorhouse, Tom

TOMBS OF ATUAN, THE. Ursula K. LeGuin. Illus. Gail Garraty. New York: Atheneum, 1971. 163 pp. American.

Because she was born the night the old Priestess died, Tenar* becomes Arha, the Eaten One, the new Priestess of the Tombs of Atuan*, where are buried the nine who ruled before Earthsea* was created. She is the old Priestess reborn, and at age five Tenar goes to Atuan and loses her name to retake the name of Arha. Arha's growing up is a loveless one; only Manan*, a eunuch, shows affection. When Arha comes of age, she is taken by Kossil*, the High Priestess of the Godking*, to the Undertomb*—a great cavern surrounded by a maze of passages—where she sentences to a sacrificial death three men who tried to kill the Godking. Though she knows it must be done, this experience upsets Arha greatly.

Because it is her domain, Arha explores the sacred Undertomb, where light is not permitted, and the less sacred Labyrinth*, a tangle of passages built to protect the Great Treasure of the Tombs. Many have come to rob the Tombs, searching for the amulet of Erreth-Akbe*, a sorcerer who was defeated in battle with the High Priest of the Twin Gods. Half of his broken ring of power lies in the Treasure; the other half was lost. Slowly Arha learns both the Labyrinth and something about those around her; Kossil, she realizes, truly worships not the nine Nameless Ones* or the gods, but power, and she would get rid of the Priestess of the Tombs if she could.

One night Arha goes into the Undertomb and finds it desecrated by light burning at the end of a staff held by a man. When he goes into the Labyrinth, she shuts its iron door behind him. Realizing that he must be a sorcerer to have gotten this far, Arha also realizes that he must be after the half of the Ring of Erreth-Akbe*. She watches through a peep-hole as he tries and fails to open the iron door and then sleeps, clutching a talisman around his neck. Though she knows he must die, Arha cannot bring herself to let him die of thirst in the Labyrinth; three days later she calls to him, sending him to another room, then in spite and fury she sends the man to the treasure room. He does not make it; Arha and Manan find him unconscious in a passageway and chain him in a chamber, taking his amulet from him.

As he recovers, he tells Arha of the wonders of the outside world, and she is an avid listener. Kossil knows of the stranger so, believing the woman will kill him, Arha takes him through the twisted maze, past the pit, to the treasure room, where Kossil cannot go. She has Manan dig a grave in the Undertomb and tells Kossil that the man has been buried alive. Kossil does not believe her, does not believe in the power of the Nameless Ones, and seems capable of destroying their worship. When Arha finds her in the Undertomb, digging to be sure the man has been buried, with a light in her hand, and realizes that the Nameless Ones will not punish her, the girl knows that Kossil is right; they are old and their power is gone. They are dead.

The man explains to her, however, that they are not dead and are not gods; they are the powers of darkness and madness and evil, and they are not her masters. He has found what he is looking for—the half of the Ring of Erreth-Akbe—which, joined with the other half—the amulet she took from him—will give the mages the Bond-Rune*. This rune, broken when the Ring was broken, will bind the lands of Earthsea and bring peace under one ruler. Long ago he had been given his half by an old woman he met on a tiny island.

The girl must make a decision: whether to be Arha or Tenar, whether to stay and be Priestess or go with the man. He trusts her and, trusting her, gives her his name—Ged*. She decides that she will go with him. Ged makes the Ring whole and gives it to Tenar. As they cross the pit, Manan is there and tries to kill Ged but falls into the dark pit. As the two travel through the passage, the caverns begin to collapse on them, and Ged holds them together with spells. Once they have escaped, the earthquake destroys the temple and the gigantic tombstones of the Nameless Ones.

The world is a wondrous place for Tenar, but she comes to feel that she is evil because she killed the three prisoners and was responsible for Manan's death. Ged will take her to Havnor*, the seat of government, to bring the Ring there, and then he will take Tenar to live with Ogion*, his old master, where she will have the silence and the time to find her own way. On a bright winter day, Ged and Tenar come into Havnor.

TOMMY BASSUMTYTE (*The Bassumtyte Treasure*). *See* Bassumtyte, Tommy

TOMS, CAPTAIN, a character mentioned in *Over Sea, Under Stone** who appears in *Greenwitch** and *Silver on the Tree**, by Susan Cooper*. He is one of the Old Ones, the forces of good. One of his ancestors, or possibly he himself, had been Roger Toms, a smuggler who had given up one of his own shipmates because the man had committed murder, and who had never again been able to live in his own village in Cornwall. Captain Toms is a retired sea captain, living in the house in Cornwall that has belonged to his family for generations. He is the owner of Rufus*, a bright, bouncy Irish setter. The Captain helps Merriman Lyon* and Will Stanton*, other Old Ones, to retrieve a grail* and a manuscript* necessary to defeat the Dark. That battle over, he departs with the rest to sail beyond the ken of men.

TOM'S MIDNIGHT GARDEN. Philippa Pearce. Illus. Susan Einzig. London: Oxford University Press, 1958. 229 pp. British. Carnegie Award, 1958.

Tom Long's* brother has the measles, so Tom is sent to stay with his uncle and aunt for the school holidays. Here he is miserable and lonely, for he is in quarantine. Unable to sleep, Tom is roused when the grandfather clock* in the hall of the flats strikes thirteen. He gets up to check the clock and finds that the door at the back of the building leads into a beautiful garden where he had been told none exists. The house has changed, and to Tom's surprise, a housemaid passes him and does not see him. Tom watches as the strange furnishings fade, and decides that he has been seeing ghosts. The next day the garden is not there; Tom realizes that the clock is his link to the garden. That night when it strikes thirteen, he goes to the garden, where it is just before dawn. Tom wanders in the lovely garden and watches the sun rise, but when he goes back to the house it is just a few minutes after midnight.

After this, Tom goes into the garden each time the clock strikes thirteen, seeing the garden at many times of its day and in many seasons. Like a ghost, he is invisible, and he cannot open doors. He can also go through walls, but it is an uncomfortable experience. Once there is a storm in the garden, and he watches as a tree is struck by lightning and falls. Terrified, he runs into the house and shuts the door, opening it once to find the storm still raging. The next time Tom opens the door, the tree is still standing.

Children sometimes play in the garden: Harriet Melbourne Bartholomew* (Hatty) and her boy cousins. Of them, only Hatty can see Tom, and they soon become companions. Hatty's parents have died, and she is unhappy in her new home and afraid of her strict aunt. Once after a terrible scene when Hatty is responsible for the geese getting loose in the yard, Tom finds himself in the garden in an earlier time, meeting a much younger Hatty who has just been orphaned. Once, after they argue on the subject, in his own time Tom proves to himself with pictures from the encyclopedia that Hatty is a Victorian ghost.

Then disaster strikes. Hatty falls from the tree house she and Tom are making and hurts her head. The gardener picks her up and shouts at Tom; he has seen the boy from the very first and thinks Tom is a demon come to hurt Hatty.

Worried, Tom goes into the house, which is still the old house, and looks for Hatty. During his search he overhears Hatty's aunt and her oldest cousin discussing the girl; the cousin decides that Hatty must have more social contacts than she does now. Finally Tom finds the girl and realizes that her room is the one he sleeps in now. She is not as hurt as he had feared, and they talk. As evening comes, Tom tries to leave but cannot get back to his own century; he sleeps beside Hatty's bed and wakes beside his own.

The next time Tom goes into the garden, there is snow. Hatty is learning to skate on the pond. At his insistence they look at the old clock and he comes to realize that neither is a ghost; they share time together. It is winter the next time Tom visits Hatty, but she is much older. Watching her skate, Tom wishes to skate, too, and he makes Hatty promise to keep her skates in a secret place in the bedroom; then he rushes upstairs to find them in his own time, but his aunt wakes before he does. The next morning he finds the skates and oils and sharpens them. That night he takes the skates with him when he goes to meet Hatty. She is going to skate alone down the river, and Tom goes with her. When they come to a village and climb the church tower, Tom is surprised to find his brother there; the brother has been dreaming of them. It is dark when Hatty and Tom get back onto the ice, and when she meets a young man who is a friend of the family, Hatty accepts a ride from him. So engrossed are they with each other that not until they reach Hatty's house does she suddenly realize that Tom is gone.

Tom has only one night left before he goes home, but that night he cannot get into the garden and cries out in anguish, waking the tenants. The next morning he goes to apologize to Mrs. Bartholomew, who owns the place and is living there, and discovers that she is Hatty. She tells him how, the night before she was to be married, she had seen him in the garden when the tree had been struck by lightning. She had bought the house long after she was married, and had it made into flats; now widowed, she lives here. Now she dreams of the past. Her dreams of the garden and his longing for companionship had made it possible for Tom to go into the garden, into her dreams. Before Tom leaves, to the surprise of Mrs. Bartholomew's tenants, she invites Tom and his brother to come visit her.

TONY MANNERING (*Peter Pan in Kensington Gardens*). *See* Mannering, Tony

TONY NICHOLAS (*Poor Tom's Ghost*). *See* Nicholas, Tony

TOPSY TARTLET (*Mary Poppins Comes Back*). *See* Tartlet, Topsy

TOSELAND (TOLLY), a character in Lucy Boston's* *The Children of Green Knowe*, *The Chimneys of Green Knowe*, *An Enemy at Green Knowe*, and *The Stones of Green Knowe*. He is the great-grandson of Mrs. Linnet Oldknow*;

his late mother's name was also Linnet. Tolly is an only child. His father remarried after his mother's death, but the child is shy around his stepmother because he does not know her. Because his parents live in Burma, Tolly does not spend school holidays with them; he goes one holiday to Green Knowe*, to stay with Mrs. Oldknow. Here Tolly meets and makes friends with those who have lived here before him: Alexander, Linnet, and Toseland Oldknow***. He later meets or learns about others, too, because Tolly spends all his holidays at Green Knowe. Tolly also meets Roger d'Aulneaux*, the first boy to live at the old house. Tolly and Hsu* help Mrs. Oldknow to defend the place against the evil Dr. Melanie Delia Powers*. Sensitive and sometimes timid, Tolly comes to feel at home at Green Knowe and grows to love it deeply. He resembles several of those who have lived here, including Roger, the other Toseland, and Tolly's grandfather, also named Toseland. His ties to the place are more than blood ties, because he has taken part in some of the events of the house, and when he inherits it, Tolly will struggle to preserve Green Knowe, as his great-grandmother has done. Tolly has a sweet voice and eventually goes to a choir school.

TOSELAND OLDKNOW (the Green Knowe books). *See* Oldknow, Toseland

TOUGH WINTER, THE. Robert Lawson. Illus. Robert Lawson. New York: Viking Press, 1954. 128 pp. American.

Though his Uncle Analdas* is prophesying a tough winter and the Folks in the house on the Hill are leaving for the winter, hiring a caretaker, Little Georgie*, a young rabbit on the Hill, does not understand the fuss. He and his family have food to last them the winter, and the winter is fine. Then, on Thanksgiving, there is snow and freezing rain. The slow old cat who lives with the Folks, Mr. Muldoon*, is trapped under the ice, but the mice take him food and Little Georgie gets a deer to break Mr. Muldoon out. The Folks leave and the caretaker comes, bringing a mean but stupid dog who will be no threat. The snow melts. The caretaker takes a few shots at the rabbits before Tim McGrath*, the gardener at the place, takes his gun away. Then, one memorable day, the dog goes after a groundhog and Georgie fetches the skunk, who is his good friend and who lets the dog have it.

Disaster strikes the Hill; cold days set in, and the caretaker's dropped cigarette burns the cover on the Hill. Worse, the fire engine sinks a wheel into the storeroom of Georgie's family and destroys their stored food. Though the rest of the mice leave because their food is gone, Willie Fieldmouse* stays with Georgie and his family. Gradually other animals leave the Hill as well. On Christmas Eve, Tim returns and spreads a good feed for the animals. All come back to eat, but there is still enough to store.

Winter comes down hard and their scanty stores are soon gone. Groundhog Day comes and so does the groundhog, who stays out long enough to cast a shadow, thus presaging six more weeks of misery. Georgie's mother is sent to stay with his sister, and Uncle Analdas sets out south for the bluegrass country to fetch back the Folks. After a hard trip following the road south, he comes to the bluegrass country—Tim's hay-filled barn. Georgie, thin and worried about his uncle, must care for his sick father, too, though Willie tries to buoy his spirits.

Then one day a spring rain melts the snow and the sun warms the air. Georgie's father gets well, the caretaker leaves, and the Folks return, as do Georgie's mother and the other animals on the Hill. Analdas comes back, too, full of tales of the bluegrass country. That night the Folks spread a feast for all. Soon things are cleaned up and back to normal. Uncle Analdas decides that he might winter again in the bluegrass country, but Georgie and Willie will stay on the Hill and fight the winter through.

TRASHBIN MACCUBBIN (*The Lost Farm*). *See* MacCubbin, Donalbain

TRAVELLER IN TIME, A. Alison Uttley. Illus. Phyllis Bray. London: Faber and Faber, 1939. 331 pp. British.

Young Penelope Taberner Cameron* has always been somewhat of a dreamer. Her mother feels that Penelope has inherited "second sight," for the girl had once seen a lady from the past going down the stairs in the house. When Penelope and her sister and brother become ill one winter, they are sent from their home in London to recuperate at Thackers*, the home of their great-uncle and -aunt—Barnabas and Cicely Ann (Tissie) Taberner**, a brother and sister who stayed on the family farm.

Thackers, now a farm, is an ancient manor that had belonged to the Babington family, whom the Taberners served generations ago. The house itself had been much larger; part of it was pulled down after Anthony Babington* was hanged for plotting against Elizabeth I to free Mary Stuart*, Queen of Scots. Thackers, with its ancient furnishings, delights Penelope.

One morning, sent back into the house for a forgotten rug, Penelope opens a door on the landing and sees four richly dressed ladies playing a game in an unfamiliar room. The ladies seem as surprised to see her as she is to see them, and when she retreats, she notices other doors on the landing. When Aunt Tissie comes up to see what is keeping Penelope, the other doors vanish. Tissie tells Penelope that the people she saw had lived at Thackers long ago. That night Penelope discovers in her great-aunt's sewing basket a "bobbin boy"*, a little wooden figure of an Elizabethan man once used to hold silk thread.

One day Penelope runs into her bedroom to find herself in the passageway of that other house. The servants, who wonder at her odd clothes, send Penelope to see Cicely Taberner*, who looks like Aunt Tissie and who accepts Penelope's explanation that she is Cicely's niece, sent by her mother to learn from Cicely. Penelope is soon accepted by all in the household but Jude*, the deaf-mute who does odd jobs and who can often sense things others cannot. Jude is at first frightened, then wary of Penelope, but he is not as frightened of her as are the household dogs, who also seem to sense that she is not of their time. The servants chatter excitedly about the return to Thackers from London of Anthony Babington, the young master of the house. Anthony is not only a Catholic under a Protestant queen, but he is sympathetic to Mary Stuart, now imprisoned at Sheffield. When Anthony is seen on the road, there is much excitement, and suddenly Penelope fades back into the twentieth century. She notes, to her astonishment, that no time has passed since she left.

This is but the first of several trips Penelope makes into Elizabethan Thackers. Gradually she comes to know these other people and to love them as well as she does those of her own century. Penelope meets Anthony, who shows her the exquisite miniature of Mary Stuart that he wears. When Penelope murmurs that the queen was executed—all she remembers, for while in Anthony's time she can remember her own only fitfully—Anthony decides that Penelope has second sight like the astrologer who had prophesied a horrible death for him. But he cannot stop trying to help Mary Stuart. Penelope comes to look on Francis Babington*, Anthony's younger brother, as a good friend. Francis is worried that Anthony is being used by his friends at court and resentful of Anthony's neglect of Thackers, for the boy loves Thackers very much and wishes he were master there.

Penelope becomes absorbed in the past life of Thackers. One day during church she slides for an instant into a hot Elizabethan day and almost faints; Aunt Tissie catches her as she staggers and takes her home, where she hears someone calling to her. It is Francis, who wants her to find the locket Anthony showed her, for he has lost it and is distraught. Suddenly all fades into the twentieth century. Days later, when it is time for Penelope to leave Thackers, she makes a tour of all her favorite places and, in the church, finds Anthony's miniature. She cannot take it to him, for she cannot get into the past, so she leaves it at Thackers.

Penelope returns to Thackers two years later, to recuperate again from an illness. Thackers has not changed, and Penelope is delighted to find that she is still able to go into the past. One day she comes into Anthony's room and finds him there. His plans to help Mary Stuart are going well. Penelope rides with Francis to the fair, where she meets Arabella Babington*, his cousin, who dislikes Penelope on the spot.

This time, when Penelope returns to her own time, it is several days before she is able to go back to the Elizabethans, whom she is coming to love more and more. Then, at the traditional celebration at the end of haymaking, Penelope sees Francis and follows him into old Thackers. There Anthony tells her how, even as a young boy, he loved the Queen of Scots, and he explains his plan for her escape from nearby Wingfield Manor*, connected with Thackers by an ancient passageway which he is clearing. Penelope hears the picks when she is in the twentieth century, but Uncle Barnabas decides that it is rats.

Penelope's parents come to Thackers and visit Wingfield, now in ruins. Penelope wanders in the ruins, remembering the Elizabethan Wingfield, and when she looks up, she sees it as it was then. She watches and listens as Mary Stuart chats with her maid. That night the twentieth century fades around Penelope and Francis takes her to help in the tunnel the men are clearing. Jude gives her a little man he has carved for her; it is her bobbin boy. When the others go to bed, Penelope walks through the Elizabethan house, silent as a ghost, and sees Anthony writing a letter that will betray him. She cannot warn him and goes back to her own time.

One rainy day Penelope is drawn to the church by strange music and finds there Arabella, who takes Penelope to an empty barn. Thinking Pelelope is a witch and a spy, Arabella imprisons her in a tunnel Anthony's men had cleared as they searched for the true passage to Wingfield. As Penelope sleeps, somehow she reaches Jude through the bobbin boy, and he rescues her. She sleeps again and wakes in the twentieth-century Thackers; she had fainted in the church, Aunt Tissie tells her, and she has been ill.

Winter comes, and Christmas, and Penelope slips into the past, where she helps with Christmas preparations there. Jude, as a reward for saving her, has been made Francis's personal servant. Suddenly Anthony rides up. Mary Stuart's guards have discovered the tunnel at Wingfield and will move her; the tunnel is still blocked at that end and they do not know where it leads, but they will search everywhere. The tunnel is filled in at Thackers, but the signs of digging are still obvious until a sudden snowfall hides all traces. In his happiness, Francis asks Penelope not to leave him, but she fades into the twentieth century.

Penelope longs for Francis and for old Thackers, and the world around her seems unreal for a time as she hears soldiers and sees shadows of men searching the house. Then she slips into the older Thackers and learns from Anthony that the searchers from Wingfield have found nothing, that Mary Stuart is to be moved, and that he will never give up trying to free her. Nothing she can say will change his mind. When she leaves, he is making his will. That night, when she goes up to bed, Penelope leans out her window to see Francis and Anthony riding away from Thackers. She knows she is seeing them for the last time, until it is her time to join Thackers's company of shadows.

TRAVERS, P[AMELA] L[YNDON] (1906-   ), British writer. She was born in Queensland, Australia, in 1906 and was privately educated. Travers has been a journalist, actress, and dancer; she worked in the British Ministry of Information during World War II. She has also been writer-in-residence at Radcliffe College, in Massachusetts, Smith College, in Massachusetts, and Scripps College, in California. In 1977 Travers received the O.B.E. (Officer, Order of the British Empire).

Of Travers's eleven works for children, the most famous are her series of Mary Poppins books*, seven episodic fantasies detailing the adventures of one of the most unforgettable characters in children's literature. *Mary Poppins*, *Mary Poppins Comes Back*, and *Mary Poppins Opens the Door* are episodic novels; *Mary Poppins in the Park* is a collection of short stories; *Mary Poppins* *from A to Z* is a small book for younger children; *Mary Poppins in the Kitchen* is a story/cook book; and *Mary Poppins in Cherry Tree Lane* is a short adventure. All have as their central character Mary Poppins*, the prim British nanny who is a catalyst for magic, and her charges, the five young Banks children. In the novels, especially, things are not always what they seem, and magic is everywhere.

Mary Poppins herself is not at all what she seems. Plain and correct, dressed in her starched aprons and smelling of toast, starch, and Sunlight Soap, reading *Everything a Woman Needs to Know*, she is the very picture of the upright nanny whose only interest is in seeing that her charges are clean, well-fed, and polite. But as the Banks children immediately find out, Mary Poppins is different, for who but she can slide *up* the banister on the stairs? Mary Poppins is different from other people in other, deeper ways, for she is the Great Exception and the laws that apply to humans do not apply to her. Her relatives are strange and exotic, and she knows exotic people; unlike most people she can remember the long journey of her birth and talks to sunlight and birds; she knows everything and tells nothing. Mary Poppins is a catalyst for the wonderful, magical happenings that take place around her, but she herself remains untouched by them, greater than they are, and offended that the Banks children should even think she has anything to do with such improper goings-on. She seems a nanny but the reality is quite different; but even the real Mary Poppins is not quite what she seems.

Their nanny is not the only thing in the Banks children's lives that is not what it seems; other things are different, too. Balloons bounce one on a wonderful ride through the air, and peppermint walking sticks behave like flying ponies; statues are not unfeeling stone but lonely boys; a piano tuner can be Methuselah's grandfather; a sweetshop proprietor can have overheard William the Conqueror and danced with Henry VIII*. Babies can chatter with the elements, and a lazy man-of-all-work can be a figure from a fairy tale.

If things are not always what they seem, then magic can be everywhere. The mysterious Bird Woman* can be the broody hen for her pigeons. A star from the heavens can come to the world to do her Christmas shopping. The spring can be the result of the woodworking skills of Nellie-Rubina Noah* and her Uncle Dodger, who craft the lambs and the daffodils, the green trees and the birds who sing in them, and put them into place. A Royal Doulton bowl* can be the doorway into the world of the past. Music can be in everything on Earth: the world sounding like a spinning top as it whirls, Buckingham Palace playing "Rule Britannia," the Thames murmuring like a drowsy flute. Wherever the Banks children look, they can see something magical, for their experiences with Mary Poppins have made them so. The stars in the sky are the gilt paper from gingerbread stars; the constellations are a circus, because they have seen them so with Mary Poppins. For the children, the world is a wonderful place full of wonderful things, for they have been taught to look beyond the surface to see what could be underneath.

The world Mary Poppins shows them is magical and wonderful, but there is an edge to the magic. Wonders may be outside in the night sky, but bedtime is always waiting. Pennies are spent at the sweetshop after all the shopping has been done, not before. Before you explore the mysterious universe, you must take care of things at home. Miss Calico's* magical peppermint walking sticks can take you home, but you cannot keep them, try as you might; the gilt paper on the gingerbread stars you buy from Mrs. Corry* is not yours to keep, either. Neither is Mary Poppins, who stays until the wind changes, until the chain on her locket breaks, or until the door opens. The Banks children have her magic for just a little while, as they have the magic of the peppermint sticks, but she never promises them forever. The only lasting magic is that of their own hearts; it is the only magic that truly belongs to them, for its source is inside them. With it they can see anew the things Mary Poppins has shown them, and see beyond the surface into each thing's secret heart. When Mary Poppins leaves them forever, she leaves behind this new awareness of the magic of the world and also, it seems, a renewal of the Banks family itself. Each time she comes to stay with them, they are at odds with each other and the world around them, and the first two times she leaves, the Banks parents are cross and complain at this treatment. But at the end of the last visit they are a family, wishing on a star together and gathering around the fire. The only lasting magic is the magic of the heart, and part of that magic is love.

Travers's works are cheerful, light, and charming, written in a brisk and lively style. Mary Poppins is wonderfully complex, at once crisp, vain, tender, and generous; though the other characters are more two-dimensional and readily fall into various patterns, they are lively and individual, each a person in his or her own right. The children are very like children everywhere, sometimes sullen, sometimes good, often imaginative.

Works

Juvenile full-length fantasy: *Mary Poppins* (1934); *Mary Poppins Comes Back* (1935); *Mary Poppins Opens the Door* (1943).

Juvenile short stories, novels, etc.: *Happy Ever After* (1940); *I Go by Sea, I Go by Land* (1941); *Mary Poppins in the Park* (1952), short stories; *The Fox at the Manger* (1962); *Mary Poppins from A to Z* (1962); *Friend Monkey* (1971), stories; *About the Sleeping Beauty* (1975); *Mary Poppins in the Kitchen: A Cookery Book with a Story* (1975); *Mary Poppins in Cherry Tree Lane* (1982).

Adult: *Moscow Excursion* (1934); *Aunt Sass* (1941); *Ah Wong* (1943); *In Search of the Hero: The Continuing Relevance of Myth and Fairy Tale* (1970), lecture.

Secondary Works

Bergsten, Staffan. *Mary Poppins and Myth*. Stockholm: Almqvist and Wiksell International, 1978.

Moore, Robert B., and P. L. Travers. "*Mary Poppins*: Two Points of View,"*Children's Literature*, 10 (1982), pp. 210-17.

Travers, P. L.. "The Heroes of Childhood: A Note on Nannies,"*The Horn Book Magazine*, 11 (Jan.-Feb., 1935), pp. 147-55.

————. Letter to the Editor. *The Horn Book Magazine*, 58 (June, 1982), p. 243.

————. "On Not Writing for Children," *Bookbird*, 6, no. 4, (1968), pp. 3-7.

————. "On Not Writing for Children," *Children's Literature*, 4 (1975), pp. 15-22.

————. "Only Connect," *Quarterly Journal of the Library of Congress*, 24 (Oct., 1967), pp. 232-48. [Reprinted in *Only Connect*, ed. Sheila Egoff, G. T. Stubbs, and L. F. Ashley (New York: Oxford University Press, 1969), pp. 183-206.]

————. "Who Is Mary Poppins?" *Junior Bookshelf*, 18 (March, 1954), pp. 45-50.

TREASURE OF GREEN KNOWE, THE. See *Chimneys of Green Knowe,The*

TREASURES, FOUR, four objects in Alan Garner's* *Elidor**. They are essential to Elidor*, a magical land, being the seeds of the fire that had created it, and once were held in four castles: Gorias, Findias, Falias, and Murias. One is the Spear of Ildana, which shines like fire; one is a shining, jeweled sword; one is a glowing stone; and one is a cauldron filled with light, the rim of which is set with pearls. When Findias, Falias, and Murias fall to the powers of darkness, their treasures are put into the Mound of Vandwy, to be rescued by David, Helen, Nicholas, and Roland Watson****, brought to Elidor by Malebron*. To keep them safe, the Treasures are taken by the children into their own world, where they become shabby parodies of themselves, though they still feel as they look in Elidor. Because the Treasures generate so much power, they cause many problems in the children's world, for they jam television and radio reception and cause things to work even though they have not been turned on or plugged in. When the Treasures are buried, their influence stops. Malebron's enemies use the powers of the Treasures to find where they are and eventually enter the children's world. At the death of Findhorn*, a unicorn, when the children see Elidor, they throw the Treasures back into it.

TRIP, JACK, a character in Penelope Lively's* *The Driftway**. This eighteenth-century orphan was taken in by an innkeeper. For ten years he is the stableboy, becoming more adept at getting out of doing work than he is at doing it. Having met so many people finer than those in the neighborhood, Jack has learned to ape their manners and their speech, and he has developed a taste for finer things. Jack plans to set himself up in London as a gentleman, and to fulfill this goal he pilfers whatever money he can. Once, when he is almost caught stealing a necklace, Jack throws suspicion on Tom Winter, a half-wit, and gets him fired. Jack overhears two drovers plotting to kill a third and make off with his share of their money, blaming "Driftway Jim," a local highwayman. Realizing that this is his chance to make a fortune, Jack poses as Driftway Jim and robs the two men, being then robbed, himself, by James Tobias Hooker*, the real Driftway Jim; Tom, in league with James, had tipped him off about Jack's plan. Poorer and a little wiser, Jack goes back to the inn. His story remains as a shadow on the driftway* he has ridden, to be re-experienced in the twentieth century by a boy named Paul*.

TROLL, a type of being in J[ohn] R[onald] R[euel] Tolkien's* *The Hobbit** and *The Lord of the Rings*. They are made of the stuff of mountains and back to stone they change if they are not underground by daylight. Trolls are large and clumsy and not terribly smart; they speak coarsely and have dreadful table manners. They eat a great deal and purloin whatever they can. A troll's purse is hard to pick, for it calls out at very inconvenient moments, as Bilbo Baggins* learns one night when he comes upon and tries to rob three trolls named William, Bert, and Tom. These three are finally turned to stone by the sun, when Gandalf*, a wizard, tricks them into arguing together until dawn. Trolls are part of the forces Sauron uses in his later war to regain his magic ring*.

TRUE, a dog in E[dith] Nesbit Bland's* *Harding's Luck**. This white dog of uncertain parentage is given in 1908 to Dickie Harding* by James Beale*; its siblings are sold. True is named by Dickie after a dog he knows when he is Richard Arden* in 1608. The dog grows up to warrant its name; when Dickie is kidnapped, True leads Edred Arden* to the cave where the boy is being kept.

TRUFFLEHUNTER, a character in C[live] S[taples] Lewis's* *Prince Caspian** and *The Last Battle**. He is one of the talking badgers in Narnia* during the reign of Miraz* and Caspian X*. Trufflehunter has his sett near Miraz's castle, though it is well enough hidden that no one knows it is there. Because he is a talking beast, Trufflehunter is persecuted by the descendants of the conquerors from Telmar* who have killed or driven into hiding the talking beasts and marvelous creatures of Narnia. The badger remembers, though, that good humans have reigned in Narnia, and that the land has never been completely right unless a human was on the throne. Thus when Caspian is knocked off his horse and found by Trufflehunter and his friends, the badger swears loyalty to him and helps him gain the throne. Trufflehunter becomes one of Caspian's trusted advisers. He is among those found in the country of Aslan*, Narnia's mystical lion-protector, when Narnia comes to an end.

TRUMPET OF THE SWAN, THE. E[lwyn] B[rooks] White. Illus. Edward Franscino. New York: Harper and Row, 1970. 210 pp. American.

While camping with his father in Canada, Sam Beaver* finds a nest of trumpeter swans. The swans, a cob* and his mate, have seen Sam watching them, but they pay no attention because he is quiet. The swans soon are glad they have tolerated Sam, for he drives away a fox menacing the female. The five eggs hatch and Sam meets the cygnets, one of which cannot talk. Because their vacation is over, Sam and his father go home to Montana.

At the lake, it becomes apparent to the parent swans that one of their sons,

Louis*, will never talk. He is not otherwise impaired, as he proves when he and the other cygnets learn to fly and wing their way to a wildlife refuge in Montana. There Louis, wishing to learn to write and thus communicate with the others, finds Sam and goes to school to learn. A year and a half later, he returns to his family, wearing around his neck a slate tied to a string. The other swans, to his chagrin, cannot read, and Louis is as helpless as ever.

Spring comes, and Louis falls in love with Serena* but cannot express his love. In desperation, the cob goes to a nearby town and steals a trumpet for his son to use to communicate. Louis appreciates the trumpet but his conscience bothers him because it was stolen. He again goes to Sam, who helps him get a job bugling at a summer camp. There Louis saves a boy from drowning and gets a medal. When Louis is paid, he has Sam slit the webbing on one foot so that he will be able to play the keys on the trumpet.

Louis's next job is in Boston, where he plays the trumpet for the swan boat riders. So popular is he that he gets an offer to play at a nightclub in Philadelphia. Here Louis lives at the zoo. The head keeper in charge of birds here wants to pinion Louis's wings to keep him, but he agrees to leave Louis alone if he plays free concerts for the visitors. The week before Christmas Serena is blown into the zoo by a storm. Louis allows her time to get herself together and one morning wakes her with a song on his trumpet. Serena falls in love with him and they plan to leave. The head keeper, however, insists they must stay, and Louis fiercely protects Serena when men come to pinion her wings. He telegraphs Sam to come, and Sam makes an agreement with the keeper whereby he will allow Louis and Serena to leave if they send a cygnet when the zoo needs one.

The two swans go home to Montana. Louis has made much more money than he needs to pay off the music store owner, but he sends it all with the cob to pay the debt. The storekeeper, frightened, shoots the cob. After much hoopla, the cob is sent to the hospital and the storekeeper gets the money, though he keeps only what will pay for the trumpet and damages and gives the rest to the Audubon Society. After a treatment for a superficial wound, the cob flies home. Louis and Serena are very happy together, traveling and raising their cygnets.

TRUMPKIN, a character in *Prince Caspian*, *The Silver Chair*, and *The Last Battle*, by C[live] S[taples] Lewis*. This kindly red dwarf* is one of those who go into hiding when conquerors from Telmar* rule Narnia* and persecute the magical creatures who live there. He is one of those who find Caspian X* when that young prince is knocked off his horse; and he takes Caspian as his own king. Caspian sends him to Cair Paravel*, a deserted castle, to guide back Edmund, Lucy, Peter, and Susan Pevensie**** should they come there after Caspian blows an ancient hunting horn*. Trumpkin is caught and, because he is a dwarf, he is almost drowned. Though he is rescued by the Pevensies, he does not think much of them until they prove their mettle to him, for he sees them only as the children they are. Once they prove themselves, Trumpkin leads them to Aslan's How, to meet Caspian. He does not believe in Aslan*, Narnia's lion-protector, until the lion appears to him and shakes him; then he believes very much indeed. Trumpkin takes part in the battle to put Caspian on the throne and later takes charge of Narnia, himself, when Caspian sails the Eastern Ocean in search of seven lost lords of Narnia, and, later, when the king goes off in search of his son. Trumpkin is one of those in Aslan's country when the end comes to Narnia.

TUCK, ANGUS (TUCK), a character in Natalie Babbitt's* *Tuck Everlasting*. He is the husband of Mae Tuck* and the father of Jesse and Miles Tuck**. At the end of the eighteenth century, when he and his family were traveling near what is now Treegap, they stopped and drank from a tiny spring*. Because in the next years they did not age, nor could they be hurt, the family realized that the spring had changed them so that they would live forever. To keep their secret, they began to move from place to place. Around 1861, Mae and Tuck settled in a cabin twenty miles from Treegap; they live here for twenty years, making things to support themselves. Tuck is a big, quiet man who rarely smiles. He has realized that life is a series of changes and that the Tucks are stuck as they are, never growing as individuals, as they were meant to. He tries to express this to Winifred Foster* (Winnie), a child who discovers their secret. When Mae kills a stranger* who tries to force Winnie to drink from the spring, Tuck seems almost to envy the man. After the family rescues Mae from jail, they leave Treegap, not to return for almost seventy years. It has changed, but they have not.

TUCK, JESSE, a character in *Tuck Everlasting*, by Natalie Babbitt*. He is the son of Angus and Mae Tuck** and the brother of Miles Tuck*. Though Jesse appears to be 17, around 1881 he is actually 104 years old; 87 years before he and his family had drunk from a tiny spring* and thereby gained everlasting life. Jesse enjoys his immortality completly, for he feels that life is to be enjoyed. He has never settled down and supports himself doing whatever job comes along. When Winifred Foster* (Winnie) meets Jesse in 1881, he seems to her a glorious young man, with his curly hair and his self-assurance. Jesse feels that Winnie is special, too, and he begs her to drink water from the spring when she becomes 17, so that they can travel the world together and have fun forever. Jesse soon realizes, however, that she has not done as he asked.

TUCK, MAE, a character in Natalie Babbitt's* *Tuck Everlasting*. She is the wife of Angus Tuck* and the mother of Miles and Jesse Tuck**. In the late eighteenth century, when they were passing by what is now Treegap, Mae and her family drank from a tiny spring* and were thereby given everlasting life. To keep their secret, the family moved from place to place. Around 1861, Mae and Tuck settled down in a small cabin twenty miles from Treegap; they lived there for twenty years, making things to sell to support themselves. Around 1881, they meet Winifred Foster* (Winnie), who learns the Tucks' secret, having sought the source of music she had heard and which had come from the music box Mae loves and carries with her everywhere. When a stranger* tries to make Winnie drink water from the spring so that he can use her to demonstrate its remarkable qualities when he tries to sell it, Mae hits him so hard with the butt of a shotgun that he dies. To Mae, immortality is something to be endured, not sought, and she does not want it forced onto an eleven-year-old girl. Mae is put into jail and will probably be hanged, though, of course, she cannot die. To prevent the hanging she is rescued by her family, and Winnie takes Mae's place in the cell. Mae does not return to Treegap for almost seventy years. It has changed drastically, but she has not.

TUCK, MILES, a character in *Tuck Everlasting**, by Natalie Babbitt*. He is the eldest son of Angus and Mae Tuck**, the brother of Jesse Tuck*, and the father of a son and of a daughter named Anna. Though Miles looks 22 around 1881, he is actually 109 years old; 87 years before, he and his family had drunk from a tiny spring* which gave them immortality. Not knowing this, Miles married and fathered two children; but when, after several years, he did not age, his wife decided that he had sold his soul to the devil and left him. Miles learned carpentry and blacksmithing and supported himself over the years by doing both. Around 1881 he meets Winifred Foster* (Winnie), a young girl who learns the Tucks' secret, and makes her realize that, though death is painful, it is necessary; for if all things lived forever, the Earth would be too crowded. Miles feels that he must do something useful and important in the world to justify his life. His special skills come in handy when Mae is put into jail for killing a stranger* who tries to force Winnie to drink from the spring; Miles removes the window from the jail so that she can escape.

TUCK EVERLASTING. Natalie Babbitt. New York: Farrar, Straus and Giroux, 1975. 139 pp. American.

The same day in 1881 that Mae Tuck* goes to meet her sons, Miles and Jesse Tuck**, eleven-year-old Winifred Foster* (Winnie) decides to run away from her overbearing mother and grandmother. That evening a stranger* stops at the Foster house. He is looking for a family but seems interested when music Winnie's grandmother had heard long before floats to them across the evening air. The next morning Winnie is not so ready to run away, but she goes into the woods to find the source of the music. Here she meets young Jesse Tuck, who will not let her drink from a small spring*. When Mae and Miles come up, they are upset to see Winnie, and the three kidnap her, saying that they will explain why later. When Winnie gets upset, Mae plays her music box for her; it plays the tune Winnie has heard the night before. As they travel, Winnie learns the Tucks' secret: eighty-seven years before, traveling through the area to find a place to settle, they had drunk from the small spring; after that, they did not age, nor could they be hurt.

Winnie is taken to a small cabin, where she meets Angus Tuck* (Tuck), Mae's husband. The Tucks have a hard time deciding what to do with Winnie, who feels comfortable here and is fond of them—especially of Jesse—though she wants to go home. Tuck explains to Winnie that no one else must know about the spring, for life is a series of changes which must not be stopped. The Tucks' horse, which is equally immortal, is stolen by the mysterious stranger, who had followed them. He goes back to see Winnie's parents, offering to trade knowledge of the child's whereabouts for the woods where the spring lies. When they agree, the stranger sets off with the constable, guiding him to the cabin where Winnie is spending the night.

Morning comes, and Miles takes Winnie fishing. The night before, Jesse had asked Winnie to drink from the spring when she is seventeen—the age he had been when he drank—so that they might be together forever. Miles makes Winnie realize that if all creatures lived forever, there would be too many creatures for the world. She still cannot stand to kill the fish, however. During breakfast the stranger, who has ridden ahead of the constable, arrives. He tries to get the Tucks' help, for he plans to sell the water of the spring. When he tries to take Winnie and force her to drink the water so that he can use her to demonstrate its qualities, Mae hits him with the stock of a shotgun, just as the constable rides up. Mae is arrested and Winnie is taken home. The stranger dies, and Mae will be hanged; Winnie realizes that she will not die, of course.

The next day Jesse visits Winnie, bringing with him water for her to drink when she is seventeen. The family is going to help Mae escape from the jail that night, and Winnie offers to take the woman's place in the cell bunk so that the Tucks will be far away before anyone knows Mae has escaped. That night all goes according to plan; Mae escapes via the cell window, which Miles works loose and replaces after the switch is made. When Winnie is discovered the next morning, all are shocked, but little happens to her. Two weeks later, to keep her favorite toad from harm, she pours on it the water Jesse gave her. There is more water in the woods.

Almost seventy years later, Tuck and Mae come into town. Things have changed drastically. The wood is gone, for the tree that grew over the spring was hit by lightning and a fire was started; the woods were bulldozed out. In the cemetery, Mae and Tuck find Winnie's grave. She had died two years before. As the Tucks leave town, they pick up a toad sitting nonchalantly in the middle of the highway and move it to safety beside the road.

TUDBELLY, DR., a character in Lloyd Alexander's* *The Cat Who Wished to Be a Man*. This balding, portly little man talks like a first year Latin text, sprinkling his conversation with Latin and Latinized phrases that do not always jibe with traditional usage. Tudbelly's pride and joy is his Armamentarium*, a chest filled with the odd ingredients he uses to create concoctions that do not always do what he hopes they will. When Tudbelly comes to the town of Brightford*, he joins the struggle of Gillian* and Lionel* to keep Gillian's inn from greedy Mayor Pursewig* and helps them with his concoctions and his talent for making the best of difficult times.

TÛL ISGRUN, a place in Jane Louise Curry's* *The Watchers**. Its name is the Ebhélic* word for "dark shrine." Tûl Isgrun lies in what is known in the twentieth century as Twilly's Green Hollow*. Until the fourth century Katóa*, a power of unending hunger and destruction, was bound here by the Aldar*; Tekla*, the queen of Kanhuan*, freed the force and set it up in a shrine at Inas Ebhélic*. When this shrine is broken in the twelfth century, the power makes its way back to Tûl Isgrun, only to be bound again by those left to watch over the shrine. The shrine at Tûl Isgrun is destroyed in the twentieth century to keep the power from being freed again.

TUMNUS, MR., a character in C[live] S[taples] Lewis's* *The Lion, the Witch, and the Wardrobe**, *The Horse and His Boy**, and *The Last Battle**. He is a faun living near Lantern Waste near the Great River in Narnia*. Mr. Tumnus lives quietly in his tidy little cave until he meets Lucy Pevensie*, a young girl from our world. He has been told by the evil White Witch* to bring to her any children of Adam he finds, but he cannot bring himself to do so and lets Lucy go home. As a result, the Witch changes Tumnus into a stone statue and as such he remains until Aslan*, the omniscient lion-protector of Narnia, releases him from this form. Mr. Tumnus later takes part in the great battle between Aslan's forces and those of the Witch. When Lucy and her brothers and sister take the throne, Mr. Tumnus stays with them as counsellor, going with them to Tashbaan, in the land of Calormen*, and helping them get out of it when its prince becomes angry at the refusal of his suit by Susan Pevensie*. Mr. Tumnus is one of those who go to Aslan's country when the end comes to Narnia.

TURVEY, ARTHUR, a character in P[amela] [Lyndon] Travers's* *Mary Poppins Comes Back** and *Mary Poppins Opens the Door**. He is the cousin of Mary Poppins*; he becomes the husband of Topsy Tartlet* and they call themselves the Topsy-Turvies. Mr. Turvey was born on the second Sunday of the month. Because his mother had wanted a girl, he had been wrong from the very first. Now, on the second Monday of every month, from three to six, everything goes wrong for him: when he wants to be in, he is out; when he wants to go upstairs, he goes down; normally cheerful, he is sad. Mr. Turvey makes his living by mending things: broken china, broken hearts, whatever is broken. On the second Monday of the month, all his mending goes awry. One second Monday Mary Poppins and her charges bring a Royal Doulton bowl* for him to mend. Because he wants to be right side up, Arthur turns upside down, and so do the children. His peevish landlady, Topsy, does too, and she turns cheerful as well. Entranced by her, Mr. Turvey asks her to marry him; together they thoroughly enjoy his second Mondays.

TUSHCLOSHÁN, a place in the Abáloc novels* by Jane Louise Curry*. In the fourth century, it is called Tuxcloshan. To this city in Cibotlán* in the twelfth century Lincoas* and his group are to be taken to be sacrificed to the Sun Serpent (Katóa*).

TWELVE AND THE GENII, THE. Pauline Clarke, Illus. Cecil Leslie. London: Faber and Faber, 1962. 185 pp. British. Carnegie Award, 1962.

When the Morleys move into their new home not far from Haworth, where the Brontës lived, eight-year-old Max Morley* discovers twelve wooden soldiers hidden under a floorboard in the attic. These antique soldiers are not ordinary toys, for they occasionally come to life. After earning their trust, Max becomes known to them as the Genie Maxii; to the soldiers, the people who invent adventures for them are genii. Max helps them downstairs from the attic. Though they are wooden soldiers, Max cannot treat them as toys; each is a person and all have dignity, and even though it would be easier for him to pick them up and carry them down the stairs, Max senses that to do so would make them forever lifeless. During the fine feast he provides for the Twelves*, as they call themselves, the soldiers recount their adventures. Suddenly the rest of the family returns from shopping and the Twelves freeze. In the confusion Max gathers all but one—Stumps*—whom he cannot find anywhere. That night Max dreams of the little soldier's escape from the kitchen and wakes to find Stumps exactly where he dreamed him. Taking Stumps to the attic, Max realizes that whatever someone makes up about the soldiers is true for them.

As the Twelves honor Stumps the next morning, Max's sister, Jane Morley*, sees them and becomes a genie herself. Butter Crashey*, the oldest of the Twelves, tells Max about the four original genii—Tallii, Annii, Emii, and Branii—who sent them on wonderful adventures long ago.

That afternoon Max and Jane and their brother, Philip Morley*, go to tea at the parson's. Mr. Howson* is a fan of the Brontës, and as he tells the children of the wooden soldiers those children had, Max realizes that the Twelves originally belonged to the Brontës. When an American professor publicly offers £5,000 for the Brontë soldiers, Philip writes to him, convinced that Max's soldiers are the toys in question, and the professor cables that he is coming to have a look. Afraid that he will have to give them up, Max decides to tell Mr. Howson about the Twelves and ask for advice. But when he goes to the attic to bring them down, Max discovers that the Twelves are gone.

Because no one will ever believe the truth, the children spread the story that they have been stolen. Max, however, realizes that Butter Crashey had heard him talking to Philip about the professor and has led the Twelves into hiding. Through his imagination, Max follows the soldiers as they ride one of his skates down the road and attempt to navigate a stream on a raft made of a small board. When the raft smashes against a rock, Stumps is swept away and saved by a rat. The next day Max's imagination leads him and Jane to the missing soldiers, who are going to Haworth parsonage, where they will be safe. The two children also find Stumps and reunite him with the others, promising to return that night to watch over the journey of the Twelves.

That night Max and Jane are followed by Philip, who is astonished and filled with wonder by the little soldiers and who becomes the Genie Philippi. The haystack where the three leave the Twelves is in a farmyard, and the next morning the Twelves watch in horror as the farmer finds Butter, who was foraging, and carries him away. Max, Jane, and Philip are equally horrified when they hear the news that night, for the soldiers are only a night's march from Haworth and it is unthinkable that they should enter it without Butter. The next day the farmer, who has recognized Butter as one of the stolen soldiers, brings him to Max.

That night is one of great excitement as Jane and Max watch over the little soldiers marching to Haworth. When they are accosted by a man who thinks they know where the valuable soldiers are, Mr. Howson comes by in time to save them and is delighted to be introduced to the Twelves as the Reverend Genie. He and the children watch over the marching soldiers until they come to Haworth. Because the children have decided that the nursery in the parsonage was the proper place for the Twelves, Philip has gotten himself locked in there so that he can open the window for the soldiers' return. The Twelves clamber up the ivy to the window and are gratified to find themselves home at last.

Mr. Howson, after a delightful chat with the Twelves one day after museum hours, convinces the museum administrators that these are indeed the soldiers the Brontës loved. The Twelves live contentedly in their old home, having adventures at night and sometimes perplexing visitors with a glimpse of their inherent liveliness.

TWELVES, THE, twelve characters in Pauline Clarke's* *The Twelve and the Genii**. These twelve wooden soldiers once belonged to Branwell Brontë, who played with them with his sisters, inventing and writing adventures for them. The Young Men, as the Brontës called them, were each given names and personalities: Parry, Ross, and sly Sneaky were kings, as once were the Duke of Wellington and brave Stumps*; dignifieid Butter Crashey* was the patriarch, being 140 years old; Monkey, Cracky, and Tracky were mischievous and adventurous midshipmen; Cheeky was a cocksure physician; Bravey was brave, and Gravey was melancholy and often jeered at by the others. Such was the power of the Brontës' creative genius that the soldiers came to life. When Branwell outgrew the little soldiers, they were collected and hidden in the attic of a nearby house, to be found in the twentieth century by eight-year-old Max Morley*. He is enchanted by the lively little men and awed by their dignity; he senses that if he were to treat them as toys they would freeze back into wooden soldiers forever and learns that the adventures he makes up for them become their reality. As they become more used to Max and his sister, Jane Morley*, the Twelves become bolder; when an American professor offering a large reward for the Brontës' toy soldiers hears about the Twelves from Philip Morley*, Max's brother, and cables that he is coming to see them, the soldiers take matters into their own hands and run away to Haworth. Their journey is watched over by Max, Jane, and, finally, Philip. The Twelves are delighted to be back in their old home, where they have adventures at night and sometimes move and startle visitors in the daytime.

TWIGLEY, FRED, a character in *Mary Poppins Opens the Door**, by P[amela] L[yndon] Travers*. He is the cousin of Mary Poppins* and the grandfather of Methuselah. Mr. Twigley's godmother gave him the power to make seven wishes come true at the first new moon after the second wet Sunday after the Third of May—a day that does not come around often. Whenever he makes a wish, music plays. Mr. Twigley is very fond of music; he tunes pianos, mends nightingales, and makes music boxes, some of which play the music in such things as in a day in the park. Mr.Twigley can hear the music of everything in the universe, from the humming-top sound of the spinning Earth to the drowsy flute of the Thames River. His landlady, Mrs. Sarah Clump*, wants to marry Mr. Twigley so that she can have his wishes, but he thwarts her by giving her all she wants— his way.

TWILLY'S GREEN HOLLOW, a place in Jane Louise Curry's* *The Watchers**. This hollow in twentieth-century West Virginia gets its name from Tûl Isgrun*, the Dark Shrine where Katóa*, an evil force, has been bound for centuries. The Hollow is inhabited by six families who keep to themselves, marrying among themselves and keeping others out. They are dark but blue-eyed and have their own songs and folk ways. These people once lived Up Top*, above the Hollow; they moved into the Hollow in order to be closer to their jobs. Though these people naturally live longer than others, something in the Hollow—probably Katóa—seems to sap their strength.

TYLWYTH TEG, Y, a race of Fair Folk* in *Beneath the Hill** and *The Change-Child**, by Jane Louise Curry*. They are also known as the Children of the Wood of the Great Dark Wood, as well as by other names. These dark, pale-eyed Folk seem to be of the same race as the Aldar*, and, like them, live long lives and are "perilous fair." The *Tylwyth Teg* stayed in Wales long after the others sailed to the Fortunate Isles, but mortal men were suspicious of them and drove them from their homes. Finally the Folk found sanctuary in a lovely valley in the center of the Great Dark Wood. When Eilian Roberts* is brought here for safety in Elizabethan times, she acts as the catalyst whereby an old curse is fulfilled, and the Folk are forced to leave this final sanctuary on Earth. They sail across the sea to Tir na'nOg*, where they will find peace and happiness. During the journey, however, some of the Folk are separated from the rest and they come instead to the shores of North America. Here they are intrigued by what they find at the City of the Moon Under the Mountain*, where others like them had lived centuries before. Trapped by encroaching civilization, this small band of Folk lives in the City until the twentieth century, when they are freed by Arthur Arthur*, Margaret Arthur*, and Stevie Griffith*, who help them to escape to the river that takes them to the sea and to Tir na'nOg.

U

U. W. UGLI (*The Enchanted Castle*). *See* Ugli, U. W.

UEEPE, a place in *The Magic Bed-Knob**, by Mary Norton*. This South Sea island is one of several sighted in 1809 by observors on board the *Lucia Cavorta*, but it has never been explored. Natives on the island of Panu, over four hundred miles away, have said that it is uninhabited, but Carey, Charles, and Paul Wilson*** and Eglantine Price* learn otherwise when they visit it in the twentieth century. This dazzling tropical island is inhabited by cannibals who threaten to eat the four; they escape only after Miss Price wins a contest of magic against the witchdoctor and turns him into a frog.

UGLI, U. W., a character in *The Enchanted Castle**, by E[dith] Nesbit Bland*. This respectable gentleman started life as an Ugly-Wugly*, a dummy made of an umbrella, a walking-stick, a gold club, and a feather duster, created to be part of the audience for a play acted by Mabel Prowse*, Gerald*, James*, and Kathleen*. When Mabel, wearing a magic ring*, wishes the Ugly-Wuglies alive, her wish comes true. Mr. Ugli is, like the others, imprisoned by the children in a secret passage in the Temple of Flora* on the grounds of Yalding Castle*; unlike the others, he finds his way down a passage to the Hall of Granted Wishes*. There his wish for a really good hotel is granted and he becomes human, with a business in London and a comfortable income. Mr. Ugli lives in London until Mademoiselle* wishes the magic done by the ring undone; his subsequent disappearance puzzles the police very much.

UGLY-WUGLIES, a group of characters in E[dith] Nesbit Bland's* *The Enchanted Castle**. These dummies are created by Mabel Prowse*, Gerald*, James*, and Kathleen* to be part of the audience for a play. When Mabel, wearing a magic ring*, wishes the dummies were alive, her wish comes true, and the children are horrified. The Ugly-Wuglies are frightening to look at, and because they have no roofs to their mouths their speech is difficult to understand. But the Ugly-Wuglies are very respectable, wishing nothing more than to find a really good hotel in which to spend the night. Mabel and Gerald (who is not afraid of them because he now wears the ring), take them to Yalding Castle* and shut them up in the secret passage behind the Temple of Flora*, knowing that eventually the magic of the ring will undo itself and the Ugly-Wuglies will become dummies again. Before this happens, however, the Ugly-Wuglies escape, injuring Lord Yalding* in the process. They do not get far before the magic ends and they become dummies again—all but one, Mr. U. W. Ugli*, who had found his way down the passage to the Hall of Granted Wishes* and become human after he spent the night in a really good hotel. When Mademoiselle* wishes undone the magic done by the ring, he too becomes a dummy.

ULFIN, a character in *Wet Magic**, by E[dith] Nesbit Bland*. He is the son of a jailer. Ulfin is one of the Under Folk*. Though Freia*, a mermaid, is a citizen of Merland* and therefore his enemy, Ulfin falls in love with her and helps her in her plan to end the centuries-long war between their peoples. Freia likes Ulfin but she will not marry him because she thinks he is ugly. Ulfin solves this problem by proving that his ugly exterior is actually armor, and the two become engaged.

UMMANODDA, a character in *The Three Mulla-mulgars**, by Walter de la Mare*. He is the son of Seelem* and Mutta-matutta and the younger brother of Thumma* and Thimbulla*. He is called "Nod." Not only is he a Mulla-mulgar, or monkey of royal descent, like his brothers; Nod is also a Nizza-neela and a favorite of Tishnar*. Years after their father leaves the family, bound for the Valleys of Tishnar* from whence he came, their mother dies, and Nod and his brothers undertake their own journey after their father. Nod, because he is a Nizza-neela, is entrusted with the lovely, magical Wonderstone*. At first Nod is more hindrance than help; he precipitates the journey by burning the house down, and he loses some of their provisions to the greedy wild pigs. However, Nod's cleverness often saves the day, as when he tricks a Gunga-mulgar* into providing blankets and food for himself and his brothers and loaning his boat. When Nod is wounded and he and his brothers are captured by the Minimuls*, he uses the Wonderstone to free them all. During Nod's sojourn with Andy Battle*, the Englishman who catches and makes friends with him, the Mulgar* saves the man by tricking the dreadful Immânala* into her own destruction. During the terrible journey across the mountains, Nod uses the Wonderstone to break through a line of gigantic Meermuts*, spirits guarding a valley, and thus he and his companions get a taste of what awaits them in the Valleys of Tishnar. Ever bewitched by beauty, near the end of his journey Nod meets a sad and beautiful Water-midden*, who makes him promise to remember her once he reaches the Valleys. Enchanted by her loveliness, once he reaches his destination he does not forget.

UNDER FOLK, a race of beings in E[dith] Nesbit Bland's* *Wet Magic**. These people live in the cold, dark waters of the deep ocean. Their land was once a republic, but its presidents were so greedy and grasping that a monarchy was established; so that no native would be jealous, the King and Queen of the Under Folk* were kidnapped from the land. The Under Folk have been at war for 3,579,308 years with the people of Merland*. The war started when one of the Under Folk accidentally stepped on the tail of a Merman and, being under a vow of silence, did not apologize. The Merpeople attacked and the war began. It ends when Mavis*, Francis*, and Bernard*, three land children, and Freia*, a Merprincess, rescue Freia's father, the king of Merland, and he makes peace. Covered with scales and having exaggerated features, the Under Folk appear hideous to the Merpeople, but this is only the appearance of the armor the Under Folk wear; beneath it, they look just like the Merpeople.

UNDERLAND, a place in C[live] S[taples] Lewis's* *The Silver Chair**. It is also called the Deep Realm. It lies beneath the surface of Narnia*, a magical land. Underland is a place of passages and caves, with underground lakes and a huge sea. Here also are strange caverns where sleep beasts that have found their way here but not the way out; Father Time* sleeps here also, until the end of Narnia. The Queen of Underland* is a lovely sorceress who, during the reign of Caspian X*, tries to dig her way to the surface and take over Narnia. She is thwarted by Jill Pole*, Eustace Clarence Scrubb*, and Puddleglum*, and at her death Underland is drowned in flood. The Narnians later come here on hot days to boat on the cool waters and tell stories of the city that lies beneath them.

UNDERTOMB, a place in Ursula K. LeGuin's* *The Tombs of Atuan**. This sacred place lies beneath the Tombstones of the Nameless Ones* on the island of Atuan*; it is the tomb of these ancient powers. Light is forbidden here. The Undertomb is a beautiful natural cavern with limestone and crystal draperies, but the Nameless Ones are strong and powerful here. Here are buried three men who try to kill the Godking* of the Kargish empire. From the Undertomb winds the great Labyrinth* designed to keep thieves from finding the Treasure of the Tombs. Only the Priestesses of the Place of the Tombs and their eunuchs are allowed in the Undertomb; no men are allowed in this sacred place, though one, Ged*, a wizard, comes here and manages to come out alive. The Undertomb is destroyed by the Nameless Ones themselves, who bring it down in an attempt to kill him and Tenar*, their Priestess, who helps him.

UP TOP, a place in *The Watchers**, by Jane Louise Curry*. This lush and lovely plateau above Twilly's Green Hollow* appears to be the top of an ancient volcano. Here there lived for hundreds of years a group of dark, blue-eyed people descended from the Aldar*; here also stands Berinir Gair*, an ancient castle. Some quality in the soil or the air makes things grow lush and tall; Up Top seems sweeter and lovelier than any other place.

URSULINA, MISTRESS, a character in Lloyd Alexander's* *Time Cat*. This old woman lives in Germany in 1600. Because she refuses to sell her land to Master Speckfresser*, and because she harbors Jason*, a boy from the twentieth century, and Gareth*, his cat, during a time when cats are believed to be demons, Ursulina is denounced by Speckfresser and found guilty of being a witch. She, Jason, and Speckfresser, who has been caught in his own web, escape with the miller, Master Johannes*, to a new place where they can start over.

UTHECAR HORNSKIN, a character in Alan Garner's* *The Moon of Gomrath*. One-eyed Uthecar is possibly one of the ugliest dwarfs* who has ever lived. He is hearty, laughing at things some others do not find at all funny, and is a good fighter. Uthecar had lost his eye in a fight with the Morrigan*, an evil witch, and had barely escaped with his life. He takes part in a later, larger battle against the witch, with Albanac*, two children named Colin* and Susan*, and an army of elves*; here Uthecar kills Pelis the False*, a traitorous dwarf.

UTTLEY, ALISON [Alice Jane Taylor] (1884–1976), British writer. She was born on 17 December 1884 in Cromford, Derbyshire. In 1906, Uttley received a B.Sc., with honors, in physics from Manchester University. She also attended Cambridge University, in 1907. From 1908 to 1911 she was a science teacher at Fulham Secondary School for Girls; in 1911 she married James A. Uttley. They had one son. Uttley received a Litt.D. in 1970 from Manchester University. She died on 7 May 1976.

Uttley was tremendously prolific, producing over 120 plays, picture books, novels, and collections of essays and short stories in about forty five years. Most of her works for children are picture books; of the rest, about seventeen are collections of her stories, five are plays, and one is a fantasy novel involving time travel. All of Uttley's works have one thing in common: a sense of place. The setting of nearly all her picture books is the countryside she knew as a child; the country is also the setting for *A Traveller in Time**, her one novel-length fantasy. Uttley's "place" is not simply a physical landscape; it is an attitude, a mood, and a position in time as well.

"Place" in *A Traveller in Time* means Thackers*. Physically it is a twentieth-century farm; it has been an Elizabethan manor. But Thackers is more than the house, the farm. It is also the attitudes of the people who have lived there and loved the place and who will live there and love it in coming years. And it is the land itself, which existed before it had a name and will endure after those who loved it are gone.

Because Thackers is so much more than the physical manor house, time here does not run in a linear fashion; time has layers, like an onion, and it is possible to step from one layer to another, as Penelope Taberner Cameron* does when she travels back and forth between the twentieth century and the sixteenth. But time is not completely nonlinear; Penelope does not visit any time other than the Elizabethan, and her visits there are strictly chronological. Time has other rules, as well; when she is in the sixteenth century, Penelope's "memories" of the twentieth are vague and haphazard and she is not able to use them to influence events. Also, the miniature Anthony Babington* loses in the Elizabethan Thackers remains lost; though Penelope finds it in the twentieth century, she cannot take it back to him because he did not regain it in his time.

Most important in *Traveller* is the sense of eternity. Thackers has always existed and will continue, absorbing its layers of time. Those who work the farm now are the descendants of those who worked the manor in the sixteenth century and will be ancestors of those who will live there in the future. Many of the furnishings in twentieth-century Thackers are those the Elizabethans used, and many of the household rituals are the same in both ages. Penelope comes to depend on the eternal, essential Thackers to give her the strength to bear her grief for the Babingtons, and she realizes that she will in turn become one of the shadows at Thackers.

Uttley's work is full of the details of everyday life of both the Elizabethan age and the twentieth century. Characters are three-dimensional and setting is well realized. Though it is a quiet book, it is full of suspense.

Works

Juvenile fantasy: *A Traveller in Time* (1939).

Juvenile non-fantasy: *The Squirrel, the Hare, and the Little Grey Rabbit* (1929); *How Little Grey Rabbit Got Back Her Tail* (1930); *The Great Adventures of Hare* (1931); *Moonshine and Magic* (1932), short stories; *The Story of Fuzzypeg the Hedgehog* (1932); *Wise Owl's Story* (1933); *Squirrel Goes Skating* (1934); *The Adventures of Peter and Judy in Bunnyland* (1935); *Candlelight Tales* (1936); *Little Grey Rabbit's Party* (1936); *Adventures of No Ordinary Rabbit* (1937); *The Knot Squirrel Tied* (1937); *Little Grey Rabbit's Washing Day* (1938); *Mustard, Pepper, and Salt* (1938), stories; *Tales of the Four Pigs and Brock the Badger* (1939); *Little Grey Rabbit's Christmas* (1940); *Moldy Warp, the Mole* (1940); *The Adventures of Sam Pig* (1941); *Sam Pig Goes to Market* (1941); *Six Tales of Brock the Badger* (1941); *Six Tales of Sam Pig* (1941); *Six Tales of the Four Pigs* (1941); *Ten Tales of Tim Rabbit* (1941); *Hare Joins the Home Guard* (1942); *Nine Starlight Tales* (1942); *Sam Pig and Sally* (1942); *Ten Candle Light Tales* (1942); *Cuckoo Cherry-Tree* (1943); *Sam Pig at the Circus* (1943); *Water Rat's Picnic* (1943); *Little Grey Rabbit's Birthday* (1944); *Mrs. Nimble and Mr. Bumble* (1944); *The Spice Woman's Basket, and Other Tales* (1944); *Adventures of Tim Rabbit* (1945); *Little Grey Rabbit to the Rescue* (1945), play; *Some Moonshine Tales* (1945); *The Speckledy Hen* (1945); *The Weathercock and Other Stories* (1945); *Washerwoman's Child* (1946), play; *Little Grey Rabbit and the Weasels* (1947); *Grey Rabbit and the Wandering Hedgehog* (1948); *John Barleycorn* (1948), stories; *Sam Pig in Trouble* (1948); *The Cobbler's Shop and Other Tales* (1950); *The Flower Show* (1950); *Little Grey Rabbit Makes Lace* (1950); *Macduff* (1950); *Snug and Serena Meet a Queen* (1950); *Snug and Serena Pick Cowslips* (1950); *Going to the Fair* (1951); *Toad's Castle* (1951); *Yours Ever, Sam Pig* (1951), stories; *Christmas at the Rose and Crown* (1952); *Hare and the Easter Eggs*

(1952); *Mrs. Mouse Spring Cleans* (1952); *The Gypsy Hedgehogs* (1953); *Little Grey Rabbit's Valentine* (1953); *Snug and the Chimney-Sweeper* (1953); *Little Grey Rabbit Goes to the Sea* (1954); *Little Red Fox and the Wicked Uncle* (1954); *Sam Pig and the Singing Gate* (1955), stories; *Hare and Guy Fawkes* (1956); *Little Red Fox and Cinderella* (1956); *Magic in My Pocket* (1957), stories; *Mr. Stoat Walks In* (1957); *Snug and the Silver Spoon* (1957); *Little Grey Rabbit's Paint-Box* (1958); *Little Red Fox and the Magic Moon* (1958); *Snug and Serena Count Twelve* (1959); *Tim Rabbit and Company* (1959); *Grey Rabbit Finds a Shoe* (1960); *John at the Old Farm* (1960); *Sam Pig Goes to the Seaside* (1960); *Something for Nothing* (1960); *Grey Rabbit and the Circus* (1961); *Snug and Serena Go to Town* (1961); *Three Little Grey Rabbit Plays* (1961): "Grey Rabbit's Hospital," "The Robber," and "A Christmas Story"; *The Little Knife Who Did All the Work* (1962), stories; *Little Red Fox and the Unicorn* (1962); *Grey Rabbit's May Day* (1963); *Tim Rabbit's Dozen* (1964), stories; *Hare Goes Shopping* (1965); *Sam Pig's Storybook* (1965); *Enchantment* (1966); *The Mouse, the Rabbit, and the Little White Hen* (1966); *Little Grey Rabbit's Pancake Day* (1967); *The Little Red Fox and the Big, Big Tree* (1968); *Lavender Shoes* (1970); *Fuzzypeg's Brother* (1971); *Little Grey Rabbit's Spring-Cleaning Party* (1972); *Fairy Tales* (1975); *Hare and the Rainbow* (1975).

Adult: *The Country Child* (1931); *Ambush of Young Days* (1937); *High Meadows* (1938); *The Farm on the Hill* (1941); *Country Hoard* (1943); *When All Is Done* (1945); *Country Things* (1946); *Carts and Candlesticks* (1948); *In Praise of Country Things* (1949), ed.; *Buckinghamshire* (1950); *Plowmen's Clocks* (1952); *The Stuff of Dreams* (1953); *Here's a New Day* (1956); *A Year in the Country* (1957); *The Swans Fly Over* (1959); *Wild Honey* (1962); *Cuckoo in June* (1964); *A Peck of Gold* (1966); *Recipes from an Old Farmhouse* (1966); *The Button Box, and Other Essays* (1970); *A Ten O'Clock Scholar, and Other Essays* (1970); *Secret Places, and Other Essays* (1972).

Secondary Works

Ayers, Lesley. "The Treatment of Time in Four Children's Books," *Children's Literature in Education*, 2 (July, 1970), pp. 69–81.

Graham, Eleanor. "Alison Uttley: An Appreciation," *Junior Bookshelf*, 5 (Dec., 1941), pp. 115–20.

V

VALE INNIS, a place in Lloyd Alexander's* *The Wizard in the Tree**. It is the Land of Heart's Desire, the Happy Land. When the enchanters and wizards left the world, they sailed to Vale Innis.

VALLEYS OF TISHNAR, a place in *The Three Mulla-mulgars**, by Walter de la Mare*. They lie on the flanks of the Mountains of Arakkaboa, where Tishnar* walks. These rich, golden, beautiful valleys are filled with flowers and fruit. Here is the Kingdom of Assasimmon*. Seelem*, who fathers Thumma*, Thimbulla*, and Ummanodda*, is from these Valleys, and to them he returns; his sons follow him.

VAUNGAYLEN (GAYLEN), the main character in *The Search for Delicious**, by Natalie Babbitt*. He becomes the husband of Medley. Gaylen is an orphan; when he was a baby he was left in a basket at the main gate of the palace. De Cree, the prime minister, lonely for a child, raised the boy, calling him Vaungaylen—"little healer"—because the child had healed him. When he is old enough, Gaylen becomes the prime minister's special assistant. Raised with great kindness and love, Gaylen sees the world as a bright garden with no weeds. When he is twelve, he is sent by the king to poll the kingdom and record the people's choices for the most delicious food. On his own in the world, Gaylen sees suspicion, hatred, and greed—enough to make him want to give up on all humans. But the alternative is indifference, which he cannot accept, for he must help those he loves. By giving back to Ardis*, a mermaid, the whistle* that allows her to retrieve her beloved doll, Gaylen gains her help and manages to stop Hemlock's* plot against the king. Eventually he marries Medley and becomes mayor of the first town in the kingdom. Every April he, his wife, and their daughter retrace Gaylen's journey through the kingdom's forests and mountains.

VAVASOUR, JOHANNA, a character in Robert Westall's* *The Devil on the Road**. She is the daughter of Major Vavasour and the goddaughter of Oliver

Cromwell; her brother, John, is a soldier. Johanna may have been born in 1630. When she gets older, she becomes a witch, learning to read signs and to manipulate the things of the earth. Johanna is a blessing-witch, able to heal with herbs and magic. She also understands people and the things of nature so well that she can predict people's actions and tell where a picked flower has come from. Johanna can also manipulate time. When in 1647 Matthew Hopkins*, witch hunter, comes to Besingtree, where Johanna's family has its manor, Johanna does what she can to discredit him. But she is herself accused of witchcraft. She manipulates time at least twice, trying to save herself; once she calls on John Michael Briarly, in 1877. Johanna also sends her familiar, a kitten named News*, into 1977 to John Webster*; by following News, he travels into the seventeenth century and, finally, rescues her by impersonating the Devil. John brings Johanna back to the twentieth century, where she is eagerly awaited by the local people, who put their faith in her cures and spells. Tiny because of poor nutrition in the seventeenth century, Johanna fairly blossoms in the twentieth, and she loves John intensely, bewitching his motorcycle so that he cannot leave her. Lovely as she is, however, John cannot love Johanna, for that would mean a permanence he does not want. Also, her powers and her reminders of the cruelty of seventeenth-century ways frighten him. When he sings a song to break her love spell, she leaves him and his century.

VERITY, MRS., a character in *The Ghost of Thomas Kempe**, by Penelope Lively*. She seems to have been raised in Ledsham, England, and never to have left it. An old woman now, she lives in a thatched cottage, with nothing to do but watch her neighbors. Mrs. Verity is a kind old woman but sometimes bothersome because she is lonely and loves to chat when she gets a chance. She is a veritable fount of knowledge about local people. When Thomas Kempe*, a seventeenth-century sorcerer whose spirit manifests itself in the house next door, decides that Mrs. Verity is a witch, a number of bewildering things happen to her, culminating with her house catching fire. Things quiet down, however, when Thomas's spirit is put to rest.

VESPUGIA, a place in Madeleine L'Engle's* *A Swiftly Tilting Planet**. This small country was once part of Patagonia, between Argentina and Chile. To what is now Vespugia Gwydyr*, an evil Welsh prince, had come in the twelfth century. Vespugia is later settled by Spaniards and Englishmen, and, in 1865, by a group of Welsh families. In the twentieth century, Vespugia's leader is Madog Branzillo*.

VETCH, a character in Ursula K. LeGuin's* *A Wizard of Earthsea**. He has several brothers and a sister named Yarrow. Vetch's real name is Estarriol. This heavyset young man from the East Reach on Earthsea* makes friends with Ged* while they are students at the wizard's school on Roke*. When he earns his sorcerer's staff, Vetch goes back to his home on Iffish to practice his trade.

When Ged, seeking the evil shadow he has loosed upon the world, comes to Iffish, Vetch joins him on his quest, to help if he can, and to warn the islands if Ged fails or make up a song about the deed if he wins.

VIOLIN, a magical instrument in *The Marvelous Misadventures of Sebastian**, by Lloyd Alexander*. This beautiful violin has a woman's face carved on the scroll and will play only for a true musician. The last of its many owners is Sebastian*, a young fiddler who thinks of music only as a livelihood until he hears the instrument's voice. This violin is said to be cursed; like other owners before him, Sebastian feels his strength flow out of him as he plays, yet he cannot keep from playing it. The violin seems to own him instead of the other way around. When Sebastian plays in the palace of the evil Count Grinssorg*, Regent of Hamelin-Loring*, Sebastian plays such music that all who hear the violin must dance; and the power of its music is so strong that it seems to kill the heartless and inhuman Regent. The violin is smashed when Presto*, Sebastian's cat, knocks him down in leaping to his shoulder as he plays.

VIVIANE. *See* Nimiane

VOGEL, WOLFGANG (DR.), a character in Lucy Boston's* *An Enemy at Green Knowe**. He is a famous scholar and alchemist in the seventeenth century; in 1630 he comes to Green Knowe* to teach Roger Oldknow, Squire Oldknow's son. He is a courtly, well-mannered man, but strange in his appearance; he has a sharp, pointed nose and a sharp, pointed forefinger, and his eyes have a slightly outward cast. He dresses richly and is a clever speaker. Dr. Vogel practices the black arts as part of his alchemy and owns many books of black magic and power. Soon Roger is morbidly fascinated by Dr. Vogel's strange mannerisms, for the man seems sometimes to speak to an invisible companion. It is rumored that the doctor is seen at night in company with a white hare-like creature larger than a hare. Roger, never strong, becomes more ill as the weeks wear on, until at last he is taken to his grandmother to recover. Finally, so frightened does Dr. Vogel become of his own black arts that he confesses to Piers Madely*, the local vicar, who helps him to burn his books and writings. That night, however, in his own house, Piers hears a terrible shriek from Green Knowe, and Dr. Vogel is never seen again. At least two of his books—a book made of a bat and a copy of *Decem Potentiae Mosio*, a book of spells—remain in the house into the twentieth century, when Dr. Melanie Delia Powers* comes to Green Knowe to find them.

VOYAGE OF QV 66, THE. Penelope Lively. Illus. Harold Jones. London: Heinemann, 1978. 172 pp. British.
    In the days following the great flood which all the people on Earth have gone to Mars to avoid, Pal*, a dog, Pansy*, a kitten, Ned*, a horse, Offa*, a dove, Freda*, a cow, and Stanley*, a monkey, get together. None of the animals—

including Stanley himself—is quite sure what Stanley is, having seen no other creature exactly like him, so they decide to go to London to see if they can find others like him. Because there is still so much water everywhere, they go in a boat labelled QV 66. After a long and sometimes hazardous journey, they come to Manchester, which has been taken over by dogs who have driven out all the other animals. Freda and Pansy, driven by the dogs into a warehouse, are rescued, and the voyagers leave.

As they travel on, they meet a tortoise who has seen animals like Stanley but cannot say where. Always clever, Stanley discovers Shakespeare and Milton, whom he improves upon, and invents music. Finding a toyshop, he blows up balloons, attaches them to a basket, and accidentally sends Pansy sailing over the landscape in it. The others follow the wind for several days, rescuing a parrot that is being tormented by other birds. At one point in their journey, Stanley gets locked behind bars in the vault of a bank; after a struggle, the others manage to rescue him. Because Offa has found someone who has seen Pansy, the voyagers go in that direction, meeting other animals going the same way because it is the proper time. They come to Stonehenge and here learn that the next day, Midsummer, an animal will be ritually killed to make sure the sun keeps rising. The next morning they learn that Pansy is to be the sacrifice. A storm comes up and, while Stanley terrifies the other animals with strange shrieks, the rest of the group rescues Pansy.

Once they have all escaped, they learn that they can follow a river to their destination. Finally they come to London. A visit to the British Museum is rather shocking; here they find stuffed creatures that look like Stanley, but they also find so many other kinds of animals that all are shocked at the variety. At last the voyagers come upon another moneky, who leads them to the zoo. After a tour of the facilities, where the monkeys act in a way that to Stanley is pointless and silly, he decides that he will not stay there, especially since his friends are not welcome and the monkeys' society is filled with rules and regulations. They leave the zoo. The others seem ready for a rest, but Stanley makes plans to discover what lies beyond the ocean.

VOYAGE OF THE "DAWN TREADER," THE. C[live] S[taples] Lewis. Illus. Pauline Baynes. London: Geoffrey Bles, 1952. 223 pp. British.

Edmund and Lucy Pevensie** are staying with their despised cousin, Eustace Clarence Scrubb*. One day as the brother and sister are discussing a picture of a ship that hangs in the Scrubbs' house, and Eustace is making himself unwanted, the picture becomes real and all three are pulled into it, landing in a cold and very wet sea. Taken onto the ship, Lucy and Edmund are delighted to find that it is the *Dawn Treader**, which has just put out from Narnia*, a magical land they have visited before. Caspian X*, the king of Narnia, is searching the sea beyond the known lands, seeking seven lords who had been sent there by his uncle years ago. With him is Reepicheep*, valiant leader of Narnia's talking mice, who feels that in the east, where the seawater is sweet, he will find his heart's desire, Aslan's* country. Edmund and Lucy are welcome aboard the *Dawn Treader*, but Eustace is a nuisance from the very beginning, complaining about everything and, once, actually swinging Reepicheep by his tail.

On the Lone Islands*, the first stop, they find one of the lords, and also an unscrupulous governor who has sanctioned slavery in the area. Caspian takes away the man's governorship, making the lord duke of the Lone Islands, and freeing all the slaves. After the *Dawn Treader* is reprovisioned, she again sets sail. After a storm, leaks are found in two water kegs and they put in at the next island they find, where a small party goes ashore to reprovision the ship.

Eustace is part of the party and, in typical fashion, he slips off to avoid work. Lost, he comes to a valley with a cave, and he watches as a dragon crawls from the cave and dies. When it rains, Eustace takes refuge in the cave, which is filled with treasure. After slipping on a diamond bracelet, he falls asleep, and when he wakes, he has become a dragon. The ensuing shock and the pain of the now too-tight bracelet make Eustace return to his companions, humble and eager to help them in his loneliness. Eustace enjoys the ensuing popularity but it soon becomes painfully clear that he must be left behind, for he is too large for the ship.

Then one night Aslan, the mystical lion who rules Narnia, comes to Eustace and takes him to a pool of water. Because he must "undress" to enter it, Eustace peels off his dragon skin, to find another and yet another underneath; Aslan peels the last one off and casts Eustace into the pool, where he discovers that he has become a boy again. The bracelet that had given him so much trouble had belonged to one of the lords Caspian seeks, but what had become of him none can tell. Eustace is a changed boy, eager to help and very popular.

When they set sail again, the ship comes upon a tiny, once-inhabited island where Reepicheep finds a small boat just right for him. Later the ship has an adventure with a singularly stupid sea monster. Finally they come to a small island where there is a curious pool of water that turns all that touch it into gold, and here they find another of the seven lords, changed into a gold statue. When a quarrel ensues over rights to the island, Aslan appears and it stops; when he vanishes they cannot remember the quarrel.

The next island is large and seemingly uninhabited, though a great house stands here. The island is the home of the Dufflepuds*, small beings so ashamed of their looks that they have made themselves invisible. In the house lives Coriakin*, the magician who had made them ugly. Now the Dufflepuds want to be visible again but are too afraid to go into Coriakin's house and read the spell that will make them so. Lucy does it for them, creeping into the lonely house and reading the spell from a beautiful book. Once she has done so, Aslan and Coriakin appear, having been made visible by the spell. When Aslan vanishes, Coriakin explains how Aslan had set him on the island to rule it and how he had punished the lazy Dufflepuds by making them dwarfs* with one leg and an enormous foot. When they discover that others do not seem to find them ugly, the Dufflepuds feel pleased about themselves.

The *Dawn Treader* sets sail again and comes on a dark island where dreams, not daydreams, come true. Here they pick up one of the seven lords and become lost in the murk until Lucy calls on Aslan and a gleaming albatross appears and leads the ship to safety. As they sail on, the winds become gentle. Finally they come to an island where is set up a table loaded as for a banquet, with the last three lords Caspian seeks asleep at one end. Caspian, Lucy, Edmund, Eustace, and Reepicheep sit at the table that night, to see what will happen. At midnight a beautiful girl comes and explains that this table has been set up at Aslan's bidding. On it lies the stone knife the White Witch* had used to slay Aslan, long ago. When the three lords had here fallen to quarrelling, one had picked up the knife, and all had instantly fallen asleep. Ramandu*, the girl's father, comes. He had once been a star and had been brought to the island, where he had grown old. Every morning a bird brings him a fire-berry from the sun, and it makes him younger. If Caspian and the others sail east and leave one person behind, the sleepers will wake.

Leaving behind the Narnian lord who had lived among his nightmares, to sleep here in dreamless sleep, the ship sails east. The sea becomes clear and sweet and seems full of light; it is all the voyagers need of food or drink. A strong current sweeps them into a sea full of water lilies, and here the water is too shallow for the ship to go on. Caspian wants to take a boat and go on by himself, but Aslan forces him to change his mind; he must go back to Narnia, and only Eustace, Edmund, Lucy, and Reepicheep can go on.

They set off in a boat, taking with them Reepicheep's coracle. Soon they come to a great wave between them and the sun, behind which is Aslan's country. When the boat grounds itself in the shallows, Reepicheep goes on in his coracle and vanishes over the great wave. The three children get out of the boat and wade along the wave until they reach land. Here Aslan, as a lamb, gives them fish to eat. There are ways into his country from all worlds, and Lucy and Edmund must learn to know Aslan in their own world; they can never come back to Narnia. Aslan opens the sky and sends them all home.

In his world Caspian marries Ramandu's daughter. And in *his* world, Eustace becomes "commonplace," according to his mother, who blames the influence of the Pevensies.

W

WALKER, THE. *See* Hawkin

WALPOLE, HEPSIBAH SAGACITY (SIBBY), a character in Jane Louise Curry's* *Parsley Sage, Rosemary & Time** and *The Magical Cupboard**. She is the aunt of Rosemary Walpole* and becomes the wife of William Wingard* (Bill). Born into a staid, practical family, Sibby felt sure that she was adopted, for she was nothing like them. When she is eight, she has a strange adventure when she is transported into eighteenth-century America, having an adventure with Goody Cakebread*, her magical cupboard*, a baby called "Wim," and a girl named Rosemary. When Sibby comes back into the twentieth century by walking between the Dreaming Trees*, Goody Cakebread's young cat, Oliver Tolliver, comes with her; she names him Parsley Sage*. Sibby has grown up to write detective stories and shock her relatives with her eccentric ways, finally buying the house at which she had had her adventure. When her niece, Rosemary, is sent to visit her and also has an adventure in the eighteenth century, the two come to realize that they shared the excitement in 1722, and that William Wingard, the young man who wants to buy Sibby's house, was "Wim." Sibby and Bill are soon married and, with Rosemary, go off in search of Goody Cakebread's cupboard. When they finally find it, they are surprised to discover that it has been kept for them for over two hundred years; Felicity Parmenter* had seen them in 1722, via the cupboard, and left word that her descendants were to keep it for them.

WALPOLE, ROSEMARY, a character in *Parsley Sage, Rosemary & Time** and *The Magical Cupboard**, by Jane Louise Curry*. Her father is Quincy Rectitude Walpole; her aunt and uncle are Hepsibah Sagacity Walpole* (Sibby) and William Wingard* (Bill). Because she is the only child of parents who pride themselves on their respectability and their pragmatic natures, Rosemary grows up level-headed and staid, more at home with facts than with imagination. When she is ten years old, Rosemary goes to stay with Sibby for a time and has a remarkable adventure during which she visits the early eighteenth century and helps an old woman there. Rosemary's adventures with an herb called "time"*, Goody Cakebread*, and her magical cupboard* change her forever, and with Sibby and Bill she goes looking for the impossible cupboard in the twentieth century, finding it, finally, in an old antique store. They are more than a little perplexed to hear that it has been kept for them for over two hundred years.

WALSH, JILL PATON. *See* Paton Walsh, Gillian Bliss

WARDROBE, an object in C[live] S[taples] Lewis's* *The Lion, the Witch, and the Wardrobe**. It looks ordinary, but it is made of the wood of an apple tree descended from a magical tree in Narnia*, a land of marvels. As such, it has properties no other wardrobe has. Made by Digory Kirke*, it sits in his great house in the country; when Edmund, Lucy, Peter, and Susan Pevensie**** visit Digory, they discover that they can walk through the wardrobe into Narnia itself, and return by the same route.

WATCH HOUSE, the title building in *The Watch House**, by Robert Westall*. It stands on a cliff overlooking the sea at Garmouth, England. The Watch House belongs to the Garmouth Volunteer Life Brigade, founded in 1870. The Brigade has operated out of this building ever since, though not much life-saving needs to be done in the twentieth century. The Watch House has gradually become the repository for souvenirs of the sea and anything else that catches the fancy of the men who work out of it: old skulls, bits of ships, clippings of rescues, and other paraphernalia. The "Old Feller," Henry Cookson*, is said to haunt the place, having died of a heart attack here; here Anne Melton*, a young girl, becomes aware of him and tries to help him. The cliff on which the Watch House stands is slowly eroding, so Anne and her friends try to draw attention to the place, hoping thereby to save the Watch House. Finally it is a long-buried legacy from Henry Cookson that provides the money to save the Watch House.

WATCH HOUSE, THE. Robet Westall. London: Macmillan, 1978. 226 pp. British.
    When her parents quarrel and her mother leaves her father, Anne Melton* is taken to live with her mother's old nanny, who lives with her brother near the sea. Bored one rainy day, Anne offers to dust the odd collection of flotsam and souvenirs of shipwrecks in the Watch House*, the ancient building which the Life Brigades still use as headquarters. As she dusts, she comes upon pleas for help written in the dust and finally watches in horror as "ANHELP" is written before her eyes. It must be, the nanny's brother tells her, the Old Feller who haunts the place. The next day, Anne finds a picture of the Old Feller in the Watch House and is startled when a huge skull retrieved from the sea somehow flings itself through the glass door of its case. When she looks at the picture again, a plea for help is written across its glass in the grime. That afternoon Anne has another strange experience when she falls into the water at the rocks

that have wrecked many ships, and thoughts about a shipwreck off Tasmania sweep into her head.

At a church youth gathering, Anne meets Timothy Jones* (Timmo) and Pat Pierson*, his girlfriend. They help as work begins on the Watch House to make it attractive to visitors coming to a local carnival. Once Timmo hypnotizes Anne in the Watch House, and while she is under she is present at the rescue of men from a wrecked ship; the rescue workers call her Henry and apparently take orders from her. When Anne tells Pat what she had seen, Pat suggests that they try to use a glass tumbler to receive messages from the ghost, but something throws the tumbler and smashes it. Then the model lighthouse in the Watch House begins to blink what Anne realizes is Morse code, though it stops when unbelieving Timmo comes. When Anne is alone in the Watch House, she deciphers a strange message to "Ware Hague." Father da Souza* and his friend, Father Fletcher*, whom Anne had met earlier, visit the Watch House; da Souza is uncomfortable there and warns Anne to stop what she has been doing. When Anne visits a nearby graveyard, she finds that the graves of five young men who all had drowned at the same time have been attacked over and over by a stray dog.

The carnival comes, and that day Anne sees the ghost of the Old Feller, who seems terrified when he sees a figure in a scarlet tunic. She learns from an old crony of his that his name had been Henry Cookson*; he seems to have died in mortal terror. Anne realizes that the Old Feller is himself haunted by an evil ghost, and when she finds a plaque dedicated to Major Scobie Hague*, a drowned soldier whose body had not been recovered, Anne decides that Hague must be that ghost. Anne and Timmo read a newspaper account of the shipwreck in which Hague had become a hero and learn that Father da Souza has also asked to see it. When Timmo again hypnotizes Anne, she relives the Old Feller's death of heart failure as he had crouched in the Watch House and seen through the window the ghost of Hague decaying and rebuilding itself to decay again. During another bout, Anne relives the scene in which ten-year-old Cookson, out to see a shipwreck, had watched the murder of Hague by five young scavengers; theirs are the graves the dog had desecrated. When Anne goes home, her mother is there, ready to take her back with her, but Anne refuses.

Timmo has realized that Anne and the Old Feller have made their respective ghosts more important than they should be, and so they have been haunted. Despite Hague's attempts to stop him, Timmo takes Hague's skull from its glass case in the Watch House and buries it in the graveyard, only to have the dog dig it up again and bring it back. Because of the incident when Anne had fallen into the water, Timmo and Pat dig there and find a skeleton which lacks a skull; it is Hague's. When part of the cliff they are standing under gives way, the bones are buried again. They will not be able to unearth the bones again and therefore cannot get rid of Hague. But Timmo reports the skeleton, and the coroner sends a bulldozer to recover it. Hague's remains are taken and an inquest held, after which the skeleton, lacking the bones of the right hand, is buried.

The writing in the dust at the Watch House does not stop, however, and Anne is again hypnotized. This time the Old Feller seems worried about digging near the village bandstand, and Timmo realizes that something must be buried there. He and Pat go to find it and discover the box Hague had been killed for, filled with gold and containing Hague's mummified right hand and a note from Henry Cookson that he has "paid in full." Anne, meanwhile, uncomfortable about the situation, has gone for Father da Souza; they arrive at the bandstand just as Hague's spirit menaces Pat and Timmo. With the help of Pat and, finally, Father Fletcher, Hague's spirit is exorcised and the hand is buried. The gold in the box, da Souza thinks, had been "repaid" to Hague after the scavengers had taken it, by Cookson, who had felt somehow guilty, perhaps because he had taken some. Anne, left alone on the beach, sees the Old Feller and reassures him before he vanishes.

WATCHERS, THE. Jane Louise Curry. New York: Atheneum, 1975. 235 pp. American.

Because he hates his stepmother, bitter, alienated Ray Siler* is sent to live with his relatives in Twilly's Green Hollow*. On his arrival, he meets Russell Boyd Moar* (Arbie), the owner of the local grocery store, who tells Ray that any information about the mysterious Twilly's Green residents might be profitable. Ray is warmly welcomed by the dark-skinned, blue-eyed Twilly's Greeners, who seem mysterious only in that they do not trust the outside world, staying in their hollow and marrying among the families that live there. Ray soon finds a mystery when he sees a strange man no one but his simple-witted young cousin can see. That night, looking out the attic window at the nearby rockhouse, Ray sees a fire lit there and, beside it, a girl dressed in strange clothes. But when Ray looks again at the rockhouse, it is empty and dark. When Ray investigates the next morning, there is no sign of a fire.

That day Ray's uncle, Durham Clewarek* (Dream), takes him to the family mine to get coal. Once the families had lived Up Top*, above the Hollow, beyond where old Penn Dreego* and his wife still live; when the men got work with the coal companies, they moved into the Hollow to be closer to where they worked. When Dream leaves Ray alone in the mine for a moment the boy has an instant of sudden hatred in himself for all his family. They uncover the head of what seems to be a huge fossil snake, and when Dream shatters it, Ray is unaccountably angry with him. Later that day Ray learns that others have seen the figures in the rockhouse; among them is Delano Mattick* (Delly). Ray sends a letter to his sister-in-law, giving her the facts about poverty-filled Twilly's Green, where he does not have to go to school unless he wants to, and he counts on her outrage to somehow get him back home.

On the day the welfare checks arrive at Arbie Moar's store, Ray goes down with the others to pick them up. Arbie is oddly excited over a piece of the fossil snake Ray finds in his pocket and Ray feels that Arbie will give him enough for the snake to buy a bus ticket home. The next day he gathers pieces of the snake in the sweet-aired cave and is stopped on the way out by the strange man he had seen the first night he was here. The man calls Ray "Ruan"* and tells him that he is buying not his freedom but the downfall of Berinir Gair*, then he vanishes. Startled but stubborn, that night Ray takes another chunk of the snake to Arbie at the church in Hoop Hollow, where he, Delly, and Dream take two cousins to sing. When Arbie hears that there is even more of the snake, he is ecstatic. Dream tells Ray that Arbie has been instrumental in starting a snake-handling ritual in the church.

As the group goes home, a wind suddenly comes up, and Ray watches in horror as Dream falls, an arrow in his chest. Ray falls, himself, and he wakes beside the body, which is not Dream's after all, but the man Ray had seen in the cave. Strangely dressed men call Ray "Ruan" and take him to the rockhouse in the Hollow. There he meets Tekla*, a priestess looking for Tûl Isgrun*, to gain the power of Katoá*, an ancient evil bound there, and conquer New Aztalán*. Captured and taken to Kanhuan* to be sacrificed, Ruan had spoken of the Shrine and led Tekla and her followers to what Ray knows as Twilly's Green Hollow. Having slain one of the Watchers over the shrine, the people from Kanhuan feel confident they will find Tûl Isgrun. Put with the other prisoners, among them the girl in the rockhouse, Ray helps her escape but fails in his own escape.

Ray wakes to find himself at the house; when the wind came up, he had tripped and fallen. The next day Arbie offers Ray money just to see the snake, but the boy is strangely reluctant. He goes to visit his uncle Penn Dreego and tells him of the dream, though not about Tekla's search. Penn tells him that there has always been a Watcher and takes the boy through the family graveyard to Up Top. As they make their way through the incredibly lush landscape Up Top, Penn explains that the long-lived Watchers had had many rules, now forgotten, and he shows Ray strange cylindrical stones with odd inscriptions on them, standing in the meadow. In the Gare, a great ruined castle with one cylindrical tower still standing, Penn shows Ray a chest filled with books in the strange language of the inscribed stones, but also one in Latin and the diary of a seventeenth-century man who had married into the family. He speaks of a translation of the Latin book but they do not find it. A day or so later Dream and the other men get a letter calling for mineworkers, but the letter does not specify which mine.

Tension builds in the Hollow. Three dogs are savaged by a mysterious creature. Though Ray gets from his father a bus ticket home, he does not really want to go. He has realized that Tûl Isgrun is Twilly's Green and that, just as Ruan had led Tekla to the Hollow, so he himself has drawn Arbie. Delly is the Watcher in the Hollow this generation. Sure that the snake he and Dream have uncovered is part of the Dark Shrine, Ray tries to translate the Latin book at the Gare, hoping to learn more. Delly takes him home and tells him that Penn's father had taught Delly about Tûl Isgrun. The congregation at Hoop Church is performing a strange ritual, as if it were calling down a dreadful thing.

Delly leaves Ray at Dream's house. As the others watch television, Ray slides into a doze in which he seems to be Ruan; bending over him is the girl he freed in the rockhouse. She runs to warn a man named Elzivir*, and Ray wakes, knowing that he must warn Delly. Four men are searching for the mine, so Delly and Ray guard it. When Ray investigates a noise he hears deeper in the cave, he is hit on the head. He wakes to find Tekla chanting to the fossil snake over a sealed crevasse in the floor of the cave. Suddenly, Elzivir—the man Ray had seen shot by an arrow—comes, warning Tekla that a curse will fall on her if she breaks the seal. As he falls, Ray watches Ruan run to him, crying that he had sought only to buy his freedom.

Ray wakes to find that Delly has defended the mine; one man had been captured but is freed by wild animals. Realizing that he and Ruan share deep ties and that perhaps he must undo something the other boy has done, Ray sends back the bus ticket. That day the men go to the reading of the will of a relative and discover that she has left a small piece of land to Hoop Church, which has sold it to a coal company owned by Arbie's wife. They also learn that the mineral rights to the Hollow and Up Top had been sold long ago by a cousin and that the Moars' company has them, too; it plans to go into the Hollow.

The inhabitants of Twilly's Green build a barricade across the dirt road into the Hollow. After the men guarding it are arrested, the women and children dam the creek running through the Hollow and wash out the road. Delly, who had spent the day seeking a lawyer's help, returns. He decides that the best way to deal with the situation is to destroy the mine; they will start a fire there and smother it later. He, Ray, and Bonethy Yanto* (Bonnie) build a bonfire in the back of the cave, dousing all with kerosene. As they labor something works on their minds, promising them the things they have longed for. As they leave the cave, Arbie runs into it and Delly goes after him. A spark from a pick Arbie swings starts the fire. Delly drags Arbie to the cave entrance.

The next day has some surprises: both the will and the deed to the mineral rights are fake. Among some papers is a translation of the Latin book, which tells how an evil thing sealed beneath the Dark Shrine had been freed in the fourth century and made its way to Inas Ebhélic*, where it had once lived. There it was worshipped as an oracle for eight hundred years, until that shrine was broken and it returned to Tûl Isgrun, to be bound again. Bonnie and Delly realize that they love one another; Dream gives Ray a letter from his father that permits him to stay with his relatives. Ray is very happy, feeling that at last he has come home.

WATER RAT, THE, a character in *The Wind in the Willows*, by Kenneth Grahame*. The Rat befriends the Mole* when that animal makes his way to the surface one spring morning, and he teaches the Mole the ways of the River. Though not unsociable, the Rat has no use for the outside world of men, preferring to live quietly in his little riverbank home, writing poetry. When he is tempted to leave home, Mole persuades the Rat to stay by reminding him of all he would leave behind. When Toad* makes a nuisance of himself and of his hobbies, the Rat helps in the attempt to curb that animal's foolishness by locking him in his room, but Toad tricks the Rat into letting him escape. After Toad returns to find his house taken over by weasels and stoats, the Rat is part of the raiding party that chases the unwelcome creatures from the hall.

WATER-BABIES, THE. Charles Kingsley. London: Macmillan and Co., 1863. 350 pp. British.

Tom* is an unlettered, unwashed chimney sweep apprenticed to brutal Mr. Grimes*. The boy looks forward to when he is grown up and can be a bullying master sweep like his master. When one day Grimes is called to clean the chimneys of a country manor, Tom gets his first look at the country. Along the way the two meet a handsome laundry woman who seems to know something about Grimes that he does not want known and who tells them that those who want to be clean will be clean and those who do not will not be, before she vanishes into the fields. The manor has so many chimneys that Tom gets lost and comes out in a pretty, white room where a little girl lies sleeping. Catching sight of an ugly, dirty figure, Tom realizes that it is his reflection in a mirror. His humiliation is complete when the girl wakes and screams, bringing her nurse running. Tom flees the house and most of the household run after him, convinced that he has stolen something.

Tom runs hard and finally loses all his pursuers but the washerwoman. Dizzy from the run in the heat, Tom scrambles down an impassible cliff to get at a stream he sees running past a cottage in the valley. Here he is cared for by an old woman who gives Tom milk and puts him to bed in a shed. His dreams send him to the stream to make himself clean. Unknown to him, the washerwoman, who has followed, is in the water before him, for she is queen of the water fairies and has brought Tom to be a little brother to them. First he must learn from the beasts, for he is a beast himself. Tom falls into the stream and turns into a water-baby*, leaving behind his body, which his pursuers find later.

Tom is happy in his new life, for he does not remember the old times. He torments the creatures in the stream until he makes friends with a dragonfly and realizes that if he is nice to others they will be nice to him. When Tom learns from an otter about the sea, he goes there when the stream floods, joining the other creatures in their mad dash to the sea.

When Tom reaches the great river he hears of other water-babies who live in the sea. One night Tom witnesses a fight between poachers and the law; one of the poachers is Grimes, who falls into the river and drowns. Terrified that Grimes will become a water-baby and torment him, Tom flees downriver and comes at last to the sea.

Even here, Tom cannot find the water-babies, though he searches for them. In the sea, Tom has an adventure with a tragic result. Ellie*, the little girl he had seen in the manor, has come to the seaside, where she spends time with the pedantic Professor Ptthmllnsprt*. The professor catches Tom, an impossible creature, in his net, and when Tom escapes Ellie falls onto some rocks trying to catch him. She dies from her injuries and the professor goes mad, cured and humbled only after he writes a book proving there are babies on the moon.

Tom, meanwhile, rescues a crotchety old lobster from a trap, and soon after this meets the water-babies. Having helped them tidy up a little rock pool, Tom goes home with them to meet the other water-babies, who are changed from children neglected while in the world.

Even with all the other water-babies to play with, Tom teases the other sea creatures until Mrs. Bedonebyasyoudid* visits and gives the water-babies sweets but gives Tom pebbles, because that is what he has given the sea anemones. Tom watches as she calls all those who have used children ill without knowing better and does to them what they have done to the children. Grimes is not there because he is in a different place, having known all along he was doing wrong.

The next day Tom tries hard to be good, and he meets Mrs. Doasyouwouldbedoneby*, the lovely sister of Mrs. Bedonebyasyoudid, who cuddles Tom and makes him promise to be good. But Tom keeps thinking about the sweets the other water-babies had got, and he gobbles up those in the cabinet of Mrs. Bedonebyasyoudid. He gets no pleasure from eating them and his discomfort increases when he gets a share of sweets the next day. When Mrs. Doasyouwouldbedoneby comes, Tom longs to be cuddled, but he is all prickly, for his "nasty tempers" are showing through. Tom asks for and receives the forgiveness of Mrs. Bedonebyasyoudid, and she sends Ellie, who teaches Tom how to get rid of his prickles. Tom wants to go where Ellie goes each Sunday, but first he must go where he does not want to go and help someone he does not want to help. Tom becomes miserable at this; he thinks he will have to help Grimes, who will turn him into a sweep again. Finally he quarrels with Ellie, who vanishes.

She has been sent away by Mrs. Bedonebyasyoudid, who tells Tom he must go out to see the world by himself. When he reluctantly agrees, she shows him what happens to people who do only what they like: the Doasyoulikes* are happy on their mountain until the mountain blows up and destroys the trees that had provided an easy living. The people live miserably and gradually evolve into apes. If Tom had not agreed to go on this journey, he would have evolved backward into an eft.

Tom starts his journey to the Other-end-of-Nowhere*, via Shiny Wall*, to find Grimes. The beasts tell him the way. In his journey, Tom sees many things, among them a ship where he sees a distraught widow with a baby. Finally some petrels take Tom part way to Shiny Wall. He again comes upon the ship. It is sinking now, and the widow's baby becomes a water-baby; a dog on board becomes a water-dog* and follows Tom. Some molly-mocks fly Tom north to the great ice pack called Shiny Wall. It has no gate, so Tom dives under it, coming out in a great pool where many whales rest. On a throne on an iceberg in the middle of the pool sits Mother Carey*, and from the foot of her throne swim millions of newborn creatures. Looking into her eyes, Tom learns the way to the Other-end-of-Nowhere, but he forgets. The dog, however, knows the way and Tom "follows" it, going backward because the dog will only go behind him. Sucked into a hole in the sea, the two come out in the Other-end-of-Nowhere.

Here Tom has many adventures in many different lands: lands where people take bad books and make worse ones out of them, where sweets are hidden from greedy children, where bad children's books are written, where foolish wisemen live. Tom meets turnips who had been children forced to study so much that their brains grew large and their bodies small, and he finds a land where people worship an ape and children must be frightened, and a lovely, quiet land where clouds are made.

Finally Tom comes to an ugly brick building guarded by policemen's truncheons who send Tom to the roof, where he finds Grimes stuck in a chimney. Tom's former master complains bitterly at being made to scramble up chimneys to sweep them. Mrs. Bedonebyasyoudid reminds him that this was the same treatment he gave Tom. She tells Grimes that his mother, who had helped Tom, is dead, and Grimes weeps, for it is too late for him to help her. His tears wash the soot from him and cause the chimney to crumble; once he is free he is sent to a volcano to help keep it cleaned out.

Mrs. Bedonebyasyoudid takes Tome back to Ellie. He has grown up and so has she, and the two fall in love. Tom and Ellie live happily, Tom going with Ellie to the place she goes on Sundays. His dog becomes the dog star, for the old one was worn out.

WATER-BABY, a type of creature in Charles Kingsley's* *The Water-babies**. Water-babies were once children who were neglected while they were alive. At their deaths, such children turn into water-babies and live at St. Brandan's Isle, caring for the creatures of the sea and being cuddled and castigated by Mrs. Doasyouwouldbedoneby* and Mrs. Bedonebyasyoudid*. Tom*, a chimney sweep, becomes a water-baby when he drowns in a stream. Lazy, nasty water-babies gradually evolve into efts, but good water-babies may eventually become land-babies or even grown men.

WATER-DOG, a creature in *The Water-babies**, by Charles Kingsley*. Once a real dog that drowned in the sinking of a ship, the water-dog follows Tom*, a water-baby*, in his search for the Other-end-of-Nowhere*. Because the dog knows the way but will only walk behind Tom, Tom must walk backward in order to watch the dog, who thereby leads him to the entrance to the Other-end-of-Nowhere. After Tom's adventures are done, the water-dog replaces the worn-out dog star and may shine there still.

WATER-MIDDEN, a type of being in *The Three Mulla-mulgars**, by Walter de la Mare*. These Water-middens—or water-maidens—are Tishnar's* maidens and as such are so achingly beautiful that they are sad. The voices of streams and cataracts are theirs. Like Tishnar's other maidens, they sometimes ride striped Zevveras. One Water-midden enchants Ummanodda* with her beauty and almost steals the Wonderstone* he carries; she makes him promise not to forget her when he comes to the Valleys of Tishnar*.

WATERSHIP DOWN. Richard Adams. London: Rex Collins, 1972. 413 pp. British. Carnegie Award, 1972.

When Fiver*, his brother, senses that death and destruction are coming for the warren but is not believed by its leader, Hazel*, a young rabbit, gathers nine other bucks, including Bigwig*, and sets out from the warren, searching for a safe place. They spend the first day in a field, and that evening Fiver shows Hazel the downs that are their distant objective. The rabbits journey all night and come to a lovely meadow, where they meet Cowslip*, a fine fat rabbit who invites them to his warren. It is a disconcerting place with a large hall and few rabbits who produce poetry and art and seem possessed with a strange sadness. Good food is left for them every day, but it is a place of unanswered questions, and Fiver can hardly control his fear. One day Bigwig runs into a snare and his friends must help him, for Cowslip and the others in the warren will not. Fiver, in a vision, sees the truth: that this warren is fed and cared for by the farmer so that he might take what rabbits he needs for meat; in despair the warren has become acquiescent and silent about its fate.

Hazel and his band, joined by a rabbit from the warren, travel hard and come at last to the downs. They find shallow burrows here but must dig others. The group is joined a day or so later by a rabbit from the warren they had come from; it has been completely destroyed. Hazel has helped a mouse escape from a hawk, and the next day, when they find Kehaar*, a wounded gull, Hazel decides to help it as well. Having realized that without does the new warren will fail, Hazel decides to persuade the gull to find some. After days spent recovering, Kehaar does, finding not only tame rabbits at a nearby farm, but a large warren two days away. Four of the band go there to find any discontented does.

Hazel, being too valuable to risk, is left behind but decides to lead a party to get the does from the farm. It is easy to persuade the others to go with him, and they get the hutch open, but the tame rabbits are unsure, and two stay behind. When Hazel goes back to get them, the farmer and his family return, and Hazel is shot, but he manages to crawl into a ditch. He is found there by the others and helped to the warren. Meanwhile the four sent to the warren return, without does. Their story is strange and terrible. The warren of Efrafa* is led by General Woundwort*, and for safety's sake, life there has been so efficiently organized that there is no freedom. Though the warren is overcrowded, no one can leave, and the four ambassadors had been treated as prisoners until they had escaped. The rabbits must get more does, and as Hazel heals, he and the others come up with a plan; Kehaar will help.

All but the farm does and a buck go near Efrafa, crossing a nearby river via a bridge and finding a boat, which Kehaar explains to them and which the rabbits decide to use to get away. Bigwig is sent to Efrafa and so impresses Woundwort that he is made an officer. He learns about life in the warren and gets the trust of discontented does, who plan with him how they and some other does will escape. As he feeds one evening, Bigwig meets Kehaar and tells him the plan. When the time comes, however, Woundwort is there, and they must miss the chance. Hazel and the others decide to go to the warren themselves if Bigwig does not return the next day. The next evening, though, Bigwig and the does make a run for it. Woundwort and his cohorts follow and are led toward the river, where they come upon Kehaar, who attacks. The does are taken onto the boat, and the rabbits get away, but their troubles are not over, for they drift downstream and lodge against a bridge and must swim to shore. The next day Kehaar leaves them and they start the journey back, coming upon an Efrafan patrol, but there is no trouble and they finally get home. The patrol, which has followed them, goes back to Efrafa to report.

Peaceful days follow until the mouse Hazel had saved tells them about rabbits coming toward the warren; it is Woundwort and his army. Hazel tries to talk with Woundwort, but the general refuses. After the warren is closed, the Efrafans try to dig into it. Suddenly Fiver has a vision that reminds Hazel of the dog at the nearby farm, and he takes two rabbits there, where he chews through the dog's rope. The dog goes after the others, who lead it to the warren, but Hazel is caught by a farm cat. Woundwort and his minions finally dig their way into a burrow, where Bigwig has hidden himself; he grabs Woundwort and they fight. Though Bigwig is horribly injured, Woundwort finds himself running away. The dog, led to the warren, catches and kills Woundwort and scatters the Efrafan army.

Hazel is saved from the cat by a little girl and eventually is taken back to the downs and set free. Five Efrafans have decided to stay at the warren; the others return to Efrafa. The rabbits live peacefully and happily, and several springs later death comes to Hazel.

WATSON, DAVID, a character in Alan Garner's* *Elidor**. He is the son of Gwen and Frank Watson and the brother of Nicholas, Roland, and Helen R. Watson***. When he and his brothers and sister go off in search of an oddly named street in London, he is the second to enter into Elidor*, a fantastical world. Here he is sent by Malebron* into a mound to retrieve three of four Treasures* but fails when he touches a crystal apple blossom and falls into a trance, broken when Roland breaks the blossom. Entrusted with a glorious sword, David goes back to his own world, to keep it safe. A year passes and David, like Nicholas and Helen, seems not to believe that their adventures in Elidor really happened. When static electricity appears in the garden over the spot where the Treasures have been buried, however, David investigates and realizes that the static is actually power leaking through from Elidor, where a great attempt is being made by Malebron's elemies to get the Treasures. David and the other children flee their house with the Treasures and eventually find Findhorn*, a unicorn; furious at Findhorn's death, David throws the sword into newly burgeoning Elidor.

WATSON, HELEN R., a character in *Elidor**, by Alan Garner*. She is the daughter of Frank and Gwen Watson and the sister of David, Nicholas, and Roland Watson***. Helen is the first to enter Elidor*, a magical land, through the abandoned church the children find. Here she is sent by Malebron* into a mound to retrieve three of four Treasures* essential to Elidor. She fails, however, when she touches a crystal apple blossom and falls into a trance broken many years later by Roland. Before Helen goes into the mound, she drops a glove; when Roland finds it, it is imbedded in quartz and has turf growing around it. Helen is entrusted with a beautiful cauldron and brings it back to her world to keep it safe; here it becomes a cracked cup. While digging a hole to bury the Treasures Helen finds and accidentally breaks an old jug with a unicorn on it, which she patches together and keeps as a treasure. A year passes, and Helen, like David and Nicholas, seems to believe that their adventures in Elidor did not really happen. When Findhorn*, a unicorn, breaks through and enemies of Malebron follow, she and the others take the Treasures and flee, eventually finding Findhorn. Because Helen is a maiden, the unicorn comes to her; with his head in her lap, he dies, singing the song that frees Elidor from the powers of darkness.

WATSON, NICHOLAS, a character in Alan Garner's* *Elidor**. He is the son of Gwen and Frank Watson and the brother of David, Helen, and Roland Watson***. When Nicholas and the other children go off in search of an oddly named street, Nicholas is the third to enter into Elidor*, a magical land. Here he is sent by Malebron* into a mound to retrieve three of four Treasures*. Nicholas touches a crystal apple blossom, however, and falls into a trance broken only when Roland breaks the blossom. Entrusted with a glowing stone, Nicholas goes back into his own world, to keep it safe. Hopeful that if the children ignore what has happened they will be left alone, in the year that follows Nicholas tries to convince himself and the others that it was mass hallucination. Events prove him false and, with the others, Nicholas takes up his responsibility when Findhorn*, a unicorn, breaks through from Elidor, followed by two of Malebron's enemies. At Findhorn's death, when the unicorn sings and the children see a newly burgeoning Elidor appear, Nicholas takes this chance to get rid of the Treasures by throwing them back into the land.

WATSON, ROLAND, a character in *Elidor**, by Alan Garner*. He is the son of Frank and Gwen Watson and the brother of Helen, David, and Nicholas Watson***. When Roland and the other children seek out an oddly named street, Roland is the last to enter Elidor*, a magical land. Here he meets Malebron*, who sends him into a mound to retrieve three of four Treasures* essential to the land; Malebron gives Roland the Spear of Ildana, the fourth Treasure. In the mound, Roland rescues his brothers and sister, who have preceded him, when he touches a magical crystal apple blossom with the spear and destroys it. Roland takes the spear back to his own world to keep it safe. Over the next year, the other children seem to believe that their adventures in Elidor never really happened, but Roland cannot deny Malebron and the charge he has laid on the children. During that year, Roland avoids the Watsons' front door, which he had visualized in order to make a way into the mound; when Malebron's enemies find the Watsons' front door, which seems sometimes to open on Elidor instead of home, Roland "uncreates" the door that exists in Elidor, blocking their entrance into his world. Even when Findhorn*, a unicorn, breaks through from Elidor, only Roland seems to believe that his song will bring life back to that land; when, at Findhorn's death, the unicorn sings and Elidor appears, glowing and burgeoning, the pain of Findhorn's death is greater than the joy of the glowing land, and in rage Roland throws his spear and Helen's cup into Elidor.

WEBSTER, JOHN, the narrator of Robert Westall's* *The Devil on the Road*. His father is Head of a school. John is good with mechanical things; he has rebuilt his motorcycle so that it runs beautifully and takes great pride in keeping it that way. He is studying civil engineering at University College, London. The summer after his first year there, John starts off on his motorcycle, going where chance will take him, as he sometimes does, for he flirts with "Lady Chance" whenever he can. This time it is almost too much for him, for John takes refuge from a storm in a barn and is catapulted into events which had taken place in the area three centuries before. Through News*, a kitten whose life John saves, he travels back in time and meets Johanna Vavasour*, a young girl accused by Matthew Hopkins* of being a witch. Always the champion of the helpless and the hurt, John helps her, appearing to Hopkins as the Devil and bringing Johanna safely to the twentieth century. Though he saves her, John cannot love her, and his unease with Johanna grows as he realizes that she has a witch's powers and had sent News to fetch him back through time. Panicked because he has been used and because he fears Johanna and her plans for him, John tries to leave her, and he sings a song that breaks her spell of love. Too late he realizes that she would have done anything but hurt him, but by this time he can do nothing.

WEIRDSTONE OF BRISINGAMEN, THE. Alan Garner. London: Collins, 1960. 224 pp. British.

Susan* and Colin* come to stay with their old nurse and her husband, Gowther Mossock*, for six months. Their first day there the children explore the area, finding several places associated with a wizard. On their way back, Selina Place, a local woman, tries to get them to get into her car but fails; Susan notices that the crystal stone her mother had given her is cloudy when Selina is near. Gowther tells them the traditional story of the wizard and how he once had bargained with a farmer for a white mare to join 139 mares belonging to an equal number of knights sleeping in a cave. That evening the children look for the gate through which the farmer had gone into the cave. They are caught by horrible creatures but are rescued by an old man, Cadellin Silverbrow*, the wizard of the legend, who takes them into the cave in the cliff and shows them the knights. Here they lie sleeping in Fundindelve* until the time of England's greatest need, when a great evil would arise; but he is worried, for the farmer had stolen Firefrost*, a fabulous stone. If the stone is destroyed the knights will wake and become mortal. Cadellin takes the children to the road, warning them about the svarts* he had rescued them from, and Gowther finds them and takes them home.

Odd things being to happen. Owls flock to the barn, the farm animals are restless, and a dwarf* appears at the farm. A few days later Colin and Susan, realizing that her stone must be Firefrost, start out to find Cadellin. A mist falls, and they are lost in it; they stumble into a circle of standing stones and are held there by the grasses growing there, as a figure cloaked in black takes Firefrost and leaves. Freed, Colin and Susan go to find Cadellin and meet instead Fenodyree*, the dwarf, who takes them to Fundindelve. The black figure, Cadellin realizes, had been Grimnir*, who, with the Morrigan*, the witch the children know as Selina Place, is seeking Firefrost for their evil master. There is no place for children in the struggle, but Fenodyree tells them to talk to the owls he has sent to the barn if they need him. Susan and Colin go home.

Fall comes, and winter. In January, they accidentally meet Cadellin again. There is hope, for Grimnir has not taken the stone to his more evil master. As Susan and Colin go home, they see a mist around Selina Place's house and investigate. Grimnir and the Morrigan are making magic to hold Firefrost for themselves. The children get inside the house and, hidden, hear the Morrigan summon creatures and then leave, waiting for the spell to take hold. Colin and Susan enter the room as the spell fails, and Susan gets Firefrost. When they hide again, they find that the cupboard they choose is an elevator that takes them down into the earth. Using their bike lamps, they wander through tunnels and caverns. When they stop to rest, Susan vanishes; running to find her, Colin is almost captured by svarts, who are killed by Durathror*, a dwarf. Durathror leads Colin to Susan, who had been taken by svarts and rescued by the dwarfs. After a dreadful journey through ancient tunnels made by dwarfs, they come out. Because Fundindelve is watched, they go to the Mossock farm to spend the night.

The next morning, when the children, Gowther, and the dwarfs set out to meet Cadellin, witches and warlocks are abroad, and crows are spying for the Morrigan, until they are shot down by silent archers. After a difficult journey through the woods, the band takes advantage of snow brought by their enemy to cross an open area to a stand of trees where they take refuge. Near nightfall they see a mara*, a troll-woman, and travel toward a lake to get away. Chased by maras, the group runs onto a small, floating island, and the maras, losing the scent, leave. As the band sleeps, its members dream of Angharad Goldenhand*, whose island this is. They dream of a feast and of warmth, and Angharad gives Susan a bracelet (the Mark of Fohla*) and all of them warm cloaks. They wake to find it all had been real. That day they travel farther.

On the appointed day, they come to the plateau where they are to meet Cadellin, but he is not there. They are attacked by birds and svarts and run to the other end of the plateau, to find there maras and the Morrigan's horrible hounds. One mara picks up Susan but accidentally touches the bracelet and melts to a rock. In the distance they see Cadellin coming, but they cannot get to him. The fight goes well for them until Fenodyree is injured; Durathror takes Firefrost and, using his magical cloak, flies toward Cadellin. But he is brought down by birds and fights against a pillar until he dies, taking many with him. Colin, Susan, Gowther, and Fenodyree are captured. Suddenly, from Grimnir's thwarted master there comes a great wolf, and the evil creatures panic and flee. Grimnir, however, gets Firefrost. After a chase, he is brought down by Cadellin's sword, and before Grimnir dies, he gives the stone to Cadellin, his brother. Cadellin sends the Morrigan back to the place from whence she had come and holds Firefrost aloft to protect them from the all-swallowing, sky-filling wolf. When the wolf is gone, the plateau is as empty as if the battle had never happened.

WENDY DARLING (*Peter and Wendy*). *See* Darling, Wendy Moira Angela

WESTALL, ROBERT [ATKINSON] (1929–   ), British writer. He was born in Tynemouth, Northumberland, on 7 October 1929, to Robert and Maggie Alexandra (Leggett) Westall. He was educated at Durham University and at Slade School, University of London. On 26 July 1958 Westall married Jean Underhill; they have one son. Westall has been an art master and an art critic as well as a writer.

Of Westall's works, two are realistic fiction and one, *The Scarecrows*, is a psychofantasy. *The Wind Eye** and *The Devil on the Road** are time fantasies and *The Watch House** is a ghost story, but in each the past reaches out and directly affects the present in one way or another, helping or harming, and in the process being helped or harmed itself.

In each work, characters of the present somehow catch the attention of someone in or of the past and are thus chosen to participate in subsequent events. In *The Wind Eye*, as Bertrand Studdard* and his family are on their way to the house he has inherited, they stop in a village and here visit the tomb of St. Cuthbert*; Madeleine Studdard*, Bertrand's wife, deliberately steps on the tomb and suddenly it seems to their daughter, Beth Studdard*, that "something" is aware of them. It is the saint himself—Cuddy, as the locals call him—who feels their needs across thirteen centuries. An ancient boat* takes them back to his century, guided by the desire of the person holding its tiller, but Cuddy appears in the twentieth century, too, and he seems sometimes to guide the boat to wherever it will do its passengers the most good. Seventeenth-century Johanna Vavasour*, in *The Devil on the Road*, kneads time, looking for a young man to help her escape witch hunter Matthew Hopkins* and the charge of witchcraft he has brought in on her. John Webster*, a twentieth-century man in search of adventure, is exactly who she needs, and she manipulates events and, later, time, to bring him to her. Frail Henry Cookson* is not a person in the past but a ghost in the present, and, in *The Watch House*, he finds in Anne Melton* someone who can help him with his peculiar need, for she needs someone to help as much as he needs someone to help him.

These encounters between the present and the past affect the lives of those in the present in many, sometimes subtle, ways. The Studdard family, on the verge of breaking apart, finds a new impetus for holding together as each member gets from Cuddy what he or she needs to live happily. Bertrand has been so afraid of the unknown that he has built a wall of logic around himself which has hemmed him in rather than keeping him safe; the events Cuddy precipitates open new vistas for him and he decides to seek the unknown and embrace it, realizing how much he hates the "dry as dust" twentieth century. Sally Studdard*, whose burned hand has caused her mental and physical pain, actively seeks out Cuddy, and he heals it. Madeleine, whose life-preserving anger is endangering her family, gets peace. The saint helps Beth realize that she must live for herself, not just her father; he gives her herself. Michael Studdard* wants and needs nothing. Anne Melton, helping Henry Cookson, finds the courage to stand up to her manipulating mother and find her own resources. John Webster needs nothing from Johanna, but she helps him learn about himself; faced with physical violence, he knows exactly what to do; what he finds impossible is a steady commitment with an individual.

Part of John's problem stems from a difficulty with belief; having seen Johanna's powers and the crudeness of her century, he cannot believe her when she says she will take care of him. He cannot love her and he cannot trust her, and in the end his disbelief is their undoing. Belief plays a part in the other works as well. Perhaps because Cuddy believes, he can do anything; Sally's belief in him heals her hand. Bertrand's blind disbelief in anything he cannot sense or measure is what must be shattered before Cuddy can help him. Anne Melton finds that believing can make something so; believing that someone has power over you gives him that power. As Henry Cookson has given Scobie Hague* power over him, even after death, so Anne and her father have given Mrs. Melton power over them. Henry himself has not been truly believed in by the members of the Garmouth Volunteer Life Brigade, so he has no power over them; Anne believes in him, and he gains power and strength.

Westall's works blend fantasy and our everyday world skillfully and suspensefully. The sense of the past in *The Wind Eye* and *The Devil on the Road* is very strong: Johanna's world is alien, with its own mood, and she could only be a product of it; Cuddy's seventh century, too, has little to remind us of the present. Characters are well realized and three-dimensional, with a life all their own.

Works

Juvenile full-length fantasy: *The Wind Eye* (1975); *The Watch House* (1977); *The Devil on the Road* (1978).

Juvenile novels and psychofantasy: *The Machine Gunners* (1975); *Fathom Five* (1979); *The Scarecrows* (1981); *Break of Dark* (1982), short stories.

Secondary Works

Westall, Robert. "The Chaos and the Track," *Signal: Approaches to Children's Books*, 25 (Jan., 1978), pp. 3–11.

WET MAGIC. E[dith] Nesbit Bland. Illus. H. R. Millar. London: T. Werner Laurie, 1913. 274 pp. British.

Francis* buys an aquarium but has no fish to put into it, so his brother, Bernard*, and his sisters, Kathleen* and Mavis*, landscape the inside of the aquarium to look as if there were water in it. Inspired, Francis speaks part of a poem* about a sea nymph and is astonished to catch a glimpse of her in the aquarium. He cannot repeat the experience for the others, however, for the next day the aquarium has been cleaned out. That day the children go to the seaside to stay with their parents; on the way they read in a newspaper of a mermaid seen at the place where they will be staying.

The day after they arrive Mavis and Francis get up early and go to the beach to find the mermaid. Francis, wading, says his poem, and his ankle is caught by a hand underwater. A sweet, mysterious voice implores the children to "save her. We die in captivity." Perplexed, the children go home to find that a mermaid has been caught and is on exhibit at the circus. They realize that they must save her. Francis, Bernard, Kathleen, and Mavis go to the circus to see the mermaid, and when Francis says the poem, she answers him tartly. The mermaid, Freia*, expects them to rescue her that night.

Bernard plans the rescue and Francis and Mavis carry it out, taking a wheelbarrow to the back of Freia's tent, bundling her into it, and starting for the beach. On the way they come across Reuben*, one of the boys in the circus, and he unexpectedly helps them, explaining that since he was stolen for revenge against his father by the gypsies in the circus, he owes them nothing. When the children get Freia to the beach, she vanishes into the waves. The children return home.

The day after the rescue, the children find in the wheelbarrow a note from Reuben; Freia wants them to come to her late that night. Reuben himself is not far away, for he has run away from the circus. Instead of going that night, the children decide to try to see Freia that day, and they go to a cave with a pool of water and say the poem. Freia appears and invites them to see her home, giving them a lock of her hair to tie around their necks so that they can breathe under water. They are reluctant, but when Freia drags Kathleen into the water, the rest follow. They swim as if they belonged in the water and follow Freia through the Cave of Learning*, where the rocks are made of books, to the gate of Freia's kingdom. Here she discards her tail and puts on a dress of seaweed.

They enter into the lovely kingdom, where they are given an ovation and a banquet for saving Freia, who is the Queen of Merland's* daughter. The children learn about Merland, a place on the sea bottom protected from the seawater by a thin bubble, and about the sea peoples, including the Under Folk*, who have been at war with Merland for 3,579,308 years. The children cannot leave Merland until someone speaks the poem and thus calls them. Though they have been told not to touch the bubble that holds back the sea, Kathleen does, and the sea pours in. The Under Folk take this opportunity to attack, and Bernard, Francis, Kathleen, and Mavis are given tails and magic jackets that make the wearer invisible and intangible. Reuben joins another group of warriors.

The Under Folk are repulsed after the first skirmish, and Bernard, Kathleen, Francis, and Mavis are sent to the gate of Merland to defend it against the Book People*, who come out of the rocks in the Cave of Learning. The villains of the books are accidentally let in, and the only way the children can save Merland is by calling out the heroes of the books, who push the villains back into their places before returning themselves. When the Under Folk attack Merland again, the children are caught and taken to the kingdom of the sad and ugly Under Folk. Here they are taken to the King and Queen of the Under Folk*, and when Francis accidentally says the poem, Freia appears among the prisoners. Immediately all but Kathleen take an antidote to the drink of oblivion which the Under Folk will give them. The Under Folk take away their jackets and their tails and give them the drink; it works only on Kathleen, who is made into a pet of the Queen. Freia and the others are locked up until the drink takes effect.

Because the prisons are filling up with Merfolk, the children and Freia are given tickets-of-leave to wander through the kingdom. The children are made to wear fetter-tails which bind their legs but do not act like real tails, so they cannot get away. Ulfin*, the jailor's son, takes them anywhere they want to go: to the archives, where they learn how the centuries-long war started, and to see a captive king, whom Freia recognizes as her long-lost father. Because the drink has made him forget who he is, Freia and the children decide to use Kathleen's antidote to bring back his memory. Ulfin takes them to the museum, where they steal their jackets and escape by wearing them and making themselves invisible. The antidote restores the king's memory and he remembers the way for Freia to remove the children's fetter-tails, which she does.

The Under Folk have lost the battle to the Merpeople, who are taking over the city, but the king goes to make real peace with the King and Queen of the Under Folk. A banquet is held to celebrate, and Reuben attends it; at the banquet Kathleen's memory is restored. The Under Folk take off the ugly armor they have been wearing all the time and reveal that they are just like the Merfolk; Ulfin and Freia become engaged. The King and Queen of the Under Folk, however, are land people whose memories have been erased, and they are allowed to leave with the children. They are given an antidote to restore their memories once they are on land. The King and Queen leave first and say the poem to recall the children; as soon as they come to land, Bernard, Mavis, Francis, Kathleen, and Reuben drink the oblivion drink to forget the people of the sea. Reuben has been told that the first people he meets on land will be his parents, and the first people he does meet are the former King and Queen. The four children forget everything about their adventure except for Reuben, who is happy with his now-happy parents.

Note: This work first appeared in *The Strand Magazine*, nos. 264–272 (Dec., 1912–Aug., 1913).

WHATSIT, MRS, a character in *A Wrinkle in Time**, by Madeleine L'Engle*. She is 2,379,152,497 years old. Once she had been a star that gave its life to overcome the powers of evil in that part of the universe. The true Mrs Whatsit is beyond human understanding, but she is very good at materializing and verbalizing. Because of these talents, she goes with Mrs Which* and Mrs Who* when they go to Earth. Mrs Whatsit is much younger than the others and is child–like in her enthusiasm, tending to chatter until she is silenced by Mrs Which. Mrs Whatsit appears on Earth as a tramp of sorts, swathed in clothes and delighted by the "haunted" house she and the others live in. With Mrs Which and Mrs Who, she helps Meg and Charles Wallace Murry** rescue their father, Mr. Murry*, from the planet Camazotz*. It is she who is responsible for explaining to the children the evil that is trying to take over the universe. Once Mr. Murry is safe, Mrs Whatsit is off with the others on another mission.

WHICH, MRS, a character in Madeleine L'Engle's* *A Wrinkle in Time**. Like her friends, Mrs Whatsit* and Mrs Who*, she is something beyond understanding, a force of good in the universe. Being insubstantial, she has trouble materializing in a corporeal fashion or even thinking in a corporeal way; her voice shimmers, as does her shape. Older than her companions, Mrs Which is more authoritative and tries to keep them in line, though she is very nice to them. Mrs Which and the others help Meg and Charles Wallace Murry** rescue Mr. Murry*, their father, from a planet that has given in to the forces of evil.

WHISPERING KNIGHTS, THE. Penelope Lively. Illus. Gareth Floyd. London: Heinemann, 1971. 160 pp. British.

At William's* insistence, he, Martha Timms*, and Susan Poulter* one day try a spell in an old barn where a witch supposedly lived long ago. Though nothing happens, that night Martha sees a shadow that stays in the room a second or two after she turns on her bedroom light. The next day when the children go to the barn a scaly thing spouting fire appears in the hay; it vanishes when they douse it with a fire extinguisher. The shaken children go to Miss Letitia Hepplewhite*, the barn's owner, who realizes that because of their spell, Morgan le Fay*, the witch who had lived there, has come back and is trying to get them. That evening she leads the children in a noisy ritual to drive Morgan away.

Days pass and all is quiet. One evening Susan finds a beautiful cake which has been left for her, and she and Martha decide to try it. When they drop a slice, the grass touching it dies; when Susan stabs the cake with a stick, the cake melts, scorching the grass. Other alarming things are also happening. The television sets in the children's houses do not work right when the children are present, and a six-lane road which was supposed to be built south of the village is suddenly planned to go right through it. Miss Hepplewhite recognizes Morgan's influence and decides that they must fight, and when they recognize the new wife of the man responsible for the road as Morgan, the children realize that she is right.

A few days later Morgan appears at the barn, though her figure changes to a pillar of stone and she escapes from the children. When Miss Hepplewhite puts the pillar in her garden and tries to drill a hole in it, it melts away. That night Martha sees from her bedroom gray shapes moving in a nearby field and knows that they are the Hampden Stones*—twenty-nine stones in a circle which people call the Whispering Knights, saying that they once drove a bad queen from the village. The next morning Martha is oddly silent. The three children go fishing, and here Martha meets a woman who seems to control her; Martha goes away with her. Susan and William, at Miss Hepplewhite's insistence, go to Morgan's house and there find Martha, who seems to be in a trance. Though they get out of the house and take a bus to town, Morgan follows them, and when the children take refuge in a church, she comes there, too, vanishing when Susan shoves a cross at her.

Susan and William take Martha to a hospital, where she wakes from her trance. She remembers seeing the Stones move, but nothing after that. When the children get on a bus to go home, Morgan's car, driverless, follows the bus. When they get off, it comes after them; they run across the fields to a river and the car, following, plunges into it. Because Morgan has seemed to Martha to be afraid of the Stones, they start toward them, quickly getting lost. An old road leading to the Stones appears, and they follow it, pursued by Morgan, who is on horseback. Miss Hepplewhite, transfigured, stands among the Stones. The children manage to get into the circle and lie with their eyes hidden, afraid to watch the awesome battle suddenly going on above them, and they hear Morgan's wail when she loses. The children seem to sleep and wake, and they go to Miss Hepplewhite, who denies having been at the Stones. Though Morgan will come back, she assures them, it will not be in their time. The next day they learn that the route of the road has been changed again, and the village is safe. The children visit the Stones to see that they are all right.

WHISTLE, an object in *The Search for Delicious**, by Natalie Babbitt*. This gray stone key-like object is made by a dwarf* named Bevel; by blowing on it, one can open or close the door of a rockhouse over a spring. When the spring floods the valley so that the dwarfs cannot get to it, the whistle is given to Ardis*, a little mermaid who is the keeper of the spring. She keeps the whistle hung on a sharp rock on the shore of the lake. One day, to her sorrow, a man comes along and takes the whistle, after blowing it and thereby shutting up Ardis's doll in the rockhouse. The whistle is handed down through the man's family as a good luck piece until it comes to Canto, a minstrel. He gives it to Vaungaylen* (Gaylen), so that the two will be able to recognize each other thirteen years hence. Discovering how important the whistle is to Ardis, Gaylen takes it to her, giving it to her only after she promises to destroy the dam which evil Hemlock* has built to trap the waters of the lake.

WHITE, E[LWYN] B[ROOKS] (1899–   ), American writer. He was born on 11 July 1899, in Mount Vernon, New York, to Jessie Hart and Samuel T. White. He was educated at Cornell University, in Ithaca, New York. White was a private in the United States Army during World War I. In 1919 he married Katharine S. Angell (died 1977); they have one son. White has been a reporter, a columnist for *Harper's* magazine, and contributing editor for *The New Yorker*.

White's works for adults include collections of essays, short stories, and poems. His three works for children are all fantasies in which both people and animals appear as characters. *Charlotte's Web*, *Stuart Little*, and *The Trumpet of the Swan* deal with issues important to us all: friendship, love, happiness, and death. In the works, relationships are essential. The characters may do what they can to get along in the world, but without relationships with others, life has little meaning, and in some cases would be well-nigh impossible.

Many times a relationship can build a bridge between animal and human. Fern Arable*, in *Charlotte's Web*, can understand the animals in the barn because, perhaps, of her love for Wilbur*. Sam Beaver* and Louis*, in *The Trumpet of the Swan*, have no trouble understanding each other, because of their friendship; Sam does not have this kind of relationship with Louis's parents and hence cannot communicate with them. Stuart Little* is born of human parents, but he has the features of a mouse, and despite this oddity he gets on well with all kinds of humans, who do not seem to find him odd at all.

In all the works, friends help each other; sometimes without this help life would be impossible. Margalo*, the little brown bird whom Stuart loves, saves his life when he is accidentally dumped, with some trash, into the sea. Less dramatically, Dr. Paul Carey*, delighted with Stuart's handling of his small model boat, helps him in his quest for Margalo by giving Stuart a little car he has made. Louis, a mute swan, turns to Sam often in his attempt to help himself; Sam takes Louis to his school, where he learns to write; Sam helps Louis get the jobs he needs to earn money to pay for the trumpet his father has taken; and Sam helps Louis negotiate for the freedom of Serena*. Louis's relationship with his father is also important, for the cob's* love helps him in his early years, when he is learning how much of a disability he has; and his father steals the trumpet that allows Louis to communicate with the other swans. Once he has won the love and admiration of Serena, their relationship sustains and nurtures him. In *Charlotte's Web*, Wilbur, the little runt pig, has two loving relationships that nurture and help him. Fern acts on impulse to keep Wilbur from being killed because he is a runt, and under her loving care he becomes a fine animal. After Wilbur is sold, he greatly enjoys Fern's visits to the barn. But it is Charlotte A. Cavatica*, the gray spider in the barn, who becomes his dearest friend and who ultimately saves his life—something Fern cannot do. At first it is difficult for Wilbur to accept Charlotte, because she has some bloodthirsty habits which make him uncomfortable. But he learns to accept or ignore the fact that she lives on the blood of insects, because Charlotte is a true and loyal friend, and at heart a kind person. Her friendship sustains him in the lonely days when Fern does not visit the barn, and the words in her web help keep Wilbur from being butchered at first frost. Though Charlotte dies, she lingers in memory, for Wilbur will never forget this true friend and good writer. Friendship is "a gamble," as Wilbur puts it, but it has great rewards.

The works are full of a sense of the world lying all about us. The natural world, especially, holds wonder. Louis makes his money in the city, but it is to the lake that he returns to live, for the lake is a peaceful place where he can be free. Margalo is from the deep countryside, and it is there that Stuart searches for her in what ultimately becomes an endless search for the elusive. The wonders of the landscape embody the beauty and wonder of the north for the telephone repairman Stuart meets, and through a description of the countryside he gives Stuart a sense of its mystery. The wonder of the countryside surrounding the farm where Wilbur lives is the wonder of the changing seasons and their sweet cycle, as things are born, grow, and die. This cycle of birth and death is one thing Wilbur must learn to accept, for it is natural; death is a part of life. Charlotte can save him from an early, unnatural death, but nothing can save her from a natural one. Fern grows up and grows away from the animals in the barn as she becomes a young adult, and this is natural, too, for it is also part of the cycle.

White's fantasies are light but meaningful, and they are always entertaining. His style is simple and descriptive; he recreates wholly the landscape through which his characters move. The characters themselves are well realized: Wilbur, Charlotte, crisp but dreamy Stuart Little, and self-serving Templeton* are among the most memorable.

Works

Juvenile fantasy: *Stuart Little* (1945); *Charlotte's Web* (1952); *The Trumpet of the Swan* (1970).

Adult: *Is Sex Necessary?* (1929), with James Thurber; *The Lady Is Cold* (1929), poems; *Ho Hum* (1931); *Another Ho Hum* (1932); *Alice Through the Cellophane* (1933); *Every Day Is Saturday* (1934); *Farewell to Model T* (1936); *The Fox of Peapack, and Other Poems* (1938); *Quo Vadimus? or, The Case for the Bicycle* (1939); *One Man's Meat* (1942); *Here Is New York* (1949); *The Second Tree from the*

Corner (1954); *The Wild Flag* (1956); *The Points of My Compass* (1962); *Letters of E. B. White* (1976); *Essays of E. B. White* (1977); *Poems and Sketches of E. B. White* (1981).

Secondary Works

Griffith, John. *"Charlotte's Web*: A Lonely Fantasy of Love," *Children's Literature*, 8 (1979), pp. 111–17.

Mason, Bobbie Ann. "The Elements of E. B. White's Style," *Language Arts*, 56 (Sept., 1979), pp. 692–96.

Rees, David. "Timor Mortis Conturbat Me: E. B. White and Doris Buchanan Smith," in *The Marble in the Water* (Boston: The Horn Book, Inc., 1980), pp. 68–77.

Weales, Gerald. "The Designs of E. B. White," *New York Times*, 24 May 1970.

WHITE, T[ERENCE] H[ANBURY] (1906–1964), British writer. He was born on 29 May 1906, in Bombay, India, to Garrick and Constance (Ashton) White, and was educated at Cheltenham College and at Queen's College, Cambridge University. White was assistant master at a preparatory school and was then head of the English Department at Stowe School, in Buckinghamshire, before becoming a free-lance writer. He died on 17 January 1964, in Athens, Greece.

White's works read primarily by children include a science fiction novel, *The Master*, and two fantasies, *Mistress Masham's Repose** and *The Sword in the Stone**. The last is part of White's five-part story of King Arthur* and was extensively rewritten to fit into the tetralogy of *The Once and Future King*, read primarily by adults. Worlds apart in subject matter, the two fantasies have as their main characters children learning to live in their worlds, becoming, if not quite adult, then at least responsible human beings. In both works, the children must understand that humans are flawed. But humans are also capable of perfection, and this the children must understand also.

In *Mistress Masham's Repose*, people are greedy and possessive, having no compunctions about using those less powerful than themselves. The tiny people of Lilliput are harried and bullied by the giants of the outside world; they are taken by Captain Biddel from their island and made to do tricks in a circus; once their descendants are found by Mr. Hater* and Miss Brown*, the only thought of the latter is how they can make the most money from the tiny people. When Maria* finds the Lilliputian* baby on the grounds of her ancestral home, her first urge is to possess it, for it is tiny and perfect and as desirable as a well-made toy. Though she soon feels guilty at taking it from its mother, Maria overcomes her guilt in a fit of rage at the woman's defense of her child, and she takes both. To Maria, the tiny people are tiny toys who are interesting and amusing, and though she overcomes this feeling for a time after being lectured by the Professor*, she soon slips back into it. Once Maria has the trust of the Lilliputians, she begins to treat them as playthings, and only after a horrible accident with one that makes it painfully clear that they are live creatures much like herself does she treat them with the dignity they deserve. Even then Maria makes plans for helping them lead happy lives, if only she were rich enough to buy them a loch with tiny islands on it, on which they could make their homes. The Professor, though he avoids the Lilliputians lest he make them feel inferior, seems to have little compunction about capturing a Brobdingnagian as much larger than he is as he is larger than the Lilliputians, and making the man into a sideshow attraction.

The Wart learns from his studies with Merlyn* in *The Sword in the Stone* that man is violent and that the might he demonstrates is not necessarily right; those who have power must control it for it to do any good for either the one who has power or those beneath him. Man, the badger tells him, is dominant over all the creatures of the world and remains potentially in God's image. But in the Dream of the Stones, the Wart watches as the last small pebble that remains of a mighty mountain is split into an arrowhead that one man uses to slay his brother; when he goes out one night, having been changed by Merlyn into a snake, the Wart hears from another snake the tale of the gentle female Atlantosaurus, the last of her kind, who has no thought of hurting anything but who is ruthlessly and thoughtlessly slain by a man. The dominant creature in the world may have the power to do whatever he wants, but this does not mean that he is right simply because he is mighty, for strength must be controlled for it to do any good. Galapas*, the mighty giant, is a bully; the pike who rules Sir Ector's moat has become a disillusioned tyrant who believes only in power, for love and pleasure are tricks not to be trusted. Those who have power must control it. The hawks in Sir Ector's mews obey not their instincts but their leader; the cobra who accidentally becomes a poisonous snake uses its power only in extremity, while the frog and the water snake who become poisonous and decide to bite whenever they like are made to lose their poison.

Having learned of human frailty, Maria and the Wart also learn to transcend them. Maria makes Malplaquet* a paradise and contents herself with visiting the Lilliputians of Mistress Masham's Repose, with the Professor at her side. The Wart, changed into a badger, meets a pathetic and helpless hedgehog he could easily snap up in his ill temper, but it is so pitiable in the face of his strength that he cannot. Those in a position of power must not abuse it but must use it to protect the helpless.

White's works are richly imaginative, filled with unforgettable characters. His style is lively and his works have an air of scholarship that is worn with gentle humor. Though parts of *The Sword in the Stone*, especially the adventure with Morgan the Fay*, are overdone, for the most part incidents are well handled.

Works

Juvenile fantasy: *The Sword in the Stone* (1939); *Mistress Masham's Repose* (1946).
Juvenile science fiction: *The Master* (1957).
Adult: *Loved Helen and Other Poems* (1929); *The Green Bay Tree* (1929), poems; *Dead*

Mr. Nixon (1931), with R. McNair Scott; *Darkness at Pemberley* (1932); *They Winter Abroad* (1932), as James Aston; *First Lesson* (1932), as James Aston; *Farewell Victorian* (1934); *Earth Stopped* (1934); *Gone to Ground* (1935); *England Have My Bones* (1936); *Burke's Steerage* (1938); *The Witch in the Wood* (1940) as *The Queen of Air and Darkness* (1958); *The Ill-Made Knight* (1940); *The Elephant and the Kangaroo* (1947); *The Age of Scandal* (1950); *The Goshawk* (1951); *The Scandalmonger* (1952); *The Once and Future King* (1958); *The Godstone and the Blackymoor* (1959) as *A Western Wind* (America); *America at Last* (1959); *The White/Garnett Letters* (1968); *The Maharajah, and Other Stories* (1981).

Secondary Works

Crane, John K. "T. H. White: The Fantasy of the Here and Now," *Mosaic*, 10 (Winter, 1977), pp. 33–46.
Irwin, W. R. "Swift and the Novelists," *Philological Quarterly*, 45 (Jan., 1966), pp. 102–13.
Langton, Jane. "A Second Look: *Mistress Masham's Repose*," *The Horn Book Magazine*, 57 (Oct., 1981), pp. 565–70.
Warner, Sylvia Townsend. *T. H. White*. New York: Viking Press, 1967.
The White/Garnett Letters, ed. David Garnett. New York: Viking Press, 1968.

WHITE RIDER, THE, a force of evil who appears in *The Grey King** and *Silver on the Tree**, by Susan Cooper*. She is one of the Dark lords and, dressed in white, rides a white horse, complementing the Black Rider*. As Blodwen Rowlands she is the wife of John Rowlands*, a Welsh shepherd. Blodwen makes friends with Bran Davies*, the son of King Arthur*, who is growing up in the twentieth century, and thus she can keep watch on him. Her life with John is happy, and he is shattered to find out her true nature, for he feels he has been living a lie. The White Rider does what she can to defeat the Light, trying hard to get Eirias*, the sword necessary for the final triumph of either the Dark or the Light. When the Dark is defeated during a final battle, the White Rider falls with the Black Rider out of time.

WHITE WITCH, THE, a character in *The Lion, the Witch, and the Wardrobe**, by C[live] S[taples] Lewis*. Her real name is Jadis; she is descended from Lilith and from giants. From the beginning of time it has been decreed by the Emperor-Beyond-the-Sea, over Narnia*, that she be given all traitors; if she does not spill their blood, all Narnia would perish in fire and water. Generations after the land is created the Witch takes the throne, claiming it as her right and plunging Narnia into an endless winter. She takes care of all those who oppose her by changing them into stone. During her reign, the Witch is fearful that true children of Adam—the rulers by right of Narnia—will come to the land and take the throne from her, so she commands that any who come into Narnia be brought to her. When Edmund and Lucy Pevensie** find their way into the magical land, the Witch gets Edmund under her enchantment and makes him betray his brother and sisters, though she does not get them. Because Edmund is a traitor she has the right to kill him, but Aslan*, the omniscient lion-protector of Narnia, persuades the Witch to take himself instead, knowing that if she kills an innocent being, death will be reversed and that person will come to life again. Resurrected, Aslan kills the Witch in a battle at the Fords of Beruna*.

WHO, MRS, a character in *A Wrinkle in Time**, by Madeleine L'Engle*. She is much more than a mortal being; like her companions, Mrs Whatsit* and Mrs Which*, she is a force of good in the universe. Mrs Who goes with the other two to Earth, here to help Meg and Charles Wallace Murry** rescue their father, Mr. Murry*, from Camazotz*, the planet on which he is imprisoned. On Earth, Mrs Who appears as a plump woman with glasses who sprinkles her conversation with quotes in several languages. When they go to Camazotz, Mrs Who gives the glasses to Meg to use as a last resort. Wearing the glasses, Meg penetrates the wall of her father's cell and rescues him.

WIGG, ALBERT, a character in P[amela] L[yndon] Travers's* *Mary Poppins** and *Mary Poppins Opens the Door**. He is the uncle of Mary Poppins* and was the nephew of a woman named Emily. Mr. Wigg was the childhood friend of Mrs. Clara Corry*, which makes him very old indeed. Portly, bald-headed Mr. Wigg is a cheerful man very disposed to laughter, sometimes laughing at things no one else would find funny. When his birthday falls on a Friday, this can be a problem, for then when he laughs he becomes so full of laughing gas that he floats in the air and cannot come down until the next day or until he thinks of something somber; once, when he had been to a circus the night before, Mr. Wigg laughed so much that he floated all day. When he mistakenly invites Mary Poppins and Jane Caroline and Michael George Banks** to tea one birthday Friday, Mr. Wigg's laughter proves so infectious that the children fill with laughing gas, too, and they must have tea in midair.

WILBUR, the main character in *Charlotte's Web**, by E[lwyn] B[rooks] White*. He is a pig, the runt of his litter, so small that he is almost killed by Mr. Arable, the farmer. Wilbur is saved, though, by Fern Arable*, Mr. Arable's eight-year-old daughter, who tenderly raises him until he is five weeks old. At that time, Wilbur is sold to Homer L. Zuckerman* for six dollars. Here he lives in the barn and is fairly happy, for Fern visits him often. After a while, though, Wilbur becomes bored and lonely, for no one in the barnyard will be his friend. When he meets Charlotte A. Cavatica*, a gray spider whose web hangs in the barn doorway, she becomes Wilbur's close friend. Wilbur enjoys his life in the barn, thriving on the lovely mixtures of garbage and table scraps with which Mr. Zuckerman feeds him and listening to Charlotte's stories and songs. He soon learns, however, that he is being fattened for slaughter in the winter, and his hysteria prompts Charlotte to save Wilbur's life by writing words and phrases descriptive of him in her web; Mr. Zuckerman takes the appearance of these words as miracles and shows Wilbur at the county fair. Here Wilbur is given a special award for being a special pig, and, because of his fame, he lives a long and contented life on Mr. Zuckerman's farm. Though Charlotte dies, Wilbur always has a friend, for, having saved and protected her egg sac, he is always kept company by her descendants, though none of them replace Charlotte in Wilbur's heart.

WILD HUNT, THE, a force in traditional lore that appears in several works. In Penelope Lively's* *The Wild Hunt of Hagworthy*, the Hunt is led by an antlered rider, who leads a pack of black, emerald-eyed hounds that breathe green fire. Traditionally the Hunt has run through the village of Hagworthy, and though it was not something to be looked on, it had not been something to be afraid of, either. Later generations had become afraid. Those who see the Hunt become part of it—on the same ground and under the same sky—as the quarry. Out of the memories of the Hunt had developed the Horn Dance*, in which someone had been pursued as a Stag, and people began to feel that the ritual of the Dance caused the Hunt to ride. In the twentieth century, this is borne out when the vicar of Hagworthy resurrects the Dance to attract tourists, and the Hunt rides at night. Kester Lang* becomes the quarry when he looks at the Hunt; when it pursues him, he escapes by holding iron and hiding his eyes.

In *The Moon of Gomrath*, by Alan Garner*, it is called the Herlathing. Thirteen riders ride in the Hunt: stag-horned Garanhir*, their leader, and his Einheriar of twelve men—the three sons of Donn, dressed all in red and with red hair and eyes, red horses, and red spears; Ulmrig, Ulmor, and Ulmbeg, the three sons of Argatron, yellow-haired and dressed in white, carrying whips as they ride white horses; Fiorn, son of Dunarth, black-bearded, on a black horse, carrying a terrible iron flail with seven chains; Fallowman, son of Melimbor, and Bagda, son of Toll, clothed in black and on black horses and bearing black swords; and Maedoc, Midhir, and Mathramil, the three sons of Orman, golden-haired warriors on golden horses, wearing sky-blue cloaks and bearing five-barbed javelins and shields that shine like the sun. The Herlathing loves slaughter and blood. Because it is of Wild Magic and thus uncontrollable, the magicians who had wielded High Magic had made it sleep for many years. Finally the Hunt is wakened accidentally when Colin* and Susan*, two children, burn a rowan fire on the mound of the Sons of Donn, on the eve of the moon of Gomrath, when time and forever mingle. Susan, because she wears the Mark of Fohla*, a bracelet that is of moon magic as the Herlathing is, can call on the Hunt to help her. Though the Herlathing should sleep again after seven days, it finally is free for ever in the land.

In Susan Cooper's* *The Dark Is Rising* and *Silver on the Tree*, the Hunt is led by stag-horned Herne*, the Hunter, who rides a white mare and leads a pack of red-eyed, red-eared white hounds: the Yell Hounds, the Yelpers, the Hounds of Doom. Every year at Twelfthnight the Wild Hunt rides, scattering all creatures it finds but killing none, for the hounds do not kill living things or eat flesh. For a thousand years the Hunt has nothing to pursue; but in the twentieth century, Herne is provided with a mare shod with shoes in the shape of the Signs of the Light*, and with a mask of the Light, by Will Stanton*, one of the forces of the Light, and the Wild Hunt pursues the Black Rider*, one of the Dark. In that encounter the Rider is scarred. At the last battle of the Light and the Dark, the Hunt is joined by the six Sleepers*, mighty warriors against the Dark. Again the Hunt harries the Black Rider until he and the White Rider*, his companion, fall out of time.

WILD HUNT OF HAGWORTHY, THE. Penelope Lively. Illus. Juliet Mozley. London: Heinemann, 1971. 149 pp. British.

When twelve-year-old Lucy Clough* goes to stay with her aunt, it seems it will be a long, dull visit, for the local girls are interested only in horses, and Kester Lang*, an acquaintance from five years back, has grown into a rude, sarcastic youth. Quiet days pass, until the vicar decides to resurrect the traditional Horn Dance* during the local fete, despite the murmurings of the villagers, who do not like the idea. Lucy is oddly frightened by the antlered masks used in the dance, which remind her of the picture of the Wild Hunt* in her aunt's house. She and Kester become friends again. Sullen and unhappy, he does not get along with anyone else. He reacts to the antlers in her aunt's house with fascinated revulsion.

During a rehearsal of the dance, the electricity goes off. That night Lucy wakes to find that one of the sets of antlers in her aunt's house is missing. The next day she hears that the Hunt had been heard; the day after that, a deformed colt is born to a mare that had been put to pasture. The next rehearsal, during which Kester baits the boy dancers, is broken up by rain, and the boys chase Kester, who easily outdistances them. The night after, Lucy again wakes to find a pair of antlers gone, but this time she follows, until she comes upon a strange black dog with emerald eyes; retreating, Lucy sees for an instant a pair of antlers silhouetted against the sky. In the morning she learns more about the Wild Hunt: that the one who sees it becomes the hunted.

Kester's relationship with the other boys is getting worse, and some of them are getting violent. Lucy, worried, follows one day when she sees some of the boys going off in their costumes. She watches as they go through the dance. To her horror, when Lucy makes a noise, they start after her. When she is caught, the boys suddenly do not understand what is happening or how they had gotten there, and they apologize. Lucy tries to talk to Kester, but he seems to want whatever will happen to happen. At the rehearsals, the boys grow more and more intense. The day of the dance draws near, and when Lucy and her aunt go out to gather flowers one morning, they find prints of a deer and hounds, though none should be there. Kester, terrified but excited, reveals to Lucy that he has seen the Hunt; he was afraid, but he had to look. He seems to have something planned for the dance. Lucy, too, makes plans, trying to hide the antler masks for the dance but getting caught by the vicar, who dismisses her attempt as an adolescent's whim. The next morning, when she gets up, a set of antlers is missing from her aunt's house.

The day of the dance comes, and the local smith, Kester's uncle, verbally abuses the vicar for reviving the ceremony, for it was never just a dance; it was a stag hunt, with someone the others disliked running as the stag and being dunked when he was caught. When Lucy tells the smith that Kester has seen the Hunt, he gives her an iron horseshoe; Kester should hold it and not look at the Hunters when they catch him. When the dance starts, there is one dancer too many, for Kester has joined. A fight starts and Kester runs, the boys chasing him. Lucy follows and manages to get them to realize that the dance is over, and they go back. Lucy finds Kester, but suddenly the Hunt is there, after him. Both hold onto the horseshoe and hear the Hunt around them until it finally leaves. Kester feels as if he has just awakened; he has been made to do things he did not want to do, such as quarrelling with everyone and joining the dance. Now, however, everything is all right.

WILD HUNT OF THE GHOST HOUNDS, THE. See *Wild Hunt of Hagworthy, The*

WILL STANTON (the Dark Is Rising Series). See Stanton, Will

WILLIAM, a character in Penelope Lively's* *The Whispering Knights**. His father is a schoolmaster. William himself is purposeful and level-headed and enjoys doing things rather than fighting and hanging around as the other boys do; he hates time-wasters. When he dreams, he dreams of adventures where he is the hero. William spends his time with Martha Timms* and Susan Poulter*, who are ready and willing to carry out his schemes. One of William's projects involves recreating the witches' spell in *Macbeth*—solely for scientific purposes, of course—and the children thereby call up Morgan le Fay*, who tries to get them into her power. After a struggle, William and the girls manage to get Morgan to the Hampden Stones*, where she is again defeated.

WILLIAM WILMER (*Mr. Wilmer*). See Wilmer, William

WILLIAM WINGARD (*Parsley Sage, Rosemary & Time; The Magical Cupboard*). See Wingard, William

WILLIE FIELDMOUSE (*Rabbit Hill; The Tough Winter*). See Fieldmouse, Willie

WILLIE KURTZ (*Mindy's Mysterious Miniature; The Lost Farm*). See Kurtz, Willie

WILLY. *See* Terwilliger

WILMER, WILLIAM, the title character in Robert Lawson's* *Mr. Wilmer*. He is the nephew of a woman named Edna; he becomes the husband of Mary Sweeney*. After he had graduated from high school, William had gotten a job at the Safe, Sane and Colossal Insurance Company. His life has settled into a safe, if dull, routine of work punctuated by quiet weekends. The only excitement in his life is his daily greeting to beautiful Miss Sweeney, who works at the insurance company as a secretary. On William's twenty-ninth birthday, he learns that he can talk to animals, and his life changes drastically. Quiet, unassuming William becomes a celebrity, gets a job he really likes—talking to animals at the zoo—becomes rich, and hires Miss Sweeney as his secretary. Through no machinations of his own, naive William manages to get the best of everyone who wants to make money from his talents. In the process he attracts the attention of Wally Wencher, a vicious gossip columnist, who makes such offensive intimations about William's relationship with Miss Sweeney that she leaves him to protect herself. William finds her, however, and they marry, honeymooning at William's new rest farm for discontented animals.

WILSON, CAREY, a character in Mary Norton's* *The Magic Bed-Knob* and *Bonfires and Broomsticks*. She is the older sister of Charles and Paul Wilson**. Carey is somewhat given to romancing and takes it in stride when she and her brothers discover that Eglantine Price*, a spinster in the village where they are spending the summer, is practicing to be a witch. Carey talks Miss Price into enchanting a bed-knob* from Paul's bed, which will transport the bed anywhere the children want to go—unless they tell about Miss Price's witchcraft. Carey and her brothers have several adventures, journeying to London and going with Miss Price to an island in the South Seas, before the children are sent home to their parents. Two years later, they again meet Miss Price and Carey talks her into allowing them to travel back in time, where they meet and bring back Emelius Jones*, a somewhat inept necromancer. When Emelius and Miss Price marry and journey back to the seventeenth century to live, Carey is the last to hear Miss Price as the children stand in the ruins of Emelius's farm on Tinker Hill; across the centuries, Miss Price orders Carey out of the lettucebed.

WILSON, CHARLES, a character in *The Magic Bed-Knob* and *Bonfires and Broomsticks*, by Mary Norton*. He is the brother of Carey and Paul Wilson**. Charles shares several adventures with his brother and sister after the children learn that Eglantine Price*, a spinster in the village where they are staying, is a witch, and she bribes them to silence by giving them an enchanted bed-knob*. With the others, Charles is transported to London and held by the police, and taken to a South Sea island, where he is almost eaten by cannibals. Two years after these adventures, Charles, Carey, and Paul meet Miss Price again, and they use the bed-knob to go into the past, where they meet Emelius Jones*, a necromancer. Charles eventually rescues the man from the stake when he is sentenced to be burnt.

WILSON, PAUL, a character in Mary Norton's* *The Magic Bed-Knob* and *Bonfires and Broomsticks**. He is the younger brother of Carey and Charles Wilson**. Six-year-old Paul is quite impressed by the practice flights of Eglantine Price*, a spinster who learns to fly on a broomstick as part of becoming a witch. Each night Paul stays awake and watches Miss Price, excited by her growing skill, until one night she falls and is discovered the next morning by the three children. To bribe them into silence about her new accomplishments, Miss Price enchants a bed-knob* Paul has taken off his brass bed; if Paul turns the knob and wishes, his bed will be magically transported anywhere in the present or the past. Carey and Charles are sometimes impatient at Paul's choice of destination, but they manage to share a few adventures before they must leave and go back home to their parents. At home, Paul is never sure exactly what part of the summer holiday he is supposed to talk about, and Carey and Charles must sometimes stop him before he reveals all to their parents. Two years after their adventures, the children again meet Miss Price and this time travel back in time, meeting and helping Emelius Jones*, a necromancer. The last time Paul twists the magic bed-knob, it is to transport Emelius and Miss Price back to the seventeenth century, where the two marry and live quietly together.

WIND EYE, THE. Robert Westall. London: Macmillan, 1976. 212 pp. British.
Bickering as usual, Bertrand, his wife, Madeleine, and their children, Michael, Beth, and six-year-old Sally Studdard*****, travel to the house Bertrand has inherited near the island where St. Cuthbert* (Cuddy) is said to have lived. On the way Madeleine insists they visit a church where Cuddy is buried, and in an act of defiance she steps on his tomb. When they get to the house, it is full of odd objects collected by Bertrand's uncle over the years, including a pair of crude boots and a loaf of mouldering bread which seem to have been important to the man. The next day the children also find a hut near the house, in which is a huge wooden boat* shaped like a Viking ship. Though Bertrand works hard to fit a mast onto it, he fails.
That night Beth wakes to find Sally standing at the window; she has heard singing and has seen a fiery ball hanging over the islands. Though atheistic Bertrand tries to sway her, Sally insists the next day that it was angels carrying a soul to heaven. Michael finds a rudder and sail that fit the boat, and he, Bertrand, Beth, and Sally take it out on the sea. An unexpected mist comes up, and everything smells cleaner; there are many more birds than the Studdards remember seeing. After Sally claims to see a man waving to her from a small island, they land on it but find no one. Once they sail back through the mist to their home, they look back to the islands and the mist is gone. That night Beth finds Sally wading in the ocean; the child explains that the man who had waved

to her on the island had waved at her again through the bedroom window and she had followed him, watching as he went into the sea and returned, singing, and two "little bendy dogs"—otters—came to him.

Michael has realized that the boat is a kind of time machine, and the next day he takes Sally and Beth out in it, Beth steering. They sail through the mist into a moonlit night. Soon dawn comes, and they see seals watching the wake of something invisible going toward the islands. As the boat reaches an island where men stand waiting, Michael panics and grabs the rudder, sailing the boat back to the children's own time. Sally has seen the man who waved to her lying on the deck of the boat, with his arms crossed over his breast. That afternoon the children again go out. Michael steers this time, having realized that the boat obeys the one who steers it. They come on invading Vikings, who attack after Michael throws a stone at them, but the children escape. That evening the local fishermen come to complain, for they do not like children using the boat, which belongs to "the Wind Eye" and was used to take drowned men away to be buried.

The man comes again that night, and Beth sees him this time, though each time she shines the flashlight on him he disappears, to return when she takes it away. Madeleine goes out to chase him away but does not see him; when he touches her on the shoulder, she wanders down the beach, unexplainedly happy and at peace. The next morning high tide reaches the boat, lifting it. When Sally jumps on board, Michael and Beth manage to follow her, though she is resentful. On the other side of the mist is a storm and they cannot steer. The boat comes to an island where a man is waiting, and almost goes aground; Sally jumps into the water and suddenly the boat is in the twentieth century. Though Beth and Michael try, they cannot get back to Sally, and she is reported missing.

Madeleine acts differently now—not angry at the world—and Michael resents it. When he tells her what has happened, they realize that Sally has been seeing Cuddy and that she must be with him. Michael and Beth take out the boat and succeed in finding Sally when they wish to be at the time when Cuddy does not want her any more. Cuddy is gone, and Sally's hand, which had been horribly burned, is whole again. Scientific Bertrand, proved wrong about the supernatural, cannot stand it; he decides that Cuddy's powers are due to his understanding of the science of Supernature. Being a pacifist, he decides to sail back and try to stop the Viking raid on the monastery, when legend has it Cuddy sank the Viking ships in a storm. First, though, Bertrand searches for the remains of the ships to prove it had really happened, precipitating a fight with the local fishermen, who do not want him meddling.

Bertrand goes off in the boat, though he leaves the rudder; fearful for his life, Beth and Michael use it to float themselves to Cuddy. When they reach the island, Michael is afraid and cannot land, so when Beth goes ashore, he goes back home. Beth finds Cuddy's hut, where he lies ill and dying. She had started the trip scantily clad and has lost those clothes, and he takes her for a devil in the form of a woman. Though Cuddy tries to use his power to drive Beth away, he does not succeed. Beth brings him water, going through the little devils that plague him, and Cuddy accepts her but sends her away. Beth finds a robe and food in the nearby hospitium and wanders about the island. At one point, Cuddy speaks to her mind and persuades her to live for herself and not for her father, as she has done. When Beth takes the robe back to the hospitium, she finds the rudder of the boat. She uses it to go home, passing on the way monks going to get Cuddy; they are sailing in the boat she and Michael had found, now new.

Bertrand, meanwhile, has come to the monastery and warned the monks, though they are so unable to defend themselves that he despises them. When the Vikings land, he tries to warn them of Cuddy's vengeance but they do not understand. As the monastery is sacked, Bertrand is forced to fight and kill the Viking leader and then to fight a second man. A storm comes up and the Vikings go for their ships. Bertrand rescues a woman they have held captive and gets her aboard the boat; they sail into the twentieth century but are quickly back again and land near the monastery, which the monks have begun to rebuild by making a temporary shelter. The woman's husband comes and is grateful to Bertrand. Tired of his own century, Bertrand decides to stay in this, but he is knocked out by the sail and wakes in his own time. Though Bertrand does not want to go home, the boat takes him there. Suddenly he realizes that his last name is similar to that of one of the monks' servants who took Cuddy's coffin to its final resting place. To find the connection, he could search all time for Cuddy, finally leaving the twentieth century forever, as had his uncle and his grandfather and generations of Studdards before him.

WIND IN THE DOOR, A. Madelein L'Engle. New York: Farrar, Straus and Giroux, 1973. 211 pp. American.

Six-year-old Charles Wallace Murry* sees "dragons" in the garden, but when he takes his teen-aged sister, Meg Murry*, to the spot, they find nothing but some strange, metallic feathers. Meg is worried, for Charles is not getting along in school because he is so bright, and his health is worsening. After dinner that night, she goes out to look again for the dragons but meets instead Mr. Jenkins*, an odious school principal. But it is not Mr. Jenkins, and before Meg's horrified eyes, it flies into the sky. Calvin O'Keefe*, Meg's dear friend, finds her, and she tells him all. Charles also comes, and suddenly there appear Blajeny*, a teacher of sorts, and the "dragons"—actually a many-eyed, many-winged cherubim named Proginoskes*. Blajeny is to teach them. Charles must learn to adapt to his school; Meg and Proginoskes together will pass three tests, and Calvin has some unknown work to do. The children are sent home.

The next morning Meg gets up early and goes to Proginoskes, who has spent the night in a nearby field. When she tells it about the appearance of Mr. Jenkins the night before, Proginoskes recognizes that an Echthros*, a thing of evil, had taken Mr. Jenkins's form. As Proginoskes is a Namer, making things more real by naming them, the Echthroi are un-Namers, Xing or annihilating them. They are part of the unreason in the world and seem to be trying to harm Charles.

Meg and Proginoskes, who has turned invisible, go to Charles's school to find Mr. Jenkins, and they do find him, but he speaks in an un-Mr.-Jenkins-like way. Suddenly there are two, then three Mr. Jenkinses and Meg must name the real one, as the first test. She must love Mr. Jenkins in order to do it, and offensive as he is, she tries. It is difficult, until Proginoskes helps her to remember a time when Mr. Jenkins had bought Calvin a pair of shoes because the boy's were not worth wearing. Suddenly Meg feels which Mr. Jenkins is real, and she names him; the others vanish. Mr. Jenkins faints when Proginoskes materializes. Blajeny comes, and when Mr. Jenkins wakes and sees them all, he decides that he is having a nervous breakdown. Charles's disease—mitochondritis—is worse, and they must help him; because Meg had Named him, Mr. Jenkins will help.

Blajeny and Proginoskes take Meg, Mr. Jenkins, and—suddenly—Calvin, to Metron Ariston*, a place in a far galaxy where they meet Sporos*, a farandola*, who is to work with Calvin, though Sporos feels that he is superior to all of them. Charles's mitochondria are dying, possibly because of the tiny farandolae that form part of them. To save Charles, they must all enter one of his mitochondria, and, because on Metron Ariston all size is irrelevant, all but Blajeny do so. Here are tree-like farae, mature farandolae, which cannot move but are at one with the universe. Sporos must Deepen, must mature, but he is holding back. Meg and Proginoskes must help him—their second test—and Mr. Jenkins may be important in getting Sporos to Deepen. The temptation for Sporos is to remain free and pleasure-seeking, no matter what the consequences, and the farandola joins other farandolae as they dance around a fara, absorbing the nourishment it needs and killing it, urged on by an Echthros which has also entered. As Meg and the others try to persuade Sporos to Deepen, the Echthros persuades him not to.

Calvin decides that he will join Sporos if the farandola joins the others in their dance of death, and he and Meg do, attempting to stop it. Meg is sucked into the ring and is saved only by Mr. Jenkins. To her horror, the man is soon surrounded by Echthroi, whirling about him to kill him. Awed by Mr. Jenkins's saving of Meg, Sporos and the other farandolae Deepen, to help him. But it is not enough, and the Echthroi enter Mr. Jenkins. Calvin tries to fight him but is being pulled in, so Meg tries to fill Mr. Jenkins—the third test—for with the Echthroi within him, he is an emptiness, a void that must be filled. But she cannot, and Proginoskes flings himself into the void to help her. Desperately Meg Names the un-Named and un-Naming Echthroi, and suddenly she, Calvin, and Mr. Jenkins are in Charles's room. The boy is much better, for the Echthroi are gone. Though Proginoskes Xed himself so that the Echthroi would not get him, he is all right; and all is well at the Murry house.

WIND IN THE WILLOWS, THE. Kenneth Grahame. London: Methuen and Co., 1908. 302 pp. British.

One lovely day the Mole* leaves his spring cleaning and escapes into the open air, where he meets the Water Rat*, who introduces him to life along the

River and invites him to stay at his house. The Mole is enthralled by his new life and by the citizens of the Riverbank, even rich and reckless Toad*, who is a slave to his whims and who conceives a passion for motorcars after a disastrous introduction to one while caravanning. Summer passes, winter comes, and their quiet lives are touched by little adventures. After a harrowing adventure in the dangerous Wild Wood, the Mole meets the secretive, unsociable Badger* who lives there. The Badger is outraged by reports of Toad's many auto accidents and brushes with the law and vows to do something about it in the spring. Having forgotten his little home in his enchantment with River life, the Mole is one day drawn back to it, and the Rat helps him to see how cosy it is and how dear to him during a little party with some field mice carolers.

When spring arrives, the Badger, the Rat, and the Mole take Toad firmly in hand, locking him in his room to watch him and keep him out of mischief. But one day he escapes, "borrows" a motorcar, and is apprehended and thrown into jail. Meanwhile, the Rat and the Mole have quieter adventures. They meet and are made to forget Pan, while they are searching for a lost otter pup; the Rat meets a Sea Rat*, who almost enchants him into leaving home, until the Mole breaks the "spell" by reminding him of all he would leave behind.

Toad's adventures are far from quiet. Gaining the sympathies of the jailor's daughter, he escapes from prison disguised as a washerwoman. His natural conceit alternately takes a beating and rises to new heights as he enlists the aid of an engine driver, steals a bargewoman's horse to teach her humility, and manages to swap the horse to a gypsy not only for money but also for a meal. Toad's disguise stands him in good stead when he is given a lift by the owners of the car he stole; before they realize who he is, Toad has seized control of their car. The crash that follows lands Toad in the River, and he washes up at the Rat's house, a bedraggled figure.

His problems are not over yet, however, for weasels and stoats from the Wild Wood have taken over Toad Hall. The Badger, the Rat, and the Mole enter the place through a secret tunnel and recapture Toad Hall. Toad's conceit gets the better of him when he writes up the invitations for the ensuing celebration; the others impose their will on him, and Toad discovers that modesty earns him almost as much attention as boasting does. Having quelled the Wild Wooders, the four live quietly in their homes near the River.

WINGARD, HEPSIBAH SAGACITY WALPOLE (*The Magical Cupboard*). *See* Walpole, Hepsibah Sagacity

WINGARD, WILLIAM (BILL), a character in Jane Louise Curry's* *Parsley Sage, Rosemary & Time** and *The Magical Cupboard**. He becomes the husband of Hepsibah Sagacity Walpole* (Sibby) and the uncle of Rosemary Walpole*. Bill is descended from the Cakebread family that built and lived for generations in Wychwood. He lived here himself until he was sixteen. When Bill, or "Wim" as he is known to them, is about two years old, he wanders into a secret garden planted long ago by Juditha Cakebread* and is transported back in time to eighteenth-century New England. There he has adventures with Sibby and Rosemary, who also at one point in their lives have wandered back in time. One of these adventures includes being shut up in Goody Cakebread's* magical cupboard* and being accidentally changed into a piglet, then changed back. When the child crawls back between the Dreaming Trees* to the twentieth century, he is still dressed in eighteenth-century clothes. Bill does not remember this adventure when he meets Sibby and Rosemary thirty-odd years later. Hearing that Sibby now owns Wychwood, he tries to talk her into selling it to him and is aghast at being reminded of the incident. Bill marries Sibby and, with Rosemary, searches in the twentieth century for the cupboard. They discover it at last in the antique shop of descendants of Felicity Parmenter* Hollybush, who have held it for over two hundred years for a member of the Cakebread family to claim.

WINGFIELD MANOR, a place in Alison Uttley's* *A Traveller in Time**. Mary Stuart*, Queen of Scots, is held here for a time. A tunnel connecting this manor with Thackers* is partially cleared by Anthony Babington* in a desperate attempt to free the queen, but his plans are thwarted when the tunnel is discovered. Wingfield has been destroyed before Penelope Taberner Cameron* sees it in the twentieth century.

WINNIE FOSTER *(Tuck Everlasting)*. *See* Foster, Winifred

WISHBONE, a magical object in *The Cat Who Wished to Be a Man**, by Lloyd Alexander*. Magister Stephanus*, a wizard, gives this wishbone to Lionel*, the young cat he has turned into a man, so that the innocent youth can help himself should he get into trouble; by breaking the wishbone, Lionel will be transported wherever he wants to go. Though tempted to use it to go back home when he almost drowns, Lionel uses the wishbone instead to go to Gillian*, the innkeeper he is trying to help; he comes to her side just in time to save her from a fire.

WITHERS, NORMAN, a character in Susan Cooper's* *Over Sea, Under Stone**. He is the brother of Polly Withers*. Norman is an antique dealer. He and his sister seem very nice, but they are servants of the Dark, forces of evil, and help the Black Rider* in his attempt to defeat Merriman Lyon*, one of the powers of good. Norman and Polly learn what they can from Barnabas, Jane, and Simon Drew***, who are seeking a mysterious grail* and a manuscript*, but they fail to stop the children.

WITHERS, POLLY, a character in *Over Sea, Under Stone**, by Susan Cooper*. She is the sister of Norman Withers*. Pretty and bright, Polly seems to be someone to like and trust. She and her brother, though, are of the forces of evil, helping the Black Rider* as he tries to defeat the forces of good. Polly tries to win the confidence of Barnabas, Jane, and Simon Drew***, but Jane instinctively dislikes her, and Polly fails.

WIX, DAVID FRANCIS, a character in *Earthfasts**, by William Mayne*. His widower father is a doctor. By his own admission more intelligent than he is clever, David is very good in school and a top athlete and is very popular, being friendly and easygoing. David seems instinctively to empathize with others and to know how they should be treated. His best friend is Keith Heseltine*. David has a presence which amazes Keith. David also has a great curiosity, and this leads him into trouble. When he and Keith investigate a strange mound which has appeared, they meet Nellie Jack John Cherry* (John), an eighteenth-century drummer boy, who comes out of the mound, bearing a strange candle* that affects time. David does a thorough investigation of the candle, learning much about it and seeming to come under its spell; he gazes long into its flame, where he sees shapes moving, and having looked into the flame, David begins to see objects and creatures others cannot. Though he cannot see the boggart* that plagues the Watson farmhouse, it seems to respect or fear him, and he can make it obey. On an October afternoon, David sees a vision, and what seems to be a butterfly appears to him, though Keith can see nothing and can only watch in horror as a crack seems to open in the air and David is swallowed up. At the inquest, a witness says he had seen a man on a horse riding down the sky toward the boy just before he vanished; the official verdict is that David and Keith had been struck by lightning and that David had been vaporized. But David is alive; the man on horseback snatches him into the chamber where King Arthur* and his knights sleep. The boy thinks he has spent only a moment there when Keith comes to set the candle back in its socket, but when they come out, it is February.

WIZARD IN THE TREE, THE. Lloyd Alexander. Illus. Laszlo Kubinehart New York: E. P. Dutton and Co., 1975. 138 pp. American.

Orphaned Mallory*, who lives now with Mr. and Mrs. Parsel** as a maid-of-all-work, loves to dream that the fairy tales her mother told her are true. When she rescues Arbican*, a testy old enchanter, from the felled oak where he has been imprisoned for centuries, Mallory thinks that she has found her fairy godfather. But Arbican mocks her preoccupation with fairy tales, and his powers seem to have vanished. Arbican is distraught, for without his powers he cannot get to Vale Innis*, where the other enchanters went long ago, and unless he gets to Vale Innis he will die, for he has outlived a lifetime in this world. Mallory hides the wizard in a cave and goes to the village to steal him some food.

There she hears some upsetting news; Squire Scrupnor*, who has inherited vast holdings after the murder of another squire, is turning tenants out of their homes so that he can mine coal under their land; and the Parsels have leagued themselves with him. Mallory watches as the local notary, not believing Scrupnor's protestations that he does not want the fortune he has inherited, has the man sign a statement saying that Scrupnor will give his inheritance to the person who finds the killer. When Scrupnor leaves, he forgets his gloves; Mrs. Parsel sends Mallory to Scrupnor's house, with his gloves and a basket of treats.

Instead, the girl goes to Arbican, who has decided to build a boat from his oak tree and sail in it to Vale Innis. In making a spell to levitate the tree and carry it to the river, Arbican accidentally turns himself into a goose, but he changes back when he seriously tries to fly. The only cure for a wizard whose powers are erratic is for a maiden to give him a "circle of gold," but Mallory does not have such a thing. Realizing that she will be punished for being slow about her errand, Arbican tries to zap Mallory to Scrupnor's house and ends up depositing them both in the man's counting room—right in front of an astonished Scrupnor. The squire decides to expose Arbican as the murderer.

Mallory and Arbican manage to escape, the enchanter turning into a stag and bearing off the girl. They spend the night in the forest, and Mallory wakes to find that Arbican has turned into a pig. This proves dangerous, for they meet Burdick Tench*, who snatches Arbican to exhibit him as a talking pig; unimpressed when the wizard refuses to talk, Burdick's father decides to slaughter him. Arbican barely escapes.

Running after the wizard, Mallory meets Mr. Parsel, who has come with a wagon to look for her. On the way to the village he is hurt in an accident, and Mallory turns back to the Tench farm for help, only to meet Bolt*, Scrupnor's gamekeeper, and another man, who have captured Arbican, now himself again. They tie up Mallory and put both in the wagon and start off. When the wagon loses a wheel, Mallory and Arbican are forced to walk, by this time Scrupnor has joined the group, and he seems irritated by Bolt's insistence that the reward is his. At the gamekeeper's cottage, Mallory and Arbican are put into the cellar, and Mallory uses a penknife Mr. Parsel has slipped her to cut their bonds. She watches through a crack in the door as Scrupnor haggles with Bolt and then murders him with a poker. When the squire opens the cellar door, Mallory attacks him, Arbican uses a spell to keep him from killing her, and the wizard and the girl get away, Mallory riding on the back of Arbican, who has changed into a stag. Scrupnor shoots at Arbican and wounds him.

The wizard manages to spirit them to Mrs. Parsel's cookshop, where that lady first seems to help them and then takes them to Scrupnor and tries to claim the reward. Scrupnor decides to kill them and, locking the three in his counting room, goes for a weapon. They realize, belatedly, that he must be the murderer. Searching for a weapon, Mallory comes upon a cache of jewels just as Scrupnor returns. Mallory finds a gold ring and gives it to Arbican, and his powers return at full force. When Scrupnor touches him, both vanish in a clap of thunder, though Scrupnor leaves behind one of his boots and his waistcoat, smouldering gently.

It is agreed that Arbican should receive Scrupnor's reward; in his absence it goes to Mallory, though she is not sure she wants it. She goes to the place where she found the wizard and there finds him again. He has built a lovely little boat from his oak tree and must leave. Fairy tales, Arbican tells Mallory, are not about wizards but about the best that is in each person. She can manage the estate she earned from Scrupnor as well as anyone could. Mallory watches as the wizard sails away toward Vale Innis.

WIZARD OF EARTHSEA, A. Ursula K. LeGuin. Drawings by Ruth Robbins. Berkeley, Calif. Parnassus Press, 1968. 205 pp. American.

On the island of Gont* in the world of Earthsea*, a child named Duny is born and grows up full of impatience and pride. As a child, he learns from his aunt some lore of herbs and healing and words of power, so that when the island is invaded, Duny is able to conceal his village in a mist filled with ghost-shapes that frighten the warriors away. In doing so, he overspends his strength and lies in a trance, to be awakened by Ogion*, a loremaster, who, when the boy is thirteen, gives him his true name, Ged*, and takes him on as apprentice.

Impatient Ged chafes under Ogion's slow, subtle method of teaching and feels that he is learning nothing. Teased by a young girl to show his skill, Ged learns a spell to summon the dead and Ogion saves him from the spell's evil effects. Aware of Ged's impatience, the mage makes him choose between his apprenticeship and study at the school for wizards at Roke*. Ged chooses to go to Roke, which he finds to be a place full of riddles. The first day there he feels slighted by Jasper*, one of the older pupils, and determines to prove himself the more powerful of the two. Ged does, however, make a friend, Vetch*. As Ged learns the wizards' arts, he becomes dissatisfied, for all the magic is illusion; one can only make real magic by knowing the true names of things, but this real magic is dangerous and not to be lightly indulged in, for it could destroy the equilibrium of the world.

During long months of study, Ged learns to work not only illusions but real magic, and he gains a pet, an untameable little otak*. Then one night he tries to prove himself better than Jasper, who is now a sorcerer, by calling up a dead spirit, using the spell Ged learned from Ogion's book. He succeeds, but through the opening between the two worlds also comes a headless shadow that attacks Ged. The Archmage, in closing the rift, overspends his strength and dies. Ged is a long time healing; he will always bear scars from the wounds the shadow gave him. Humbled now by fear of the shadow, still at large in the world, he becomes a sorcerer and is appointed wizard on a small island needing protection from dragons.

His life here is quiet and sweet. When the child of a friend dies, Ged sends his spirit after it into the land of the dead. The child eludes him, and when his spirit turns back to the land of the living, he finds the shadow in his path. Ged's spirit gets past it, but his body lies in a trance until he is brought completely back to the living by the touch of the otak. Realizing that the shadow seeks to take him over, Ged also knows that he cannot stay for it to find him. Determined to rid the islanders of their peril, he goes to Pendor* and seeks out the dragons that live there, killing most and binding the others to the island by a vow, despite the oldest dragon, who offers to tell Ged his shadow's name and thus give him mastery over it. Pursued by his shadow, Ged makes his way to Osskil*, to the Court of the Terrenon*, where, he has been told, he might gain that which would protect him from his shadow. On Osskil, he is attacked by a sailor whom the shadow has taken over, and, escaping, loses his otak and comes to the Court. Here he meets Serret* and her husband, the lord of the keep built over the Terrenon, a stone in which is imprisoned an ancient evil power. He is to be the stone's master, they tell him, and it will tell Ged his shadow's name; but he knows that he will instead become the stone's slave, and he refuses. Enraged at his wife's perfidy, the lord of the stone threatens her and, when Ged and Serret flee the castle, sends after them hideous beasts that kill Serret. Ged escapes in the form of a hawk.

He flies to Ogion, his old master, who makes Ged realize that he must hunt down the shadow and destroy it. Though he fears that it will enter him and use his skills for evil, Ged pursues his shadow across the ocean of Earthsea. Because it has taken power from him, the shadow has a man's shape. During the pursuit, Ged is shipwrecked on a tiny island where he finds an old man and an old woman; they were children of a royal house, abandoned here by a usurper. Ged rebuilds his boat with spells and leaves them, bearing with him the half of a broken ring the old woman gives him, and leaving behind a spell to sweeten the island's salty spring.

Again Ged pursues his shadow, almost catching it once but unable to grasp it. He gets a new boat and comes at last to the island where Vetch, his old friend, is wizard, and together they chase the shadow, which now has Ged's shape. In the sea beyond the last island in the east, they come to a place where the water seems to be land. Here Ged leaves the boat and meets his shadow on the sand. Each recognizes the other; each speaks the other's name—"Ged"— and, touching, the two become one. The sand becomes water again, and Ged and Vetch sail home. Ged has accepted the shadow of his pride and has become whole, a man who knows his true self.

WOLDWELLER, a traditional figure in Celtic lore who appears as a character in Natalie Babbitt's* *The Search for Delicious*. This wizened little old man lives alone in the forest and cannot be found unless one is lost. He will answer questions because he is very wise. People in the kingdom where Vaungaylen* (Gaylen) lives once believed in woldwellers and sought them out, but by Gaylen's time they no longer do so. In his poll of the kingdom to find out the people's choice for most delicious food, Gaylen comes upon a woldweller, nine hundred years old, and learns from him of the bid for power of the queen's brother, Hemlock*. Though he knows Hemlock is evil, the woldweller is indifferent to the knowledge and to whatever effect what he tells Hemlock will have on the rest of the world. The woldweller's favorite food is rabbit.

WOLFGANG VOGEL (*An Enemy at Green Knowe*). *See* Vogel, Wolfgang

WOLVES OF AAM, a race of creatures in Jane Louise Curry's* *The Wolves of Aam**. These wolves were bred by Tion, the Wolf King, and they are special in that they are able to communicate with beings who are not of their kind. They also can camouflage themselves; their fur darkens or lightens to help them blend with their surroundings. They gained these gifts when one of them helped Tion to imprison Katóa*, an evil force. Few of the wolves still have these powers, however, when they help Runner-to-the-Sky's-Edge* rescue Lek*, a conjuror, from the mountain fortress at Gzel* and keep Mirelidar*, a powerful skystone*, out of the hands of power-hungry Lord Naghar*. One of the wolves, Findral*, leads Lek on his quest for the City of the Moon Under the Mountain* while the other wolves take Mirelidar to a place of safety.

WOLVES OF AAM, THE. Jane Louise Curry. New York: Atheneum, 1981. 192 pp. American.

Lek*, a conjuror, is hiding in a tomb from pursuers when Runner-to-the-Sky's-Edge* (Runner), one of the small, wandering Tiddi*, comes upon him. Surprised by wolves, Runner has injured himself, and Lek tends him, discovering as he does so Mirelidar*, one of the twelve mysterious skystones*, in the Tiddi's pouch. Because he was held responsible for the disappearance of another of these powerful stones, Lek has undertaken a journey to the City of the Moon Under the Mountain*, where he hopes to learn where to find a replacement for the stone. When his pursuers come near the next morning, he leads them away from the tomb, leaving Runner to be found by the other Tiddi, who also find grim evidence that there has been a fight.

That night Runner is kidnapped, and Cathound* (Cat), a strange girl adopted by the Tiddi as a child, and Fith*, Runner's friend, set out to find him. Runner wakes from a drugged sleep to discover himself among a mismatched band of rough men, a gigantic Iceling* named Ghagra* and the horrifying, goblin-like Illigan*, their Rokarrhuk* leader. They are looking for Lek and have captured Runner because he might know where the man has gone. But Runner cannot remember, so the band starts for Nagharot*, where their master, Lord Naghar*, waits. Along the way the Illigan reveals that they are also after the skystone Runner carries and is furious to find that it has been replaced by a pebble; Runner realizes that Lek must have made the switch. When the band comes to a Rokarrhuk camp and learns that Lek has been captured and is being taken to Gzel*, a mountain fortress, the Illigan commands Ghagra to dispose of Runner, who is no longer needed. Instead, the Iceling sets him free, and Runner finds himself with the mysterious talking Wolves of Aam*, who are descended from those bred by the Wolf King, whose tomb sheltered Lek and Runner.

Fith and Cat are attacked by the Rokarrhuk and their wolf mounts. Pursuing one of the wolves into a cave, they meet two scouting Icelings who agree to help them, having no love for Naghar and his deeds. The four soon come upon Runner and the wolves. Though Fith wants to go home, having found Runner, Runner wants his stone back and feels that he must help Lek. Renga* and the other wolves will help him, for Renga realizes that Runner's "dreamstone" is the powerful Mirelidar, which must be kept from the Illigan and his master. The Tiddi, the Icelings, and the wolves make the hard journey to Gzel only to watch helplessly as a well-guarded Lek is taken into the mountain fortress.

The citadel at Gzel is not impenetrable, however; the Icelings, who lived here when the land was warm and green, lead the group into the castle through a secret way. They come out above the many-storeyed hall where the Illigan is questioning Lek, and Runner and Cat climb higher in order to hear what is said. Using a magical mirror, the Illigan exacts the confession that Lek had left the stone with "the Wolves of Aam" before the young man collapses and is taken to his cell. The Illigan goes to send men to capture some Tiddi to get more information, leaving behind a set of keys. Runner climbs down to get them, for they might unlock Lek's iron bonds. Spotted by one of the dreadful wolves that guard the place, he runs further into the fortress and comes at last upon his friends. Unknown to Runner, Cat is captured by the Illigan.

Runner and the others rescue Lek and are on their way out when they realize that Cat and Renga are missing. There is no time to wait, however, for the Icelings, intent on revenge, have set fires to destroy the citadel. In anguish, the little group leaves the fortress and watches as the sleeping fires of the mountain stir and it explodes into a volcano. Their sadness is short-lived, for Cat and Renga join them. Ghagra is with them; he has killed the Illigan and led the two to safety.

Lek is desperate, for he is convinced that Lord Naghar will find the skystone. When he is introduced to the Wolves of Aam, his despair turns to elation; he had not realized that they still existed. Lord Naghar will be looking for the wrong wolves. The "Wolves of Aam" with which Lek left the stone are the wolves carved into the granite walls of the Wolf King's tomb, where he met Runner. Journeying back to the tomb, Lek finds the skystone exactly where he left it, in the mouth of one of the stone wolves. The living Wolves of Aam set off to take the skystone to safety at an Iceling camp, leaving behind one of their number, Findral*, who will guide Lek to the City of the Moon. Cat, Fith, and Runner set out after their nomadic people, full of stories of their own to tell.

WONDERSTONE, a magical stone in Walter de la Mare's* *The Three Mulla-mulgars*. This is the Wonderstone of Tishnar*, and it has great powers. This lovely stone is milk-white and carved all over with figures of birds and beasts and strange cyphers; to use it, one must spit on it and rub it three times with the left thumb, Samaweeza, that is, counter-clockwise. This stone is brought out of the Valleys of Tishnar* by Seelem*, a monkey of royal descent, and is inherited by his youngest son, Ummanodda* (Nod), because he is a Nizza-neela. Because Nod bears the Wonderstone on the journey he and his brothers make to the Valleys of Tishnar, the fierce Minimuls* and Mishcha*, the Quatta hare, do not harm him. Nod uses the Wonderstone to rescue his brothers and himself from the Minimuls and to help the small band of Mulgars* pass the ghoulish

Meermuts* they meet in the mountains. Several times the Wonderstone is almost lost; once it falls into the hands of a lovely Water-midden*, and it frightens her when it crackles and glows with Tishnar's anger.

WOOD, ROBIN (ROBIN HOOD), a legendary figure who appears as a character in T[erence] H[anbury] White's* *The Sword in the Stone**. He is the sweetheart of Maid Marian. Robin is over six feet tall and pulls a hundredweight bow; he is one of two people in the world to shoot an arrow the distance of a mile with an English longbow. He gets his name from the woods he loves, for Robin lives free in the Forest Sauvage*, chief of a band of one hundred outlaws. Tales of him are told far and wide. When Friar Tuck, one of his band, is captured, with two men and a dog, by Morgan the Fay*, Robin and his men rescue them, taking along two boys, Kay* and the Wart (Arthur*), to enter Morgan's castle. After this adventure, the two boys often visit Robin and his men. Though he is an outlaw, Robin leads the king's huntsmen on a hunt for wild boar, for he knows the forest better than any. At the Wart's coronation as king of Britain, Robin and Marian send him a gown of the skins of pine martens. Robin lives to be eighty seven, which he attributes to smelling the turpentine in the pines of the forest.

WOOD BETWEEN THE WORLDS, a place in C[live] S[taples] Lewis's* *The Magician's Nephew**. This dreamy wood is filled with trees and with pools of water that are each a way into a world. When that world dies, its pool dries up. Still and warm and dreamy, the Wood affects each who visits it in a different way: to Digory Kirke* and Polly Plummer*, it is rich and very soothing; to Jadis*, an evil queen, it is oppressive and deadly. So dreamy is the Wood that it is possible to forget one's past here. Dust from this Wood is made into rings* by Andrew Ketterley*; the dust is attracted or repelled by the Wood and thus it is possible to travel between the worlds by wearing the right ring and leaping into the right pool. One of Andrew's experimental guinea pigs lives here in great contentment.

WOUNDWORT, GENERAL, a character in Richard Adams's* *Watership Down**. This rabbit was the strongest of a litter of five and its only survivor after a man had shot Woundwort's father and dug out the burrow. Found nuzzling the body of his mother, who was killed before his eyes, Woundwort was raised by an elderly schoolmaster, but he had grown up wild, biting whenever he could and savaging the schoolmaster's cat. One night Woundwort escaped. Coming to a small warren, he violently made himself its leader, but Woundwort longed for greater power and took some followers to found a new warren, Efrafa*, set up and ruled with heartless efficiency. Under Woundwort's absolute rule, the warren prospers, soon becoming overcrowded. Woundwort is a leader terrible in ambition, in ferocity, and in efficiency. He institutes Wide Patrols, leading and sending out patrols of rabbits to kill predators in the neighborhood and to bring in any stray rabbits who might attract the attention of men. Despite his violent nature, Woundwort inspires great loyalty in his followers, who accept his dictatorship because he makes them feel greater than they had been. Unafraid of anything, he makes them unafraid, too. But Woundwort meets his match in Bigwig*, a rabbit from another warren, who successfully gets some does away from Efrafa. During an attack on Bigwig's warren, Woundwort battles Bigwig and must get away to survive. When he and his forces are attacked by a dog lured to them by the rabbits they attack, Woundwort is probably killed. His body is never found. Legend has it, though, that he still lives, driving off predators and feeding in the sky, that he will return to fight for those who honor him, and that he is the first cousin of the Black Rabbit of death.

WRINKLE IN TIME, A. Madeleine L'Engle. New York: Ariel Books, 1962. 211 pp. American. Newbery Award, 1963.

Teen-aged Meg Murry* is miserable, for she feels like a misfit, ugly and stupid and over-emotional. She wishes she could be more like her beautiful, brilliant mother, who is able to control herself even though Mr. Murry* has disappeared. One stormy night, Meg learns from her five-year-old brother, Charles Wallace Murry*, that he has met Mrs Whatsit*, Mrs Who*, asnd Mrs Which*, the three inhabitants of a supposedly empty house. Mrs Whatsit, in fact, pays them a brief visit that night. The next day Meg and Charles go to visit the three women, joined by Calvin O'Keefe*, a bright, hitherto unapproachable student at Meg's school. The three meet Mrs Who, who sends them home to ''rest up.'' When Calvin meets the rest of the Murrys, he feels at home, among people like himself, for the first time. As Meg starts to walk Calvin home that night, they stop to talk and are interrupted by Charles; they are going to find Mr. Murry. Mrs Who, Mrs Which, and Mrs Whatsit, who are more than they appear to be, come, and suddenly there is darkness.

They come out in a sunlit field, having ''wrinkled'' space and come to another planet. Here Mrs Whatsit shows the children a terrible shadow obscuring the stars; Mr. Murry, fighting the shadow, is on the other side. The children are being taken to him in hopes he will be able to do for them what he cannot do for himself: get free. The children and the three Mrs W's travel to another planet, where the children are shown Earth, in a crystal ball. The powers of darkness cloud Earth, as evil has invaded all the universe, but everywhere it is being fought, and it can be overcome.

Next all travel to Camazotz* where Mr. Murry is, a planet which has given in to the powers of darkness. Here the children are left alone, after Mrs Who gives Meg a pair of glasses and Mrs Which warns them not to separate. The children enter a town where all the houses are identical, as are the actions of all their inhabitants, except for one boy. Everyone the children speak to seems interested only in the papers they should be carrying. The children come to the city's CENTRAL Central Intelligence Center, and though Calvin feels that they should not, they enter the building. Here they are sent to a red-eyed man who tries to get them into his power. Realizing that the man is only being used by someone else, Charles allows himself to be hypnotized in order to find out what is controlling the man, until Meg stops him. Though Calvin and Meg try to close their minds to the man, they cannot quite; Charles can, but to find their father, he allows himself to be subsumed by whatever the man represents. Suddenly he is like the controlled people they have already met.

Charles leads Meg and Calvin to Mr. Murry, explaining that Camazotz is happy and peaceful because all its inhabitants are alike, all of the same mind, having given in to IT*. On the way to Mr. Murry they see the odd little boy they had seen earlier, being horribly corrected. Then they come to Mr. Murry, imprisoned in a transparent column they cannot enter. Meg puts on Mrs Who's glasses and enters her father's cell. Wearing the glasses, he takes her back through the wall. Charles takes them all to IT, a great disembodied brain that pulses with an inescapable rhythm. Though she struggles to be free of its rhythm, Meg cannot, and Mr. Murry "wrinkles" space to get them away.

They land on a dark, cold planet without Charles, whom Mr. Murry could not get away. Mr. Murry had been part of a team of scientists who had worked out "wrinkling" years before, and he had landed on Camazotz by mistake and not been able to get away. Now he must warn Earth about the dangers of using science without understanding. The three are found and cared for by the "beasts"* who inhabit the planet. Unable to get back to Camazotz, they call the three Mrs W's, who explain that only Meg can save Charles, for she is closest to him. Mrs Which takes her to Camazotz, explaining that Meg has something IT does not, that she must find out for herself. Fearful but determined, Meg goes to IT and there finds Charles. She realizes that, though IT knows hate, IT does not have love, which she has in abundance. Meg loves Charles with all her strength, and he runs to her, suddenly himself again. Suddenly they are whirled home by Mrs Whatsit with Calvin and Mr. Murry. Mrs Who, Mrs Which, and Mrs Whatsit appear but are too busy to say goodbye before they vanish.

YALDING, LORD, a character in *The Enchanted Castle**, by E[dith] Nesbit Bland*. He becomes the husband of Mademoiselle*. This young man fell in love with her and wanted to marry her, in spite of his uncle's objections. She was sent into a convent, however, and Lord Yalding could not find her. When his uncle died, out of spite the old man left Yalding Castle* to Lord Yalding and his money to the lord's second cousin, so that Lord Yalding could not afford to keep the castle open but lived elsewhere. During his visit to Yalding Castle, the lord has several adventures when he meets Mabel Prowse*, Gerald*, James*, and Kathleen*, who have discovered a magic ring* in the castle and who are using it to make their wishes come true. He uses the ring to reunite himself with his lover, now a French teacher at a local school, and the price he pays for its use is to think he is going mad. The children reveal to him the hidden treasure in the castle's tower; Lord Yalding and his sweetheart are married, and they live in the castle on money from the sale of the treasure.

YALDING CASTLE, a place in E[dith] Nesbit Bland's* *The Enchanted Castle**. The present Lord Yalding's* ancestor built it to remind his wife of her home, but she did not live to see it completed; her death was the price exacted for his use of the magic ring* she gave him. The castle is huge and magnificent, and its grounds are a garden filled with statues that come alive at sunset. Here are the Temple of Flora* and the Hall of Granted Wishes*. Here, too, is the Temple of Strange Stones*, where one perfect ray of light falls at the time of harvest. Because he was angry with his nephew, the present Lord Yalding's uncle left the castle to him but did not leave him enough money to live there; consequently the impoverished young man tries to rent the castle to an American millionaire. When this scheme fails, Lord Yalding is delighted and surprised to learn from Mabel Prowse*, Gerald*, Kathleen*, and James* of a great treasure hidden in one of the towers. Lord Yalding and his bride live comfortably at the castle on the proceeds from the sale of the treasure. When Mademoiselle* undoes the magic done by the ring, the parts of the castle built through its use vanish and must be replaced.

YANTO, BONETHY (BONNIE), a character in *The Watchers**, by Jane Louise Curry*. She is the daughter of Roney and Fae Yanto and the sister of Merle. Bonnie has lived all her life in Twilly's Green Hollow*, in West Virginia; she longs for other things and intends to become a country singer. Bonnie helps Delano Mattick* (Delly) and Ray Siler* destroy the shrine at Tûl Isgrun*, sealing an evil force that is bound there. Secretly in love with Delly for some time, she is thrilled when he returns her love; the two will probably move Up Top*, above the Hollow, to live where their ancestors lived for hundreds of years.

YELLOW EAGLE, a character in *Five Children and It**, by E[dith] Nesbit Bland*. This native American is chief of the tribe of Rock-dwellers. He and his bloodthirsty band appear one morning when the Psammead* grants Cyril's* wish that there were Indians in England. Yellow Eagle is a noble savage; his speech is flowery and immensely dignified. When he wishes that he and his followers were in their native land, the Psammead obliges him.

ZARA-PETRA, a place in *The First Two Lives of Lukas-Kasha**, by Lloyd Alexander*. This small town is the home of Lukas-Kasha*, who is the village ne'er-do-well.

ZILLAH LLAWCAE (*A Swiftly Tilting Planet*). *See* Llawcae, Zillah

ZILLIE, a character in Madeleine L'Engle's* *A Swiftly Tilting Planet**. She is descended from Gwydyr*, a twelfth-century Welsh prince who had come to what is now Vespugia*, a South American country. Zillie is the sister of Gedder*. She was born in nineteenth-century Vespugia. Her mother having died, Zillie was raised with her brother by an English sheep rancher. She becomes a beautiful young woman. In 1865, when Welsh settlers come to Vespugia, Gedder tries to force Zillie on Bran Maddox*, one of the settlers, though another, Llewellyn Pugh, is in love with her. In one time line, he succeeds, and one of their descendants is Madog Branzillo*, a Vespugian leader who tries to destroy the world. Charles Wallace Murry*, however, travels through time and alters events; and Bran marries his childhood sweetheart. Zillie probably marries Llewellyn.

ZUCKERMAN, HOMER L., a character in E[lwyn] B[rooks] White's* *Charlotte's Web**. He is the husband of Edith Zuckerman and the uncle of Fern Arable*. He is a farmer. Mr. Zuckerman buys a five-week-old piglet, Wilbur*, to fatten up and slaughter in the winter. When a gray spider named Charlotte A. Cavatica* begins to write words and phrases flattering the pig, in her web, Mr. Zuckerman begins to have second thoughts about the matter, feeling that the words are appearing as a result of divine intervention. After Wilbur wins a special award at the county fair, Mr. Zuckerman lets him live a long and contented life in the barn.

ZYLL, a character in Madeleine L'Engle's* *A Swiftly Tilting Planet**. She is the daughter of Reschal; she becomes the wife of Madoc*, a twelfth-century Welsh prince who comes to North America. Zyll is one of the People of the

Wind native to North America. One day when she is searching for rare herbs in the forest, she finds Madoc and brings him back to her village. A year later they marry. Their wedding day is spoiled by Gwydyr*, Madoc's brother, who wants Zyll for his own, but Madoc defeats him. Among Zyll's descendants are Zillah Llawcae* and Gwen, Matthew, and Bran Maddox***.

ZYLLE LLAWCAE (*A Swiftly Tilting Planet*). *See* Llawcae, Zylle

WORKS ABOUT FANTASY

Alexander, Lloyd. "Wishful Thinking—Or Hopeful Dreaming?" *The Horn Book Magazine*, 44 (Aug., 1968), pp. 383-90.

Anderson, William, and Patrick Groff. "Fantasy," in *A New Look at Children's Literature*. Belmont, Calif.: Wadsworth Publishing Company, 1972, pp. 66-92.

Astbury, E. A. "Other and Deeper Worlds," *Junior Bookshelf*, 39 (Oct., 1975), pp. 301-5.

Attebery, Brian. *The Fantasy Tradition in American Literature*. Bloomington, Ind.: Indiana University Press, 1980.

Ayers, Lesley. "The Treatment of Time in Four Children's Books," *Children's Literature in Education*, 2 (July, 1970), pp. 69-81.

Bisenicks, Dainis. "Children, Magic, and Choices," *Mythlore*, 6 (Winter, 1979), pp. 13-16.

Blount, Margaret. *Animal Land: The Creatures of Children's Fiction*. New York: William Morrow and Company, 1975.

Bodem, Marguerite M. "The Role of Fantasy in Children's Reading," *Elementary English*, 52 (April, 1975), pp. 470-71.

Cameron, Eleanor. " 'The Dearest Freshness Deep Down Things,' " *The Horn Book Magazine*, 40 (Oct., 1964), pp. 459-72.

———. *The Green and Burning Tree*. Boston: Little, Brown and Company, 1969.

———. "Why *Not* for Children?" *The Horn Book Magazine*, 42 (Feb., 1966), pp. 21-33.

Colbath, Mary Lou. "Worlds as They Should Be: Middle-earth, Narnia and Prydain," *Elementary English*, 48 (Dec., 1971), pp. 937-45.

Crouch, M. S. "Experiments in Time," *Junior Bookshelf*, 20 (Jan., 1956), pp. 5-11.

Curry, Jane. "On the Elvish Craft," *Signal: Approaches to Children's Books*, 2 (May, 1970), pp. 42-49.

De Luca, Geraldine, and Roni Natov. "The State of the Field in Contemporary Children's Fantasy: An Interview with George Woods," *The Lion and the Unicorn*, 1 (Fall, 1977), pp. 4-15.

Drury, Roger W. " 'Realism Plus Fantasy Equals Magic,' " *The Horn Book Magazine*, 48 (April, 1972), pp. 113-19.

Eaton, Anne. " 'Extensions of Reality,' " *The Horn Book Magazine*, 3 (May, 1927), pp. 17-22.

Egoff, Sheila. "The New Fantasy," in *Thursday's Child*. Chicago: American Library Association, 1981, pp. 80-129.

Ellis, Alec. "Little Folk and Young People," *Junior Bookshelf*, 30 (April, 1966), pp. 97-102.

Gagnon, Laurence. "Philosophy and Fantasy," *Children's Literature: The Great Excluded*, 1 (1972), pp. 98-103.

Helson, Ravenna. "Fantasy and Self-Discovery," *The Horn Book Magazine*, 46 (April, 1970), pp. 121-34.

———. "The Psychological Origins of Fantasy for Children in Mid-Victorian England," *Children's Literature: The Great Excluded*, 3 (1974), pp. 66-76.

Hieatt, Constance B. "Analyzing Enchantment: Fantasy After Bettelheim," *Canadian Children's Literature*, 15/16 (1980), pp. 6-14.

Higgins, James E. *Beyond Words: Mystical Fancy in Children's Literature*. New York: Teachers College Press, 1970.

Hoffeld, Laura. "Where Magic Begins," *The Lion and the Unicorn*, 3 (Spring, 1979), pp. 4-13.

Hunter, Mollie. "One World (Part I)," *The Horn Book Magazine*, 51 (Dec., 1975), pp. 557-63.

———. "One World (Part II)," *The Horn Book Magazine*, 52 (Feb., 1976), pp. 32-38.

Hürlimann, Bettina. "Fantasy and Reality," in *Three Centuries of Children's Books in Europe*, trans. Brian W. Alderson. Cleveland and New York: The World Publishing Company, 1968, pp. 76-92.

Inglis, Fred. *The Promise of Happiness: Value and Meaning in Children's Fiction*. New York: Cambridge University Press, 1981.

Irwin, William Robert. *The Game of the Impossible: A Rhetoric of Fantasy*. Urbana: University of Illinois Press, 1976.

Jacobs, James S. "The Focus of Fantasy," *Arizona English Bulletin*, 18 (April, 1976), pp. 199-202.

Jago, Wendy. " 'A Wizard of Earthsea' and the Charge of Escapism," *Children's Literature in Education*, 8 (July, 1972), pp. 21-29.

Klingsberg, Göte. "The Fantastic Tale for Children—Its Literary and Educational Problems," *Bookbird*, no. 3 (1967), pp. 13-20.

Lanes, Selma G. "America as Fairy Tale," in *Down the Rabbit Hole*. New York: Atheneum, 1971, pp. 91-111.

Lang, Andrew. "Modern Fairy Tales," in *A Peculiar Gift: Nineteenth Century Writings on Books for Children*, ed. Lance Salway. Harmondsworth, England: Penguin Books, Kestrel Books, 1976, pp. 133-36. [Reprinted from *Illustrated London News*, 3 Dec. 1892, p. 714.]

Laurence, M. J. P. "Fantasy and Fashion," *Junior Bookshelf*, 18 (Oct., 1954), pp. 169-74.

L'Engle, Madeleine. "Childlike Wonder and the Truths of Science Fiction," *Children's Literature*, 10 (1982), pp. 102-10.

Lochhead, Marion. *The Renaissance of Wonder in Children's Literature*. Edinburgh: Canongate, 1977.

Lynn, Ruth Nodelman. *Fantasy for Children: An Annotated Checklist*. New York and London: R. R. Bowker Company, 1979 [rev. 1983].

MacDonald, George. "The Fantastic Imagination," in *A Peculiar Gift: Nineteenth Century Writings on Books for Children*, ed. Lance Salway. Harmondsworth, England: Penguin Books, Kestrel Books, 1976, pp. 162-67. [Reprinted from *A Dish of Orts*. Edwin Dalton, 1908.]

Manlove, C. N. *Modern Fantasy: Five Studies*. New York: Cambridge University Press, 1975.

Maxwell, Margaret. "The Perils of the Imagination: Pre-Victorian Children's Literature and the Critics," *Children's Literature in Education*, 13 (1974), pp. 45-52.

Meigs, Cornelia, et al. *A Critical History of Children's Literature*, rev. ed. New York: Macmillan Publishing Co., 1969.

Millar, John Hepburn. "On Some Books for Boys and Girls," in *A Peculiar Gift: Nineteenth Century Writings on Books for Children*, ed. Lance Salway. Harmondsworth, England: Penguin Books, Kestrel Books, 1976, pp. 154-61. [Reprinted from *Blackwood's Magazine*, 159 (March 1896), pp. 389-95.]

Mobley, Jane. "Toward a Definition of Fantasy Fiction," *Extrapolation*, 15 (May, 1974), pp. 117-27.

Morris, John S. "Fantasy in a Mythless Age," *Children's Literature: The Great Excluded*, 2 (1973), pp. 77-86.

Nichols, Ruth. "Fantasy and Escapism," *Canadian Children's Literature*, 4 (1976), pp. 20-27.

Philip, Neil. "Fantasy: Double Cream or Instant Whip?" *Signal*, 35 (May, 1981), pp. 82-90.

Pickering, Samuel F., Jr. "Notions of *Spirits* and *Goblings*: The Dangerous World of Fairy Tales," in *John Locke and Children's Books in Eighteenth-Century England*. Knoxville, Tenn.: The University of Tennessee Press, 1981, pp. 40-69.

Poskanzer, Susan Cornell. "A Case for Fantasy," *Elementary English*, 52 (April, 1975), pp. 472-75.

Prickett, Stephen. *Victorian Fantasy*. Bloomington and London: Indiana University Press, 1979.

Ruskin, John. "Fairy Stories," in *A Peculiar Gift: Nineteenth Century Writings on Books for Children*, ed. Lance Salway. Harmondsworth, England: Penguin Books, Kestrel Books, 1976, pp. 127-32. [Reprinted from *German Popular Stories*, ed. Edgar Taylor. London: John Camden Hotten, 1868.]

Sale, Roger. *Fairy Tales and After: From Snow White to E. B. White*. Cambridge, Mass.: Harvard University Press, 1978.

Smith, Lillian H. "Fantasy," in *The Unreluctant Years*. Harmondsworth, England: Penguin Books, 1953, pp. 150-62.

Terry, June S. "To Seek and to Find: Quest Literature for Children," *The School Librarian*, 18 (Dec., 1970), pp. 399-404.

Thompson, Hilary. "Doorways to Fantasy," *Canadian Children's Literature*, 21 (1981), pp. 8-16.

Tolkien, J. R. R. "On Fairy Stories," in *Essays Presented to Charles Williams*. London and New York: Oxford University Press, 1947, pp. 38-89. [Reprinted in *The Tolkien Reader*. New York: Ballantine Books, 1966, pp. 33-99.]

Toothaker, Roy E. "What's Your Fantasy I. Q.?" *Language Arts*, 54 (Jan., 1977), pp. 11-13.

Tymn, Marshall B., Kenneth J. Zahorski, and Robert H. Boyer. *Fantasy Literature*. New York and London: R. R.Bowker Company, 1979.

Waggoner, Diana. *The Hills of Far Away*. New York: Atheneum, 1978.

Whetton, Betty B. "In This Year of the Dragon: An Invitation to a Retrospective of Fantasy Literature or a New Look at an Age-old Genre Many Thought to Have

Been Replaced by Realistic Fiction," *Arizona English Bulletin*, 18 (April, 1976), pp. 110-15.

Yep, Laurence. "Fantasy and Reality," *The Horn Book Magazine*, 54 (April, 1978), pp. 137-43.

Yolen, Jane. *Touch Magic: Fantasy, Faerie and Folklore in the Literature of Childhood.* New York: Philomel Books, 1981.

Zanger, Jules. "Goblins, Morlocks, and Weasels: Classic Fantasy and the Industrial Revolution," *Children's Literature in Education*, 27 (1977), pp. 154-62.

CHRONOLOGY

1819	Charles Kinglsey born
1820	Jean Ingelow born
1824	George MacDonald born
1839	Mary Louisa Molesworth born
1858	Edith Nesbit Bland born
1859	Kenneth Grahame born
1860	James M. Barrie born
1863	*The Water-babies*
1865	Rudyard Kipling born
1869	*Mopsa the Fairy*
1870	"At the Back of the North Wind" serialized in *Good Words for the Young*
1871	*At the Back of the North Wind*
	The Princess and the Goblin
1873	Walter de la Mare born
1875	Charles Kingsley dies
	Carolyn Sherwin Bailey born
1877	*The Cuckoo Clock*
1879	*The Tapestry Room*
1882	*The Princess and Curdie*
1884	Alison Uttley born
1892	Lucy M. Boston born
	Robert Lawson born
	J. R. R. Tolkien born
1893	"In the Rukh" published in *Many Inventions* (first Mowgli story)
1894	*The Jungle Book*
1895	*The Second Jungle Book*
1897	Jean Ingelow dies
1898	C. S. Lewis born
1899	E. B. White born
1902	"The Psammead" serialized in *The Strand Magazine* and published in book form as *Five Children and It*
	The Little White Bird [Peter Pan in Kensington Gardens]
1903	Mary Norton born
	"The Phoenix and the Carpet" begins serialization in *The Strand Magazine*

1904   Play *Peter Pan* produced
            The Phoenix and the Carpet
1905   George MacDonald dies
            "The Amulet" begins serialization in *The Strand Magazine*
1906   P. L. Travers born
            T. H. White born
            Peter Pan in Kensington Gardens
            The Story of the Amulet
            "The Enchanted Castle" begins serialization in *The Strand Magazine*
1907   *The Enchanted Castle*
1908   *The Wind in the Willows*
            "The House of Arden" serialized in *The Strand Magazine* and
            published as a book
1909   "Harding's Luck" serialized in *The Strand Magazine* and published as a book
1910   *The Three Mulla-mulgars*
            "The Magic City" serialized in *The Strand Magazine* and published
            as a book
1911   *Peter and Wendy*
1912   Eleanor Cameron born
            "Wet Magic" begins serialization in *The Strand Magazine*
1913   *Wet Magic*
1914   Randall Jarrell born
1918   Madeleine L'Engle born
            Robert O'Brien born
1920   Richard Adams born
            Philippa Pearce born
1921   Pauline Clarke born
            Mary Louisa Molesworth dies
1924   Lloyd Alexander born
            Edith Nesbit Bland dies
1928   William Mayne born
1929   Ursula K. LeGuin born
            Robert Westall born
1932   Natalie Babbitt born
            Jane Louise Curry born
            Kenneth Grahame dies
1933   Penelope Lively born
1934   *Mary Poppins*
1935   Susan Cooper born
            Alan Garner born
            Mary Poppins Comes Back
1936   Rudyard Kipling dies
1937   James M. Barrie dies
            The Hobbit
1938   *The Sword in the Stone*
1939   Jill Paton Walsh born
            A Traveller in Time
            Ben and Me

1943	*The Magic Bed-Knob*
1944	*Rabbit Hill*
	Mary Poppins Opens the Door
1945	*Mr. Wilmer*
	Stuart Little
1946	*Mistress Masham's Repose*
	Miss Hickory
1947	*Mr. Twigg's Mistake*
	Bonfires and Broomsticks
1949	*The Fabulous Flight*
1950	*The Lion, the Witch, and the Wardrobe*
1951	*Prince Caspian*
	The Hobbit revised
1952	*The Voyage of the ''Dawn Treader''*
	The Borrowers
	Charlotte's Web
1953	*The Silver Chair*
1954	*The Horse and His Boy*
	The Children of Green Knowe
	The Tough Winter
1955	*The Magician's Nephew*
	The Borrowers Afield
1956	Walter de la Mare dies
	The Last Battle
1957	Robert Lawson dies
1958	*Tom's Midnight Garden*
	The Chimneys of Green Knowe
1959	*The Borrowers Afloat*
	The River at Green Knowe
1960	*The Weirdstone of Brisingamen*
1961	Carolyn Sherwin Bailey dies
	The Borrowers Aloft
1962	*The Twelve and the Genii*
	A Wrinkle in Time
1963	C. S. Lewis dies
	Time Cat
	The Moon of Gomrath
1964	T. H. White dies
	The Book of Three
	An Enemy at Green Knowe
1965	Randall Jarrell dies
	The Black Cauldron
	The Animal Family
	Elidor
1966	*The Castle of Llyr*
	Over Sea, Under Stone
	Earthfasts
1967	*Beneath the Hill*

Taran Wanderer
The Owl Service

1968 *The Sleepers*
The High King
A Wizard of Earthsea

1969 *The Change-Child*
The Search for Delicious

1970 *The Daybreakers*
Mindy's Mysterious Miniature
The Marvelous Misadventures of Sebastian
The Trumpet of the Swan

1971 *Over the Sea's Edge*
Mrs. Frisby and the Rats of NIMH
The Tombs of Atuan
The Wild Hunt of Hagworthy
The Whispering Knights

1972 *Watership Down*
The Farthest Shore
The Driftway

1973 Robert O'Brien dies
J. R. R. Tolkien dies
The Cat Who Wished to Be a Man
The Court of the Stone Children
The Ghost of Thomas Kempe
The Dark Is Rising
A Wind in the Door

1974 *The Lost Farm*
Greenwitch

1975 *The Watchers*
Parsley Sage, Rosemary & Time
The Wizard in the Tree
The Grey King
Tuck Everlasting
Are All the Giants Dead?

1976 Alison Uttley dies
The Magical Cupboard
The Stones of Green Knowe
The Wind Eye

1977 *The Birdstones*
Poor Tom's Ghost
Silver on the Tree

1978 *A Chance Child*
A Swiftly Tilting Planet
The Devil on the Road
The Bassumtyte Treasure
The Voyage of QV 66

ILLUSTRATORS

Adshead, Mary
    Bonfires and Broomsticks (1947)
Allen, James
    The Princess and Curdie (1882)
Babbitt, Natalie
    The Search for Delicious (1969)
Baynes, Pauline
    The Lion, the Witch, and the Wardrobe (1950)
    Prince Caspian (1951)
    The Voyage of the "Dawn Treader" (1952)
    The Silver Chair (1953)
    The Horse and His Boy (1954)
    The Magician's Nephew (1955)
    The Last Battle (1956)
    The Borrowers Avenged (1982)
Bedford, F. D.
    Peter and Wendy (1911)
Bernstein, Zena
    Mrs. Frisby and the Rats of NIMH (1971)
Boston, Peter
    The Children of Green Knowe (1954)
    The Chimneys of Green Knowe (1958)
    The River at Green Knowe (1959)
    An Enemy at Green Knowe (1964)
    The Stones of Green Knowe (1976)
Bray, Phyllis
    A Traveller in Time (1939)
Cober, Alan E.
    The Dark Is Rising (1973)
Crane, Walter
    The Cuckoo Clock (1877)
    The Tapestry Room (1879)
Eichenberg, Fritz
    Mistress Masham's Repose (1946)
Einzig, Susan

Tom's Midnight Garden (1958)
Floyd, Gareth
    The Sleepers (1968)
    The Change-Child (1969)
    The Whispering Knights (1971)
Franscino, Edward
    The Trumpet of the Swan (1970)
Froud, Brian
    Are All the Giants Dead? (1975)
Gannett, Ruth
    Miss Hickory (1946)
Garraty, Gail
    The Tombs of Atuan (1971)
    The Farthest Shore (1972)
Gill, Margery
    Over Sea, Under Stone (1966)
Gobbato, Imero
    Beneath the Hill (1967)
Heslop, Michael
    Greenwitch (1974)
    The Grey King (1975)
Hughes, Arthur
    At the Back of the North Wind (1871)
Jones, Harold
    The Voyage of QV 66 (1978)
Keeping, Charles
    Elidor (1965)
Kipling, J. Lockwood
    The Jungle Book (1894)
    The Second Jungle Book (1895)
Kubinyi, Laszlo
    The Wizard in the Tree (1975)
Lawson, Robert
    Ben and Me (1939)
    Rabbit Hill (1944)
    Mr. Wilmer (1945)
    Mr. Twigg's Mistake (1947)
    The Fabulous Flight (1949)
    The Tough Winter (1954)
Leslie, Cecil
    The Twelve and the Genii (1962)
Maitland, Antony
    The Ghost of Thomas Kempe (1973)
Millar, H. R.
    Five Children and It (1902)
    The Phoenix and the Carpet (1904)
    The Story of the Amulet (1906)
    The Enchanted Castle (1907)

The House of Arden (1908)
Harding's Luck (1909)
The Magic City (1910)
Wet Magic (1913)
Monsell, E. A.
The Three Mulla-mulgars (1910)
Mozley, Juliet
The Wild Hunt of Hagworthy (1971)
Peirce, Waldo
The Magic Bed-Knob (1943)
Rackham, Arthur
Peter Pan in Kensington Gardens (1906)
Robbins, Ruth
A Wizard of Earthsea (1968)
Robinson, Charles
The Daybreakers (1970)
Mindy's Mysterious Miniature (1970)
Over the Sea's Edge (1971)
The Lost Farm (1974)
Parsley Sage, Rosemary & Time (1975)
The Magical Cupboard (1976)
Sendak, Maurice
The Animal Family (1965)
Shepard, Mary
Mary Poppins (1934)
Mary Poppins Comes Back (1935)
Mary Poppins Opens the Door (1944)
Sokol, Bill
Time Cat (1963)
Stanley, Diana
The Borrowers (1952)
The Borrowers Afield (1955)
The Borrowers Afloat (1959)
The Borrowers Aloft (1961)
Tolkien, J. R. R.
The Hobbit (1937)
Williams, Garth
Stuart Little (1945)
Charlotte's Web (1952)

Index

Index entries that represent entries in the body of the book are set in all capital letters; the entry numbers are set in italics.

Calavar, 19
Caledvwlch. *See* Excalibum
CALICO, MISS, *91-92*, 356, 357, 550
California, 149, 233, 476, 502
Callista Rivers (*The Daybreakers*; *The Birdstones*). *See* Rivers, Callista Lee
CALORMEN, 20, 28, *92*, 161, 395, 437, 438, 444, 557; in *The Horse and His Boy*, 17, 19, 84, 125, 126, 239, 249, 250, 251, 256, 295, 327, 467, 537; in *The Last Battle*, 90, 172, 206, 272, 296, 297, 479, 488, 524, 536
Calvin O'Keefe (the Time trilogy). *See* O'Keefe, Calvin
CAMAZOTZ, 50, *92-93*, 263, 306, 390, 408, 591, 598, 616, 617
CAMERON, ELEANOR, *93-95*; *The Court of the Stone Children*, 127-29
CAMERON, PENELOPE TABERNER, xiii, xvi, 68, *95*, 508, 528, 564, 565, 608; acquaintances of, 35, 275; adventures of, 546-48; relatives of, 519
Camha, 14
Campion, 167
Canada, 50, 501
canal, 103-5, 130
CANDLE, 26, 69, *95*, 108, 163, 164, 240, 273, 358-59, 609
candles of winter, 139
cannibal, 561, 602
Cannibal Isles, 461
Canto, 593
Cantrev Cadiffor (Prydain), 201, 210, 459, 497
Captain (dog), 401
Captain Kidd's Cat (Lawson), 298
Caradog Prichard (*The Grey King*). *See* Prichard, Caradog
CAREY, MOTHER, 51, *95-96*, 153, 489, 580
CAREY, PAUL (DR.), *96*, 316, 509, 593
Carey Wilson (*The Magic Bed-Knob*; *Bonfires and Broomsticks*). *See* Wilson, Carey
CAROLANNA, 91, *96*, 424
Carondel, Hyppolyte Calome, 113
carp. *See* Neptune (carp)

carpet, Persian. *See* carpet, wishing
CARPET, WISHING, 56, 64, 67, 87, *96-97*, 122, 439, 441, 460; owners of, 17, 135, 268, 294, 478
Carved Lions, The (Molesworth), 374
Caspian IX, 97
CASPIAN X, 56, 90, *97*, 143, 255, 309, 322, 395, 468, 504, 525, 563; adventures of, 452-54, 490, 492, 570-72; and his friends, 126, 207, 399, 437, 438, 439, 470, 552, 553, 554; relatives of, 368, 473
Caspian the Conqueror, 525
Caspian the Navigator. *See* Caspian X
Caspian the Seafarer. *See* Caspian X
castle, 120, 268, 330, 455, 520; in Earthsea, 612; in England, 26, 163, 197, 358, 430; in Fairyland, 382; in the Land of Cockayne, 2, 159; in the Lost Land, 493; in Narnia, 552; in Wales, 416; in Zargonia, 179; sand, 339, 460. *See also* Annuvin; Anvard; Arden Castle; Berinir Gair; Caer Colur; Caer Dathyl; Cair Paravel; Dinas Rhydnant; Falias; Findias; Glorietta, the; Gorias; Harfang; Murias; Oeth-Anoeth; Siege of Air and Darkness, the; Spiral Castle; Yalding Castle
CASTLE COX, *97*, 117, 198, 398, 399, 446, 447, 448
CASTLE OF LLYR, THE (Alexander), *97-99*, 113
Castle of Yew, The (Boston), 79
Cat. *See* Cathound
CAT (character), *99*, 120, 121, 356
cat, 69, 87, 176, 230, 250, 253, 282, 364, 441; in *Time Cat*, 194, 257, 271, 323, 326, 396, 533, 534. *See also* Dragon; Dulcinea; Gareth; Ginger; Lionel; Lisabetta; Llyan; Muldoon, Mr.; News; Pansy; Presto; Sage, Parsley; Snowbell; Windy
CAT WHO WISHED TO BE A MAN, THE (Alexander), 9, *100-101*
"Cathay." *See* Kathleen (*Wet Magic*)
CATHOUND (CAT), *101*, 188, 204, 258, 481, 532, 613, 614
cathound (animal), 101

About the Author and Editor

PAT PFLIEGER is a Teaching Associate of English Composition at the University of Minnesota. She is currently earning a Ph.D. in American Studies with a concentration in children's literature.

HELEN M. HILL is Professor of English at Eastern Michigan University and a leading authority on the subject of children's literature.